P9-DET-344

PENGUIN BOOKS
THE PORTABLE
RENAISSANCE READER

Each volume in The Viking Portable Library either presents a representative selection from the works of a single outstanding writer or offers a comprehensive anthology on a special subject. Averaging 700 pages in length and designed for compactness and readability, these books fill a need not met by other compilations. All are edited by distinguished authorities, who have written introductory essays and included much other helpful material.

"The Viking Portables have done more for good reading and good writers than anything that has come along since I can remember."
—Arthur Mizener

Some Volumes in

THE VIKING PORTABLE LIBRARY

SHAKESPEARE
015.008 0

POE
Edited by Philip Van Doren Stern.   015.012 9

RABELAIS
Selected and translated by Samuel Putnam.   015.021 8

BLAKE
Edited by Alfred Kazin.   015.026 9

DANTE
Edited by Paolo Milano.   015.032 3

SWIFT
Edited by Carl Van Doren.   015.037 4

VOLTAIRE
Edited by Ben Ray Redman.   015.041 2

MILTON
Edited by Douglas Bush.   015.044 7

MEDIEVAL READER
Edited by James Bruce Ross and Mary Martin McLaughlin.   015.046 3

COLERIDGE
Edited by I. A. Richards.   015.048 x

ROMAN READER
Edited by Basil Davenport.   015.056 0

CERVANTES
Translated and edited by Samuel Putnam.   015.057 9

GIBBON
Edited by Dero A. Saunders.   015.060 9

RENAISSANCE READER
Edited by James Bruce Ross and Mary Martin McLaughlin.   015.061 7

THE GREEK HISTORIANS
Edited by M. I. Finley.   015.065 x

VICTORIAN READER
Edited by Gordon S. Haight.   015.069 2

THOMAS JEFFERSON
Edited by Merrill D. Peterson.   015.080 3

CHAUCER
Edited and translated by Theodore Morrison. Revised edition.   015.081 1

The Portable

RENAISSANCE
READER

Edited, and with an Introduction, by
JAMES BRUCE ROSS AND
MARY MARTIN McLAUGHLIN

PENGUIN BOOKS

Penguin Books Ltd, Harmondsworth,
Middlesex, England
Penguin Books, 40 West 23rd Street,
New York, New York 10010, U.S.A.
Penguin Books Australia, Ltd, Ringwood,
Victoria, Australia
Penguin Books Canada Limited, 2801 John Street,
Markham, Ontario, Canada L3R 1B4
Penguin Books (N.Z.) Ltd, 182–190 Wairau Road,
Auckland 10, New Zealand

First published in the United States of America
by The Viking Press 1953
Paperbound edition published 1958
Revised edition published 1968
Reprinted 1968 (twice), 1969, 1970, 1972 (twice),
1973, 1974, 1975, 1976
Published in Penguin Books 1977
Reprinted 1978 (twice), 1980, 1981, 1982, 1983, 1985

Copyright 1953 by The Viking Press, Inc.
Copyright © The Viking Press, Inc., 1968
All rights reserved

BRARY OF CONGRESS CATALOGING IN PUBLICATION DATA
Ross, James Bruce, 1902–   ed.
The portable Renaissance reader.
Reprint of the 1953 ed. published by The Viking
Press, New York, which was issued as no. 61 of the
Viking portable library.
1. European literature—Renaissance, 1450–1600.
I. McLaughlin, Mary Martin, 1919–   joint ed.
II. Title. III. Title: Renaissance reader.
[PN6014.R67 1977]   808.8′002′4   77–7967
ISBN 0 14 015.061 7

Printed in the United State of America by
Kingsport Press, Inc., Kingsport, Tennessee
Set in Linotype Caledonia

Some of the selections in this book are used by permission of the holders
of copyright and publication rights, listed among the Acknowledgments,
pages 755–56, and may not be reproduced without their consent. The
portions translated by the editors may be reprinted only with the
authorization of Viking Penguin Inc.

Except in the United States of America,
this book is sold subject to the condition
that it shall not, by way of trade or otherwise,
be lent, re-sold, hired out, or otherwise circulated
without the publisher's prior consent in any form of
binding or cover other than that in which it is
published and without a similar condition
including this condition being imposed
on the subsequent purchaser

Contents

Introduction   1
Suggestions for Further Reading (Revised, 1967)   42
Biographical List of Authors   50
Chronological Table   59

PART ONE: AN AGE OF GOLD

THIS OUR AGE

War and the Golden Age	*Jean de Montreuil*	65
The Turkish Menace	*Cardinal Bessarion*	70
A Bleak Prospect	*Pope Pius II*	74
The Golden Age in Florence	*Marsilio Ficino*	79
An Age of Gold	*Erasmus of Rotterdam*	80
The Restoration of the Gospel	*Jacques Lefèvre d'Étaples*	84
The Necessary Evils	*Richard Eden*	87
The Golden Age	*Torquato Tasso*	89
The Excellence of This Age	*Loys Le Roy*	91
The Evils of the Times	*Justus Lipsius*	109
Don Quixote and the Golden Age	*Miguel de Cervantes Saavedra*	116

The Return of the Muses

The Man of Letters	*Francesco Petrarca*	120
The Return of the Muses	*Giovanni Boccaccio*	123
Petrarca and the Art of Poetry	*Leonardo Bruni*	127
The Glory of the Latin Language	*Lorenzo Valla*	131
Germany Invokes the Muses	*Joachim von Watt*	135
The Arts Reborn	*Giorgio Vasari*	140

The New-Found World

The Golden World	*Pietro Martire d'Anghiera*	146
Joyful News from the New-Found World	*Nicolas Monardes*	152
Avarice	*Luis de León*	156
The Old World and the New	*Michel de Montaigne*	157
Tobacco, Tobacco	*Anonymous*	161

PART TWO: THE CITY OF MAN

The Pursuit of Profit

The Prosperity of Florence	*Benedetto Dei*	165
Venice, Mistress of the Seas	*Arnold von Harff*	168
The Hapsburgs and the Fuggers	*Maximilian I* / *Jakob Fugger*	175
Jack of Newberie, an English Clothier	*Thomas Deloney*	181
Antwerp, the Great Market ·	*Ludovico Guicciardini*	185
The Dearness of Things	*Jean Bodin*	202

THE MANNER OF THE WORLD

Life in Vienna   *Pope Pius II*   208
The Plight of the French Poor   *Cahier of the*
                                  Estates General   214
Life among the English   *Venetian Relazione*   218
The Manner of the World
  Nowadayes   *John Skelton (?)*   224
A Painter's Travels   *Albrecht Dürer*   227
The Peasants' War in Tyrol   { *Georg Kirchmair*
                                  Michael Geismayr }   234
A House in Venice   *Pietro Aretino*   241
Observations on the Turks   *Ogier Ghiselin de*
                                  Busbecq   244
The Judgment of a Witch   *Fugger News-*
                                  Letter   258

THE EDIFICE OF POWER

The Circle of Governments   *Niccoló Machiavelli*   263
A Portrait of Lorenzo de' Medici *Francesco*
                                  Guicciardini   267
The Balance of Power in Italy   *Francesco*
                                  Guicciardini   279
Henry VII, A New Monarch   *Francis Bacon*   284
Charles V and Philip His Son   *Marino Cavalli*   294
The Strength and Weakness of
  France   *Michele Suriano*   305

THE SEARCH FOR PERFECTION

On Virtù and Fortune   *Leon Battista*
                                  Alberti   328

The Perfect Country House   *Leon Battista
                                  Alberti*   332

The Perfect Gentleman   *Giovanni della Casa* 340
The Relief of the Poor   *Juan Luis Vives*   347
The Reform of the Common-
    wealth   *Thomas Starkey*   354
War and the Law of Nations   *Francisco de
                                  Vitoria*   365
The Concord of the World   *Guillaume Postel*   372

            PART THREE: THE STUDY OF MAN

                LEARNING OF THE BEST SORT

The Ruins of Rome   *Poggio Bracciolini*   379
The Restoration of Rome   *Bartolommeo
                                  Platina*   385
The Soul of Man   *Marsilio Ficino*   387
The Immortality of the Soul   *Pietro Pomponazzi*   392
The Life of a Scholar-Printer   *Aldus Manutius*   396
On the New Testament   *Erasmus of
                                  Rotterdam*   401
Pythagoras Reborn   *Johann Reuchlin*   409
Gargantua's Advice to
    Pantagruel   *François Rabelais*   414

                   THE ORPHIC LYRE

In Praise of Poetry   *Giovanni Boccaccio*   421
Music and the Courtier   *Baldassare
                                  Castiglione*   424
A Complaint by Night of the
    Lover Not Beloved   *Francesco Petrarca*   429
On the Death of the Lady Laura   *Francesco Petrarca*   430

A Ballata	*Angelo Poliziano*	431
A Carnival Song	*Lorenzo de' Medici*	432
Astolpho's Journey to the Moon	*Ludovico Ariosto*	435
Love's Justification	*Michelangelo Buonarroti*	440
To Vittoria Colonna: The Model and the Statue	*Michelangelo Buonarroti*	440
Mass of Love: A Spanish Ballad	*Anonymous*	441
A Sonnet	*Luis Vaz de Camões*	442
Night of Stars	*Luis de León*	443
To the Moon	*Pierre de Ronsard*	446
Of His Lady's Old Age	*Pierre de Ronsard*	447
Happy Who Like Ulysses	*Joachim du Bellay*	447
A Sonnet to Heavenly Beauty	*Joachim du Bellay*	448
Poor Loving Soul	*Louise Labé*	449
My Lute Awake	*Sir Thomas Wyatt*	449
Thou Blind Man's Mark	*Sir Philip Sidney*	451
Weep You No More, Sad Fountains	*Anonymous*	452

THE THEATER OF LIFE

Orfeo	*Angelo Poliziano*	453
A Theatrical Performance	*Baldassare Castiglione*	460
Lazarillo de Tormes	*Anonymous*	466

THE DIGNITY OF MAN

The Dignity of Man	*Giovanni Pico della Mirandola*	476

Self-Portrait of a Universal Man   *Leon Battista*
                                          Alberti   480
St. Thomas More   *Nicholas Harpsfield*   492
Michelangelo Buonarroti   *Ascanio Condivi*   501
On Himself and His Life   *Girolamo Cardano*   512

PART FOUR: THE BOOK OF NATURE

THE ARTS AND NATURE

The Art of Building   *Leon Battista*
                                          Alberti   527
Nature, Art, and Science   *Leonardo da Vinci*   531
The Casting of the "Perseus"   *Benvenuto Cellini*   540
On Landscape Painting   *Karel van Mander*   548
The Art of Paracelsus   *Paracelsus*   552
A Surgeon in the Field   *Ambroise Paré*   558
Anatomy and the Art of
    Medicine   *Andreas Vesalius*   563
The Health of the Mind   *Girolamo*
                                          Fracastoro   572
On Nature and Experience   *Bernard Palissy*   574

REVOLUTIONS OF THE SPHERES

The Diurnal Rotation of the
    Earth   *Nicole Oresme*   580
The Nature of the Universe   *Nicholas of Cusa*   584
The Revolutions of the Celestial   *Nicholas*
    Spheres   *Copernicus*   589
The New Star   *Tycho Brahe*   593
Comrades in the Pursuit of   ⎧*Galileo Galilei* ⎫
    Truth   ⎩*Johannes Kepler*⎭   597
The Starry Herald   *Galileo Galilei*   608

PART FIVE: THE KINGDOM OF GOD

THE CONGREGATION OF THE FAITHFUL

The Trial of Jerome of Prague	*Poggio Bracciolini*	615
The Unity of the Church	*Nicholas of Cusa*	624
The Election of a Pope	*Pope Pius II*	630
A Preacher of Reform	*Girolamo Savonarola*	644
Savonarola, A Portrait	*Francesco Guicciardini*	647
The Lutheran Revolt	*Alfonso de Valdés*	652
An Anabaptist View of the Church	*Peter Rideman*	661
An Appeal to the Council of Trent	*Reginald Pole*	665
The True Kirk and Its Signs	*John Knox*	672

FREEDOM OF THE WILL

On Free Will	*Erasmus of Rotterdam*	677
The Bondage of the Will	*Martin Luther*	694
Free Will and Predestination	*John Calvin*	704

TRUE CHRISTIAN PIETY

The Brethren of the Common Life	*Thomas a Kempis*	712
Members of One Body	*Erasmus of Rotterdam*	717
The Faith of a Christian	*Martin Luther*	721
The Self-Knowledge of a Christian	*Juan de Valdés*	727

The Fervent Spirits   Pietro Paolo
                                   Vergerio   730
The Livery of Christ   Hugh Latimer   733
Good Christian Discipline   John Calvin   738
The Lord's Labour   St. Teresa of Avila 742
The Obscure Night of the Soul St. John of the
                                   Cross   753

Acknowledgments   755

Introduction

I

"IMMORTAL GOD," exclaimed Erasmus of Rotterdam in 1517, "what a world I see dawning! Why can I not grow young again?" In two famous letters of the same year, the great humanist, in many ways a touchstone of the spirit of his time, described his vision more clearly. He saw the "near approach of a golden age," in which, he predicted, "three of the chief blessings of humanity are about to be restored to her"—true Christian piety, learning of the best sort, and, finally, the public and lasting concord of Christendom. Some years earlier Erasmus's outlook had been more gloomy, and he had complained, "Who being a good man in deed, does not see and lament this marvelous corrupt world? When was there ever more tyranny? When did avarice reign more largely and less punished? When did our iniquity so largely flow with more liberty? When was ever charity so cold?" A similar view, inspired by the "disaster" following so closely on his optimistic prophecy, is expressed in a letter to Martin Luther in 1526, lamenting the "irremediable confusion of everything," for which, he remarked, "we have to thank only your uncontrollable nature."

Erasmus would perhaps not be surprised to know that his debate with himself concerning the character of his world has never ended. For no time in Western history has been more glorified, and more disputed and deplored, than the two centuries which were bridged by his lifetime. A choir of rhapsodists, hailing the "re-

birth of the human spirit" and the "emancipation of the
mind," has sung hymns of praise to this age and its discovery of "new horizons"; while a crowd of mourners
has intoned dirges over its upheavals, social, intellectual,
and religious, discerning in them the origins of our as-
sorted woes.

Even among those who have studied them more
objectively, the fifteenth and sixteenth centuries have
provoked sharp disagreement. Some have sought in
their complexity a unified meaning, or a common main-
spring that set in motion the processes of change in
every area. To others, these changes seem to have produced only diversity, a mélange of movements, and a
galaxy of "divided and distinguished worlds." Testify-
ing to the efforts of many explorers to mark trails
through the forest of these centuries with conveniently
labeled signposts are the three familiar abstractions,
Renaissance, Reformation, and Counter Reformation.
But even these labels are disputable; a good many
people, for example, prefer "Protestant Revolt" to "Reformation," and others reject both the name and the
idea of a "Renaissance." The signposts themselves have
sometimes loomed so large that they have obscured
the lines of connection between religious and cultural
movements, which were not only contemporaneous but
closely related. And they have often obstructed a wider
view of this age, a view that would embrace the plains
and foothills as well as the peaks of its landscape.

The magnifying of one or another of its features has
created problems which are perhaps best illustrated by
the case of the Renaissance, the most comprehensive of
these abstractions. The ingredients of a picture enlarged
and embellished by later ages were supplied by the
writers of the fifteenth and sixteenth centuries, peerless

propagandists of their own interests and attainments. Long regarded as a cultural movement—the revival of art, letters, and learning that they described—the Renaissance is, as a historical period, the creation of nineteenth-century historians. In its classic portrayal, Jacob Burckhardt's brilliant essay, *The Civilization of the Renaissance in Italy*, certain figures and facets of Italian culture from Dante to Michelangelo are drawn in sharp perspective, while others are shadowy or not apparent.

"My starting point," Burckhardt said, "has to be a vision," and, though he called it the "Renaissance," what he saw was "the first mighty surging of a new age." Its characteristics—a new kind of state, a "work of art," a new type of individual, the self-aware and many-sided personality, a new culture molded by the recovery of the ancient past and the "discovery of the world and of man," a society marked by immorality and religious indifference—are displayed in a carefully constructed mosaic. For all its high qualities, it is the idealized portrait of an age, glowing with worldly individualism and novelty, but static and foreshortened in time and space.

Its creator himself warned his readers that "in the wide ocean upon which we venture the ways and directions are many," and that the same studies which had served for his work might easily lead to essentially different conclusions. But his picture was so appealing, and his techniques so useful, that, extended to other areas of Europe, they shaped the modern conception of the Renaissance. Through the catchwords of textbooks and the colorful clichés of romances, his insights have filtered down in the common notion of a "golden age" populated by glamorous figures somewhat larger than life. Only in this century have numerous critics in-

quired whether the vision of Burckhardt and his followers was perhaps an optical illusion.

The controversy they have touched off is ironically
sketched by one of its participants in a dialogue between a Dreamer who sees the Renaissance as a glorious
world, splendid in purple and gold, and a Questioner
who voices the objections of more critical scholars. Beholding "the rise of individualism, the awakening of a
desire for beauty, the triumph of worldly pleasure and
the joy of life," the Dreamer sees in his reverie a procession of painters and poets like Michelangelo and
Ariosto, Dürer and Ronsard, even catching sight of St.
Francis of Assisi and Jan van Eyck. The Questioner,
laughing, challenges this Renaissance, declaring that it
does not stand firm in time or space, in content or
meaning, that it is too vague, too incomplete, and hap-
hazard.

Many of the Questioners whose protests have undermined the traditional idea of the Renaissance have attacked with special vigor the notion of its novelty, of a
break with earlier traditions. Students have found in the
medieval centuries the worldliness, individualism, and
humanistic interest in antiquity once regarded as characteristic of the "Renaissance," and in the fifteenth and
sixteenth centuries much that had seemed peculiarly
"medieval." Historians of science, tracing the diverse
currents of thought that merged in the "scientific revolution" of the sixteenth and seventeenth centuries—
to many the real origin of the modern world and the
modern mentality—have shown that if its effects were
revolutionary, its development was long and tortuous.
Others have seen the major turning point of our civilization in the powerful surge of economic life, which,
transforming European society from the eleventh cen-

tury, brought to flowering both "medieval" and "Renaissance" culture. To some of those who stress the continuity of history, the ideas of rebirth or sudden change are utterly repugnant, and they resist what is in their opinion an attempt to "give to airy nothing a local habitation and a name."

Such assaults as these have made the boundary line between "Middle Ages" and "Renaissance," if not nonexistent, vaguer than ever. Yet to many of its students the Renaissance still bears a distinctive physiognomy, though not perhaps the face that Burckhardt saw. They have not agreed on its character, but their scrutiny, discovering many new facts concerning its individual features—its art and literature, politics and economy, science, philosophy, and religion—has made important corrections of perspective in the old picture.

The cultural primacy of Italy, though still acknowledged, has been modified by an awareness that the relationship between Italy and the North was not a one-way traffic but a process of cross-fertilization. An age that had appeared to many joyous, pagan, secular, and optimistic has been revealed as also serious, religious, and profoundly pessimistic. Its intellectual life, in which classical humanism once seemed dominant, is now regarded as a whirlpool of currents so conflicting that a "Counter Renaissance" has recently been created, to serve as sanctuary for a motley crowd of refugees from the main or classical Renaissance, for such figures as Machiavelli and Montaigne, Luther and Calvin, Bruno and Bacon. Those to whom the Renaissance was the "Sunday dress" of society in these centuries, a minority movement of a few artists and scholars who were patronized by princes and rich merchants, have been challenged by others who would reconcile the interests of an intellectual and artistic elite with the common assumptions and experience of the time.

The fifteenth and sixteenth centuries have, in fact, undergone a fate comparable to that of many of their great paintings. Modern techniques, including the use of X-ray and the microscopic examination of cross-sections, have demonstrated that these familiar works of art are often distorted versions of the originals, which, as their colors faded, were more than once touched up and restored. Now, after the layers of hard modern colors and glossy veneers that flattened perspective have been removed, the true features of the artists' work are uncovered. A painting like Van Eyck's "Adoration of the Mystic Lamb," which was altered not only by later hands but by the artist's own brush, now appears different in shading and emphasis from the picture long seen, but fresher and more beautiful, more vivid in color and plastic in form.

Although the explorations stimulated by the Renaissance controversy can never lay bare in the same way the true features of the past, they have revealed a time perhaps less highly colored than it formerly appeared, but far more complex and interesting in itself and in its ties to its past and our present. In the *Renaissance Reader*, the troubled and exciting world of the fifteenth and sixteenth centuries is portrayed in some fragments of its reality, in selections from those contemporary writings which "enable men born in a distant age to have past events as much before their eyes as those in whose presence they occurred."

II

The disease of writing, as Petrarca was pleased to note, is highly contagious, and it spread more widely than ever in the centuries following his own. By the time of Erasmus, who wrote "standing on one foot," and sometimes with his printers waiting to snatch the sheets from his hands, the man of letters and the printer often worked in close alliance to produce the multitude of books which enhance the difficulties of those who now "undertake to choose things worthy to be known." From the mass of writings illuminating the life and thought of this age, we have tried to make selections which have the power to draw the reader into their world; the sound of the living voice, the personal and immediate response to experience, the direct statement of ideas and ideals, have been the objects of our search. These records we have drawn not only from the literature of imagination, but from letters, which were often works of art, from memoirs, journals, and biography, from history and chronicles, and from treatises ranging in subject from mystical theology and astronomical theory to landscape painting and the high cost of living.

Assembling a collection of this kind is in many ways like attempting to pack the crown jewels into a hatbox. It can be done only by leaving out the settings and even many of the stones, and those who choose must hope that the brightness of the gems they have put in will compensate for the beauty of those which have been left out. Adequately to represent, for example, even in several volumes the size of this, the abundant literary treasures of centuries that produced Ariosto and Tasso, Ronsard and Rabelais, Spenser and Shakespeare, would be extremely difficult. We have sought instead to illustrate certain characteristic tendencies, themes, and seminal forms of the self-expression of this age; among them, its lyric and dramatic qualities, its devotion to the sonnet, the pastoral, and the romantic epic, and the mutual influences of poetry and music. If our selections invite readers to discover, or to rediscover, the riches that await them, much more amply, in the works of the makers of Renaissance literature, one of our purposes will be fulfilled.

The claims of the many great spokesmen who demand a hearing and of those humbler voices which have often been muted have made the task of selection still more formidable. We have tried to do justice to both, and merchants, artisans, and peasants have found a place in the *Renaissance Reader,* as well as the "giants," who are well represented though sometimes not by their best-known writings. Since brief excerpts can do nothing but violence to such works as More's *Utopia,* Erasmus's *Praise of Folly,* and Machiavelli's *Prince,* we have presented their authors in selections exhibiting other facets of their personalities and thought. Erasmus may be encountered in his letters and in his debate with Martin Luther; More in the life by Nicholas Harpsfield, the first formal biography in the English language; and Machiavelli in his *Discourses* and in the political reality of his time.

Though a great many books were written in the fifteenth and sixteenth centuries, many have not been reprinted or translated since that time, some were never printed, and others have never been translated into English. In translations from Latin and several modern languages, and in modernized English texts, we offer here some significant records which are not ordinarily available. A number of these newly translated selections are from works long considered essential to an understanding of this age; they include the self-portrait of Leon Battista Alberti, Burckhardt's many-sided man of the early fifteenth century, and the writings of his contemporaries, humanists like Leonardo Bruni, Lorenzo Valla, and Poggio Bracciolini; the historical works of Francesco Guicciardini, the peer of Machiavelli as a political realist and his superior as a historian, and the famous description of the Low Countries by Guicciardini's nephew, Ludovico.

In other translations, perhaps less familiar individuals and phases of thought and action are represented; among them, the activities of Bernard Palissy, the philosophical potter, and the ideas of Loys Le Roy, a pioneer in the comparative study of civilizations, and of Guillaume Postel, whose many works and several journeys to the East were dedicated to realizing a single vast dream, the concord of the world. The hopes and fears of the lowlier members of society, which in an aristocratic age were more often expressed in actions than in words, are revealed in the moving plea of the "little people" of France to the Estates General of 1484, and in a brief account of the German peasants' war.

To impose limits where temporal boundaries are shadowy and much disputed, and spatial ones rapidly changing, is a peculiarly difficult and unsatisfactory task. Those we have set are tentative, and, though partly the outcome of practical exigencies, they are in keeping with the untidy reality of this time. After a long period of expansion the world of Latin Christendom was, by the fifteenth century, narrowed and long to be menaced by the advance of the Ottoman Turks. The great adversary which overthrew Constantinople in 1453 and was ultimately to reach the gates of Vienna had earlier still absorbed the shrunken lands of the Byzantine Empire and a considerable part of Eastern Europe. Yet, by the century's end, the voyages of the

Portuguese and Spanish, looking for Christians and spices, had opened new worlds in East and West. The impact on European society of these tremendous adventures of exploration and conquest, and of the long struggle and more peaceful encounters with the Turks, is evident in a number of selections in this volume. But its focus is the area of Europe that shared a common tradition and historical experience, the culture of Western Christendom.

The absence of sharp dividing lines in the evolution of this culture is suggested in the close kinship between this book and its predecessor, *The Medieval Reader*. Both exhibit, most directly in selections from the same individuals—Petrarca and Boccaccio, Pope Pius II and Nicholas of Cusa—the mingling of old and new in certain aspects of the life and thought of the fourteenth and fifteenth centuries. It has been said that, from the beginning of the fifteenth century, the balance between particular forces—society, state, church, art, science— began to shift slowly, with new forces pressing up and altering the previous equilibrium. But it is also true that the processes of change in these different spheres followed no well synchronized timetable, and if any pattern is to be discerned in their movement, it is that of a series of waves, each breaking in a different time and place. In the *Renaissance Reader* we have followed more closely the course of those advancing waves, often beginning far back in the past, which swelled most vigorously in the late fifteenth and sixteenth centuries. At the same time, we have watched the receding waves whose force was by no means spent in a time when men were still closely bound to the ideals and institutions and patterns of the past.

The framework in which our selections are placed

represents a comprehensive view of these centuries, large enough to embrace Castiglione's Urbino, the Antwerp of merchants and bankers, and the Wittenberg of Martin Luther, and to link the world of Pope Pius II and Nicholas of Cusa with that of Kepler and Galileo. "An Age of Gold," presenting some significant themes in the thought of these centuries, offers an introduction also to their larger aspirations and to those aspects of their experience which were most stimulating to the self-awareness of which the name "Renaissance" is one expression. In the "City of Man," selections portray more fully the social, economic, and political reality, and some of the ideals and programs through which men sought the "good life" and the improvement of their society. Their search for truth and beauty in learning and literature, in the arts and sciences, their inquiries into the nature of man and the universe, are illustrated in "The Study of Man" and "The Book of Nature." The religious quests which grew so pressing in this age, the condition of the Church and efforts to reform it, and the conflicts that shattered its unity, are depicted in the section entitled "The Kingdom of God," which ends with some varied expressions of a common Christian piety.

III

To many men of these centuries the contrast between the promise and the reality of their time posed the dilemma trenchantly expressed in Erasmus's conflicting views of his age. Drawing up balance sheets of the excellences and flaws of their society was a favorite occupation of writers, who were torn between admiration for its achievements and dismay at its upheavals. Few judgments are as penetrating as the account of Loys Le Roy, a more sanguine Toynbee of the sixteenth century, with the catalogues of men and events which proved him an "abyss of learning," and provide the modern reader with a valuable summary. But a persistent and self-conscious concern with "this our age," and its relation to the past and future, has left numerous revelations of the hopes and fears of men, and varied estimates of the great problems and issues they faced. Such records, as important to our understanding of the past as the more prosaic details of its life, often make its experience more meaningful to the present.

Perhaps the most striking quality of these writings is the remarkable range of their optimism and pessimism, the response to an environment in which Fortune was the most common symbol of change and instability. To many, from those humanists who considered themselves to be living in the "end and dregs of time" to the six-teenth-century reformers for whom theirs were "the last and most wicked days," the outlook was prevailingly bleak. Pessimism, nourished by the traditional Christian contempt of the world, was strengthened by unblinking scrutiny of man and his frailties and follies. It was deepened also by contemplation of the more depressing marvels of the age, the new instruments of warfare, the "new disease," whose many names gave way finally to the poetic epithet, syphilis, and the new religious sects. A veritable cult of gloom found in death an engrossing theme, most vividly elaborated by the poets and painters who depicted the dance of death, or its triumph, or, like Holbein, its "images and storied faces."

Those who surveyed the larger spectacle of Europe at the beginning and the end of this period would have found little to lighten the dark view. For an observer of the early fifteenth century would have looked upon a society in the throes of a long depression, a world in which the older forms of order, feudal and urban, were slowly disintegrating, a divided and competitive Europe in which a few great kingdoms and a multitude of petty states were the actual centers of political authority. For their rulers, self-interest was a more compelling motive than allegiance to the old ideals of unity which were most comprehensively embodied in a Church whose weaknesses were flagrantly exposed in the long years of the Great Schism. The picture of this same Europe might have appeared still less bright to one who regarded it from the vantage point of the late sixteenth century, when religious revolution had made permanent the schism of Christendom, and added religious struggles to the conflicts of more powerful states, when an unprecedented flow of wealth had served not only to enrich a few, but to produce an economic crisis in which inflation impoverished whole classes.

Yet in spite of the dismal features of their society men found much to foster the irrepressible optimism that reached its peak in the brief years of the early sixteenth century, when many, sharing the vision of Erasmus, could feel that they were living in the dawn of a better world. There were strong grounds for optimism in the "many fine things newly discovered," and almost all good things, even those which, like printing, were the fruit of long development, were claimed as the "new" discoveries of the age. Among these novelties the voyages and explorations, which gave to Europeans a new conception of their place in a larger world, were clearly "such great adventures as Fate had to no former age allowed." If the "joyful news from the new-found world" brought access to new commodities, profits, and comforts of life, it also confronted more Europeans than ever before with the revelation of strange societies and races of men, through which they came to see themselves more objectively, and sometimes more critically.

But the hopes of those who tried, as men had for centuries, to reform society and the Church, to revivify Christian piety to attain, even in an age of combat, the "concord of Cnristendom," were most actively sustained by the achievements of their time in literature, learning, and art. Poets and scholars found new modes of expression in the literature of Rome and Greece, and fresh significance in those ancient disciplines they called the "studies of humanity." Following the models of antiquity, but, more closely, nature herself, artists were portraying and adorning the visible environment of man in forms of unsurpassed beauty. These signs of Europe's creative vigor, drawing inspiration from both the more remote and the more recent past, fostered the belief that past glories might be equaled or even surpassed.

The passion of this age for the exploration of antiquity, opening to many minds the way to a world far more real and meaningful than either of the Indies, was but a more intense and more widely diffused expression of an unceasing devotion. For centuries men had lived on the ancient patrimony like a family on a somewhat dilapidated ancestral estate, cherishing and constantly refurbishing its treasures. Their recovery was the perennial task of Western Christendom. But where a humanist of the twelfth century might use the metaphor of dwarfs on the shoulders of giants to express his view of the continuity of his age with the ancient past, the followers of Petrarca and Boccaccio delighted in the proliferation of images involving the restoration of the ancient treasures from darkness to light or from death to life. Considering themselves the true heirs of Roman culture, of

which they had been dispossessed by the barbarians
of the North, Italian men of letters of the late fourteenth and fifteenth centuries approached antiquity with
the self-consciousness of exiles.

"The return of the Muses," a recurrent theme in their
writings, expresses the spirit of a literary movement that,
initiating a change of intellectual fashion, profoundly
influenced the thought of this time and its conception of
itself. From their journeys of exploration the Italian
humanists brought back not only the ancient patronesses
of the arts they esteemed most highly, but the elements
of a new view of history. For if they saw the vision of
the classical past more clearly, they saw it more re-
motely, over the gulf of time on which their perspective
grew darker and more distorted, the centuries which
were not "antique" but simply "old." Hoping devoutly
that ancient history would repeat itself, these writers
found, in the old cyclical theories which they revived,
and in the still vigorous Christian ideas of religious and
political renewal, support for their ideal of a renewal of
culture after earlier darkness and decay. From the repetition of their slogans and symbols, which were elaborated with variations by scholars in other fields and other
lands, there ultimately emerged the modern conceptions
of a "Middle Age" and a "Renaissance" in the conventional division of Western history.

How deeply writers who prided themselves on knowing fifty different ways to say "thank you for your
letter," admired "copiousness of expression," the reader
of their works will soon discover. The appeal of metaphor and symbol was especially strong in a time that not
only drew on the treasuries of the Christian tradition
and classical literature and mythology, but invented the
new "sign-language" which was one of its real inno-

vations. Vast ingenuity was exercised in the creation of the hieratic emblems that decorate the paintings and sculpture, the medals and books, of the Renaissance. The great printers of the time, like Aldus Manutius with his famous dolphin and anchor mark, identified their wares with such emblems (one of their descendants is the Viking ship which decorates this book). Others were personal badges, like Lorenzo de' Medici's three feathers in a diamond ring and the Sforzas' burning brand; even Rabelais' Gargantua had his emblem, a gold plate weighing some forty-five pounds, bearing his motto, "Love conquers all."

If there is a symbol that can comprehend the varied expressions of the self-awareness of these centuries, the diversity of their hopes and strivings, their doubts and disillusionments, it is the idea of a "golden age." Few themes are more often repeated, by poets, scholars, and reformers, by humanists, naturalists, and realists, than the ancient myth of a time when man and the world had been gloriously young and innocent, before the reign of Saturn ended and man deteriorated through a series of ages from gold to iron. In antiquity the poet Vergil had prophesied a "new beginning of the great sequence of the ages," the return of the maid Justice, and the restoration of Saturn's reign. This promise, echoing through all the Christian centuries, spoke more eloquently than ever to those who represented the latest of many efforts to restore the great traditions of Western culture. Their ideals of renewal and reform and rebirth, their utopian visions of a better society, shone most brightly in the dream of a time when there was no war, no greed, no "mine and thine."

Christian humanists from Jean de Montreuil to Erasmus envisaged a peaceful and orderly society, ruled by devout princes and illuminated by a purer Christian faith and by the "best sort of learning." Scholars and reformers who labored to restore the Gospel and its teachings, to revive the spirit and life of early Christianity, saw in the primitive Church the golden age of the religion they hoped to purify. Others, looking to nature rather than to classical reason and Christian faith, longed for an age of freedom from custom, convention, and law, an Abbey of Thélème, where men might do as they pleased. Theirs was the ancient vision of an earthly paradise, the "golden world" of which a living model was presented in accounts of the newly discovered lands whose inhabitants were not yet corrupted by European vices. The ideal of a happier condition of society had meaning, if only as an expression of their disillusionment, even for hard-eyed realists, who thought that in the beginning men were "little different from beasts" and who saw no great change since.

A "golden age" was the most poignant dream of a troubled time, an unbalanced world in which men sought eagerly for new forms of order and perfection, and for new ways to attain the old ideals. It was also the most revealing mirror of an increasingly acquisitive society, in which the pursuit of wealth and other varieties of self-interest were not only the sources of corruption and change, but the largest obstacles to reform. The contrast was stated with devastating simplicity in Thomas More's description of Utopia, where gold was used to make chains for slaves and chamberpots for citizens. In More's Europe gold and silver were "the blood of the whole body social," whose parts depended on their circulation.

IV

To accompany Albrecht Dürer on his travels in the
Low Countries is to explore through the artist's eyes
some of the "noble and beautiful cities" which were the
vital centers of this social organism. Its mightiest arteries moved not through the most powerful states, but
along the routes of an international commerce that had
brought first the cities of Italy and Flanders, then those
of other lands, to prosperity and cultural eminence. By
the sixteenth century Antwerp, the goal of Dürer's
journey, had become the richest heir of the medieval
economic revolution, to which the cities of Europe owed
their flourishing life and city-dwellers their rapidly
growing importance in the scale of society. This great
international market and financial clearing house,
into which poured the new world-trade opened up by
the discoveries, was now, as Venice had been earlier,
"the microcosm that reflected the soul of commercial
Europe." It was a major focus of the economic energies
which were most actively shaping the environment of
these centuries.

To Antwerp's bourse flocked the merchants and
bankers of every land and tongue, so that, as Guicciardini remarked, "in a single city you might observe
the nature, way of life, and customs of many peoples."
The many-sided activities of this city, in fact, summed
up the economic expansion of several centuries, from
the emergence of the guilds in which most craftsmen
and small traders were still organized, to the rise of an
aristocracy of wealth whose greatest representatives
were financial dynasties like the Medici and Chigi,
Fuggers and Welsers.

These financiers drawing huge incomes from in-

vestments in land and mines, in banking and voyages
to the Indies, were only the most notable exponents of
the capitalism that was now a dynamic force. Its spirit
and methods were well developed by the thirteenth century, especially in Italy, where the rapid extension of
commercial enterprise had early stimulated the more aggressive pursuit of profit characteristic of the economic
life of this age. In the hands of its "money-masters,"
capital, invading agriculture and the old industries once
protected by the guilds, also supplied loans and financed
new enterprises on an ever larger scale. But, though
the power of money appeared in its quintessence in
these activities and at Antwerp, the steady expansion
of a money economy had for centuries been challenging
the traditional ideals of the Christian commonwealth
and transforming its institutions.

In a time when the majority of men still lived and
worked in the older patterns of a predominantly agri-
cultural society, the impact of economic forces was
sharply felt, if dimly understood. The mirror of change,
for most contemporary observers, was the varied "manner of the world," reflecting in the lives of individuals
and groups, in city and countryside, alterations which
were sometimes fruitful and often destructive. The
larger lines of change were by no means new, but in
the undermining of a social order divided—more
effectively in theory than in practice—into a hierarchy
of classes, they were now more evident than they had
been earlier.

"New-come gentlemen," whose gentility was derived
from goods, not blood, rose at the expense of an older
nobility, now confronted by newer forms of wealth as
well as by new ways of government and warfare. To
salvage their declining fortunes and preserve their

social prestige, many of its members became the servants of rulers and the ornaments of their courts. Others experienced the decay or ruin that drove a few—like Michael Geismayr, who dreamed of the destruction of cities—to lead the wars and rebellions of peasants. For the discontent of those who worked on the land often grew more active as their freedom increased, and if for many the disabilities of serfdom had been removed, they were frequently replaced by the harsher exactions of landlords and kings.

Nobles, peasants, and small burghers alike felt the heavy pressures of a more competitive economy, sharpening the cleavage between rich and poor and producing those dislocations which intensified the social and religious ferment of the age, the quest for new forms of security, both earthly and heavenly. The confusions and disorders of a world where violence was common, war almost incessant, and poverty endemic, gave impetus also to the spread of the two social diseases that became epidemic in the sixteenth century, syphilis and the witchcraft delusion. The belief in witchcraft, and its persecution, laying bare the deep springs of unreason in this society, grew into a mass neurosis of a kind which was not to be seen again until our own day.

Yet to those who could withstand its rigors the social climate was invigorating. For the pursuit of profit, which aggravated the worst features of society, and its most serious crises, also fostered its most promising achievements. The accumulation of riches in the cities of Italy and the North supported those aristocracies of wealth and talent in whose activities the urban culture of the age attained its consummate expression. And the happy union of money, leisure, and talent bore fruit also in the wider diffusion of literature and learning, in the broadening of the lay public, most strikingly exemplified by the development of printing. The rapid growth of this new enterprise, highly capitalized from the first, reflects the more favorable conditions of life in these centuries—the still small but increasing numbers of those who enjoyed the education, the larger leisure, and the higher standard of living, the houses more spacious and better lighted—which made possible the appeal of the printed book. Its varied powers, which were to revolutionize the cultural life of Europe, were early displayed in the woodcuts and engravings of Dürer and others, in the unparalleled influence of Erasmus's writings, and the tracts, broadsides, and cartoons of the reformers. With printing, the city was more than ever the "quickforge and working house of thought."

The stimulus of an urban environment is evident in other ways. Dürer's record of his tireless sightseeing and souvenir hunting, his collections of sugarcane and sweetmeats, porcelain and buffalo horns, his wonder at the first exhibit of American art he saw in Brussels, are a revelation of the new ideas that might strike the minds of city-dwellers, the new products that might enrich their lives or, like tobacco, soothe their troubled spirits. Among novelties and curiosities, the rare animals and plants which were to encourage the studies of naturalists exercised a special fascination. Florence was entranced by the shipment of strange animals sent to Lorenzo de' Medici by the Sultan, as was the Rome of Pope Leo X by the papal zoo, which featured, until it died prematurely of the effects of nervous strain, an elephant posthumously immortalized by Raphael. From distant journeys travelers—such as Busbecq, who brought with other treasures from Turkish lands the tulip, the lilac, and the horse chestnut—returned with the exotic plants that soon adorned the gardens of Europe.

Like the new plants, culture in the urban society of the Renaissance served a variety of ends, practical as well as aesthetic and intellectual. The splendors of art and architecture, the delights of literature, enhanced the prestige of their patrons, whether merchants and bankers or princes and prelates, and competition for their services helped to raise the social status of artists and men of letters. For the gifted and enterprising of whatever origins, culture was a passport admitting its bearer to the higher realms of society. Its possession made possible even a career like that of Aretino, whose house in Venice and other appurtenances of an elegant life were maintained largely by the proceeds of literary blackmail. For the newer aristocracies, which had emerged victorious from earlier social struggles, the investment in culture became both a visible sign of success and the most useful measure of gentility in a time when older standards of nobility were losing their meaning.

If the expansion of economic power was a fundamental factor in the changing life of these centuries, the growing consolidation of political strength was equally impressive. Following Machiavelli's "circle of governments," most states, whether former urban republics like Florence and Milan, or feudal kingdoms like France and England, were by the late fifteenth century well advanced on the path to despotism. Devotion, or at least submission, to the strong ruler who provided stern remedies for disorder was replacing both the larger and the lesser loyalties of Christendom. Out of the great diversity of political forms inherited from the Middle Ages was emerging the "new order" of the sovereign territorial state, which was to become an end in itself, attempting to subdue or conquer all opposing forces within its boundaries.

In the financial difficulties of Lorenzo de' Medici and in the relations of the Hapsburgs with Jakob Fugger, the "paymaster" of kings and popes, whose money underwrote the more fantastic and the shrewder schemes of the Emperor Maximilian, the golden bond between the courts of rulers and the counting houses of merchants is clearly revealed. Both "new" princes and old, bent on constructing and enlarging the edifice of power, required a free flow of revenue to maintain more highly centralized governments and more lavish courts, to pay for the wars which drained off the wealth of Europe. Not only for the "felicity of full coffers," but for the support and execution of their policies, monarchs turned often to those middle classes which benefited from the weakening of the nobility and the creation of larger and stronger states.

Though the work of Henry VII of England, the ablest of the new monarchy's "three wise men," and others, presaged the eventual triumph of the national states which could most effectively dispose their resources in wealth and men, their victory was not entirely certain. For the fate of France in the sixteenth century showed how precarious, in the struggle for power within states, was the strength of even the greatest kingdoms. And the ancient commercial republic of Venice was still a model of political stability and a past mistress of the statecraft manifested in the reports of ambassadors like Cavalli and Suriano, whose detailed accounts of their missions are as illuminating to the modern reader as they were to the Venetian Senate. Through their diplomacy and their wars, rulers now tried more consciously to achieve the equilibrium reached in late fifteenth-century

Italy, to prevent the domination of a single state. By the sixteenth century the balance of power was most heavily weighted by the dynastic imperialism of the Hapsburgs, whose hegemony over lands as widely separated as Spain and Bohemia dominated the map of Europe and the diplomacy of its states. The sprawling "empire" of Charles V was, in its striving for a larger unity and in the pluralism that defeated this effort, a massive microcosm of the political life of Europe.

When Erasmus deplored "avarice" and "tyranny" as the salient qualities of a "marvelous corrupt world," he was taking a common view of the forces that seemed to dominate the environment of his age. Yet awareness of the growing gap between the ideal and the reality, nowhere wider than in the spheres of economic and political activity, was a powerful stimulus to the persistent endeavor to achieve a better society, to improve everything from the individual to the world. Even Machiavelli, after looking long at man as he was, and perceiving the shape of his political future with depressing clarity, turned in the *Discourses* to thoughts of what he might be.

In Castiglione's courtier, who was not only the soldier skilled in arms but poet and philosopher, artist and musician, the new ideal of the perfectly cultivated man, which emerged from the life of the Italian cities and their courts, reached its peak of refinement. In less exalted and more attainable form, as in the practical precepts of the amusing *Galateo*, it was to be the basis of the modern conception of the gentleman. The eager search for social perfection was expressed also in larger programs designed to implement the dream of a golden age by the attainment of more limited goals within the framework of existing institutions. Such at-

tempts to cure the major ills of society are represented
by Vives' wise proposals for the relief of the poor, by
Thomas Starkey's prescriptions for the reform of Henry
VIII's England, and by the significant efforts of the
Spaniard Vitoria to provide a foundation in international
law for the peace that so many idealists passionately
desired. The belief of Guillaume Postel—who, with
many of his contemporaries, was deeply impressed by
Moslem culture and its tolerance—that the concord of
the world might be achieved by the mutual knowledge
and understanding of its peoples may seem to disillu-
sioned moderns either touching or absurd. But his is
simply a transcendent expression of the faith in education, in the application of learning to life, on which all
the social aspirations of the age were founded.

v

Although this confidence in the powers of education
was widely shared, what is the "best sort of learning"—
a problem that still concerns a great many people—was
a hotly debated question. In the universities of Europe
the old disciplines of theology and law, medicine and
natural philosophy, were still vigorous, and their dev-
otees might claim that, among their advantages, they
trained men for useful and often lucrative careers. But
these studies and their methods seemed arid and old-
fashioned to scholars who rediscovered, in the still older
tradition of literary humanism, in the languages and
literature of the great urban culture of antiquity, the
"disciples worthy of free men." The study of "good
letters" became the basis of a new ideal of education,
developed in the schools of humanist teachers like
Vittorino da Feltre and in innumerable treatises, stress-
ing that familiar goal of educators, the well-rounded

personality, harmoniously cultivated in body, mind, and soul. To be "well-polished in the workshop of Minerva," was ultimately, in Rabelais' lively statement of the ideal, to be the paragon of learning that Gargantua hoped to make of Pantagruel.

In their enthusiasm for a culture that seemed to them vitally significant for their own society, nostalgic spirits labored to restore the "vast ruins and broken buildings" of antiquity and, by more critical studies, the texts of its literature, while their patrons built libraries and museums to house the remains of the ancient world. The nets with which these zealous fishermen dragged the sea of the past brought up, with many of its riches, some strange fish, like the mystical doctrines of the Jewish cabala, which appealed so strongly to Pico della Mirandola and his disciple Johann Reuchlin. At its worst the "New Learning" added one form of pedantry to another, replacing an overrefined logic with an overelaborate rhetoric. But at its best the humanism of this age meant a return to the founts of ancient wisdom and beauty, both classical and Christian, which powerfully refreshed the currents of contemporary life and thought.

The "lost world" of Greek literature, whose recovery was the most exciting intellectual adventure of fifteenth-century Italy, became a source of inspiration in many fields. A renewed interest in the thought of Plato and his followers encouraged artists and writers of many lands to take flight on the wings of Platonic mysticism and it spurred on those thinkers who, hoping to reconcile "Plato and Moses, Socrates and Christ," looked for the one truth underlying all the diversity of religions and philosophies. To the efforts of this age to create a new synthesis of classical learning and Christian faith, to the scholarship that shaped the social and religious ideals of the Christian humanists, perhaps the greatest monument is Erasmus's edition of the Greek New Testament, which he hoped that all men might read and understand.

No one did more than this ruler of the republic of letters, this scholarly journalist whose works have been called a retail shop of classical knowledge, to spread the "heavenly manna of fine learning." And his friend, Aldus Manutius, who wittily describes a publisher's aims and vexations, is a distinguished representative of the scholar-printers who also worked zealously at the task of popularization, the humanists' most enduring contribution. Aldus himself invented the inexpensive pocket-size, or portable, book, which made good editions of the classics available to the growing public of his day.

A larger knowledge of ancient writings, a sharper perception of their formal beauty, and an emphasis on style and elegance helped to shape a new aesthetic ideal that attained its fullest expression in the venacular literatures. In Italy the "fervor of poesy," which had inspired Petrarca and Boccaccio, though dampened in their scholarly successors, surged up again when Poliziano, Lorenzo de' Medici, and others turned once more to the language of the people and earlier themes. Their "singing of songs to the Orphic lyre" resounded with greater depth and vigor in other lands, in France and Spain and England, where the sonnets of Petrarca and the lyrics of later Italian poets were models often as closely followed as the odes and elegies of the ancients.

The lyre and the theater are appropriate symbols for what was, despite its more popular aspects, in many ways the culture of an aristocracy at play. Its creators often played in art and literature, and sometimes in life, an elaborate game of make-believe, donning the

togas of antiquity, or the rustic garb of shepherds and
shepherdesses, or, mock-heroically, the knightly armor of
the feudal past. For they loved to poke fun at medieval
traditions and themes, which were still vital under newer
forms. Though the true centers of this culture were rich
and bustling cities, it flourished to perfection in villas
and gardens and courts, where the joys of life were enhanced by the making of music for pleasure, the singing
of madrigals to the lute and the viol, and by the splendid
pageants and spectacles which delighted the age.

The spirit that lives most brilliantly in the paintings
of a Mantegna or a Ghirlandaio is distilled also in
Poliziano's *Orfeo*, the first secular drama in Italian,
celebrating the beloved myth of Orpheus, who civilized
the world through poetry and song. In its union of the
lyric, the drama, and music in a pastoral setting, this
charming minor work embodies or prefigures many of
the qualities which were to characterize the later literature of the Renaissance; it contains the promise fulfilled
in the achievements of Elizabethan England and Spain's
"golden century." A reminder that the drama of life had
many settings, and other modes of expression, is the
picaresque tale of the engaging young rascal Lazarillo
de Tormes, and his adventures in the world of beggars
and blind men, foreshadowing in irony and realism such
magnificent descendants as Don Quixote.

The greatest writers of this time were, in their different ways, most serious when they were most playful.
The ironic laughter of Ariosto, the boisterous guffaws of
Rabelais, the wit of Erasmus and More, were not only
an outlet for the conflicts and tensions of their society, but a weapon against the vices and follies of
a world that seemed to its more sensitive spirits a

"theater stuffed and crammed with swarms of fools."
Perhaps the nearest approach to the golden age in
these centuries lay in the idyllic moments of serenity
and harmony when friends and kindred spirits, the
members of an intellectual elite, escaped briefly into
the better world that many of them hoped to mold.
Indeed the culture of the Renaissance appears sometimes as a constellation of the "bright, elect lights"
who revolved around one another in circles and groups,
endlessly writing, painting, building, and, above all,
talking. Even when they wrote, these lovers of eloquence and oratory often continued the conversation
in their favorite literary forms, the dialogue and the
letter. Although their discussions ranged over many
subjects, their central theme was man, his nature, his
life in society, his soul and its relation to God.

Studying this "most fortunate creature" in the light of
both ancient and contemporary models, a cloud of
witnesses testified to his "excellent dignity." Made in
God's image, "the temporary dwelling-place and instrument of the immortal soul," man was a little world, the
microcosm of the universe in which he was the vicar of
God. In Pico della Mirandola's praise of man's liberty
and universality, the exaltation of his capacity to make
and mold himself reaches a crescendo that St. Thomas
Aquinas would certainly have thought presumptuous.
But the great theologian would have affirmed with Ficino and Erasmus and many others a conception of man
and the primacy of his reason which represents centuries of the mingling of Christian and classical ideas.
If in the conflicts of the age this optimistic view was
contradicted by skeptics, and by those theologians to
whom man was "a withered fruit stinking in the nostrils

of the Lord," it was still the resource of the scholars and philosophers, poets and artists, who added luster to the "sparkle of divinity" in man.

For the study of man is more brightly illumined by the lives and works of many men and women of these centuries than by their ideas, which were rarely original. In the self-portrait of Leon Battista Alberti, humanist, artist, and citizen, whose proficiency in all skills, from ball-playing to church-building, demonstrated his conviction that "men can do anything with themselves if they will," the unique qualities of a personality are as sharply drawn as the features of the portrait-medals of his time. The versatility of the individual is displayed with special clarity also in the lives of two men who appeared to their contemporaries, and to posterity, to have added new dimensions to the measure of human dignity. Thomas More, that "Christian English Cicero," the man of affairs and servant of the commonwealth, clever scholar, social reformer, and saint, was, in all, perhaps, ¹ ut his martyrdom, the humanists' ideal fulfilled. And Michelangelo, who "loved not only human beauty, but universally every beautiful thing," manifested in its noblest forms the artist's struggle for perfection.

But the many-sidedness of man, and of the age, is revealed in a number of other selections, both biographical and autobiographical. Few individuals have ever left so unreserved a record of themselves, so rich a quarry for the study of human nature, as St. Teresa of Avila, whose cyclonic energy was expended not only in the mystic's quest for God and in the practical work of religious reform, but in the incessant writing that set forth her every act and thought. The self-scrutiny of Montaigne is more familiar than the masterly self-dissection of his no less fascinating contemporary, the physician Girolamo Cardano, man of science and magic, gambler and mathematician, who portrayed himself "warts and all," even to his favorite dishes and the size of his feet; his autobiography is an almost perfect mirror of "man considering himself, the great prodigy of nature."

VI

The "Book of Nature," no less than the books of men, inspired the "illustrious discoveries" which demonstrated the powers of man and enhanced his dignity. For the rivalry, and the mingling, of various traditions, which reinvigorated learning and literature, philosophy and theology, were nowhere more fruitful than in the study of nature. The old framework of the arts and sciences, and the old divisions between theoretical and practical arts, were dissolving, and the new lines which were to separate them had not yet been sharply drawn. Theology was losing her hold as queen of the sciences, and architecture hers as mistress of the arts. But the arts and sciences, whose common source was nature, could now be regarded as communicating rooms in a house of universal wisdom. In this house magic—to many "the most secret of the arts and the highest wisdom," and still, as it had been for centuries, the close comrade of experimental science—had by no means the least important place. Through every means, artists and astronomers, physicians and philosophers, alchemists and astrologers, seeking to read nature's secrets and to extend their domination over her, carried on the long explorations which were eventually to revolutionize the traditional conceptions of the universe and man. From the interpenetration of the arts and sciences, the closer union of theory and practice, which characterized this period, were to come some of its most significant innovations in both art and science.

In style, and often in spirit, art and architecture showed the pervasive influence of their classical models. But artists also believed that "art stands firmly fixed in nature, and that he alone possesses her who can rend her thence." It was with the aid of the sciences which made possible the new art of focused perspective and its faithful reproduction of nature, that painting became the universal art of this age, the "mistress of all works and arts and sciences." Only painting could embrace man and nature in the unity most fully achieved in the great landscapes of Brueghel, which inspired Van Mauder's poetic treatise. Not content simply to fill their world with beauty, painters, sculptors, and architects also undertook, from the early fifteenth century, to analyze the arts and to define their laws, to make them sciences and fit companions of the old liberal arts. The outcome was not only a new theory of art, which Alberti was the first to elaborate, but the exaltation of the artists and the arts. For as the visual arts advanced from the status of crafts to that of fine arts, artists, once ranked with manual workers, became members of the intellectual aristocracy, and were to be raised higher still by those who considered the great artist, like Michelangelo, a "divine genius."

While the arts were growing more theoretical, the sciences, often drawing on the techniques of arts and crafts and on magic, grew more empirical. This frequently obscure process, which had been going on for centuries, took many forms. Through the observation of nature, an artisan like Palissy the potter, who learned about the earth and its products while grubbing for his clays, and a barber-surgeon like Paré, who gained his knowledge of the treatment of wounds on the battle-field, contributed to the discoveries and the technical improvements which were gradually to fertilize the scholarly traditions of science. Paracelsus, charlatan and genius, was a fantastic representative of the numerous intellectual vagabonds who wander through these centuries; wishing, like Leonardo da Vinci, to work miracles, he thought to renovate man through the arts, chiefly magical, of which he was the "monarch of the age." But he also applied his knowledge of alchemy to medicine, in the preparation of chemical substances for use as drugs. And in his belief that physicians should treat the whole man, "inner and outer," as well as in Fracastoro's recognition of the intimate relation between the health of mind and body, there is more than a glimpse of the "psychosomatic" approach of our own day.

The mingling of arts and science is perhaps most familiar in the work of Leonardo, whose prodigious versatility as artist and theorist, inventor and engineer, seems to epitomize the creative forces of his time. This "magician of the Renaissance" was not a scientist, though his notebooks are a wonderful, if disorderly, storehouse of the more important ideas of late medieval science and of his own brilliant insights into the "anatomy of nature." His recently discovered letter to the Sultan, offering to build a bridge over the Golden Horn—which displays incidentally his customary willingness to work for the highest bidder—is symbolic also of his significant role as a builder of bridges between the various arts, the several traditions of knowledge. When, for example, he discussed anatomy, a study as fundamental to the arts of painting and sculpture as to medicine, Leonardo stressed among the gifts necessary to an anatomist, besides a strong stomach, the mastery of perspective drawing, by which observations might be recorded in accurate and permanent form. The crucial importance of illustration for the descriptive sciences was demonstrated also by Vesalius, when he joined to his famous treatise on the structure of the human body the meticulous drawing which laid before the reader's eyes a dissected corpse.

As the work of Vesalius suggests, science is not simply the appeal to nature and experience, not flashes of insight, but an "organized and cumulative body of knowledge." The main currents of this science, despised by most humanists, had been developing for centuries in such universities as Paris and Oxford and Padua, which was in this age the "most famous gymnasium of the whole world," where Fracastoro and Vesalius, Cardano and Galileo, studied and taught. It was in these centers that the efforts of many scholars, in physics and astronomy and mathematics, were slowly to rend asunder the old closed and finite cosmos of Aristotle and Ptolemy, a universe of concentric spheres revolving around a motionless earth, and to reveal finally a universe of infinite space and dynamic motion.

By the late fourteenth century, when Nicole Oresme, the inventor of analytic geometry, played "for fun," as he said, with the idea of the earth's daily rotation, physical science was in many ways as far advanced as it was when Copernicus, in the sixteenth century, was moved to reverse the positions of sun and earth and to assert that the earth not only rotates on its axis but also revolves around the sun. But neither earlier scientists, like Oresme and Nicholas of Cusa, who were playing also with ideas of relativity, nor Copernicus himself, who was still imprisoned in a fantasia of circles and spheres, realized the riches that lay within their grasp. To explore the universe Copernicus had glimpsed, to solve the massive problem of how and why it moved, was the work of more than a century.

Few records reveal the spirit and adventures of a great sixteenth-century man of science as intimately and honestly as the letters of Johann Kepler, the brilliant mathematician and astronomer, who, though he often earned his living casting horoscopes and still listened for the music of the spheres, was finally to discover the laws of planetary motion. His arduous pursuit of truth through speculation and observation, through astronomy and astrology, mathematics and mysticism, his struggle to find proof for the Copernican theory, sums up one long phase of the movement which was, more than any other in these centuries, to determine the outlook of the modern world. Galileo, looking through his newly invented telescope, opened a new stage in the investigation of the universe, whose dynamic motion he demonstrated, a stage which was to end with Newton's vast cosmological machine operating by uniform physical laws. But Copernicus and Kepler, like the painters and Platonists, were seeking, above all, the beauty and order, the "wonderful symmetry and harmony," of nature. In the fifteenth and sixteenth centuries the universe was still a work of art, in which men looked for the reflection of its Sublime Artisan, its Great Architect.

VII

Where the "ways and directions are many," we have followed in this introduction some of the broader paths leading into the life of these centuries, and especially the paths opened by those contemporary themes and symbols which are among the most effective keys to the character of a culture. Of all the "magic words" of this age, there are few that occur more frequently in its writings, and there is none that bears a heavier freight of meaning, than the word "Christendom." In its various forms—in phrases like "the common corps of Christendom," the "Christian commonwealth," and Erasmus's "concord of Christendom"—it represented most comprehensively the ideal of unity and order, which was still the great goal of Western culture. This ideal, always unachieved, became more elusive than ever, though no less potent in its appeal, in a time when medieval "Christendom" was slowly turning into modern "Europe," when in every sphere the old strings of order and degree were untuned.

But "Christendom" also corresponded with a reality, both physical and spiritual, which was no less real because it was undergoing vast changes. For in this word was embodied all that had for more than a millennium made men of the West, in spite of their diversity and divisions, "members of one body"; it stood for a common culture founded on the memories and traditions of Rome and Greece, and for the common Christian faith which was the encompassing bond of a unity essentially religious. The strength of the ideal of "Christendom," and of its reality, help to explain the urgency of those religious quests which can with justice be described as the "last great upsurge of medieval religion," yet in whose outcome can also be observed the triumph of the newer forces of the time, the victory of the sovereign state and of the urban middle classes. The prolonged religious crisis of these centuries reveals most clearly a society rent by conflicts, a society in which the pursuit of earthly perfection in all its varied forms grew more ardent and exuberant as the claims of this world became more insistent, yet a society whose transcendent goal was still the Kingdom of God.

In selections ranging from the vivid picture of Jerome of Prague's defiance of the Council of Constance and his heroic death to the mystical poetry of St. John of the Cross, our aim has been to illustrate not the course of the religious movements and upheavals of this time, but some aspects of their character and spirit. We have attempted to suggest both their fundamental divergences and those common needs and ideals of Christians which, in a divided Christendom, have been less often stressed than their differences; above all, we have tried to convey a sense of the depth and variety, and the complexity, of a religious experience which is not adequately encompassed by the conventional categories of "Reformation" and "Counter-Reformation."

Nicholas of Cusa eloquently describes the order and bonds of unity of the Church, which had for centuries offered men, in the sacraments administered by a priestly hierarchy, the means of salvation. But Pope Pius II's frank account of his own election, in circumstances more appropriate to a modern political campaign than to the highest office in Christendom, sums up most graphically the corruption and anarchy of a Church gravely compromised by its life in the plains. The spiritual mission of this enormous institution, involved in every sphere of society, had long been threatened by the changes which fostered the more aggressive pursuit of wealth and power. Its authority was challenged in the fifteenth century, as it had been earlier, by the growing strength of secular states and worldly interests, by discontent in all ranks of society, and by the assaults of those who were led by religious zeal to reject its doctrines—by all the forces which were in the next century to be catalyzed by Luther's revolt.

Yet this same Pope Pius, the acute observer of a divided society faced by a powerful external enemy, was also a devoted exponent of the traditional ideals of unity and reform, which he tried to strengthen not only by the old means of the council and the crusade, but by the more novel device of the international meeting. The spiritual vitality manifested in the efforts of such reforming churchmen was apparent also in the appeal of Savonarola's harsh asceticism and of various pietistic movements such as the Brethren of the Common Life, who united a simpler and more direct devotion with the study of the Bible and the classics. It found still broader expression in the work of the Christian humanists who, putting the "New Learning" in the service of religion, endeavored to purify the Church without destroying its unity, to restore an uncorrupted Christianity, to "teach Christ in simplicity." If their ideals were not realized, their influence on the diverse religious movements of the sixteenth century, from Catholic reform to the groups representing the "left wing" of Protestantism, can hardly be overestimated.

By their criticism of the contemporary Church, by their appeal to the Bible and to early Christianity, the humanists stimulated the religious strivings of those for whom the reason and learning of an intellectual aristocracy were not enough, of the reformers who were to lead a revolution in which the tensions formerly confined within a single Church erupted in the conflicts of churches and sects. Against the authority of a visible Church these reformers, who considered themselves not innovators but the restorers of true Christianity, asserted the superiority of inward conviction and the authority of the Scriptures "rightly interpreted." Yet the influence of the old ideals was still powerful, and Christians were still seeking a church to house the "congregation of the faithful." Though the visible shape of the new churches was largely determined by the political and territorial divisions of Europe, Protestants found a larger unity in the ideal of a spiritual aristocracy, "God's peculiar people," who were members of the "Church invisible," embracing, as John Knox says, "the elect of all the ages."

For at its heart the revolution was religious, and its strength was derived not only from Luther's "uncontrollable nature" but from many similar natures seeking the certainty of salvation. That the crux of the struggle was man's immortal soul is evident in the debate between Erasmus and Luther on the question of the freedom of man's will. This problem—laying bare the gulf that separated the humanists from the more radical reformers, and demonstrating the truth of Luther's statement that he attacked "not the life but the doctrine" of the Church, not its abuses but its very foundations— brings into focus the many issues that "convulsed the Christian world" in the sixteenth century. In this question of man's spiritual freedom—which in other forms continues to this day to be a most vital one—were crystallized the eternal problems of good and evil, liberty and bondage, the relation of man to God.

Erasmus, the great spokesman of the ideals of humanism and the dignity of man, here defends the view of free will essential to the conception of a sacramental Church. Luther, who proclaimed the liberty of the Christian from servitude to "works," here upholds a conception of God and man wrested from the depths of his own spiritual agony, but also firmly established in Christian theology. His is an all-powerful God confronting sinful and powerless man, for whom the way to salvation is through "faith alone," the faith which only God can grant and which He grants only to some. Luther thus champions those doctrines of predestination and election which Calvin, seeing man still more darkly, was to carry to their extremes, reasoning himself so logically into the chains of predestination that half of Europe was constrained to follow him. As Luther's justification by faith supplied an answer to the problem of salvation outside the sacraments and priesthood of the Church, so in Calvinism the doctrine of predestination eliminated concern over this problem. To the followers of Calvin, as to the disciples of Karl Marx, determinism was not a counsel of despair but a creed for action, an inspiration to the efforts of the elect to establish the Kingdom of God on earth.

What is still most vital in the religious experience of this age is the outcome of that renewal of Christian piety which was, amid all the struggles that ruptured the unity of Christendom, an indisputable achievement. As to the nature of "true Christian piety," St. Teresa would have disagreed most heartily with "those Lutherans" whom she deplored; the impulse to serve God and to show forth His praises was expressed more diversely than ever in a time when the role of the layman in religion was exalted and the "priesthood of all believers" emphasized. But a resurgent piety produced the many great expressions of the religious spirit which still speak to the modern mind and heart, not only with the power of Luther or Loyola, but with the eloquence of those who held to the vision of Erasmus. Their circles, representing most broadly the Christianity of their time, included such "fervent spirits" as Juan de Valdés and Vergerio and Marguerite of Navarre, Cardinal Pole and Vittoria Colonna and Michelangelo, who cared little for dogma "whether cold from Rome or hot from Wittenberg or Geneva," who wanted to be neither Lutherans nor Calvinists nor Zwinglians but simply Christians.

In the experience of the Christian humanists, the dilemmas of this age, and its achievements and failures, appear perhaps most poignantly. Pursuing in the larger spheres of society and the Church the dream of perfection most fully attained in art and literature, they made the last great attempt, not to renew severally the classical and the Christian pasts, but to reconcile these two ancient traditions that lie at the roots of our culture. In the ideals of those who stood between "the priests of the old and the prophets of the new," who hoped by making better men to make a better world, the secular and religious aspirations of these centuries, often in conflict, are most completely harmonized. In their works, and in the diverse records of their time, the reader may look freshly at this age in which many sought, and a few found, an "age of gold," may participate most directly in this crucial phase of the great debate which is Western culture.

For counsel in our search for materials for this Reader, and in preparing our translations, we are indebted to many friends and fellow explorers of these centuries. Our thanks are due once more to Professor Henry F. Schwarz of Wellesley College for contributing his translation of letters of the Emperor Maximilian, and to Smith College, especially to Professors Leona C. Gabel and Florence A. Gragg, for their generous permission to use selections from their translation of *The Commentaries of Pope Pius*

II, in the *Smith College Studies in History.* We owe again a special debt of gratitude to the staff of the Vassar College Library, whose friendly interest and assistance have greatly lightened our labors. We are grateful, finally, to Clarice L. Pennock for her help with problems of translation, and to all those who assumed the burden of typing our manuscript, especially to Angela Bachman Riedel, who typed the greater part of it.

Suggestions for Further Reading
(Revised, 1967)

In bringing up to date these suggestions for reading, we have tried, within the limits of a highly selective list, to take account as fully as possible of the large number of significant works published or made more widely available in inexpensive editions since the *Renaissance Reader* first appeared in 1953. Although both their number and their importance justify our emphasis on recent studies, some still essential older works are also included. Our revised selection, like our earlier list, has been drawn largely from books written in or translated into English; wherever possible, the best paperback edition of both older and newer items has been chosen and is identified within parentheses. In general, individual sources, works of purely national scope, and textbooks have been omitted. Owing to exigencies of space, the bibliographic form has been abbreviated.

An indispensable guide to the interpretation of the Renaissance throughout five centuries is W. K. Ferguson's *The Renaissance in Historical Thought* (Boston, 1948) and its accompanying bibliography. The rock on which all the waves of controversy have broken since 1860 is the classic work of the Swiss historian Jacob Burckhardt, *The Civilization of the Renaissance in Italy* (available in the illustrated Phaidon edition, New York, 1950), whose ideas were amplified and popularized by J. A. Symonds in *The Renaissance in Italy* (first published from 1875 to 1886 and now a Random House Modern Library Giant, 2 vols.).

As works of reference the first two volumes of the *New Cambridge Modern History* are valuable, though they have not entirely supplanted the same volumes in the original *Cambridge Modern History*. Also useful are certain chapters in the first three volumes of the *Cambridge Economic History*. Several volumes in French series of collaborative scholarship now appearing are among the most original works of synthesis dealing with this period: the outstanding series are the "Destins du Monde," the "Collection historique," edited by P. Lemerle, and the "Nouvelle Clio," edited by R. Boutruche and P. Lemerle. In collections of sources, a large number of relevant texts are available: a few in the "Records of Civilization," published by the Columbia University Press, many in the "Library of Christian Classics," and many, especially in literature, in the Penguin Classics and Everyman Library. Included in the Viking Portable Library, along with *The Medieval Reader* and *The Elizabethan Reader,* are volumes devoted to Cervantes, Rabelais, and Shakespeare.

I. WORKS OF BROAD SCOPE

Ady, C. M. *Lorenzo dei Medici and Renaissance Italy.* (Macmillan: Collier Books).

Cheyney, E. P. *The Dawn of a New Era, 1250-1453.* (Harper Torchbooks).

Ferguson, W. K. *et al. Facets of the Renaissance.* (Harper Torchbooks).

———. *The Renaissance: Six Essays.* (Harper Torchbooks).

Gilmore, M. P. *The World of Humanism, 1453-1517.* (Harper Torchbooks).

Hale, J. R. *et al. Europe in the Late Middle Ages.* London, 1965.

Hay, Denys. *The Italian Renaissance in Its Historical Background.* (Cambridge University Press).

———. *Europe: The Emergence of an Idea.* (Harper Torchbooks).

Helton, Tinsley, ed. *The Renaissance: A Reconsideration of the Theories and Interpretations of the Age.* (University of Wisconsin).

Huizinga, Johan. *The Waning of the Middle Ages.* (Doubleday Anchor).

Jacob, E. F., ed. *Italian Renaissance Studies.* London, 1960.

Mattingly, Garrett, *et al. Renaissance Profiles.* Ed. J. H. Plumb. (Harper Torchbooks).

Plumb, J. H. *The Italian Renaissance: A Concise Survey of Its History and Culture.* (Harper Torchbooks).

Schevill, Ferdinand. *Medieval and Renaissance Florence.* (Harper Torchbooks, 2 vols.).

———. *The Medici.* (Harper Torchbooks).

Vaughn, Dorothy. *Europe and the Turks: A Pattern of Alliances, 1350-1700.* Liverpool, 1966.

II. SOCIETY AND POLITICS

Bennett, H. S. *Six Medieval Men and Women.* (Atheneum).

Brucker, G. A. *Florentine Politics and Society, 1343-1378.* Princeton, 1962.

Cipolla, C. M. *Money, Prices and Civilization in the Mediterranean World, X-XVII Century.* Princeton, 1956.

Chabod, Federico. *Machiavelli and the Renaissance.* (Harper Torchbooks).

Davies, R. T. *The Golden Century of Spain, 1501-1621.* (Harper Torchbooks).

Elliott, J. H. *Imperial Spain, 1469-1716.* (New American Library).

Elton, G. R. *The Tudor Revolution in Government.* Cambridge, England, 1960.

Gilbert, Felix. *Machiavelli and Guicciardini: Politics and History in Sixteenth-Century Florence.* Princeton, 1965.

Hale, J. R. *Machiavelli and Renaissance Italy.* (Macmillan: Collier Books).

Heers, Jacques. *L'Occident ou xiv° et xv° siècles.* Paris, 1963.

Lynch, John. *Spain under the Habsburgs.* Vol. I: *Empire and Absolutism.* New York, 1964.

von Martin, Alfred. *Sociology of the Renaissance.* (Harper Torchbooks).

Martines, Lauro. *The Social World of the Italian Humanists, 1390-1460.* Princeton, 1963.

Mattingly, Garrett. *Renaissance Diplomacy.* (Penguin).

Neale, J. E. *The Age of Catherine de Medici.* (Harper Torchbooks).

Origo, Iris. *The World of San Bernardino.* New York, 1962.

Pirenne, Henri. *Early Democracies in the Low Countries*. (Harper Torchbooks).

de Roover, Raymond. *The Rise and Decline of the Medici Bank*. (Norton).

Rubenstein, Nicolai. *The Government of Florence under the Medici, 1434-1494*. Oxford, 1966.

Vespasiano da Bisticci. *Renaissance Princes, Popes, and Prelates: Lives of Illustrious Men of the XVth Century*. (Harper Torchbooks).

III. LITERATURE, LEARNING, AND PHILOSOPHY

Adams, R. P. *The Better Part of Valor: More, Erasmus, Colet and Vives on Humanism, War and Peace, 1469-1535*. University of Washington, 1962.

Baker, Herschel. *The Image of Man: A Study of the Idea of Human Dignity in Classical Antiquity, the Middle Ages, and the Renaissance*. (Harper Torchbooks).

Baron, Hans. *The Crisis of the Early Italian Renaissance*. Princeton, 1966.

Bolgar, R. R. *The Classical Heritage and Its Beneficiaries*. (Harper Torchbooks).

Cassirer, Ernst, *et al.*, eds. *The Renaissance Philosophy of Man*. (University of Chicago Press: Phoenix).

Cassirer, Ernst. *The Individual and the Cosmos in Renaissance Philosophy*. (Harper Torchbooks).

Chambers, R. W. *Thomas More*. (University of Michigan Press: Ann Arbor Books).

Copleston, Frederick. *History of Philosophy*. Vol. III: *Late Mediaeval and Renaissance Philosophy*. (Doubleday Image Books).

Cunningham, J. V., ed. *The Renaissance in England*. (Harcourt: Harbinger).

Garin, Eugenio. *Italian Humanism: Philosophy and Civic Life in the Renaissance*, tr. Peter Munz. Oxford, 1966.

Geanokoplos, D. J. *Greek Scholars in Venice*. Cambridge, Mass., 1962.

Goldschmidt, E. P. *The Printed Book of the Renaissance*. Cambridge, England, 1950.

Green, O. H. *Spain and the Western Tradition: The Castilian Mind in Literature from El Cid to Calderon*. Madison, Wisconsin. Vols. I-II, 1963-1966.

Hexter, J. H. *More's Utopia: The Biography of an Idea*. (Harper Torchbooks).

Huizinga, Johan. *Erasmus and the Age of Reformation.* (Harper Torchbooks).

Kristeller, P. O. *Renaissance Thought: The Classic, Scholastic, and Humanist Strains.* (Harper Torchbooks).

———. *Renaissance Thought II: Papers on Humanism and the Arts.* (Harper Torchbooks).

———. *Eight Philosophers of the Renaissance.* Stanford, 1964.

Klibansky, R., and H. J. Paton, eds. *Philosophy and History.* (Harper Torchbooks).

Lind, L. R. *Lyric Poetry of the Italian Renaissance: An Anthology of Verse Translations.* (Yale University Press).

Miles, Leland. *John Colet and the Platonic Tradition.* (Open Court).

Phillips, M. M. *Erasmus and the Northern Renaissance.* (Macmillan: Collier Books).

Popkin, R. H. *The Philosophy of the Sixteenth and Seventeenth Centuries.* (Macmillan: Free Press).

Spitz, W. *The Religious Renaissance of the German Humanists.* Cambridge, Mass., 1963.

Weiss, Roberto. *The Spread of Italian Humanism.* London, 1964.

IV. SCIENCE

Boas, Marie. *The Scientific Renaissance, 1450-1630.* (Harper Torchbooks).

Butterfield, Herbert. *The Origins of Modern Science, 1300-1800.* (Macmillan: Free Press).

Crombie, A. C. *Medieval and Early Modern Science.* (Doubleday Anchor, 2 vols.).

Hall, A. R. *The Scientific Revolution, 1500-1800.* (Beacon).

Koyré, Alexander. *From the Closed World to the Infinite Universe.* (Harper Torchbooks) .

Kuhn, T. S. *The Copernican Revolution.* (Random House-Vintage).

Sarton, George. *Six Wings: Men of Science in the Renaissance.* (World: Meridian Books).

Thorndike, Lynn. *A History of Magic and Experimental Science,* 8 vols., New York, 1923-1958 (especially Vols. IV-VI).

V. THE ARTS

Benesch, Otto. *The Art of the Renaissance in Northern Europe.* Cambridge, 1945.

Berenson, Bernard. *The Italian Painters of the Renaissance.* (World: Meridian Books).

Blunt, Anthony. *Artistic Theory in Italy 1450-1600.* (Oxford University Press).

Bukofzer, M. F. *Studies in Medieval and Renaissance Music.* (Norton).

Chastel, André, and R. Klein. *The Age of Humanism, 1480-1530.* New York, 1964.

———. *The Studies and Styles of the Renaissance: Italy, 1460-1500,* tr. J. Griffin. London, 1966.

Clark, Kenneth. *Leonardo da Vinci.* (Penguin).

Freedberg, Sidney. *Painting of the High Renaissance in Rome and Florence.* 2 vols. Cambridge, Mass., 1961.

Holt, E. G., ed. *Literary Sources of Art History.* (Doubleday Anchor, 2 vols.).

Klein, Robert, and Henri Zerner. *Italian Art, 1500-1600: Sources and Documents.* (Prentice-Hall).

Lowry, Bates. *Renaissance Architecture.* (Braziller).

Meiss, Millard. *Painting in Florence and Siena after the Black Death.* (Harper Torchbooks).

Michelangelo Buonarroti. *The Complete Works of Michelangelo,* foreword by Mario Salmi. New York, 1965.

Murray, Peter and Linda. *The Art of the Renaissance.* (Praeger).

Panofsky, Erwin. *Studies in Iconology: Humanistic Themes in the Art of the Renaissance.* (Harper Torchbooks).

———. *Albrecht Dürer.* 2 vols. Princeton, 1943.

Pelican History of Music. Vol. II: *Renaissance and Baroque.*

Pevsner, Nikolaus. *Outline of European Architecture.* (Penguin).

Pope-Hennessy, John. *Italian High Renaissance and Baroque Sculpture.* 3 vols. Phaidon Press, 1963.

Seznec, Jean. *Survival of the Pagan Gods: The Mythological Tradition and Its Place in Renaissance Humanism and Art.* (Harper Torchbooks).

Stechow, Wolfgang. *Northern Renaissance Art: Sources and Documents.* (Prentice-Hall).

Strunk, W. O., ed. *Source Readings in Music History.* New York, 1950.

Vasari's Lives of the Artists, ed. B. Burroughs. (Simon and Schuster).

Wölfflin, Heinrich. *The Art of the Italian Renaissance.* (Schocken Books).

VI. RELIGION: PIETY AND REFORM

Bainton, R. H. *The Reformation of the 16th Century.* (Beacon).

Chadwick, Owen. *The Reformation.* Pelican History of the Church, Vol. 3.

Cohn, Norman. *The Pursuit of the Millennium.* (Harper Torchbooks).

Desiderius Erasmus: Christian Humanism and the Reformation, Selected Writings, ed. J. C. Olin. (Harper Torchbooks).

Dickens, A. G. *Reformation and Society in Sixteenth Century Europe.* New York, 1966.

Elton, G. R. *Reformation Europe, 1517-1559.* (Harper Torchbooks).

Erikson, Eric. *Young Man Luther.* (Norton).

Fevre, Lucien. *Au Coeur religieux du 16° siècle.* Paris, 1957.

Harbison, E. H. *The Christian Scholar in the Age of the Reformation.* (Scribner).

Holborn, Hajo. *Ulrich von Hutten and the German Reformation.* (Harper Torchbooks).

Huizinga, Johan. *Erasmus and the Age of Reformation.* (Harper Torchbooks).

Hughes, Philip. *The Church in Crisis: A History of the General Councils.* (Doubleday Image Books).

Hurstfield, Joel, ed. *The Reformation Crisis.* (Harper Torchbooks).

Jedin, Herbert. *History of the Council of Trent.* 2 vols. Edinburgh, 1957-1961.

John Calvin and Jacopo Sadoleto, a Reformation Debate, ed. J. C. Olin. (Harper Torchbooks).

Jones, R. M. *Spiritual Reformers of the 16th and 17th Centuries.* (Beacon).

Lecler, J. *Toleration and the Reformation,* 2 vols. London, 1965.

Leith, J. H., ed. *Creeds of the Churches.* (Doubleday Anchor).

Mollat, G. *The Popes at Avignon, 1305-1378.* (Harper Torchbooks).

Peers, E. A. *The Mystics of Spain*. London, 1951.

Powicke, F. M. *The Reformation in England*. (Oxford University Press).

Rupp, Gordon. *Luther's Progress to the Diet of Worms*. (Harper Torchbooks).

Roth, Cecil. *The Jews in the Renaissance*. (Harper Torchbooks).

Samuelson, Kurt. *Religion and Economic Action: A Critique of Max Weber's The Protestant Ethic and the Spirit of Capitalism*. (Harper Torchbooks).

Troeltsch, Ernst. *The Social Teachings of the Christian Churches*. (Harper Torchbooks, 2 vols.).

Williams, George. *The Radical Reformation*. Philadelphia, 1962.

VII. TRAVEL AND DISCOVERY

Boxer, C. R. *Four Centuries of Portuguese Expansion, 1415-1825*. Chester Springs, Pa., 1961.

Newton, A. P., ed. *The Great Age of Discovery*. London, 1932.

Parry, J. H. *The Establishment of the European Hegemony, 1415-1715*. (Harper Torchbooks).

Penrose, Boies. *Travel and Discovery in the Renaissance, 1420-1620*. (Atheneum).

Rowse, A. L. *The Expansion of Elizabethan England*. (Harper Torchbooks).

SOURCES

Many valuable primary sources have never been translated into English or even re-edited in modern times; some of these are represented by selections in the present book. A few anthologies on special topics are mentioned above. Some important individual works now available in inexpensive editions are: Castiglione, *The Book of the Courtier;* Cellini, *Memoirs;* Erasmus, *Praise of Folly;* Leonardo da Vinci, *Notebooks;* Luther, *Three Treatises;* Machiavelli, *The Prince* and *The Discourses;* Montaigne, *Essays;* More, *Utopia.*

BIOGRAPHICAL LIST OF AUTHORS

Alberti, Leon Battista (1404-1472). Italian humanist, art theorist, architect, and moralist, whose most influential works were his treatises on painting, sculpture and architecture.

d'Anghiera, Pietro Martire (1459?-1526). Italian humanist, identified with the court of Spain, which he served as teacher, soldier, diplomat; notable as "the first historian of America" in *The Decades of the New World.*

Aretino, Pietro (1492-1556). Versatile Italian satirist and poet, who lived lavishly on the gifts of those who feared his tongue and pen.

Ariosto, Ludovico (1474-1533). Italian courtier, diplomat, and poet at the court of Ferrara, best known for his romantic epic, *Orlando Furioso.*

Bacon, Francis (1561-1626). English philosopher, essayist, historian, and statesman, who attained and lost the position of Lord Chancellor.

du Bellay, Joachim (1525?-1560). French lyric poet, member of the Pléiade, the group of seven who defended the new French poetry.

Bessarion, John, Cardinal (1403-1472). Greek Archbishop of Nicaea, delegate to the Council of Florence, who adhered to Rome; Platonist, collector and translator of Greek works, patron of Greek scholars in the West.

Boccaccio, Giovanni (1313-1375). Italian poet and creator of Italian prose in the *Decameron,* who turned to Latin scholarship under the influence of Petrarca and produced invaluable compendia for classical students.

Bodin, Jean (1530-1596). French lawyer, scholar, and political theorist, the first to understand the inflationary effects of American gold and silver on the European economy.

Bracciolini, Poggio (1380-1459). Italian papal secretary, chancellor of Florence, an indefatigable hunter and discoverer of classical manuscripts.

Brahe, Tycho (1546-1601). Danish astronomer, notable for his devotion to the improvement of astronomical instruments and for regular and systematic observation, e.g., of the new star of 1572.

Bruni, Leonardo (1370-1444). Italian humanist, papal secretary, chancellor of Florence, whose many works include translations from the Greek, notably Aristotle, and a history of Florence.

Buonarroti, Michelangelo (1475-1564). Italian painter, sculptor, architect, and poet, universal genius, whose greatest works were commissioned by the popes.

Busbecq, Ogier Ghiselin de (1522-1592). Flemish diplomat in the service of the Hapsburgs, representative of Ferdinand of Austria to the Turkish sultan, humanist and naturalist, known through his letters.

Calvin, John (1509-1564). French theologian, dominant influence in Geneva and over the "reformed" churches of Europe, whose *Institutes of the Christian Religion* was the first systematic exposition of Protestant doctrine.

Camões, Luis Vaz de (1524?-1580). Portuguese courtier and soldier of fortune, whose poem *The Lusiads* is the national epic of Portugal, celebrating its heroic exploits in the East.

Cardano, Girolamo (1501-1576). Italian mathematician, physician, astrologer, encyclopedic writer, who left a unique self-revelation in his autobiography.

della Casa, Giovanni (1503-1556). Italian bishop, distinguished as poet, diplomat, and orator, author of the influential courtesy book, *Galateo*.

Castiglione, Baldassare (1478-1529). Italian courtier, diplomat, and writer, who immortalized the court of Urbino in his famous *Book of the Courtier*.

Cavalli, Marino. Ambassador of the Venetian Republic, who gave a notable account (*relazione*) of his mission to the Emperor Charles V in 1551.

Cellini, Benvenuto (1500-1571). Florentine goldsmith, sculptor, and egotistical adventurer, famous for his frank autobiography.

Cervantes Saavedra, Miguel de (1547-1616). Spanish wandering soldier and minor official, novelist, poet, dramatist, who acquired fame and immortality with *Don Quixote*.

Condivi, Ascanio (1525?-1574). Italian minor artist, whose fame rests solely on his authoritative biography of Michelangelo, his friend and teacher.

Copernicus, Nicholas (1473-1543). Polish astronomer whose heliocentric hypothesis, gradually accepted, undermined the traditional (Ptolemaic) geocentric conception of the universe.

Dei, Benedetto (fl. c.1470). Florentine burgher and merchant, author of a defense of the commerce of Florence against Venice.

Deloney, Thomas (1543?-1600?). English silk-weaver, the most popular ballad-journalist of his day in London and one of the creators of the English novel in his success stories such as *Jack of Newberie*.

Dürer, Albrecht (1471-1528). German painter, humanist, and art theorist, who best epitomizes the "northern Renaissance," and whose use of popular graphic media, engravings and woodcuts, won him fame.

Eden, Richard (1521?-1576). English scholar and man of science, translator of contemporary works on exploration.

Erasmus of Rotterdam (1466?-1536). Dutch monk who left the cloister and acquired international fame and influence as classical and Biblical scholar, man of letters, and advocate of reform.

Ficino, Marsilio (1433-1499). Florentine Platonist, translator of Plato and neo-Platonic writers, central figure of the "Platonic Academy" under the patronage of the Medici.

Fracastoro, Girolamo (1478-1533). Italian physician and poet, whose medical and scientific poem *Syphilis* treated the origin and character of the "new disease."

Fugger, Jakob (1459-1525). Head of the famous South German family of merchants, bankers, and international financiers.

Galilei, Galileo (1564-1642). Paduan mathematician, physicist, astronomer, whose work in these fields was crucial in achieving the intellectual revolution leading to the acceptance of the Copernican theory.

Geismayr, Michael (d. 1528). Tyrolean noble, leader in the Peasants' War, bold and original revolutionary.

Guicciardini, Francesco (1483-1540). Florentine lawyer, diplomat, and historian, whose histories of Florence and Italy are a landmark in the development of critical history.

Guicciardini, Ludovico (1523-1589). Nephew of Francesco, Florentine diplomat and banker, acute observer of social and economic conditions in the Low Countries.

Harff, Arnold von (1471-1505). German nobleman, known chiefly for the vivid account of his pilgrimage to the Holy Land and travels in the Near East.

Harpsfield, Nicholas (1519-1575). English Catholic priest, theologian, and scholar, author of the first complete biography of Thomas More, written in the time of Queen Mary.

Jean de Montreuil (1350?-1418). French humanist, theologian, sent by King Charles VI to Italy on diplomatic missions, slain during the Hundred Years' War.

St. John of the Cross (1542-1591). Spanish Carmelite, monastic reformer, renowned mystic, who "challenges Luis de León for the title of Spain's greatest poet."

Kepler, Johannes (1571-1630). German mathematician and astronomer, who worked out the laws of planetary motion in harmony with the theory of Copernicus.

Kirchmair, Georg (d. 1554). Austrian chronicler, especially of the Peasants' War.

Knox, John (1505-1572). Scottish reformer and historian, militant Calvinist, opponent of Mary Queen of Scots.

Labé, Louise (1526-1566). French lyric poet of the circle of Lyons, famous for her military exploits, her learning, and her loves.

Latimer, Hugh (1485?-1555). Bishop of Worcester, famous preacher, one of the chief promoters of the Reformation in England, died at the stake under Queen Mary.

Lefèvre d'Étaples, Jacques (1455-1536?). French cleric, humanist, Biblical scholar, and advocate of ecclesiastical reform; protected by Marguerite of Navarre.

Leonardo da Vinci (1452-1519). Italian painter, student and observer of nature, engineer and inventor, whose notebooks reveal his universal genius.

Le Roy, Loys (1510?-1577). French humanist, scholar, notable as an acute judge of his contemporaries and as a pioneer historian of comparative culture.

Lipsius, Justus (1547-1606). Belgian humanist and neo-Stoic philosopher, editor of Tacitus and Seneca.

Luis de León (1528?-1591). Spanish Augustinian friar, theologian, and professor, distinguished writer of both prose and poetry, "greatest lyric poet in Castilian."

Luther, Martin (1483-1546). Augustinian friar who became the founder of Protestantism in Germany and one of the creators of modern German prose in his translation of the Bible.

Machiavelli, Niccoló (1469-1527). Florentine republican statesman, Italian patriot, historian, and political theorist, known primarily as the author of *The Prince* and *The Discourses.*

Mander, Karel van (1548-1606). Flemish minor painter, historian of Northern art in his *Painter's Book,* often called "the Northern Vasari."

Manutius, Aldus (1449-1515). Italian scholar-printer of Venice, friend and publisher of many scholars; his press was the first to issue the Greek authors.

Maximilian I (1459-1519). Holy Roman Emperor by elec-

tion, hereditary Hapsburg ruler, gifted but erratic statesman, writer, and patron.

Medici, Lorenzo de' (1449-1492). Florentine citizen-prince,
Italian statesman, enlightened patron, and gifted poet.

Monardes, Nicolas (1493-1588). Spanish physician, notable
for his description of the plants and medicines of the
West Indies, including tobacco.

Montaigne, Michel de (1533-1592). French official, moral
philosopher, skeptical self-scrutinizer, who in his *Essays*
created a new literary form.

Nicholas of Cusa (1401-1464). German cardinal and ecclesiastical statesman, one of the most profound thinkers of
the fifteenth century, theologian, philosopher, humanist,
mathematician.

Oresme, Nicole (1320?-1382). French bishop and counselor
to King Charles V, theologian and natural philosopher,
who wrote on economics, mathematics, and mechanics.

Palissy, Bernard (1510?-1590). French Huguenot artisan,
potter to the queen, empirical student of nature, early
scientific collector and lecturer.

Paracelsus (Theophrastus Bombastius) (1493-1541). Eccentric, wandering German physician, encyclopedic writer
on scientific and pseudo-scientific subjects, especially
medicine, alchemy, and astrology.

Paré, Ambroise (1510?-1590). French barber-surgeon whose
military experience led to important discoveries concerning the treatment of gunshot wounds, etc.

Petrarca, Francesco (1304-1374). Italian lyric poet in the
vernacular, who turned to Latin scholarship and became
"the most renowned scholar and moral philosopher of
his age."

Pico della Mirandola, Giovanni (1463-1494). Italian scholar
and philosopher, learned in Hebrew and Arabic, whose
goal was to reconcile all knowledge and religion.

Pius II, Pope (Aeneas Silvius Piccolomini) (1405-1464).
Italian cosmopolitan scholar and man of letters, diplomat,
ecclesiastical politician who became bishop, cardinal, and

pope; devoted to the task of unifying Christendom against the Turks.

Platina, Bartolommeo (1421-1481). Italian scholar and papal secretary, member of the Roman Academy, author of the valuable *Lives of the Popes.*

Pole, Reginald, Cardinal (1500-1558). Cousin of Henry VIII, English Catholic exile in Italy, member of reforming circles, cardinal and Archbishop of Canterbury under Queen Mary.

Poliziano, Angelo (1454-1494). Florentine humanist of the Medicean circle, teacher of Greek and Latin literature, whose poetry in both Latin and Italian attained a high level of excellence.

Pomponazzi, Pietro (1462-1525). Italian philosopher, influential teacher at Padua and Bologna, notable exponent of the Aristotelian tradition.

Postel, Guillaume (1510-1581). French scholar and linguist, orientalist, theologian and mystic, writer on many subjects, whose goal is best revealed in *The Concord of the World.*

Rabelais, François (1495?-1553?). French friar, monk, and priest, humanist of Erasmian temper, physician, romancer and humorist in *Gargantua and Pantagruel.*

Reuchlin, Johann (1455-1522). German lawyer, humanist, Hebraist, founder of the scientific study of Hebrew, involved in a famous controversy over the study of Jewish literature.

Rideman, Peter (1505-1556). German elder of the Hutterian Brotherhood, a branch of the Anabaptist movement in Moravia.

Ronsard, Pierre de (1524-1585). French courtier, humanist, and supreme lyric poet in the vernacular, leader of the Pléiade, exponents of the new poetry.

Savonarola, Girolamo (1452-1498). Italian friar and preacher of reform, prior of St. Mark's, Florence, 1491, and unofficial dictator of the city from 1494 to May 1498, when he was burned at the stake by a hostile signory.

Sidney, Sir Philip (1554-1586). English courtier, statesman, and soldier; notable lyric poet.

Skelton, John (1460?-1529). English cleric, tutor to Henry VIII, humanist, and perhaps the most notable poet between Chaucer and Spenser.

Starkey, Thomas (1499?-1538). English cleric, chaplain to Henry VIII, intermediary between the king and Reginald Pole; concerned with the reform of society in his *Dialogue*.

Suriano, Michele. Ambassador of the Venetian Republic, who delivered notable accounts of his missions to the courts of Spain (1559) and France (1561).

Tasso, Torquato (1544-1595). Italian courtier, master of poetry in many forms, known especially for the pastoral drama *Aminta*, and the epic *Jerusalem Delivered*.

St. Teresa of Avila (1515-1582). Spanish Carmelite nun, tireless founder of reformed convents and profound writer on the mystical life; friend of St. John of the Cross.

Thomas a Kempis (1380?-1471). German Augustinian canon, celebrated mystic, identified with the pietistic movement in the Low Countries, probable author of the *Imitation of Christ*.

Valdés, Alfonso de (1500?-1532). Spanish Erasmian humanist, Latin secretary to the Emperor Charles V, known for his *Dialogues* written in defense of Imperial policies.

Valdés, Juan de (1500?-1541; perhaps twin brother of Alfonso). Spanish Erasmian humanist and theologian, exile from the Inquisition in Naples, where he became center of a reforming religious circle.

Valla, Lorenzo (1406-1457). Italian humanist, papal secretary, philologist, whose critical scholarship applied to the Donation of Constantine and the Vulgate had far-reaching influence.

Vasari, Giorgio (1512-1574). Italian painter and architect, student of Michelangelo; the "first art historian" by virtue of his *Lives of the Excellent Painters, Sculptors and Architects*.

Vergerio, Pietro Paolo (1498-1563). Italian bishop, active

reforming spirit, who fled to northern Europe and died in exile; not identified with any sect.

Vesalius, Andreas (1514-1564). Belgian physician and anatomist, court physician to Charles V and Philip II, author of the epoch-making *De fabrica corporis humani* (1543).

Vitoria, Francisco de (1486?-1546). Spanish Dominican, theologian, and jurist, who in his lectures expounded the concept of an international community and principles of international law.

Vives, Juan Luis (1492-1540). Spanish humanist of practical temper, identified with the Low Countries and England, notable for works on education, psychology, social reform, and peace.

Watt, Joachim von (Vadianus) (1484-1551). Swiss humanist and poet, geographer, religious reformer, friend and patron of Paracelsus.

Wyatt, Sir Thomas (1503?-1542). English courtier and diplomat, distinguished as soldier, scholar, linguist, musician, and poet, who introduced the sonnet form into English literature.

Chronological Table, 1400–1600

Fifteenth Century

POLITICAL TRENDS	ECONOMIC, SOCIAL TRENDS	RELIGION	CULTURE
Continuation of 100 Years' War Battle of Agincourt, 1415 Treaty of Troyes, 1420 Jeanne d'Arc, 1429-31 End of Anglo-Burgundian alliance, 1435	Beginning of Portuguese expansion Capture of Ceuta, 1415 Cape Verde Islands, 1456 Henry the Navigator, d. 1460	Pietistic movement in Low Countries Brethren of Common Life Monastic reform	Humanism, especially in Italy Extension of knowledge of Latin antiquity: discovery of manuscripts, formation of libraries; translation, imitation, critical study; archaeology, philology, education
Consolidation of greater Italian states Venetian expansion on mainland, from 1405 Medici in Florence, from 1434 Aragonese in Naples, from 1435 Sforza in Milan, from 1450	Continuance of economic contraction Exploitation of mines in central Europe Increase of bullion Technological improvements Development of South German cities	Conciliar period Council of Pisa, 1409 Council of Constance, 1414-18: executions, John Hus, Jerome of Prague Council of Basel, 1431-49 Pragmatic sanction of Bourges, 1438 Council of Ferrara-Florence, 1438-1442 "Re-union" of churches Hussite Wars, 1420-33	Extension of knowledge of Greek antiquity: importation of manuscripts and scholars; translations; Platonic revival in Florence, Ficino Hebrew scholarship begun Pico della Mirandola

59

			Theology and science	*Vernacular literature*	*Art and architecture*
Fall of Constantinople to Turks, 1453 End of 100 Years' War, 1453 Creation of "balance of power" in Italy, 1454 Wars of Roses in England, from 1455	Invention of printing with movable types Gutenberg Bible, 1454 Decline of Hanseatic League Decline of Bruges, rise of Antwerp	Last Crusade, Varna, 1444 Recovery of papal authority Nicholas V, 1447-55 Pius II, 1458-64 Sixtus IV, 1471-84 Innocent VIII, 1484-92	Nicholas of Cusa Toscanelli Peuerbach Regiomontanus	Revival in Italy: Poliziano, Lorenzo de' Medici, Pulci, Boiardo	Late Gothic realism in north, Flemish-Burgundian school, the Van Eycks Study of nature and antiquity in Italy, preeminence of Florence: Brunelleschi, Donatello, Botticelli, Leonardo da Vinci, etc.
Dynastic consolidation Burgundy, height and fall (1477) Hapsburgs, marriage of Maximilian and Mary of Burgundy, 1477 France, acquisitions of Louis XI, 1461-1483 Spain, marriage of Ferdinand and Isabella, 1469; conquest of Granada, 1492 England, establishment of Tudors, 1485 Poland, defeat of Teutonic Knights, 1466 Muscovy, expansion under Ivan III, 1462-1505	*Changes in agrarian economy* Decay of manorial organization *Portuguese expansion* Diaz rounds Cape of Good Hope, 1488 Da Gama reaches India, 1498 *Spanish expansion* Voyages of Columbus, 1492-1504 Papal demarcation line, 1493	Establishment of Spanish Inquisition, 1478 Bull of Innocent VIII against witches, 1484 Death of Lorenzo de' Medici, 1492 Reforms of Savonarola in Florence, 1494-98 Expulsion of Jews from Spain, 1492			

Sixteenth Century

POLITICAL TRENDS	ECONOMIC, SOCIAL TRENDS	RELIGION	CULTURE
European expansion French invasion of Italy Italian wars, Hapsburg-Valois struggle for Italy to 1559	Building of empires overseas Portugal in East and Brazil Spain in New World	Reforming movements Spain, under royal direction Italy, new monastic orders France, reforming bishops	Christian humanists, especially in north Wide influence of Erasmus: Colet, More, Valdés, Lefèvre Biblical scholarship: corrected texts—Ximenes, Erasmus, etc.; translations into vernaculars
Extension of royal control over Church Francis I by Concordat of Bologna, 1516 Henry VIII by break with Rome, from 1534 North German and Scandinavian princes by establishment of Lutheran churches	Spread of syphilis in Europe Economic expansion "Commercial revolution" Growth of industrial capitalism Gradual inflation of prices	Renaissance papacy Alexander VI, 1492-1503 Julius II, 1503-13 Leo X, 1513-21 Clement VII, 1523-34 Lutheran revolt, from 1517 Diet of Worms, 1521 Confession of Augsburg, 1530	Classical scholarship: critical editions and translations—Scaliger, Lipsius Vernacular literature France: the Pléiade, Rabelais, Montaigne Italy: Castiglione, Ariosto, Tasso Spain: Garcilaso, Luis de León, Cervantes
Expansion of Hapsburg domain under Charles V, 1519-56 Sack of Rome, 1527 Election of Hapsburgs in Hungary and Bohemia, 1526	Depression of agrarian workers Peasants' War in Germany, 1524-25 Displacement from land; enclosures in England	Establishment of state churches Religious peace of Augsburg, 1555 Zwingli in Zurich, 1518-31	England: Spenser, Sidney, Shakespeare

Abdication of Charles V and division of Hapsburg domain, 1556

Treaty of Cateau-Cambrésis, 1559

Hapsburg hegemony of Philip II, 1556-98
Revolt of Netherlands, 1568-1609
Civil and religious wars in France, 1562-98

Consolidation of states
Elizabeth I of England, 1558-1603
Henry IV of France: Edict of Nantes, 1598
Emergence of Dutch Republic, 1581

Northern and Eastern Europe
Independence of Sweden: Gustavus Vasa, 1523-60
Ivan IV, Tsar of "all the Russias," 1547-84

Technological advances
Cannon and small arms
Cartography: Mercator's projection, 1569

Economic leadership of Atlantic states
Height of Antwerp
Gradual decline of Venice
Growth of economic nationalism

Witchcraft mania

Decline of Portuguese Empire under Spanish rule, 1580-1640

Gregorian reform of calendar, 1582

Calvin in Geneva, 1541-64
Growth of "reformed" churches, France, Low Countries, Scotland

Persecution of Anabaptists and independents

Program of Catholic Reform
Reforming papacy from Paul III, 1534-49
Society of Jesus, 1540
Roman Inquisition, 1542
Council of Trent, 1545-63
Reorganization of curia

Spanish mystics and reformers
St. Teresa

Music
Perfection of counterpoint and polyphony
Improved instruments

Art and architecture
Pre-eminence of Venice and Rome: Titian, Michelangelo, etc.
Holbein, Dürer, and Brueghel in the North

Science
Aristotelian tradition at Padua
Advances in astronomy, physics, and mathematics: Copernicus, Brahe, Kepler, Galileo
Advances in biological sciences: anatomy—Vesalius; botany and zoology—Fuchs, Gesner, Rondelet; medicine and surgery—Fracastoro, Cardano, Paré
Continuation of astrology and alchemy

I. AN AGE
OF GOLD

This Our Age

War and the Golden Age

JEAN DE MONTREUIL

1395

TO JOHN BEAUFORT, EARL OF SOMERSET (?)

You will wonder, illustrious and most magnificent prince, how it has happened that I, a man of modest birth and as completely French as a man of my clerical rank can be, should presume to write to you, a prince of the highest and most noble royal line of Britain, and related to that of Spain. Know then that I speak the truth, I do not lie; I am moved to do this by the glorious renown of your name, which has reached not only those close to you and the great of this world, but also more distant peoples and those of lowly condition, proclaiming you a distinguished lover of truth and peace and justice. From earliest boyhood I have always admired and cultivated such men, and I have ever followed them with the greatest affection, but my desire to praise them is greater, I fear, than my ability.

The subject about which I am going to write also moves me, namely peace, encompassing all good in a single monosyllable. I am further inspired, most kind

65

prince, by the fact that I have heard that you love letters, and especially that you often meditate upon the Sacred Scripture, qualities which are certainly deserving of praise, and that you are also vigorous in action; in fact, that you excel in all things, although very many modern nobles despise the knowledge of letters, and spurn what was once to other men both honourable and glorious. Were not Alexander of Macedon, King David, Joshua, Judas Maccabeus, and the wise Solomon and the Queen of Saba, who came from the ends of the earth in order to acquire knowledge, were not Julius Caesar, and Augustus, and the other Caesars, and, among the Christians, Charles the Great and very many other most powerful kings and nobles (whom I shall not mention because of their number and because I think that you have read the works of history more thoroughly than I)—were not all these deeply devoted to letters, and at the same time men of action? Indeed, in the first age men very seldom advanced to the highest dignities if they had not been instructed and perfected in liberal studies. May, therefore, that age return which then and for this reason was called golden. But, in order not to prolong my plea, let me come now, O kindest of princes, to what it is that I long for.

There have now elapsed, as I have gathered from our elders, almost sixty years in which the most extensive war has raged between our kings [The Hundred Years' War], and with such hostility that one ruler— and this I call to mind with the most bitter sorrow that it could be true of those joined by so strong a bond of kinship—that one ruler strives to destroy the other rather than to crush the infidel. In these unbelievers and servants of Satan, this enmity inspires exultation and rejoicing; indeed, it fosters not a little, they say,

the increase and progress of their most wicked religion
and the weakening of our own most true law and faith.
And it is not to be doubted that, if one of our kings
should turn against the infidel attacks like those which
he directs against his fellow ruler, besides the service
which would be rendered to Christ crucified, he would
deserve glory, fame, and praise which would endure
through all time, and he would be able to conquer
more lands and possessions than the most noble kingdoms of both rulers now encompass or possess. As the
most elegant of poets writes, the great sequence of the
ages would begin anew for me; I would take up a more
exalted theme. But if I wish to relate the evils which
follow from the war that now rages, I am compelled to
exclaim with Vergil: "What opening words shall I
choose first?" . . .

For who shall describe the slaughter, especially of
so many nobles of the highest rank and even of kings?
Who shall tell of the robbery and the burning even of
sacred places? Who shall set forth the sacrilege, the
raping, the violence, the oppression, the extortion, the
plundering, the pillaging, the banditry, and the rioting?
Finally, to embrace many crimes in a few words, who
will portray the inhuman savageries . . . committed
in this horrible and most cruel war? Indeed, as Sallust
says, how can I relate things which no one would believe unless he had seen them? How can these crimes
be exaggerated enough, even if, as Vergil says, there
were a hundred tongues and a hundred mouths? But
who, most sweet Jesus, will tell with dry eyes how
children are snatched from the embraces of their parents, some slain on the very bosoms of their mothers,
and others cruelly slaughtered at their parents' feet,
how mothers and daughters are subjected to enemy
lust, how many people of the highest rank are carried

off into servitude, and how many are put up for sale
like animals? O savage spirits, O cruel deeds, O men
forsaken by humanity! . . .

But who, I say, if he has not a heart of iron, shall
refrain from tears when he describes or hears the cries
of so many infants, languishing and dying of hunger
and cold on the breasts of their mothers, among brambles and thornbushes. . . . Some, alas, were born prematurely, to be devoured by their own mothers after
the manner of cattle, a thing horrible to relate! They
were finally driven to this by the madness of hunger
and desperation. Many of these innocents, moreover,
lay half dead or dying from the mangling of vultures,
and were slain and destroyed by the fangs of wild
beasts, and many others—alas, how dreadful!—were
greedily devoured by savage wolves. O heavens, O
earth, O Neptunian seas, as the venerable Terence exclaimed, indeed I may call on all the elements! So now
it comes back to this: why have we been born in times
when Christians so cruelly persecute Christians and
cause them to die such monstrous deaths? For if a just
man will hardly be saved, what an entrance to hell
have you made for your souls, O you who die in such
acts! Truly you little heed, you heed not at all, the
command of our Saviour, Jesus, saying to you: "Thou
shalt not kill, thou shalt not commit adultery, thou
shalt not steal," forbidding all these crimes under pain
of perpetual damnation.

For these reasons, most high prince and lord, and
because a far more favourable opportunity to make
peace offers itself now than ever before, I beg, pray,
and beseech you to consider very carefully, through
your devotion to the good of the commonwealth, the
many arguments that plead the cause of peace, . . .
so that by your intervention such a wholesome, neces-

sary, and beautiful end may be achieved and these kingdoms may rest in the sweetness of peace and tranquility. Consider the truce which has been made for a period of four years; this offers the image and likeness of peace, an interval of time in which you will be able to exhort and urge your king, a man of good will, and others who are, with you, of his own most noble blood, to seek those things which are for the peace of Jerusalem. I say Jerusalem, since from the most glorious peace of kings the reformation of the holy Church, our best mother, may follow without delay; she is truly our best mother, in that when we were born, receiving us in the embrace of sincerity, she conferred upon us the water of regeneration in holy baptism. . . .

Withdraw then from your other cares, and devote yourself to this purpose as your manly portion, exhorting your king and highest lord, and other princes and lords of his blood and yours, to this end, which I know our king, now that we have suffered every horror, is also most willing and ready to seek, even to the jeopardizing of his body and his goods. Then finally, when peace has been made among kings, let peace be made also, by their efforts, in the Church of God, for no one will resist them if they agree in this one purpose. Then will this age flourish and its spirit grow strong.

From Epistola II, in Martène and Durand, *Amplissima collectio veterum scriptorum* (Paris, 1714); trans. M.M.M.

The Turkish Menace

CARDINAL BESSARION

July 13, 1453

TO FRANCESCO FOSCARI, DOGE OF VENICE

Most illustrious and excellent prince, I have put off until this day commending to your highness my unhappy and wretched city of Constantinople. This I have done partly because I was restrained by a certain provincial modesty, lest in asking something for her advantage and welfare, I should seem to seek my own profit; I have also held back because, of its own accord, your renowned Senate, as it has been most merciful to all those who are suffering, had prepared so much aid and assistance that all doubtless might think it sufficient, indeed more than enough, to save this city, to hold back the barbarians from the walls, to contain the attack of a most cruel enemy. Would that it might have been brought to bear at the proper time! Would that we had not been deprived of hope and deceived in our judgment; but truly it was not through any negligence on your part, of which, in so great a crisis, there was never a shadow.

But it so happened, because of the proximity of the enemy and the unfavourable season of the year, and by the will of the fates, that, while your fleet was in midcourse, while in hope of victory fresh forces were being brought against the enemy, the barbarians conquered the city [May 29, 1453]. This city which was most heavily protected by its situation, its walls and supplies, and by all manner of defence, this city which, it was hoped, would be able to withstand a total siege for an entire year, the barbarians stormed and overthrew. A thing terrible to relate, and to be deplored by all who have in them any spark of humanity, and especially by Christians.

Wretched me! I cannot write this without the most profound sorrow. A city which was so flourishing, with such a great empire, so many illustrious men, such very famous and ancient families, so prosperous, the head of all Greece, the splendour and glory of the East, the school of the best arts, the refuge of all good things, has been captured, despoiled, ravaged, and completely sacked by the most inhuman barbarians and the most savage enemies of the Christian faith, by the fiercest of wild beasts.

The public treasure has been consumed, private wealth has been destroyed, the temples have been stripped of gold, silver, jewels, the relics of the saints, and other most precious ornaments. Men have been butchered like cattle, women abducted, virgins ravished, and children snatched from the arms of their parents. If any survived so great a slaughter, they have been enslaved in chains so that they might be ransomed for a price, or subjected to every kind of torture, or reduced to the most humiliating servitude. The sanctuaries and shrines of the saints have been defiled by curses, scourgings, bloodshed, and all kinds of shameful acts. They have made camps of the churches of God, and have exposed the sacred things of God in their camps. O unhappy, O wretched, and so swift and manifold a transformation of a city! If anyone reads this, ignorant of what has been done, he will not believe that these things have happened.

But I do not wish to lament the calamities of my

fatherland to you, to whom these things are perhaps better known than to me, and especially lest I should seem to reopen your wound, whom the fates decreed should share our miseries. So many Venetian citizens and most noble gentlemen were besieged in that city, so many men of patrician rank. Would that they have experienced better fortune than ours, and may return unharmed to their native city. Certainly it is to be feared that, tossed in the same tempest, they may have perished in the same way.

To me, however, has been given the opportunity freely to implore aid, not for my fatherland, not for the good of my city, but for the safety of all, for the honor of Christians. On this occasion I could explain in great detail how much danger threatens Italy, not to mention other lands, if the violent assaults of the most ferocious barbarians are not checked. But I am not sure that these arguments are not better known to your Senate than to me. And this letter hastens to its close. I say but this one thing briefly. One of two things must happen; either your Highness, together with other Christian princes, must curb and crush the violence, not to say madness, of the barbarian, in these very beginnings, not only to safeguard yourselves and your own, but also in order to take the offensive against the enemy; or the barbarian, when he has shortly become master in what remains of Greece, which is now still subject to our rule, and in all our islands and also in Pannonia and Illyricum, may bring Italian affairs to a most dangerous crisis.

There is no one who may not hope, however, that Christian princes will take the offensive the more readily, seeing that there are such important reasons, so grave, so serious, so urgent. They would act for the common good, for the Christian religion, and for the glory of Christ, especially if they were summoned by your Highness and your Senate, whose authority is very great.

Therefore I exhort you, renowned and most illustrious prince, and I entreat, beseech, and implore you, with what prayers I can, that, when Italian affairs have finally been settled, and those wars ended in which Christian princes have attacked each other, you will direct your attention to greater matters and behold the enemy raging on the boundaries of Christian territories and destroying everything savagely.

Why do you think the barbarian has burst forth with such great insolence? Doubtless because he has learned that Christian princes, waging wars against each other, have stained their hands with the blood of their own people, have defiled their arms with the blood of Christians. These things make the enemy bold; relying on them, he has lately assaulted the chief city of Greece, and has conquered, ravaged, and destroyed it. But if he should learn that, with our own hostilities resolved, united and harmonious as Christian princes should be, we would rise up to defend the Christian religion, believe me, he would not only refrain from invading foreign lands, but would withdraw to that place within his own territories which is most favourable for defence.

Rise up then, renowned prince, and when the mutual animosities of Christians have been extinguished (and this will be easy for you, who are exceedingly influential in authority and wisdom), awaken, awaken at once, and arouse their peaceful and tranquil spirits. Exhort them, challenge them, induce them to join you, before the enemy takes the Peloponnesus, in dedicating themselves to avenging the violence of the barbarian, to destroying the enemy of the Christian faith, to recovering that city which formerly belonged to your republic, and which would be yours again once victory had been achieved. Nothing you could do would be more profitable for your empire, more advantageous for Italy, and for the whole commonwealth of Christians; nothing more acceptable to the immortal God; nothing more glorious for your own fame. If your highness knows anything that my smallness can contribute to this task, either by calming the spirits of our people or by exhorting them to wage war on the barbarians, I shall spare no labour, no care or solicitude.

In H. Vast, *Le Cardinal Bessarion* (Paris, 1878); trans. M.M.M.

A Bleak Prospect

POPE PIUS II

1454

TO LEONARDO DI BENTIVOGLIO

You have written that many were summoned from Italy to the Congress at Regensburg [April-May, 1454], and you thought it would be like the Council of Constance, not to mention that of Basel, which lasted for twenty years. But our meeting ended within a month. Another has been announced, to be held at Frankfort [Autumn, 1454], to which the King of Aragon, the Venetians, the Genoese, the Florentines, the Sienese, and the Luccans are called again from Italy. Although Count Francesco Sforza has not yet been invested with the duchy of Milan, he has also been summoned, and the Duke of Modena and the Marquesses of Mantua, Montferrat, and Saluzzo. We shall

see how great the fervour of our Italians will be. Letters
have gone also to the kings of France, England, Bohemia, Hungary, Poland, Denmark, Sweden, Norway,
and Scotland, inviting them to the meeting. The princes
of Germany have been ordered to be present, and the
counts to send envoys. If it is a long congress, there is
high hope of accomplishing matters successfully; if
only a few should come, you may say that it is because
of inertia.

How do you feel? What do you think will happen?
I prefer to say nothing, and I would rather be considered a false prophet than a true one. Yet I must say that
I am full of foreboding. I do not expect that what I
desire will happen; I cannot persuade myself that
there is anything good in prospect. You will ask why,
and I answer: "Why should I hope for anything
better?" Christendom has no head whom all will obey
—neither the pope nor the emperor receives his due.
For there is no reverence and no obedience. We regard
"pope" and "emperor" only as empty titles and figure-
heads. Every city has its own king, and there are as
many princes as there are households. How can you
persuade the many rulers of the Christian world to take
up arms under a single standard? And if you gave the
word and all the kings assembled in arms, to whom
would you entrust the leadership? What kind of order
would there be in such an army? What military discipline? What obedience? Who would be the shepherd
of such a mixed flock? Who could command their diverse languages? Who would be able to regulate their
varied customs? Who will make the English love the
French? Who will unite the Genoese and the Aragonese?
Who will reconcile the Germans with the Hungarians
and Bohemians? If you lead a small army against the
Turks, you will easily be overcome; if a large one, it

will soon fall into confusion. Everywhere there are difficulties.

You have only to survey the state of Christendom. Italy, you say, is at peace, and with affairs quiet at home she will readily take up arms against the foreigners. But I do not know how peaceful she is. There are still vestiges of war between the Genoese and the Aragonese. And one cannot believe that these Genoese, who are said to pay tribute to the Turks, are ready to go to war against them. The Venetians have made a treaty with the Turks, and yet they say they will take up arms for our faith, if other Christians will go to war against the Turks. Who will fulfil this condition? It will be necessary now to ask, to beg, and to arouse the Venetians, who may imitate the others, if there is no peace between them and the Turks. What can you do with the Italians when the two naval powers, and indeed the greater states, fail in their duty? Although the King of Aragon is very powerful, and zealous for the common good, he will hardly undertake alone a naval war against the Turks. You are aware how large a fleet the pope has! We lack, therefore, one major arm of warfare. For since the proposal is to attack the Turks on land and sea, it is to be hoped that the Italians would lack nothing necessary for maritime warfare. The Hellespont will lie open before the Asiatics, and if war is waged on land, the Turks will bring an infinite number of troops into Greece from Asia.

You know how many kings there are in Spain, and how unequal they are in power, government, will, and judgment. And those lying in the extreme west are not drawn to the north. Then there is the question of what they would do with the people of Granada at home. If the King of France has driven out the enemy from his whole kingdom, his shores are still subject to attack,

and he will not dare to send an army outside his kingdom while he fears the renewed attacks of English
fleets. The English have nothing in mind but to avenge
their expulsion from France. The Scots, the Danes, the
Swedes, and the Norwegians are situated on the most
remote shores of the world, and there is nothing they
can do outside their homelands.

The Germans, divided among themselves, find no
center of unity anywhere. The cities quarrel with the
princes, and the princes themselves are not joined by
any bond of concord. The Swiss maintain their ancient
hatred of the dukes of Austria. The Count Palatine has
been attacked by the Archbishop of Mainz. The possession of the duchy of Luxembourg is in dispute between
the King of Bohemia and the Duke of Burgundy, although there is a truce in this affair until the calends of
November. The dukes of Saxony are quarrelling with the
Bohemians over sixty castles. When the people of Brati-
slava were asked by the King of Bohemia to do homage
to him, they refused, unless the king should come to
them. The Prussians, who were ruled by the Teutonic
Order, have thrown off the authority of the prior and
gone over to the King of Poland. And now, having
entered this region, King Casimir and his wife have
received their oaths of fealty. The people of Liegnitz,
which King Ladislas turned over to the governor of
Bohemia, George Podiebrad, refuse to surrender. . . .
In Austria nothing is peaceful. The Austrians rebel
against the government of the Baron von Eizing, they
love the cities, and frequent insurrections occur. The
Bohemian Vuancho with two thousand bandits lays
waste the region far and wide. In Vienna fires are frequently set, and nobody knows who starts them. In
Hungary the prelates and the magnates are opposed
by John Hunyadi, who formerly was governor and now

has the title of captain and holds the greatest part of the kingdom. . . . Although the despot of Rascia is thought to be united with the Turks, he has asked for aid from the King of Hungary and reported that the Turks are prepared for war. Yet the Hungarians are not moved by these threats, but are believed to be ready to make a truce or a treaty with the enemy rather than go to war.

You see now what may be expected or feared in so great a variety of affairs. Observe the habits of men and look at the actions of our princes, behold the huge and yawning maw of avarice, see how much inertia and how much greed there are. No one is devoted to letters or to the studies of the good arts. And do you think that an army of Turks could be destroyed by men of such morals? I could wish that you would turn out to be right and I wrong. However things go, I shall be at Frankfort on the day which has been set, and if I do not advance the cause of the Christian commonwealth, I shall in any case torment myself, and as a punishment for my sins I shall be miserable in body and mind. If anything results for the common good I shall welcome it the more gladly, the more it exceeds my expectation.

From *Opera omnia* (Basel, 1571); trans. M.M.M.

The Golden Age in Florence

MARSILIO FICINO

1492

TO PAUL OF MIDDELBURG

What the poets once sang of the four ages, lead, iron, silver, and gold, our Plato in the *Republic* transferred to the four talents of men, assigning to some talents a certain leaden quality implanted in them by nature, to others iron, to others silver, and to still others gold. If then we are to call any age golden, it is beyond doubt that age which brings forth golden talents in different places. That such is true of this our age he who wishes to consider the illustrious discoveries of this century will hardly doubt. For this century, like a golden age, has restored to light the liberal arts, which were almost extinct: grammar, poetry, rhetoric, painting, sculpture, architecture, music, the ancient singing of songs to the Orphic lyre, and all this in Florence. Achieving what had been honoured among the ancients, but almost forgotten since, the age has joined wisdom with eloquence, and prudence with the military art, and this most strikingly in Federigo, Duke of Urbino, as if proclaimed in the presence of Pallas herself, and it has made his son and his brother the heirs of his virtue. In you also, my dear Paul, this century appears to have perfected astronomy, and in Florence it has recalled the Platonic teaching from darkness into light. In Germany in our times have been invented the instruments for printing books, and those tables in which in a single hour (if I may speak thus) the whole face of the heavens for an entire century is revealed, and one may mention also the Florentine machine which shows the daily motions of the heavens.

From *Opera omnia* (Basel, 1576); trans. M.M.M.

❧

An Age of Gold

ERASMUS OF ROTTERDAM

1517

TO CAPITO

It is no part of my nature, most learned Wolfgang, to be excessively fond of life; whether it is that I have, to my own mind, lived nearly long enough, having entered my fifty-first year, or that I see nothing in this life so splendid or delightful that it should be desired by one who is convinced by the Christian faith that a happier life awaits those who in this world earnestly attach themselves to piety. But at the present moment I could almost wish to be young again, for no other reason but this, that I anticipate the near approach of a golden age, so clearly do we see the minds of princes, as if changed by inspiration, devoting all their energies to the pursuit of peace. The chief movers in this matter are Pope Leo and Francis, King of France.

There is nothing this king does not do or does not suffer in his desire to avert war and consolidate peace; submitting, of his own accord, to conditions which might be deemed unfair, if he preferred to have regard to his own greatness and dignity rather than to the general advantage of the world; and exhibiting in this, as in everything else, a magnanimous and truly royal character. Therefore, when I see that the highest sovereigns of Europe—Francis of France, Charles the King Catholic, Henry of England, and the Emperor Maximilian—have set all their warlike preparations aside and established peace upon solid and, as I trust, adamantine foundations, I am led to a confident hope that not only morality and Christian piety, but also a genuine and purer literature, may come to renewed life or greater splendour; especially as this object is pursued with equal zeal in various regions of the world—at Rome by Pope Leo, in Spain by the Cardinal of Toledo, in England by Henry, eighth of the name, himself not unskilled in letters, and among ourselves by our young King Charles. In France, King Francis, who seems as it were born for this object, invites and entices from all countries men that excel in merit or in learning. Among the Germans the same object is pursued by many of their excellent princes and bishops, and especially by Maximilian Caesar, whose old age, weary of so many wars, has determined to seek rest in the employments of peace, a resolution more becoming to his own years, while it is fortunate for the Christian world. To the piety of these princes it is due, that we see everywhere, as if upon a given signal, men of genius are arising and conspiring together to restore the best literature.

Polite letters, which were almost extinct, are now cultivated and embraced by Scots, by Danes, and by Irishmen. Medicine has a host of champions; at Rome, Nicolas of Leonice; at Venice, Ambrosius Leo of Nola; in France, William Cop and John Ruelle; and in England, Thomas Linacre. The Imperial Law is restored at Paris by William Budé, in Germany by Udalric Zasy; and mathematics at Basel by Henry of Glaris.

In the theological sphere there was no little to be done, because this science has been hitherto mainly professed by those who are most pertinacious in their abhorrence of the better literature, and are the more successful in defending their own ignorance as they do it under pretext of piety, the unlearned vulgar being induced to believe that violence is offered to religion if anyone begins an assault upon their barbarism. For in the presence of an ignorant mob they are always ready to scream and excite their followers to stone-throwing, if they see any risk of not being thought omniscient. But even here I am confident of success if the knowledge of the three languages continues to be received in schools, as it has now begun. For the most learned and least churlish men of the profession do in some measure assist and favour the new system; and in this matter we are especially indebted to the vigorous exertions of James Lefèvre of Étaples, whom you resemble not only in name but in a number of accomplishments.

The humblest part of the work has naturally fallen to my lot. Whether my contribution has been worth anything I cannot say; at any rate, those who object to the world regaining its senses are as angry with me as if my small industry had had some influence; although the work was not undertaken by me with any confidence that I could myself teach anything magnificent, but I wanted to construct a road for other persons of higher aims, so that they might be less impeded by pools and stumbling blocks in carrying home those fair and glorious treasures.

Why should I say more? Everything promises me the happiest success. But one doubt still possesses my mind. I am afraid that, under cover of a revival of ancient literature, paganism may attempt to rear its

head—as there are some among Christians that acknowledge Christ in name but breathe inwardly a
heathen spirit—or, on the other hand, that the restoration of Hebrew learning may give occasion to a revival
of Judaism. This would be a plague as much opposed
to the doctrine of Christ as anything that could happen. . . . Some books have lately come out with a
strong flavour of Judaism. I see how Paul exerted himself to defend Christ against Judaism, and I am aware
that some persons are secretly sliding in that direction.
I hear also that some are intent upon other schemes,
which do nothing for the knowledge of Christ, but
only cloud men's eyes with smoke. So much the more
do I wish you to undertake this province; I know that
your sincere piety will have regard to nothing but
Christ, to whom all your studies are devoted. . . .

TO POPE LEO X

While on the one hand, as a private matter, I
acknowledge my own felicity in obtaining the approbation not only of the Supreme Pontiff but of Leo, by his
own endowments supreme among the supreme, so on
the other hand, as a matter of public concern, I congratulate this our age—which bids fair to be an age
of gold, if ever such there was—wherein I see, under
your happy auspices and by your holy counsels, three
of the chief blessings of humanity are about to be restored to her. I mean, first, that truly Christian piety,
which has in many ways fallen into decay; secondly,
learning of the best sort, hitherto partly neglected and
partly corrupted; and thirdly, the public and lasting
concord of Christendom, the source and parent of piety
and erudition. These will be the undying trophies of
the tenth Leo, which, consecrated to eternal memory
by the writings of learned men, will forever render your

pontificate and your family illustrious. I pray God that he may be pleased to confirm this purpose in you, and so protract your life, that after the affairs of mankind have been ordered according to your designs, Leo may make a long-delayed return to the skies.

Epistles 522 and 530, from *The Epistles of Erasmus*, trans. F. M. Nichols (London: Longmans, Green & Co., 1901).

The Restoration of the Gospel

JACQUES LEFÈVRE D'ÉTAPLES

1522

O YOU whom God has truly loved, and who are especially dear to me in Christ, know that only those are Christians who love our Lord Jesus Christ and His Word with perfect purity. Their name is holy and venerable, and, as Ignatius said to the Magnesians, whosoever calls himself by any other name does not belong to God.

For the Word of Christ is the Word of God, the Gospel of peace, liberty, and joy, the Gospel of salvation, redemption, and life; the Gospel of peace after continuous warfare, of liberty after the most harsh servitude, of joy after constant sadness, of salvation after complete perdition, of redemption after the most dreadful captivity, and finally of life itself as an escape from eternal death. If this Word is called the Gospel, the "good news," it is because, for us, it is the herald of all good things, and of the infinite blessings which are prepared for us in heaven. How could those be Christians who do not love Christ and His Word with perfect purity? Their portion is quite different. I wish that none would be found among their number, and that all would be found among those who love Christ. A lawful hope, indeed, for God wills that all men should be saved, should attain to the knowledge of the truth, and come to the love of the evangelical life. . . .

And pray God that the model of faith may be sought in the primitive Church, which offered to Christ so many martyrs, which knew no other rule than the Gospel, and no other end than Christ, and which rendered its devotion to only one God in three Persons! If we rule our life by this example, the eternal Gospel of Christ will flourish now, as it flourished then. The faithful then depended in everything on Christ; we ourselves should also depend entirely on Him. All their faith was concentrated on Him, all their trust, all their love; it is to Him that we also should address the same sentiments. No one then lived by his own spirit, but by the Spirit of Christ; we also should live by this Spirit; we should finally depart this life to go to Him, as those before us departed, for whom Christ was everything, those whom we love and glorify for the sake of Christ, in offering with them all worship and all glory to God alone.

Why may we not aspire to see our age restored to the likeness of the primitive Church, when Christ received a purer veneration, and the splendour of His Name shone forth more widely? . . . As the light of the Gospel returns, may He Who is blessed above all grant also to us this increase of faith, this purity of worship: as the light of the Gospel returns, I say, which at this time begins to shine again. By this divine light many have been so greatly illuminated that, not to speak of other benefits, from the time of Constantine, when the primitive Church, which had little by little declined, came to an end, there has not been greater knowledge of languages, more extensive discovery of new lands, or wider diffusion of the name of Christ in the more distant parts of the earth than in these times.

The knowledge of languages, and especially of Latin and Greek (for afterwards the study of Hebrew letters was stimulated by Johann Reuchlin), began to return about the time when Constantinople was captured by the enemies of Christ, and when a few Greeks, notably Bessarion, Theodore of Gaza, George of Trebizond, and Manuel Chrysoloras, took refuge in Italy.

Soon afterwards the new lands were discovered, and thereupon the name of Christ was propagated, by the Portuguese in the east, and in the southwest by the Spaniards, under the leadership of a Genoese, and in the northwest by the French. Would that the name of Christ might have been, and may henceforth be, proclaimed purely and sincerely so that soon the word may be fulfilled: "O Lord, may the whole earth adore Thee." Yes, may it offer Thee a religion evangelical and pure, a religion of the spirit and of truth! It is this above all which is to be desired.

From *Commentarii initiatorii in IV evangeliis praefatio* (Meaux, 1522); trans. M.M.M.

The Necessary Evils

RICHARD EDEN

1555

To this book of the Indies and navigations I have thought good to add the book of metals, for three causes which especially moved me: of these the first is, that it seems to me a thing indecent to read so much of gold and silver, and to know little or nothing of the natural generation thereof, being nevertheless things not only most desired, but also such without which in this age the life of man cannot be passed over without many adversities, forasmuch as poverty is hateful to all men, and virtue no further esteemed than it is supported by riches, since now that lady that reigned in Saturn's days is become the slave to him that was then her bondman in that golden world; so named not for the desire that men had for gold, but for the innocence of living in those days, when Mars was of no power, and men thought it cruelty by breaking the bones of our mother the earth, to open a way to the court of infernal Pluto, from thence to get gold and silver, the seeds of all mischief and angels of such a god, whom antiquity (not without good consideration) painted blind, affirming also that of him gold and silver have received the property to blind the eyes of men.

But since it is now so that we shall be forced to seek aid by that which was sometimes a mischief, it remains to use the matter as do cunning physicians that can minister poison in proportion with other things, in such sort qualifying the maliciousness thereof, that none shall thereby be intoxicated. Forasmuch, therefore, as gold and silver have obtained this prerogative that they are such necessary evils which the life of man cannot lack without detriment, not only they but other metals also, perhaps more necessary although not so precious, are things worthy to be better known than only by name, since they are the instruments of all arts, the prices of all things, the ornaments of all dignities, and not the least portion of nature, whereby the contemplation of them is no less pleasant than necessary.

But forasmuch as it is not here my intent to entreat much of metals, I will speak of the second cause: which is, that if in travelling strange and unknown countries any man's chance shall be to arrive in such regions where he may know by the information of the inhabitants or otherwise, that such regions are fruitful of rich metals, he may not be without some judgment to make search for the same. The third cause is, that although this our realm of England is full of metals not to be contemned and much richer than men suppose, yet are there few or none in England that have any great skill thereof, or anything written in our tongue, whereby men may be well instructed of the generation and finding of the same.

Preface to the *Booke of Metals*, in *The First Three English Books on America, 1511-1555*, ed. Edward Arber (Birmingham, Eng., 1885).

The Golden Age

TORQUATO TASSO

1572

O lovely age of gold!
Not that the rivers rolled
With milk, or that the woods wept honeydew;
Not that the ready ground
Produced without a wound,
Or the mild serpent had no tooth that slew;
Not that a cloudless blue
Forever was in sight,
Or that the heaven, which burns
And now is cold by turns,
Looked out in glad and everlasting light;
No, nor that even the insolent ships from far
Brought war to no new lands nor riches worse than
    war:

But solely that that vain
And breath-invented pain,
That idol of mistake, that worshipped cheat,
That Honour—since so called
By vulgar minds appalled—
Played not the tyrant with our nature yet.
It had not come to fret
The sweet and happy fold
Of gentle humankind;
Nor did its hard law bind
Souls nursed in freedom; but that law of gold,

That glad and golden law, all free, all fitted,
Which Nature's own hand wrote— What pleases is per-
    mitted.

Then among streams and flowers
The little winged powers
Went singing carols without torch or bow;
The nymphs and shepherds sat
Mingling with innocent chat
Sports and low whispers; and with whispers low,
Kisses that would not go.
The maiden, budding o'er,
Kept not her bloom uneyed,
Which now a veil must hide,
Nor the crisp apples which her bosom bore;
And oftentimes, in river or in lake,
The lover and his love their merry bath would take.

'Twas thou, thou, Honour, first
That didst deny our thirst
Its drink, and on the fount thy covering set;
Thou bad'st kind eyes withdraw
Into constrained awe,
And keep the secret for their tears to wet;
Thou gather'dst in a net
The tresses from the air,
And mad'st the sports and plays
Turn all to sullen ways,
And putt'st on speech a rein, in steps a care.
Thy work it is—thou shade, that wilt not move—
That what was once the gift is now the theft of Love.

Our sorrows and our pains,
These are thy noble gains.
But, O, thou Love's and Nature's masterer,

Thou conqueror of the crowned,
What dost thou on this ground,
Too small a circle for thy mighty sphere?
Go, and make slumber dear
To the renowned and high;
We here, a lowly race,
Can live without thy grace,
After the use of mild antiquity.
Go, let us love; since years
No truce allow, and life soon disappears;
Go, let us love; the daylight dies, is born;
But unto us the light
Dies once for all; and sleep brings on eternal night.

From *Aminta*, trans. Leigh Hunt.

The Excellence of This Age

LOYS LE ROY

1575

Now just as the Tartars, Turks, Mamelukes, and Persians have by their valour drawn to the East the glory of arms, so we here in the West have in the last two hundred years recovered the excellence of good letters and brought back the study of the disciplines after they had long remained as if extinguished. The sustained industry of many learned men has led to such success that today this our age can be compared to the most learned times that ever were. For we now see the languages restored, and not only the deeds and writings of the ancients brought back to light, but also many fine things newly discovered. In this period grammar, poetry, history, rhetoric, and dialectic have been illumined by expositions, annotations, corrections, and innumerable translations. Never has mathematics been so well known, nor astrology, cosmography, and navigation better understood. Physics and medicine were not in a state of greater perfection among the ancient Greeks and Arabs than they are now. Arms and military instruments were never so destructive and effective, nor was there equal skill in handling them. Painting, sculpture, modelling, and architecture have been almost wholly restored. And more could not possibly have been done in eloquence and jurisprudence. Even politics, including and controlling everything, which seemed to have been left behind, has recently received much illumination. Theology, moreover, the most worthy of all, which seemed to be destroyed by the sophists, has been greatly illuminated by the knowledge of Hebrew and Greek; and the early fathers of the Church, who were languishing in the libraries, have been brought to light. Printing has greatly aided this work and has made easier its development.

Since in the course of our discussion and the succession of times we have now arrived at this age, we shall consider it henceforth, not with respect to the special excellence of different countries, but as a whole with regard to the memorable deeds and events within this space of time throughout Europe, Asia, Africa, the new lands, in the Orient, the Occident, the North, the South, and with regard to the blessings which it has pleased God to distribute among persons notable in the same period throughout the various countries of the habitable earth.

Now since we have distinguished the other ages by some illustrious warrior and by the great power which existed in each mutation, it seems that the marvels of this age should begin with the great and invincible Tamerlane, who frightened the world by the terror of his name about the year A.D. 1400, and by his incredible army of twelve hundred thousand seasoned and obedient warriors acquired the empire of Asia. He had planned to pass into Europe to subjugate it entirely as far as Spain, from which he would have gone over into Africa and returned to Asia by that route, but he was prevented by the pestilence which broke out in his army. . . .

During the reign of Tamerlane there began the restoration of the languages and of all the disciplines. The first to apply himself to this work was Francesco Petrarca, who opened up libraries which had long been closed and removed the dust and filth from the good books and ancient writers. Being a man of great understanding and excellent learning, he not only embellished the Italian tongue, of which he, together with his disciple Boccaccio, is revered as an exemplar and principal author, but also laudably stimulated Latin poetry and prose. Then Giovanni of Ravenna, grammarian, who as a youth had known Petrarca as an old man, greatly advanced the progress of the Latin language, instructing and exhorting to the love of good letters many who became very learned. Among these were Leonardo Bruni, Francesco Filelfo, Lorenzo Valla, Guarino da Verona, Poggio, Ognibene of Lonigo, Niccoló Perotti, Vittorino da Feltre, Francesco Barbaro, Pietro Paolo Vergerio, Maffeo Vegio, Leonardo Giustiniani, Gregorio and Lilio Tifernas, Antonio of Panormo, Giovanni Aurispa, Pietro Candido, Flavio Biondo. Then Manuel Chrysoloras, a gentleman of Constantinople, a personage famous for his learning and for every virtue, was sent by the Emperor John Paleologos

[Manuel II, 1393] to the kings of Europe to implore
their aid for the rescue of Greece, which was perishing.
After he had fulfilled this onerous duty he stayed at
Venice, seeing his fatherland delivered from the fear
of Bayazid whom Tamerlane held as prisoner. Here he
taught for the first time the Greek language, neglected
and unknown for more than seven hundred years in
Italy; and later, in Florence, Rome, and Pavia, he
taught most of the disciples of Giovanni of Ravenna
mentioned above. He succeeded in this so well that
by virtue of his instruction, continued for a few years,
it came to pass that henceforth those ignorant of the
Greek language were considered less learned among
the Latins. But other Greeks coming later to Italy
marvellously advanced the work so happily begun by
him: such as Bessarion the cardinal, great philosopher
and theologian, who left to Venice his fine Greek library, Gemistos Plethon, George Trapezuntios, the
learned Aristotelian who in his extreme old age completely forgot literature, Theodore of Gaza, most excellent translator, Andronicus of Thessalonica, John
Argyropulos, Constantine and John Lascaris, Demetrios
Chalcondyles, Sophianos, Marullus the poet, Marcus
Musurus. These men God raised up to preserve in these
parts the Greek language and Greek learning, oppressed in Greece by Turkish arms, and they have
summoned to the knowledge of their literature not only
the Italians, but also the French, Germans, Flemings,
English, Scots, Poles, Hungarians, Spanish, all of whom
gave themselves to it with great ardour and affection. . . .

But we should rather note the celebrated personages
of this age according to their functions and professions,
as we have done in the other periods. Now the most
renowned captains and warriors have been Tamer-

lane, . . . Murad and Mohammed his son, Selim and
Suleiman the Ottomans, King Charles VIII of France,
King Ferdinand of Spain, called the Catholic, Gonsalvo
the Great, Emperor Charles V, Charles of Bourbon, the
Shah Ismail, the Sheriff of Fez, Francis Duke of Guise.
On the sea, Andrea Doria, Adriano Bassa, called Bar-
barossa, Dragut and Salec Rez, Strozzi prior of Capua.

The most renowned Platonic philosophers have been
Bessarion, Gemistos, Ficino; the Aristotelians, Trapezuntios, Argyropulos, Lefèvre, Nifo, Pomponazzi, Con-
tarini, Grynaeus. Giovanni Pico proposed to harmonize
these two sects and to reconcile Plato and Aristotle, as
Boethius had undertaken to do earlier. But the one
like the other died before fulfilling this promise. Among
the eloquent imitators of the ancients and students of
Cicero, the first in rank is Lorenzo Valla, who brought
Latin oratory back to the ancient manner of speaking;
he was a great admirer of Quintilian, as Cardinal Hadrian was of Cicero, and likewise Nizzoli and Dolet.
The most Ciceronian writers are Bembo, Sadoleto, Lon-
gueil, Périon, Flaminio. The Latin, Italian, and French
poets are Petrarca, Antonio of Panormo, Pontano, Ma-
rullus, Sonnazzaro, Vida, Fracastoro, Molza, Navagero,
Flaminio, Capito, Paleario, More, Bourbon, Macrin,
Eobanus Hessus, Sabinus, Buchanan, Ariosto, Ronsard,
Joachim du Bellay. . . . Among the Italian historians
are Machiavelli and Guicciardini; among the French,
Jean Froissart, Enguerrand de Monstrelet, Philippe
de Commines. Among the jurisconsults, Zasius, Alciati,
Oldendorp, Baron. . . . Among the physicians, . . .
Fernel, Rondelet, Jacobus Sylvius, Amatus Lusitanus,
Vesalius, Martin Acakia. . . . Among the mathema-
ticians Pierre d'Ailly, Regiomontanus, the Cardinal of
Cusa, Peuerbach. . . .

Among the painters were Giotto the Florentine, who

restored painting, neglected for a long time, and made it very illustrious; also Bellini, who because of his excellence was sent by the signory of Venice to Sultan Mohammed, Emperor of Constantinople. Also Piero della Francesca, Raphael of Urbino, Albrecht Dürer, who wrote on painting in German, as Jean Cousin did in French, and Leon Battista Alberti in Latin. Among the sculptors and carvers were Donatello, Michelangelo, Andrea of Cremona, Cristoforo of Mantua, Lorenzo Ghiberti, who spent fifty years in making the doors of the Baptistery of Florence, on which by marvellous skill are modelled in bronze the stories of the Old and New Testaments. Among the architects were Leon Battista Alberti, who composed a very learned work on architecture, Giovanni Giocondo of Verona, who built the great bridge of Paris and was the first to publish Vitruvius complete with drawings, and similarly the commentaries of Caesar. Also Filippo Brunelleschi, who made the great church of Florence, the vaulting of which, thanks to unusual artifice, is not sustained by any pillars, Aristotile of Bologna moved without damage some stone towers from one place to another by cleverly placing sliding wheels under the foundations. Sebastiano Serlio of the same city wrote books of architecture in Italian. Pierre Lescot, called Claigny, was director of the work on the Louvre and its repair, begun under King Francis I, while Philibert de l'Orme undertook the construction of the Tuileries, of Anet and St. Maur; the latter left books on his art and invented a new kind of roofing for covering houses.

The philologists and investigators of antiquity and the properties of languages, correctors of books, translators and commentators, included Lorenzo Valla, Perotti, Gaza, Trapezuntios, Pomponio Leto, . . . Cristoforo Landino, Lebrixa, Budé, Erasmus, Sigonio, Grouchy. . . . Antoine du Noiroy translated into French the whole natural history of Pliny; Jean Martin, the architecture of Vitruvius and of Leon Alberti; Jacques Amyot, the lives and short works of Plutarch with a part of Diodorus Siculus. Claude Seyssel translated Appius of Alexandria, and the voyage of the young Cyrus; Hugues Salel, the *Iliad* of Homer. Loys Le Roy translated the *Republic* of Plato, the *Timaeus*, the *Phaedo* and the *Symposium*, illuminated by annotations, and the *Politics* of Aristotle clarified by commentaries; he also translated the political orations of Demosthenes with some books of Isocrates and Xenophon. And there have been countless other translations in many tongues and nations. Among the illustrious travellers, pilots, navigators, discoverers, and conquerors of new lands were Cristoforo Colombo of Genoa, Amerigo Vespucci of Florence, Prince Henry of Portugal, Magellan, Cortés, Pizzaro, Alfonso Albuquerque, Cabot.

The princes who have done most to revive the arts are Pope Nicholas V and Alfonso King of Naples, who welcomed honourably and rewarded liberally those who presented to them Latin translations of Greek books. The King of France, Francis I, paid the salaries of public professors in Paris, and created a sumptuous library at Fontainebleau, full of all the good books. Without the favour and liberality of the kings of Castile and Portugal, the discovery of the new lands and the voyage to the Indies would not have come about. The Medici lords of Florence, Cosimo and Lorenzo, helped very much, receiving the learned men who came to them from all parts, supporting them honourably; and, sending scholars at their own expense to hunt throughout Greece for the good and ancient books which were being lost, they built up magnificent libraries for the common good.

Besides the restoration of ancient learning, now almost complete, the invention of many fine new things, serving not only the needs but also the pleasure and adornment of life, has been reserved to this age. Among these, printing deserves to be put first, because of its excellence, utility, and the subtlety of craftsmanship from which has come the cutting of matrices and fonts, the distribution and composing of type, the making of ink and of balls for putting it on the form, the setting of presses and the way of handling them, of dampening the paper, placing, taking out, and drying the leaves, then gathering them into volumes, going over and correcting the proof, which has already been spoken of. Thus more work is accomplished in one day than many diligent scribes could do in a year. On this account, books, formerly rare and dear, have become common and easy to procure. The invention has greatly aided the advancement of all disciplines. For it seems miraculously to have been discovered in order to bring back to life more easily literature which seemed dead. The invention is attributed to the Germans and began in Mainz; it was then employed in Venice and subsequently spread over all Latin Christendom, brought to its perfection by Nicholas Jenson, Aldus, the Giunti, Froben, Badius, Robert Estienne, and others. The Portuguese, however, who have sailed all over the world, trading in the remote East and North, in China and Cathay, have brought back books printed in the language and writing of the country, saying that printing had long been in use in those parts. This fact has led some to believe that the invention was carried through Tartary and Muscovy to Germany and then communicated to other Christians, to whom the providence of God has especially entrusted the consummation of divine and human wisdom. Deprived of this grace, the Mohammedans have entirely rejected printing, not using it at all among themselves, nor permitting the importation of books on their own affairs printed elsewhere in Arabic.

Second praise must be given to the invention of the marine compass, the rose, and the steel needle which, when touched or rubbed on the lodestone, always indicates the point corresponding to the direction where the arctic pole is supposed to be. Aristotle did not understand this property, nor Galen, nor Alexander of Aphrodisias, nor Avicenna, a very curious observer of natural things. For if they had known such a miracle of nature and such a useful aid to navigation, they would not have been silent about it in their books, having treated many other things of less importance. It was also unknown to the Romans, who suffered so many shipwrecks when fighting at sea against the Carthaginians, and under Octavian lost a great fleet of vessels fighting against Sextus Pompey. By this skill the whole ocean has been navigated, innumerable islands found, and a great part of *terra firma* discovered in the West and South, unknown to the ancients, and therefore called "the new world," which has been not only conquered but also converted to the Christian religion under the power of Spain. This enterprise was begun by Cristoforo Colombo the Genoese, and by Amerigo Vespucci the Florentine, a person of excellent understanding and fine judgment who deserves no less praise than the famous Hercules of Greece; then it was continued by the Castilians, rivals for the same honour and eager for gain, who by great courage and incomparable endurance have continued to make other discoveries. Some of these have been drowned in the vast sea not yet explored, others eaten by the cannibals, leaving a pitiful record of their wretched audacity. But there have been three of them, more favoured by fortune, who made very notable discoveries: Cortés of the kingdom of Mexico and the great city of Tenochtitlán, similar to Venice in site, construction, and number of inhabitants; Pizarro of Peru and Cuzco, rich in gold; Magellan of the Moluccas where the spices grow. At the same time the Portuguese, dividing the world with the Castilians according to the bull of Pope Alexander VI, by the same knowledge of navigation sailed through the Atlantic and the Canaries, conquering several cities on the coast of Barbary from the Saracens. Then, traversing the zone formerly called Torrid, and falsely considered a desert, they journeyed beyond Capricorn, conquering Brazil and other lands. Later, turning toward the East, they sailed along the coast of the whole of Africa and the shores of Ethiopia, passed beyond the Arabian and Persian Gulfs, and, having reached India, conquered by arms the kings of Cambay, Cananor, and Calicut; they built fortresses in their lands in order to safeguard the eastern trade of which they had made themselves masters. In addition, passing beyond the Ganges and Indus Rivers, they travelled as far as Taproban [Ceylon] and the Golden Chersonese [the Malay Peninsula], making the King of Malacca their tributary. Thence, setting sail for the North, they went to China and Cathay, where they set the limits of their navigation in this direction, entering into friendship and alliance with the great Cham in order to have freedom to trade safely in his country, heretofore not accessible to strangers except under imminent peril of death. And thus, through Spanish industry, today the whole world is known which in great part remained unknown for such a long time; and the extremes of the East, West, North, and South communicate with one another, and men separated by so many seas, so remote and different from one another, now go back and forth, thanks to the fact that navigation has been made safer and easier, chiefly by this invention.

I should willingly give third place to "bombard" or cannonry—which has brought an end to all other military instruments of the past, which it surpasses in force of motion, violence, and speed—if it were not for the fact that it seems invented rather for the ruin than the utility of humankind, the enemy of generous virtue, which it attacks without distinction, breaking and destroying everything it encounters. It was first invented in Germany by a worker in alchemy, and from there it has been carried all over the world; and it seems today to be brought almost to perfection, since they have discovered how to shoot in volleys of several pieces simultaneously, which knock down any place no matter how strong it is in site or height or depth of walls and ramparts. The cannon which was first called "bombard" because of the noise it makes, or "mortar," was of iron bound together in several pieces, heavy and clumsy, throwing big balls of stone with a great quantity of power, composed of saltpetre, sulphur, and charcoal, the invention of which is no less wonderful than that of the cannon itself. Then iron was succeeded by bronze, out of which there were made at first huge pieces placed on wheels, more manageable than the mortar, with balls of iron in their barrels; to them have been given the names of birds and other animals frightful in appearance, such as culverins, serpents, basilisks, falcons, and other names, given according to the diversity of their proportions, shapes, and range, at the pleasure of the craftsmen or the princes who order them. Subsequently smaller and lighter pieces have been made for firing with balls of lead, such as harquebuses, pistols, and pistolets. . . .

This age has brought forth many other great and notable inventions on which, however, I shall not insist, inasmuch as they are rather accessories to ancient things and do not go beyond the understanding of our forebears, whereas all antiquity has nothing to show comparable to these three inventions. But among the marvels of our century there has manifested itself a new and strange malady unknown to the ancients, and never considered by any Greek, Arab, or Roman physician, as if there were not enough maladies dispersed throughout the world, up to the number of three hundred and more, without speaking of the discomforts experienced every day through the excesses of men! Anyone who considers it well will certainly conclude that it is the true punishment of God, sent to chastise the excessive lewdness of human beings, inasmuch as it is acquired by immodest contact and begins in the shameful parts, rising straightway to the countenance, which it sullies with ugly spots, and covering the body with pustules, at first hard and then bloody. It eats into the place where it attacks clear to the bone, which it penetrates with its venom, causing intolerable pains in the head, shoulders, and other members without cease, night and day, thus preventing rest and sleep. It was more virulent in the beginning than it is now, since it was then impossible to find any proper remedy for it. But it abated day by day after there were found more appropriate remedies for curing it by means of diet or massage; and in addition, the influences of the heavens, which seem to have caused it, seem now to be weakened. Thus it is likely that it will disappear in the course of time, as did the *mentagra*, similar to it, which greatly afflicted Rome in the reign of the Emperor Tiberius, and the lichen, which under Claudius his successor molested not only Italy but all Europe. Some have believed that it came from Brazil, where it is common, and is cured by the decoction of guaiacum, and that from there it was carried to Spain and to Italy, where it appeared when the King of France, Charles VIII, went to conquer Naples, being for this reason called by the French the Neapolitan disease, and by the Italians the French disease. Others call it the great pox, common to all nations. Fracastoro, the excellent poet of Verona, has written verses about its origin. . . .

In addition, sects have sprung up in all countries, which have greatly disturbed the public peace and chilled the mutual charity of human beings. Some more curious persons wish to attribute the cause of this to celestial movements, in view of the fact that at about the same time Luther in Saxony, Techel Cuselbas, and the Shah [Ismail] in Persia, and others elsewhere have presumed to reform the established ceremonies of the religions, and to change their accepted doctrines. For as we have observed throughout the past, in the most noteworthy mutations of the human race, in which nature has made its greatest efforts, extreme malice is encountered along with excellent virtue, and extraordinary calamities have accompanied great felicity. So one could not imagine any kind of misfortune or vice which is not found in this century at the very time when good letters are revived and the arts restored. There is no one among all Christians and barbarians who has not greatly suffered. No part of the habitable earth, no person, is free from afflictions, which increase from day to day and are too well known, to our loss and confusion.

Everywhere states have been afflicted, disturbed, or ruined; everywhere religions have been troubled by heresies. Not only the whole of Europe, but also the remote regions of Asia and Africa, the inhabitants of the new lands and of the East and West Indies, innumerable in multitude and scattered in countless places, have been torn by foreign and civil war, long continued. From this has followed the excessive price of everything, together with famine and frequent pestilence. One must believe that God, in wrath against mortals, sends such calamities both in general and in particular, to correct our vices and to lead us back to greater knowledge of Him and reverence for Him. Not for a long time has there been more malice in the world, more impiety and disloyalty. Piety is extinguished, simplicity and innocence are mocked, and only the shade of justice remains. Everything is pell-mell and in confusion; nothing is as it should be. . . .

Having set forth succinctly the excellence of this century, we shall now compare it with the most famous ones of the past in respect to arms, artillery, captains, armies, battles, sieges, empires and other states, travels by sea and land, discoveries of countries, wealth, customs and disciplines, in order to learn in what respects it is superior or inferior or equal to them. . . .

Great minds endowed with a capacity for letters have always been rare, even in the most learned centuries and among the most gifted peoples. Consequently the excellence of knowledge has likewise been rare, and so much the more admirable. In order to achieve it, there must be men of happy character, laborious diligence, and constant perseverance, who are advanced, honoured and rewarded by princes. The latter, however, in general care little about letters and support them meagrely. Students, if they are poor,

apply themselves to gainful arts in order to have something to live on, after profiting only moderately from
letters. If they are rich, they want pleasure, seeking the
easy surface of learning and not its painful depths.
Most instructors use routine methods and digests, fulfilling their duties perfunctorily. Most of those who
write only repeat or copy grammars, works on rhetoric,
dialectic, texts, introductions, epitomes, annotations,
corrections, translations, epistles, orations, eclogues, dialogues, adages, elegies, odes, vernacular rhymes, and
other similar versification.

It is necessary, moreover, to learn from books in
schools the Latin, Greek, Hebrew, Chaldean, and Arabic, which were native languages to the ancients who
learned them in the cradle by speaking. These use up
a great deal of time and the best of one's life, which
would be better employed in the knowledge of things
and the understanding of the disciplines. There is still
another difficulty among scholars which is not slight,
that they spend their lives sheltered by the academic
shade without acquiring any poise and without having
any experience of practical affairs, although learning is
imperfect without application. That is why today we
do not have such eminent persons in philosophy as Pythagoras, Thales, Plato, Aristotle, Theophrastus; in eloquence as Demosthenes and Cicero; in medicine as
Hippocrates, Galen, and Avicenna; in law as Servius,
Sulpicius, Papinian, and Ulpian; in history as Herodo-
tus, Thucydides, Polybius, Sallust, Titus Livius, Tacitus;
in mathematics as Euclid, Eudoxius, Archimedes, and
Ptolemy. In the latter, however, there have been a
number of very excellent men in this age. For from the
time when the mathematical sciences died out in Egypt
and were neglected by the Greeks and Arabs, they
were never more illustrious than they are today, espe-

cially astrology and cosmography. For the ancients scarcely understood half of the heavens, the earth, and the sea, knowing nothing in the West beyond the Canaries and in the East beyond Catigare. Today the whole of the earth and sea is known and travelled over.

Thales, Pythagoras, Aristotle, Hipparchus, Artemidorus, Eratosthenes, Strabo, Pliny, Macrobius, Capellus, Vergil, and generally all the ancient authors except Ptolemy, Avicenna, and Albertus Magnus, thought that of the five zones of the heavens only two were inhabited, and that the other three remained empty because of excessive heat or extreme cold. Today nothing is more certain than that they are all inhabited. Pliny, Lactantius and St. Augustine believed there were no Antipodes, but now we control them and trade normally with them. Those who formerly looked at the heavens found few movements there and were scarcely able to comprehend ten of them. Now, as if the knowledge of both the one and the other world had been by some destiny reserved to our age, movements have been observed in greater number and more wonderful, and two other principal ones added to serve to prove with certainty various things appearing in the stars and to discover the secret mysteries of nature. So greatly has the whole of cosmography, together with astrology, been illuminated that if Ptolemy, father of both, returned to life he would not recognize them, augmented as they are by recent observations and navigations. Regiomontanus is considered the best mathematician of this time, and judged to be scarcely below Anaximander of Milesia or Archimedes of Syracuse. Peuerbach his teacher, Cardinal Cusa, and Copernicus, all Germans, have excelled in these disciplines. Also Gioviano Pontano has worked well in astrology, not less happily in prose than in poetry. . . . George Agricola, the German, has acquitted himself so well in the investigation of metals that Aristotle, Theophrastus, Pliny, and other ancients seem to have understood nothing in comparison with him. Count Giovanni Pico della Mirandola was the honour of this century, and could have been comparable to the whole of antiquity, Egyptian, Chaldean, Persian, Greek, Roman, and Arabic, if he had lived.

But now it is time to put an end to this discourse by which we have clearly shown the vicissitude in all human affairs, arms, letters, languages, arts, states, laws, and customs, and how they do not cease to rise and fall, growing better or worse alternately.

For if the memory and knowledge of the past serve as instruction to the present and warning to the future, it is to be feared that since they have now arrived at such great excellence, the power, wisdom, disciplines, books, industry, works, and knowledge of the world may in the future decline as they have done in the past and be destroyed; that the order and perfection of today will be succeeded by confusion, refinement by crudity, learning by ignorance, elegance by barbarism. I foresee already in my mind certain peoples, strange in form, colour, and habits, pouring in upon Europe, as did formerly the Goths, Huns, Lombards, Vandals, and Saracens, who destroyed our towns, cities, castles, palaces, and churches. They will change our customs, laws, languages, and religion; they will burn our libraries, ruining everything noble they find in the countries they occupy in order to destroy their honour and virtue. I foresee wars springing up in all parts, civil and foreign; factions and heresies arising which will profane all that they touch, human and divine; famine and pestilence menacing mortals; the order of nature, the regulation of the celestial movements, and the harmony of the elements breaking down with the advent of floods on the one hand, excessive heat on the other, and violent earthquakes. And I foresee the universe approaching its end through the one or other form of dislocation, carrying with it the confusion of all things and reducing them to their former state of chaos.

Although things proceed in this way, as the physicists tell us, according to the inevitable law of the world, and have their natural causes, nevertheless their coming about depends chiefly on divine providence, which is above all nature and alone knows the times determined in advance for their decline. For this reason men of good will should not be astounded but should rather take courage, each working faithfully in the vocation to which he is called, in order to preserve as many as possible of the fine things restored or recently invented, the loss of which would be irreparable, and to transmit them to those who come after us just as we have received them from our ancestors; likewise good letters insofar as it shall please God for them to endure. We shall pray Him to preserve from indignities those who worthily profess letters in order that they may persevere in this honourable study, improving the arts and clarifying the truth to His praise, honour, and glory.

From *De la vicissitude ou variété des choses en l'univers*, ed. B. W. Bates (Princeton: Princeton University Press, 1944); trans. J.B.R.

The Evils of the Times

JUSTUS LIPSIUS

1584

A FEW YEARS past, as I travelled towards Vienna in Austria, I turned aside (not without God's direction) to the town of Liége, being not far out of my way, and where I had some friends, whom both for custom and good will I was persuaded to salute. Among whom was Charles Langius, a man (simply and without boasting be it spoken) for virtue and learning the chief of the Flemings. Who having received me into his house, tempered my entertainment, not only with courtesy and good will, but also with such communication as was profitable to me and will be while I live. For he was the man who opened my eyes by driving away the clouds of some vulgar opinions; he showed me the pathway whereby I might directly come (as Lucretius says):

> To the lofty temple of sages right
> By the clear beams of learning's light.

For, as we walked in the porch of his house after noon, the hot sun towards the end of June being in its full force, he asked me friendly of my journey, and the causes thereof.

When I had spoken to him much of the troubles of the Low Countries, of the insolence of the governors and soldiers, I added lastly that I pretended other excuses, but this in truth was the cause of my departure.

For (said I) who is of so hard and flinty a heart that he can any longer endure these evils? We are tossed, as you see, these many years with the tempest of civil wars; and like seafaring men are we beaten with sundry blasts of troubles and sedition. If I love quietness and rest, the trumpets and rattling of armour interrupt me. If I take solace in my country gardens and farms, the soldiers and murderers force me into the town. Therefore, Langius, I am resolved, leaving this unfortunate and unhappy Belgica (pardon me, my dear country) to change land for land, and to fly to some other part of the world, where I may neither hear of the name or facts of a Pelops' brood.

Hereat Langius much marvelling and moved: "Yea, friend Lipsius, and will you thus leave us?" "Yes, truly," said I, "I will either leave you, or this life. How can I fly from these evils but only by flight? For, to see and suffer these things daily as heretofore, I cannot, Langius; neither have I any plate of steel about my heart." Langius sighed at these words, and therewithal said unto me, "O foolish youth, what childishness is this? Or how think you to seek safety by flying away? Your country, I confess, is tossed and turmoiled grievously. What part of Europe is at this day free? So you may conjecture that saying of Aristophanes to prove true: 'Thundering Jupiter will turn all things upside down.'

"Wherefore, Lipsius, you must not forsake your country, but your affections. Our minds must be so confirmed and conformed that we may be at rest in troubles, and have peace even in the midst of war." Hereto I, rashly enough, replied, "Nay, surely, I will forsake my country, knowing that it is less grief to hear report of evils than to be an eyewitness to them. Besides that, thereby we ourselves shall be without danger of the lists. Mark you not what Homer wisely warns? 'Be out of the weapons' reach, lest that haply some man add one wound to another.'"

Langius, beckoning somewhat with his head: "I hear you, Lipsius, but I had rather you would hearken to the voice of wisdom and reason. For these mists and clouds that thus encompass you do proceed from the smoke of opinions. Wherefore I say with Diogenes, 'You have more need of reason than of a rope.' That bright beam of reason, I mean, which may illuminate the obscurity of your brain. Behold, you forsake your country; tell me, in good sooth, in forsaking it, can you forsake yourself also? See that the contrary does not happen: and that whithersoever you go, you carry not in your breast the fountain and food of your own grief. As they that are held in a fever do toss and turn themselves unquietly, and often change their beds through a vain hope of remedy; in like case are we, who being sick in our minds do, without any fruit, wander from one country to another. This is indeed to betray our grief, but not to allay it. To discover this inward flame, but not to quench it: very fitly said that wise Roman (Seneca), 'It is proper to a sick person not to suffer anything long, but to use mutations instead of medicines. Hereof proceed wandering peregrinations and walkings on sundry shores, and our inconstancy, always loathing things present, at one time will be on the sea, then incontinently desires the land.' Therefore you fly from troubles always, but never escape them. . . .

"You say, this age is the unhappiest that ever was. This has been an old lay, long ago used. I know your grandfather said so, and likewise your father. I know also that your children and children's children will sing the same note. It is a thing naturally given unto men to cast their eyes narrowly upon all things that are grievous, but to wink at such as are pleasant. As flies and such-like vile creatures do never rest long upon smooth and fine polished places, but do stick fast to rough and filthy corners, so the murmuring mind does lightly pass over the consideration of all good fortune, but never forgets the adverse or evil. It handles and pries into that, yes, and oftentimes augments it with great wit. Like as lovers do always behold something in their mistress whereby they think her to excel all others, even so do men that mourn, in their miseries. Yea, moreover we imagine things that are false, and bewail not only things present, but also such as are to come. And what gain we by this fore-reaching wit of ours? Surely nothing else, but that as some spying afar off the dust raised by an army, do thereupon forsake their tents for fear; so the vain shadow of future danger casts us down into the pit of desperation. . . .

"But you, Lipsius, let pass these vulgar matters, and follow me now to that comparison which you so much desire. Thereby it shall most plainly appear unto you that the miserable desolations of old time were not only in all respects equal to these of our age but did far surpass them; and that we who live in these days have cause to rejoice rather than to grudge. You say we are tossed with wars. What then? Were not they of old time likewise? Yes, Lipsius, they had their beginning with the world, and shall never be at an end so long as the world lasts. But perhaps theirs were not so great nor so grievous as ours are. Nay, but it is so far otherwise that all ours are mere jestings and toys (I speak in good earnest), if they are compared with the ancient ages. I shall hardly find an entrance in, or a way out, if once I throw myself into this deep sea of examples. . . .

"Finally you accuse, moreover, the tyranny of these

times, and the oppressions of body and mind. It is not my purpose ambitiously to extol this our age, or to afflict and grieve it. For what good would come thereof? I will speak of that which makes for my purpose of comparison. When were not these evils rife? And where not? Name me any age without some notable tyranny, or any country? If you can do so (let me abide the danger of this hazard), I will confess that we are the most wretched of all wretches. Why do you hold your peace? I see that the old taunting by-word is true, 'That all good princes may be written at large in the compass of our ring.' For it is naturally given to men's dispositions to use imperial authority insolently, nor can they easily keep a mean in that thing which is above mediocrity. Even we ourselves who thus complain of tyranny do bear in our breasts some seed thereof, and many of us do not want will to perform it, but ability. The serpent being benumbed with cold has yet his poison within him, but does not cast it out. So it is with us, whom only imbecility keeps back from doing harm, and a certain coldness of Fortune. Give strength, give fit opportunity or instruments, and I fear me that they who now are so querulous against mighty men will be most unruly themselves. We have examples in the common course of our life. See how this father tyrannizes over his children, that master over his servants, another schoolmaster over his scholars. . . .

"You reply yet that all these are only oppressions of the body, but now this passes all the rest, that we endure also servile oppression of our minds. Is it so indeed? Of our minds? Take heed this be not spoken more enviously than truly. He seems to me to know neither himself, nor the celestial nature of the mind, who thinks it may be oppressed or constrained. For no outward force can ever make you to will what you will not, or to believe that you believe not. A man may have power upon this bond or fetter of the mind, but not over the mind itself. A tyrant has power to loose it from the body, but not unloose the nature thereof. Such things as are pure, everlasting, and of fiery nature set nought by all external and violent handling.

"But, say you, it is not lawful for me to express my mind freely. Be it so; herein your tongue alone is bridled, not your mind. Your judgment is not restrained, but your acts. But this is a strange course, and never before heard of. Alas, good man, how are you deceived? How many could I recount unto you, who for their unadvised tongues have suffered punishment of all their senses under tyrants? How many of them have endeavoured to force and constrain men's judgments? Yea, their judgments, I say, in matters of religion. . . .

"Neither will I add any more touching comparison; I come now to the last troop of my legion, which fights against novelty, but briefly, and with contempt of it. For it shall rather gather up the spoils of the conquered enemies than be forced to any fierce grappling with them. For in very truth, what is there here that can be accounted new to any man, unless that you yourself, being new-born, are a novice in human affairs? Well spoke Crantor, and wisely, who had ever this verse in his mouth: 'Woe is me, what woe is me? We have suffered but things pertaining to men.' For these miseries do but wheel about continually, and circularly run about this circle of the world. Why do you sigh for the happening of these heavy accidents? Why do you marvel at them? . . .

"This rather is a thing to be wondered at, if any man were lawlessly exempted from this common law, and carried none of that burden, whereof every man bears a part. Solon, seeing a very friend of his at Athens mourning piteously, brought him into a high tower, and showed him underneath all the houses in that great city, saying to him, 'Think with yourself how many sundry mournings in times past have been in all these houses, how many at this present are, and in time to come shall be, and leave off to bewail the miseries of mortal folk, as if they were your own.'

"I would wish you, Lipsius, to do the like in this wide world. But because you cannot in deed and fact, go to, do it a little while in conceit and imagination. Suppose, if it please you, that you are with me in the top of that high hill Olympus. Behold from thence all towns, provinces, and kingdoms of the world, and think that you see even so many enclosures full of human calamities. These are but only theatres and places for the purpose prepared, wherein Fortune plays her bloody tragedies. Neither cast your eyes far from here. Do you see Italy? It is not yet full thirty years ago since it had rest from cruel and sharp wars on every side. Do you behold the large country of Germany? There were lately in her great sparks of civil dissension, which do begin to burn again, and, unless I am deceived, will grow to a more consuming flame. Britain? In it there have been continual wars and slaughters, and in that now it rests awhile in peace, must be referred to the government of a peaceable sex. What of France? See, and pity her. Even now a festered gangrene of bloody war creeps through every joint thereof. So is it in all the world besides. Which things think well upon, Lipsius, and by this communication or participation of miseries, lighten your own. And like as they who rode gloriously in triumph had a servant behind their backs, who in the midst of all their triumphant jollity cried out often-times, 'Thou art a man,' so let this be ever as a prompter by thy side, 'That these things are human,

or appertaining to men.' For as labour being divided
between man is easy, even so likewise is sorrow."

From *Two Bookes of Constancie*, trans. John Stradling (London
1594).

Don Quixote and the Golden Age

MIGUEL DE CERVANTES SAAVEDRA

1605

THE GOATHERDS did not understand all this jargon
about squires and knights-errant; they did nothing
but eat, keep silent, and study their guests, who very
dexterously and with much appetite were stowing away
chunks of meat as big as your fist. When the meat
course was finished, they laid out upon the sheepskins
a great quantity of dried acorns and half a cheese,
which was harder than if it had been made of mortar.
The drinking horn all this while was not idle but went
the rounds so often—now full, now empty, like the
bucket of a water wheel—that they soon drained one
of the two wine bags that were on hand. After Don
Quixote had well satisfied his stomach, he took up a
handful of acorns and, gazing at them attentively, fell
into a soliloquy.

"Happy the age and happy those centuries to which
the ancients gave the name of golden, and not because
gold, which is so esteemed in this iron age of ours,
was then to be had without toil, but because those who
lived in that time did not know the meaning of the
words 'thine' and 'mine.' In that blessed era all things
were held in common, and to gain his daily sustenance

no labour was required of any man save to reach forth
his hand and take it from the sturdy oaks that stood
liberally inviting him with their sweet and seasoned
fruit. The clear-running fountains and rivers in magnificent abundance offered him palatable and transparent
water for his thirst; while in the clefts of the rocks and
the hollows of the trees the wise and busy honey-
makers set up their republic so that any hand whatever
might avail itself, fully and freely, of the fertile harvest
which their fragrant toil had produced. The vigorous
cork trees of their own free will and grace, without the
asking, shed their broad, light bark with which men
began to cover their dwellings, erected upon rude
stakes merely as a protection against the inclemency of
the heavens.

"All then was peace, all was concord and friendship;
the crooked plowshare had not as yet grievously laid
open and pried into the merciful bowels of our first
mother, who without any forcing on man's part yielded
her spacious fertile bosom on every hand for the satisfaction, sustenance, and delight of her first sons. Then
it was that lovely and unspoiled young shepherdesses,
with locks that were sometimes braided, sometimes flowing, went roaming from valley to valley and hillock to
hillock with no more garments than were needed to
cover decently that which modesty requires and always
has required should remain covered. Nor were their
adornments such as those in use today—of Tyrian
purple and silk worked up in tortured patterns; a few
green leaves of burdock or of ivy, and they were as
splendidly and as becomingly clad as our ladies of the
court with all the rare and exotic tricks of fashion that
idle curiosity has taught them.

"Thoughts of love, also, in those days were set forth
as simply as the simple hearts that conceived them,

without any roundabout and artificial play of words
by way of ornament. Fraud, deceit, and malice had not
yet come to mingle with truth and plain-speaking. Justice kept its own domain, where favor and self-interest
dared not trespass, dared not impair her rights, becloud,
and persecute her as they now do. There was no such
thing then as arbitrary judgments, for the reason that
there was no one to judge or be judged. Maidens in
all their modesty, as I have said, went where they
would and unattended; whereas in this hateful age of
ours none is safe, even though she go to hide and shut
herself up in some new labyrinth like that of Crete;
for in spite of all her seclusion, through chinks and
crevices or borne upon the air, the amorous plague
with all its cursed importunities will find her out and
lead her to her ruin.

"It was for the safety of such as these, as time went
on and depravity increased, that the order of knights-
errant was instituted, for the protection of damsels, the
aid of widows and orphans, and the succouring of the
needy. It is to this order that I belong, my brothers, and
I thank you for the welcome and the kindly treatment
that you have accorded to me and my squire. By natural law, all living men are obliged to show favor to
knights-errant, yet without being aware of this you
have received and entertained me; and so it is with
all possible good will that I acknowledge your own
will to me."

This long harangue on the part of our knight—it
might very well have been dispensed with—was all
due to the acorns they had given him, which had
brought back to memory the age of gold; whereupon
the whim had seized him to indulge in this futile
harangue with the goatherds as his auditors. They
listened in open-mouthed wonderment, saying not a

word, and Sancho himself kept quiet and went on munching acorns, taking occasion very frequently to pay a visit to the second wine bag, which they had suspended from a cork tree to keep it cool.

From *The Ingenious Gentleman Don Quixote de la Mancha*, trans. Samuel Putnam (New York: The Viking Press, 1949).

The Return of the Muses

The Man of Letters

FRANCESCO PETRARCA

1352

Is IT then true that this disease of writing, like other malignant disorders, is, as the Satirist claims, incurable, and, as I begin to fear, contagious as well? How many, do you reckon, have caught it from me? Within our memory, it was rare enough for people to write verses. But now there is no one who does not write them; few indeed write anything else. Some think that the fault, so far as our contemporaries are concerned, is largely mine. I have heard this from many, but I solemnly declare, as I hope sometime to be granted immunity from the other ills of the soul—for I look for none from this—that I am now at last suddenly awakened for the first time by warning signs to a consciousness that this may perhaps be true; while intent only upon my own welfare, I may have been unwittingly injuring, at the same time, myself and others. I fear that the reproaches of an aged father, who unexpectedly came to me, with a long face and almost in tears, may not be without foundation. "While I," he said, "have always honoured your name, see the return

120

you make in compassing the ruin of my only son!" I
stood for a time in embarrassed silence, for the age of
the man and the expression of his face, which told of
great sorrow, went to my heart. Then, recovering myself, I replied, as was quite true, that I was unac-
quainted with either him or his son. "What matters it,"
the old man answered, "whether you know him or not?
He certainly knows you. I have spent a great deal in
providing instruction for him in the civil law, but he
declares that he wishes to follow in your footsteps. My
fondest hopes have been disappointed, and I presume
that he will never be either a lawyer or a poet." At this
neither I nor the others present could refrain from
laughter, and he went off none the better humoured.
But now I recognize that this merriment was ill-timed,
and that the poor old man deserved our consolation,
for his complaints and his reproaches were not un-
grounded. Our sons formerly employed themselves in
preparing such papers as might be useful to themselves
or their friends, relating to family affairs, business, or
the wordy din of the courts. Now we are all engaged
in the same occupation, and it is literally true, as
Horace says, "learned or unlearned, we are all writing
verses alike."

It is after all but a poor consolation to have companions in misery. I should prefer to be ill by myself.
Now I am involved in others' ill-fortune as well as in
my own, and am hardly given time to take breath. For
every day letters and poems from every corner of our
land come showering down upon my devoted head.
Nor does this satisfy my foreign friends. I am overwhelmed by floods of missives, no longer from France
alone, but from Greece, from Germany, from England.
I am unable to judge even my own work, and yet I
am called upon to be the universal critic of others.

Were I to answer the requests in detail, I should be the busiest of mortals. If I condemn the composition, I am a jealous carper at the good work of others; if I say a good word for the thing, it is attributed to a mendacious desire to be agreeable; if I keep silence altogether, it is because I am a rude, pert fellow. They are afraid, I infer, that my disease will not make away with me promptly enough. Between their goading and my own madness I shall doubtless gratify their wishes.

But all this would be nothing if, incredible as it may seem, this subtle poison had not just now begun to show its effects in the Roman Curia itself. What do you think the lawyers and doctors are up to? Justinian and Aesculapius have palled upon them. The sick and the litigious cry in vain for their help, for they are deafened by the thunder of Homer's and Vergil's names, and wander oblivious in the woody valleys of Cirrha, by the purling waters of the Aonian fountain. But it is hardly necessary to speak of these lesser prodigies. Even carpenters, fullers, and ploughmen leave the implements of their calling to talk of Apollo and the Muses. I cannot say how far the plague, which lately was confined to a few, has now spread.

If you would find an explanation for all this, you must recollect that although the delights of poetry are most exquisite, they can be fully understood only by the rarest geniuses, who are careless of wealth and possess a marked contempt for the things of this world, and who are by nature especially endowed with a peculiar elevation and freedom of soul. Consequently, as experience and the authority of the most learned writers agree, in no branch of art can mere industry and application accomplish so little. Hence—and you may find it comical, although it disgusts me—all the poets are nowadays to be found on the street corner,

and we can descry scarcely one on Helicon itself. They
are all nibbling at the Pierian honeycomb, but no one
can manage to digest it. How delightful indeed must
this gift be to those who really possess it, when it can
exercise such a fascination over sluggish minds, and in
our vain and degenerate age can induce even the most
avaricious to leave the pursuit of gain! On one thing,
at least, our country may be congratulated: in spite of
all the tares and sterile stalks which cumber the earth,
some signs of true youthful genius are to be discovered.
Some, if I am not misled by my hopes, will not drink
in vain of the Castalian spring. I felicitate thee, Mantua,
beloved of the Muses, thee, Padua, thee, Verona, thee,
Cimbria, thee, Sulmo, and thee, Parthenope, home of
Maro, when I see elsewhere the thirsty herd of upstart
poetasters wandering drearily among uncertain byways!

In J. H. Robinson and H. W. Rolfe, *Petrarch, the First Modern
Scholar and Man of Letters* (New York and London: G. P. Putnam's Sons, 1898).

The Return of the Muses

GIOVANNI BOCCACCIO

c. 1370

TO JACOPO PIZZINGHE

In our age, if I observe well, more illustrious men
have come from heaven, generous spirits who wish to
raise up again with all their strength the oppressed art
of poetry, and to recall it from exile into its former
abode; and not in vain. But we see, as you will not be
displeased to read, or we could have seen, that in ad-

vance of others who are worthy of note, a famous man, our Dante Alighieri, who dwelt in the house of Philosophy, had drunk the honied waters at that fount which was lost many centuries ago. We see also that he reached it, not by the path that the ancients had followed, but by certain byways entirely unknown to our ancestors, seeking it not without anxious effort; and then, exalted to the stars, he ascended the mountain and arrived at the place where this fount began. There he awakened those half-sleeping sisters, the Muses, and drew Phoebus back to his lyre, and dared to urge them to take up the maternal song. . . . And it is indeed to be lamented that, when the writing of his glorious work had been finished, Dante departed uncelebrated, carried off to well-deserved honour by a premature death. He left, besides his sacred poem, the heritage that, after the long-hidden fame of poetry had been spread abroad, those who wished could learn from a new poet what the nature of poetry is and with what its function is concerned.

Then, after Dante, his fellow citizen of Florence, that illustrious man, Francesco Petrarca, my teacher, rejecting the principles of writers who, as has already been said, had hardly touched on the threshold of poetry, began to follow the ancient path, with such fortitude of heart, such ardour of spirit, and such acuteness of talent that no hindrances could stop him, and no obstacles of the way could frighten him. Indeed, by clearing away the brambles and thickets with which he found the path encumbered through the negligence of mortals, and piling up in a solid heap the half-eroded rocks which had descended in an avalanche, he opened the way for himself and for those who wished to ascend after him.

For Petrarca cleansed the fount of Helicon, swampy

with mud and rushes, restoring its waters to their former purity, and reopened the Castalian cave which was overgrown with the entwining of wild vines. Clearing the laurel grove of briars, he restored Apollo to his ancient temple and brought back the Muses, soiled by rusticity, to their pristine beauty. Then he ascended to the topmost peaks of Parnassus.

From there he brought back to his own age the laurel wreath which had not been seen for perhaps a thousand years or more, and displayed it to the citizens of Rome, amid the applause of the Senate. He forced the rusted hinges of the ancient Capitol to turn in the opposite direction, and the extreme joy of the Romans sealed their annals with an unaccustomed triumph. O admirable honour! O memorable deed! By his mighty efforts and by those meticulous writings which are now renowned everywhere, by his lofty song which sounds forth swiftly as if through the whole world, this man has spread the fame of poetry which he recalled from its hiding place. He has revived in noble spirits the hope which had almost died, and showed that contrary to the belief of many, the way to Parnassus is open and its summit accessible. And I do not doubt that he has inspired many to ascend it. . . .

Advance then, and with good and favourable omen, ascend with high courage even to the peak, so that wreathed with laurel you may be seen in your own glory by those panting in the ascent, and from the watchtower of the Capitoline citadel you may make yourself known to the whole world. Make joyful the Italy of those who mourn. Turn, I beg you, filial eyes on her, and this I want to say also to other Italians. Behold how the Roman Empire fell. Think what it is like to see Rome herself, once mistress of the world, now torpid under the harsh yoke of the Pharisees.

Think what it is to remember the notable triumphs of the generals, to see the statues and the monuments bearing witness to illustrious deeds, to reflect upon the famous works of the philosophers, and the myrtle and laurel wreaths of the poets, surpassing those of Greece herself, to recall to memory the military discipline in which Rome excelled other nations, and the authority of the laws by which the whole world was governed, and the striking example of morals.

All these achievements, not to mention others, and to say nothing of the rest of Italy, our ancestors, to their very great dishonour, neglected with godlike irresponsibility and allowed them to be defiled, to be snatched away or shamefully destroyed by foreign peoples. And if all the glories of Rome may not be restored, at least, in the splendour of your poetic fame take pity on these immense misfortunes, and ease them as much as you can by taking them upon your dutiful shoulders . . . so that among the barbarian nations Rome can display at least something of her ancient majesty. . . . And mingling with the choruses of the rejoicing, I shall add my voice to those who are extolling your name with well-deserved praise: "Now Justice, the Maid, returns, the reign of Saturn is now restored."

From *Lettere edite ed inedite di Giovanni Boccaccio*, ed. Corazzini (Florence, 1877); trans. M.M.M.

Petrarca and the Art of Poetry

LEONARDO BRUNI

1436

THE Latin language, in all its perfection and greatness, flourished most vigorously in the time of Cicero, for its first state was not polished or refined or subtle, but, mounting little by little to perfection, it reached its highest summit in the time of Cicero. After his age it began to sink and to descend, as until that time it had risen, and many years had not passed before it experienced a great decline and diminution; and it can be said that letters and the studies of the Latin language went hand in hand with the condition of the Roman Republic, which had also grown in power until the age of Cicero.

After the liberty of the Roman people had been lost through the rule of the emperors, who did not desist from killing and eliminating the men of excellence, the flourishing condition of studies and of letters perished, together with the welfare of the city of Rome. Augustus, who was the least evil of the emperors, had thousands of Roman citizens slain; Tiberius, Caligula, Claudius and Nero did not leave anyone alive who had the face of a man. There followed, then, Galba, Otho, and Vitellius, who killed off each other within a few months. After them there were no more emperors of Roman blood, since the country had been so ruined by the preceding emperors that no one of any excellence remained. . . . Why am I relating all this? Simply to

demonstrate that as the city of Rome was destroyed by
the emperors, who were perverse tyrants, so studies and
Latin letters experienced a like ruin and decay, to such
an extent that finally almost no one could be found who
understood Latin literature with any refinement. Then
Italy was invaded successively by the Goths and the
Lombards, barbarian and foreign peoples, who almost
completely extinguished all knowledge of letters, as appears in the documents drawn up in that time, than
which nothing could be found more coarse and crude.

From the time when the liberty of the Italian peoples
was recovered, by the defeat of the Lombards who had
occupied Italy for two hundred and four years, the
cities of Tuscany and elsewhere began to revive, and
to take up studies, and somewhat to refine the coarse
style. So little by little these came to recover vigour,
but very feebly, and without any true sense of refinement, paying more attention to writing in vernacular
rhymes than to other forms. And so until the time of
Dante few knew the cultivated style, and those few
understood it rather badly, as we have said in the life
of Dante.

Francesco Petrarca was the first who had such grace
of talent, and who recognized and restored to light the
ancient elegance of style which was lost and dead, and
although in him it was not perfect, nevertheless by
himself he saw and opened the way to this perfection,
by recovering the works of Cicero, by enjoying them,
by understanding them, and by adapting himself as
much as he could, and he learned the way to that most
elegant and perfect fluency. Certainly he did enough
merely by showing the way to those who came after
him. Thus, devoted to these studies and manifesting
his talent even as a youth, Petrarca was much honoured
and renowned, and was asked by the pope to act as

secretary of his court, but he never consented or
sought his own gain; nevertheless, in order to live in
ease and in an honourable fashion, he accepted benefices and became a secular cleric. This he did not so
much of his own will as constrained by necessity, since
little or nothing remained of the inheritance from his
father, and in marrying off one of his sisters he spent
almost all of the paternal inheritance. His brother,
Gerardo, became a Carthusian monk, and died persevering in the religious life.

The honours of Petrarca were such that no man of
his age was more highly esteemed than he, not only
beyond the Alps but in Italy herself. For, coming to
Rome, he was solemnly crowned poet laureate. He
wrote in one of his letters that in 1350 he came to
Rome for the Jubilee, and in returning from Rome
made his way to Arezzo to see the place where he was
born, and when they learned of his coming all the
citizens came out to meet him, as if a king had come
to them. In conclusion, so great was his fame and the
honour accorded him by all cities and states and by all
the people throughout Italy, that it seemed an incredible and wonderful thing. Not only was he sought after
and revered by the populace and the middle class, but
he was provided with lavish pensions by the highest and
greatest princes and lords. He spent some time with
Messer Giangaleazzo Visconti, who begged him most
graciously to deign to remain with him; and he was
greatly honoured likewise by the lords of Padua. So
great was his reputation and the reverence in which he
was held by these lords that oftentimes they argued at
length with him to persuade him to take precedence in
entering or leaving a place, and to take the place of
honour. So honoured and rewarded in this life, Petrarca
lived until the very end of his days.

He had in his studies a singular gift, that he was highly skilled in both prose and poetry, and in both forms he wrote a great many works. His prose was graceful and flowery, his poetry was refined and full and very lofty. And this grace in both forms of writing has existed in few or in none except him, because it seems that nature inclines either toward the one or the other and man is wont to dedicate himself to that one in which he excels by nature. Hence it happened that Vergil, who was most excellent in poetry, accomplished nothing in prose, or wrote nothing; and Cicero, who was the greatest master of style in prose, achieved nothing in poetry. We see the same thing in other poets and orators, that they won high praise in one of these forms of writing, but none of them, that I remember having read about, in both. Petrarca alone excelled by his singular gift in both forms of writing, and he composed many works in prose and poetry, which there is no need to enumerate since they are well known.

Petrarca died at Arquà, a castle of Padua, to which he had retired in his old age for peace and a leisurely life, removed from all disturbance. As long as he lived he maintained the very closest friendship with Giovanni Boccaccio, who was famous in that age in the same studies. So that when Petrarca died, the Florentine Muses, as if by hereditary succession, passed to Boccaccio, and in him dwelt the fame of the aforesaid studies. And this succession was also temporal, for when Dante died, Petrarca was seventeen years old, and when Petrarca died, Boccaccio was nine years younger than he, and thus by succession went the Muses.

From "Vita di Messer Francesco Petrarca," in P. Villani, Liber de civitatis Florentinae famosis civibus, ed. G. C. Galletti (Florence, 1847); trans. M.M.M.

The Glory of the Latin Language

LORENZO VALLA

c. 1430-1440

As OUR ANCESTORS, winning high praises, surpassed other men in military affairs, so by the extension of their language they indeed surpassed themselves, as if, abandoning their dominion on earth, they had attained to the fellowship of the gods in Paradise. If Ceres, Liber, and Minerva, who are considered the discoverers of grain, wine, oil, and many others have been placed among the gods for some benefaction of this kind, is it less beneficial to have spread among the nations the Latin language, the noblest and the truly divine fruit, food not of the body but of the soul? For this language introduced those nations and all peoples to all the arts which are called liberal; it taught the best laws, prepared the way for all wisdom; and finally, made it possible for them no longer to be called barbarians.

Why would anyone who is a fair judge of things not prefer those who were distinguished for their cultivation of the sacred mysteries of literature to those who were celebrated for waging terrible wars? For you may most justly call those men royal, indeed divine, who not only founded the republic and the majesty of the Roman people, insofar as this might be done by men, but, as if they were gods, established also the welfare of the whole world. Their achievement was the more amazing because those who submitted to our rule knew that they had given up their own government, and, what is more bitter, had been deprived of liberty, though not perhaps by violence. They recognized, however, that the Latin language had both strengthened and adorned their own, as the later discovery of wine did not drive out the use of water, or silk expel wool and linen, or gold the other metals, but added to these other blessings. And just as the beauty of a jewel set in a golden ring is not diminished but enhanced, so our language, in uniting with the vernacular speech of others, conferred splendour: it did not destroy it. For not by arms or bloodshed or wars was its domination achieved, but by benefits, love, and concord. Of this achievement (so far as I can conjecture) the sources have been, as I have said, first, that our ancestors perfected themselves to an incredible degree in all kinds of studies, so that no one seems to have been pre-eminent in military affairs unless he was distinguished also in letters, which was a not inconsiderable stimulus to the emulation of others; then, that they wisely offered honourable rewards to the teachers of literature; finally, that they encouraged all provincials to become accustomed to speak, both in Rome and at home, in the Roman fashion.

But since this is sufficient, I shall say no more about the comparison between the Roman Empire and its language. The Roman dominion, the peoples and nations long ago threw off as an unwelcome burden; the language of Rome they have thought sweeter than any nectar, more splendid than any silk, more precious than any gold or gems, and they have embraced it as if it were a god sent from Paradise. Great, therefore, is the sacramental power of the Latin language, truly great is its divinity, which has been preserved these many centuries with religious and holy awe, by strangers, by barbarians, by enemies, so that we Romans should not grieve but rejoice, and the whole listening earth should glory. We have lost Rome, we have lost authority, we have lost dominion, not by our own fault but by that of the times, yet we reign still, by this more splendid sovereignty, in a great part of the world. Ours is Italy, ours Gaul, ours Spain, Germany, Pannonia, Dalmatia, Illyricum, and many other lands. For wherever the Roman tongue holds sway, there is the Roman Empire.

But now the Greeks are going around, boasting about the abundance of their languages. Impoverished as they say it is, our one language is more effective than five of their dialects, which, according to them, are so much richer than ours. The Latin language is a single tongue, like one law, for many peoples; in one Greece there is not a single language (which is a scandalous thing), but many dialects, like factions in a state. Moreover, foreigners agree with us in speaking as we do; the Greeks cannot agree among themselves, much less hope to induce others to speak their language. Among the Greeks, various authors write in Attic, Aeolic, Ionic, Doric, Koiné; with us, that is among many nations, no one writes except in Latin, in the language that embraces all disciplines worthy of a free man, just as among the Greeks they are diffused in many dialects. Who does not know that when the Latin language flourishes, all studies and disciplines thrive, as they are ruined when it perishes? For who have been the most profound philosophers, the best orators, the most distinguished jurisconsults, and finally the greatest writers, but those indeed who have been most zealous in speaking well?

But when I wish to say more, sorrow hinders and torments me, and forces me to weep as I contemplate the state which eloquence had once attained and the condition into which it has now fallen. For what lover of letters and the public good can restrain his tears when he sees eloquence now in that state in which it was long ago when Rome was captured by the Gauls; everything was overturned, burned, destroyed, so that the Capitoline citadel hardly survived. Indeed, for many centuries not only has no one spoken in the Latin manner, but no one who has read Latin has understood it. Students of philosophy have not possessed, nor do they possess, the works of the ancient philosophers; nor do rhetoricians have the orators; nor lawyers the jurisconsults; nor teachers the known works of the ancients, as if after the Roman Empire had fallen, it would not be fitting to speak or understand in the Roman fashion, and the glory of Latinity was allowed to decay in rust and mould. And many, indeed, and varied are the opinions of wise men on how this happened. I neither accept nor reject any of these, daring only to declare soberly that those arts which are most closely related to the liberal arts, the arts of painting, sculpture, modelling, and architecture, had degenerated for so long and so greatly and had almost died with letters themselves, and that in this age they have been aroused and come to life again, so greatly increased is the number of good artists and men of letters who now flourish.

But truly, as wretched as were those former times in which no learned man was found, so much the more this our age should be congratulated, in which (if we exert ourselves a little more) I am confident that the language of Rome will shortly grow stronger than the city itself, and with it all disciplines will be restored. Therefore, because of my devotion to my native Rome and because of the importance of the matter, I shall arouse and call forth all men who are lovers of eloquence, as if from a watch tower, and give them, as they say, the signal for battle.

From *De elegantiis linguae latinae*, in F. A. Gragg, *Latin Writings of the Italian Humanists* (New York: Charles Scribner's Sons, 1927); trans. M.M.M.

Germany Invokes the Muses

JOACHIM VON WATT

1518

ALTHOUGH the splendour and dignity of the three tongues, Hebrew, Greek, and Latin, have developed a special and fitting art of poetry for utterances of the highest beauty, yet it can be shown that there are many other peoples who have practised this art, when nature has called it forth in their souls, as we have said, and it is evident that they have achieved in it their own special delights. To pass over other peoples for a time, I have often reflected, brother, on the great care, zeal, and effort the Germans have exercised in cultivating this art of poetry in their own language, a language most capable of elegance and copiousness of expression. Today the humbler sort of men still sing their poems on various themes, composed appropriately in the most precise rhythms, and arranged in the most regular sequence of syllables, and these indeed are very ancient songs, the work of only the most learned masters of varied subjects. . . .

Our own Germanic writers, during the common calamity of studies, were so wisely devoted to the art of poetry that they would have preferred to be accused of negligence in writing badly than of laziness in not writing at all. But no one has ever edited what is valuable of their work. For the poems of Rabanus [Rabanus Maurus, c. 784-856] on the mystery of the cross and other subjects are resplendent with an amazing art and skill. . . . His teacher Bede [673-735] was also extremely gifted and agreeable in poetry, as is revealed in two hymns of his which I published in years past, after I had found them in the very ancient library of the abbey of St. Gall. A little book on the cultivation of gardens by the monk Strabo [Walafrid Strabo, 809-849], of which I made a copy five years ago in the same library, shows that this pupil of Rabanus also loved and composed poetry. Many of his epigrams, dedicated to his master Rabanus, and to many others, would be most worthy of public reading, except that they are redolent indeed of the ruin of his time. I have observed the same thing in the works of the monk Notker [Notker Balbulus, 840-912], who composed what they call sequences with much learning and grace. He earlier wrote in hexameters some books concerning the life of St. Gall and his deeds and miracles. . . . To these works circumstances were so opposed that this very learned father, Notker, was unable to polish them and give them the finishing touches. The same thing is true of Bishop Aldhelm [c. 639-709], whose epigrams and riddles survive. Although these may seem crude to the more learned, I shall publish them shortly, after they have been corrected slightly, because there appears in them a certain measure of excellence. Who does not marvel, moreover, at Rosvitha [of Gandersheim, c. 935?-973?] and her works, which were recently edited by Conrad Celtes? Although these writings may be barbarous, if they are compared with those of the ancients, as I remember hearing Celtes himself say, yet if one keeps in mind her sex, place, and time it is certainly amazing how such skill in writing came to a womanly soul in such an unfavourable time. . . . This is especially surprising because it seems that the new Christian religion, which was almost entirely spread in barbarian or German lands by means of the monasteries, would have hindered, indeed despised and rejected, the art of poetry. Nevertheless, we know from the most ample testimony that this art was cultivated in German lands in that age when in its own native abode there was neither safety nor leisure for the pursuit of Latin letters. . . .

For it seems to me that the more refined studies lay prostrate, just as did that city which was the parent of elegance and of studies, after the Sennonian Gauls had invaded it and had destroyed everything. But as, by the will of the gods, Rome was defended and delivered from the final calamity by the leadership of Camillus, and later ascended to the greater glory of the Empire, so in this later age the best and highest God has ordained that one by one new Camilli have been born, and having pity on the republic of letters, they have dared to take up arms against any barbarous enemy whatsoever, and to fight steadfastly for the achievement of glory. The victory greatly longed for by all has rewarded their steadfastness, and has renewed and restored in us the well-deserved remembrance of things done in ages long past. For unless the divine splendour of languages should succumb again to the barbarians who were driven back by Camillus, this renewal and restoration of a great part of learning and knowledge, of the very largest part indeed of elegance, urbanity, and manners, has been achieved. . . .

Among the Germanic peoples, Rudolph Agricola the Frisian is most justly the first to be named, for he was

the first who by the brilliance of his own spirit summoned the noble Muses to cross the Alps themselves,
into those German lands which had earlier shown no
power of acquiring a knowledge of letters. This was
partly owing to the remoteness and inaccessibility of
these lands, qualities which were as advantageous to
the Roman Empire, according to Pliny, as they seemed
certainly most harmful to us, since they cut off the
opportunity for learning; partly (and I speak truly)
owing to the victorious power of arms among the Germans, which prevented or greatly hindered, according
to Caesar and Tacitus, communication with foreign
peoples. Thus it was that facility in the Latin language
could not exist in Germany, except insofar as it crept
in through the monasteries here and there, fostered by
the approved religion; for the monasteries were the
only schools of scholarship and erudition for our ancestors. . . .

Most happy, therefore, was Agricola, who wished to
lead the Muses from Italy into Germany, as if eternal
splendour flowed from them, so that at last they might
strive to conquer by the beauty of language where
once men had contended for glory with arms, and
might hold their colonies in elegance and grace rather
than in slavery. Teaching Greek and Latin literature in
the University of Heidelberg, Agricola advanced most
successfully the task which he had earlier undertaken
at Ferrara with the highest glory. He was a man of
very great learning in all honourable arts, and his
teaching produced many who were both erudite and
famous. . . .

A worthy pupil of his master Agricola was Conrad
Celtes, the Franconian, the best of German poets, who
was crowned laureate. He is not to be mentioned without an introduction of honour as the preceptor of my

youth, and I would discuss him more fully here, except
that, as is well known, I have recently written his life.
Celtes was exceedingly dear to those most fortunate
rulers, the Emperors Frederick III and his son Maximilian, because of his active advancement of Latin culture in their dominions. On receiving a ducal stipend,
he established the public teaching of poetry and oratory in the University of Vienna, and he himself began
this instruction, after he had taught literature there
for some years in the most praiseworthy fashion. Indeed, I do not know whether he displayed greater
grace or diligence in his teaching, for he was graceful
and orderly in exposition, and he was most careful in
explaining matters pertaining to antiquity, and to both
aspects of teaching he added the highest authority. He
was neither sharp nor haughty in manner, and he did
not claim a great deal of credit for censoring and correcting grammatical errors, as many are wont to do
nowadays, but he considered the height of glory to lie
in the advancement of truth in his auditors. He may be
named among the best scholars in astronomy and
physics, among the liberal arts, and, to sum it all up
in a word, he was perfectly accomplished.

From *De poetica et carminis ratione*, in H. Rupprich, *Humanismus
und Renaissance in der deutschen Städten und an den Universi-
täten* (Leipzig, 1935); trans. M.M.M.

The Arts Reborn

GIORGIO VASARI

1550

I DO NOT believe that I wandered far from the true solution when I suggested that the origin of these arts was nature herself—the first image or model, the most beautiful fabric of the world—and the master [was] that divine light infused into us by special grace, which has made us not only superior to all other animals, but has exalted us, if it be permitted so to speak, to the similitude of God Himself. This is my belief, and I think that every man who shall maturely consider the question will be of my opinion. And if it has been seen in our times—as I hope to demonstrate presently by various examples—that simple children, rudely reared in the woods, have begun to practise the arts of design with no other model than those beautiful pictures and sculptures furnished by nature, and no other teaching than their own genius—how much more easily may we believe that the first of mankind, in whom nature and intellect were all the more perfect in proportion as they were less removed from their first origin and divine parentage—that these men, I say, having nature for their guide, and the unsullied purity of their fresh intelligence for their master, with the beautiful model of the world for an exemplar, should have given birth to these most noble arts, and from a small beginning, ameliorating them by slow degrees, should have conducted them finally to perfection? I do not intend to deny that there must have been one who made the first commencement, for I know perfectly well that the first principle must have proceeded from some given time, and from some one person; neither will I deny the possibility that one may have assisted another, thus teaching and opening the way to design, to colour, and to relief; for I know that our art is altogether imitation, of nature principally, but also, for him who cannot soar so high, of the works of such as he esteems better masters than himself . . . Let us proceed to matters of which we have better knowledge, the perfection of the arts, namely, their decay and restoration, or rather second birth, of which we can speak on much better grounds.

The rise of art in Rome must have taken place at a late epoch, if it be true, as we find asserted, that among her first statues was the bronze figure of Ceres, formed from the spoils of Spurius Cassius, who was deliberately put to death by his own father, for having aspired to become king. And although the arts of sculpture and painting continued to be practised to the close of the reign of the twelve Caesars, yet they did not maintain themselves in that degree of excellence and perfection which they had previously displayed; so that, in all the buildings erected by the emperors, one after another, the arts may be gradually seen to decline, until all perfection of the art of design was ultimately lost. To the truth of this assertion, the works in sculpture and architecture, executed in Rome under Constantine, bear ample testimony, more particularly the triumphal arch, raised to him by the Roman people, near the Colosseum, where we perceive that, for the want of good masters, they not only availed themselves of sculptures executed in the time of Trajan, but also of the spoils brought to Rome from other parts of the empire. . . .

After the departure of Constantine, the Caesars whom he left in Italy continued building in Rome and elsewhere, and did their best for the execution of such works as they constructed; but, as we see, not only sculpture, but painting and architecture, fell constantly from bad to worse, and this, perhaps, because human affairs, when they begin to decline, never cease to sink, until they have reached the lowest depths of deterioration. . . .

So it chanced that, after these things, the barbarous nations of the world arose, in divers places, in rebellion against the Romans; whence there ensued, in no long time, not only the decline of that great empire, but the utter ruin of the whole, and more especially of Rome herself, when all the best artists, sculptors, painters, and architects were in like manner totally ruined, being submerged and buried, together with the arts themselves, beneath the miserable slaughters and ruins of that much renowned city. . . .

But infinitely more ruinous than all other enemies to the arts above named, was the fervent zeal of the new Christian religion, which, after long and sanguinary combats, had finally overcome and annihilated the ancient creeds of the pagan world, by the frequency of miracles exhibited, and by the earnest sincerity of the means adopted; and ardently devoted, with all diligence, to the extirpation of error, nay, to the removal of even the slightest temptation to heresy, it not only destroyed all the wondrous statues, paintings, sculptures, mosaics, and other ornaments of the false pagan deities, but at the same time extinguished the very memory, in casting down the honours, of numberless excellent ancients, to whom statues and other monuments had been erected, in public places, for their virtues, by the most virtuous times of antiquity. Nay, more than this, to build the churches of the Christian faith, this zeal not only destroyed the most renowned temples of the heathens, but, for the richer ornament of St. Peter's, and in addition to the many spoils previously bestowed on that building, the tomb of Adrian, now called the castle of St. Angelo, was deprived of its marble columns, to employ them for this church, many other buildings being in like manner despoiled, and which we now see wholly devastated. And although the Christian religion did not effect this from hatred to these works of art, but solely for the purpose of abasing and bringing into contempt the gods of the Gentiles, yet the result of this too ardent zeal did not fail to bring such total ruin over the noble arts, that their very form and existence was lost. . . .

It is to the masters of those times that we owe the fantastic images and absurd figures still to be seen in many old works. And a similar inferiority is perceptible in architecture, for it was necessary to build; but all good methods and correct forms being lost by the death of good artists and the destruction of their works, those who devoted themselves to that employment were in no condition to give either correct proportion or grace of any kind to their designs. Then arose new architects, and they, after the manner of their barbarous nations, erected the buildings in that style which we now call Gothic, and raising edifices that, to us moderns, are rather to the discredit than glory of the builders, until at a later period there appeared better artists, who returned, in some measure, to the purer style of the antique; and this may be seen in most of the old (but not antique) churches throughout Italy, which were built in the manner just alluded to by these last-named artists. . . .

It was only by slow degrees that those who came after, being aided in some places by the subtlety of the air around them, could begin to raise themselves from these depths; when, towards 1250, Heaven, moved to pity by the noble spirits which the Tuscan soil was producing every day, restored them to their primitive condition. It is true that those who lived in the times succeeding the ruin of Rome, had seen remnants of arches, colossi, statues, pillars, storied columns, and other works of art, not wholly destroyed by the fires and other devastations; yet they had not known how to avail themselves of this aid, nor had they derived any benefit from it, until the time specified above. When the minds then awakened, becoming capable of distinguishing the good from the worthless, and abandoning old methods, returned to the imitation of the antique, with all the force of their genius, and all the power of their industry.

But that my readers may the better comprehend what it is that I call "old," and what "antique," I add that the antique are works executed before the time of Constantine, in Corinth, Athens, Rome, and other far-famed cities, down to the times of Nero, Vespasian, Trajan, Hadrian, and Antoninus; "old" are such as were executed from the days of St. Silvester downwards, by a certain residue of the Greeks, whose profession was rather that of dyeing than painting. For the greater part of the excellent earlier artists being extirpated in those times of war, there remained, as I have said, nothing to these Greeks ("old," but not "antique") save only the first rude outlines on a ground of colour, as is made sufficiently manifest by a crowd of mosaics

executed throughout Italy by these Greeks and which
may be seen in any old church of whatsoever city you
please, through all the land. . . .

Thus much I have thought it advisable to say respecting the first commencement of sculpture and
painting, and may perhaps have spoken at greater
length than was here needful; but this I have done not
so much because I was carried on by my love of art, as
because I desire to be useful and serviceable to the
whole body of artists, for they, having here seen the
manner in which art proceeded from small beginnings,
until she attained the highest summit, and next how
she was precipitated from that exalted position into
the deepest debasement; and considering that it is the
nature of art, as of human existence, to receive birth, to
progress, to become old, and to die, may thus more
perfectly comprehend and follow the progress of her
second birth to the high perfection which she has once
more attained in these our days.

From *Lives of the Most Eminent Painters, Sculptors, and Architects*, trans. Mrs. Jonathan Foster (London: George Bell's Sons,
1890).

The New-Found World

The Golden World

PIETRO MARTIRE D'ANGHIERA

1511

WE HAVE DECLARED in the book here before, how the Admiral [Christopher Columbus] passed by the coasts of the Cannibals to the island of Hispaniola with his whole navy. But now we intend further to show what he found concerning the nature of this island, after he had better searched the secrets of the same; likewise of the island of Cuba near unto it, which he yet supposed to be the firm land. . . . [Hispaniola] reaches in length from the east to the west, seven hundred and fourscore miles. . . . The form of the island resembles the leaf of a chestnut tree. Upon a high hill on the north side of the island, he built a city, because this place was most apt for that purpose by reason of a mine of stones which was near to the same, serving well both to build with, and also to make lime. At the bottom of this hill there is a great plain of threescore miles in length. . . . Through this plain run divers fair rivers of wholesome waters. But the greatest of them which is navigable falls into the haven of the city for the space of half a furlong. How fertile

146

and fruitful this valley is, you shall understand by
these things which follow. On the shore of this river,
they have limited and enclosed certain ground to make
gardens and orchards, in which all kinds of bigger
herbs, such as radishes, lettuce, cabbages, borage, and
others, wax ripe within sixteen days after the seed is
sown. Likewise melons, gourds, cucumbers, and others,
within the space of thirty-six days. These garden herbs
they have fresh and green all the whole year. Also the
roots of the canes or reeds, of the liquor whereof sugar
is made, grow a cubit high within the space of fifteen
days, but the liquor is not yet hardened. The like they
affirm of plants or loppings of young vines, and say
that the second year they have gathered ripe and sweet
grapes of the same. . . . Furthermore, a man of the
country sowed a little wheat about the calends of
February, and brought with him to the city a handful
of the ripe ears of the same the third day before the
calends of April. . . . Also all kinds of pulse, such as
beans, peas, sytches, vetch, and others, are ripe twice
in the year. . . .

In the meantime, while these things were going on,
the Admiral sent out a company of thirty men to search
the region of Cipanga, otherwise called Cibana. This
region is full of mountains and rocks, and the middle
back of the whole island in which there is great plenty
of gold. When they that went to search the region returned, they reported marvellous things as touching the
great riches of this region. . . . The day before the
ides of March, the Admiral himself with all his horsemen and four hundred men on foot marched directly
toward the south side of the golden region. Thus passing over the river, the plain, and the mountain which
environed the other side of the plain, he chanced upon
another vale in which a river much bigger than the

first and many other medium-sized rivers run through. When he had also conveyed his army over the river and passed the second vale, which was in no part inferior to the first, he made way through the third mountain, where there was no passage before, and descended into another vale which was now the beginning of Cibana. Through this also run many floods and rivers, out of every hill, and in the sands of them all there is found great plenty of gold. And when he had now entered threescore and twelve miles into the golden region from the city, he intended to build a fortress upon the top of a hill, standing by the shore of a certain great river, that he might the better and more safely search the secrets of the inner parts of the region. This he called the fortress of St. Thomas. In the meantime, while he was building this, the inhabitants being desirous of hawk bells and other of our things, resorted daily thither. To whom the Admiral declared that if they would bring gold they should have whatsoever they would like. Forthwith turning their backs and running to the shore of the next river, they returned in a short time, bringing with them their hands full of gold. Amongst the others, there came an old man bringing with him two pebble stones of gold, weighing an ounce, desiring them to give him a bell for the same. He, when he saw our men marvel at the bigness thereof, made signs that they were but small and of no value in respect of some that he had seen. And taking in his hands four stones the least of which was as big as a walnut, and the biggest as big as an orange, he said that there were found pieces of gold so big in his country, being but half a day's journey from thence, and that they had no regard to the gathering thereof. Whereby we perceive that they care not much for gold inasmuch as it is gold only, but so far esteem it, as the hand of the artificer has fashioned it in some comely form. For who does greatly esteem rough marble or unwrought ivory? But if they be wrought by the cunning hand of Phidias or Praxiteles, and shaped to the similitude of the fair nymphs or fairies of the sea (called Nereides) or the fairies of the woods (called Hamadryades) they shall never lack buyers. Besides this old man, there came also divers others, bringing with them pebble stones of gold weighing ten or twelve drams and feared not to confess that in the place where they had gathered that gold there were found sometimes stones of gold as big as the head of a child. . . .

At length . . . [the Admiral] returned to the shore of Cuba by the same way which he came. Here a multitude of the inhabitants, women as well as men, resorted to him with cheerful countenance and without fear, bringing with them parrots, bread, water, and coneys, but especially stock doves much bigger than ours, which he affirms, in savour and taste, to be much more pleasant than our partridges. . . . As the Admiral heard Mass on the shore, there came towards him a certain governor [native ruler], a man of fourscore years of age and of great gravity, although he was naked saving his privy parts. He had a great train of men waiting on him. All the while the priest was at Mass, he showed himself very humble and gave reverent attention with grave and demure countenance. When the Mass was ended, he presented to the Admiral a basket of the fruits of his country, delivering the same with his own hands. When the Admiral had gently entertained him, desiring leave to speak, he made an oration in the presence of Didacus, the interpreter, to this effect. "I have been advised, most mighty prince, that you have of late with great power subdued

many lands and regions hitherto unknown to you, and
have brought no little fear upon all the people and
inhabitants of the same. Your good fortune you shall
bear with less insolence, if you remember that the souls
of men have two journeys after they are departed from
this body. The one foul and dark, prepared for such as
are injurious and cruel to mankind; the other pleasant
and delectable, ordained for them who in their lifetime
loved peace and quietness. If therefore you acknowledge yourself to be mortal, and consider that every
man shall receive condign reward or punishment for
such things as he has done in this life, you will wrongfully hurt no man."

When he had said these words and others like, which
were declared to the Admiral by the interpreter, he,
marvelling at the judgment of the naked old man, answered that he was glad to have his opinion as touching the sundry journeys and rewards of souls departed
from their bodies, supposing that neither he nor any
other of the inhabitants of those regions had had any
knowledge thereof. He declared further that the chief
cause of his coming thither was to instruct them in
such godly knowledge and true religion, and that he
was sent into those countries by the Christian King of
Spain (his lord and master) for the same purpose; and
especially to subdue and punish the cannibals and such
other mischievous people, and to defend innocents
against the violence of such evildoers, willing him and
all others who embraced virtue in no case to be afraid
but rather to open his mind unto him, if either he or
any other such quiet men as he was had sustained any
wrong of their neighbours, and that he would see the
same revenged. These comforting words of the Admiral
so pleased the old man that, notwithstanding his ex-

treme age, he would gladly have gone with the Admiral, as he would have done indeed, if his wife and children had not hindered him of his purpose. But he marvelled not a little that the Admiral was under the dominion of another, and much more when the interpreter told him of the glory, magnificence, pomp, great power, and accoutrements of war of our kings, and of the multitudes of cities and towns which were under their dominions.

Intending therefore to have gone with the Admiral, his wife and children fell prostrate at his feet, with tears desiring him not to forsake them and leave them desolate. At their pitiful requests, the worthy old man, being moved, remained at home to the comfort of his people and family, satisfying rather them than himself. For not yet ceasing to wonder, and of heavy countenance because he might not depart, he demanded often times if that land were not heaven, which brought forth such a kind of men. For it is certain that among them [the natives], the land is as common as the sun and water, and that Mine and Thine (the seeds of all mischief) have no place with them. They are content with so little that in so large a country they have rather superfluity than scarceness. So that (as we have said before) they seem to live in the golden world, without toil, living in open gardens, not entrenched with dikes, divided with hedges, or defended with walls. They deal truly one with another, without laws, without books, and without judges. They take him for an evil and mischievous man who takes pleasure in doing hurt to others. And albeit that they delight not in superfluities, yet they make provision for the increase of such roots whereof they make their bread, such as maize, cassava, and gourds, contented with such simple diet, whereby health is preserved and diseases avoided.

From *The Decades of the New World*, trans. by Richard Eden, in *The First Three English Books on America, 1511-1555*, ed. Edward Arber (Birmingham, Eng., 1885).

Joyful News from the New-Found World

NICOLAS MONARDES

1569-1571

IN THE YEAR of our Lord God 1492, our Spaniards were led by Sir Christopher Colon, being naturally born of the country Genoa, to discover the Occidental Indies, that is called at this day the new world, and they did discover the first land thereof, the eleventh day of October, of the said year; and from that time unto this, they discovered many and sundry islands, and much firm land, as well in that country which they call the new Spain, as in that which is called the Peru, where there are many provinces, many kingdoms, and many cities that have contrary and diverse customs in them, where have been found out things that never in these parts nor in any other parts of the world have been seen, nor unto this day known. And of other things which are now brought unto us in great abundance, that is to say, gold, silver, pearls, emeralds, turquoises, and other fine stones of great value, great is the excess and quantity that have come, and every day does come, and especially of gold and silver. And it is a thing of admiration that the great number of millions which have come, besides the great quantity of pearls, has filled the whole world; also they bring from those parts popinjays, griffons, apes, lions, gerfalcons and other kinds of hawks, tiger's wool, cotton wool, grain to dye colors withal, hides, sugars, copper, brazil, the wood ebony, anil. And of all these there is such great quantity that there come every year one hundred ships laden thereof, that it is a great thing and an incredible riches.

And besides these great riches, our Occidental Indies send unto us many trees, plants, herbs, roots, juices, gums, fruits, liquors, stones that are of great medicinal virtues, in which there be found, and have been found in them, very great effects that surpass others in value and price. All the aforesaid, by so much as corporal health is more excellent and necessary than temporal goods, which things all the world lacks, the want thereof is not a little hurtful, according to the great profit which we see follows, by the use of them, not only in our Spain but in the whole world. . . .

And as there are discovered new regions, new kingdoms, and new provinces by our Spaniards, they have brought unto us new medicines and new remedies wherewith they cure and make whole many infirmities, which if we lack them, were incurable, and without any remedy; which things although some have knowledge of them, yet they be not common to all people. For which cause I intend to treat and to write of all things that they bring from our Indies which serve for the art and use of medicine, and the remedy of the hurts and diseases that we suffer and endure; whereof no small profit follows to those of our time and also unto them that shall come after us; and I shall be the first, so that the followers may add thereunto with this beginning, that which they shall know more about and by experience shall find.

And as in this city of Seville, which is the port and market of all the Occidental Indies, we know about them more than in any other parts of all Spain, because all things come first hither, where with narration and greater experience it is known. I do it with experience and use of them this forty years that I cure in this city, where I have informed myself from those who have brought these things out of those parts with much care, and I have made experience thereof with many and divers persons, with all diligence and foresight possible, and with much happy success. . . .

This herb which commonly is called tobacco, is a herb of much antiquity and known amongst the Indians, and especially among those of the new Spain, and after those countries were gotten by our Spaniards, being taught of the Indians, they did avail themselves of those things, in the wounds which they received in their wars, healing themselves therewith, to their great benefit.

Within these few years it has been brought to Spain, more to adorn gardens with the fairness thereof, and to give a pleasant sight, rather than that it was thought it had the marvellous medicinal virtues which it has; now we use it more for its virtues than for its fairness. For surely they are such as to cause admiration. . . .

The Indians of our Occidental Indies use the tobacco to take away the weariness and to take lightsomeness of their labour, for in their dances they be so much wearied, they remain so weary, that they can scarcely stir. And so that they may labour the next day and return to that foolish exercise, they take at the mouth and nose the smoke of the tobacco and they remain as dead people. And being so, they be eased in that sort that when they be awakened of their sleep, they remain without weariness and may return to their labour as much more, and so they do always when they have need of it. For with that sleep they receive their strength and be much the lustier.

The black people that have gone from these parts to the Indies have taken the same manner and use of the tobacco that the Indians have, for when they see themselves weary, they take it at the nose and mouth, and it happens unto them as unto our Indians, lying as though they were dead three or four hours. And afterwards they remain lightened, without any weariness, to labour again, and they do this with such great pleasure that although they be not weary yet, they are very desirous to do it. And the thing is come to so much effect that their masters chasten them for it and burn the tobacco, because they should not use it; whereupon they go to the deserts and secret places to do it, because they may not be permitted to drink themselves drunk with wine, and therefore they are glad to make themselves drunken with the smoke of tobacco. I have seen them do it here and happen to them as is said. And they do so that when they come out of the same trance or dream, they find themselves very lusty, and they rejoice to have been after the same sort and manner, seeing that thereof they receive no hurt.

From *Joyful Newes out of the Newe Found Worlde*, trans. John Frampton (1577).

Avarice

LUIS DE LEÓN

Portugal's ships in vain
Plough the wide seas; for not Moluccas' spice
Nor gold of Persian main
Can with false lure entice
Whom sweet content without riches doth suffice.

For India brings no rest
Unto man's heart, nor can the emerald rare,
Philip, our woes arrest,
But wrinkled with more care
Is he who holds of wealth a larger share.

The Persian treasure left
The Roman's thirst unsatisfied, nay first
Him of his life bereft,
And Tantalus, immersed
In waters deep, is evermore athirst.

Such thirst and even worse
Befalls the miser everlastingly
Toiling, who fast his purse
Keeps closed, to cross the sea
Most bold, not bold in generosity.

For what avails for me
The hoarded gold that murders gentle sleep,
If 'tis but slavery

And clouded still doth keep
Its owner's brow, poor though he treasure heap?

Trans. A. F. G. Bell.

The Old World and the New

MICHEL DE MONTAIGNE

1588

IF WHATSOEVER has come unto us by report of what
is past were true, and known by any body, it would
be less than nothing in respect to that which is unknown. And even of this image of the world, which
while we live therein glides and passes away, how
wretched, weak, and how short is the knowledge of the
most curious? Not only of the particular events which
fortune often makes exemplary, and of consequence,
but of the state of mighty commonwealths, large monarchies, and renowned nations, there escapes our knowledge a hundred times more than comes unto our
notice. We make a to-do and wonder at the miraculous
invention of our artillery and are amazed at the rare
device of printing, when, unknown to us, other men,
and at the other end of the world named China, knew
and had perfect use of both a thousand years before. If
we saw as much of this vast world as we see but a
least part of it, it is very likely we should perceive a
perpetual multiplicity and an ever-changing vicissitude
of forms. Therein is nothing singular and nothing rare,
if regard be had unto nature, or to say better, if relation be had unto our knowledge which is a weak

foundation of our rules, and which does commonly present us a right false image of things. How vainly do we nowadays conclude the decline and decrepitude of the world by the fond arguments we draw from our own weakness, drooping and decline.

> "And now both age and land
> So sick affected stand."

And as vainly did another conclude its birth and youth, by the vigour he perceived in the wits of his time, abounding in novelties and invention of divers arts.

> "But all this world is new, as I suppose,
> Worlds nature fresh, nor lately it arose:
> Whereby some arts refined are in fashion,
> And many things now to our navigation
> Are added, daily grown to augmentation."

Our world of late has discovered another (and who can warrant us whether it be the last of his brethren, since both the demons, the sybils, and we ourselves have hitherto been ignorant of this?), no less large, fully peopled, yielding in all things, and mighty in strength than ours; nevertheless so new and infantile that he is yet to learn his ABC. It is not yet full fifty years since he knew neither letters, nor weights, nor measures, nor apparel, nor corn, nor vines. But he was all naked, simply pure, in nature's lap, and lived only upon such means and food as his mother-nurse afforded him. If we rightly conclude about our end, and the aforesaid poet about the infancy of this age, this late world shall only come to light when ours shall fall into darkness. The whole universe shall fall into a palsy or convulsion of sinews; one member shall be maimed or shrunken, another nimble and in good plight. I fear that by our contagion we shall directly have furthered his decline and hastened his ruin, and that we shall too dearly have sold him our opinions, our new fangles and our arts. It was an unpolluted, harmless, infant world; yet we have not whipped and submitted the same unto our discipline, or schooled him by the advantage of our valour or natural forces, nor have we instructed him by our justice and integrity, nor subdued him by our magnanimity. Most of their answers, and a number of the negotiations we have had with them, witness that they were nothing short of us, nor beholding to us for any excellence of natural wit or perspicuity concerning pertinency. The wonderful, or as I may call it, amazement-breeding magnificence of the never-like seen cities of Cuzco and Mexico, and among an infinite number of such things, the admirable garden of that king where all the trees, the fruits, the herbs and plants, according to the order and greatness they have in a garden, were most artfully framed in gold, as also in his cabinet all the living creatures that his country or his seas produced, were cast in gold; and the exquisite beauty of their works in precious stones, in feathers, in cotton, and in painting show that they yielded as little unto us in cunning and industry. But concerning unfeigned devotion, aweful observance of laws, unspotted integrity, bounteous liberality, due loyalty and free liberty, it has greatly aided us that we had not so much as they, for by this advantage they have lost, cast away, sold, undone, and betrayed themselves.

Touching hardiness and undaunted courage, and as for matchless constancy, unmoved assurance, undismayed resolution against pain, smarting, famine, and death itself, I will not fear to oppose the examples which I may easily find among them to the most famous ancient examples that we may with all our industry discover in all the annals and memories of our known old world. For, as for those who have subdued them, let them lay aside the wiles, the policies, and stratagems which they have employed to cozen, to catch by cunning, and to circumvent them; and the just astonishment which those nations might justly conceive by seeing so unexpected an arrival of bearded men, divers in language, in habit, in religion, in behaviour, in form, in countenance, and from a part of the world so distant and where they had never heard there was any habitation; mounted upon great and unknown monsters against those who had never so much as seen a horse and less any beast whatsoever apt to bear or taught to carry either man or burden; covered with a shining and hard skin and armed with slicing-keen weapons and glittering armour against them who for the wonder of the glittering of a looking-glass or of a plain knife would have changed or given inestimable riches in gold, precious stones, and pearls; and who had neither the skill nor the matter with which at any leisure they could have pierced our steel; to which you may add the flashing-fire and thundering roar of shot and harquebus, able to quell and daunt even Caesar himself, had he been so suddenly surprised and as little experienced as they were, and thus to come against and assault silly-naked people, saving where the invention of weaving cotton cloth was known and used, for the most altogether unarmed, except some bows, stones, staves, and wooden bucklers, unsuspecting poor people, surprised under colour of amity and well-meaning faith, overtaken by the curiosity to see strange and unknown things: I say, take this disparity from the conquerors, and you deprive them of all the occasions and cause of so many unexpected victories. When I consider the stern, untamed obstinacy and undaunted vehemence with which so many thousands of men, of women and children, at countless times present themselves unto inevitable dangers for the defence of their gods and liberty; this generous obstinacy to endure all extremities, all difficulties, and death more easily and willingly than basely to yield unto the domination of those by whom they have been so abominably used, some of them choosing rather to starve with hunger and fasting on being taken rather than to accept food at their enemies' hands, so basely victorious: I perceive that whoever had undertaken them man to man, without odds of arms, of experience or of number, should have had as dangerous a war, or perhaps more, than any we see amongst us.

From "On Coaches," in *The Essayes of Montaigne*, trans. John Florio (1600).

Tobacco, Tobacco

ANONYMOUS

1605

Tobacco, tobacco, sing sweetly for tobacco!
　　Tobacco is like love, oh love it;
　　For you see, I will prove it.
Love maketh lean the fat men's tumour,
　　So doth tobacco.
Love still dries up the wanton humour,
　　So doth tobacco.
Love makes men sail from shore to shore,
　　So doth tobacco.

'Tis fond love often makes men poor,
      So doth tobacco.
Love makes men scorn all coward fears,
      So doth tobacco.
Love often sets men by the ears,
      So doth tobacco.
      Tobacco, tobacco,
    Sing sweetly for tobacco.
    Tobacco is like love, oh love it;
    For you see I have proved it.

        In Tobias Hume's *Musical Humours* (1605).

II. THE CITY OF MAN

The Pursuit of Profit

The Prosperity of Florence

BENEDETTO DEI

1472

LETTER TO A VENETIAN

Florence is more beautiful and five hundred forty years older than your Venice. We spring from triply noble blood. We are one-third Roman, one-third Frankish, and one-third Fiesolan. . . . We have round about us thirty thousand estates, owned by noblemen and merchants, citizens and craftsmen, yielding us yearly bread and meat, wine and oil, vegetables and cheese, hay and wood, to the value of nine hundred thousand ducats in cash, as you Venetians, Genoese, Chians, and Rhodians who come to buy them know well enough. We have two trades greater than any four of yours in Venice put together—the trades of wool and silk. Witness the Roman court and that of the King of Naples, the Marches and Sicily, Constantinople and Pera, Broussa and Adrianople, Salonika and Gallipoli, Chios and Rhodes, where, to your envy and disgust, in all of those places there are Florentine consuls and merchants, churches and houses, banks and offices, and whither go more Florentine wares of all kinds, espe-

165

cially silken stuffs and gold and silver brocades, than from Venice, Genoa, and Lucca put together. Ask your merchants who visit Marseilles, Avignon, and the whole of Provence, Bruges, Antwerp, London, and other cities where there are great banks and royal warehouses, fine dwellings, and stately churches; ask those who should know, as they go to fairs every year, whether they have seen the banks of the Medici, the Pazzi, the Capponi, the Buondelmonti, the Corsini, the Falconieri, the Portinari, and the Ghini, and a hundred of others which I will not name, because to do so I should need at least a ream of paper. You say we are bankrupt since Cosimo's death. If we have had losses, it is owing to your dishonesty and the wickedness of your Levantine merchants, who have made us lose thousands of florins; it is the fault of those with well-known names who have filled Constantinople and Pera with failures, whereof our great houses could tell many a tale. But though Cosimo is dead and buried, he did not take his gold florins and the rest of his money and bonds with him into the other world, nor his banks and storehouses, nor his woolen and silken cloths, nor his plate and jewellery; but he left them all to his worthy sons and grandsons, who take pains to keep them and to add to them, to the everlasting vexation of the Venetians and other envious foes whose tongues are more malicious and slanderous than if they were Sienese. . . . Our beautiful Florence contains within the city in this present year two hundred seventy shops belonging to the wool merchants' guild, from whence their wares are sent to Rome and the Marches, Naples and Sicily, Constantinople and Pera, Adrianople, Broussa, and the whole of Turkey. It contains also eighty-three rich and splendid warehouses of the silk merchants' guild, and furnishes gold and silver stuffs, velvet, brocade, damask, taffeta,

and satin to Rome, Naples, Catalonia, and the whole
of Spain, especially Seville, and to Turkey and Barbary.
The principal fairs to which these wares go are those
of Genoa, the Marches, Ferrara, Mantua, and the whole
of Italy; Lyons, Avignon, Montpelier, Antwerp, and
London. The number of banks amounts to thirty-three;
the shops of the cabinet-makers, whose business is carving and inlaid work, to eighty-four; and the workshops
of the stonecutters and marble workers in the city and
its immediate neighbourhood, to fifty-four. There are
forty-four goldsmiths' and jewellers' shops, thirty gold-
beaters, silver-wire-drawers, and a wax-figure maker.
. . . Go through all the cities of the world, nowhere
will you ever be able to find artists in wax equal to
those we now have in Florence, and to whom the figures in the Nunziata can bear witness. Another flourishing industry is the making of light and elegant gold and
silver wreaths and garlands, which are worn by young
maidens of high degree, and which have given their
names to the artist family of Ghirlandajo. Sixty-six is
the number of the apothecaries' and grocer shops;
seventy that of the butchers, besides eight large shops
in which are sold fowls of all kinds, as well as game
and also the native wine called Trebbiano, from San
Giovanni in the upper Arno Valley; it would awaken
the dead in its praise.

In Gertrude R. B. Richards, *Florentine Merchants in the Age
of the Medici* (Cambridge: Harvard University Press, 1932).

Venice, Mistress of the Seas

ARNOLD VON HARFF

1497

ITEM at Venice I was taken by the merchants to the German house, which is called in the Lombard speech Fondigo Tudisco, into the counting house of Anthony Paffendorp, who now lives in Cologne behind St. Mary's. He obtained for me an honourable reception there and showed me much friendship and conducted me everywhere to see the city.

Item to describe first this trading house. As I stayed there for some time I was able to see daily much traffic in spices, silks, and other merchandise packed and dispatched to all the trading towns, since each merchant has his own counting house there—from Cologne, Strassburg, Nuremberg, Augsburg, Lubeck, and other German cities of the Empire. The merchants told me that the counting houses paid daily to the lords of Venice a hundred ducats free money, in addition to which all merchandise was bought there and dearly paid for. Item from this German house one goes over a long wooden bridge on the right hand. Then one reaches a small square called the Rialto. Here the merchants assemble daily about nine or ten o'clock for their business, so that each one can be found without delay. Item this square is built round about and is about as large as [that at] Düren. Close by the square sit the money-changers who have charge of the merchants' cash, which they keep with the money-changers so that they may have less money to handle. When a merchant buys from another he refers him to the bankers, so that little money passes between the merchants. Item leading from the Rialto are long streets where the merchants have their shops, such as goldsmiths and jewellers selling pearls and precious stones. Item one street contains tailors, cobblers, rope-sellers, linen and cloth dealers, and others, trading there without number. Item above the shops is a place like a monastery dormitory, so that each merchant in Venice has his own store full of merchandise, spices, rare cloths, silk draperies, and many other goods, so that it can be said that the wealth of Venice lies in this square.

Item from here we went to the chief church of St. Mark through many narrow streets, in some of which were apothecaries, in some bookbinders, in others all kinds of merchants driving a thriving trade. Item St. Mark's is a very beautiful but low church, above which are many round vaults covered with lead. Item this church, below and above and on both sides, is covered with marble stones, and in addition above and on both sides it is covered with gold. Item as one enters the church from the square there is, on the left hand, an altar enclosed with a railing against a pillar, upon which stands a wooden crucifix which was struck by a disappointed gambler and which has performed many miracles. . . .

Item close by St. Mark's Church, southwards, stands the Doge's Palace, which is very fine and is daily being made more beautiful by the Doge Augustin Barbarigo, who is now having the palace covered with marble and gilt. He was also building a whole marble staircase with beautiful carving, which at this time was not half complete, the half having cost ten thousand ducats. Item as one first enters the palace, stand two four-cornered

marble columns carved with flowers, on the left close
by St. Mark's Church. These two columns, so placed
that an iron bar can be laid on them, are called the
Doge's Gallows. If he does evil, he is forthwith hanged
between the two columns, and I was told as a truth
that within a hundred years one person has been
hanged there. Item as one first enters on the right hand
one climbs a staircase to a round hall in which justice
is administered. Also in this hall hangs an innumerable
collection of arms of pilgrims who have been to the
Holy Land. Item from this hall one ascends by a stone
staircase to a very large hall which is the council chamber of the lords of Venice. In this council are seven
hundred persons who are nobles called gentlemen, and
I counted them at one time in this hall. Item in this
council chamber there is, finely pictured, the story of
the Emperor Frederick Barbarossa, which I have already related. In this council chamber there are pictures also of all who have been doges of Venice. Item I
asked a gentleman and told him that it seemed to me
that there were a great number of councillors on the
day when I counted them. He answered and said that
if there were as many councillors as the land and
people [could send] there would be seven thousand in
the council. But the seven hundred who went daily to
council were gentlemen—that is, nobles, all fine men,
handsomely dressed in long gowns to the feet, the
heads all shaved and on the head a small bonnet; all
usually wear grey beards. They wear generally girdles
round the gown. The sleeves of this gown are narrow
at the hand, but behind they hang down about an ell
wide, like a sack, just as we make clothes for jesters in
our country. The gentlemen have to wear these cloaks
and to go about like this.

Item Venice is a very beautiful city with many inhabitants. It lies in the middle of the salt sea, without walls, and with many tidal canals flowing from the sea, so that in almost every street or house there is water flowing behind or in front, so that it is necessary to have little boats, called barks, in order to go from one house, from one street, or from one church to another, and I was told as a fact that the barks at Venice number more than fifty thousand.

Item in this city or lordship they elect from the seven hundred gentlemen twelve chief lords, and from the twelve they choose a doge who has in the council only two votes. He must live in the palace and cannot leave the city or the palace without the permission of the eleven lords. Item this doge with the government has very many towns, countries, and kingdoms under him, since their dominion extends as far as Milan and to Jaffa, a port of the Holy Land, which I reckon is more than five hundred German miles, to name also many beautiful towns in Lombardy, Padua, Vicentia, Verona, Brescia, Tervicium [Treviso], Ravenna, Mestre, with other countless towns and castles. Item they have also fine towns in Poyen [Apulia] in Calabria. Also many towns in Wendish lands. Item many towns in Slavonia. Item many towns and castles in Albania. Item many towns and castles in Greece. Item innumerable islands on which are beautiful towns and castles. Item the kingdom of Candia. Item the kingdom of Cyprus, with many other remarkable towns in Turkish lands. Item also many towns and castles in the kingdom of Dalmatia. All which they govern with wisdom, sending every year new governors to these towns, castles, islands, and countries from among the gentlemen of Venice.

Item the doge at this time was Doge Augustin Barbarigo, an old man of more than seventy years. I saw

him going in state to St. Mark's Church in this manner.
Item first they carried before him eight golden banners,
of which four were white and four brown. Item then
came a picture which was borne on a golden standard.
Item next was carried a golden chair with a cushion
which was made of golden stuff. Item next they carried
his hat with which he is made a doge, which is valued
at a hundred thousand ducats. Item then came the doge,
most gorgeously dressed. He had a long grey beard and
had on his head a curious silk hat shaped like a horn
behind, reaching upwards for a span's length, as he is
pictured here. This hat must be worn by every doge.
Item before the doge was carried also a white lighted
candle in a silver candlestick.

Item there preceded him also fourteen minstrels,
eight with silver bassoons, from which hung golden
cloths with the arms of St. Mark, and six pipers with
trumpets, also with rich hangings. Item behind the
doge was carried a sword with a golden sheath. Item
there followed him the eleven chief lords with the
other gentlemen richly attired, fine stately persons.

Item on Ascension Day the doge celebrates a festival
each year before the haven on the high sea. He then
throws a golden finger ring into the wild sea, as a sign
that he takes the sea to wife, as one who intends to be
lord over the whole sea. Item the ship in which he celebrates is a small stately galley, very splendidly fitted
out. In front of this ship is a gilt maiden: in one hand
she holds a naked sword and in the other golden scales,
a sign that as the virgin is still a maid, so the government is still virgin and was never taken by force. The
sword in the right hand signifies that she will do
justice: for the same reason the maiden holds the scales
in the left hand.

Item this lordship of Venice has inside the city a

great house of weapons called the arsenal, which is
about as big as Düren. I was taken in with the help of
two gentlemen and by means of certain presents. Item
first at the entrance, travelling with the sun, we ascended some stairs to a great hall thirty feet wide and
quite a hundred long which is full of arms hanging on
both sides in three rows, one above the other, very
orderly disposed, with everything that belongs to a
soldier, such as a coat-of-mail, a sword, a dagger, a
spear, a helmet, and a shield. In addition, as part of
the arrangement of this hall, there are stored there more
than three or four thousand swords, daggers, and innumerable numbers of long pikes, with many more
accoutrements for war, and above in the roof are crossbows hanging side by side, touching each other, six
rows deep. Item we were taken higher, up still another
staircase, to a fine hall which was also arranged like
the first and was no smaller. Item from these halls we
went out and came to a large high building which has
thirty arches under one roof, each arched space being
one hundred and fifty paces long and ten broad, beneath which they build the great ships. Also close by
stands another building with arches, in which they also
build ships. Between the two runs deep water, and
when the ships are ready they are rolled on round
wooden wheels into the water. Item we went further
into another building in which were very fine cannon,
namely five main pieces of copper. They measured by
one of my feet twenty-four feet long, and each cannon
had three pieces which could be screwed into each
other. As we were about to look into one of them, out
crept a boy with a vegetable basket, who had hidden
himself in it. I was told that each piece had cost seven
thousand ducats and that each piece discharges a stone
of a thousand pounds. Item close by in two rows were

more than four hundred copper half-slings, which had just been mounted on two strong wheels. Item close by were also many carthouns, slings, half-slings, and chamber-guns, which are all used on the ships. Item close by were also three copper mortars. Item I was told as a fact by a gentleman who had made an inventory that there were thirty-eight main pieces, one hundred and sixty large copper slings, forty-four copper carthouns, and more than five hundred half copper slings. Further that in every town under their dominion was more artillery than we saw there, since in his opinion Venice did not need so much, as she had only to arm the ships. And I can say in truth that having seen many armaments in such towns as Brescia, Verona, Padua, Treviso, Mestre, Vienna, Modon, Corfu, Roumania, Candia, Cyprus, and in many other towns, I had not seen even a part. . . .

Item at Venice I had to change all my money for new Venetian ducats called *de zecca,* since the money in Greece, Turkey and in heathen lands is differently coined from Christian money. Item since it was in my mind to travel in the lands of unbelievers I had to see that my money was not stolen or taken, which often happened to me. I was taken therefore with the help of the German merchants to a gentleman of Venice who traded in all countries overseas, who gave bills of exchange in the cities of Alexandria, Damietta, Damascus, Beiruth, Antioch, Constantinople, and other towns, so that I could supply my needs, for which the other merchants of the counting house of Anthony Paffendorp of Cologne were my sureties, that they would make good what I spent in other countries. Item when I came to a heathen town and presented these bills to the person to whom they were made out, although I could not speak with him, I nodded my head at him and kissed my finger in order to show my respect, and gave him the bills. Whereupon he would stare at me and disappear into the back of his house, returning at once and paying me my money, indicating with his finger that I should write down how much I had received. I was told this by the gentleman in Venice, and in truth they keep to it although they are heathens.

From *Pilgrimage of Arnold von Harff, Knight . . . 1496-1499*, trans. Malcolm Letts (London: Hakluyt Society, 1946).

The Hapsburgs and the Fuggers

September 1511

MAXIMILIAN I TO PAUL VON LIECHTENSTEIN

We do not doubt that you still hold in fresh remembrance our notification, given you some time ago, concerning the reasons for which we desired and intended to seek the papacy, if we can achieve it; about which we have thought from time to time. Now we find in our heart, and indeed it is true, that nothing would more honourably, highly, or better become us than to receive the said papal office.

And since now Pope Julius, who just a short time ago was most deathly ill and, as has been reported to you by our court and Tyrolean Chancellor, Cyprian von Seretin, everyone in Rome was of the opinion that he had died, we have therefore decided to pursue our intention as far as possible and have taken actions and steps to attain the papacy; and thereupon we have now suggested the plan to Cardinal Adrian, who for some time, as you know, has been out here in Germany with us. He advises us strongly in favour of it, and believes there will be no difficulty with the cardinals, and on hearing of our plan he wept for joy.

Since, as you yourself may well imagine and realize, the pope may now die, which is wholly to be expected (for he eats little, and what he does eat is nothing but fruit, and he drinks so much more that as a result his life seems precarious), since, as I say, he may die, the bishop of Gurk has been dispatched by us to post to Rome to help us behind the papal throne. But since this matter cannot well be carried through without a notable sum of money which we must place and invest in it, we have decided, to fulfil our aforesaid purpose, and on the agreement and promise of assistance from the cardinal and various other persons, to raise up to three hundred thousand ducats, and to transmit, order, and agree to the same only through the Fugger Bank in Rome. You know, however, that at the present time we do not have the money on hand, and also that it is not in our power to satisfy the said Fugger for this sum of money except by depositing our crown jewels as security. We therefore command with all earnestness that from this hour and most expeditiously you shall inform Fugger of these matters in the most fitting manner (as you well know how to do), secretly, and in consideration of the duty with which he is bound to us as our councillor, and our great concern with them, and that he should thereupon with the greatest and best diligence, to our honour and satisfaction, arrange it that the aforesaid three hundred thousand ducats for this business be deposited in his bank in Rome. He should also make sure that his agents will certainly give out and pay the money to those who are presented to them by our princes and dear reverent Matthias, Bishop of Gurk, and other of our ambassadors whom we shall send to Rome. And you shall agree and promise to give reasonable interest as is mentioned, and for that purpose give him promissory notes from the bank, as is customary.

In return we shall give him as security the four best chests of treasure, including our robes of investiture, those that do not belong to the Empire but to the house of Austria, and which, if we get the papacy, we will no longer need—for if for the greater honour we have ourselves crowned emperor beforehand, we will use the robes of the sainted Duke Charles, which we intend to take with us. And you are to arrange that he shall send immediately to Rome, to the hands of the said Bishop of Gurk, ten thousand ducats in cash or bills of exchange, either on account of the above determined sum or on your promise (for which we will guarantee you), and that for the above mentioned reasons and because of our special reliance on him, he shall not refuse or delay. We therefore will send you, as soon as you gain our wish from Fugger—write to us immediately and quickly, day or night—sufficient instructions, receipts, and other documents to transfer quickly to Fugger the chests and robes mentioned above.

And if Fugger during these negotiations wishes to know how we will again redeem these our treasures and robes, which he will have in his possession, you shall inform and indicate to him that we intend to pay the said sum of three hundred thousand ducats, and in addition we are willing to give him one hundred thousand ducats for his three jewels which we also wish to have from him—although they are not worth the said sum—but still as secret interest on his loan; which then will make a grand total of five hundred and thirty-three thousand florins Rhenish. This sum will be drawn from the imperial aids, which we will get from the estates of the Empire at the next Reichstag; similarly from the future aids of our hereditary principalities and lands, and taxes, and in addition the money which is always sent us annually by our dear brother the King of Spain, and it will all be allocated to the redemption of our treasure. But if all this should not reach the required sum, we shall then, for the rest, transfer a third of all our income from the papacy until it is all paid. Therefore, let him send one of his friends, whoever he pleases, to us at our court. We will make him our treasurer or master of the exchequer to handle our income and also to receive and collect his third part, and we will also use him in other of our affairs. . . .

We add also for your information that our secretary, Johann Colla, wrote us today by a special post that the Orsini, the Colonna, and the Roman populace have wholly decided and determined not to have or to accept any pope who is French or Spanish or who is supported by one of these states.

September 1511

MAXIMILIAN I TO THE ARCHDUCHESS MARGARET

Very dear and well-beloved daughter:

I have in hand the report which you have sent me by Guillaume Pingeon, our chamberlain, about which we have thought still further. And we do not find it good for any reason that we should marry again, but have earlier set our determination and will never more to have anything to do with a naked woman. We are today sending my Lord of Gurk, the bishop, to Rome to the pope, to find means by which we could come to an agreement with him to take us as a coadjutor, to the end that after his death we could be assured of having the papacy, and becoming a priest, and afterwards being canonized; so you will be under the necessity, after my death, of being required to adore me, which seems to me most glorious.

I am sending by this same post to the King of Aragon [Ferdinand] to pray him to aid us in achieving this project, concerning which he also will be satisfied, since I shall relinquish the Empire to our common grandson, Charles. I am satisfied also to do this.

The people and gentry of Rome have made an alliance against the French and Spanish, and there are twenty thousand soldiers; and we are told that they are in favor of creating a pope from my office and from the Empire of Germany, and that they do not wish to have a Frenchman, an Aragonese, or even any Venetian. I am also beginning to work on the cardinals, where two or three thousand ducats do me a great service, considering the partiality which is already apparent among them.

The King of Aragon has told his ambassador that he will order the Spanish cardinals to support the project of giving the papacy to us.

I beg you, keep this matter a bit secret; even so I fear that in a few days it will happen that the whole world will know it; for it is hardly possible to keep such a great matter secret, for which it is necessary to have the help and labour of so many people, and so much money, and the aid of God.

Done by the hand of your dear father, Max, future pope.

P.S. The pope has double fevers again and cannot live long.

In A. Schulte, *Kaiser Maximilian I als Kandidat für den papstlichen Stuhl*, 1511, trans. H. F. Schwarz.

[*This ambitious project was not achieved, but Maximilian's grandson became the Emperor Charles V with the help of Fugger money, as is clear in the following letter.*]

1523

JAKOB FUGGER TO CHARLES V

Your Imperial Majesty is doubtless well aware how I, and my nephews, have been devoted to the service of the house of Austria and have promoted its welfare and its progress in all humility. On that account we had dealings with the late Emperor Maximilian, your Imperial Majesty's grandfather, and promised our help in acquiring the Roman Crown for your Imperial Majesty against some of the electors, which should establish your faith and trust in me, and perhaps in no one else. Also for the consummation of the aforesaid project which we undertook we supplied a fine sum of money which I raised, not only from my own resources and from my nephews, but also, with great loss, from among my other good friends, in order that so praiseworthy a purpose of your Imperial Majesty for high honour and the public good might win success.

It is also well known and clear as day that your Imperial Majesty could not have acquired the Roman Crown without my help, as I can demonstrate by documents of all your Imperial Majesty's commissioners. Nor have I sought my own profit in this undertaking. For if I had remained aloof from the house of Austria and had served France, I would have obtained much profit and money, which was then offered to me. Your Majesty may well ponder with deep understanding the damage which would have resulted for your Imperial Majesty and the house of Austria.

Considering all this, I humbly petition your Imperial Majesty, graciously to consider my faithful and humble services, which have advanced your Majesty's welfare, and to decree that the sum of money due me together with the interest should be discharged and paid to me without further delay. I shall always be found ready to serve your Majesty in all humility, and I humbly remain at all times your Imperial Majesty's to command.

Your Imperial Majesty's most humble servant,
Jakob Fugger

In J. Strieder, *Das reiche Augsburg* (Munich, 1938); trans. M.M.M.

Jack of Newberie, an English Clothier

THOMAS DELONEY

Sixteenth century

IN THE DAYS of King Henry VIII, that most noble and victorious prince, in the beginning of his reign, John Winchcomb, a broadcloth weaver, dwelt in Newberie, a town in Berkshire; who for that he was a man of a merry disposition and honest conversation, was wondrous well-beloved of rich and poor, especially because in every place where he came, he would spend his money with the best, and was not at any time found a churl of his purse. Wherefore, being so good a companion, he was called of old and young Jack of Newberie, a man so generally well-known in all his country for his good fellowship that he could go in no place but he found acquaintance, by means whereof, Jack could no sooner get a crown but straight he found means to spend it. Yet had he ever this care, that he would always keep himself in comely and decent apparel; neither at any time would he be overcome in drink but so discreetly behave himself with honest mirth and pleasant conceits that he was every gentleman's companion.

After that Jack had long led this pleasant life, being (though he were but poor) in good estimation, it was his master's chance to die and his dame to be a widow, who was a very comely ancient woman and of reasonable wealth. Wherefore she, having a good opinion of her man John, committed unto his government the guiding of all her workfolks for the space of three years together, in which time she found him so careful and diligent that all things came forward and prospered wondrous well. . . . The report was all over the town that Jack had married his dame. . . . They lived long together in most godly, loving, and kind sort, till in the end she died, leaving her husband wondrous wealthy.

Now Jack of Newberie, being a widower, had the choice of many wives, men's daughters of good credit and widows of great wealth. Notwithstanding, he bent his only like to one of his own servants whom he had tried in the guiding of his house a year or two, and knowing her carefulness in her business, faithful in her dealing, an excellent good housewife, thought it better to have her with nothing than some other with much treasure. And beside as her qualities were good, so was she of very comely personage, of a sweet favour and fair complexion. In the end he opened his mind to her and craved her good will. The maid (though she took this motion kindly) said she would do nothing without consent of her parents. Whereupon a letter was written to her father, being a poor man dwelling at Alesbury in Buckinghamshire, who being joyful of his daughter's good fortune, speedily came to Newberie where of her master he was friendly entertained; who, after he had made him good cheer, showed him all his servants at work and every office in his house.

> Within one room being large and long,
> There stood two hundred looms full strong;
> Two hundred men the truth is so,
> Wrought in these looms all in a row.
> By every one a pretty boy,
> Sat making quills with mickle joy:
> And in another place hard by,
> A hundred women merrily,
> Were carding hard with joyful cheer,
> Who singing sat with voices clear.
> And in a chamber close beside,
> Two hundred maidens did abide,
> In petticoats of stammel red,
> And milk-white kerchiefs on their head;
> Their smock sleeves like to winter snow,
> That on the western mountains flow,
> And each sleeve with a silken band,
> Was featly tied at the hand.
> These pretty maids did never lin,
> But in that place all day did spin:
> And spinning so with voices meet,
> Like nightingales they sung full sweet.
> Then to another room came they,
> Where children were in poor array:
> And every one sat picking wool,
> The finest from the coarse to cull:
> The number was seven score and ten,
> The children of poor silly men:
> And these their labours to requite,

Had everyone a penny at night,
Beside their meat and drink all day,
Which was to them a wondrous stay.
Within another place likewise,
Full fifty proper men he spies,
And these were shearmen every one,
Whose skill and cunning there was shown:
And hard by them there did remain,
Full fourscore rowers taking pain.
A dye-house likewise had he then,
Wherein he kept full forty men:
And likewise in his fulling mill,
Full twenty persons kept he still.
Each week ten good fat oxen he
Spent in his house for certainty:
Beside good butter, cheese, and fish,
And many another wholesome dish.
He kept a butcher all the year,
A brewer eke for ale and beer:
A baker for to bake his bread,
Which stood his household in good stead.
Five cooks within his kitchen great,
Were all the year to dress his meat.
Six scullion boys unto their hands,
To make clean dishes, pots, and pans,
Beside poor children that did stay,
To turn the broaches every day.
The old man that did see this sight,
Was much amaz'd, as well he might:
This was a gallant clothier sure,
Whose fame forever shall endure.

When the old man had seen this great household
and family, then was he brought into the warehouses,
some being filled with wool, some with flocks, some

with woad and madder, and some with broadcloths and kerseys ready dyed and dressed, beside a great number of others, some stretched on the tenters, some hanging on poles, and a great many more lying wet in other places. "Sir," said the old man, "I see that you're 'bominable rich, and I'm content that you shall have my daughter, and God's blessing and mine light on you both."

From *Jack of Newberie* (1596), in *The Works of Thomas Deloney*, ed. F. O. Mann (Oxford: Clarendon Press, 1912).

Antwerp, the Great Market

LUDOVICO GUICCIARDINI

1560

LET US CONSIDER in a few words by what ways and means this city has risen to such rank and pre-eminence. The first of her most notable advantages began, I believe, with the fairs for merchandise which her princes long ago granted her with extensive privileges which have since been confirmed by the authority and favour of popes and emperors. But Jean II, Duke of Brabant, having conceived some hatred for this city, took from her part of that franchise which he granted to the city of Malines in 1300. Henry VII of Luxembourg, however, returned it to her in its entirety in 1309. But Louis Count of Flanders, to whom this city had been bound and pledged by the Duke of Brabant as a dowry, once again took it away from Antwerp and gave it to Malines in 1358; and it was for this reason that the people of Antwerp and Malines on many oc-

casions took to arms, and notably in 1410. But, to be
brief, by agreement two fairs finally remained at Antwerp, which still flourish, and they are highly privileged, as I have said.

The privileges in substance consist of the following:
that during the time of the franchise anyone may
come and stay in Antwerp, and then return home
with his goods and merchandise in complete safety
without being hindered in any way on account of
debt, or having anything at all exacted of him during
his whole journey. . . .

The second of the notable advantages which have
made the city of Antwerp so great, rich, and famous,
began about the year 1503-1504, when the Portuguese,
by marvellous and amazing navigation, and with
warlike equipment, having, just before, occupied Calicut, made a treaty with the king of that region. They
began to transport spices and drugs from India to
Portugal and then to carry them from Portugal to the
fairs in this city. These spices and drugs were formerly brought by way of the Red Sea to Beirut and
Alexandria, and from these places carried by the Venetians to Venice to supply Italy, France, Germany,
and other Christian provinces. But once this commerce had been intercepted by the Portuguese, and
they had sent an agent to Antwerp in the name of
their king, little by little this trade attracted the Germans. First the Fuggers, the Welsers, and Hochstätters
became interested, and perhaps before all of these
Nicholas Rechtergem, already mentioned, who was the
first to make an agreement at Antwerp with the agent
of the King of Portugal concerning spices, and the
first to send them from here to Germany, where, not
yet knowing anything about the new voyage of the
Portuguese, the Germans were so astounded that they

doubted the quality of the said spices, and suspected that they were adulterated. This was because the Germans had been accustomed to furnish the people of these lands with the same drugs which came overland from Venice. At this time there were several honourable families of Spaniards in this city, such as those of Diego d'Aro, of Diego di Sanian, of Ferrando di Bernui, and Antonio del Vaglio. And thus about the year 1516 all the foreign merchants who had been living at Bruges, one after the other (except some Spaniards who remained there) came to this place, with no less damage to Bruges than great profit and advantage to Antwerp. And the first who withdrew from Bruges were the Gualterotti, and after them the Buonvisi, then the Spinoli, families of great consequence who controlled a great deal of trade. . . .

The inhabitants of this city are for the most part engaged in commerce, and indeed they are great merchants and very rich, some here being worth two hundred thousand, others up to four hundred thousand crowns a man, and more. They are courteous, civil, ingenious, quick to imitate foreigners, and to intermarry with them. They are capable of dwelling and carrying on business throughout the world. Most of them, and even the women (though they may not have been out of the country), know how to speak three or four languages, not to mention those who speak five and six and seven; this is something to marvel at as well as a great advantage. They have artisans proficient in every kind of art and craft, for they work so well that they sell their products even before these are finished, and, as everyone knows, continual work brings perfection.

Now as to the kind and number of crafts exercised in this city, one can almost say in a single word—all.

For here they make cloth, linens of every kind, tapestry, Turkish carpets and fustians; armour and all other munitions of war; they carry on tanning, painting, dyeing, color-making, gilding, silvering, glass-making in the Venetian style; they make every kind of mercery, of gold, of silver, of silk, of thread, of wool, and small wares of metals of all kinds and other things beyond number. They also make here all kinds of silk cloth, such as velvet, satin, damask, sarsenet, taffeta, and others; but what is more, from their own silkworms, and contrary almost to nature and to the climate of this country, they produce and weave silk itself, although in small quantity. This, in addition to what comes to them from outside (which is of inestimable value), they work up in all ways and manners. They refine in quantity, with great industry and skill, metals, wax, sugar, and other merchandise. And it is only here that vermilion, which we call "cinnabar," is made.

For other minor and major crafts there are a great many artisans in the city, so that to show you the greatness of this city, it seems good to me to specify the number of heads and masters of shop of some crafts, the most common and most necessary which are now to be found here, so that from the knowledge of these you may more easily imagine how many others there are. There are, then, 169 master bakers, 78 butchers, 75 sellers of sea fish and 16 or 17 of freshwater fish; 110 barbers and surgeons; tailors and bootmakers, 594. There are 124 goldsmiths, not to mention a great number of cutters of jewels and other precious stones, who produce, in truth, marvellous works with the purchase of stupendous and incredible jewels. So that there are to be found more such men in this city alone than in many entire provinces. As to painters and sculptors of various professions of painting and sculpture, there are about 300 masters. Of shopkeepers, large and small, the number is infinite.

All of these persons, being people who are earning money, invest it not only in commerce but also in building, in buying lands and properties, and in every way improving their position, and thus from day to day the city keeps on growing, and flourishes, and increases marvellously.

Moreover, although a part of the lesser folk and some others more austere live in accordance with the old custom of eating sparingly, it is nonetheless a fact that at present the people live sumptuously, and perhaps better than is seemly. Both men and women of all ages go about very well dressed, each according to his resources and rank, always following new and tasteful fashions, but many of them much more richly and more sumptuously than decorum and respectability can or should permit. You can see here at all hours weddings, feastings, and dances. You hear everywhere the sounds of instruments, songs, and the noise of merrymaking. To conclude, in all possible ways appear the wealth, power, pomp, and magnificence of this city.

Since we have talked and discoursed both of the government of the city and of the habits and way of life of its inhabitants, it is right that we say something about the trade, business, and way of doing things which prevail among the foreign merchants trading in this city, considering that her principal foundation consists of commerce and that she is made famous and increased by foreigners. I shall say in the first place, then, that in Antwerp, in addition to the people of this country, who in great numbers throng and dwell here, and in addition to the French merchants who in time of peace come here every day, there are six principal nationalities, who reside here both in war and peace, and who number more than a thousand merchants, including their principal managers and assistants. There are the Germans, the Danes together with the Hanseatic merchants from all parts, the Italians, Spanish, English, and Portuguese, but there are, perhaps, more Spaniards than any other nationality, and certainly without question more who are married and settled here.

All these merchants observe the laws and ordinances of the city, and, moreover, live, dress, and conduct themselves freely according to their desires. To tell the truth, foreigners live in greater liberty here in Antwerp, and in all the Low Countries, than in any other part of the world. So that it is a marvellous thing to see such a mixture of men, of so many kinds, and even more marvellous to hear among them such a variety of languages, so different from one another, so that, without going abroad, in a single city you can observe and imitate, if you wish, the nature, way of life, and customs of many nations. And thus it happens that in Antwerp, because of the presence of so many foreigners, one always has news of the whole world.

The richest and most renowned among all these merchants are the Fuggers, Germans of Augsburg; the head of this family, Lord Anton, truly the prince of all the merchants, who died recently in his own country, left by will to his heirs an estate of more than six million gold crowns, not to mention all the other wealth which abounds in this illustrious and splendid family, and which was earned during the space of seventy years in commercial activity. The result is that

the Fuggers have risen to honours and dignities, bestowed by states and signories, not only in Germany
but also in many other parts of Europe and even in
the New World.

But before going on I should add this, that neither
the Catholic King, nor the King of Portugal, nor the
Queen of England disdains to place in this company
of merchants highly qualified men, who negotiate and
trade for the needs of their majesties; these managers
are called factors. First of all, the Catholic King keeps
two here, each having a separate function and establishment for himself, and agents and assistants to serve
him; one of these at present is Lord Gaspar Schetz,
and the other is Lord Juan Lopez Gallo, Baron of
Male, a gentleman, rich, and of good reputation. These
have very broad powers of attorney from the king,
which provide in substance that they may take on deposit, exchange, or in any other way they please, any
sum of money for a fixed time, and bind the king in
general and specifically with regard to certain of his
assignments in this and in that province. The result
is that not long ago his representatives drew from the
Exchange an infinite sum of money, which they returned at the proper time and place. The King of
Portugal keeps here only one factor but one highly
honoured, such as the present one, Francesco Pesoa.
He likewise has complete power of attorney, enabling
him to borrow whatsoever sum and quantity he wishes
both of money and goods, binding the crown of Portugal, and by this means the king recently raised on
this Exchange all he wanted. . . .

As for the Queen of England, for some years she has
kept here as representative Sir Thomas Gresham,
highly honoured knight, also with sufficient power of

attorney, who has raised for her on this Exchange very great sums of money, which she goes about paying back nobly.

Coming now to discuss the handling of and traffic in merchandise which commonly goes on every day in Antwerp, I may say that all these merchants, whether foreign or native, carry on a commerce and trade which is unbelievable and marvellous, in exchange and in deposit as well as in merchandise, and we shall describe briefly how it is done, which is as follows. Morning and evening they go at a certain hour to the English Exchange, and there for more than an hour at a time, by means of brokers speaking every language, of whom there is a very great number, they negotiate principally the buying and selling of every sort and kind of merchandise. A little later they go to the New Exchange, and likewise for an hour and by means of brokers they negotiate especially exchanges and deposits.

Now there is exchange at Antwerp on several exchanges in Italy, as on Rome, Venice, Milan, Florence, and Genoa; on many exchanges in Germany, as on Augsburg, Nuremberg, and Frankfurt; on exchanges in Spain, namely on the four fairs, two at Medina del Campo, one at Villalon, and one at Riosecco; also there is some exchange on Burgos, Cadiz, and Seville. They exchange also on many exchanges in France, such as on the four fairs of Lyons, on Paris and Rouen, and finally also on London and Besançon, and occasionally something on Lisbon. And this exchange consists in substance of giving or receiving here at Antwerp as many groats as make a crown, ducat, or angelet, in order to recover or pay out the same value on the exchanges of Italy or the other places mentioned above. And so, giving or taking here in order to recover or pay out there, that is properly called "exchange." And this practice was invented principally for the convenience of trade, but out of cunning some merchants, and especially the richest, not satisfied with this convenience but impelled by avarice and insatiable thirst for extraordinary gain, have altered and corrupted this honest method of exchange. For, by borrowing money or by giving or taking sums for which they have no need, in many arbitrary ways they cause money either to be scarce or plentiful artificially, for their own profit and to the general harm and loss. And yet this custom of exchange ordinarily is not only bearable but very convenient, nor can it, according to the theologians, be called unjust gain, if it is well used, inasmuch as most often one gains little and at great risk and peril, and sometimes one loses one's capital thereby.

But let us say a word about what the merchants call "deposit." At present they call it deposit (in order to cloak with fine words the ugliness of the facts) when one gives a sum of money to someone for a fixed time at a determined and fixed price and interest, for example, following the ordinance and permission of the Emperor Charles V, confirmed by his son, King Philip, at twelve per cent annually. This interest was permitted by their majesties to the merchants in difficult times to obviate greater inconveniences, but time and experience, in addition to former examples, show sufficiently that this exorbitant interest, being continually corrupted and increased by the cunning of men by many ways and means, is a grievous thing, and of great harm to poor men and to commerce and trade in merchandise. Certainly this way of contracting would redound to the public good if the lenders would be content with an honest rate, such as the six or six and a quarter per cent, which, according to the permission of the said emperor and king, is allowed to the nobles and others who live on fixed incomes, or even a bit more, up to eight per cent. But not content with this gain, they more often go beyond the limits of reason and honesty and in many ways transform negotiations for loans into something troublesome and violent. Formerly gentlemen of means used to invest their money in lands and properties, in cultivation, in livestock and such things, by which many were employed and the country made bountiful. The merchants too, who were wealthy in merchandise, sent out and brought in commodities in abundance, and they supplied them here and there where they saw need required it; and in this great and abundant trade many men of all kinds were given gainful employment. And thus since the land was filled with plenty and the cities well supplied with every kind of merchandise, they saw their revenues increased and those of the princes also. At present, part of the nobility who have ready money, enticed and corrupted by such a great and certain profit as that which comes now by means of those excessive and usurious loans, put their money out at interest secretly (for that is forbidden them by the laws of the nobility), or have it lent for them by others. And similarly, many rich merchants, impelled by the same opportunity and to avoid labour, and troubles and risks, lend their money at a rate of interest fixed and exorbitant or exchange money at the highest price. And thus it comes about with regard to the nobility that many lands lie uncultivated and without a sufficient number of livestock, a condition which results in scarcity of victuals and sometimes misery to the public. And as for the merchants, the country is no longer sufficiently

supplied with goods and merchandise, a condition
which, in addition to other ills, causes what goods
exist in the country frequently to be expensive and
sometimes some of them excessive in price; and all
this redounds to the great and extreme damage of the
public welfare and especially of the poor, who are in
many ways devoured by the rich. One could cite
plenty of clear examples of this, but because one only
too often sees the effect of it, with many bankruptcies
and disorders, and in order not to offend anyone, we
shall speak no more about it.

Rather, coming back to the subject of commerce,
since we have already told how some merchants gain
unjustly and injure the public, we should also say
that an infinite number of them gain justly, and are
of use to the world, and this merely by means of the
trade in merchandise which they buy in abundance
and sell in good faith, and import from everywhere
and send out to all places and countries. We should
also mention some of the most important kinds of
merchandise which come and go in this country every
day from Europe and other parts of the universe, by
sea and by land, since it is a matter of such consequence and managed chiefly by the merchants resident
in Antwerp and carried on in this same city; especially
since the knowledge of such variety and abundance
of everything can bring, if not pleasure, something of
advantage for the reader. In the first place, let us say
that there comes here by land an infinite quantity of
fine merchandise from Italy, worth an inestimable sum
of money, and from here are sent to those parts other
kinds of merchandise which are worth a fortune. But
let us be specific and, beginning with the Papal States,
follow the preferences of states and not the geography
of regions.

From Rome no merchandise of any great value is brought, but to Rome are sent woollen cloth of many kinds, tapestry, serges, worsteds and half worsteds, linens, and many other goods and commodities. . . .

From Ancona are sent here incredible quantities of camlets, grograms and mohairs of many kinds; spices, drugs, silks, cottons, felts, carpets, cordovan leather, and the colour indigo, all commodities secured from the Levant. In return are sent a great quantity of woollen cloth, such as kersey, and other cloth from England, as well as much cloth from this country, especially that made of four colours from Armentière, serges in good number, worsteds, linens, and some tapestry, and dyes of crimson called "cochineal," which comes from Spain and is worth a good sum of money.

From Bologna are sent here many cloths of silk, much spun and raw silk, and organzine of half gold and half silver, and cloths likewise of gold and silver, and similar things. From here are sent serges of all kinds, half worsteds, tapestry, linens, small wares, and some little woollen cloth.

The Venetians dispose in these parts of spices such as clove, cinnamon, nutmeg, ginger, and numerous drugs such as rhubarb, cassia, agaric, dragon's blood, mummy, senna-leaf, colocynth, scammony, tutty, mithridate, and treacle. They draw almost all these spices and drugs from the Levant. Before the King of Portugal had intercepted that trade, the Venetians were accustomed to transport by sea all the spices and nearly all the drugs which came to these parts. In fact I find that in the year 1318 there arrived in this port of Antwerp five Venetian galleys loaded with spices and drugs, coming here to the fairs. From Venice likewise are brought here much very beautiful and rich silk cloth, spun and raw silk, camlets, grograms and mohairs, carpets, samites marvellously well made; excellent scarlets, cottons, cumin, and other small wares of silk and other material. In addition they send indigo and other colours suitable for dyeing and painting. From here are sent to Venice precious stones and many pearls, woollen cloths and wool from England in quite good quantity, although the Venetians supply themselves by sea with a large part of these things. To Venice is sent cloth of the fashion of these regions, and of many kinds, such as serges of Hondschote, Lille, Arras, Valenciennes, Mons, and other places; worsteds and half worsteds, an infinite quantity of linens, tapestry, the colour crimson, worth a large sum; and various kinds of small wares and household furnishings in quantity. In addition sugar is often sent there, and sometimes pepper.

From the kingdom of Naples are sent here some silk cloth, and spun and raw silk, and in addition a few kinds of fine fur, and saffron from Aquila, and excellent manna. To those parts are sent from here considerable cloth both of this country and of England, an infinite quantity of linens, serges, worsteds and half worsteds, tapestry and numerous small wares of metal and other kinds.

From the kingdom of Sicily is brought here, both by sea and by land, a great quantity of gallnuts, cumin, cotton, and silk; sometimes also wines of various kinds, such as *vernaccia* and other similar ones. And to those parts are sent a great quantity of woollen cloth, and linens, and serges, and innumerable small wares of metal and various other kinds.

From Milan and the subject region there come many goods, such as gold and silver thread worth a large sum, cloths of silk and gold of many kinds, an infinite amount of fustian of varying quality, scarlets, estamins,

and other fine fabrics; very good rice and in great
quantity; excellent armour and many kinds of wares
worth much money, even Parmesan cheese, which is
a commodity of importance. To Milan are sent pepper
and sugar; precious stones, musk, and other scents; a
quantity of woollen cloth from here and from England;
and abundance of serges of every kind, worsteds and
half worsteds, an infinite quantity of linens, the colour
crimson, and also English and Spanish wool.

From Germany are sent here by land silver bullion
and quicksilver, crude and refined copper in incredible
quantity, very fine wool from Hesse, and glassware; a
fortune's worth of fustian, woad, madder, saffron for
dyeing, saltpetre, small wares, and beautiful and
marvellous household furnishings of every kind of metal
and worth a great deal. Also sent are arms for defence
and offence, of every kind and price, and of the greatest
importance, and many kinds of white Rhine wines,
likewise of great importance, excellent in taste and
very good for the health and digestion. To them are
sent precious stones and pearls and a very large
quantity of spices and of drugs, saffron, sugar, a fortune's worth of fine English woollen cloth, and in addition serges, worsteds, half worsteds, tapestry, and
linens in quantity.

From Denmark, the Hanseatic lands, Norway, Sweden, Poland, and other northern regions and provinces
is sent by sea an inestimable quantity of merchandise;
first a large amount of wheat and rye, much copper,
saltpetre, woad, wallwort, excellent wool from Austria,
flax, honey, pitch, wax worth much, sulphur, potash,
which is an important commodity, amber from Danzig;
very beautiful and fine furs of every kind, such as
sable, marten, ermine, vair, lynx, leopard, skunk, very
beautiful silver fox and ordinary fox, marvellous silver

and ordinary wolf, and even many skins from many different kinds of fish; and then leather in quantity from all kinds of animals, especially buffalo, and finally many bear skins for use in war; very beautiful and good wood of every kind, ship timbers for the most part, and a certain kind called "wainscot," truly beautiful and with a grain almost like walnut, which is used here for a thousand things because it is beautiful and durable and furthermore does not crack or get worm-eaten except when extremely old, and this is sent to Italy. There is also brought from these countries much fine beer, salted meat, and salted fish in considerable amount, and fish dried by smoke, sun, wind, and even the cold, and in addition much more merchandise in quantity, which, if we wanted to list it all, we would neither know the names of the items nor have the time to do it.

To those parts are sent a huge quantity of spices, drugs, saffron, sugar, salt, much English and Flemish cloth, serges, worsteds, half worsteds, fustians, and linens, and in addition precious stones, cloths of silk and of gold, camlets, grograms and mohairs, some tapestry, much wine, particularly Spanish wines, alum, Brazil wood, small wares, and a large quantity of household furnishings. . . .

From England are sent here cloths in very great quantity, including kerseys and many other kinds of fine and coarse cloth, cottons, friezes, and other goods worth much; very fine wool, excellent saffron, although not in great quantity, tin and lead worth much, a very great quantity of sheep and coney skins and some other fine furs and some hides; much beer, cheese, and other victuals in large amounts, and even malmsey brought there every year by sea from Candia.

And thither are sent precious stones, silver bullion,

and quicksilver, cloth of gold and silver, of silk, gold and silver thread, camlets, grograms and mohairs; spices, drugs, sugar, cotton, cumin, galls, fine and coarse linens, serges, half worsteds, tapestry, madder, hops in very great amount, much glassware, salted fish, small wares of every kind of metal and of other types worth very much; arms of every kind, and in addition an infinite number of household furnishings. . . .

From Spain are brought here innumerable kinds of merchandise, precious stones and pearls of various quality and prices, which the Spaniards bring from their West Indies and from Peru called "America," and the New World. These precious stones and pearls that come from there are large and beautiful but not as perfect as those from the Orient. They bring here a large amount of gold, of pure silver in bullion and hand wrought, which is likewise brought for the most part from that new and happy world; likewise the colour crimson called by them "cochineal," and in addition are brought the root called sarsaparilla which is highly medicinal, and also guaiacum wood, which has among its excellent virtues that of curing the disease which we Italians wrongly call the "French disease." This wood comes from the same country of the Indies from which that illness was brought into Europe about 1492 through the navigations of the Genoese Christopher Columbus.

From Spain itself are sent much saffron, some drugs, grains [for red dye], much crude silk, many kinds of silk cloth, primarily the velvets of Toledo and sarsenets, salt, alum from Mazzeron, orchil [for red dye] from the Canary Islands, called by the Florentines *raspa,* very good wool, iron, cordovan leather, sumach,

ANTWERP, THE GREAT MARKET

many kinds of white wine, such as bastard [a sweet wine], *romanie*, and other good and healthful varieties; sweet oils and heavy oils for cloth, vinegar, honey, molasses, gum arabic, soap, and a great quantity of legumes of every kind, and fresh and dried fruits such as oranges, lemons, pomegranates, olives, capers, dates, figs, raisins, almonds, in which there is great traffic. There is also brought sugar from the Canary Islands, which are those islands called by the ancients the "Isles of the Blest," by the meridian of which Ptolemy and the other mathematicians take the longitude of the earth. They belong at the present time to the crown of Spain.

To Spain is sent quicksilver, although it was customary formerly to receive quantities of it from Spain; this is due to the fact that some of the veins and the mines have dried up, and also to the fact that they themselves are using more of it than was their wont formerly. Also sent there are copper, bronze, crude and wrought brass, tin and lead, a very large quantity of many kinds of cloth which are made in these countries, especially in Flanders, and a few in England, serges of every kind and price, worsteds, half worsteds, tapestry, a fortune's worth of fine and coarse linens, camlets, grograms and mohairs, flax, yarn, wax, pitch, madder, tallow, sulphur, and often grain, meat and salted fish, and even cheese and butter; and then small wares of every kind of metal, and of silk from the silkworm, and other goods worth a marvellous sum of money, much silverplate, many arms for defence and offence, and every kind of munitions; and an infinite number of household furnishings from the smallest to the largest. In conclusion it can be said that Spain in large part supplies itself from these countries with almost all of those things which are manufactured for common use and which consist in the industry and toil of man, to which toil the Spaniards of low condition are hostile, at least in their own country. . . .

From *Descrittione di tutti i Paesi Bassi* (Antwerp, 1567); trans. J.B.R. and C. Pennock.

The Dearness of Things

JEAN BODIN

1568

I FIND that the high prices we see today are due to some four or five causes. The principal and almost the only one (which no one has referred to until now) is the abundance of gold and silver, which is today much greater in this kingdom than it was four hundred years ago, to go no further back. Moreover, the registers of the court and of the chamber do not go back more than four hundred years; the remainder has to be obtained from old histories with little assurance of accuracy. The second reason for the high prices arises in part from monopolies. The third is scarcity, caused partly by export and partly by waste. The fourth is the pleasure of kings and great lords, who raise the price of the things they like. The fifth has to do with the price of money, debased from its former standard. I will treat all these points briefly.

The principal reason which raises the price of everything, wherever one may be, is the abundance of that which governs the appraisal and price of things. . . .

But, someone will say, where did so much gold and

silver come from since that time? I find that the
merchant and the artisan, who cause the gold and
silver to come, were inactive at that time; for the
Frenchman, having one of the most fertile countries
in the world, devoted himself to tilling the soil and
feeding his cattle, which is the greatest industry
[*mesnagerie*] in France, neglecting the trade with
the Levant, because of fear of the Barbary pirates,
who hold the coast of Africa, and of the Arabs, whom
our fathers called Saracens, who controlled the whole
Mediterranean Sea, treating the Christians they captured
like galley slaves. And as for the trade with the West,
it was entirely unknown before Spain had sailed the
Indian Sea. There was also the fact that the English,
who held the ports of Guyenne and of Normandy, had
closed the routes to Spain and the Isles to us. On the
other hand, the quarrels of the houses of Anjou and of
Aragon cut us off from the ports of Italy. But a hundred fifty years ago our fathers drove out the English;
and the Portugese, sailing the high seas by the compass, made himself master of the Gulf of Persia, and
to some extent of the Red Sea, and by this means
filled his vessels with the wealth of the Indies and of
fruitful Arabia, outwitting the Venetians and Genoese,
who obtained the merchandise from Egypt and from
Syria, whither it was brought by the caravans of the
Arabs and Persians, to sell it to us in small lots and
for its weight in gold. At the same time the Castilian,
having gained control of the new lands full of gold
and silver, filled Spain with them, and prompted our
citizens to make the trip around Africa with a marvellous profit. It is incredible, and yet true, that there
have come from Peru since the year 1533, when it
was conquered by the Spaniards, more than a hundred
millions of gold, and twice as much silver. The ransom

of King Atubalira brought 1,326,000 pesans of gold.
At that time in Peru cloth hose cost three hundred
ducats; a cloak, a thousand ducats; a good horse, four
or five thousand; a bottle of wine, two hundred ducats:
as the history of the Indies testifies. And yet Augustín
de Zarate, master of accounts of his Catholic Majesty,
found that the officers of his Catholic Majesty in Peru
showed a balance in their accounts rendered of eighteen hundred thousand pesans of gold, and six hundred
thousand livres of silver; not counting the incredible
profit which the King of Portugal makes by trade in
the Moluccas, where cloves, cinnamon, and other
precious drugs grow, which he obtained from the
Emperor Charles V as a pledge for three hundred
fifty thousand ducats, when he went through Boulogne,
to be crowned emperor; which the Italians wished to
redeem and pay the sum in cash, but the emperor
would not consent, on account of the alliance of the
two houses.

Now the fact is that the Spaniard, who gets his
subsistence only from France, being compelled by un-
avoidable necessity to come here for wheat, cloths,
stuffs, dyestuffs, paper, books, even joinery and all
handicraft products, goes to the ends of the earth to
seek gold and silver and spices to pay us with.

On the other hand, the English, the Scotch, and
all the people of Norway, Sweden, Denmark, and the
Baltic coast, who have an infinity of mines, dig the
metals out of the center of the earth to buy our wines,
our saffron, our prunes, our dye, and especially our
salt, which is a manna that God gives us as a special
favour, with little labour: for the heat being lacking
for people north of the forty-seventh degree, salt cannot be made there, and below the forty-second degree
the excessive heat renders the salt more corrosive;

especially the salt of the mines in Spain, Naples, and
Poland, which often injures persons and things, so that
the salt works of Franche Comté and the rock salt in
Spain and Hungary are nowhere nearly equal to ours
in quality. This often causes the English, the Flemings,
and the Scotch, who carry on a large trade in salt fish,
to load their vessels with sand, in default of other
merchandise, in order to come and buy our salt with
good hard cash.

The other cause of the great amount of wealth that
has come to us in the last hundred and twenty or
thirty years is the huge population which has grown up
in this kingdom, since the civil wars between the
houses of Orléans and Bourgogne were ended: which
allowed us to experience the sweetness of peace, and
enjoy the fruit thereof for a long time, down to the
religious troubles; for the foreign war which we have
had since then was only a purging of bad humours
necessary for the whole body of the republic. Formerly
the open country was deserted and the cities nearly
so, as a result of the ravages of the civil wars, during
which the English had sacked cities, burned villages,
murdered, pillaged, killed a good part of the people
of France, and gnawed the remainder to the bones:
which led to the breakdown of agriculture, trade, and
all mechanical arts. But in the last hundred years we
have cleared a vast territory of forests and moors,
built several villages, peopled the cities, so that the
greatest wealth of Spain, which otherwise is a wilder-
ness, comes from the French settlers who go into Spain
in a steady stream, and principally from Auvergne and
from Limousin: to such an extent that in Navarre and
Aragon almost all the vine-dressers, labourers, carpenters, masons, joiners, stone-cutters, turners, wheel-
wrights, waggoners, carters, rope-makers, quarrymen,

saddlers, harnessmakers are French. For the Spaniard is astonishingly indolent, except in arms and trade, and therefore likes the active and willing Frenchman; as he made plain in the case of the prior of Capouë's enterprise in Valencia, where there were ten thousand French servants and artisans, who were threatened with trouble for having had a part in the conspiracy against Maximilian, then lieutenant general in Spain: but it turned out that the masters and inhabitants of Valencia warned them all. There are also many in Italy.

Another cause of the riches of France is the trade with the Levant, which was opened to us as a result of the friendship between the house of France and the house of the Ottomans in the time of King Francis the First; so that French merchants since that time have done business in Alexandria, in Cairo, in Beirut, in Tripoli, as well as the Venetians and Genoese; and have as good standing at Fez and at Morocco as the Spaniard, which was discovered when the Jews, driven out of Spain by Ferdinand, withdrew into the country of Languedoc, and accustomed the French to trading in Barbary.

Another cause of the abundance of gold and silver has been the bank of Lyons, which was opened, to tell the truth, by King Francis the First, who began to borrow money at the twelfth penny, and his successor at the tenth, then the sixth, and up to the fifth in emergencies. Suddenly the Florentines, Luccans, Genoese, Swiss, Germans, attracted by the high profit, brought a vast amount of gold and silver into France; and many settled here, partly because of the mildness of the climate, and partly because of the natural goodness of the people and the fertility of the country. By the same means, the annuities charged upon the city of Paris, which amount to three million three hundred thousand livres every year, have enticed the foreigner, who brought his money hither to make a profit, and eventually settled here: which has greatly enriched this city. It is true that the mechanical arts and merchandise would flourish much more, in my opinion, without being diminished by the traffic in money which is carried on, and the city would be much richer, if people did as they do in Genoa, where the house of Saint George takes the money of all who wish to bring any, at the twentieth penny, and lends it to merchants to trade with, at the twelfth or fifteenth penny; which is one of the causes of the grandeur and wealth of that city, and which seems to me very expedient for the public and for the individual. . . .

These, Sir, are the means which have brought us gold and silver in abundance in the last two hundred years. There is much more in Spain and Italy than in France, owing to the fact that in Italy even the nobility engage in trade, and the people of Spain have no other occupation; and so everything is dearer in Spain and in Italy than in France, and dearer in Spain than in Italy. This is true even of servants and artisans, which attracts our Auvergnats and Limousins into Spain, as I learned from them myself, because they earn three times as much as they do in France, for the rich, proud, and indolent Spaniard sells his labour very dear, as Clenard testifies, who writes in his letters, in the chapter on expenses, in a separate entry: for being shaved in Portugal, fifteen ducats per year. It is therefore the abundance of gold and silver which causes, in part, the high prices of things.

From *Reply to the Paradoxes of Malestroit*, in *Early Economic Thought*, ed. A. E. Monroe (Cambridge: Harvard University Press, 1924)

The Manner of the World

Life in Vienna

POPE PIUS II

c. 1458

VIENNA is surrounded by a wall two thousand paces in circumference, but it has large suburbs with moats encompassing them, and a palisade all around. The city also has a great moat and rising from it a very high rampart. Then there are thick and lofty walls with numerous towers and defences prepared for war. The houses of the citizens are roomy and richly adorned, yet solid and strong in construction. Everywhere there are arched doorways and broad courts. In the houses there are stoves in the living rooms, which are called *Stube* by the Viennese. By this means they tame the harshness of winter. Windows of glass let in the light from all sides, and the gates of the houses are made mostly of iron. On these many birds sing. In the houses there is a great deal of elegant furniture. The stables are full of horses and domestic animals of all kinds. The high façades of the houses make a magnificent sight. Only one thing produces an unpleasant effect; they very often cover the roofs with wooden shingles, and few are tiled. For the rest, the houses

208

are built of stone, and they shine with paint inside and out. Whatever house you enter, you will think you are in the palace of a prince.

Over the houses of the nobles and the prelates, the magistrates of the city exercise no jurisdiction. The wine cellars are so deep and so spacious that it is said that Vienna has as many buildings under the earth as above it. The streets are paved only with hard stone, so that the wheels of vehicles are not easily worn out. The churches, which are dedicated to the saints who have attained Paradise and to the most high God himself, are both large and splendid, built of dressed stone, full of light, and admirable for their rows of columns. The numerous precious relics of the saints are bedecked with silver, gold, and jewels; the churches are beautifully adorned and richly furnished. The priests abound in worldly wealth. He who is chief priest at St. Stephen's is second only to the Roman prince. This city is in the diocese of Padua, but the daughter is in this case greater than the mother. Many people in the city possess consecrated chapels in their houses, with their own priests. The four orders of mendicants are very far from poor. The Irish monks and the canons of St. Augustine also possess great wealth. . . . There is also a nunnery called St. Jerome's, in which former prostitutes are received as lay sisters; day and night they sing hymns in the German language; and if any of them is found to have relapsed into her former ways of sin she is thrown into the Danube. Thus they live there a modest and holy life; an evil rumour is rarely heard of them.

There is also a university here, with faculties of liberal arts, canon law, and theology; it is new, however, and established by papal charter. A great crowd of students flocks to it from Hungary and the upper

regions of Germany. I have found out that two distinguished theologians flourished here; one was Henry
of Hesse, who was educated at Paris and migrated here
on the foundation of the university, and was the first
regent master in theology. He wrote a great many
volumes which are worthy of note. The other was
Nicholas Dinckelsbühl the Swabian, who was virtuous
in his life and very famous for his teaching; his sermons
are avidly read today by the learned. There also is in
Vienna today a fairly well-known theologian, who, they
say, has written some histories which are not unprofitable. I would praise his teaching, if he had not lectured
for two and twenty years on the first chapter of Isaiah
and never yet come to the end. But the greatest flaw
in this center of learning is that they give too much
attention to dialectic and too much time to a study
which is not very fruitful. Those who are honoured
with the title of master of arts are examined especially
in this one art. For the rest, they have no concern for
music or rhetoric or the metrical art, although they
require that certain verses and letters unskilfully edited
by others should be taught. Oratory and poetry are
almost unknown among them; for them, all study in
logic is futile disputation, with hardly a solid foundation
anywhere. You rarely find anyone who owns the works
of Aristotle and other philosophers, but they use commentaries for the most part. The students largely devote
themselves to pleasure, and are avid for food and wine;
few come out with any learning, nor are they restrained
by any discipline. Day and night they roam about, in-
flicting grave injuries on citizens, and their wits are
completely addled by the shamelessness of the women.

It is believed that the city numbers fifty thousand
communicants. Eighteen men are chosen as magistrates,
and there is a judge whose duty it is to interpret the

law, and a master of citizens, who has charge of civic affairs. The prince chooses those who are considered the most loyal citizens, and exacts an oath from them. There are no other magistrates except those who collect the taxes on wine, which everyone must pay; these officials hold office for one year.

It is really incredible how much produce is brought into the city day after day. Many wagons come in loaded with eggs and crayfish. Flour, bread, meat, fish, and poultry are brought in tremendous masses; nevertheless, by evening nothing is left to be bought. The wine harvest lasts here for forty days, and every day three hundred carts full of wine are brought in two or three times, and twelve hundred horses are harnessed daily to bring in the harvest. In the villages outside Vienna, up to the feast of St. Martin, liberty is granted to all to bring wine into the city; it is unbelievable how much wine is brought in, which is either drunk in Vienna or sent to those outside by way of the Danube, with great effort and against its current. From the wine which is sold in Vienna in small quantities, one tenth of a penny goes to the prince; this amounts to twelve thousand gold coins which are delivered to the treasury every year and constitute only a slight burden on the citizens.

On the other hand, in so large and so noble a city, there are many irregularities. Night and day, brawls are fought like military engagements: now the craftsmen against the students, then the citizens against the workers, and again some workers take up arms against others. Hardly a celebration goes by without a manslaughter; numerous murders are committed. When there is a brawl, there is no one to separate the contending parties; neither the magistrates nor the princes try, as they should, to prevent such great evils.

To sell wine in the home is in no way damaging
to the reputation. Almost all citizens operate taverns
for wine-drinking. They heat up the stoves, prepare
food, fetch in the drunkards and the harlots, and give
them free some of the food that they have cooked so
that they will drink more, but then they are given
shorter measure in wine. The common people worship
their bellies and are gluttonous. What a man has earned
during the week by the work of his hands, he squanders
down to the last penny on Sunday. This is a ragged,
boorish lot, and there is a very great number of whores.
Rare is the woman who is content with one husband.
The nobles, when they come to visit the citizens, draw
their wives off for secret meetings; when the husbands
leave home, full of wine, their wives yield to the
nobles. Most girls choose their husbands without the
previous knowledge of their fathers. Widows remarry
as they wish, even during the period of mourning. Few
people live in the city whose ancestors lived in the
vicinity; old families are rare, and practically all the
inhabitants are immigrants or foreigners. Rich old
merchants marry young girls and soon leave them
widows. These then choose young men, with whom in
any case they have frequently had adulterous relations,
from among the associates of the family. And thus he
who yesterday was still poor, today blossoms out as
a rich man.

So also those husbands who outlive their wives take
new ones, and the whole business moves in a circle;
rarely does a son inherit from his father. Among the
Viennese the law is that the surviving spouse receives
half of the property of the deceased. Wills are not
restricted, so that husbands may make wills in favour
of their wives, and wives in favour of their husbands.
There are numerous legacy hunters, who by fawning

upon the old get themselves written down as heirs.
And they say that there are many women who will
remove by poison husbands who are troublesome to
their wives. It is well known that often citizens, who
have alarmed their wives by a word, have been slain
by the nobles who were their lovers.

The Viennese live, moreover, without any written
law; they say that they live according to ancient customs, which they often distort or interpret as they
wish. Justice is wholly venal. Those who have the
means sin without punishment; the poor and unpro-
tected are punished with the full rigour of the law.
Oaths which have been sworn publicly are observed to
the letter, because an oath which can be denied has no
force. Those who lend money for a certain period, if
they should suffer any loss after the term of the agreement has expired, extort whatever sum they wish, and
impose the highest penalty on the debtors. Pledges
which are given for loans, if they are accepted, are not
considered usurious. The Viennese fear excommunication only insofar as it is harmful to the reputation or
may bring material disadvantages. Stolen goods which
are discovered in the possession of the thief are surrendered to the judge. The Viennese do not, moreover,
observe the ecclesiastical holidays strictly; meat is sold
in the city on every fast day. The draymen never take
a holiday.

From *Historia Frederici III imperatoris*, in *Opera geographica
et historica* (1699); trans. M.M.M.

The Plight of the French Poor

CAHIER OF THE ESTATES GENERAL

1484

FOR THE third and common estate, the people of the three estates declare that this kingdom is at present like a body which has been drained of its blood by various wounds, to such an extent that all its members are empty. And just as the blood is the nourishment of the corporal life, so the finances of the kingdom are the nourishment of the commonwealth. The members are the clergy, the nobles, and people of the third estate, who are drained and denuded of resources; and there is no longer a bit of gold or silver in the said members except for those who have been near the king and have shared in his benefactions. And to understand the cause of this extreme poverty of the kingdom, it should be known that for eighty or a hundred years this poor French body has been drained almost continuously in various and pitiable ways. . . .

As for the little people, one could not imagine the persecution, poverty, and misery they have suffered and still suffer in many ways.

First of all, since that time [1461, the death of Charles VII] no region has been free from the continual going and coming of armed men, living off the poor people, now the standing companies, now the feudal levies of nobles, now the free archers, sometimes the halberdiers and at other times the Swiss and pikemen, all of whom have done infinite harm to the people.

And one should note and consider with pity the injustice and iniquity suffered by this poor people, for the men of arms are hired to defend them from oppression and yet it is they who oppress them the most. It is necessary for the poor labourer to pay and hire those who beat him, dislodge him from his house, make him sleep on the ground, deprive him of his substance; and yet securities are granted to the men of arms to preserve and defend them, and to protect their goods!

And the iniquity of this practice is clear enough. For when the poor labourer has worked all day long in weariness and sweat of his body, and has gathered the fruit of his labour, from which he expects to live, they come to take from him part of the fruit of his labour, to hand over to someone who will perhaps beat him before the end of the month, and will come to remove the horses who have tilled the land which bore the fruit with which the man of war is paid. And when the poor labouring man has paid with great difficulty the quota he owes as tallage, for the hire of the men of arms, and when he takes comfort in what is left to him, hoping it will be enough to live on for the year, or to sow, there suddenly come men of arms who eat up or waste this little reserve which the poor man has saved to live on.

And there is still worse. For the man of war is not satisfied with the goods which he finds in the hut of the labourer but forces him by blows with stick or spear to go to town to get wine, white bread, fish, spices, and other luxuries. And, in truth, if God did not counsel the poor and give them patience, they would succumb in despair. And if in times past there were many evils, it has been even worse since the death of the king. And if the people had not felt the hope of some relief on the accession of the new king, they would have abandoned their labours.

And as for the intolerable burden of tallage and taxes which the poor people of this kingdom have not carried, to be sure, for that would have been impossible, but under which they have died and perished from hunger and poverty, the mere description of the grievousness of these imposts would cause infinite sadness and woe, tears of pity, great sighs and groans from sorrowing hearts; not to mention the enormity of the evils which followed and the injustice, violence, and extortion with which these taxes were imposed and seized.

And to consider these burdens which we may call not only intolerable but even deadly and pestiferous, who would ever have thought or dreamed of seeing this poor people so badly treated, who were formerly called free [*françoys*]. Now we may call them a people in worse condition than serfs, for serfs are nourished and this people has been crushed by intolerable burdens, such as securities, duties, impositions, and excessive tallage. While in the time of King Charles VII the quotas of the tallage imposed by the parish officials were counted only in twenties, such as twenty, forty, sixty pounds, after his death they began to be levied by hundreds, and since, they have grown from hundreds to thousands. And in many parishes where in the time of the late King Charles only forty or sixty pounds of tallage a year were levied, up to a thousand pounds were imposed in the year of the death of the last king [Louis XI]. And in the time of King Charles, in the duchies, Normandy, Languedoc, and others, the tallage was only in thousands but now it is in millions. And in the province of Normandy . . . there have followed many great and pitiable consequences, for some have fled and sought shelter in England, Brittany, and elsewhere, others in great numbers have died of hunger, others in despair have killed their wives and children and themselves, seeing they had nothing left to live on. And many men, women, and children, having no animals, are forced to work yoked to the plough, and others labour at night out of fear that in daylight they will be seized and apprehended for the said tallage. And as a result parts of the land have remained unploughed, and all because they have been subject to the will of those who wish to enrich themselves with the substance of the people, and without the consent and deliberation of the three estates. . . .

And as to the manner of raising these tallages and taxes, great pillage and robbery have been committed which everyone knows about. Among great abuses and injustices, all notorious, it has happened that the individuals of a parish who had already paid their quota and share have been imprisoned to pay what their neighbours owe, and even more than the other parishioners owed. And they were not through after paying the quota and share of the others but must also pay the sergeant, jailer, and clerk, or else suffer harm and the loss of their earnings. These things considered, it seems to the said estates that the king should take pity on his poor people, and relieve them of the said tallage and taxes, as he has proclaimed, in ordered that they may be able to live under him. And this they beg of him very humbly. . . .

And may it please my lords who take pensions to content themselves with the income from their own lords, without taking any extraordinary pensions or sums of money. Or at least if some receive them, let the pensions be reasonable, moderate, and bearable, out of regard for the afflictions and miseries of the poor people. For these pensions and monies are not taken from the domain of the king, nor could he supply them, but they are taken entirely from the third estate; and it is only the poor labourer who contributes to paying the said pensions. And thus it often happens that the poor labourer and his children die of hunger, for the subst ince on which he was to live was taken for the said pensions. And there is no doubt that in the payment of these there is sometimes a piece of money which has come out from the purse of a labourer whose children beg at the gates of those who receive the said pensions. And often the dogs are fed with bread bought with the pennies of the poor labourer on which he was to live.

From the *Journal des états généraux de France tenus à Tours en 1484*, ed. A. Bernier. (Paris, 1835); trans. J.B.R.

Life among the English

VENETIAN *RELAZIONE*

c. 1500

THE ENGLISH are, for the most part, both men and women of all ages, handsome and well proportioned; though not quite so much so, in my opinion, as it had been asserted to me before your Magnificence went to that kingdom; and I have understood from persons acquainted with these countries that the Scotch are much handsomer; and that the English are great lovers of themselves, and of everything belonging to them; they think that there are no other men than themselves, and no other world but England; and whenever they see a handsome foreigner, they say that "he looks like an Englishman," and that "it is a great pity that he should not be an Englishman"; and when they partake of any delicacy with a foreigner, they ask him "whether such a thing is made in *their* country?" They take great pleasure in having a quantity of excellent victuals, and also in remaining a long time at table, being very sparing of wine when they drink it at their own expense. And this, it is said, they do in order to induce their other English guests to drink wine in moderation also; not considering it any inconvenience for three or four persons to drink out of the same cup. Few people keep wine in their own houses, but buy it, for the most part, at a tavern; and when they mean to drink a great deal, they go to the tavern, and this is done not only by the men but by ladies of distinction. The deficiency of wine, however, is amply supplied by the abundance of ale and beer, to the use of which these people are become so habituated that, at an entertainment where there is plenty of wine, they will drink them in preference to it, and in great quantities. Like discreet people, however, they do not offer them to Italians, unless they should ask for them; and they think that no greater honour can be conferred, or received, than to invite others to eat with them, or to be invited themselves; and they would sooner give five or six ducats to provide an entertainment for a person than a groat to assist him in any distress.

They all from time immemorial wear very fine clothes, and are extremely polite in their language; which, although it is, as well as the Flemish, derived from the German, has lost its natural harshness, and is pleasing enough as they pronounce it. In addition to their civil speeches, they have the incredible courtesy of remaining with their heads uncovered, with an admirable grace, whilst they talk to each other. They are gifted with good understandings, and are very quick at everything they apply their minds to; few, however, excepting the clergy, are addicted to the study of letters; and this is the reason why anyone who has learning, though he may be a layman, is called by them "a clerk." And yet they have great advantages for study, there being two general universities in the kingdom, Oxford and Cambridge; in which are many colleges founded for the maintenance of poor scholars. And your Magnificence lodged at one named Magdalen, in the University of Oxford, of which the founders having been prelates, so the scholars are also ecclesiastics.

The common people apply themselves to trade, or to fishing, or else they practise navigation; and they are so diligent in mercantile pursuits that they do not fear to make contracts on usury.

Although they all attend Mass every day, and say many Paternosters in public (the women carrying long rosaries in their hands, and any who can read taking the office of Our Lady with them, and with some companion reciting it in the church verse by verse, in a low voice, after the manner of churchmen), they always hear Mass on Sunday in their parish church, and give liberal alms, because they may not offer less than a piece of money, of which fourteen are equivalent to a golden ducat; nor do they omit any form incumbent upon good Christians; there are, however, many who have various opinions concerning religion.

They have a very high reputation in arms; and from the great fear the French entertain of them, one must believe it to be justly acquired. But I have it on the best information, that when the war is raging most furiously, they will seek for good eating, and all their other comforts, without thinking of what harm might befall them.

They have an antipathy to foreigners, and imagine that they never come into their island but to make themselves masters of it, and to usurp their goods; neither have they any sincere and solid friendships amongst themselves, insomuch that they do not trust each other to discuss either public or private affairs together, in the confidential manner we do in Italy. And although their dispositions are somewhat licentious, I never have noticed anyone, either at court or amongst the lower orders, to be in love; whence one must necessarily conclude either that the English are the most discreet lovers in the world or that they are incapable of love. I say this of the men, for I understand it is quite the contrary with the women, who are very violent in their passions. Howbeit the English keep a very jealous guard over their wives, though anything may be compensated, in the end, by the power of money.

The want of affection in the English is strongly manifested towards their children; for after having kept them at home till they arrive at the age of seven or nine years at the utmost, they put them out, both males and females, to hard service in the houses of other people, binding them generally for another seven or nine years. And these are called apprentices, and during that time they perform all the most menial offices; and few are born who are exempted from this fate, for everyone, however rich he may be, sends away his children into the houses of others, whilst he, in return, receives those of strangers into his own. And on inquiring their reason for this severity, they answered that they did it in

order that their children might learn better manners.
But I, for my part, believe that they do it because they
like to enjoy all their comforts themselves, and that
they are better served by strangers than they would
be by their own children. Besides which the English,
being great epicures and very avaricious by nature,
indulge in the most delicate fare themselves and give
their household the coarsest bread, and beer, and
cold meat baked on Sunday for the week, which,
however, they allow them in great abundance. That
if they had their own children at home, they would
be obliged to give them the same food they made use
of for themselves. That if the English sent their children away from home to learn virtue and good
manners, and took them back again when their appren-
ticeship was over, they might, perhaps, be excused;
but they never return, for the girls are settled by their
patrons, and the boys make the best marriages they
can, and, assisted by their patrons, not by their fathers,
they also open a house and strive diligently by this
means to make some fortune for themselves; whence it
proceeds that, having no hope of their paternal inheritance, they all become so greedy of gain that they feel
no shame in asking, almost "for the love of God," for
the smallest sums of money; and to this it may be
attributed, that there is no injury that can be committed
against the lower orders of the English, that may not be
atoned for by money. . . .

The riches of England are greater than those of any
other country in Europe, as I have been told by the
oldest and most experienced merchants, and also as I
myself can vouch, from what I have seen. This is
owing, in the first place, to the great fertility of the soil,
which is such that, with the exception of wine, they
import nothing from abroad for their subsistence. Next,

the sale of their valuable tin brings in a large sum of money to the kingdom; but still more do they derive from their extraordinary abundance of wool, which bears such a high price and reputation throughout Europe. And in order to keep the gold and silver in the country, when once it has entered, they have made a law, which has been in operation for a long time now, that no money, nor gold nor silverplate, should be carried out of England under a very heavy penalty. And everyone who makes a tour in the island will soon become aware of this great wealth, as will have been the case with your Magnificence, for there is no small innkeeper, however poor and humble he may be, who does not serve his table with silver dishes and drinking cups; and no one who has not in his house silverplate to the amount of at least a hundred pounds sterling, which is equivalent to five hundred golden crowns with us, is considered by the English to be a person of any consequence. But above all are their riches displayed in the church treasures; for there is not a parish church in the kingdom so mean as not to possess crucifixes, candlesticks, censers, patens, and cups of silver; nor is there a convent of mendicant friars so poor as not to have all these same articles in silver, besides many other ornaments worthy of a cathedral church in the same metal. Your Magnificence may therefore imagine what the decorations of those enormously rich Benedictine, Carthusian, and Cistercian monasteries must be. These are, indeed, more like baronial palaces than religious houses, as your Magnificence may have perceived at that of St. Thomas of Canterbury. And I have been informed that, amongst other things, many of these monasteries possess unicorns' horns, of an extraordinary size. I have also been told that they have some splendid tombs of English saints, such as St.

Oswald, St. Edmund, and St. Edward, all kings and
martyrs. . . .

A *Relation . . . of the Island of England . . . c. 1500*, trans.
C. A. Sneyd (London: Camden Society, 1847).

The Manner of the World Nowadayes

JOHN SKELTON (?)

c. 1500

So many pointed caps
Laced with double flaps,
And so gay felted hats,
   Saw I never:
So many good lessons,
So many good sermons,
And so few devotions,
   Saw I never.

So many gardes[1] worn,
Jagged and all to-torn,
And so many falsely forsworn,
   Saw I never:
So few good policies
In townes and cities
For keeping of blind hostries,
   Saw I never.

So many good workes,[2]
So few well-learned clerkes,

[1] trimmings
[2] i.e., books

And so few that goodness markes,
   Saw I never:
Such pranked coats and sleeves,
So few young men that preves,[3]
And such increase of thieves,
   Saw I never.

So many garded hose,
Such horned shoes,
And so many envious foes,
   Saw I never:
So many inquests sit
With men of smalle wit,
And so many falsely quit,
   Saw I never.

So many gay swordes,
So many altered wordes,
And so few covered boardes,
   Saw I never:
So many empty purses,
So few good horses,
And so many curses,
   Saw I never.

Such boasters and braggers,
So new fashioned daggers,
And so many beggers,
   Saw I never:
So many proper knives,
So well apparelled wives
And so ill of their lives,
   Saw I never.

[3] turn out well

. . .

Sometime we sang of mirth and play,
But now our joy is gone away,
For so many fall in decay,
   Saw I never:
Whither is the wealth of England gone?
The spiritual saith they have none,
And so many wrongfully undone,
   Saw I never.

It is great pity that every day
So many bribers go by the way,
And so many extortioners in each countrey,
   Saw I never:
To thee, Lord, I make my moan,
For thou may'st help us every one:
Alas, the people is so woe-begone,
   Worse was it never!

Amendment
Were convenient,
But it may not be;
We have exiled veritie.
God is neither dead nor sick;
He may amend all yet,
And trow ye so indeed,
As ye believe ye shall have mede.
After better I hope ever,
For worse was it never.

A Painter's Travels

ALBRECHT DÜRER

1520

AT ANTWERP I went to Jobst Plankfelt's inn, and the same evening the Fuggers' factor, Bernhard Stecher, invited me and gave us a sumptuous meal. My wife, however, dined at the inn. I paid the driver 3 gold florins to bring us there, and 1 stiver I paid for carrying the goods.

On Saturday after the feast of St. Peter in Chains my host took me to see the burgomaster's [Arnold van Liere] house at Antwerp. It is newly built and beyond measure large, and very well ordered, with spacious and exceedingly beautiful chambers, and many of them, a tower splendidly ornamented, a very large garden— altogether a noble house, the like of which I have nowhere seen in all Germany. The house also is reached from both sides by a very long street, which has been quite newly built according to the burgomaster's liking and at his charges.

I paid 3 stiver to the messenger, 2 pfennig for bread, 2 pfennig for ink.

On Sunday, it was St. Oswald's day, the painters invited me to the hall of their guild, with my wife and maid. All their service was of silver, and they had other splendid ornaments and very sumptuous meats. All their wives also were there. And as I was being led to the table the company stood on both sides as if they were leading some great lord. And there were amongst them men of very high position, who all behaved most respectfully towards me with deep courtesy, and promised to do everything in their power agreeable to me that they knew of. And as I was sitting there in such honour the syndic [Adrian Horebouts] of Antwerp came, with two servants, and presented me with four cans of wine in the name of the town councillors of Antwerp, and they had bidden him say that they wished thereby to show their respect for me and to assure me of their good will. Wherefore I returned them my humble thanks and offered my humble service. After that came Master Peter [Frans], the town carpenter, and presented me with two cans of wine, with the offer of his willing services. So when we had spent a long and merry time together till late in the night, they accompanied us home with lanterns in great honour. And they begged me to be ever assured and confident of their good will, and promised that in whatever I did they would be all-helpful to me. So I thanked them and laid me down to sleep.

I have also been in Master Quentin Massys' house, and to the three great shooting places. I received a sumptuous feast at Lorenz Staiber's, and another time at the Portuguese factor's [Francisco Brandan], whose portrait I drew in charcoal. Of my host, Jobst Plankfelt, I have also made a portrait; he gave me a branch of white coral. Paid 2 st. for butter, 2 st. to the joiner at the painters' warehouse. . . .

On the Sunday after our dear Lady's Assumption I saw the great procession from the Church of Our Lady at Antwerp, when the whole town of every craft and rank was assembled, each dressed in his best according to his rank. And all ranks and guilds had their signs, by which they might be known. In the intervals great costly pole-candles were borne, and their long old

Frankish trumpets of silver. There were also in the German fashion many pipers and drummers. All the instruments were loudly and noisily blown and beaten.

I saw the procession pass along the street, the people being arranged in rows, each man some distance from his neighbour, but the rows close one behind another. There were the goldsmiths, the painters, the masons, the broiderers, the sculptors, the joiners, the carpenters, the sailors, the fishermen, the butchers, the leatherers, the clothmakers, the bakers, the tailors, the shoemakers —indeed workmen of all kinds, and many craftsmen and dealers who work for their livelihood. Likewise the shopkeepers and merchants and their assistants of all kinds were there. After these came the shooters with guns, bows, and crossbows, and the horsemen and foot-soldiers also. Then followed a great crowd of the lords magistrates. Then came a fine troop all in red, nobly and splendidly clad. Before them, however, went all the religious orders and the members of some foundations very devoutly, all in their different robes.

A very large company of widows also took part in this procession. They support themselves with their own hands and observe a special rule. They were all dressed from head to foot in white linen garments, made expressly for the occasion, very sorrowful to see. Among them I saw some very stately persons. Last of all came the chapter of Our Lady's Church, with all their clergy, scholars, and treasures. Twenty persons bore the image of the Virgin Mary with the Lord Jesus, adorned in the costliest manner, to the honour of the Lord God.

In this procession very many delightful things were shown, most splendidly got up. Wagons were drawn along with masques upon ships and other structures. Among them was the company of the prophets in their order and scenes from the New Testament, such as the Annunciation, the Three Holy Kings riding on great camels and on other rare beasts, very well arranged; also how Our Lady fled to Egypt—very devout—and many other things, which for shortness I omit. At the end came a great dragon, which St. Margaret and her maidens led by a girdle; she was especially beautiful. Behind her came St. George with his squires, a very goodly knight in armour. In this host also rode boys and maidens most finely and splendidly dressed in the costumes of many lands, representing various saints. From beginning to end the procession lasted more than two hours before it was gone past our house. And so many things were there that I could never write them all in a book, so I let it well alone.

I have been into Fugger's house at Antwerp. He has newly built it in very costly fashion, with a noteworthy tower, broad and high, and with a beautiful garden. I saw also his fine horses. Tomasin gave my wife fourteen ells of good thick arras for a mantle and three and a half ells of half-satin to line it. I drew a design for a lady's forehead-band for the goldsmith. The factor of Portugal sent me Portuguese and French wine to the inn. Senhor Rodrigo Fernandez of Portugal has given me a small cask full of all sorts of sweetmeats, amongst them a box of sugar candy, besides two large dishes of barley-sugar, marzipan, and many other kinds of sugar work, some sugar canes also as they grow. I gave his servant in return 1 florin for a tip. I have again changed for my expenses 1 light florin for 12 st. . . .

On Sunday after Bartholomew's I travelled with Herr Tomasin from Antwerp to Mechlin, where we lay for the night. There I bade Master Konrad Meyt and a painter with him to supper. And this Master Konrad is the good carver in Lady Margaret's service. From

Mechlin we passed through the little town Vilvorde and
came to Brussels on Monday at midday. I have paid
the messenger 3 st. I dined with my lords [of Nurem-
berg] at Brussels, also once with Herr [Jacob de] Bannisis, and I gave him a "Passion" in copper. I gave the
Margrave Jan van Ymmerseele at Brussels the letter of
recommendation which my Lord of Bamberg wrote for
me, and I gave him a "Passion" engraved in copper by
which to remember me. I have also dined again with
my lords of Nuremberg. In the golden chamber in the
town hall at Brussels I saw the four paintings which the
great Master Roger van der Weyden made. And I saw
out behind the king's house at Brussels the fountains,
labyrinth, and beast garden; anything more beautiful
and pleasing to me and more like a paradise I have
never seen. Erasmus is the name of the little man who
wrote out my supplication at Herr Jacob de Bannisis'
house. At Brussels is a very splendid town hall, large,
and covered with beautiful carved stonework, and it
has a noble, open tower. I took a portrait at night by
candlelight of Master Konrad of Brussels, the host of
my lords; I drew at the same time Doctor Lamparter's
son in charcoal, also the hostess.

I saw the things which have been brought to the
king from the new land of gold [Mexico], a sun all of
gold a whole fathom broad, and a moon all of silver
of the same size, also two rooms full of the armour of
the people there, and all manner of wondrous weapons
of theirs, harness and darts, very strange clothing, bed-
covers, and all kinds of wonderful objects of human
use, much better worth seeing than prodigies. These
things were all so precious that they are valued at a
hundred thousand florins. All the days of my life I have
seen nothing that rejoiced my heart so much as these
things, for I saw amongst them wonderful works of art,

and I marvelled at the subtle *ingenia* of men in foreign
lands. Indeed I cannot express all I thought there. . . .

When I reached Bruges, Jan Prevost took me in to
lodge in his house and prepared the same night a
sumptuous meal and bade much company to meet me.
Next day Marx, the goldsmith, invited me and gave
me a sumptuous meal and asked many to meet me.
Afterwards they took me to see the emperor's house,
which is large and splendid. I saw the chapel there
which Roger painted, and some pictures by a great old
master; I gave 1 st. to the man who showed us them.
Then I bought two ivory combs for 30 st. They took
me next to St. Jacob's and showed me the precious pictures by Roger and Hugo, who were both great masters.
Then I saw in Our Lady's Church the alabaster Ma-
donna, sculptured by Michelangelo of Rome. After that
they took me to many more churches and showed me
all the good pictures, of which there is an abundance
there; and when I had seen the Jan van Eyck and all
the other works, we came at last to the painters' chapel,
in which there are good things. Then they prepared a
banquet for me, and I went with them from it to their
guild hall, where many honourable men were gathered
together, both goldsmiths, painters, and merchants, and
they made me sup with them. They gave me presents,
sought to make my acquaintance, and did me great
honour. The two brothers Jacob and Peter Mostaert, the
councillors, gave me twelve cans of wine; and the whole
assembly, more than sixty persons, accompanied me
home with many torches. I also saw at their shooting
court the great fish-tub on which they eat; it is nineteen
feet long, seven feet high, and seven feet wide. So early
on Tuesday we went away, but before that I drew with
the metalpoint the portrait of Jan Prevost, and gave his
wife 10 st. at parting.

From Bruges we travelled to Ursel, and breakfasted there; on the way there are three villages. Thence we went on through three villages more to Ghent and I paid 4 st. for the journey and 4 st. for other expenses. On my arrival at Ghent the Dean of the Painters came to me and brought with him the first masters in painting; they showed me great honour, received me most courteously, offered me their good will and service, and supped with me. On Wednesday they took me early to the Beffroi of St. John, whence I looked over the great wonderful town, yet in which even I had just been taken for something great. Then I saw Jan van Eyck's picture (the "Adoration of the Mystic Lamb"); it is a most precious painting, full of thought, and the Eve, Mary, and God the Father are specially good. Next I saw the lions and drew one with metalpoint. And I saw at the place where men are beheaded on the bridge, the two statues erected (in 1371) as a sign that there a son beheaded his father. Ghent is a fine and remarkable town; four great waters flow through it. I gave the sacristan [at St. Bavon's] and the lions' keepers 3 st. as a tip. I saw many wonderful things in Ghent besides, and the painters with their Dean did not leave me alone, but they ate with me morning and evening and paid for everything and were very friendly to me. I gave away 5 st. at the inn at leaving.

On Whitsuntide I set out from Ghent and passed through some villages to the inn called the Swan, where we breakfasted. Then we went on through a fine village and came to Antwerp and the fare was 8 st.

From Dürer's "Travel Diary," in W. M. Conway, *Literary Remains of Albrecht Dürer* (Cambridge: University Press, 1889); text slightly revised by J.B.R.

The Peasants' War in Tyrol

GEORG KIRCHMAIR'S ACCOUNT

1525

THERE arose in this country a cruel, terrible, and inhuman insurrection of the common peasant folk; I was there at the time and beheld strange and wondrous things. Certain factious and noisy people had undertaken to rescue by force from the judge a condemned rebel who had done wrong and who had justly been sentenced to punishment. After they had done this on a Wednesday, on Whitsunday the peasants, young and old, flocked together from all the mountains and valleys, although they did not know what they would do. Then when a great crowd of them had gathered together in the Mühland meadow in the Eisack valley, they concluded that they would deliver themselves of their burdens. A noble lord, Sigmund Brandisser, who was bailiff in Rodenegg, went to the assembled peasants and pointed out to them all the danger, mockery, damage, trouble, and care that would ensue. Although they promised him not to take action, but to present their grievances before their rightful prince, who was then at Innsbruck, they did not keep their promise, and on Whitsunday night they attacked Brixen, and in defiance of God and right they plundered and robbed all the priests, canons, and chaplains. Then they assembled before the bishop's courtyard and drove away all his councillors and servants with great violence, and in such an inhuman way that it cannot be described.

The people of Brixen forgot their duty to their Bishop Sebastian no less quickly than the peasants of Neustift had forgotten theirs to their lord, the Provost Augustine. In sum, no one thought of duty, loyalty, promises, or anything else. The people of Brixen and the peasants were of one mind. Each group had its leaders. Without any notice, without any reason, these leaders with five thousand men marched on the monastery of Neustift, and fell on the church on Friday, May 12, 1525. Of the wantonness of which they were guilty there one could write a whole book. The Provost Augustine, a pious man, was driven out and pursued, and the priests were so insulted, mocked, and tortured that each must have been made ashamed of the name and sign of priest. The peasants did more than twenty-five thousand florins' worth of damage to the church, in destroying the building and in looting silver, ornaments, furnishings and vessels, documents and books. The insolence, drunkenness, blasphemy, and sacrilege with which the house of God was desecrated at this time no one can describe. It would also have been burned, but God would not suffer this to happen.

On Saturday, May 13, the peasants chose a leader, Michael Geismayr, a squire's son from Sterzing, a malicious, evil, rebellious, but crafty man. As soon as he was chosen their leader, the plundering of priests went on through the whole land. There was no priest in the land so poor but that he must lose all he possessed. Afterwards they fell upon many of the nobility, and destroyed many of them, for no one was able to arm himself for defence. Even the Archduke Ferdinand and his excellent wife knew that they were safe nowhere. For in the whole country, in the valley of the Inn and on the Etsch, in the towns and among the peasants, there was such rioting, such an uproar and tumult, that an honest man might hardly walk in the streets. Robbing, plundering, and thieving were so common that even many pious men were tempted, who afterwards bitterly repented. And yet, to tell the truth, no one grew rich from the robbing, plundering, and stealing.

In J. Janssen, *Geschichte des deutschen Volkes seit dem Ausgang des Mittelalters* (Freiburg-im-Breisgau, 1915); trans. M.M.M.

MICHAEL GEISMAYR'S PLAN OF REFORM

1526

At the very outset you must pledge your lives and property, not to desert each other but to cooperate at all times; always to act advisedly and to be faithful and obedient to your chosen leaders. You must seek in all things, not your own welfare, but the glory of God and the commonweal, so that the Almighty, as is promised to those who obey Him, may give us His blessing and help. To Him we entrust ourselves entirely because He is incorruptible and betrays no one.

All those godless men who persecute the Eternal Word of God, who oppress the poor and who hinder the common welfare, shall be extirpated.

The true Christian doctrines founded on the Holy Word of God shall be proclaimed, and you must zealously pledge yourselves to them.

All privileges shall be done away with, as they are contrary to the Word of God, and distort the law which declares that no one shall suffer for the misdeeds of others.

All city walls, castles, and fortresses shall be demolished. From now on cities shall cease to exist and all shall live in villages. From cities result differences in station in the sense that one deems himself higher and more important than another. From cities come dissension, pride, and disturbances; whereas in the country absolute equality reigns.

All pictures, images, and chapels that are not parish churches (which are a horror unto God and entirely un-Christian) shall be totally abolished throughout the land.

The Word of God is to be at all times faithfully preached in the empire, and all sophistry and legal trickery shall be uprooted and all books containing such evil writings burned.

The judges, as well as the priests in the land, shall be paid only when they are employed, in order that their services may be obtained at the least expense.

Every year each community shall choose a judge and eight sworn jurors who shall administer the law during that year.

Court shall be held every Monday, and all cases shall be brought to an end within two days. The judges, sworn scribes, advocates, court attendants, and messengers shall not accept money from those concerned in the lawsuit, but they shall be paid by the community. Every Monday all litigants shall appear before the court, present their cases, and await decision.

There shall be only one government in the land, which should be located at Brixen as the most suitable place, because it is in the center of the empire, and contains many monasteries and other places of importance. Hither shall come the officials from all parts of the land, including several representatives from the mines, who shall be chosen for that purpose.

Appeals shall be taken immediately to this body and never to Meran, where it is useless to go. The administration at Meran shall be forthwith abolished.

At the seat of government there shall be established a university wherein the Word of God alone shall be taught. Three learned members of this university, well versed in Holy Scriptures (from which alone the righteousness of God can be taught), shall be appointed members of the government. They shall judge all matters according to the commands of God, as is proper among a Christian people.

Each province shall, after consulting with the others, decide whether the taxes are to be abolished from now on or whether a "free year" shall be established as is ordained in the Bible. In the meanwhile taxes should be collected for public purposes. We must remember that the empire will need money for carrying on war.

It is in the general interest to abolish customs tariffs in the interior but to permit them at the frontiers; this will establish the principle of taxing imports and not exports.

Every man shall pay the tithe according to the Word of God; it shall be spent in the following manner: In each parish there shall be a priest to preach the Scriptures, and he shall be supported from the tithe in a respectable fashion. The rest of the tithe shall be given to the poor; but such regulation shall be made as will do away with house-to-house begging, so that idle loafers may no longer be permitted to collect charity.

The monasteries and houses of the Teutonic Knights shall be turned into asylums. In some of these only sick people shall be housed; and they must be well cared for with food and medicines. In others old people who can no longer work shall be maintained; and in some, poor uneducated children shall be respectably brought up. The poor who remain at home shall be assisted on the advice of the district judge, since he is best informed. Such people shall be provided for, according to their needs, from the tithe or by charity. If the tithe be not enough for the support of the priests and the poor, then let each man loyally give charity according to his ability, and any shortage shall be made up from the public treasury. One official shall do nothing else except look after the asylums and the poor. Every judge, each in his own district, shall, by the means of the tithe, charity, and public appeals, be helpful to the poor at their homes. They shall be provided not only with meat and drink, but with clothing and other necessities as well, so that good morals prevail in the land. . . .

No one shall engage in business, and so avoid being contaminated with the sin of usury. Good regulations shall be enacted to prevent scarcity as well as to prohibit overcharging and cheating; so that all things may be sold at an honest and fair price. Let some place in the land be fixed upon (Trent, for example, on account of its central location) where all the manufactured articles shall be made. Silk, cloth, velvet, and shoes shall be produced there under the supervision of an official. Whatever cannot be grown in our country, as spices, shall be imported; shops shall be opened in several appointed places where all sorts of things shall be sold. No profit is to be made, as all things are to be sold at cost. By such means will all deceit and trickery be prevented and all things be bought at their proper value. Money will remain in the country, and this will be for the benefit of the common man. The official and his assistants, charged with the duty of enforcing these regulations, shall be paid fixed salaries. . . .

All smelting houses and mines of tin, silver, copper, and other metals found in the country, which belong to the nobles or to associations of foreign merchants, such as the Fuggers, Hochstätters, Baumgartners, and others like them, shall be confiscated and given over to public ownership; in all justice, they have forfeited them as they have acquired the mines by unjust and cruel means. The workmen were paid their wages in bad wares and bad money, though in appearance they were given more in amount than their earnings. The prices of spices and other wares rose because of bad currency. All coiners of money who bought silver of these monopolists had to pay their arbitrary prices. This indirectly resulted to the disadvantage of the poor man, who found that the rewards of his labour had decreased. All the merchants through whose hands the bad coins passed demanded still higher prices. As a result the whole world was entangled in this un-Christian usury. In such manner were the princely fortunes made, which, in all fairness, should be forfeited.

There shall be a superintendent over all the mines in the country who must be resworn every year. He shall have power to supervise every transaction and shall permit no smelting to be done except by the government. The metals shall be bought when prices are low. The miners shall be paid their wages in cash and not in goods, in order that peace and satisfaction may exist among the workers. If the mines are worked in an orderly and systematic manner there will be enough profit from them to pay the running expenses of the government. If the income is not sufficient for this purpose, a penny tax shall be laid on all to equalize the burden. Every effort should be made, however, to get the most out of the mines. The profits of one mine should be used to open another, because, through mining, the country can get the largest income with the least labour.

This is Geismayr's constitution when he dreams in his chimney corner and imagines himself a prince.

In J. S. Schapiro, *Social Reform and the Reformation* (New York: Columbia University Press, 1909).

A House in Venice

PIETRO ARETINO

1537

TO DOMENICO BOLANI

It would appear to me, honored gentleman, a sin of ingratitude, if I did not pay in praises the debt I owe to the divinity of the place in which your house is situated, where I dwell with all the pleasure that there is in life, for its site is the most proper, being neither too high up nor too low down. I am as timorous about entering upon its merits as one is about speaking of those of the emperor. Certainly he who built it picked out the best spot on the Grand Canal. And since it is the patriarch of streams and Venice the popess of cities, I can say with truth that I enjoy the finest street and the pleasantest view in the world. I never go to the window that I do not see a thousand persons and as many gondolas at the hour of market. The *piazze* to my right are the Beccarie and the Pescaria [meat and fish markets]; as well as the Campo del Mancino, the Ponte and the Fondaco dei Tedeschi; and where these meet there is the Rialto, crowded with men of business. Here, we have the grapes in barges, the game and pheasants in shops, the vegetables on the pavement.

Nor do I long for meadow streams, when at dawn I wonder at the waters covered with every kind of thing in its season. It is good sport to watch those who bring in the great stores of fruit and vegetables passing them out to those who carry them to their appointed places! All is bustle, except the spectacle of the twenty or twenty-five sailboats, filled with melons, which, huddled together, make, as it were, an island in the middle of the multitude; but then comes the business of counting, sniffing, and weighing them, to judge their perfection. Of the beautiful housewives, shining in silk and superbly resplendent in gold and jewels, not to appear to be indulging in an anticlimax, I refrain from speaking. But of one thing I shall speak, and that is of how I nearly cracked my jaws with laughter when the cries, hoots, and uproar from the boats were drowned in that of grooms at seeing a bark-load of Germans, who had just come out of the tavern, capsized in the cold waters of the canal, a sight that the famous Giulio Camillo and I saw one day. He, by the way, used to take delight in remarking to me that the entrance to my house from the landside, being a dark one and with a beastly stair, was like the terrible name I had acquired by revealing the truth. And then he would add that anyone who came to know me would find in my pure, plain, and natural friendship the same tranquil contentment that was felt on reaching the portico and coming out on the balconies above.

But that nothing might be lacking to my visual delights, behold, on one side, I have the oranges that gild the base of the Palazzo dei Camerlinghi, and, on the other side, the *rio* and the Ponte di San Giovan Crisostomo. Nor does the winter sun ever rise without entering my bed, my study, my kitchen, my other apartments, and my drawing room. But what I prize

most is the nobility of my neighbours. I have opposite
me the eloquent, magnificent, and honoured Maffio
Lioni, whose supreme virtues have taught learning, science, and good manners to the sublime intellect of
Girolamo, Piero, and Luigi, his wonderful sons. I have
also his Serene Highness, my sacramental and loving
godfather, and his son. I have the magnanimous Francesco Moccinico, who provides a constant and splendid
board for cavaliers and gentlemen. At the corner I see
the good Messer Giambattista Spinelli, under whose
paternal roof dwell my friends, the Cavorlini (may
God pardon fortune for the wrong done them by fate).
Nor do I regard as the least of my good fortune the fact
that I have the dear Signora Iacopa, to whom I am so
used, for a neighbour.

In short, if I could feed the touch and the other
senses as I feed the sight, this house which I am praising would be to me a paradise; for I content my vision
with all the amusement which the objects it loves can
give. Nor am I at all put out by the great foreign
masters of the earth who frequently enter my door, nor
by the respect which elevates me to the skies, nor by
the coming and going of the bucentaur, nor by the
regattas and the feast days, which give the Canal a
continuously triumphal appearance, all of which the
view from my windows commands.

And what of the lights, which at night are like
twinkling stars, on the boats that bring us the necessities for our luncheons and our dinners? What of the
music which by night ravishes my ears? It would be
easier to express the profound judgment which you
show in letters and in public office than to make an end
of enumerating all the delights my eyes enjoy. And so,
if there is any breath of genius in my written chatter-
ings, it comes from the favour you have done me—

not the air, not the shade, not the violets and the greenery, but the airy happiness I take in this mansion of yours, in which God grant I may spend, in health and vigour, the remainder of those years which a good man ought to live.

From *The Works of Aretino*, trans. Samuel Putnam (New York: Covici, Friede Inc., 1933).

Observations on the Turks

OGIER GHISELIN DE BUSBECQ

1555-1562

I UNDERTOOK, when we parted, to give you a full account of my journey to Constantinople, and this promise I now hope to discharge with interest; for I will give you also an account of an expedition to Amasia, which is by far the rarer treat of the two.

To an old friend like yourself I shall write very freely, and I am sure you will enjoy some pleasant passages which befell me on my way; and as to the disagreeables which are inseparable from a journey so long and so difficult, do not give them a thought, for I assure you that, though they annoyed me at the time, that very annoyance, now they are past and gone, only adds to my pleasure in recalling them.

You will remember that, after my return home from England, where I attended the marriage of King Philip and Queen Mary, in the train of Don Pedro Lasso, whom my most gracious master, Ferdinand King of the Romans, had deputed to represent him at the wedding, I received from the last-mentioned sovereign a summons to undertake this journey. . . .

At Buda I made my first acquaintance with the janizaries; this is the name by which the Turks call the infantry of the royal guard. The Turkish state has twelve thousand of these troops when the corps is at its full strength. They are scattered through every part of the empire, either to garrison the forts against the enemy, or to protect the Christians and Jews from the violence of the mob. There is no district with any considerable amount of population, no borough or city, which has not a detachment of janizaries to protect the Christians, Jews, and other helpless people from outrage and wrong.

A garrison of janizaries is always stationed in the citadel of Buda. The dress of these men consists of a robe reaching down to the ankles, while, to cover their heads, they employ a cowl, which, by their account, was originally a cloak sleeve, part of which contains the head, while the remainder hangs down and flaps against the neck. On their forehead is placed a silvergilt cone of considerable height, studded with stones of no great value.

These janizaries generally came to me in pairs. When they were admitted to my dining room they first made a bow, and then came quickly up to me, all but running, and touched my dress or hand, as if they intended to kiss it. After this they would thrust into my hand a nosegay of the hyacinth or narcissus; then they would run back to the door almost as quickly as they came, taking care not to turn their backs, for this, according to their code, would be a serious breach of etiquette. After reaching the door, they would stand respectfully with their arms crossed, and their eyes bent on the ground, looking more like monks than warriors. On receiving a few small coins (which was what they wanted) they bowed again, thanked me in loud tones, and went off blessing me for my kindness. To tell you the truth, if I had not been told beforehand that they were janizaries, I should, without hesitation, have taken them for members of some order of Turkish monks, or brethren of some Moslem college. Yet these are the famous janizaries, whose approach inspires terror everywhere.

During my stay at Buda a good many Turks were drawn to my table by the attractions of my wine, a luxury in which they have not many opportunities of indulging. The effect of this enforced abstinence is to make them so eager for drink that they swill themselves with it whenever they get the chance. I asked them to make a night of it, but at last I got tired of the game, left the table, and retired to my bedroom. On this my Turkish guests made a move to go, and great was their grief as they reflected that they were not yet dead drunk, and could still use their legs. Presently they sent a servant to request that I would allow them access to my stock of wine and lend them some silver cups. With my permission, they said, they would like to continue their drinking bout through the night; they were not particular where they sat; any odd corner would do for them. Well, I ordered them to be furnished with as much wine as they could drink, and also with the cups they asked for. Being thus supplied, the fellows never left off drinking until they were one and all stretched on the floor in the last stage of intoxication.

To drink wine is considered a great sin among the Turks, especially in the case of persons advanced in life: when younger people indulge in it the offence is considered more venial. Inasmuch, however, as they think that they will have to pay the same penalty after death whether they drink much or little, if they taste one drop of wine they must needs indulge in a regular debauch; their notion being that, inasmuch as they have already incurred the penalty, appointed for such sin in another world, it will be an advantage to them to have their sin out, and get dead drunk, since it will cost them as much in either case. These are their ideas about drinking, and they have some other notions which are still more ridiculous. I saw an old gentleman at Constantinople who, before taking up his cup, shouted as loud as he could. I asked my friends the reason, and they told me he was shouting to warn his soul to stow itself away in some odd corner of his body, or to leave it altogether, lest it should be defiled by the wine he was about to drink, and have hereafter to answer for the offence which the worthy man meant to indulge in. . . .

After stopping one day at Adrianople, we set out to finish the last stage of our journey to Constantinople, which is not far distant. As we passed through these districts we were presented with large nosegays of flowers, the narcissus, the hyacinth, and the tulipan (as the Turks call this last). We were very much surprised to see them blooming in midwinter, a season which does not suit flowers at all. There is a great abundance of the narcissus and hyacinth in Greece; their fragrance is perfectly wonderful, so much so that, when in great profusion, they affect the heads of those who are unaccustomed to the scent. The tulip has little or no smell; its recommendation is the variety and beauty of the colouring.

The Turks are passionately fond of flowers, and though somewhat parsimonious in other matters, they do not hesitate to give several aspres for a choice blossom. I, too, had to pay pretty dearly for these nosegays, although they were nominally presents, for on each occasion I had to pull out a few aspres as my acknowledgment of the gift. A man who visits the Turks had better make up his mind to open his purse as soon as he crosses their frontier, and not to shut it till he quits the country; in the interval he must sow his money broadcast, and may thank his stars if the seed proves fruitful. But even assuming that he gets nothing else by his expenditure, he will find that there is no other means of counteracting the dislike and prejudice which the Turks entertain towards the rest of the world. Money is the charm wherewith to lull these feelings in a Turk, and there is no other way of mollifying him. But for this method of dealing with them, these countries would be as inaccessible to foreigners as the lands which are condemned (according to the popular belief) to unbroken solitude on account of excessive heat or excessive cold. . . .

I must now return to my subject. A messenger was despatched to Suleiman, with a letter announcing my arrival. During the interval, while we were waiting for his answer, I had an opportunity of seeing Constantinople at my leisure. My chief wish was to visit the Church of St. Sophia; to which, however, I only obtained admission as a special favour, as the Turks think that their temples are profaned by the entrance of a Christian. It is a grand and massive building, well worth visiting. There is a huge central cupola, or dome, lighted only from a circular opening at the top. Almost all the Turkish mosques are built after the pattern of St. Sophia. Some say it was formerly much bigger, and that there were several buildings in connection with it, covering a great extent of ground, which were pulled down many years ago, the shrine in the middle of the church alone being left standing.

As regards the position of the city, it is one which nature herself seems to have designed for the mistress of the world. It stands in Europe, Asia is close in front, with Egypt and Africa on its right; and though these last are not, in point of distance, close to Constantinople, yet, practically, the communication by sea links them to the city. On the left are the Black Sea and the Sea of Azov. Many nations live all round the coasts of these seas, and many rivers pour into them; so that, through the length and breadth of these countries, which border on the Black Sea, there is nothing grown for man's use which cannot, with the greatest ease, be brought to Constantinople by water. On one side the city is washed by the Sea of Marmora, on the other the creek forms a harbour which, from its shape, is called by Strabo "the Golden Horn." On the third side it is united to the mainland, so that its position may be described as a peninsula or promontory formed by a ridge running out between the sea on one side and the firth on the other. Thus from the centre of Constantinople there is a most exquisite view over the sea, and of Mount Olympus in Asia, white with perpetual snow. The sea is perfectly crowded with shoals of fish making their way, after the manner of their kind, from the Sea of Azov and the Black Sea through the Bosporus and the Sea of Marmora into the Aegean and Mediterranean, or again returning to the Black Sea. . . .

If I had not visited the Black Sea, when I had an opportunity of sailing thither, I should have deserved to be blamed for my laziness, since the ancients held it to be quite as great an exploit to have visited the Black Sea as to have sailed to Corinth. Well, we had a delightful voyage, and I was allowed to enter some of the royal kiosks. On the folding doors of one of these palaces I saw a picture of the famous battle between

Selim and Ismael King of the Persians, executed in masterly style, in tesselated work. I saw also a great many pleasure grounds belonging to the Sultan, situated in the most charming valleys. Their loveliness was almost entirely the work of nature; to art they owed little or nothing. What a fairyland! What a landscape for waking a poet's fancy! What a retreat for a scholar to retire to! I do declare that, as I said just now, these spots seem to grieve and ask for Christian help and Christian care once more; and still truer are these words of Constantinople, or rather of the whole of Greece. That land was once most prosperous; today it is subject to an unnatural bondage. It seems as if the country, which in ancient times discovered the fine arts and every liberal science, were demanding back that civilization which it gave to us, and were adjuring us, by the claim of a common faith, to be its champion against savage barbarism. But it is all in vain. The princes of Christendom have other objects in view; and, after all, the Greeks are not under heavier bondage to the Turks than we are to our own vices—luxury, intemperance, sloth, lust, pride, ambition, avarice, hatred, envy, malice. By these our souls are so weighed down and buried that they cannot look up to heaven, or entertain one glorious thought, or contemplate one noble deed. The ties of a common faith and the duty we owe our brethren ought to have drawn us to their assistance, even though glory and honour had no charm for our dull hearts; at any rate, self-interest, which is the first thing men think of nowadays, should have made us anxious to rescue lands so fair, with all their great resources and advantages, from the hand of the barbarian, that we might hold them in his stead. At present we are seeking across the wide seas the Indies and Antipodes. And why? It is because in those lands there are simple, guileless creatures from whom rich booty may be torn without the cost of a single wound. *For these expeditions religion supplies the pretext and gold the motive.*

This was not the fashion with our ancestors. They scorned to place themselves on the level of a trader by seeking those lands where gold was most plentiful, but deemed that land most desirable which gave them the best opportunity of proving their valour and performing their duty. They, too, had their toil; they, too, had their dangers; they, too, had their distant expeditions; but honour was the prize they sought, not profit. When they came home from their wars, they came home not richer in *wealth,* but richer in *renown.*

These words are for your private ear, for perhaps some may hold it foul wrong for a man to suggest that the moral tone of the present day leaves aught to be desired. However that may be, I see that the arrows are being sharpened for our destruction; and I fear it will turn out that if we *will* not fight for glory, we shall be *compelled* to fight for existence. . . .

Angora [Ankara] formed our nineteenth halting place from Constantinople. It is a town of Galatia, and was, at one time, the headquarters of the Tectosages, a Gallic tribe. Pliny and Strabo both mention it, but it is not improbable that the present city covers only a part of the ancient town. The Kanuns call it Anquira.

Here we saw a very beautiful inscription, [the Monumentum Ancyranum] containing a copy of the tablets in which Augustus gave a summary of his achievements. We made our people copy out as much as was legible. It is engraven on the marble walls of a building now ruinous and roofless, which formerly may have formed the official residence of the governor. As you enter the building one half of the inscription is on the right, and the other on the left. The top lines are nearly perfect;

in the middle the gaps begin to present difficulties; the
lowest lines are so mutilated with blows of clubs and
axes as to be illegible. This is indeed a great literary
loss, and one which scholars have much reason to regret;
the more so as it is an ascertained fact that Ancyra was
dedicated to Augustus as the common gift of Asia. . . .

On our arrival at Amasia we were taken to call on
Achmet Pasha (the chief vizier) and the other pashas
—for the Sultan himself [Suleiman the Magnificent]
was not then in the town—and commenced our negotiations with them touching the business entrusted to us
by King Ferdinand. The pashas, on their part, apparently wishing to avoid any semblance of being prejudiced with regard to these questions, did not offer any
strong opposition to the views we expressed, and told
us that the whole matter depended on the Sultan's
pleasure. On his arrival we were admitted to an audience; but the manner and spirit in which he listened
to our address, our arguments, and our message were
by no means favourable.

The Sultan was seated on a very low ottoman, not
more than a foot from the ground, which was covered
with a quantity of costly rugs and cushions of exquisite
workmanship; near him lay his bow and arrows. His
air, as I said, was by no means gracious, and his face
wore a stern, though dignified, expression.

On entering we were separately conducted into the
royal presence by the chamberlains, who grasped our
arms. This has been the Turkish fashion of admitting
people to the sovereign ever since a Croat, in order to
avenge the death of his master, Marcus, Despot of
Servia, asked Amurath for an audience, and took advantage of it to slay him. After having gone through
a pretence of kissing his hand, we were conducted
backwards to the wall opposite his seat, care being

taken that we should never turn our backs on him.
The Sultan then listened to what I had to say; but the
language I held was not at all to his taste, for the
demands of his Majesty [Ferdinand] breathed a spirit
of independence and dignity, which was by no means
acceptable to one who deemed that his wish was law;
and so he made no answer beyond saying in a tetchy
way, *"Giusel, giusel,"* i.e., well, well. After this we were
dismissed to our quarters.

The Sultan's hall was crowded with people, among
whom were several officers of high rank. Besides these
there were all the troopers of the Imperial Guard,
Spahis, Ghourebas, Ouloufedgis, and a large force of
janizaries; but there was not in all that great assembly
a single man who owed his position to aught save his
valour and his merit. No distinction is attached to birth
among the Turks; the deference to be paid to a man is
measured by the position he holds in the public service. There is no fighting for precedence; a man's place
is marked out by the duties he discharges. In making
his appointments the Sultan pays no regard to any pre-
tensions on the score of wealth or rank, nor does he
take into consideration recommendations or popularity;
he considers each case on its own merits, and examines
carefully into the character, ability, and disposition of
the man whose promotion is in question. It is by merit
that men rise in the service, a system which ensures
that posts should only be assigned to the competent.
Each man in Turkey carries in his own hand his ancestry and his position in life, which he may make or
mar as he will. Those who receive the highest offices
from the Sultan are for the most part the sons of
shepherds or herdsmen, and so far from being ashamed
of their parentage, they actually glory in it, and consider it a matter of boasting that they owe nothing to

the accident of birth; for they do not believe that high
qualities are either natural or hereditary, nor do they
think that they can be handed down from father to son,
but that they are partly the gift of God, and partly
the result of good training, great industry, and un-
wearied zeal; arguing that high qualities do not descend from a father to his son or heir any more than
a talent for music, mathematics, or the like; and that
the mind does not derive its origin from the father, so
that the son should necessarily be like the father in
character, but emanates from heaven, and is thence
infused into the human body. Among the Turks, therefore, honours, high posts, and judgeships are the rewards of great ability and good service. If a man be
dishonest, or lazy, or careless, he remains at the bottom of the ladder, an object of contempt; for such
qualities there are no honours in Turkey!

This is the reason that they are successful in their
undertakings, that they lord it over others, and are
daily extending the bounds of their empire. These are
not our ideas; with us there is no opening left for
merit; birth is the standard for everything; the prestige
of birth is the sole key to advancement in the public
service. But on this head I shall perhaps have more to
say to you in another place, and you must consider
what I have said as strictly private.

For the nonce, take your stand by my side, and look
at the sea of turbaned heads, each wrapped in twisted
folds of the whitest silk; look at those marvellously
handsome dresses of every kind and every colour; time
would fail me to tell how all around is glittering with
gold, with silver, with purple, with silk, and with
velvet; words cannot convey an adequate idea of that
strange and wondrous sight: it was the most beautiful
spectacle I ever saw. . . .

From this you will see that it is the patience, self-denial, and thrift of the Turkish soldier that enable him to face the most trying circumstances, and come safely out of the dangers that surround him. What a contrast to our men! Christian soldiers on a campaign refuse to put up with their ordinary food, and call for thrushes, becaficos, and such-like dainty dishes! If these are not supplied they grow mutinous and work their own ruin; and, if they are supplied, they are ruined all the same. For each man is his own worst enemy, and has no foe more deadly than his own intemperance, which is sure to kill him, if the enemy be not quick. It makes me shudder to think of what the result of a struggle between such different systems must be; one of us must prevail and the other be destroyed; at any rate we cannot both exist in safety. On their side is the vast wealth of their empire, unimpaired resources, experience and practice in arms, a veteran soldiery, an uninterrupted series of victories, readiness to endure hardships, union, order, discipline, thrift, and watchfulness. On ours are found an empty exchequer, luxurious habits, exhausted resources, broken spirits, a raw and insubordinate soldiery, and greedy generals; there is no regard for discipline, licence runs riot, the men indulge in drunkenness and debauchery, and, worst of all, the enemy are accustomed to victory, we, to defeat. Can we doubt what the result must be? The only obstacle is Persia, whose position on his rear forces the invader to take precautions. The fear of Persia gives us a respite, but it is only for a time. When he has secured himself in that quarter, he will fall upon us with all the resources of the East. How ill prepared we are to meet such an attack it is not for me to say. . . .

As to your inquiries about Greek books and your

writing that you hear I have brought back many curiosities and some rare animals, there is nothing among them that is much worth mentioning. I have brought back a very tame ichneumon, an animal celebrated for its hatred to the crocodile and asp, and the internecine war it wages with them. I had also a remarkably handsome weasel, of the kind called sables, but I lost him on the journey. I also brought with me several beautiful thoroughbred horses, which no one before me has done, and six she-camels. I brought back some drawings of plants and shrubs, which I am keeping for Mattioli, but as to plants and shrubs themselves I have few or none. For I sent him many years ago the sweet flag (*Acorus calamus*) and many other specimens. Carpets too, and linen embroidered in Babylonian fashion, swords, bows, and horse-trappings, and many knick-knacks elegantly made of leather, which is generally horse leather, and other trifling specimens of Turkish workmanship I have, or rather, to speak more correctly, I ought to say, I had. For, as in this great assemblage of sovereigns, both male and female, here at Frankfort, I give, of my own accord, many presents to many people as compliments, and am ashamed to refuse many others who ask me, what I have left for myself is but little. But, while I think my other gifts have been well bestowed, there is one of which I regret having been so lavish, namely, the balsam, because physicians have thrown doubts on its genuineness, declaring that it has not got all the properties which, according to Pliny, mark the true balsam, whether because the strength of the very old plants, from which it flows, has been in some degree impaired by age, or for some other reason. This much, at any rate, I know for certain, that it flowed from the shrubs which are cultivated in the gardens of Matarieh, near Cairo. . . .

I am also bringing back a great medley of ancient coins, of which I shall present the most remarkable to my master.

I have besides, whole wagonfuls, whole shiploads, of Greek manuscripts. There are, I believe, not much fewer than two hundred and forty books, which I sent by sea to Venice, to be conveyed from there to Vienna, for their destination is the Imperial Library. There are some which are not to be despised and many common ones. I ransacked every corner to collect, in a sort of final gleaning, all that remained of such wares. The only one I left at Constantinople was a copy of Dioscorides, evidently a very ancient manuscript, written throughout in uncial characters and containing drawings of the plants, in which, if I am not mistaken, there are also some fragments of Cratevas and a treatise on birds. It belongs to a Jew, the son of Hamon, who was Suleiman's physician, and I wanted to buy it, but was deterred by the price. For he demanded a hundred ducats, a sum suiting the Imperial purse, but not mine. I shall not leave off pressing the emperor till I induce him to ransom so famous an author from such foul slavery. The manuscript is in very bad condition from the injuries of age, being so worm-eaten on the outside that hardly anyone, if he found it on the road, would take the trouble of picking it up.

But my letter is too long already; expect to see me in person very shortly; if anything remains to be told, it shall be kept for our meeting. But mind you invite men of worth and learning to meet me, so that pleasant company and profitable conversation may serve to rub off the remains of the rust I have contracted during my long sojourn among the Turks. Farewell.

From "Turkish Letters," in *The Life and Letters of Ogier Ghiselin de Busbecq*, trans. C. T. Forster (London: C. Kegan Paul & Co., 1881).

The Judgment of a Witch

FUGGER NEWS-LETTER

1587

THE HEREIN mentioned, malefic and miserable woman, Walpurga Hausmännin, now imprisoned and in chains, has, upon kindly questioning and also torture, following on persistent and fully justified accusations, confessed her witchcraft and admitted the following. When one-and-thirty years ago she had become a widow, she cut corn for Hans Schlumperger, of this place, together with his former servant, Bis im Pfarrhof by name. Him she enticed with lewd speeches and gestures, and they convened that they should, on an appointed night, meet in her, Walpurga's, dwelling, there to indulge in lustful intercourse. So when Walpurga in expectation of this sat awaiting him at night in her chamber, meditating upon evil and fleshly thoughts, it was not the said bondsman who appeared unto her, but the Evil One in the latter's guise and raiment and indulged in fornication with her. Thereupon he presented her with a piece of money, in the semblance of half a thaler, but no one could take it from her, for it was a bad coin and like lead. For this reason she had thrown it away. After the act of fornication she saw and felt the cloven foot of her whoremonger, and that his hand was not natural, but as if made of wood. She was greatly affrighted thereat and called upon the name of Jesus, whereupon the Devil left her and vanished.

On the ensuing night the Evil Spirit visited her again in the same shape and whored with her. He made her many promises to help her in her poverty and need, wherefore she surrendered herself to him body and soul. Thereafter the ·Evil One inflicted upon her a scratch below the left shoulder, demanding that she should sell her soul to him with the blood that had flowed therefrom. To this end he gave her a quill and, whereas she could not write, the Evil One guided her hand. She believes that nothing offensive was written, for the Evil One only swept with her hand across the paper. The script the Devil took with him, and whenever she piously thought of God Almighty, or wished to go to church, the Devil reminded her of it.

Further, the above-mentioned Walpurga confesses that she oft and much rode on a pitchfork by night with her paramour, but not far, on account of her duties. At such devilish trysts she met a big man with a grey beard, who sat in a chair, like a great prince, and was richly attired. That was the Great Devil to whom she had once more dedicated and promised herself body and soul. Him she worshipped and before him she knelt, and unto him she rendered other such-like honours. But she pretends not to know with what words and in which fashion she prayed. She only knows that once she heedlessly pronounced the name of Jesus. Then the above-mentioned Great Devil struck her in the face and Walpurga had to disown (which is terrible to relate) God in heaven, the Christian name and belief, the blessed saints and the Holy Sacraments, also to renounce the heavenly hosts and the whole of Christendom. Thereupon the Great Devil baptized her afresh, naming her Höfelin, but her paramour-devil, Federlin. . . .

Since her surrender to the Devil, she had seemingly

oft received the Blessed Sacrament of the true Body and Blood of Jesus Christ, apparently by the mouth, but had not partaken of it, but (which once more is terrible to relate) had always taken it out of her mouth again and delivered it up to Federlin, her paramour. At their nightly gatherings she had oft with her other playfellows trodden underfoot the Holy and Blessed Sacrament and the image of the Holy Cross. The said Walpurga states that during such-like frightful and loathsome blasphemies she at times truly did espy drops of blood upon the said Holy Sacrament, whereat she herself was greatly horrified. . . . She confesses, also, that her paramour gave her a salve in a little box with which to injure people and animals, and even the precious fruit of the field. He also compelled her to do away with and to kill young infants at birth, even before they had been taken to Holy Baptism. This she did, whenever possible. . . .

She rubbed with her salve and brought about the death of Lienhart Geilen's three cows, of Bruchbauer's horse, two years ago of Max Petzel's cow, three years ago of Duri Striegel's cow, two years ago of Hans Striegel's cow, of the cow of the governor's wife, of a cow of Frau Schötterin, and two years ago of a cow of Michel Klingler, on the village green. In short, she confesses that she destroyed a large number of cattle over and above this. A year ago she found bleached linen on the common and rubbed it with her salve, so that the pigs and geese ran over it and perished shortly thereafter. Walpurga confesses further that every year since she has sold herself to the Devil she has on St. Leonard's Day exhumed at least one or two innocent children. With her devil-paramour and other playfellows she has eaten these and used their hair and their little bones for witchcraft.

She was unable to exhume the other children she had slain at birth, although she attempted it, because they had been baptized before God.

She had used the said little bones to manufacture hail; this she was wont to do once or twice a year. Once this spring, from Siechenhausen, downwards across the fields. She likewise manufactured hail last Whitsun, and when she and others were accused of having held a witches' revel, she had actually held one near the upper gate by the garden of Peter Schmidt. At that time her playfellows began to quarrel and struck one another, because some wanted to cause it to hail over Dillingen Meadows, others below it. At last the hail was sent over the marsh towards Weissingen, doing great damage. She admits that she would have caused still more and greater evils and damage if the Almighty had not graciously prevented and turned them away.

After all this, the Judges and Jury of the Court of this Town of Dillingen, by virtue of the Imperial and Royal Prerogative and Rights of his Right Reverence, Herr Marquard, bishop of Augsburg, and provost of the Cathedral, our most gracious prince and lord, at last unanimously gave the verdict that the aforesaid Walpurga Hausmännin be punished and dispatched from life to death by burning at the stake as being a maleficent and well-known witch and sorceress, convicted according to the context of Common Law and the Criminal Code of the Emperor Charles V and the Holy Roman Empire. All her goods and chattels and estate left after her to go to the Treasury of our most high prince and lord. The aforesaid Walpurga to be led, seated on a cart, to which she is tied, to the place of her execution, and her body first to be torn five times with red-hot irons. The first time outside the town hall in the left breast and the right arm, the second time at the lower gate in the right breast, the third time at the mill brook outside the hospital gate in the left arm, the fourth time at the place of execution in the left hand. But since for nineteen years she was a licensed and pledged midwife of the city of Dillingen, yet has acted so vilely, her right hand with which she did such knavish tricks is to be cut off at the place of execution. Neither are her ashes after the burning to remain lying on the ground, but are thereafter to be carried to the nearest flowing water and thrown thereinto. Thus a venerable jury have entrusted the executioner of this city with the actual execution and all connected therewith.

From *The Fugger News-Letters*, ed. Victor von Klarwell, trans. P. de Chary (London: John Lane, The Bodley Head Ltd., 1924).

The Edifice of Power

The Circle of Governments

NICCOLÓ MACHIAVELLI

c. 1517

H AVING PROPOSED to myself to treat of the kind of
government established at Rome, and of the
events that led to its perfection, I must at the beginning observe that some of the writers on politics
distinguished three kinds of government, viz. the mon-
archical, the aristocratic, and the democratic; and maintain that the legislators of a people must choose from
these three the one that seems to them most suitable.
Other authors, wiser according to the opinion of many,
count six kinds of governments, three of which are very
bad, and three good in themselves, but so liable to be
corrupted that they become absolutely bad. The three
good ones are those which we have just named; the
three bad ones result from the degradation of the other
three, and each of them resembles its corresponding
original, so that the transition from the one to the
other is very easy. Thus monarchy becomes tyranny;
aristocracy degenerates into oligarchy; and the popular government lapses readily into licentiousness. So
that a legislator who gives to a state which he founds

either of these three forms of government, constitutes it but for a brief time; for no precautions can prevent either one of the three that are reputed good from degenerating into its opposite kind; so great are in these the attractions and resemblances between the good and the evil.

Chance has given birth to these different kinds of governments amongst men; for at the beginning of the world the inhabitants were few in number, and lived for a time dispersed, like beasts. As the human race increased, the necessity for uniting themselves for defence made itself felt; the better to attain this object, they chose the strongest and most courageous from amongst themselves and placed him at their head, promising to obey him. Thence they began to know the good and the honest, and to distinguish them from the bad and vicious; for seeing a man injure his bene-factor aroused at once two sentiments in every heart, hatred against the ingrate and love for the benefactor. They blamed the first, and on the contrary honoured those the more who showed themselves grateful, for each felt that he in turn might be subject to a like wrong; and to prevent similar evils, they set to work to make laws, and to institute punishments for those who contravened them. Such was the origin of justice. This caused them, when they had afterwards to choose a prince, neither to look to the strongest nor bravest, but to the wisest and most just. But when they began to make sovereignty hereditary and non-elective, the chil-dren quickly degenerated from their fathers; and, so far from trying to equal their virtues, they considered that a prince had nothing else to do than to excel all the rest in luxury, indulgence, and every other variety of pleasure. The prince consequently soon drew upon himself the general hatred. An object of hatred, he naturally felt fear; fear in turn dictated to him precautions and wrongs, and thus tyranny quickly developed itself. Such were the beginning and causes of disorders, conspiracies, and plots against the sovereigns, set on foot, not by the feeble and timid, but by those citizens who, surpassing the others in grandeur of soul, in wealth, and in courage, could not submit to the outrages and excesses of their princes.

Under such powerful leaders the masses armed themselves against the tyrant, and, after having rid themselves of him, submitted to these chiefs as their liberators. These, abhorring the very name of prince, constituted themselves a new government; and at first, bearing in mind the past tyranny, they governed in strict accordance with the laws which they had established themselves; preferring public interests to their own, and to administer and protect with greatest care both public and private affairs. The children succeeded their fathers, and ignorant of the changes of fortune, having never experienced its reverses, and indisposed to remain content with this civil equality, they in turn gave themselves up to cupidity, ambition, libertinage, and violence, and soon caused the artistocratic government to degenerate into an oligarchic tyranny, regardless of all civil rights. They soon, however, experienced the same fate as the first tyrant; the people, disgusted with their government, placed themselves at the command of whoever was willing to attack them, and this disposition soon produced an avenger, who was sufficiently well seconded to destroy them. The memory of the prince and the wrongs committed by him being still fresh in their minds, and having overthrown the oligarchy, the people were not willing to return to the government of a prince. A popular government was therefore resolved upon, and it was so organized that the authority should not again fall into the hands of a prince or a small number of nobles. And as all governments are at first looked up to with some degree of reverence, the popular state also maintained itself for a time, but which was never of long duration, and lasted generally only about as long as the generation that had established it; for it soon ran into that kind of licence which inflicts injury upon public as well as private interests. Each individual only consulted his own passions, and a thousand acts of injustice were daily committed, so that, constrained by necessity, or directed by the counsels of some good man, or for the purpose of escaping from this anarchy, they returned anew to the government of a prince, and from this they generally lapsed again into anarchy, step by step, in the same manner and from the same causes as we have indicated.

Such is the circle which all republics are destined to run through. Seldom, however, do they come back to the original form of government, which results from the fact that their duration is not sufficiently long to be able to undergo these repeated changes and preserve their existence. But it may well happen that a republic lacking strength and good counsel in its difficulties becomes subject after a while to some neighbouring state, that is better organized than itself; and if such is not the case, then they will be apt to revolve indefinitely in the circle of revolutions. I say, then, that all kinds of government are defective; those three which we have qualified as good because they are too short-lived, and the three bad ones because of their inherent viciousness. Thus sagacious legislators, knowing the vices of each of these systems of government by themselves, have chosen one that should partake of all of them, judging that to be the most stable and solid. In fact, when there is combined under the same constitution a prince, a nobility, and the power of the people, then these three powers will watch and keep each other reciprocally in check.

From *The Discourses*, trans. C. E. Detmold (Boston: J. R. Osgood & Co., 1882).

A Portrait of Lorenzo de' Medici

FRANCESCO GUICCIARDINI

1509

THE CITY was in a state of perfect peace, the citizens of the state united and bound together, and the government so powerful that no one dared to oppose it. Every day the populace delighted in spectacles, feasts, and novel diversions. The city was sustained both by its abundant supplies and its flourishing and well-established business enterprises; men of talent and ability were rewarded through the recognition and support given to all letters, all arts, all gifts. And finally when the city was in a state of profound tranquility and quiet within, and at the height of glory and reputation without—as a result of having a government and a head of the greatest authority, of having recently extended its dominion, of having been in great part responsible for the salvation of Ferrara and then of King Ferrante, of controlling completely Pope Innocent, of being allied with Naples and Milan, and of being a kind of balance for Italy as a whole—something happened which turned everything upside down, to the confusion not only of the city but of all Italy.

And this was the fact that in the said year, Lorenzo de' Medici, having had a long illness, but one which was at first diagnosed by the doctors as of slight importance, and perhaps not looked after with adequate care, but which nevertheless had secretly taken hold of him, finally on the . . . day of April, 1492, passed from this life.

This death was marked out as one of the greatest consequence by many omens: a comet had appeared a short time before; wolves had been heard to howl; a mad woman in Santa Maria Novello had cried out that an ox with fiery horns was burning up the whole city; some lions had fallen into a fight and the most beautiful had been killed by the others; and finally a day or two before his death lightning had struck at night the lantern of the dome of Santa Liparata [Reparata] and knocked down some enormous stones, which fell toward the house of the Medici. And some also considered it a portent that Master Piero Lione of Spoleto, by reputation the leading Italian physician, who had taken care of Lorenzo, threw himself as if in despair down a well and drowned there, although some say he had been thrown in.

Lorenzo de' Medici was forty-three years old when he died, and he had been in the government of the city twenty-three years, because when his father Piero died in 1469 he was twenty years old. And although he was so young and supposedly under the control of Messer Tommaso Soderini and other elders of the state, nevertheless, in a short time he gained such strength and reputation that he governed the city in his own way. Since his authority multiplied every day and then reached its height through the political crisis of 1478 and later on his return from his successful mission to Naples, he continued until his death to govern the city and to arrange matters entirely according to his own will, as if he were the sole and absolute master. And because the greatness of this man was of the highest order, and Florence never had a citizen equal to him, and his fame was very widespread both after his death and while he lived, it does not seem to me out of place but rather most suitable to give a detailed account of his habits and his character. Such a portrait I can draw not from experience, because I was a boy when he died, but from persons and places that are reliable and worthy of credence, and of such a kind that, unless I deceive myself, what I write will be the pure truth.

There were in Lorenzo many and most excellent virtues; there were also in him some vices, due partly to nature, partly to necessity. He possessed such great authority that one could say that in his time the city was not free although it abounded in all the glory and felicity that a city can have; free in name, but in fact and in truth tyrannized over by one of its citizens. His deeds, although they can be censured in part, were very great nonetheless, and so great that they win much more admiration from careful consideration of the facts than from mere hearsay, because they are lacking in those feats of arms and in that military art and discipline for which the ancients are so famous. This was due not to any fault of his but to the age and the customs of the time. One does not read in his life about a single masterly defence of a city, not a single remarkable storming of a fortress, nor a stratagem in battle and victory over the enemy. And yet, although his deeds do not shine with such brilliance of arms, there will certainly be found in him all those signs and evidences of ability which one can see and consider in civil life.

No one, even among his adversaries and those who maligned him, denies that there was in him a very great and extraordinary genius. To have governed the city for twenty-three years, and always with increasing power and glory, is such proof of it that anyone who denies it is mad; especially since this is a city most free in speech, full of the most subtle and restless talents, such a small dominion as to make it impossible to sustain all its citizens with its resources, making it necessary, after having contented a small number, to exclude the others. Proof also is the friendship and great reputation he enjoyed with many princes both inside and outside Italy, with Pope Innocent, with King Ferrante, with Duke Galeazzo, with King Louis of France, and finally with the Great Turk and with the Sultan, by whom in the last years of his life he was presented with a giraffe, a lion, and some rams. This reputation sprang from nothing else than knowing how to keep the friendship of these princes with great dexterity and skill. Proof also to those who heard him was his public and private discourse, full of acumen and subtlety, by which in many times and places, and especially in the Diet of Cremona, he gained very great advantage. Proof also are the letters dictated by him, full of such art that one could not ask for more; these seemed the more beautiful inasmuch as they were accompanied by a great eloquence and a most elegant style.

He had the good judgment of a wise man, but nevertheless not of a quality comparable to his genius; and he was seen to commit various acts of rashness, such as the war with Volterra, which, through his desire to win out over the people of Volterra in regard to the alum mines, forced her to rebel and lit a fire capable of turning all Italy upside down, although in the end it turned out well. Also, after the revolt of 1478, if he had borne himself gently with the pope and king, perhaps they would not have broken out into war against him, but by wishing to act the injured one and not wishing to conceal the injury received, he precipitated a war which caused the greatest damage and danger to himself and to the city. Again, the mission to Naples was considered too heated and hasty an undertaking, considering that he put himself into the hands of a king who was most restless, faithless, and hostile to him. And if, indeed, the necessity for peace in which he and the city found themselves excused him, nevertheless it was believed he could have achieved it with greater security and not less advantage by staying in Florence.

He desired glory and excellence beyond that of anyone else, and in this he can be criticized for having had too much ambition even in regard to minor things; he did not wish to be equalled or imitated by any citizen even in verses or games or exercises, turning angrily against any who did so. He was too ambitious even in great affairs, inasmuch as he wished in everything to equal or emulate all the princes of Italy, which was very displeasing to Lord Ludovico. In general, however, such ambition was praiseworthy and was responsible for making his renown celebrated everywhere, even outside Italy, because he strove to bring it about that in his time all the arts and talents should be more excellent in Florence than in any other city of Italy. Chiefly for the sake of letters he refounded in Pisa a university of law and the arts, and, having been shown that for many reasons not so large a number of students could assemble there as in Padua and Pavia, he said it was enough for him that the College of Lecturers should surpass the others. And therefore there always taught in Pisa in his time, with the highest salaries, all the most excellent and famous men of Italy, whom he did not spare expense or trouble to secure. And similarly there flourished in Florence the studies of the humanities under Messer Agnolo Poliziano, of Greek under master Demetrios and later Lascaris, and the studies of philosophy and of art under Marsilio Ficino, Messer Giorgio Benigno, the Count of Mirandola, and other excellent men. He showed the same favour to vernacular poetry, to music, architecture, painting, sculpture, and all the fine and mechanical arts, so that the city was overflowing with all these graces. These arts developed all the more because he, being most versatile, could pass judgment on them and distinguish among men, with the result that all strove with one another in order to please him the more. Of advantage also was the boundless generosity with which he showered pensions on talented men and supplied them with all the tools necessary to their arts. For example, when he wanted to create a Greek library, he sent Lascaris, a most learned man who taught Greek in Florence, as far as Greece to seek out ancient and good books.

This same liberality preserved his renown and his friendship with the princes outside Italy, since he neglected no show of magnificence, even at the greatest expense and loss, by which he might influence great men. And so, through such display and lavishness, his expenditures multiplied in Lyons, Milan, Bruges, and in the various centres of his trade and his company, while his profits diminished from being neglected by incompetent agents, such as Lionetto de' Rossi, Tommaso Portinari, and others. His accounts were not well kept because he did not understand commerce or pay enough attention to it, and as a result his affairs more than once fell into such disorder that he was on the point of bankruptcy, and it was necessary for him to help himself out both with money from his friends and with public funds.

In 1473, therefore, he borrowed from the sons of Pierfrancesco de' Medici sixty thousand ducats, which, not being able to return, he paid back gradually by turning over to them the villa of Cafaggiuolo with the property he owned in Mugello. He ordered that in the war of that year the soldiers should be paid at the bank of the Bartolini, in which he held shares; and by his order there was withheld from the payments such a large commission that it amounted to about eight per cent interest. This caused a loss to the commune because the *condottieri* were lacking so many men through defection, and the commune had to enter into so many more military contracts. And later at another time he availed himself of public funds to take care of his needs and necessities, which were often so urgent that in 1484, to avoid bankruptcy, he was forced to borrow from Lord Ludovico four thousand ducats and to sell for another four thousand a house he owned in Milan, which had been given by Duke Francesco to Cosimo, his grandfather. One can well believe that he did this with tears in his eyes, considering his nature, so generous and magnificent. When he found himself left behind by the changes in commerce, he tried to secure an income from landed property of fifteen or twenty thousand ducats; and he so expanded his earlier holdings in Pisan property that the income must have come to ten thousand.

He was very proud by nature, so much so that, besides desiring that men should not oppose him, he even wished them to understand him intuitively, using few and ambiguous words in important affairs. In ordinary conversation he was very witty and agreeable; in domestic life, refined rather than sumptuous, except in the banquets at which he honoured magnificently the many noble foreigners who came to Florence. He was licentious, and very amorous and constant in his loves, which usually lasted several years. In the opinion of many this so weakened his body that it caused him to die relatively young. His last love, which lasted many years, was for Bartolomea de' Nasi, wife of Donato Benci, who was by no means beautiful but with a style and grace of her own. He was so infatuated with her that one winter when she stayed in the country he would leave Florence at five or six o'clock in the evening on horseback with several companions to go to her, departing, however, in time to be back in Florence in the morning before daybreak. When his companions, Luigi della Stufa and Butta de' Medici, complained, she, perceiving this, brought them into such disfavour with Lorenzo that to satisfy her he sent Luigi as ambassador to the Sultan and Butta to the Great Turk. What foolishness that one of such great reputation and prudence, forty years old, should be so taken with a woman, who was not beautiful and already well along in years, that he was led to do what would be disgraceful to any boy!

He was considered by some as naturally cruel and vindictive because of the harshness he showed in dealing with the Pazzi conspiracy, imprisoning the innocent young men of the family and not wishing the young girls to be married, after so much slaughter had taken place in those days. This event was so bitter, however, that it was no wonder he was extraordinarily angered by it. And it was seen later that, softened by time, he gave permission for the girls to be married and ·vas willing for the Pazzi to come out of prison and go to live outside the territory of Florence. It was seen also in his other dealings that he did not employ cruelty and that he was not a bloodthirsty person.

But the trait in him which was more serious and annoying than anything else was suspicion. This came perhaps not so much from his nature as from the knowledge that he had to hold down a free city, and one in which what was done had to be done by magistrates and according to the laws of the city and under the appearance and form of liberty. In the beginning, therefore, when he first began to gain a foothold, he set about holding down as much as possible all those citizens whom he knew to be commonly esteemed either because of noble birth, or wealth, or power, or reputation. And although these men, if they were of families and ancestry faithful to the state, were generously granted magistracies, embassies, commissions, and similar honours, nevertheless, not trusting them, he appointed as supervisors of the scrutinies [election lists] and taxes, and confided his intimate secrets to, men whom he convinced that they were of such quality that without his help they would not have succeeded.

This same suspicion led him to take care that many men powerful in themselves should not become related by marriage, and he did his best to arrange matches in such a way that they would not cause him any reason for suspicion; sometimes, in order to prevent these unions, forcing youths of rank to take as wives those whom they would not have chosen. And finally things reached the point where no marriage alliance at all, except the most unimportant, was established without his intervention and permission.

This same suspicion accounts for the fact that in order to prevent the ambassadors who went abroad from passing beyond his control he ordered secretaries, paid by the state, to be established in Rome, Naples, and Milan, who were in the service of the resident ambassadors and from whom he received separate reports and was informed about current affairs.

I do not wish to attribute to suspicion the fact that he was escorted by a large number of armed guards, whom he favoured considerably, giving to some hospitals and places of refuge, because the conspiracy of the Pazzi was the reason for it. Nevertheless this was not a free city and a private citizen, but a city in servitude and a tyrant. And finally one must conclude that under him the city was not free, but, nevertheless, it would have been impossible for it to have had a better or more pleasing tyrant. From his inclination and natural goodness came infinite advantages, but through the necessity of tyranny some evils, although they were restrained and limited as much as necessity permitted; there were very few inconveniences through his intention and free will. And although those whom he had held down rejoiced at his death, nevertheless it was a source of sorrow to men in the government and even to those who had sometimes been injured, not knowing what would happen to them. It caused great grief also to the city in general and to the common people, whom he had continuously kept in abundance, supplied with pleasures, delights, and festivals. It caused the greatest anguish to all men in Italy of excellence in letters, painting, sculpture, or similar arts, either because they had been encouraged by him with great rewards or because they had been the more esteemed by other princes who feared that if they were not caressed they would go over to Lorenzo.

He left three sons: Piero, the first, about twenty-one years old; Messer Giovanni the Cardinal, the second, who a few weeks before Lorenzo's death had received the hat and had been established in the dignity of the cardinalship; Giuliano, the third, still a boy. Lorenzo was of medium height, his countenance coarse and dark in colour and yet with an air of dignity; his pronunciation and voice were harsh and unpleasing because he talked through his nose.

There are many who seek to know which was more excellent, Cosimo or Lorenzo, because Piero, although superior to them both in piety and mercy, was beyond doubt inferior to them in the other virtues. In this inquiry it seems to be agreed that Cosimo had more firmness and judgment, because he created the state, and after he had created it he enjoyed it for thirty years, securely, one can say, and without opposition, handling equally well the Blacks and the others of whom he had some fear, without coming to a break with them, and nevertheless in such a way that he was safe. And amid so many occupations of state he did not neglect the management of business and of his private affairs but governed them with such diligence and intelligence that his wealth was always greater than that of the state, which was very great indeed, and he was not constrained by need to manipulate the public income or to usurp private funds. In Lorenzo there was not such good judgment, although he had only the trouble of preserving the state because he found it already created; nevertheless he preserved it through great dangers, such as the crisis of the Pazzi and the expedition to Naples. He did not have ability in business and in private affairs, so that when things went badly he was forced to avail himself of public funds, and perhaps in some cases of private funds, to his great shame and blame. But there abounded in him eloquence, cleverness, and universal capacity to delight in all virtuous things and to favour them. In eloquence

Cosimo was entirely lacking; he was said, as a youth especially, to be rather inept in speaking.

The magnificence of both was very great but in different ways. Cosimo built palaces and churches inside and outside the fatherland and things which were intended to be permanent and always witness to his fame. Lorenzo began at Poggio in Caiano a most magnificent fortification but did not finish it because of death; and although it was in itself a great thing, nevertheless, in comparison with the many great walls of Cosimo, one can say that Lorenzo was no great builder of walls. But he was a very great donor, and by his gifts and liberality he made great friendships with princes and with the men who were near to them. From such things I believe one can conclude that, all things considered, Cosimo was the more excellent man; and yet through ability and fortune both were so great that perhaps, from the decline of Rome to the present, Italy has never had private citizens like them.

When the news of Lorenzo's death was heard in Florence, for he died in Careggi in his villa, immediately a great multitude of citizens thronged there to visit Piero, his son, to whom, as the eldest, the state pertained by succession. And later his obsequies were celebrated in Florence without pomp and luxury, but with a coming together of all the citizens of the city, all with some sign of mourning, thus showing that there had died a father of the people and a protector of the city. As in his lifetime the city had been happy with everything under his control, so after his death it fell into such calamity and misfortune that both his reputation and the desire for him increased beyond measure.

From *Storie fiorentine*, ed. R. Palmarocchi (Bari: Laterza e figli, 1931); trans. J.B.R.

The Balance of Power in Italy

FRANCESCO GUICCIARDINI

1536

I HAVE DETERMINED to relate the things which happened in Italy within our memory from the time when the French armies, called in by our own princes, began to disturb it by their great invasion. This subject, in its variety and grandeur, is most memorable and full of the most atrocious events, because for so many years Italy suffered all those calamities with which wretched mortals are wont to be tormented, sometimes through the just wrath of God, sometimes from the impiety and wickedness of other men. From the knowledge of these incidents, so various and grievous, everyone will be able to draw salutary precepts both for his own and for the public good. It will become clearly apparent from innumerable examples to what great instability human affairs are subject, not unlike a sea stirred by the winds. And it will be seen how destructive, almost always to themselves but always to the people, are the poorly considered counsels of rulers when, bearing only in mind either vain errors or current greed, they do not remember the frequent changes of fortune, and, turning to the harm of others the power granted them for the common welfare, make themselves the authors of new commotions either from insufficient prudence or excessive ambition.

But the calamities of Italy (in order that I may note what was then its condition and likewise the causes from which so many evils sprang) inspired so much greater grief and fear in the minds of men because things in general were at that time joyous and happy. It is clear that from the time when the Roman Empire, weakened chiefly by the change in its ancient customs, began to decline—already more than a thousand years ago—from that greatness to which it had risen by marvellous ability and fortune, Italy had never known such great prosperity nor experienced a state of affairs so desirable as that in which she rested securely in the year of our Christian salvation, 1490, and the years just before and after. In a condition of the greatest peace and tranquility, cultivated no less in the more mountainous and arid places than in the plains and more fertile regions, not subjected to any rule except that of her own, she not only abounded in inhabitants, merchandise, and riches, but was highly renowned for the magnificence of many princes, for the splendour of many most noble and beautiful cities, for the seat and majesty of religion. She also flourished in men most distinguished in the administration of public affairs, and of noble talents in all branches of learning and in every art and skill. Since she did not lack military glory, in accordance with the custom of the age, and was adorned by such great gifts, she deservedly bore a most splendid name and fame among all the nations.

In this state of felicity, achieved by means of various opportunities, she was preserved by many factors. But among others not a little credit was attributed, by general consent, to the industry and ability of Lorenzo de' Medici, a citizen so far above private rank in the city of Florence that by his counsels there were governed the affairs of that republic, which was powerful more by the advantage of its location, the capacities of its men, and the readiness of its money than by the extent of its dominion. And having recently become related by marriage to Pope Innocent VIII and influenced the pope to trust not a little in his advice, Lorenzo's name was great throughout all Italy and his authority accepted in the deliberations on common affairs. Knowing that it would be very dangerous to the Florentine republic and to himself if anyone of the greater potentates should extend farther his own power, he strove with great effort to bring it about that the affairs of Italy were maintained as if in a balance, so that they did not incline more to one side than to another. This could not be done without preserving the peace and without being diligently on the alert against every mishap, even the slightest.

There concurred in the same desire for the common tranquility Ferrante of Aragon, King of Naples, a prince certainly most prudent and of the highest esteem, despite the fact that many times in the past he had revealed ideas which were ambitious and foreign to the counsels of peace, and at this time was much urged on by Alfonso, Duke of Calabria, his eldest son. The latter took it ill that Giovanni Galeazzo Sforza, duke of Milan, his son-in-law, more than twenty years old, although very deficient in intellect, held only the ducal name, being humbled and held down by Ludovico Sforza, his uncle. More than ten years before, Ludovico, as a result of the imprudent and dissolute habits of the mother, Lady Bona, had assumed tutelage over his nephew, and thanks to this opportunity had little by little brought under his own power the fortresses, the armed forces, the treasury, and all the foundations of the state. Now he continued in the government not as guardian or regent but, except for the title of Duke of Milan, with all the outward show and actions of a prince.

Ferrante, nevertheless, having more in mind present

advantage than former ambition or indignation, however just, about the youth, desired that Italy should not be changed. Perhaps he feared that Italian discord would afford an opportunity to the French to attack the realm of Naples, having experienced a few years before, in the gravest peril, the hatred directed against himself by his barons and his people, and knowing the affection which many of his subjects felt for the name of the French dynasty from the memory of past events. Or perhaps he recognized that union with the others was necessary, and especially with the states of Milan and Florence, in order to counteract the power of the Venetians, then formidable to the whole of Italy.

Nor could any other counsel appeal to Ludovico Sforza, although he was restless and ambitious in spirit, since the danger from the Venetian Senate threatened no less those who ruled Milan than the others, and because it was easier for him to preserve his usurped authority in the tranquility of peace than in the troubles of war. And although the intentions of Ferrante and Alfonso of Aragon were always suspect to him, nevertheless, recognizing the desire of Lorenzo de' Medici for peace and likewise the fear which Lorenzo also had of their greatness, he was persuaded that, because of the difference in spirit and the ancient hatred between Ferrante and the Venetians, it was vain to fear that any alliance would be established between them. And so he considered it fairly certain that the Aragonese would not be accompanied by others in attempting against him what they were not competent to achieve alone.

Since, then, there was present in Ferrante, Ludovico, and Lorenzo, partly for the same, partly for different reasons, the same inclination to peace, there was easily maintained an alliance, contracted in the name of Ferrante, King of Naples, Giovanni Galeazzo, Duke of

Milan, and the Florentine republic, for the defence of their states. This relationship, begun many years before and interrupted thereafter by various accidents, had been renewed in the year 1480 for twenty-five years, with the adherence of almost all the minor powers of Italy, having as its chief end to prevent the Venetians from becoming more powerful. The latter, greater without doubt than any one of the allies but lesser than all of them together, followed their own counsels, apart from the common counsels, and, awaiting the opportunity to derive advantage from the divisions and troubles of the others, stood by attentive and ready to avail themselves of any chance that might open the way to their dominion over the whole of Italy. This aspiration had been very clearly recognized at various times, especially when, seizing the occasion of the death of Filippo Maria Visconti, Duke of Milan, they had tried to make themselves lords of that state under pretence of defending the liberty of the Milanese; and more recently, when in open warfare they strove to occupy the duchy of Ferrara.

This alliance easily held in check the cupidity of the Venetian Senate, but it did not unite the allies in sincere and faithful friendship, inasmuch as, full of competition and jealousy among themselves, they did not cease to watch carefully one another's movements, mutually undermining all the plans by which any one of them might grow in power or reputation. This, however, did not make the peace less stable; on the contrary, it aroused in all of them the greater readiness to try to extinguish carefully all the sparks which might prove to be the origin of a new fire.

Such was the state of affairs, such were the foundations of the tranquility of Italy, disposed and balanced in such a way that not only was there no fear of present change, but no one could easily guess from what counsels or through what chances or by what arms such a great quiet could possibly be disturbed. Then, in the month of April 1492, there came about unexpectedly the death of Lorenzo de' Medici, a death bitter to him on account of his age, because he died before finishing his forty-fourth year; bitter, too, for the fatherland [Florence], which, through his renown and wisdom, and through his genius skilled in all worthy and excellent things, flourished marvellously in riches and in all those goods and ornaments with which a long peace is wont to be accompanied in human affairs. But it was a death most unfortunate for the rest of Italy as well, both on account of the other activities which he carried on continually for the common security, and because he was the mediator and almost like a brake in the disagreements and suspicions which for various reasons often sprang up between Ferrante and Ludovico Sforza, princes of ambition and almost equal in power.

From *Storia d'Italia*, ed. C. Panigada (Bari: Laterza e figli, 1929); trans. J.B.R.

Henry VII, A New Monarch

FRANCIS BACON

1622

THIS KING (to speak of him in terms equal to his deserving) was one of the best sort of wonders; a wonder for wise men. He had parts (both in his virtues and his fortune) not so fit for a commonplace as for observation. Certainly he was religious, both in his affection and observance. But as he could see clear (for those times) through superstition; so he would be blinded now and then by human policy. He advanced churchmen. He was tender in the privilege of sanctuaries, though they wrought him much mischief. He built and endowed many religious foundations, besides his memorable hospital of the Savoy: and yet was he a great almsgiver in secret; which showed that his works in public were dedicated rather to God's glory than his own. He professed always to love and seek peace; and it was his usual preface in his treaties, that when Christ came into the world peace was sung, and when he went out of the world peace was bequeathed. And this virtue could not proceed out of fear or softness, for he was valiant and active; and therefore no doubt it was truly Christian and moral. Yet he knew the way to peace was not to seem to be desirous to avoid wars. Therefore would he make offers and fames of wars, till he had mended the conditions of peace. It was also much, that one that was so great a lover of peace should be so happy in war. For his arms, either in foreign or civil wars, were never infortunate; neither did he know what a disaster meant. The war of his coming in, and the rebellions of the Earl of Lincoln and the Lord Audley, were ended by victory. The wars of France and Scotland by peaces sought at his hands. That of Brittaine by accident of the duke's death. The insurrection of the Lord Lovell, and that of Perkin at Exeter and in Kent, by flight of the rebels before they came to blows. So that his fortune of arms was still inviolate. The rather sure, for that in the quenching of the commotions of his subjects he ever went in person: sometimes reserving himself to back and second his lieutenants, but ever in action. And yet that was not merely forwardness, but partly distrust of others.

He did much maintain and countenance his laws; which (nevertheless) was no impediment to him to work his will. For it was so handled that neither prerogative nor profit went to diminution. And yet as he would sometimes strain up his laws to his prerogative, so would he also let down his prerogative to his Parliament. For mint and wars and martial discipline (things of absolute power) he would nevertheless bring to Parliament. Justice was well administered in his time, save where the king was party; save also that the counsel table intermeddled too much with *meum* and *tuum*. For it was a very court of justice during his time; especially in the beginning. But in that part both of justice and policy which is the durable part, and cut as it were in brass or marble, which is the making of good laws, he did excel. And with his justice he was also a merciful prince: as in whose time there were but three of the nobility that suffered—the Earl of Warwick; the Lord Chamberlain; and the Lord Audley: though the first two were instead of numbers in the dislike and obloquy of the people. But there were never so great rebellions expiated with so little blood drawn by the hand of justice as the two rebellions of Blackheath and Exeter. As for the severity used upon those which were taken in Kent, it was but upon a scum of people. His pardons went ever both before and after his sword. But then he had withal a strange kind of interchanging of large and inexpected pardons with severe executions: which (his wisdom considered) could not be imputed to any inconstancy or inequality; but either to some reason which we do not now know, or to a principle he had set unto himself, that he would vary, and try both ways in turn. But the less blood he drew the more he took of treasure: and as some construed it, he was the more sparing in the one that he might be the more pressing in the other; for both would have been intolerable. Of nature assuredly he coveted to accumulate treasure; and was a little poor in admiring riches. The people (into whom there is infused for the preservation of monarchies a natural desire to discharge their princes, though it be with the unjust charge of their councillors and ministers) did impute this unto Cardinal Morton and Sir Reignold Bray; who as it after appeared (as councillors of ancient authority with him) did so second his humours, as nevertheless they did temper them. Whereas Empson and Dudley that followed, being persons that had no reputation with him otherwise than by the servile following of his bent, did not give way only (as the first did) but shape him way to those extremities, for which himself was touched with remorse at his death; and which his successor renounced, and sought to purge. This excess of his had at that time many glosses and interpretations. Some thought the continual rebellions wherewith he had been vexed had made him grow to hate his people: Some thought it was done to pull down their stomachs and to keep them low: Some, for that he would leave his son a golden fleece: Some suspected he had some high design upon foreign parts. But those perhaps shall come nearest the truth that fetch not their reasons so far off; but rather impute it to nature, age, peace, and a mind fixed upon no other ambition or pursuit: whereunto I should add, that having every day occasion to take notice of the necessities and shifts for money of other great princes abroad, it did the better by comparison set off to him the felicity of full coffers. As to his expending of treasure, he never spared charge which his affairs required: and in his buildings was magnificent; but his rewards were very limited. So that his liberality was rather upon his own state and memory than upon the deserts of others. He was of an high mind, and loved his own will and his own way; as one that revered himself, and would reign indeed. Had he been a private man he would have been termed proud: but in a wise prince, it was but keeping of distance; which indeed he did towards all; not admitting any near or full approach either to his power or to his secrets. For he was governed by none. His queen (notwithstanding she had presented him with divers children; and with a crown also, though he would not acknowledge it) could do nothing with him. His mother he reverenced much, heard little. For any person agreeable to him for society (such as was Hastings to King Edward the Fourth, or Charles Brandon after to King Henry the Eighth), he had none; except we should account for such persons Foxe and Bray and Empson, because they were so much with him. But it was but as the instrument is much with the workman. He had nothing in him of vainglory, but yet kept state and majesty to the height; being sensible that majesty maketh the people bow, but vainglory boweth to them.

To his confederates abroad he was constant and just; but not open. But rather such was his inquiry and such his closeness, as they stood in the light towards him, and he stood in the dark to them; yet without strangeness, but with a semblance of mutual communication of affairs. As for little envies or emulations upon foreign princes (which are frequent with many kings), he had never any, but went substantially to his own business. Certain it is, that though his reputation was great at home, yet it was greater abroad. For foreigners that could not see the passages of affairs, but made their judgments upon the issues of them, noted that he was ever in strife and ever aloft. It grew also from the airs which the princes and states abroad received from their ambassadors and agents here; which were attending the court in great number; whom he did not only content with courtesy, reward, and privateness; but (upon such conferences as passed with them) put them in admiration to find his universal insight into the affairs of the world: which though he did suck chiefly from themselves, yet that which he had gathered from them all seemed admirable to every one. So that they did write ever to their superiors in high terms concerning his wisdom and art of rule. Nay when they were returned, they did commonly maintain intelligence with him; such a dexterity he had to impropriate to himself all foreign instruments.

He was careful and liberal to obtain good intelligence from all parts abroad; wherein he did not only use his interest in the liegers here, and his pensioners which he had both in the court of Rome and the other courts of Christendom, but the industry and vigilancy of his own ambassadors in foreign parts. For which purpose his instructions were ever extreme curious and articulate; and in them more articles touching inquisition than touching negotiation: requiring likewise from his ambassadors an answer, in particular distinct articles, respectively to his questions.

As for his secret spials which he did employ both at home and abroad, by them to discover what practices and conspiracies were against him; surely his case required it; he had such moles perpetually working and casting to undermine him. Neither can it be reprehended; for if spials be lawful against lawful enemies, much more against conspirators and traitors. But indeed to give them credence by oaths or curses, that cannot be well maintained; for those are too holy vestments for a disguise. Yet surely there was this further good in his employing of these flies and familiars; that as the use of them was cause that many conspiracies were revealed, so the fame and suspicion of them kept (no doubt) many conspiracies from being attempted.

Towards his queen he was nothing uxorious; nor scarce indulgent; but companiable and respective, and without jealousy. Towards his children he was full of paternal affection, careful of their education, aspiring to their high advancement, regular to see that they should not want of any due honour and respect; but not greatly willing to cast any popular lustre upon them.

To his council he did refer much, and sat oft in person; knowing it to be the way to assist his power and inform his judgment: in which respect also he was fairly patient of liberty both of advice and of vote, till himself were declared.

He kept a strait hand on his nobility, and chose rather to advance clergymen and lawyers, which were more obsequious to him, but had less interest in the people; which made for his absoluteness, but not for his safety. Insomuch as I am persuaded it was one of the causes of his troublesome reign. For that his nobles, though they were loyal and obedient, yet did not co-operate with him, but let every man go his own way. He was not afraid of an able man, as Lewis [Louis] the Eleventh was. But contrariwise he was served by the ablest men that then were to be found; without which his affairs could not have prospered as they did. For war, Bedford, Oxford, Surrey, Dawbeny, Brooke, Poynings. For other affairs, Morton, Foxe, Bray, the Prior of Lanthony, Warham, Urswick, Hussey, Frowick, and others. Neither did he care how cunning they were that he did employ: for he thought himself to have the master-reach. And as he chose well, so he held them up well. For it is a strange thing, that though he were a dark prince, and infinitely suspicious, and his times full of secret conspiracies and troubles; yet in twenty-four years' reign he never put down or discomposed councillor or near servant, save only Stanley the Lord Chamberlain. As for the disposition of his subjects in general towards him, it stood thus with him; that of the three affections which naturally tie the hearts of the subjects to their sovereign—love, fear, and reverence—he had the last in height; the second in good measure; and so little of the first, as he was beholding to the other two.

He was a prince, sad, serious, and full of thoughts and secret observations; and full of notes of memorials of his own hand, especially touching persons; as whom to employ, whom to reward, whom to inquire of, whom to beware of, what were the dependencies, what were the factions, and the like; keeping (as it were) a journal of his thoughts. There is to this day a merry tale, that his monkey (set on, as it was thought, by one of his chamber) tore his principal notebook all to pieces, when by chance it lay forth: whereat the court which liked not those pensive accounts was almost tickled with sport.

He was indeed full of apprehensions and suspicions. But as he did easily take them, so he did easily check them and master them; whereby they were not dangerous, but troubled himself more than others. It is true, his thoughts were so many, as they could not well always stand together; but that which did good one way, did hurt another. Neither did he at some times weigh them aright in their proportions. Certainly that rumour which did him so much mischief (that the Duke of York should be saved and alive) was (at the first) of his own nourishing, because he would have more reason not to reign in the right of his wife. He was affable, and both well and fair spoken; and would use strange sweetness and blandishments of words, where he desired to effect or persuade any thing that he took to heart. He was rather studious than learned; reading most books that were of any worth in the French tongue. Yet he understood the Latin, as appeareth in that Cardinal Hadrian and others, who could very well have written French, did use to write to him in Latin.

For his pleasures, there is no news of them. And yet by his instructions to Marsin and Stile touching the Queen of Naples, it seemeth he could interrogate well touching beauty. He did by pleasures as great princes do by banquets, come and look a little upon them, and turn way. For never prince was more wholly given to his affairs, nor in them more of himself: insomuch as in triumphs of justs and tourneys and balls and masks (which they then called disguises) he was rather a princely and gentle spectator than seemed much to be delighted.

No doubt, in him as in all men (and most of all in kings) his fortune wrought upon his nature, and his nature upon his fortune. He attained to the crown, not only from a private fortune, which might endow him with moderation; but also from the fortune of an exiled man, which had quickened in him all seeds of observation and industry. And his times being rather prosperous than calm, had raised his confidence by success, but almost marred his nature by troubles. His wisdom, by often evading from perils, was turned rather into a dexterity to deliver himself from dangers when they pressed him, than into a providence to prevent and remove them afar off. And even in nature, the sight of his mind was like some sights of eyes; rather strong at hand than to carry afar off. For his wit increased upon the occasion; and so much the more if the occasion were sharpened by danger. Again, whether it were the shortness of his foresight, or the strength of his will, or the dazzling of his suspicions, or what it was; certain it is that the perpetual troubles of his fortunes (there being no more matter out of which they grew) could not have been without some great defects and main errors in his nature, customs, and proceedings, which he had enough to do to save and help with a thousand little industries and watches. But those do best appear in the story itself. Yet take him with all his defects, if a man should compare him with the kings his concurrents in France and Spain, he shall find him more politic than Lewis the Twelfth of France, and more entire and sincere than Ferdinando of Spain. But if you shall change Lewis the Twelfth for Lewis the Eleventh, who lived a little before, then the consort is more perfect. For that Lewis the Eleventh, Ferdinando, and Henry, may be esteemed for the *tres magi* [Three Wise Men] of kings of those ages. To conclude, if this king did no greater matters, it was long of himself; for what he minded he compassed.

He was a comely personage, a little above just stature, well and straight limbed, but slender. His countenance was reverend, and a little like a churchman: and as it was not strange or dark, so neither was it winning or pleasing, but as the face of one well disposed. But it was to the disadvantage of the painter, for it was best when he spake.

His worth may bear a tale or two, that may put upon him somewhat that may seem divine. When the Lady Margaret his mother had divers great suitors for marriage, she dreamed one night that one in the likeness of a bishop in pontifical habit did tender her Edmund Earl of Richmond (the king's father) for her husband. Neither had she ever any child but the king, though she had three husbands. One day when King Henry the Sixth (whose innocency gave him holiness) was washing his hands at a great feast, and cast his eye upon King Henry, then a young youth, he said, "This is the lad that shall possess quietly that that we now strive for." But that that was truly divine in him, was that he had the fortune of a true Christian as well as of a great king, in living exercised and dying repentant. So as he had an happy warfare in both conflicts, both of sin and the cross.

He was born at Pembroke Castle, and lieth buried at Westminster, in one of the stateliest and daintiest monuments of Europe, both for the chapel and for the sepulchre. So that he dwelleth more richly dead, in the monument of his tomb, than he did alive in Richmond or any of his palaces. I could wish he did the like in this monument of his fame.

From *History of The Reign of King Henry VII*, in *The Works of Francis Bacon*, ed. James Spedding (London: Longmans & Co., 1890).

Charles V and Philip His Son

MARINO CAVALLI

1551

THE COURT of the emperor follows the usage of the court of Burgundy, as does that of his son, which is exactly alike and almost equal in size to that of the father, so that in speaking of one, your Highness will gain knowledge of both. His Majesty has from thirty to forty pages, sons of counts and lords who are his vas-

sals, and also a few of other rank, for the support of
whom his Majesty pays every day one-sixth of a crown
apiece to the one in charge, and moreover clothes
them every year, not very richly but abundantly. His
Majesty maintains for them masters who teach them
to dance, fence, ride, perform feats of horsemanship,
and who give them a little learning. These pages, if
they continue in service fifteen or twenty years, are
promoted to the rank of gentlemen with a third of a
crown a day for allowance, and there may be twenty
to thirty of these gentlemen. Then both these and others
from outside are made gentlemen of the household,
who receive two-thirds of a crown a day; they are
about three hundred in number, obliged to serve with
arms and horses on every occasion when it is appropriate to their rank. Among these, according to their merit,
are chosen those who are called "gentlemen of the
mouth"; there are about fifty of them with an allowance
of one crown a day each. Besides service with arms
and horses like the others, they serve at the table of the
emperor as cup-bearers, carvers, stewards, butlers, and
in carrying the dishes from the kitchen.

Then his Majesty has thirty-six gentlemen of his
chamber, to whom not more than a crown a day is
given as allowance. These for the most part are princes
or related to princes. They perform no service; the
things which are needed for the chamber are all performed by six or eight lower servants of the chamber.
At the head of all these is the grand chamberlain, a
place which is at present vacant, but there is an acting
official called "the steward of the body," who sleeps in
the chamber of the emperor. He is a knight of the
Order of the Fleece and has a thousand crowns a
month to expend, counting all the perquisites which he
draws from the emperor; and with this amount he is

responsible for maintaining a regular table for the gentlemen of the emperor's chamber. With about as much, at the expense of his Majesty, however, he maintains the table of the "gentlemen of the mouth" and of some others of the household. And because the said majordomos do not have to incur any expenses except for themselves, they receive only about a thousand crowns of ordinary income.

Above all these majordomos stands the Duke of Alva, who is the greater majordomo and captain general of his Majesty, and master of the whole court. He receives an ordinary income of twelve thousand crowns and in addition he draws eight thousand with the obligation of maintaining a table for the soldiers and other gentlemen of the most honourable court, and he enters into all the secret councils with the highest authority. He has beneath him the masters of the lodgings with their marshal and wardens, who are the judges of the court in civil and criminal cases, with their bailiffs and sergeants.

Then there are at the court one hundred German halberdiers on foot, one hundred Spaniards on foot, and one hundred Burgundian archers on horseback, for the Imperial bodyguard. These are under various captains of their own nationalities, with a stipend of three crowns monthly for the foot soldiers and ten for the horsemen. There is also the stable of his Majesty which does not exceed seventy or eighty horses and sixty mules, and this has its own ministers and ordinary officials, such as bailiffs, marshals, riding masters, and others. Then there are armourers, saddlers, buglers, heralds, custodians of tents, and other equipment of war, who are all under the direction of the great shield-bearer who is a knight of the Order of the Fleece and has also a thousand crowns a month to spend regularly.

He is obliged to arm the emperor with his own hands and to lace his boots for him whenever it is necessary.

His Majesty maintains ordinarily forty chaplains, each at two crowns a month, and they are the second-born of the leading personages of his states. When they have served six, eight, ten, or more years they are rewarded with pensions, abbeys, and bishoprics as it suits his Majesty. These are obliged to go to the chapel in their surplices and to sing vespers like private priests. There is also the almoner, who besides his office of dispensing alms (about a thousand crowns a year) serves also as master of ceremonies in the chapel and always stands at the canopy of his Majesty, telling him when he should rise, and when kneel, and when to go to the offertory, pointing out to him on certain books and missals the prayer, and all that is said in the Mass.

There are singers, perhaps as many as forty, the most accomplished and excellent choir in Christendom, chosen from all the Low Countries, which are today the fountainhead of music. There are also inferior officials attached to the choir, in charge of the song books, the canopy of his Majesty and other ornaments of the chapel; everything is well ordered and regulated. There are two preachers, one French and one Spanish, and all these are under the confessor, who is ordinarily a Dominican friar of the observance, and receives two hundred crowns a month for his expenses, and some other extraordinary donations for pious expenses. This confessor enters into all councils where matters pertaining to conscience are treated, and because of this he is admitted whenever war and justice are discussed, and especially when nominations for benefices are reported and considered. This confessor almost always ends up as bishop and sometimes as cardinal, and deservedly, because I assure your Highness that he bears a very heavy responsibility in discussing, and almost in determining, matters concerning heretics, the new Christians in Spain, the Moors, usury, war against Christians and infidels, benefices, councils, and almost everything the emperor does, because everything concerns conscience. And in this it is necessary that he should not fail to express his opinion soundly and reasonably, and take care to express it so modestly that the truth will be received without reflection on his modesty; otherwise he may accomplish little and greatly lessen his authority.

The affairs which pertain to business are divided in this way. His Majesty has three chancelleries which always follow the court, with a secretary in chief for each and many lesser officials and scribes. The first is that of the Empire, through which pass all the documents and affairs of Germany and Italy that are dependent upon it; the second is the Spanish, which settles the affairs of Spain and the Indies; the third is that of Naples and Sicily, and this one also has the responsibility of the concessions of favours that are commonly made. All these affairs are settled after infinite delay and length of time.

Then there is another separate set of treasurers or exchangers who are trained in accounts, and with the advice of some of these his Majesty borrows money on the exchange and at interest, and thus makes provision for whatever he needs in time of war and peace. And it is remarkable that although in the past wars they have borrowed at from ten up to twenty-five and thirty per cent yearly, the emperor has never wished to fail in his word to the merchants. The result is that if he has indeed suffered some inconvenience, he has, nevertheless, so well preserved his credit that in any great war which might occur the merchants would never fail him. Such a thing is of the greatest importance to a prince,

in my opinion, because in any case of need he can say
that he has in reserve as much money as he wants.

For the government of his states his Majesty maintains a council made up of various experienced regents,
one for Sicily, one for Naples, one for Milan, one for
Burgundy, one for the Low Countries, one for Aragon,
and one for Castile, with two or three other experts,
who all together, in matters of highest importance, consult and pass judgment on every concern of the emperor
which pertains to the states. Then separately each one
of them informs himself about his own province and
consults the others, seeking their cooperation. The chief
of them all is my Lord of Arras, and they have an
income from his Majesty of one thousand to fifteen
hundred crowns a year.

In affairs of state and in every other detail the emperor makes use solely of the advice of the Lord of
Granvelle. It is true that for the sake of form, more than
anything else, the Duke of Alva is admitted; and in
the absence of the Lord Granvelle and for the execution
of business, my Lord of Arras enters into every consultation. And because in the deliberations of state or with
other princes matters pertaining to conscience are
treated, the confessor of the emperor enters into every
consultation, as said previously. But the matter is decided entirely between the emperor and the Lord of
Granvelle, between whom there is such great harmony
of procedure that rarely, indeed very rarely, are there
any differences of opinion or conclusions between them.
This is because his Majesty, through the experience of
many years, has found this lord most zealous not only
in the affairs of state but in anything else that he may
have to do, such as going, doing, staying, coming, permitting, and arranging everything. And so every evening Granvelle sends to the emperor on a sheet of

paper his opinion concerning the affairs of the following day, which his Majesty has to take up, his Majesty having previously without deciding anything, sent every bit of information and every detail of the negotiations with the ambassadors and others to his lordship. The result is that we ambassadors have noticed, on being referred to Lord Granvelle, that his Excellency has learned every detail and almost every word which has previously passed between us and the emperor.

This lord receives twelve thousand crowns a year as salary; he has a stipend from the Order of Calatrava which is worth four thousand crowns, and often receives extraordinary gifts which may amount to another four thousand crowns or more a year. He does not have the title of Grand Councillor, but of Keeper of the Great Seal, because since the death of Cardinal Gattinara his Majesty has not wished to give that title to anyone else.

My Lord of Arras, his son, has an income from the Church of four thousand crowns, and from other sources about twelve thousand crowns a year, besides some extraordinary donations which he, too, obtains from the emperor, so that, without anything else, these two have more than fifty thousand crowns a year. They have so enriched their house in a few years that at present their capital reaches millions.

The emperor is now fifty-one years of age, in ill health because of the gout, which distresses him terribly all winter and sometimes at other seasons; the doctors say that since it has begun to go up into his head it is so dangerous that it may carry him off at any time. He suffers often from asthma, and it is even said that he shows slight symptoms of the French disease [syphilis], so that if it were not for drugs and special diets, and the water of the wood [guaiacum], which he takes with so many medicines, he would be dead at this time, and everyone foretells a brief life for him.

But when his Majesty was in sound health he was most accomplished in all bodily exercises and a most excellent horseman. He jousted well in the lists and in the open field, he fought at the bar, he rode in the ring, he killed bulls, and, in short, did everything that one can do on horseback, with a jennet and bridle. He has as great a knowledge of horses, of artillery, of quartering armies, of storming cities, and of every detail pertaining to war as any man alive today, and not only on land but also in matters of the sea. He uses great care in understanding every detail of his affairs, nor is a crown spent in his household which he does not know about or see a receipt for. He does not dress ostentatiously, nor has he ever done so, but he is wont to wear now a doublet and cloak, now a short garment reaching to the knees; and he is as well groomed and trim as it is possible to be. . . .

His Majesty is very religious; he hears two Masses every day, vespers and sermons on feast days only; he says many prayers; he goes to confession and Holy Communion four times a year; and in the public eye he lives like a Christian, in private like a knight. He has no defects at all because he abstains from all vices; and in all his actions, even the most trivial, he is so well composed and ordered, so well informed and so judicious that no one could desire more; with certain gestures and certain words so prudent that they deserve to be admired by everyone. He always speaks kindly, never grows angry or threatens, but always with justice in his mouth, with hope in God, and founding his policies on legal right; so that it is said that he has, up to this time, never uttered a word worthy of blame nor one which could have harmed his own interests. He never determines upon any reply by himself but wishes first the advice of the Lord of Granvelle. In negotiating he uses words very ambiguously when it is a matter of importance, so that if the ambassadors are not very wary, his Majesty and councillors can say with a certain dubiety of words, "We understand the matter in this way and this other way." . . .

He is severe concerning points of honour and concerning every detail contained in the treaties of peace and alliances which he has made with others. He forgives or ignores for the time being wrongs to himself or his people when it is worth his while for some greater gain. He is fixed in his opinions, but he apparently never does anything by force, and he will let the world go to ruin rather than do something in violence. He keeps very careful account of the princes or private persons who can be useful to him or do him harm, but outwardly, for the sake of discretion, he does not reveal this.

He is not bloodthirsty nor revengeful to the point of seeking the utter ruin of his enemies; he weakens but does not destroy them. He rarely punishes any of those who serve him, often even enduring things which he should not, and he is a sharp defender of his own spokesmen, even in matters done contrary to his order. He is extremely well informed, and secretly, from all sides; he discusses affairs four or five hours continuously at a time, sitting on a chair, and sometimes he writes down the reasons for and against a point in order to see better how it is reasoned. He deliberates slowly and is then resolute. Sometimes he will hold up the courier for two days in order to see in cold blood if the deliberation is coming out well. In summary, his diplomacy is so well conceived, so well reasoned, and altogether so well planned and executed that anyone who approves the beginning can scarcely with honour fail to admit the conclusion which he draws. He knows thoroughly the nature of all the princes with whom he negotiates and spends a great deal of time in informing himself better about them; he is therefore almost never wrong in the predictions he makes.

Of this most excellent republic [Venice] he is as sure, in matters of importance, of her basic policies as he is of his own, because he knows what she is now planning and what she waits for. It is the same with the other princes; and therefore he negotiates with them, using the best and soundest arguments, not generalities and trifles. He always keeps the negotiations alive on all sides, awaiting a favourable moment and the ripeness of time and the opportunity for execution, so that there is coming to pass now what he has dreamed of and has hoped to accomplish for perhaps twenty-five or thirty years. And therefore it cannot be wondered at if affairs have succeeded and are still turning out happily for a prince so prudent and so expert in affairs of state and of war, who gives so much thought thereto. . . .

At times his Majesty goes hunting with eight or perhaps ten horses, and he returns often with a great bag of one or two deer, or it may be wild boar. At other times he will go shooting in the forests, and when big game fails him he takes pleasure in shooting at rooks, doves, and similar things. In this hunting his Majesty does not spend one hundred crowns a year, and he does not consider it shameful to be surpassed in this, or in dressing, or in similar things, by any other prince in the world; for he has turned his thought and attention to matters of importance, in which he has made such great progress that he has surpassed everyone else.

And because in the time I have been at court there

was also present for about a year and a half his most
serene Highness, the Prince of Spain [the future King
Philip II], it seems to me I should also say something
about him, since it is likely that on account of his youth
your Serenity [the Senate of Venice] will have to negotiate for many years with that prince.

His Highness is now in his twenty-fourth year, of
very delicate complexion and medium stature. In both
face and mind he resembles his father. He never eats
fish or anything else that is not of good nourishment. He
is not very strong in body, but since he has been engaged in Flanders in the exercises of those Burgundian
lords he has become a fair horseman. He appears to
be generous but in such a way that one can predict he
will soon grow tired of it. He very rarely goes out in
company but takes pleasure in staying in his chamber
with four or six favourites and talking of private affairs;
and if at times the emperor sends for him, he excuses
himself in order to enjoy his usual quiet. He dresses
sumptuously and ornately with great style.

He takes excessive pleasure in being revered, and he
maintains with everyone, no matter who he may be, a
greater haughtiness than his father, a fact which his
subjects, except for the Spaniards, are not happy about.
And, indeed, they have good reason, being used to his
father, who knows extremely well how to adjust himself by various ways to all kinds of people. It seems as
if nature had made the emperor capable of satisfying
the Flemings and Burgundians by his habits of familiarity and informality, the Italians by his talents and wisdom, the Spaniards by his reputation and severity. His
subjects, who now see the son behaving otherwise, feel
not a little displeasure at this change. In dealing with
matters of importance, since the emperor makes him
spend two or three hours a day in his chamber, partly

in council and partly for private instruction, it is said
that he has made considerable progress and gives promise of going farther. But owing to the greatness of his
father, and the fact that he was born great and has
not yet proved himself in any work, he will never appear in the last analysis as the equal of the emperor;
and this is the misfortune of those who are too fortunate.

One may judge that when this prince succeeds to
the government of his states he will be served wholly
by Spanish ministers, for he is inclined towards that
people more than is fitting in a prince who wishes to
rule over various peoples, and therefore it is believed
that the Lord of Arras and all the others who are not
Spanish will not be called on to deal with any affair
of state; and if in war or government he has to make
use of Italians or Burgundians, he will do it out of sheer
necessity and with the attitude that if he could find
Spaniards of equal valour, or even less, he would gladly
give up the others.

In *Relazioni degli ambasciatori veneti al senato*, ed. Eugenio
Albèri; Series I, Vol. II (Florence, 1840); trans. J.B.R.

The Strength and Weakness of France

MICHELE SURIANO

1561

STATES are like men in that their vigour and prosperity do not last forever; they mature, they grow
old, they succumb. All things in this world, both great
and small, were made by God with this instability and

uncertainty, in order that every man should humble
himself and recognize that his happiness comes from
Him; and that he who governs others should learn
never to trust so much in success that he abandons the
path of prudence which alone can preserve great things
and elevate small ones. Various examples of this vari-
ability of fortune have been seen in every age. Many
ancient kingdoms and many rich republics which once
governed the world have been extinguished so completely that nothing now remains of them but the
memory of history; and many powers which are at
present great were nothing in reputation or in name
only a little while ago.

But no greater and more striking example of this
instability of human greatness can be shown than that
of the kingdom of France, whose greatness and fortune
made it only yesterday the firm hope of its friends and
the greatest terror of its enemies. Now, if I am to tell
the truth, this great edifice rests on such weak shoulders
that it is not only incapable of sustaining others but is
in a state of such great peril that it trembles at the
slightest shock and is shaken throughout. Since it is
my duty to describe the condition of France, and what
I have been able to see and learn in the fourteen continuous months of my embassy, I shall try so far as
possible to paint from life the true picture of the good
and bad fortune of this kingdom, treating especially,
not in the form of history but in simple commentary and
brief discourse, the causes of its greatness and those accidents which have made it recently fall into the perils
in which it finds itself. . . .

To begin with, I say that the kingdom of France, by
universal opinion, was reputed the first kingdom of
Christendom by reason of its dignity and power and the
authority of its kings. As to its dignity, it was inde-

pendent from the very beginning and has never recognized any superior authority except God. . . . Of its power there can be no doubt, because it is the most extensive kingdom and exceeds any other European kingdom in population, arms, and wealth. It includes eleven great provinces, like eleven members of a body, which, joined together and united, lend strength and energy to one another. . . .

The kingdom of France stands as if at the center of Christendom, more conveniently and suitably placed than any other to unite and divide at will the forces of the most powerful princes and the most warlike peoples. It has Italy in front of it, England behind; Spain at its right, Germany at its left; on one side the Swiss, on the other the Flemings. It lies, moreover, between two seas, the Mediterranean and the ocean, and hence both by land and by sea can easily favour or impede any enterprise and plan of any prince or power in the world. As for itself, France is most secure on all sides, thanks to nature and art, for it is defended from Spain and Italy by mountains, from England and more remote kingdoms by the sea, from Flanders and Germany by rivers. And at the most important points along the frontiers, as well as throughout the kingdom, there are strongholds and great supplies of arms and artillery and everything necessary for war, and men skilled in placing and handling and utilizing the equipment of war. . . .

But because the chief foundation of the greatness and power of a state lies in its men, whose courage and industry are worth more in offence and defence than artillery or arms or fortresses, I shall discuss briefly the people of France, their number and condition, the use which the king makes of them, and the qualities for which they are so renowned in the world.

The population of France is very large. It has one

hundred and forty episcopal cities, and an infinite number of other lands, castles, and villages, and every place is as full as it can be. In Paris alone there are believed to be from four hundred to five hundred thousand souls. The condition and quality of the people are threefold, and hence there are three estates of the realm. The first is that of the clergy; the second of the nobility; the third has no special name, but because it is composed of various ranks and professions one can give it the general name of "the estate of the people."

The clergy includes many of the third estate and many foreigners who, because of services to the crown or by special favour of the king, are named to benefices in the kingdom. A considerable part, however, comes from the nobility, because the second- and third-born sons of princes and lords, having little share in the family inheritance, which goes mostly by primogeniture, enter the Church in order to acquire wealth and reputation at the same time.

By nobles are meant those who are free and do not pay any kind of tax to the king; they have only the obligation of personal service in time of war. Among these are the princes and barons. And among the princes, those of the blood, because of their relationship to the crown, are of more importance than the others, although some of them, on account of poverty, cannot live in the splendour suitable to such high rank. Eighty years ago these princes of the blood were numerous, within the houses of Orléans, Angoulême, Anjou, Burgundy, Alençon, and Bourbon, . . . but now the house of Bourbon stands alone; all the others have either been united to the crown or extinguished. Once the last, it has now by good fortune become the first, and is nearest to the succession after my Lord of Orléans and my Lord of Anjou, brothers of the king, and thus it has arrived at a greater position than ever before. The head of this house is at present the King of Navarre [Anthony], who has a son of eight years [the future Henry IV]. After him comes the Prince of Condé, his brother, because the cardinal does not count, being a cleric. . . .

The estate of the people includes men of letters—who are called "men of the robe"—merchants, artisans, plebeians, and peasants. Among the men of the robe, whoever has the rank of judge or councillor or a similar office is considered as noble and privileged and is so treated throughout his life. The merchants, being in these times the money-masters, are favoured and caressed, but they have no distinction of dignity because any pursuit of gain in this kingdom is held to be unworthy of the nobility. Therefore even this rank of men is counted in with the lesser people and the plebeians, and pays taxes like the non-nobles and the peasants, who are more oppressed than any other class, both by the king and by the privileged. The Emperor Maximilian used to say that the King of France was a king of asses because his people endured every kind of burden without ever complaining.

These three estates are used in various ways for the benefit of the kingdom. The third estate of the people always has in its hands four important offices, either by virtue of law or ancient custom, or because it does not seem honourable to the nobles to be burdened with such responsibilities. The first is the office of the great chancellor, who enters into all the councils and holds the great seal; without his presence nothing of importance is considered, or if anything is considered it is not carried out. The second is that of the secretaries of state, each of whom in his own sphere is entrusted with the execution of affairs and the safeguarding of documents and of the most important secrets. The third office is that of the presidents, councillors, judges, advocates, and others who have jurisdiction both in criminal and civil cases throughout the kingdom. The fourth is that of the treasurers, collectors, receivers general, and special receivers, through whose hands passes the whole fiscal administration of the revenues and expenses of the crown. Now since the people have in their hands all these offices, which carry with them reputation and riches, and since two of them always go to men of letters or "of the robe," that of the chancellor and the administration of justice (which is most extensive and controls many posts), every father tries to send one of his sons to the university. That is why there are so many students in France, more than in any other Christian kingdom. In Paris alone there are more than five thousand. And for some time the princes also have been sending their sons to the university, especially the second and third born, not indeed to put them in these offices but to make clerics of them, because now some effort is being made not to give bishoprics to ignorant persons. Would to God this concern had been shown much earlier, for the good of Christianity!

The government of the state is in the hands of the nobles and prelates. The prelates advise on affairs but do not carry them out, whereas the nobles do both. The latter are often content to leave all the honour of deliberation to the prelates, knowing that the execution of affairs will be theirs, and this arrangement suits everyone. The nobles, who are usually not very rich, are ruined when they come to court, where everything is dear, by the great cost of servants, horses, food, and clothing. On the contrary, when they stay in their châteaux and lead a private and simple life, they have all they need without livery, sumptuous garments, expensive horses, banquets, and other things necessary to a courtier. For this reason there has grown up the service of the king "by quarters"; whoever serves is obliged to stay at court only three months in the year. Thus he can spend the rest of the year at home and cut down his expenses so much that he can afford the luxury which he must have in his three months of service.

The prelates, however, do not have to consider this aspect of expense because they have to bear the cost of their households and vestments wherever they are. Although living at court is more expensive, nevertheless their hope of constantly acquiring more wealth and reputation by always staying near the king leads them to disregard this loss. And many of them, although they would like to stay in residence (as they are obliged to do by recent decrees), would not be permitted to stay away from the court for long because of the service expected of them, especially those who have served as ambassadors abroad, such as my Lord of Orléans and others. But this will not be the case in the future, because the council has recently forbidden bishops to serve as ambassadors, and especially to the pope.

The proper function of the nobles, and that which is of greatest value to king and people, is military service. Of this there are two kinds, on land and on sea. Not much can be said about the latter because there have never been enough ships and equipment or sailors and captains to put together a force adequate to make an effective attack on anyone. This is why in the time of Francis I the practice of using Turkish forces in war was first introduced. . . . But the heart of the military in France is the land force, and rather the cavalry than the infantry, because the ease of acquiring Germans and Swiss and the dislike of putting arms in the hands of plebeians and peasants have given the cavalry so much greater a reputation that it is composed entirely of nobles. It is, therefore, made up of men of courage and talent, unlike that of other countries, which is composed of persons of all conditions. This cavalry is of two kinds, partly paid and partly obligatory. The latter is called the *arrière-ban*, that is, companies of nobles obliged to serve the king in person with a certain number of horses according to the quality of their fiefs. And because the nobles are numerous, this troop is great in numbers, but in numbers only, partly because of the greed and negligence of the feudatories, who have only to produce so many horses, good or bad, and partly because the best are enrolled among the ordinary paid companies and are counted among them and not with the *arrière-ban*. And hence when the *arrière-ban* is called it is a sign of the great need of the kingdom but not a sign of great strength. . . .

This is all I have to say about the number and character of the people of France and of the service which the crown derives from the three estates. As long as they were united, each performing its office without envying the others, and contributing its share to the public welfare and aiding the king, one estate by giving counsel, another by giving its wealth, and the last by giving its life, they made this kingdom invincible and formidable to all the world. But since this curse of the new religious sects has begun to sow dissension between the clergy and the nobles, and among the nobles themselves, and between the people and the others, everything has fallen into disorder, to the great damage of all, and of the king in particular, as I shall soon show. . . .

With regard to the authority of him who rules (which was the third point I proposed earlier), I say that this most extensive and powerful kingdom, full of people and abounding in commodities and wealth, depends wholly on the supreme will of the king, who is the natural prince, loved and obeyed by the people, and of absolute authority. The king of France is a prince by natural right because this kind of government is ancient and not new; for more than a thousand years no other kind has ever been known in this kingdom. He does not succeed to the crown by the election of the people and therefore does not have to curry their favour; nor does he succeed by force, and hence he does not have to be cruel and tyrannical. The succession is rather by law of nature, from father to eldest son, or to that one who is most closely related, excepting bastards and women. The first-born succeeds, or, failing that, the nearest blood kin, because the kingdom does not suffer division but always goes to a single person. It is customary in France, not only with regard to the crown but in all the great families, for the eldest to inherit everything; the others receive only enough to enable them to live according to their rank. This practice preserves the greatness and wealth of families and estates, whereas the division of inheritance by head, as in Germany, reduces them to practically nothing. St. Bernard spoke well when he said that of the three estates including all men of active life, princes and lords should always succeed by primogeniture, citizens and those who live on incomes should divide their inheritance by head, and plebeians and peasants should hold everything in common.

In France bastards are not admitted to the succession of their fathers, except sometimes by grace. But it is prohibited by law to take account of bastards of kings, and this has been in force since the end of the line of Charlemagne. . . . Women are excluded by the Salic Law, as they call it, or by an established custom which has the force of law. And therefore the king of France is always a Frenchman and can never be of another nationality. For this reason there never happens here what often happens in other kingdoms where the succession through women causes uncertainty as to who will become king, and where often the king comes from a hated and hostile people. In this way Spain fell under the power of the Flemings, and Naples and Sicily of the Spanish. And so it comes about that there is no kingdom in the world to which some prince does not have the pretext of a claim; and claimants vying against claimants, each one tries to support his claims by arms or by the aid of partisans, with the result that kingdoms are divided against themselves, becoming the victims of one or another usurper. It is this which has introduced so many foreign arms and customs into Italy. But France is free from this calamity because by the exclusion of women there is excluded any claim which a foreigner could assert to this kingdom.

All these factors are the foundation and root of the love and obedience of the French. Accustomed for so long to being governed by a king, they have no desire for any other kind of government. And recognizing that they were born to the role of serving and obeying one king, they willingly serve the one who was born to rule them, who, in order to reach the throne, has used no fraud or force, and who, having no reason to harm his subjects out of suspicion, on the contrary always preserves them for his greater glory and grandeur. This explains the familiarity which prevails between the king and his subjects, all of whom he treats as companions. No one is ever excluded from his presence; even lackeys, people of the lowest sort, dare to penetrate the inner chamber of the king, to see all that is going on and hear what is being discussed. And so anyone who has an important matter to take up must have the patience to find a place where there is not such a crowd and to speak softly in order not to be overheard. This familiarity, although it makes the people insolent and presumptuous, nevertheless makes them more loving, devoted, and faithful towards their prince.

But what best preserves and increases this affection of the people is their own interest and hope of something useful, for the king of France, being able to distribute so many places, offices, and magistracies, so much wealth of the Church, so many appointments, pensions, and emoluments, and so many other privileges and honours, which are infinite in this kingdom, divides everything among his own Frenchmen. And therefore it does not happen in France, as in other kingdoms, and especially in the kingdom of Naples, that the people are discontented and disgruntled because the honours and offices which ought to be distributed among them are all in the hands of foreigners. Although the king of France favours some Italians and other foreigners, they are few in number, and the favour depends on merit acquired in the service of the crown.

For this reason there has never been a time in France when the people rebelled against the king to call another prince to the throne. Insurrections are very rare; as for conspiracies, none are known except the recent one of Amboise. Few Frenchmen go abroad to serve other princes. Everyone loves, even adores, his king; everyone promptly expends his goods, risks his life in the royal service, subordinates convenience to trouble, pleasure to peril, leisure to toil, in order either to make an example of himself or out of hope of reward. As the king is loved, obeyed and served by everyone, he has supreme and absolute authority in the kingdom, because on his will depends every decision of war and peace, the imposition of taxes and tributes, the concession of favours and benefices, of offices and magistracies, throughout the realm. In brief, the king is recognized as true monarch and absolute lord of everything.

And there is no council or magistrate of such authority as to circumscribe his actions, nor any prince or lord in the kingdom of such audacity as to oppose his will, as often happens in other kingdoms. The princes of the blood and the other great nobles are so poor and so lacking in authority, as compared to the king, that even if they tried to turn against him they would not be supported. They are poor, I say, because all the lands and wealth of importance of the greater families of the kingdom have fallen at various times into the hands of the crown, some through the failure of male heirs, as was the case of Provence, Anjou, Berri, Alençon, Guienne, and Britanny; some by the succession of the house to the throne, as in the case of Orléans and Angoulême, and before that, of Valois; some by confiscation, as was the land of Burgundy in the time of King Louis XI and of King Francis I. They have little authority because there is no prince in the realm who has jurisdiction over the people except the king. Although brothers of the king are called "Duke of Orléans" and "Duke of Anjou," they enjoy nothing but the titles and incomes from the duchies; the king rules, and not they.

As for the councillors and magistrates, it is enough to say that the king directs and chooses them at his will; and the council of affairs, which considers matters of state, is made up of few heads, and of those most close and dear to the king, sometimes of one only, as was the Constable in the time of King Henry II and the Cardinal of Lorraine in the time of Francis I. This council is new, and was established by Francis I, who detested a large council and was the first king of

France to arrive at great decisions independently. It is called the "council of affairs" because while the king was rising from bed and going about his toilet, which is properly referred to as "his affairs," he had near him those whom he most trusted; and the place where he took up the most important matters gave to the council the name which it has since preserved although the manner of holding it has changed. Now it has become a regular council to which are always admitted the leading and most trusted personages. And to the private council, where formerly great matters were discussed, which are at present taken over by the council of affairs, are now referred only those things which have to be determined according to the constitution of the kingdom, or which the king turns over to it out of boredom. Thus in the council of affairs the king exercises his absolute power, whereas in the private council he exercises his ordinary power. And so it sometimes happens that the parliaments, which have supreme authority in the administration of justice and laws, especially the Parliament of Paris, modify, interpret, or even veto the decisions of the private council, but no one dares to touch those of the other council.

But if any authority in France can moderate the absolute authority of the king it is the assembly of the three estates, which represents the whole body of the kingdom, like the general parliament in England and Scotland, and the diet in Germany. Formerly it assembled almost every year, and always when there was any matter of importance to consider. This was called holding the estates, a custom which the former kings willingly supported when the world was not yet sunk in ambition and pride, and when it was considered more suitable for a king to govern his people with moderation and equity than to extend his kingdom by force.

But since kings have lost these true virtues and each one has begun to want more than he should have, they have gradually discontinued the practice of holding the estates in order to free themselves little by little from this yoke. In the time of Louis XI anyone who proposed to call the estates was considered a rebel; and the king was wont to say that he had passed beyond the status of page and minor and was no longer in tutelage. Since his time the estates have been called properly only twice, once in 1483 when Charles VIII succeeded to the crown, because, since he was a minor, it was necessary to make arrangements for the government of the realm; the second time last year, in 1560, when they were called by King Francis II on the advice of the Cardinal of Lorraine for reasons which I shall reveal. On the death of this king and the succession of the present king, Charles IX, of tender age, the sessions of the estates were continued. But because the consequence seems to be disorder rather than the order which they once contributed to the kingdom, it is likely that the estates will finally break down completely and the authority of the king will continue steadily to grow greater.

These are the foundations, these the columns, which support the great edifice of the kingdom of France. The great size of the state, the number of its cities and provinces, the strength of its location and frontiers, the number, unity, and obedience of the people and military forces, the supreme authority of the king and the unrestricted government—these are the chief reasons why this crown has reigned so long, has fought so many wars with such great glory, has acquired such reputation and dominion, has preserved its friends, frightened its enemies, and has become known in recent times as the sole refuge of the oppressed. And it would be able to achieve even greater things if there had not befallen those accidents and disorders of which I have to speak; these have weakened the strength on which was founded and established every aspect of the glory and greatness of this realm.

I must now speak of the defects and disorders in the kingdom of France, very great indeed and very grave, because if it is true, as reason and experience teach us, that every change and alteration in states is always perilous, what state was ever in greater peril than one which at the same time, and almost the same moment, experienced a change in its head, its principal members, and its whole body? As for the head of the kingdom of France, on the death of King Francis II, who possessed real authority, Charles IX succeeded, who has only the name of king. As for the members, the government of such a great kingdom has fallen into the hands of women or inexperienced men, and there is no agreement among them. And into the whole body there has been introduced the curse of the new sects which has totally confused the religion of the realm, which is the sole means of holding a people united and obedient to its prince. Since this is the subject which excites most interest, I shall speak first of religion; I shall not, however, discuss opinions and dogmas (this is not the place for such matters) but shall consider only the origins of such a great disturbance, its progress, and the disastrous results that spring from it.

The beginning of every great evil is always slight, and mixed with some appearance of good, which deceives men, just as poison in delicate dishes deceives the palate. Nothing is more true than the saying that one must keep one's eyes open at the beginning, because when the evil is weak one does not consider the danger, and when it is grown strong one can find no remedy. It will not be difficult for me to show how slight was the beginning of this evil, because everyone knows that it was one man alone [Martin Luther], and of very lowly condition, who revived the old heresies and was the source of the new sects of our times. And yet he alone in a few years has infected such a great part of the world that he has not only changed the religion in Germany, where he was born, but in Denmark, Switzerland, Prussia, Poland, and all the northern countries. He has, moreover, ruined England and Scotland, corrupted France and Flanders, thrown Italy and Spain into confusion, and even affected the Indies. There is no part of Christianity which is free from this pestilence. And although from the three branches sprung from this root—Lutherans, Sacramentarians, and Anabaptists—there have now grown more than thirty sects, each one different from the others, all go back to this one man alone. . . .

Although it now seems that God may wish to give some hope of aid to this kingdom, nevertheless things are still in a very bad state, because this disease has too much strength and encounters too little resistance. Those who could, do not wish to repress it, and those who wish to repress it, cannot or know not how. That is why it has made such great progress in a short time and has given birth to worse consequences than have ever been experienced in any other kingdom. I shall speak of these now, not of all because that would be long and tedious, but of the three principal ones.

First, it lessens the fear of God, which should always take precedence over all other considerations, because on that rests the rule of life, the concord of men, the preservation of the state, and all greatness. And how can there be fear of God where there is no observation of divine law, no obedience to magistrates, either ecclesiastical or civil; where everyone dares to conceive God after his own fashion, interpreting Holy Scripture not according to the ancient tradition of the Church and the Holy Fathers, but according to his own understanding, as if one whose vision reaches only a span should presume to measure things a thousand miles away?

The second evil consequence of this change in religion is that it destroys the control and order of the government, because from it springs a change in the usual habits and customs of life, contempt for the laws and authority of magistrates and finally even for the prince. Already in various parts of France judges have been driven out of the land and new ones set up at the will of the seditious. In other places they have not wished to permit the publication of royal edicts, and in others they have begun to disseminate among the crowd the idea that the king holds his authority from the people and that subjects are not obliged to obey the prince when he commands something which is not stated in the Holy Gospels. This is the path that is leading to the reduction of this land to a popular state like Switzerland and the destruction of the monarchy and kingdom.

To these two disorders is added a third, the division of the people, the seditions, and civil wars which always spring from religious confusion. Many can remember the rising of the peasants in Germany against the nobles, in which more than fifty thousand persons were put to the sword. Everyone knows the tumult of the Anabaptists, the wars of the Protestants, and so many other calamities of that land which are more recent. Everyone knows the condition of England and how much blood has been shed on account of religion in that kingdom. In Scotland, finally, the queen has had the greatest difficulty in securing from her subjects the right to live according to the Catholic faith. The insolence of these rebels has become so great that nature is turned upside down; where the head was wont to rule the members, the members now rule the head.

Although such serious effects have not yet been seen in France, one hears every day of murders and wounds and other acts of violence. In every part of the kingdom this sect is found organized and with connections in Flanders, England, Scotland, and other countries. It is known that it spends freely and supports not only its preachers and ministers, but also many princes and other great men who favour it. And so it grows every day in insolence and becomes more difficult to repress. And since the disturbance springs from the lower class, which, being envious and poor, aspires to the wealth and honours of the rich, everyone is in a state of suspicion; trade ceases, contracts are broken, and there is no merchant in Paris or Lyons or anywhere in the kingdom who feels secure in his house. Although not a tenth of the kingdom (according to calculation) is yet infected, everything is so disturbed that one can imagine what would happen if the corruption spread to the rest.

This grave malady, sprung from small beginnings, and strengthened by the negligence or ineptitude of those who have governed the realm, has produced all these evil consequences: contempt for the majesty of God, detriment to the authority of the king, division of the people, and disturbance of the public peace.

After speaking of the religious disorder which has brought general disorder and confusion to the body of the kingdom, I shall speak now of two other misfortunes of less importance that occurred at the same time. One concerns the head, which is the king; the other the chief members, who are those of authority in the government. It seems as if all the evils that cause the destruction of kingdoms have conspired together for the ruin of France.

As to the first, everyone knows that a change of kings always produces some alteration in kingdoms, because it rarely happens that a new king has the same ideas as the old. And in France it has been seen that the son does not follow the path of his father, and has no love for those who served him. Out of this come public confusion and private discontent. As for public affairs, what was done is now undone, what was begun is not finished, what was turned in one direction is continued in another. As for individuals, one is exalted, another brought low; one is rewarded, another persecuted; one loses hope, another gains it; and, in general, whoever hopes pursues his interest, and whoever fears seeks to insure himself. All this breeds sedition and tumult. And when the new king lacks ability and authority, so much greater is the change. What happens to other kings from lack of wisdom has happened to the present king, Charles IX, because of his tender age, and because like an innocent lamb he is subject to the influence of those who control him. If it has always been considered a calamity for a kingdom to have a boy king (as is proved by His words, "Woe to the land whose king is a child"), how much more miserable is a kingdom full of disorders, division, and rivalry, oppressed by debts and poverty, exhausted by a long and expensive war, and where one boy has succeeded another and neither of them was able to learn how to govern from the instruction and example of his father, owing to the brevity of the latter's life! Because when King Francis succeeded to the crown he was scarcely fifteen years, and the present king not yet ten; now he is eleven and a half. It is true that he is of fine and noble intelligence, that he shows in his actions gravity and modesty, in his words sweetness and humanity, in his countenance grace and gaiety, and indeed lacks no kingly quality. One can entertain great hope of his Majesty, if he lives and does not change, and if in the future he does not find all his interests so destroyed and ruined that he is forced to accept the results of the negligence and evil-doing of others. I say "if he lives and if he does not change" because both of these conditions are uncertain. As for living, it is the opinion of many that he has not long to live, both because of his feeble and delicate constitution and because he is not taken care of as regularly as he should be. What increases this suspicion is the fact that the astrologer Nostradamus, who for many years has always predicted accurately the calamities of France (and in this way acquired the confidence of many), has told the queen that she will see all her sons become king. She has already seen two, Francis and Charles, and two remain, Alexander Duke of Orléans, and Hercules Duke of Anjou, one ten and the other seven. If she is to see them as kings, Charles must die soon, and that would mean the total destruction of the kingdom. While it continues so long in the hands of boys (who until their majority are governed by guardians), it delays too long in acquiring a king with supreme authority, who would be feared by his subjects, respected by his neighbours, and esteemed by all, and who by some notable action would restore greatness and glory to the crown. . . .

Let us speak now of the particular defects of those who have the chief responsibility, the queen [Catherine de' Medici] and the King of Navarre [Anthony of Bourbon]. As to the queen, it is enough to say that she is a woman, but, I should add, a foreigner as well, and even more, a Florentine, born in a private family, very unequal to the grandeur of the kingdom of France. On this account she does not have the reputation or authority which she would have, perhaps, if she had been born in the kingdom or of more illustrious blood. It cannot be denied that she is a woman of great worth and intelligence; and if she had greater experience in matters of state, and were a bit more firm, she might well achieve great things. But in the time of King Henry, her husband, she was held down; and although after the succession of King Francis she seemed to have supreme authority, it was only apparently so because the Cardinal of Lorraine did everything by himself. For this reason her Majesty has need of good advisers, but she has no one in whom she can trust; dissension in religion and discord among the great have made everyone suspect to her. . . .

As for the intentions of her Majesty in matters of religion, opinions differ. . . . I can affirm, however, from what I have seen, although I do not know what her Majesty's true sentiments are, that she does not suffer willingly these tumults in the kingdom. If she has not shown herself as zealous in repressing them as one could desire, she has been restrained by fear that the necessity of using force would tear France to pieces. . . . I know that she is trying to hold all her sons safely in the Catholic faith and in Christian ways of life; she speaks earnestly to this effect with many persons. And therefore I believe one should think well of her Majesty rather than otherwise. If her actions do not bear out her desires, the reason is perhaps that she does not have all the authority or experience that are needed. So much for the queen.

The King of Navarre, to speak freely, is a very weak character; although he is a gallant prince, gracious and agreeable, he does not have the experience or judgment essential for the burden of such an important government. As for experience, it is known that he has never had any responsibility of state until now, but has been concerned only with his own convenience and pleasure. As for his judgment, I shall not go into the fact that he wears finger rings and earrings like a woman, although his beard is white and his years many, nor that in great matters he listens to the advice of the many flatterers and worthless men who surround him, nor that he lets himself be ruled by a wife who can do anything with him. But I say that in matters of religion he has shown himself neither firm nor wise, moving now in one direction, now in another, now favouring the Catholics in order to stand in well with the pope, now the Huguenots to secure a following in the kingdom, now the Lutherans to keep the friendship of Germany. And although this inconstancy is not without design, it reveals a weak and irresolute spirit. Sitting on so many stools is never comfortable. . . .

Such then is the present state of France: the king a boy, without experience or authority; the council full of discord; supreme authority in the hands of the queen, a wise woman, although timid and irresolute, and always a woman; the King of Navarre, a noble and gracious prince, but inconstant and little skilled in government; the people in open discord and disunity, full of insolent and seditious elements, who under pretext of religion have disturbed the public peace, corrupted the old customs and ways of life, spoiled discipline, stifled justice, defied the magistrates, and finally undermined the authority of the king and the safety of all. Anyone who wishes to compare the present state of the kingdom with the past, when it was so formidable to the great kings and emperors of the world, will find it so weak and infirm that there is not a single sound member left in it.

From *Commentarii del regno di Francia*, from *Relations des ambassadeurs vénetiens sur les affaires de France au XVI siècle*, ed. M. N. Tommaseo (Paris, 1838); trans. J.B.R.

The Search for Perfection

On Virtù and Fortune

LEON BATTISTA ALBERTI

1434

WHEN I call to mind from ancient histories and from the memory of our elders, and when I see in our own times, both elsewhere and in Italy, that not a few families once supremely happy and glorious are now lost and extinguished, I often wonder and grieve. Could iniquitous and malign fortune have so prevailed against men? Could hers be the responsibility, in her fickleness and temerity, that families so full of the most talented men, abounding in goods cherished and desired by mortals, adorned with honour, reputation, praise, authority, and grace, have been deprived of every felicity, thrown into poverty, solitude, and misery; reduced from many elders to a handful of grandsons, from immeasurable wealth to dire necessity, from brightest splendour of glory submerged in such misfortune and cast down into darkness and stormy adversity?

Alas, how many families are to be seen, fallen and ruined! It would be impossible to name them or tell how many (like the Fabii, Decii, Drusii, Gracchi, Marcelli, and the other noble families of antiquity) there have been, even in our own land, who once maintained liberty for the public good and preserved the dignity and authority of the fatherland, who were temperate in peace and war, and so full of wisdom and strength that they were feared by their enemies and felt themselves loved and respected by their friends. Of all these families, not only the magnificence and wealth but even the men have been reduced and brought low, and not only the men but the very name, as if every memory and reminder had been lost and destroyed. It seems to me not unreasonable, therefore, to wish to know whether fortune ever possesses such power over human affairs or if to her was granted the excessive right to plunge into ruin the greatest and most excellent families by her instability and inconstancy.

When I contemplate this, without prejudice and free from all passion, and when within myself, oh, young Albertis, I consider our family, noting how many adversities it withstood in times past by its courageous spirit, and with what sound reason and wisdom our forefathers knew how to drive off, and with what constancy to sustain, both harsh misfortune and the furious assaults of iniquitous fate, I realize that many persons often blame fortune without just cause. And I perceive many who, fallen on evil days through their own stupidity, blame fortune and complain of being tossed about by those stormy waves into which the fools have actually cast themselves! Just so, many foolishly attribute their own errors to the power of others. But if anyone wishes to investigate carefully what it is that exalts and increases families and also maintains them at a high peak of honour and felicity, he will clearly see that men are themselves the source of their own fortune and misfortune; nor indeed will he ever conclude that the power of gaining praise, wealth, and reputation should be attributed to fortune rather than to ability.

And if one considers republics and passes in mind all past principalities, he will find that in acquiring and increasing, in maintaining and conserving majesty and glory already achieved, in none did fortune ever avail more than good and sound discipline in living. Who can doubt it? Just laws, virtuous princes, prudent and firm counsels, steadfast deeds, love of the fatherland, faith, diligence, courteous and praiseworthy relations among citizens, these will enable states even without fortune to win and seize fame, and with fortune greatly to extend and spread their glory and to commend themselves to posterity and immortality. . . .

I believe the wise man will judge that what is true of principalities is also true of families, and will agree that families have rarely fallen into a state of misery through anything else than their own lack of prudence and diligence. I recognize this happens either because in prosperity they do not know how to control and restrain themselves, or because in adversity they are not wise enough to sustain and support themselves; and hence fortune engulfs and submerges families in those cruel waves into which they actually abandon themselves. And since I do not doubt that good government, watchful and diligent fathers of families, good customs, honourable ways, refinement, ease and courtesy render families most affluent and happy, I have decided to investigate with zeal and diligence what instructions there may be for the good regulation and direction both of fathers and the whole family, useful for achieving the ultimate and supreme felicity and preventing a collapse before iniquitous and strange fortune. What leisure I have been able to steal from my other labours I have spent entirely in searching through the ancient writers to see what precepts they have left that are apt and suitable for the well-being, honour, and growth of families. Finding in them many and most excellent instructions, I consider it my duty to collect them and put them together so that you, finding them in one place thanks to me, will expend less effort in knowing them, and once knowing them, in following them. And I believe that you, when you have with me reviewed the sayings and examples of those good men of antiquity, and noted the fine customs of our ancestors, the Alberti, will be of the same mind, and will decide for yourselves that as ability goes, so goes our fortune. Nor will it please you less, as you read, to see the good old ways and customs of our house, the Alberti, than to approve and accept them, recognizing that the counsels and sayings of our ancestors were all necessary and perfect. You will see from them how a family multiplies, by what arts it becomes fortunate and blessed, in what ways it acquires grace, good will, and friendship, by what disciplines honour, fame, and glory grow and spread, and how the name of the family wins eternal praise and immortality.

From Proemio to *Della famiglia*, in *Opere volgari*, ed. A. Bonucci (Florence, 1844); trans. J.B.R.

The Perfect Country House

LEON BATTISTA ALBERTI

1450

I NOW COME to treat of private edifices. I have already
observed elsewhere that a house is a little city. We
are therefore in the building of it, to have an eye almost
to everything that relates to the building of a city; that
it be healthy, furnished with all manner of necessaries,
not deficient in any of the conveniences that conduce
to the repose, tranquility, or delicacy of life. . . . A
private house is manifestly designed for the use of a
family, to which it ought to be a useful and convenient
abode. It will not be so convenient as it ought, if it has
not everything within itself that the family has occasion
for. There is a great number of persons and things in
a family, which you cannot distribute as you would in
a city so well as you can in the country. In building a
house in town, your neighbour's wall, a common gutter,
a public square or street, and the like, shall all hinder
you from contriving it just to your own mind; which
is not so in the country, where you have as much freedom as you have obstruction in town. For this, and
other reasons, therefore, I shall distinguish the matter
thus: that the habitation for a private person must be
different in town from what it is in the country. In
both there must again be a difference between those
which are for the meaner sort of citizens and those which
are for the rich. The meaner sort build only for necessity; but the rich for pleasure and delight. I shall set

down such rules as the modesty of the wisest men may approve of in all sorts of buildings, and for that purpose shall begin with those which are most easy. Habitations in the country are the freest from all obstructions, and therefore people are more inclined to bestow their expense in the country than in town. We shall therefore first take a review of some observations which we have already made, and which are very material with relation to the chief uses of a country house.

They are as follows: we should carefully avoid a bad air and an ill soil. We should build in the middle of an open champian, under the shelter of some hill, where there is plenty of water, and pleasant prospects, and in the healthiest part of a healthy country. . . . A country house ought to stand in such a place as may lie most convenient for the owner's house in town. Xenophon would have a man go to his country house on foot, for the sake of exercise, and return on horseback. It ought not therefore to lie far from the city, and the way to it should be good and clear, so as he may go to it either in summer or winter, either in a coach, or on foot, and if possible by water. It will be also very convenient to have your way to it lie through a gate of the city that is not far from your town house, but as near as it may be, that you may go backwards and forwards from town to country, and from country to town, with your wife and family, as often as you please, without being too much observed by the people, or being obliged in the least to consult your dress. It is not amiss to have a villa so placed, that when you go to it in the morning the rays of the rising sun may not be troublesome to your eyes, nor those of the setting sun in the evening when you return to the city. Neither should a country house stand in a remote, desert, mean corner, distant from a reasonable neighbourhood; but in a situation where you may have people to converse with, drawn to the same place by the fruitfulness of the soil, the pleasantness of the air, the plentifulness of the country, the sweetness of the fields, and the security of the neighbourhood. Nor should a villa be seated in a place of too much resort, near adjoining either to the city, or any great road, or to a port where great numbers of vessels and boats are continually putting in; but in such a situation, as though none of those pleasures may be wanting, yet your family may not be eternally molested with the visits of strangers and passengers. . . .

Some are of opinion that a gentleman's country house should have quite different conveniences for summer and for winter; and the rules they give for this purpose are these: the bedchambers for the winter should look towards the point at which the sun rises in winter, and the parlour, towards the equinoctial sun-setting; whereas the bedchambers for summer should look to the south, the parlours, to the winter sun-rising, and the portico or place for walking in, to the south. But, in my opinion, all these conveniences ought to be varied according to the difference of the country and climate, so as to temper heat by cold and dry by moist. I do not think it necessary for the gentleman's house to stand in the most fruitful part of his whole estate, but rather in the most honourable, where he can uncontrolled enjoy all the pleasures and conveniences of air, sun, and fine prospects, go down easily at any time into his estate, receive strangers handsomely and spaciously, be seen by passengers for a good way round, and have a view of some city, towns, the sea, an open plain, and the tops of some known hills and mountains. Let him have the delights of gardens, and the diversions of fishing and hunting close under his eye.

We have in another place observed, that of the different members of a house, some belong to the whole family in general, others to a certain number of persons in it, and others again only to one or more persons separately. In our country house, with regard to those members which belong to the whole family in general, let us imitate the prince's palace. Before the door let there be a large open space, for the exercises either of chariot or horse racing, much longer than a youth can either draw a bow or throw a dart. Within the house, with regard to those conveniences necessary for a number of persons in the family, let there not be wanting open places for walking, swimming, and other diversions, courtyards, grass plots, and porticoes, where the old men may chat together in the kindly warmth of the sun in winter, and where the family may divert themselves and enjoy the shade in summer.

It is manifest some parts of the house are for the family themselves, and others for the things necessary and useful to the family. The family consists of the following persons: the husband, the wife, their children and relations, and all the different sorts of servants attendant upon these; besides which, guests too are to be reckoned as part of the family. The things useful to the family are provisions and all manner of necessaries, such as cloths, arms, books, and horses also. The principal member of the whole building is that which (whatever names others may give it) I shall call the courtyard with its portico; next to this is the parlour, within this the bedchambers, and lastly, the private rooms for the particular uses of each person in the family. The other members of the house are sufficiently known by their uses. The courtyard therefore is the principal member, to which all the other smaller members must correspond, as being in a manner a public

marketplace to the whole house, which from the courtyard derives all the advantages of communication and
light. For this reason everyone desires to have his courtyard as spacious, large, open, handsome, and convenient as possible. . . . Exactly answering the middle of your courtyard, place your entrance, with a
handsome vestibule, neither narrow, difficult, nor obscure. Let the first room that offers itself be a chapel
dedicated to God, with its altar, where strangers and
guests may offer their devotions, beginning their
friendship by religion; and where the father of the
family may put up his prayers for the peace of his
house and the welfare of his relations. Here let him
embrace those who come to visit him, and if any
cause be referred to him by his friends, or he has any
other serious business of that nature to transact, let
him do it in this place. Nothing is handsomer in the
middle of the portico than windows of glass, through
which you may receive the pleasure either of sun or
air, according to the season. . . .

From the courtyard we proceed to the parlours,
which must be contrived for different seasons, some
to be used in summer, others in winter; and others as
we may say in the middle seasons. Parlours for summer
require water and the verdure of gardens; those for
winter must be warm and have good fireplaces. Both
should be large, pleasant, and delicate. There are many
arguments to convince us that chimneys were in use
among the ancients; but not such as ours are now. . . .
In Germany, Colchos, and other places, where fire is
absolutely necessary against the extreme cold, they
make use of stoves; of which we shall speak elsewhere.
Let us return to the chimney, which may be best
made serviceable in the following manner. It must be
as direct as possible, capacious, not too far from the

light, it must not draw the wind too much, but enough, however, to carry up the smoke, which else would not go up the tunnel. For these reasons do not make it just in a corner, nor too far within the wall, nor let it take up the best part of the room where your chief guests ought to sit. Do not let it be incommoded by the air either of doors or windows, nor should it project too far out into the room. . . .

To the parlours we must accommodate the kitchen, and the pantry for setting by what is left after meals, together with all manner of vessels and linen. The kitchen ought to be neither just under the noses of the guests, nor at too great a distance; but so that the victuals may be brought in neither too hot nor too cold, and that the noise of the scullions, with the clatter of their pans, dishes, and other utensils, may not be troublesome. The passage through which the victuals are to be carried should be handsome and convenient, not open to the weather, nor dishonoured by any filth that may offend the stomachs of the guests.

From the parlour the next step is to the bedchamber; and for a man of figure and elegance, there should be different ones of these latter, as well as of the former, for summer and winter. This puts me in mind of Lucullus's saying, that it is not fit a great man should be worse housed than a swallow or crane. However, I shall only set down such rules, with relation to these apartments, as are compatible with the greatest modesty and moderation. I remember to have read in Aemilius Probus the historian, that among the Greeks it was never usual for the wife to appear at table, if anybody was there besides relations; and that the apartments for the women were parts of the house where no men ever set foot except the nearest kindred. And indeed I must own I think the apartments for the ladies ought to be sacred, like places dedicated to religion and chastity. I am besides for having the rooms particularly designed for virgins and young ladies, fitted up in the neatest and most delicate manner, that their tender minds may pass their time in them with less regret and be as little weary of themselves as possible. The mistress of the family should have an apartment in which she may easily hear everything that is done in the house. However, in these particulars, the customs of every country are always to be principally observed.

The husband and wife should each have a separate chamber, not only that the wife, either when she lies in, or in case of any other indisposition, may not be troublesome to her husband; but also that in summertime either of them may lie alone whenever they see fit. Each of these chambers should have its separate door, besides which there should be a common passage between them both, that one may go to the other without being observed by anybody. The wife's chamber should go into the wardrobe; the husband's into the library. Their ancient mother, who requires tranquility and repose, should have a warm chamber, well secured against the cold, and out of the way of all noises either from within or without. Be sure particularly to let it have a good fireplace, and all other conveniences necessary for an infirm person, to comfort and cheer both the body and mind. Out of this chamber let there be a passage to the place where you keep your treasure. Here place the boys; and by the wardrobe the girls, and near them the lodgings for the nurses.

Strangers and guests should be lodged in chambers near the vestibule or fore-gate, that they may have full freedom both in their own actions and in receiving visits from their friends, without disturbing the rest of the family. The sons of sixteen or seventeen years old should have apartments opposite to the guests, or at least not far from them, that they may have an opportunity to converse and grow familiar with them. The strangers too should have some place to themselves, where they may lock up anything private or valuable, and take it out again whenever they think fit. Next to the lodgings of the young gentlemen should be the place where the arms are kept. Stewards, officers, and servants should be so lodged asunder from the gentlemen, that each may have a convenient place, suitable to his respective business. The maidservants and valets should always be within easy call, to be ready upon any occasion that they are wanted for. The butler's lodging should be near both to the vault and pantry. The groom should lie near the stable. The saddlehorses ought not to be kept in the same place with those of draught or burthen; and they should be placed where they cannot offend the house with any smells, nor prejudice it by their kicking, and out of all danger of fire.

It is worth observing how careful birds are, and particularly swallows, to keep their nests clean and neat for their young ones. The example nature herein sets us is wonderful. Even the young swallows, as soon as ever time has strengthened their limbs will never mute, but out of the nest; and the old ones, to keep the filth at a still greater distance, will catch it in their bills as it is falling, to carry it further off from their own nest. Since nature has given us this excellent instruction, I think we ought by no means to neglect it.

From *The Architecture of Leon Batista Alberti*, trans. James Leoni (London, 1755).

The Perfect Gentleman

GIOVANNI DELLA CASA

c. 1555

THERE IS no doubt, but who so disposes himself to live, not in solitary and desert places, as hermits, but in fellowship with men and in populous cities, will think it a very necessary thing to have skill to put himself forth comely and seemly, in his fashions, gestures, and manners. The lack of these parts does make those other virtues lame, and little or nothing can they work to good effect without other helps, whereas this civility and courtesy, without other relief or patrimony, is rich of itself and has substance enough, as a thing that stands in speech and gestures alone.

And that you may now more easily learn the way unto it, you must understand it behooves you to frame and order your manners and doings, not according to your own mind and fashion but to please those with whom you live, and after that direct your doings. And this must be done by discretion and measure. For who so applies himself too much to feed other men's humours in his familiar conversation and behaviour with men, is rather to be thought a jester, a juggler, or flatterer than a gentleman well taught and nurtured. As contrariwise, whoso has no care or mind to please or displease, is a rude, untaught, and uncourteous fellow. Forasmuch then, as our manners have some pleasure in them when we respect other men and not our own pleasure, if we diligently search forth what those things be that most men do generally like or dislike, we shall in such sort wisely and easily find out the means and ways to choose and eschew those fashions and manners we are to leave or take, to live amongst men.

We say then, that every act that offends any of the common senses, or overthwarts a man's will and desire, or else presents to the imagination and conceit matters unpleasant, and that likewise which the mind does abhor, such things I say be naught, and must not be used. For we must not only refrain from such things as be foul, filthy, loathsome, and nasty, but we must not so much as name them. And it is not only a fault to do such things but against good manner by any act or sign to put a man in mind of them. And therefore it is an ill-favoured fashion that some men use, openly to thrust their hands in what part of their body they list.

Likewise, I like it ill to see a gentleman settle himself to do the needs of nature in presence of men, and after he has done to truss himself again before them. Neither would I have him (if I may give him counsel), when he comes from such an occupation, so much as wash his hands in the sight of honest company, for that the cause of his washing puts them in mind of some filthy matter that has been done apart. And by the same reason, it is no good manner when a man chances to see, as he passes the way (as many times it happens) a loathsome thing that will make a man to cast his stomach, to turn unto the company and show it them. And much worse I like it, to reach some stinking thing unto a man to smell unto it, as it is many a man's fashion to do with importunate means, yes, thrusting it unto their nose, saying, "Foh, see I pray you, how this does stink," where they should rather say, "Smell not unto it, for it has an ill scent."

And as these and like fashions offend the senses to which they appertain, so to grind the teeth, to whistle, to make pitiful cries, to rub sharp stones together, and to file upon iron do much offend the ears and would be left in any case. Neither must we refrain from those things alone, but we must also beware we do not sing, and specially alone, if we have an untuneful voice, which is a common fault with most men; and yet, he that is of nature least apt unto it, does use it most.

So there be some kind of men that in coughing and sneezing make such noise that they make a man deaf to hear them; some others use in like things so little discretion that they spit in men's faces that stand about them. Besides these there be some that in yawning bray and cry like asses. And yet such, with open mouth, will ever say and do what they list, and make such noise, or rather such roaring, as the dumb man does, when he strives with himself to speak. All these ill-favored fashions, a man must leave, as loathsome to the ear and the eye. . . .

And when you have blown your nose, use not to open your handkerchief, to glare upon your snot, as if you had pearls and rubies fallen from your brains, for these be slovenly parts, enough to cause men, not so much not to love us, as if they did love us, to unlove us again. . . .

When a man talks with one, it is no good manner to come so near, that he must needs breathe in his face; for there be many that cannot abide to feel the air of another man's breath, albeit there come no ill savour from him. These and like fashions be very unseemly, and would be eschewed, because their senses with whom we acquaint ourselves, cannot brook nor bear them.

Now, let us speak of those things which (without

any hurt or annoyance to the senses) offend the minds of most men, before whom they be done. . . . So that it is a rude fashion (in my conceit) that some men use, to lie lolling asleep in that place where honest men be met together, of purpose to talk. For his so doing shows that he does not esteem the company, and little reckons of them and their talk. And more than that, he that sleeps (and especially lying at little ease, as he must) wonts (for the most part) to do some foul thing, to behold or hear; and many times they awake sweating and drivelling at the mouth. And in like manner, to rise up where other men do sit and talk, and to walk up and down the chamber, it is no point of good manner. Also there be some that so shift themselves about, reach, stretch, and yawn, writhing now on one side, and then another, that a man would wean they had some fever upon them, a manifest sign that the company they keep does weary them.

Likewise do they very ill that now and then pull out a letter out of their pocket to read it, as if they had great matters of charge and affairs of the commonwealth committed unto them. But they are much more to be blamed, that pull out their knives or their scissors, and do nothing else but pare their nails, as if they made no account at all of the company, and would seek some other solace to pass the time away. This fashion too must be left, that some men use, to sing between the teeth, or play the drum with their fingers, or shuffle their feet. For these demeanours show that a body is careless of any man else.

Besides, let not a man so sit that he turn his tail to him that sits next to him, nor lie tottering with one leg so high above the other that a man may see all bare that his clothes would cover. For such parts be never played but amongst those to whom a man need use

no reverence. It is very true, that if a gentleman should
use these fashions before his servants, or in the presence of some friend of meaner condition than himself,
it would betoken no pride, but a love and familiarity. . . .

Such manner of people, with their rude behaviours
and fashions, make men with whom they live, suspect
they do esteem them but light. And that causes them
worse welcome wheresoever they come and ill beloved
amongst men.

But there be some besides these, that deserve more
than bare suspicion; their deeds and their doings be
so intolerable that a man cannot abide to live amongst
them by any means. For they be ever a let, a hurt and
trouble to all the company, they be never ready, ever
a trimming, never well dressed to their minds. But
when men be ready to sit down to the table, the meat
at the board, and their hands washed, then they must
write or make water or have this exercise to do, saying, "It is too early, we might have tarried a while;
what haste is this, this morning?" And thus they dis-
quiet all the company, as men caring for themselves
alone and their own matters, without consideration in
the world of other men. Besides this, they will in all
things be preferred above others; they must have the
best bed and best chamber; they must take upon them
the highest place at the table, and be first set and
served of all men. And they be so dainty and nice that
nothing pleases them but what they themselves devise;
they make a sour face at anything else. And they be
so proud-minded that they look that men should wait
upon them when they dine, ride, sport, or solace
themselves. . . .

It ill becomes a man when he is in company to be
sad, musing, and full of contemplation. And albeit it

may be suffered perchance in them that have long beaten their brains in these mathematical studies, which are called (as I take it) the liberal arts, yet without doubt it may not be borne in other men. For even these studious fellows, at such time, when they be so full of their muses, should be much wiser to get themselves alone. . . .

In speech a man may err many ways. And first in the matter itself, that is in the talk, which may not be vain or filthy. For they that do hear it will not abide it; as you talk they take no pleasure to hear but rather scorn the speech and the speaker both. Again, a man must not move any question of matters that be too deep and too subtle, because it is hardly understood of the most. And a man must watchfully foresee that the matter be such as none of the company may blush to hear it, or receive any shame by the tale. Neither must he talk of any filthy matter, albeit a man would take a pleasure to hear it; for it ill becomes an honest gentleman to seek to please but in things that be honest.

Neither in sport nor in earnest must a man speak anything against God or His saints, how witty or pleasant soever the matter be. Wherein the company that Giovanni Boccaccio has brought to speak in his novels and tales has erred so much that methinks every good body may justly blame them for it. . . .

And they do as much amiss, too, that never have other things in their mouth than their children, their wife, and their nurse. "My little boy made me so laugh yesterday; hear you, you never saw a sweeter babe in your life. My wife is such a one, Cecchina told me; of truth you would not believe what a wit she has." There is none so idle a body that will either intend to answer or abide to hear such foolish prittle-prattle. For it irks a man's ears to hearken unto it.

There be some again so curious in telling their dreams from point to point, using such wonder and admiration withal, that it makes a man's heart ache to hear them, and especially because (for the most part) they be such kind of people as it is labour lost to hear, even the very best exploits they do when they be most awake and labour most to show their best. Wherefore we must not trouble men with so base and absurd matter as dreams be, especially such foolish things as most times men have. . . .

Neither must a man boast of his nobility, his honour or riches, much less vaunt of his wit, or gloriously rehearse too much of his deeds and valiant acts, or what his ancestors have done, nor upon every occasion, fall in rehearsal of such things, as many men do. For in such case a man would wean they seek either to contend with the company (if they be, or will take upon them to be, as good gentlemen and of as much wealth and worthiness as they be), or else to overcrow them (if they live in meaner condition and calling, than they do), and as it were to upbraid them their poor and mean condition of life. . . .

We say that those be good manners and fashions which bring a delight or at least offend not their senses, their minds and conceits with whom we live. And of these we have spoken enough. But you must understand with all this that men be very desirous of beautiful things, well proportioned and comely. And of counterfeit things foul and ill-shapen, they be as squeamish again on the other side. And this is a special privilege given to us, that other creatures have no capacity to understand what beauty or measure means. And, therefore, as things not common with beasts but proper to ourselves, we must embrace them for themselves and hold them dear; and yet those, much more, that draw nearest to the knowledge of man as which are most apt and inclined to understand the perfection which nature has left in man. . . .

It is not enough for a man to do things that be good but he must also have a care he does them with a good grace. And good grace is nothing else but such a manner of light (as I may call it) as shines in the aptness of things set in good order and well disposed, one with another, and perfectly knit and united together. Without which proportion and measure, even that which is good is not fair, and the fairness itself is not pleasant. And as meats, though they be good and savoury, will give men no mind to eat them if they have no pleasant relish and taste, so fares it with the manners of men other while (although in themselves in no respect they be ill but foolish a little and fond), if a man does not season them with a certain sweetness which you call (as I take it) grace and comeliness.

From *Galateo*, trans. Robert Peterson (1576).

The Relief of the Poor

JUAN LUIS VIVES

1526

THEY HAVE no conception of the duty of a government who wish to limit it to the settling of disputes over money or to the punishment of criminals. On the contrary, it is much more important for the magistrates to devote their energy to the producing of good citizens than to the punishment and restraint of evildoers. For how much less need would there be to punish, if these matters were rightly looked after beforehand! . . .

Surely it is a shame and disgrace to us Christians, to whom nothing has been more explicitly commanded than charity—and I am inclined to think that is the one injunction—that we meet everywhere in our cities so many poor men and beggars. Whithersoever you turn you encounter poverty and distress and those who are compelled to hold out their hands for alms. Why is it not true that, just as everything in the state is restored which is subject to the ravages of time and fortune—such as walls, ditches, ramparts, streams, institutions, customs, and the laws themselves—so it would be suitable to aid in meeting that primary obligation of giving, which has suffered damage in various ways? Certain salutary measures have been devised by very eminent men who have sought to further the welfare of the state: taxes have been eased, public lands turned over to the poor to cultivate, certain surplus funds have been distributed by the state—things which we have seen even in our own time. But measures of this nature need special conditions, which rarely arise in these days. Recourse must therefore be had to other remedies, more suitable and of more lasting effect.

Someone may ask me: How do you propose to relieve so great a multitude? If true charity dwelt in our hearts, if it were really a law unto us—though compulsion is not an element that concerns one who loves—it would make all things common, nor would a man regard the distress of another otherwise than his own. As it is, no one extends his interest beyond his home, and sometimes not beyond his own chamber, nor even beyond himself, while many are not sufficiently faithful to parents and children and brothers and wife. Therefore, whenever human remedies must be employed, especially among those for whom the divine commands have too little weight, I propose the following plan.

Some of the poor live in those institutions commonly called hospitals . . . ; others beg publicly; still others bear their hardships as best they can, each one in his own home. I call "hospitals" those places where the sick are fed and cared for, where a certain number of paupers is supported, where boys and girls are reared, where abandoned infants are nourished, where the insane are confined, and where the blind dwell. Let the governors of the state realize that all these institutions are a part of their responsibility. . . .

In the next place, there is nothing so free in the state that it is not subject to inquiry by those who administer the government; for it does not constitute freedom to yield no obedience to common magistrates; but rather an encouragement to savagery and opportunity for widespread licence in whatever direction a whim may lead. Nor can anyone remove his property from the oversight and control of the state, unless he gives up his citizenship. Nor indeed can he free his own life, which is of more consequence and dearer to everyone than property, especially since everyone has acquired his property with the help of the state, as if it were a gift, and can keep and hold it only by the help of the state.

Therefore, let the senators, by twos, with a secretary, visit each of these homes, and inspect it, and write a full account of its condition, of the number of its inmates and their names, likewise from what cause each one has come there. Let all these things be reported to the councillors and the Senate in assembly.

Let those who suffer poverty at home be registered, both they and their children, by two senators for each

parish; their needs ascertained, in what manner they
have lived hitherto, and by what ill chance they have
fallen into poverty. It will be easy to learn from the
neighbours what sort of men they are, how they live
and what their habits are. Evidence about one poor
person should not be taken from another, for he would
not be free from jealousy. Let the councillors and the
Senate be informed of all these things. If any man suddenly fall into some ill fortune, let him notify the
Senate through some senator, and let his case be
decided according to his condition and circumstances.

Then in regard to the beggars who wander about
with no fixed dwelling places; let those who are in
health declare their name and the reason for their
mendicancy in the presence of the Senate, in some open
place or vacant lot, that their filth may not pollute
the Senate chamber; let those who are sick do likewise
in the presence of two or four senators and a physician,
that the eyes of the Senate may be spared. Let witnesses be sought by them to testify in regard to their
manner of life.

Upon those whom they appoint to make these ex-
aminations and perform these duties, let the Senate
confer the authority to coerce and exact obedience, even
to the point of imprisonment, that the Senate may have
knowledge of those who show themselves refractory.

Before everything else this principle must be accepted, which the Lord imposed upon the human race
as a punishment for its sin: that each man should eat
bread that is the fruit of his own labour. When I say
"eat" or "nourished" or "supported" I do not mean to
imply food alone, but clothes, shelter, fuel, candles; in
fine, everything which is involved in the sustenance of
the body.

Let no one among the poor, therefore, be idle, provided of course he is fit for work by his age and the condition of his health. The Apostle Paul writes to the Thessalonians: "For even when we were with you, this we commanded you, that if any would not work, neither should he eat. For we hear that there are some which walk among you disorderly, working not at all, but are busybodies. Now them that are such we command and exhort by our Lord Jesus Christ, that with quietness they work, and eat their own bread." . . .

Health and age must be taken into consideration; but in order that you may not be imposed upon by a pretence of sickness or infirmity—which not infrequently happens—let the opinion of physicians be sought, and let impostors be punished. Of the able-bodied vagrants the foreign-born should be returned to their native country—which indeed is provided for in the Imperial law—with travelling money, for it would be inhuman to send a destitute man on a journey without any money, and would be nothing less than commanding him to rob. But if they are from villages or towns afflicted with war, then the teaching of Paul must be borne in mind, that among those who have been baptized in the blood of Christ there is neither Greek nor barbarian nor Gaul nor Fleming, but a new creature; and they must be treated even as if they were native-born.

Should the native poor be asked whether they have learned a trade? Yes; and those who have not, if they are of suitable age, should be taught the one to which they say they are most strongly inclined, provided it is feasible. If it is not feasible, let them be taught some similar trade; for example, let him who cannot sew garments sew what they call *caligas* [soldiers' boots].

But if this trade is too difficult, or he is too slow in learning, let an easier one be assigned to him, all the way down to those which anyone can learn thoroughly in a few days: such as digging, drawing water, bearing loads, pushing a wheelbarrow, attending on magistrates, running errands, bearing letters or packets, driving horses.

Even those who have dissipated their fortunes in riotous living—by gambling, harlots, extravagance, and gluttony—must be relieved, for no one must die of hunger. But to them more irksome tasks should be assigned, and smaller rations, that they may be an example to others, and may repent of their former life and may not relapse easily into the same vices, being restrained both by lack of food and by the severity of their tasks. They must not die of hunger, but they must feel its pangs.

Nor would I allow the blind either to sit idle or to wander around in idleness. There are a great many things at which they may employ themselves. Some are suited to letters; let them study, for in some of them we see an aptitude for learning by no means to be despised. Others are suited to the art of music; let them sing, pluck the lute, blow the flute. Let others turn wheels and work the treadmills; tread the winepresses; blow the bellows in the smithies. We know the blind can make little boxes and chests, fruit baskets, and cages. Let the blind women spin and wind yarn. Let them not be willing to sit idle and seek to avoid work; it is easy enough to find employment for them. Laziness and a love of ease are the reasons for their pretending they cannot do anything, not feebleness of body. . . .

And this reminds me of the insane. Since there is

nothing in the world more excellent than man, nor in man than his mind, particular attention should be given to the welfare of the mind; and it should be reckoned the highest of services, if we either restore the minds of others to sanity or keep them sane and rational. Therefore, when a man of unsettled mind is brought to a hospital, first of all it must be determined whether his insanity is congenital or has resulted from some misfortune; whether there is hope of his recovery or not. One ought to feel compassion for so great a disaster to the health of the human mind, and it is of the utmost importance that the treatment be such that the insanity is not nourished and increased, as may result from mocking, exciting, and irritating madmen, approving and applauding the foolish things which they say or do, inciting them to act more ridiculously, applying fomentations, as it were, to their stupidity and silliness. What could be more inhuman than to drive a man insane just for the sake of laughing at him and amusing oneself at such a misfortune?

Remedies suited to the individual patient should be used. Some need medical care and attention to their mode of life; others need mild and friendly treatment, that like wild animals they may gradually grow gentle; others, instruction. There will be some who will require force and chains, but these must be so used that the patients are not made more violent by them. Above all, as far as possible, tranquility must be introduced into their minds, for it is through this that reason and sanity return.

Let the investigators make their examination into the needs of the poor humanely and kindly. Let nothing be given if the judgment is unfavourable. Intimidation should not be used unless they deem it necessary in dealing with persons who are refractory and who disparage the government.

From *Concerning the Relief of the Poor*, trans. M. M. Sherwood, *Studies in Social Work*, No. 11 (New York School of Philanthropy, Feb., 1917).

The Reform of the Commonwealth

THOMAS STARKEY

c. 1535

LUPSET: Much time past, Master Pole, I have greatly desired to commune with you, being moved thereto by the great friendship and familiarity which of youth growing between us, is now so by virtue increased and confirmed, that nature has not so sure a band and knot to couple and join any hearts together in true love and amity. Wherefore I am right glad, Master Pole, that I have now at this time here found you, both, as it seems to me, at convenient leisure to commune and talk, and also in this place of Bisham, where the image and memory of your old ancestors of great nobility, shall, as I trust, stir and move your heart and mind to the same purpose that I would now and long have desired to communicate unto you.

Pole: Truth it is that leisure here, as you say, is not at all lacking; but I pray you, what is that, good Master Lupset, that you seem so earnestly to will? It appears to be, by your beginnings, some great matter, and weighty.

Lupset: Truth it is a great matter indeed, and, as it seems to me, touching the whole order of your life,

Master Pole; and shortly to show you, without long circumstance, thus it is. I have much and many times marvelled, reasoning with myself, why you, Master Pole, after so many years spent in quiet study of letters and learning, and after such experience of the manners of man, taken in diverse parts beyond the sea, have not before this settled yourself and applied your mind to the handling of the matters of the common weal here in our own nation; to the intent that both your friends and country might now at the last receive and take some fruit of your long studies, wherein you have spent your whole youth, as I ever took it, to the same purpose and end. You know right well, Master Pole, that to this all men are born and of nature brought forth, to communicate such gifts as be given to them, each one to the profit of other, in perfect civility; and not to live to their own pleasure and profit without regard of the weal of their country, forgetting all justice and equity. . . . Wherefore it seems to me, whosoever he be who, drawn by the sweetness of his studies and moved by his own quietness and pleasure, leaves the care of the common weal and policy, he does manifest wrong to his country and friends, and is plainly unjust and full of iniquity, as one who regards not his office and duty, to which above all he is most bound by nature. . . . Wherefore, Master Pole, now at last wake out of this dream; remember your country, look to your friends, consider your office and duty that you are most bound to. And so now thus you have briefly heard the cause of my coming and purpose at this time. . . .

Pole: Well, Master Lupset, if you like it well, after this manner we shall devise, because every man speaks so much of the common weal, and many more, I fear me, do know it indeed. And because the common weal is the end of all parliaments and common councils, first therefore (to keep a certain process in order), we will search out, as nearly as we can, what is the very and true common weal, wherein it stands and when it most flourishes, that we may, having this plainly set before our eyes, ever resolve and refer all our counsels to this point. Second, we will search out thereby the decay of our common weal, with all the common faults and disorders of the same. Thirdly, we will devise of the cause of this same decay and of the remedy and means to restore the common weal again. And this shall be the process of our communication.

Lupset: Sir, this process pleases me well, but here of one thing, I pray you, take heed, that in this your plan of your communication, you follow not the example of Plato, whose order of common weal no people upon earth to this day could ever yet attain. Wherefore it is reputed by many men but as a dream and vain imagination, which never can be brought to effect; and by some others it is compared to the Stoic philosopher who never appeared yet to the light; such virtue and wisdom is attributed to him, that it can be found in no mortal man. Therefore look you to the nature of our country, to the manner of our people, not without respect both of time and place, that your plan hereafter, by the help of our most noble prince, may the sooner obtain its fruit and effect. . . .

Pole: A very and true common weal is nothing else but the prosperous and most perfect state of a multitude assembled together in any country, city, or town, governed virtuously in civil life, according to the nature and dignity of man. The nature whereof now, I think, you may clearly perceive, and how seemingly it arises out of three things, alike and proportionable to those wherein stands the weal of every particular man. For just as a man is wealthy and has high felicity when he has health, strength, and beauty of body, with sufficiency of friends and worldly goods to maintain the same, and has also thereto joined honest behaviour both toward God and man; so a country, city, or town has its common weal and most perfect state when first the multitude of people and politic body is healthy, beautiful, and strong, able to defend themselves from outward injuries; and then plenteously nourished with abundance of all things necessary and pleasant for the sustenance and quietness of man's life—and so, thirdly, live together in civil order, quietly and peaceably passing their life, each one loving the other as parts of one body, every part doing his duty and office required thereto. Then, I say, there is the very and true common weal; there is the most prosperous and perfect state that in any country, city, or town, by policy and wisdom may be established and set. . . .

Well, Master Lupset, then let us proceed. First, if you remember, after we had declared what it is that we call the true common weal, and after we began to search out such common faults and lacks as we could find in our country concerning the same, we agreed that we have, considering the place and fertility thereof, a great lack of people, the multitude whereof is, as it were, the ground and foundation of this our common weal; which lack we called, as it were, a consumption of the politic body, of which now first it is required to search out the cause, which, Master Lupset, shall not be hard to do. For this is a necessary truth: inasmuch as man grows not out of rocks or of trees, as fables do feign, but springs by natural generation, this lack must needs come as from a principal cause, that man does not apply his study to natural procreation. For though it be so that there may be many other exterior causes thereof, such as battle and pestilence, hunger and dearth, which have in too many countries brought penury of people, as we may by experience see in many countries desolated thereby; yet now, to our purpose, the principal cause of our lack of people cannot be attributed thereto. And yet, if perchance it were so indeed, the way and mean to suffice, multiply and increase them again to a convenient number, is only natural generation. How say you, Master Lupset, is it not so?

Lupset: Sir, there is no doubt; this is the only way to increase not only man by the course of nature, but all other living creatures here upon earth which are not engendered by putrefaction.

Pole: Well, Master Lupset, then we must now devise the means for removing such impediments and hindrances—as there be to this cause, and so to allure man to this natural procreation, after a civil order and politic fashion. For though nature has given to man, as to all other beasts, natural inclination to his increase, yet because man only is born to civility and politic rule, therefore he may not, without order or respect, study to the satisfaction of this natural affection. And for this cause it has been ordained, I trow, from the first generation of man, that he should couple himself in lawful matrimony, and so thereby multiply and increase. So that this remains, Master Lupset, in this matter, now especially to us, having the light of Christ's Gospel, to devise some way to entice men to this lawful marriage and coupling together. . . . Seeing that matrimony is the only or chief means politic to increase this multitude to a just number again, we must both by privilege and pain induce men thereto, and study to take away all obstacles and hindrances which we find thereto; in which thing, Master Lupset, let me hear something of your mind.

Lupset: Sir, because you will so, this I shall say as touching the obstacles and hindrances whereof you speak. You put me in remembrance of a thing which to you I dare speak; for I know not whether I may speak this abroad, but in that I submit myself to your judgment. The thing is this: I have thought long and many a day a great hindrance to the increase of Christian people the law of chastity ordained by the Church, which binds so great a multitude of men to live thereafter, as all secular priests, monks, friars, canons, and nuns, of which, as you know, there is no small number, by reason whereof the generation of man is marvellously hindered and diminished. Wherefor, except for the ordinance of the Church (against which I would never gladly rebel) I would plainly judge that it should be very convenient something to release the band of this law. . . .

Pole: Well, Master Lupset, this which you say is not all without reason. . . . Wherefore in this matter I think it were necessary to temper this law, and at the least to give and admit all secular priests to marry at their liberty, considering now the great multitude and number of them. But as touching monks, canons, friars, and nuns, I hold for a thing very convenient and meet, in all well-ordered common weals, to have certain monasteries and abbeys to which all such as, after lawful proof of chastity before had, may retire, and from the business and vanity of the world may withdraw themselves, wholly giving their minds to prayer, study, and high contemplation. This occasion I would not have to be taken away from Christian policy, which is a great comfort to many feeble and weary souls, which have been oppressed with worldly vanity. But as touching the secular priests, I utterly agree with you, and so to take away that obstacle which hinders in many ways the increase of our people, as many other things do more also; among which another chief, after my mind, is this: the great multitude of serving men, which in service spend their lives, never finding means to marry conveniently, but living always as common corrupters of chastity. Wherefore there would be, as I think, an ordinance that no gentleman, nor other of the nobility, take to his service a greater number of men than he is able to promote and set forward to some honest fashion of living and lawful matrimony; and so by this means the multitude of them should be greatly diminished. . . .

We noted, if you call to remembrance, in the chief part of the body, that is, the head, an appropriate disease, which we called then a frenzy, which disease if we could find the means to cure, all the disorders in the rest of the party should easily be helped; for all hang on this. . . . The point I speak of is this: to have a good prince to govern and rule. This is the ground of all felicity in the civil life. This is the foundation of all good policy in such a kind of state as is in our country. The prince institutes and makes almost all under-officers. He has authority and rule of all. Therefore, if we could find a means to have a good prince commonly, this should be a common remedy, almost, as I said, for all the rest of the disorders in the policy.

Lupset: Marry, Sir, that is truth; but this lies in God only, and not in man's power.

Pole: Master Lupset, though this be truth, that all goodness comes of God, as out of the fountain, yet God requires the diligence of man in all such things as pertain to his felicity. The providence of God has this ordained, that man shall not have anything perfect, nor attain to his perfection, without care and travail, labour and diligence, by which, as by money, we may buy all things of God, who is the only merchant of all things that are good. . . . The goodness of God, out of which spring all things that are good, has made man, of all creatures on earth, most perfect, giving unto him a sparkle of His own dignity—that is to say, right reason —whereby he should govern himself in civil life and good policy, according to his excellent nature and dignity. But with this same sparkle of reason, thus given to man, are joined by nature so many affections and vicious desires, by reason of this earthly body, that (unless man with care, diligence, and labour resist the same) they overrun reason, this little sparkle, and so bring man, consequently, from his natural felicity and from that life which is convenient to his nature and dignity; insomuch that he is then as a brute beast, following not the ordinance of God, which gave him reason to subdue his affections as much as the nature of the body would suffer. For if He had given him so much reason and wisdom that he should never have been overcome with affections and vain desires, He should have made man above man, and made him as an angel; and so there should have lacked here in this world the nature of man. . . .

And now to our purpose. Even as every particular man, when he follows reason, is governed by God, and contrary, blinded with ignorance by his own vain opinion; so whole nations, when they live together in civil order, instituted and governed by reasonable policy, are then governed by the providence of God, and be under His tuition. As, contrary, when they are without good order and politic rule, they are ruled by the violence of tyranny; they are not governed by His providence nor celestial ordinance, but as a man governed by affections, so they are tormented in infinite ways, by reason of such tyrannical power; so that of this you may see that it is not God that provides tyrants to rule in cities and towns, any more than it is He that ordains ill affections to overrun right reason. But now to the purpose, Master Lupset. It is not man that can make a wise prince of him that lacks wit by nature, nor make him just that is a tyrant for pleasure. But this is in man's power, to elect and choose him that is both wise and just, and make him a prince, and so to depose him that is a tyrant. Wherefore, Master Lupset, this I may truly say, to which all this reasoning now tends, that if we will correct this frenzy in our common weal, we may not at a venture take him to our prince, whatsoever he be that is born of his blood and comes by succession, which, and you remember, we noted before also to be one of the greatest faults, as it is indeed, in our policy; which fault, once corrected, shall also take away this frenzy. . . .

But here you must remember, Master Lupset, . . . that albeit we have now in our days, by the providence of God, such a prince [Henry VIII] and of such wisdom that he may right well and justly be subject to no law —whose prudence and wisdom are living law and true policy—yet we now . . . may not deny but that in our order here is a certain fault, and to the same now devise some remedy. Wherein the first and best mean is this, after my mind and opinion, here in our country to be taken; after the decease of the prince, by election of the common voice of the parliament assembled to choose one most apt to that high office and dignity, which should not rule and govern at his own pleasure and liberty, but ever be subject to the order of his laws. . . . This has been ever used among them which have ever lived under a prince with liberty, whereby they have been governed by living reason, and not subject to deadly affection. The second means, as it seems to me, may well be this, if we will that the heir of the prince shall ever succeed, whatsoever he be, then to him must be joined a council, by common authority; not such as he will, but such as by the most part of the parliament shall be judged to be wise and meet thereunto.

Lupset: Why, but then by this means our parliament should have much to do, if, when so ever there lacked any councillors, it should be called to subrogate others and set in their place.

Pole: Nay, Master Lupset, I would not so; but for that a provision must be had, and that might be this. For as much as the great parliament should never be called but only at the election of our prince, or else for some other great urgent cause concerning the common state and policy, I would think it well if at London there should ever remain (because it is the chief city of our realm) the authority of the parliament, which ever there should be ready to remedy all such causes, and repress seditions, and defend the liberty of the whole body of the people, at all such times as the king or his council tended to anything hurtful and predjudicial to the same. This council and authority of parliament should rest in these persons: first, in four of the greatest and ancient lords of the temporalty; two bishops, as of London and Canterbury; four of the chief judges; and four of the most wise citizens of London. These men, jointly together, should have authority of the whole parliament in such time as the parliament were dissolved. This authority should be chiefly instituted to this end and purpose: to see that the king and his proper council do nothing against the ordinance of his laws and good policy; and they should have also power to call the great parliament whensoever to them it should seem necessary for the reformation of the whole state of the commonalty. By this council also should pass all acts of leagues, confederation, peace, and war. All the rest should be ministered by the king and his council. But this, above all, as a ground, should be laid, that the king should do nothing pertaining to the state of his realm without the authority of his proper council appointed to him by this authority. This council should be of two bishops, four lords, and four of the best learned and politic men, expert in the laws, both spiritual and temporal. And so this council, though we took our prince by succession, to avoid sedition, should deliver us from all tyranny, setting us in true liberty. And so we should have, consequently, the ground of this frenzy taken away; for, by the council of those appointed to the king, all bishoprics and great offices should be distributed and given; and all great faults and enormities openly committed should be, by their prudence, justly punished. all other inferior lords, knights, and gentlemen, who did not their office and duty in administration of justice with equity towards their subjects in such things as they had jurisdiction of, should be called to count, and before them give reckoning of all things done by them, whereof by any man they were accused.

This band of reckoning before the council of higher authority should make the under-officers to be wary and diligent to do their duty; which if they did, by and by should follow the correction of the other particular faults which we noted to be in the parts resembling the feet and hands of the commonwealth; which faults were nothing else but other negligence of the people, or else, at the least, springing out of the same. For, as touching this, that the ground lies so untilled and crafts be so ill occupied here in our nation, it comes of nothing chiefly but of negligence of the people or vain occupation.

Wherefore, if such negligence, perceived and proved at courts openly in every village and town, both of ploughmen and artisans, were by the officers punished by certain penalty forfeited, prescribing the same, you should have both the crafts better occupied, and also the ground more diligently tilled; especially if the statute of inclosure were put in execution, and all such pasture put to the use of the plough as before time has been so used; for in many places herein there is evidently perceived much negligence and great lack in the applying of the ground to the plough. This must be amended, and then you shall see both all things in more abundance and the politic body more lively and active.

From *A Dialogue between Cardinal Pole and Thomas Lupset, Lecturer in Rhetoric at Oxford*, ed. J. M. Cowper (London: Early English Text Society, 1878).

War and the Law of Nations

FRANCISCO DE VITORIA

c. 1532

INASMUCH as the seizure and occupation of those lands of the barbarians whom we style Indians can best, it seems, be defended under the law of war, I propose to supplement the foregoing discussion of the titles, some just and some unjust, which the Spaniards may allege for their hold on the lands in question, by a short discussion of the law of war, so as to give more completeness to that *Relectio*. As, however, the other claims on my time will not allow me to deal with all the points which arise out of this topic, the scope which I can give my pen must be proportionate, not to the amplitude and dignity of the theme, but to the shortness of the time at my disposal. And so I will merely note the main propositions of this topic, together with very brief proofs, and will abstain from touching on the many doubtful matters which might otherwise be brought into this discussion. I will deal with four principal questions. First, Whether Christians may make war at all; secondly, Where does the authority to declare or wage war repose; thirdly, What may and ought to furnish causes of just war; fourthly, What and how extensive measures may be taken in a just war against the enemy? . . .

What may be a reason and cause of just war? It is particularly necessary to ask this in connection with the case of the Indian aborigines, which is now before us. Here my first proposition is: Difference of religion is not a cause of just war. This was shown at length in the preceding *Relectio,* when we demolished the fourth alleged title for taking possession of the Indians, namely, their refusal to accept Christianity. And it is the opinion of St. Thomas (*Secunda Secundae,* qu. 66, art. 8), and the common opinion of the doctors—indeed, I know of no one of the opposite way of thinking.

Second proposition: Extension of empire is not a just cause of war. This is too well known to need proof, for otherwise each of the two belligerents might have an equally just cause and so both would be innocent. This in its turn would involve the consequence that it would not be lawful to kill them and so imply a contradiction, because it would be a just war.

Third proposition: Neither the personal glory of the prince nor any other advantage to him is a just cause of war. This, too, is notorious. For a prince ought to subordinate both peace and war to the common weal of his state and not spend public revenues in quest of his own glory or gain, much less expose his subjects to danger on that account. Herein, indeed, is the difference between a lawful king and a tyrant, that the latter directs his government towards his individual profit and advantage, but a king to the public welfare, as Aristotle says (*Politics*, bk. 4, ch. 10). Also, the prince derives his authority from the state. Therefore he ought to use it for the good of the state. Also, laws ought "not to be enacted for the private good of any individual, but in the common interest of all the citizens," as is ruled in can. 2, dist. 4, a citation from Isidore. Therefore the rules relating to war ought to be for the common good of all and not for the private good of the prince. Again, this is the difference between freemen and slaves, as Aristotle says (*Politics*, bk. 1, ch. 3 and 4), that masters exploit slaves for their own good and not the good of the slaves, while freemen do not exist in the interest of others, but in their own interest. And so, were a prince to misuse his subjects by compelling them to go soldiering and to contribute money for his campaigns, not for the public good, but for his own private gain, this would be to make slaves of them.

Fourth proposition: There is a single and only just cause for commencing a war, namely, a wrong received. . . .

Fifth proposition: Not every kind and degree of wrong can suffice for commencing a war. The proof of this is that not even upon one's own fellow countrymen is it lawful for every offence to exact atrocious punishments, such as death or banishment or confiscation of property. As, then, the evils inflicted through war are all of a severe and atrocious character, such as slaughter and fire and devastation, it is not lawful for slight wrongs to pursue the authors of the wrongs with war, seeing that the degree of the punishment ought to correspond to the measure of the offence (Deuteronomy, ch. 25).

The fourth question is about the law of war, namely what kind and degree of stress is lawful in a just war. Here let my first proposition be: In war everything is lawful which the defence of the common weal requires. This is notorious, for the end and aim of war is the defence and preservation of the state. Also, a private person may do this in self-defence, as has been proved. Therefore much more may a state and a prince.

Second proposition: It is permissible to recapt everything that has been lost and any part of the same. This is too notorious to need proof. For war is begun or undertaken with this object.

Third proposition: It is lawful to make good out of enemy property the expenses of the war and all damages wrongfully caused by the enemy. This is clear, for the enemy who has done the wrong is bound to give all this redress. Therefore the prince can claim it all and exact it all by war. Also, as before, there is the argument that, when no other way lies open, a private creditor can seize the amount of his debt from the debtor. Also, if there were any competent judge over the two belligerents, he would have to condemn the unjust aggressors and authors of wrong, not only to make restitution of what they have carried off, but also to make good the expenses of the war to the other side, and also all damages. But a prince who is carrying on a just war is as it were his own judge in matters touching the war, as we shall forthwith show. Therefore he can enforce all these claims upon his enemy.

Fourth proposition: Not only are the things just named allowable, but a prince may go even further in a just war and do whatever is necessary in order to obtain peace and security from the enemy; for example, destroy an enemy's fortress and even build one on enemy soil, if this be necessary in order to avert a dangerous attack of the enemy. This is proved by the fact that, as said above, the end and aim of war is peace and security. Therefore a belligerent may do everything requisite to obtain peace and security. Further, tranquility and peace are reckoned among the desirable things of mankind and so the utmost material prosperity does not produce a state of happiness if there be no security there. Therefore it is lawful to employ all appropriate measures against enemies who are plundering and disturbing the tranquility of the state. Also, all measures of this kind may be taken against internal foes, that is, against bad citizens. Therefore they are lawful against external foes. The antecedent is clear, for if one citizen does a wrong to a fellow citizen, the magistrate not only compels the wrongdoer to make amends to the injured party, but, if the former is a source of fear to the latter, he is compelled to give bond or quit the city, so as to remove the danger of which he is the cause. This shows that even when victory has been won and redress obtained, the enemy may be made to give hostages, ships, arms, and other things, when this is genuinely necessary for keeping the enemy in his duty and preventing him from becoming dangerous again. . . .

All this can be summarized in a few canons or rules of warfare. First canon: Assuming that a prince has authority to make war, he should first of all not go seeking occasions and causes of war, but should, if possible, live in peace with all men, as St. Paul enjoins on us (*Romans*, ch. 12). Moreover, he should reflect that others are his neighbours, whom we are bound to love as ourselves, and that we all have one common Lord, before whose tribunal we shall have to render our account. For it is the extreme of savagery to seek for and rejoice in grounds of killing and destroying men whom God has created and for whom Christ died. But only under compulsion and reluctantly should he come to the necessity of war.

Second canon: When war for a just cause has broken out, it must not be waged so as to ruin the people against whom it is directed, but only so as to obtain one's rights and the defence of one's country and in order that from that war peace and security may in time result.

Third canon: When victory has been won and the war is over, the victory should be utilized with moderation and Christian humility, and the victor ought to deem that he is sitting as judge between two states, the one which has been wronged and the one which has done the wrong, so that it will be as judge and not as accuser that he will deliver the judgment whereby the injured state can obtain satisfaction, and this, so far as possible, should involve the offending state in the least degree of calamity and misfortune, the offending individuals being chastised within lawful limits; and an especial reason for this is that in general among Christians all the fault is to be laid at the door of their princes, for subjects when fighting for their princes act in good faith and it is thoroughly unjust, in the words of the poet, that "For every folly their kings commit the punishment should fall upon the Greeks." . . .

No war is just the conduct of which is manifestly more harmful to the state than it is good and advantageous; and this is true regardless of any other claims or reasons that may be advanced to make of it a just war. The proof is: that if the state has no power to make war except for the purpose of defending itself, and protecting itself and its property, it follows that any war will be unjust, whether it be begun by the king or by the state, through which the latter is not rendered greater, but rather is enfeebled and impaired. Nay more, since one nation is a part of the whole world, and since the Christian province is a part of the whole Christian State, if any war should be advantageous to one province or nation but injurious to the world or to Christendom, it is my belief that, for this very reason, that war is unjust. If, for example, the Spanish should undertake against the French a war which, in other respects, was just, and which was, besides, advantageous to the Spanish kingdom, but which involved Christendom as a whole in still greater harm and loss (suppose, for instance, that the Turks in the meantime take possession of Christian provinces), then the Spanish should cease from waging that war. And these are the points which pertain to the exposition of the first conclusion. . . .

From all that has been said, a corollary may be inferred, namely: that international law has not only the force of a pact and agreement among men, but also the force of a law; for the world as a whole, being in a way one single state, has the power to create laws that are just and fitting for all persons, as are the rules of international law. Consequently, it is clear that they who violate these international rules, whether in peace or in war, commit a mortal sin; moreover, in the gravest matters, such as the inviolability of ambassadors, it is not permissible for one country to refuse to be bound by international law, the latter having been established by the authority of the whole world.

From *De jure belli* and *De potestate civili*, in J. B. Scott, *The Spanish Origin of International Law*, Part I (Oxford: Clarendon Press, 1934).

The Concord of the World

GUILLAUME POSTEL

1560

IT SEEMS true that God has put man in this world to be a social animal (one man helping another), or a creature who delights in being assembled with others. Since it is impossible, because of the diversity of customs, languages, opinions, and religions, to achieve a community and union of diverse men before they truly understand each other, it is very certain that the most beautiful, useful, and necessary work in this world, for the perfect reconciliation of men, can be accomplished only by actually giving to men this knowledge of one another. By means of such knowledge, through an understanding of the vice and virtue of individuals or peoples hitherto unknown to one another, everyone in the world, tolerating the vice of others and approving their virtue, would be able to come to agreement.

There has never been, in written memory, a nation, people, or language greater in extent and dominion than is the Mohammedan or Arabic today, which altogether is comprehended under the name of Ismael, the bastard son of Abraham, and there has never been a power which has longer or with less reason opposed Christianity than this one, or for whom likewise the Christians have had greater hatred, as for sovereign enemies. Since they comprise so many peoples, spread all around the earth, I judge that there is no people about whom it is more necessary to inform Christendom than this.

In the past, on my return from my first journey to the East, I discussed this subject and history, and many others have tried to illuminate it. Yet since none of the others had a knowledge of the Arabic language, on which this history and its truth depend, and because when I first wrote on the subject I had less than at present, I have decided to discuss it briefly once more, and to repeat the beginning of this history, not at length, but only with respect to its origins and institutions. Thus, by means of this original history, the Christians, possessing the knowledge which up to now has been veiled by very great ignorance, may begin to understand their most powerful adversaries as they really are, and not as opinion or passion have until now caused them to be judged in many respects, more or less according to the truth. And when the Christians, and especially their chief leaders and princes, are duly informed of that truth, I am sure that a very easy way will be found to bring the whole human race into perfect concord, since it will be possible to reconcile the two greatest powers of the world, and to bring them into agreement by mutual or reciprocal knowledge. . . .

After the Jews and Christians had failed as true children of Abraham, since they had become bastardized and had ceased to do their duty, it was necessary for God to raise up in their place and earthly prosperity the bastard line of Abraham. Although the latter have not done the work of perfection, nevertheless they have, in the first place, wiped out, and kept from arising anew in the world, the power and religion of the pagan peoples and their law, for the destruction of which both the Christian and the Jewish religions, each in its time, were instituted and favoured by God. Thus everywhere, although the Ismaelites [Mohammedans] allow the Christians and Jews to live according to their own law and ceremonies, which they could prevent if they wished to, or to speak more correctly, if God permitted them to, nevertheless they wage such war on all idolators and temples of idols over which they have power, that in no way do they suffer them to exist. And this was the principal reason for which God had granted the crown of spiritual power and also of temporal power to the Christians and Jews, to the end that, if they could not bring it about that in the whole world good should be done, at least they should force everyone to refrain from evil—namely, the greatest evil in the world, which is not to know God, and in His place to worship and adore idols and the works of man's hands. In this Ismael, Mohammed, and the whole sect that believes in the Koran is truly the legitimate heir of Abraham, although their mother Hagar was a bastard and empty and devoid of truly good works. . . . We must conclude that the good which the Moslems have introduced by destroying idolatry is infinitely greater than any evil which they have brought upon the world by the error of their false religion. . . .

For though the falsity of the bastard doctrine of the Ismaelites has caused very great ruin and violent damage in the world, as much in customs and letters as in religion, nevertheless the good which they have done in humbling the pride of Christians, Jews, and pagans, as in destroying idolatry and in preserving the fragrance and the distant remembrance of the sacred histories and doctrines, is infinitely greater than has been the evil brought about by their law. And besides, God, without anyone being conscious of it, has brought it to pass that in seven-tenths of the world the inhabitants are already half-converted and almost Christians, and so jealous of that which they think pertains to the divine honour that there are found among them those who die to sustain such truth of Christ as they can understand from their Koran, while waiting to be better informed. And this is the greatest good that could be offered, in any conceivable way, for the love of God. For seeing how they die for an imperfect and shadowy knowledge of the truth, what do we think that they would do if they had as perfect knowledge as we do? . . .

And thus it may and should be judged that since the most wicked of Moslems or Ismaelites are less sinful towards God, because of their ignorance, than are the least of Christians, who offend the more because of their knowledge and grace, God has ordained that the Moslems should be allowed to come to an imperfect knowledge, and to die or to lose their goods, their life, and honour for what they know, rather than to let those live who know too much, and by knowing too much, have denied Him by their works. Not only do they not wish to expend their goods or life or honour, but they would prefer to lose all truth in order to gain temporal goods, both of body and of soul—that is to say, temporal and not eternal glory. For these reasons, we see today that the greater number of Christians have renounced all truth.

From *De la république des Turcs* (Poitiers, 1560); trans. M.M.M.

III. THE STUDY
OF MAN

Learning of the Best Sort

The Ruins of Rome

POGGIO BRACCIOLINI

1430

NOT LONG AGO, after Pope Martin left Rome shortly before his death for a farewell visit to the Tuscan countryside, and when Antonio Lusco, a very distinguished man, and I were free of business and public duties, we used to contemplate the desert places of the city with wonder in our hearts as we reflected on the former greatness of the broken buildings and the vast ruins of the ancient city, and again on the truly prodigious and astounding fall of its great empire and the deplorable inconstancy of fortune. And once when we had climbed the Capitoline hill, and Antonio, who was a little weary from riding, wanted to rest, we dismounted from our horses and sat down together within the very enclosures of the Tarpeian ruins, behind the great marble threshold of its very doors, as I believe, and the numerous broken columns lying here and there, whence a view of a large part of the city opens out.

Here, after he had looked about for some time, sighing and as if struck dumb, Antonio declared, "Oh, Poggio, how remote are these ruins from the Capitol

379

that our Vergil celebrated: 'Golden now, once bristling with thorn bushes.' How justly one can transpose this verse and say: 'Golden once, now rough with thorns and overgrown with briars.' I remember the story of Marius, once the pillar of the Roman Empire, later arraigned and banished from his native city, how when he had arrived in Africa, they say that he sat down amid the ruins of Carthage, marvelling at once at his own fortune and that of Carthage, comparing them and pondering whether his fate or the city's offered a more striking spectacle of the instability of fortune. But truly I cannot compare the tremendous ruin of Rome to that of any other city; this one disaster so exceeds the calamities of all other cities, whether these were brought about in the natural course of things or wrought by the hand of man.

"You may turn all the pages of history, you may read all the long-drawn-out records of the authors, you may examine all the historical annals, but you will find that fortune offers no more striking example of her own mutability than the city of Rome, the most beautiful and magnificent of all those that either have been or shall be, the city which was described by Lucian, the learned Greek author, when he was writing to a friend of his who wanted to see Rome, as not so much a city as a bit of Paradise. How much the more marvellous to relate and bitter to behold, how the cruelty of fortune has so transformed its appearance and shape, that, stripped of all beauty, it now lies prostrate like a giant corpse, decayed and everywhere eaten away.

"Surely this city is to be mourned over which once produced so many illustrious men and emperors, so many leaders in war, which was the nurse of so many excellent rulers, the parent of so many and such great virtues, the mother of so many good arts, the city from

which flowed military discipline, purity of morals and
life, the decrees of the law, the models of all the virtues,
and the knowledge of right living. She who was once
mistress of the world is now, by the injustice of fortune,
which overturns all things, not only despoiled of her
empire and her majesty, but delivered over to the basest
servitude, misshapen and degraded, her ruins alone
showing forth her former dignity and greatness. Let
us pass over the empire which was snatched away, the
kingdoms which were broken up, the lost provinces;
both in conferring them and in taking them away fortune exercised her dominion according to her own law.
What, it seems, is more to be lamented is that the lust
of fortune raging within the walls of the city has been
so violent in the work of destruction and devastation
that if one of the early citizens of the ancient city should
come back to life, to behold the men of other times, he
would exclaim that he had long ago dwelt in another
city. For its appearance and the city itself are so demolished that he would recognize almost nothing which
represented the city as it was.

"And indeed, at the nod of fortune, kingdoms are
utterly transformed, empires pass into other hands, nations decline, and peoples are set in motion (for the
fickle mind of man is always seeking something new),
so that it hardly seems unusual that Rome should submit
to her will. Yet truly these buildings of the city, both
public and private, which it seemed would vie with
immortality itself, now in part destroyed entirely, in
part broken and overturned, since very few are left
which preserve their original greatness—these buildings
were believed to lie beyond the reach of fortune. Astounding indeed are her power and inconstancy, which
have brought it about that since the very foundations
of these edifices, which their builders considered beyond

the reach of calamity, have been utterly destroyed, almost nothing is left of such great achievements. For what has the world seen greater than the many buildings of Rome—the temples, the arcades, the baths, the amphitheatres, the aqueducts, the porticos, the palaces —which have suffered her fate, and now of so large a number of splendid edifices none or very few remain?"

Then I answered, "You may well wonder, Antonio, at the injury wrought by fortune on this mother of cities, now so cruelly damaged that, as I wander through it today, surveying it, I am compelled not only to marvel but o lament that almost nothing survives intact, that there are so few remains of the ancient city, and those half-consumed and lying in ruins. For of all the public and private buildings of this once free city, only some few broken remnants are seen. There survive on the Capitoline the double tier of arcades set into a new building, now a receptacle of the public salt, on which is written in very ancient letters, greatly corroded by the moisture of the salt, that Q. Lutatius, Q. F., and Q. Catulus, the consuls, had charge of making the substructure and the *Tabularium;* this is an edifice to be revered for its very antiquity. There is also the sepulchre in the Capitol of C. Poplicius, in which he and his descendants are interred; this was granted for virtue and honour by the decree and order of the Senate. Then there is the bridge across the Tiber to the island, of very ancient construction, which, according to the inscription, was built under the supervision of L. Fabricius C. F., the overseer of the public thoroughfares, and approved by M. F., consul. Also surviving is the arch of Tiburtine stone over the street between the Aventine hill and the bank of the Tiber; this, it is evident from the letters inscribed on it, was constructed and approved by P. Lentulus Scipio and

T. Quinctius Crispinus, at the decree of the Senate. There are also certain early monuments which today are called 'Cimbron,' the temple built by C. Marius from Cimbrian spoils, in which his trophies are still seen. The pyramid set in the walls of the city near the Porta Ostia may be added; this is the noble tomb of C. Cestius, a member of the college of priests, and the letters inscribed on it refer to it as a work completed in one hundred and thirty days, from the will of Ponthus Clamela. I am the more amazed, since this inscription still survives entire, that the most learned Francesco Petrarca wrote in one of his letters that this is the tomb of Remus. . . .

"This will perhaps seem trivial, but it moves me greatly, that to these monuments I may add—of the once almost innumerable *colossi* and statues, of both marble and bronze (for it is less surprising that silver and gold statues were melted down), which were erected in honour of illustrious men because of their greatness of character, not to mention the various figures set up by the state for the sake of art and public enjoyment—only these five marble statues, four in the baths of Constantine, two standing beside horses— the work of Phidias and Praxiteles—two reclining, and the fifth in the forum of Mars, a statue which today bears the name of this forum. And there is only one gilded bronze equestrian statue, which was presented to the Lateran basilica by Septimius Severus. We see that so little has survived that the loss of these monuments alone, if one is concerned with numbers, constitutes the greatest part of the ruin of the city.

"It is indeed most grievous and scarcely to be related without great amazement that this Capitoline hill, once the head and center of the Roman Empire and the citadel of the whole world, before which every king and prince trembled, the hill ascended in triumph by so many emperors and once adorned with the gifts and spoils of so many and such great peoples, the cynosure of all the world, now lies so desolated and ruined, and so changed from its earlier condition, that vines have replaced the benches of the senators, and the Capitol has become a receptacle of dung and filth. Look at the Palatine, and there accuse fortune, which has laid low the palace built by Nero, after the burning of the city, from the plunder of the whole world, and splendidly embellished with the assembled riches of the empire, the dwelling which, enhanced by trees, lakes, obelisks, arcades, gigantic statues, amphitheatres of vari-coloured marble, was admired by all who beheld it; all this is now so ruined that not a shadow remains that can be identified as anything but wild wasteland. Look at the other hills of the city. You see them all lying forsaken, their buildings ruined and overgrown with vines. The forum, which, properly speaking, was the most famous place in the city, after the laws had been passed which called the people together and created the magistracy and the distinguished assembly, has become, by the malignity of fortune, a neglected desert, here the home of pigs and wild deer, and there a vegetable garden."

From *The Inconstancy of Fortune*, in *Latin Writings of the Italian Humanists*, ed. F. A. Gragg (New York: Charles Scribner's Sons, 1927); trans. M.M.M.

The Restoration of Rome

BARTOLOMMEO PLATINA

1460

THEN Pope Nicholas, whether through the weariness of spirit by which he was grievously afflicted after the fall of Constantinople, or by the fever and gout which sorely troubled him, died in the eighth year of his pontificate, in 1455, and was buried in the basilica of St. Peter with the most solemn and honourable pomp. On his sepulchre this epitaph is fittingly inscribed:

Here lie the bones of the fifth pope Nicholas, who restored the golden age to you, O Rome. Illustrious in wisdom, he was more splendid in virtue; learned himself, he favoured learned men. He removed the error by which schism had infected the world; he restored morals, buildings, churches, and homes. Amid the holy ceremonies of the Jubilee, he canonized St. Bernardino of Siena. Upon the head of Frederick, at the same time a bridegroom, he set the golden crown of empire. On Italian affairs he imposed the bond of peace. He had many Greek works translated into the Roman tongue. Cast incense, then, upon his holy tomb!

Praiseworthy indeed is the liberality which he manifested towards everyone, especially towards scholars, whom he supported wonderfully with money and curial offices and benefices. For with rewards he so incited them to public lectures, to the composition of original works, and to the translation of Greek authors into Latin, that Greek and Latin letters, which had then lain hidden in mould and darkness for six hundred

years, have now at last attained a certain splendour.
He also sent cultivated men through all of Europe, to
hunt out industriously those books which had been lost
through the negligence of our ancestors and the plundering of the barbarians. It was thus that Poggio discovered Quintilian, and Enoch of Ascoli the works of
Marcus Caelius Apicius and Pomponius Porphyrio, who
was a distinguished commentator on the works of
Horace.

Pope Nicholas built magnificently and splendidly,
moreover, both in the city and on the Vatican. In Rome
itself he reconstructed the papal palace adjoining Santa
Maria Maggiore. He restored also the church of San
Stefano Rotondo on the Caelian hill; and from its very
foundations he rebuilt the church of San Teodoro, which
is situated on the plain between the Palatine and the
Capitoline hills. The Pantheon, which is a very ancient
temple, built by M. Agrippa and lying in the center of
the city, was rebuilt with a leaden roof. On the Vatican
he sumptuously restored the papal palace in the form
in which we now see it, and after the unsound foundations for the towers had been razed, he began to construct the very high and broad walls of the Vatican and
the greater citadel which was built over them, as a
defence against enemies, so that the papal palace and
the church of St. Peter should not be damaged, as had
often happened before. He also began the great vault
for the apse of St. Peter's, popularly called a tribune,
by which the church itself is made more splendid and
capable of holding more people. He restored the Milvian
bridge and erected a princely palace to house the baths
of Viterbo. And it was by his decree that almost all the
streets of Rome were cleared and paved. . . .

So free of avarice was he that he neither sold any
office nor was he led by the sin of simony to confer any

benefice for a price. Towards those who were deserving he expressed his own gratitude and that of the Church of God. He was a lover of justice, an author and keeper of the peace, merciful to transgressors, and most diligent in the observance of ceremonies; he overlooked nothing which might pertain to our holy religion. There may still be seen the gold and silver vessels, the crosses adorned with jewels, the priestly vestments decorated with gold and pearls, the hangings and tapestries splendidly embroidered with gold and silver, and the pontifical crown; all these display to us the munificence of this man. I pass over the numerous sacred books copied at his command, and bound in gold and silver. And one can now behold the papal library splendidly established by his zeal and liberality.

From *The Life of Pope Nicholas V,* in *Latin Writings of the Italian Humanists,* ed. F. A. Gragg; trans. M.M.M.

The Soul of Man

MARSILIO FICINO

c. 1474

MAN IS really the vicar of God, since he inhabits and cultivates all elements and is present on earth without being absent from the ether. He uses not only the elements, but also all the animals which belong to the elements, the animals of the earth, of the water, and of the air, for food, convenience, and pleasure, and the higher, celestial beings for knowledge and the miracles of magic. Not only does he make use of the animals, he also rules them. It is true, with the

pure rational Angels —
rational/passion Man — Almost Angelic
pure passion Animals

388 THE STUDY OF MAN

weapons received from nature some animals may at times attack man or escape his control. But with the weapons he has invented himself man avoids the attacks of wild animals, puts them to flight, and tames them. Who has ever seen any human beings kept under the control of animals, in such a way as we see everywhere herds of both wild and domesticated animals obeying men throughout their lives? Man not only rules the animals by force, he also governs, keeps, and teaches them. Universal providence belongs to God, who is the universal cause. Hence man who provides generally for all things, both living and lifeless, is a *kind* of god. Certainly he is the god of the animals, for he makes use of them all, rules them all, and instructs many of them. It is also obvious that he is the god of the elements, for he inhabits and cultivates all of them. Finally, he is the god of all materials, for he handles, changes, and shapes all of them. He who governs the *body* in so many and so important ways, and is the vicar of the immortal God, he is no doubt immortal.

But these arts, although they shape the material of the world, rule the animals, and thus imitate God the artisan of nature, are yet inferior to those arts which, imitating the divine rule, take care of human government. Individual animals are hardly capable of taking care of themselves or their young. Man alone abounds in such a perfection that he first rules himself, something that no animals do, and thereafter rules the family, administers the state, governs nations, and rules the whole world. As if he were born to rule, he is unable to endure any kind of slavery. Moreover, he undergoes death for the common weal, a thing which no animal does. For man despises these mortal blessings, being confident in the firmness of the common and eternal good.

Some may think that these arts pertain to the present life, and that so much care is not necessary for the present life but should be devoted to the imitation of the divine providence. Let us therefore consider those arts which are not only unnecessary for bodily life, but are most harmful to it, such as all the liberal arts, the study of which weakens the body and impedes the comfort of life: the subtle reckoning of numbers, the curious drawing of figures, the obscure movements of lines and the awe-inspiring consonance of music, the long-continued observation of the stars, the inquiry into natural causes, the investigation of things long past, the eloquence of orators and the madness of poets. In all these arts the mind of man despises the service of the body, since the mind is able at times, and can even now begin, to live without the help of the body.

One point above all should be noted, that not every man can understand how and in what manner the skilful work of a clever artisan is constructed, but only he who possesses a like artistic genius. Certainly no one could understand how Archimedes constructed his brazen spheres and gave them motions like the heavenly motions unless he were endowed with a similar genius. He who can understand it because he has a like genius could doubtless, as soon as he has understood it, also construct another, provided he did not lack the proper material. Now, since man has observed the order of the heavens, when they move, whither they proceed and with what measures, and what they produce, who could deny that man possesses as it were almost the same genius as the Author of the heavens? And who could deny that man could somehow also make the heavens, could he only obtain the instruments and the heavenly material, since even now he makes them, though of a different material, but still with a very similar order?

We have shown that our soul in all its acts is trying with all its power to attain the first gift of God, that is, the possession of all truth and all goodness. Does it also seek His second attribute? Does not the soul try to become everything just as God is everything? It does in a wonderful way; for the soul lives the life of a plant when it serves the body in feeding it; the life of an animal, when it flatters the senses; the life of a man, when it deliberates through reason on human affairs; the life of the heroes, when it investigates natural things; the life of the daemons, when it speculates on mathematics; the life of the angels, when it inquires into the divine mysteries; the life of God, when it does everything for God's sake. Every man's soul experiences all these things in itself in some way, although different souls do it in different ways, and thus the human species strives to become all things by living the lives of all things. This is what Hermes Trismegistus was admiring when he said: Man is a great miracle, a living creature worthy of reverence and adoration, for he knows the genus of the daemons as if he were by nature related to them, and he transforms himself into God as if he were God himself.

Moreover, all things that exist, insofar as they exist, are true; and insofar as they possess some force, order, and purpose they are good. We have already shown that the soul seeks all true and all good things. Hence it seeks all things. What else does the soul seek except to know all things through the intellect and to enjoy them all through the will? In both ways it tries to become all things. One of the senses, for instance, sight, cannot perceive colours unless it assumes the forms of those colours, and unless a single thing is produced from the power of seeing and the actualizing of the

visible form, just as a single thing is produced from air
and light. In the same way the intellect does not know
things themselves unless it is clothed with the forms of
the things to be known, and unless a single thing results from the power of thinking and the actualizing of
the intelligible form, and their union is accompanied
by a single action. . . .

Finally, since the mind is more excellent than matter,
it also receives and unites to itself the desired form
much more effectively than does matter. We must not
believe that the mind is less able to unite to itself what
it takes in than is the body. For the body transforms
the most diverse foods, the soul digesting them. The
mind also transforms into itself what it receives or conceives, and much more so. For corporeal extension prevents a mutual union in bodies, whereas spiritual things
are much more adapted to union. Hence, according to
Plotinus, the ideas (*rationes*) of things intellectually
known pass into the substance of the intellect much
more than do foods into the substance of the body. . . .

To conclude, our soul by means of the intellect and
will, as by those twin Platonic wings, flies toward God,
since by means of them it flies toward all things. By
means of the intellect it attaches all things to itself; by
means of the will, it attaches itself to all things. Thus
the soul desires, endeavours, and begins to become
God, and makes progress every day. Every movement
directed towards a definite end first begins, then proceeds, then gradually increases and makes progress, and
is finally perfected. It is increased through the same
power through which it was begun; it makes progress
through the same power through which it was increased; and finally, it is perfected through the same
power through which it made progress. Hence our soul

will sometime be able to become in a sense all things; and even to become a god.⌟

From *Platonic Theology*, trans. by J. L. Burroughs, *Journal of the History of Ideas*, April 1944.

The Immortality of the Soul

PIETRO POMPONAZZI

1516

Now I hold that the beginning of our consideration should be made at this point. Man is clearly not of simple but of multiple, not of certain but of ambiguous (*ancipitis*) nature, and he is to be placed as a mean between mortal and immortal things. This is plain to see if we examine his essential operations, as it is from such operations that essences are made known. For in performing the functions of the vegetative and of the sensitive soul, which, as is said in *De anima*, Book II, and in *De generatione animalium*, Book II, chapter 3, cannot be performed without a bodily and perishable instrument, man assumes mortality. However, in knowing and willing, operations which throughout the whole *De anima* and in *De partibus animalium*, Book I, chapter 1, and in *De generatione animalium*, Book II, chapter 3, are held to be performed without any bodily instrument, since they prove separability and immateriality, and these in turn prove immortality, man is to be numbered among the immortal things. From these facts the whole conclusion can be drawn, that man is clearly not of a simple nature, since he includes three souls, so to speak—the vegetative, the sensitive, and the intellective—and that he claims a twofold nature for himself, since he exists neither unqualifiedly (*simpliciter*) mortal nor unqualifiedly immortal but embraces both natures.

Therefore the ancients spoke well when they established man between eternal and temporal things for the reason that he is neither purely eternal nor purely temporal, since he partakes of both natures. And to man, who thus exists as a mean between the two, power is given to assume whichever nature he wishes. Hence there are three kinds of men to be found. Some are numbered with the gods, although such are but few. And these are the men who, having subjugated the vegetative and the sensitive, have become almost completely rational. Some from total neglect of the intellect and from occupying themselves with the vegetative and the sensitive alone, have changed as it were, into beasts. And perhaps this is what the Pythagorean fable means when it says that men's souls pass into different beasts. Some are called normal men; and these are the ones who have lived tolerably according to the moral virtues. They have not, however, devoted themselves entirely to the intellect or held entirely aloof from the bodily powers. Each of these two latter sorts has a wide range, as is plain to see. With this agrees what is said in the Psalm: "Thou hast made him but a little lower than the angels," etc. . . .

And it must be considered that many men have thought the soul mortal who nevertheless have written that it is immortal. But they did so on account of the proneness to evil of men who have little or no intellect, and neither knowing nor loving the goods of the soul devote themselves to bodily things alone. Whence it is

necessary to cure them by devices of this sort, just as
the physician acts towards the sick man and the nurse
towards the child lacking reason.

By these reasons, I think, other points also can be
resolved. For although it is commonly said that, if the
soul is mortal, man ought to give himself over completely to bodily pleasures, commit all evils for his own
advantage, and that it would be vain to worship God,
to honour the divine, to pour forth prayers to God,
to make sacrifices, and do other things of this sort,
the answer is clear enough from what has been said.
For since happiness is naturally desired and misery
shunned, and by what has been said happiness consists in virtuous action, but misery in vicious action,
since to worship God with the whole mind, to honour
the divine, to raise prayers to God, to sacrifice are
actions in the highest degree virtuous, we ought hence
to strive with all our powers to acquire them. But on
the contrary, thefts, robberies, murders, a life of pleasures are vices, which make man turn into a beast and
cease to be a man; hence we ought to abstain from
them. And note that one who acts conscientiously, expecting no other reward than virtue, seems to act far
more virtuously and purely than he who expects some
reward beyond virtue. And he who shuns vice on
account of the foulness of vice, not because of the fear
of due punishment for vice, seems more to be praised
than he who avoids vice on account of the fear of
punishment, as in the verses:

> The good hate sin from love of virtue,
> The evil hate sin from fear of punishment.

Wherefore those who claim that the soul is mortal
seem better to save the grounds of virtue than those
who claim it to be immortal. For the hope of reward

and the fear of punishment seem to suggest a certain servility, which is contrary to the grounds of virtue, etc. . . .

Now since these things are so, it seems to me that in this matter, keeping the saner view, we must say that the question of the immortality of the soul is a neutral problem, like that of the eternity of the world. For it seems to me that no natural reasons can be brought forth proving that the soul is immortal, and still less any proving that the soul is mortal, as very many scholars who hold it immortal declare. Wherefore I do not want to make answer to the other side, since others do so, St. Thomas in particular, clearly, fully, and weightily. Wherefore we shall say, as Plato said in the *Laws* I, that to be certain of anything, when many are in doubt, is for God alone. Since therefore such famous men disagree with each other, I think that this can be made certain only through God. . . .

Wherefore, if any arguments seem to prove the mortality of the soul, they are false and merely seeming, since the first light and the first truth show the opposite. But if any seem to prove its immortality, they are true and clear, but not light and truth. Wherefore this way alone is most firm, unshaken, and lasting; the rest are untrustworthy.

From "On the Immortality of the Soul," trans. by W. H. Hay II in E. Cassirer et al., *The Renaissance Philosophy of Man* (Chicago: University of Chicago Press, 1948).

The Life of a Scholar-Printer

ALDUS MANUTIUS

1514-15

TO ANDREA NAVAGERO

All those who devote themselves to the composition of new works, or the restoration and correction of ancient ones, not only for their own benefit but for that of others (for, as Plato has wisely said, we are not born for ourselves alone, but partly for our native land, partly for our parents, and partly for our friends), all those, I say, need peace and quiet, and betake themselves from the concourse and company of men into solitude, as into harbour. For the sacred studies of letters and the Muses themselves always require leisure and solitude, and especially when one would write works which he wishes to be "worthy of being smeared with cedar oil and preserved in smooth cypress." This indeed you, my Navagero, have done frequently and happily; for, leaving the city and the company of men, you take yourself off to the country, to places ruled by peace and tranquility, as in former years to the laurel and olive groves of Lake Garda, "when the gates of war, grim with iron and close-fitting bars, have been closed." There, free of all those cares and troubles which hinder the excellent studies of letters, "such music makest thou as the Cynthian god modulates with fingers pressed upon his well-skilled lyre."

But as for me, there are two things especially, not to mention some six hundred others, which interrupt and hinder my zealous studies: first of all, the numerous letters of learned men which are sent to me from all over. If I were to answer them, I would spend all my days and nights writing letters. Then there are those who visit me, some to greet me, some to find out what is new, and others (and this is by far the largest number) for lack of anything else to do—for then they say, "Let's go to see Aldus." They come in droves and sit around idly, "like a leech that will not let go the skin, till gorged with blood." I pass over those who come to recite their poetry, or some prose composition they want published by our press, and this very often clumsy and unpolished, since they "cannot brook the toil and tedium of the file," and they put off giving their attention to the poem which should be corrected, which "many a day and many a blot has not restrained and refined ten times over to meet the test of perfection."

I have begun at last to protect myself from those who pester and interrupt me. For to those who write to me I either reply not at all, when the letter is not very interesting, or, if it is important, I answer very briefly. Since I do this not from pride or rudeness, but simply so that I may use whatever time I have in publishing good books, I ask that no one should take it too hard, but accept it in the spirit in which I do it. And so that those who come to say "hello," or for any other reason, may not continue to interrupt my work and serious study, I have taken care to warn them, by putting up a notice, like an edict, on the door of my office, to this effect:

WHOEVER YOU ARE, ALDUS BEGS YOU ONCE AND FOR ALL TO STATE BRIEFLY WHAT YOU WANT, AND THEN LEAVE QUICKLY, UNLESS YOU HAVE COME, LIKE HERCULES, TO SUPPORT THE WEARY ATLAS ON YOUR SHOULDERS, FOR

THAT IS WHAT YOU WILL DO WHEN YOU ENTER THIS WORKSHOP

But, on the other hand, there are men who are learned in both Greek and Latin, who by frequent and diligent visits to my office render Herculean service to me. Of these you, most excellent Navagero, have enabled me to rest as Atlas did, by your most accurate collation of these very books of Cicero, *On Precepts for Orators,* and *On Fullness of Expression,* and *On the Study of Eloquence,* with those ancient manuscripts which have been discovered. And now you are zealously performing the same task with his orations and his divine books on philosophy, and so felicitously that soon some of these, which for a long time were only to be found here and there, may go out into the hands of scholars in a more correct form. I do not say how diligently, how skilfully, how learnedly you have been untiring in correcting, by the good exemplars which you possess, not only certain prose works, but especially the best works of the poets, which you have most kindly promised to give to me, such is your generosity and your love of good letters, because, when they are finished, I want to publish them from my press.

Indeed, you have often urged me, even saying: "Aldus, what are you thinking of? Why don't you ask me for Vergil, Horace, Tibullus, Ovid, and others? You can hardly believe how carefully I have emended them from ancient manuscripts!" Thus you have so bound me to you that I love you not less than myself, and I greatly desire a very long life for both of us. For, since as a young man you have become so accomplished in both prose and poetry that you are almost the equal of those ancients who won the highest praise for their work in both forms, I do not doubt that you will be the greatest ornament of our age, and, with our Bembo, "another hope of great Rome."

Although it does not escape me that you, in your modesty, will not listen to this willingly, yet because I know that I speak the truth and because you know from your own experience how very rightly that famous phrase "Know thyself" is used not only to lessen arrogance, but also that we may become aware of our blessings, I wish to speak thus to you about yourself, following the example of many and learned men. And not to mention others, both Greek and Roman, who were wont to do this very thing, Pliny the Younger—in that most skilful and divine panegyric which, when he was about to begin his consulship under the Emperor Trajan, he delivered to the assembled Senate—thought it most honourable and appropriate to utter the highest praises of that emperor in his presence, because he knew both that these were certainly very true and that this ruler was fully aware of his own virtues. For Trajan was not only an emperor but the best of men. Whence it is that now, when an emperor is being crowned, they say this to him first of all: "May you be happier than Augustus and better than Trajan." It may be added that our epistles or prefaces are of such a kind that it seems to us proper, for the same reason, that although we seem to write privately to one man, we nevertheless write publicly for all who read our words in friendly fashion. For this reason also, we consider it permissible to say something to him to whom we are writing, by way of introduction concerning those works to which we add epistles or prefaces of this kind—not in order to instruct him (for this would be arrogant), but so that he may examine our words, and may be their judge, and so that those who do not know these things (for we want always to make

them known) may learn them from us. We have resolved, therefore, that this should be done here. And
we have chosen you, most learned Navagero, as judge,
both for other reasons and because you know, as well
as you know your own fingers and fingernails, the matters which are treated in these books on the knowledge
of speaking. For those works that at great pains we
have prepared for publication we ought to recite or
submit in writing to those who are qualified to praise
them if they are good, and to criticize them if they
are bad, as Quintilian used to have poems recited to
him, and would say, when he did not approve of something, "Pray correct this and that." . . .

You then, my Navagero, will readily allow us to say
these things to you, since you are at once very learned
and very kind, and also because when they are said to
you they are spoken to all those into whose hands these
books of ours may come. You will, therefore, read the
brief introductory discussions we have written for these
books of Cicero, and not reproachfully, as Hannibal did
Phormio (as a barbarian indeed), but you will let me
off kindly, as you usually do, when you have read
them. . . .

I regard what I have said about these works as written casually. For I have been even more pressed and
harassed by business than perhaps anyone else. May
God help me and deliver me from these wicked and
most grievous vexations by which I am pursued, and
may He ordain that, when my lands have been lost and
I thus lament:

Behold to what a pass strife has brought our unhappy citizens! For these have we sown our fields!

or thus:

We have lived to see the day—an evil never dreamed—when a stranger, holder of our little farm, could say, "This is mine, begone, ye old tenants!"

you, who are also a divine poet (for you are another like Vergil), will sing these lines, or others like them, to console me, your compatriot:

Happy old man, so these lands will still be yours . . . and you will be allowed to quit your long slavery, and elsewhere find the gods ready to aid you.

For after I have finally reached the point when like Sisyphus I have at last brought to the summit of the mountain the rock which I have untiringly rolled for so many years, "lying under the spreading beech's shade," I myself may be able to say, "It is a god who wrought for us this peace."

"Preface to Cicero's *De arte rhetorica*," in *Latin Writings of the Italian Humanists*, ed. F. A. Gragg; trans. M.M.M.

On the New Testament

ERASMUS OF ROTTERDAM

1516

TO HENRY BULLOCK

I AM TRULY glad to hear that the New Testament, as restored by our industry, is approved at Cambridge by the best people; although I have been told by some credible persons that one of the most theological of your colleges, composed of pure Areopagites, has passed a serious resolution that no one shall either by horse, or boat, or cart, or porter bring that volume within the precincts of the college. I beseech you, most learned Bullock, ought one to laugh or weep over such proceedings?

They say it is wrong to attempt such a work unless by the authority of a general council. But I should like to have an answer from them to this question. Was that very version, of which they are so fond, undertaken by the translator under the authority of a general council, or was it first published, and afterwards approved by the judgment of the Fathers? I believe it was written first, and approved afterwards; and the same may take place with respect to my edition, though that is a thing I neither solicit nor expect. But I have conceded too much; it is more probable that the received version crept into use, and only gained strength by the progress of time. For if it had been approved and promulgated by the public judgment of a council, it would have been in universal use. As it is, one text is cited by Ambrose, another by Augustine, another by Hilary, and another by Jerome. Indeed the copies now in use do not agree. So that, if they think the Christian religion is upset if there is any variation in any part of the book, we were already subject to that risk, though we may have been sleeping through it.

But, say they, the received version is used by the Fathers in their synods. But it remains to be proved that the passages cited in the acts of councils differ from our emendation; while it must be remembered that most of the proceedings of councils were conducted in Greek. And finally it may well be that passages originally cited in another form have been changed by some copyist to our present version, as we constantly find has been done in the Commentaries of Jerome and Ambrose. About twenty years ago the

Missal and Book of Hours were being printed at Paris according to the usage of the Church of Treves; but the printer, who had but a smattering of learning, when he found there were many discrepancies, corrected everything according to our usual version, as he himself confessed to me, thinking he was doing a fine thing! Again, I do not think it absurd to suppose that an error may pass unnoticed by a general council, especially in matters not necessary to salvation. It is enough that what is enacted in the synod itself cannot be censured. Finally, why are we more alarmed at a various reading in the Sacred Books than we are at a various interpretation? Surely there is equal danger in both cases. And we constantly find that the explanations given are not only different but conflicting.

Again, let them clear up, if they can, this dilemma. Do they allow any change to be made in the sacred text, or absolutely none at all? If any, why not first examine whether a change is rightly made or not? If none, what will they do with those passages where the existence of an error is too manifest to be concealed? Will they desire to follow the example of the priest who, having been used to say *mumpsimus* for twenty years, refused to change his practice when told that he ought to read *sumpsimus?*

Suppose I had explained all the Sacred Books in a Paraphrase, so that they might, without injury to the sense, be read with less stumbling and be more easily apprehended, would your friends bring me to book for this? Juvencus, who ventured to turn the Gospel history into verse, gained some praise by his work. And who calls to account that great divine, Aegidius Delphus, who embraced almost all the Scriptures in a poem? The Psalms are sung every day in church according to the old edition; and yet there is Jerome's recension, and also his translation after the Hebrew original. The former is read in choirs, the latter in schools or at home; and the one does not interfere with the other. Indeed Felix Pratensis has lately issued a new translation of the whole Psalter, differing considerably from all the former ones, and who has raised any outcry against him? My friend, Jacques Lefèvre of Étaples, had already done for St. Paul what I have done for the whole New Testament; and why are some people disturbed on this occasion, as if nothing of the kind had happened before? Do they intend to refuse to me alone a liberty they allow to everyone else? Lefèvre, however, has ventured much further than I. He has set up his own translation in opposition to the old, and that in Paris, the queen of all the universities. I, professing only to be a reviser, either correct or explain a few passages. In saying this, I have no intention of casting any reflection upon Lefèvre, who by his high reputation has long raised himself above reflection; I wish only to make it manifest, how unfair it is, when a thing has been constantly done by a number of people without any blame, to reproach me for doing it, as if it were something unprecedented.

What have the Aristotelians lost, since Argyropulos, Leonardus Aretinus, and Theodorus Gaza brought out a new edition? Will it be held that their version ought to be suppressed or abolished, to save those earlier professors of Aristotelian philosophy from the appearance of having been ignorant of some particulars? Or is William Cop prevented from translating the books of Galen and Hippocrates by the fear of letting the world know that former physicians have put a false interpretation on many passages?

But it will be said that what is expedient in human science is a serious danger, if applied to the Sacred

Books in all parts and by anyone who pleases. Now in the first place I do not change all parts, for there is only a question about a few passages, the main substance remaining unaltered. Neither do I quite think that I am to be regarded, with reference to this matter, as one of the ordinary crowd. I show how in some places Hilary has been mistaken. So of Augustine, and Thomas Aquinas. And this I do, as it ought to be done, reverently and without contumely, so that, if they were themselves alive, they would thank me, whatever I might be, for setting them right in such a way. They were men of the highest worth, but they were men. Let my opponents prove that they were right, and refute me by argument, and I shall be greatly obliged to them.

But they think it beneath them to descend to these small details of grammarians. For so they call those who have learned Good Letters, thinking the name of grammarian a severe reproach, as if it were a credit to a theologian not to know grammar. It is true that the mere knowledge of grammar does not make a theologian; still less does ignorance of it; and certainly some scholarship conduces to a knowledge of theology, while the want of it impedes such knowledge. Indeed it cannot be denied that Jerome, Ambrose, and Augustine, on whose authority our theological system mainly rests, belonged to the class of grammarians. For at that time Aristotle had not yet been received in the theological schools, and the Philosophy which is now in use there was not yet born. But a modest man will not object to be set right by anyone. "Though he be blind that shows the way, you still may pay him some regard," as Flaccus says.

Again, those who make the whole question depend not on judgment but on authority cannot find any great

defect in my case. It was provided in the late Lateran
Council that a book, before it is published, shall be
approved by the Ordinary or his delegates. Now our
book was both written and published with the knowledge and approbation of the bishop of the place, and
that no common bishop, but one who, not to speak of
the reverence due to his age or of the dignity of his
birth, is distinguished by a singular integrity of life
and no common learning. Indeed he not only approved
my work but made me every possible offer, if I had
been willing to remain with him; and when I left,
pursued me with such kind offices and with so much
munificence that I am ashamed to recall the circumstances. Not content with this, he wrote of his own
accord to the Archbishop of Canterbury, both commending me in most honourable terms and thanking
him on my behalf. So that, if my labour has not been
approved by a synod, it has at any rate been approved
according to the ordinance of a synod. And the person
approving is of such authority that he alone may well
stand in the place of many; while his vote ought to
have all the more weight, as it was not obtained by
any solicitation or obsequious attentions, but was spon-
taneously offered and almost forced upon me. And if
the authority of a single person is wanting in weight,
the bishop's judgment has been backed by two professors of theology, who are at the head of that profession. One of these is Louis Bère, a man so practised in
the theological arena as to have earned the first place
at Paris among the doctors of that faculty. He disap-
proved our work so much that he offered to share with
me all his fortune, which is most ample; and has spon-
taneously put at my disposal one of the two prebends
which he holds. The other is Wolfgang [Capito], who
on account of his distinguished theological knowledge

has been chosen one of the Chapter of Basel Cathedral, where he fills the office of public preacher, a man who, besides other accomplishments, is pre-eminently skilled in three tongues, Greek, Latin, and Hebrew, and finally is a person of so much integrity and piety that I have never seen anything more stainless. These were the witnesses to the publication of my book, in whose judgment the bishop upon the gravest matter would not hesitate to confide, if he was not certain of his own.

Neither indeed have any other theologians condemned our work. Only some have lamented that they did not learn Greek when they were boys, and that for them the book has come into the world too late. . . .

We sent last winter one volume to Leo [Pope Leo X], to whom it is dedicated, and if it has been delivered, I do not doubt that he will requite our vigils with the highest rewards.

What is it, then, that these people find deficient in me? I have not been the first to take this matter in hand; I have not done it without consideration; and I have followed the rule of the synod. If anyone is influenced by learning, my work is approved by the most learned; if by virtue, it is approved by the most upright; if by authority, it is approved by bishops, by archbishops, by the pope himself. Nevertheless I do not desire to obtain any advantage from their support, if it be found that I have solicited the favour of any of them. Whatever support is given, has been given to the cause, and not to the man.

Are your friends perhaps afraid that, if students are attracted to these subjects, their schools will be emptied? Let them take these facts into consideration. About thirty years ago nothing was taught at Cambridge but Alexander, the *Parva Logicalia*, as they are called, those old "dictates" of Aristotle, and questions from Scotus. In process of time Good Letters were introduced; the study of Mathematics was added, and a new or at least a renovated Aristotle. Then came some acquaintance with Greek, and with many authors, whose very names were unknown to the best scholars of a former time. Now I ask, what has been the result to the university? It has become so flourishing that it may vie with the first schools of the age, and possesses men compared with whom those old teachers appear mere shadows of theologians. This is not denied by the senior men, where you find any of a candid character. They congratulate others on their good fortune, and lament their own infelicity.

Are your friends displeased that in future the Gospels and Apostolic Epistles will be read by more persons and with more attention? Are they grieved to see even this portion of time devoted to studies, on which all our time would be well bestowed? And would they prefer that our whole life should be consumed in the useless subtleties of "Questions"? Is it not well to recall such divines to the original sources?

I have a sure presentiment that posterity will form a more candid judgment of my lucubrations, such as they are; though I have no cause to complain even of my own age. It has rated me higher—I do not say than I ask, but than I either deserve or can justify.

I approve of your having adopted the practice of public preaching, and congratulate you on your success, especially as you teach Christ in simplicity, without any display of the subtleties of men.

Epistle 441, from *The Epistles of Erasmus*, trans. F. M. Nichols (London: Longmans, Green & Co., 1904).

Pythagoras Reborn

JOHANN REUCHLIN

1517

TO POPE LEO X

Most blessed Pope Leo X, the Italian philosophy of
the Christian religion, which was once handed down
from Pythagoras, the first parent of its fame, to great
men of excellent minds, submitted for many years to the
loud barking of the sophists, and lay buried for a long
time in darkness and dense night, until by the favour
of the gods there rose the Sun of all the best kinds of
studies, your renowned father, Lorenzo de' Medici, the
successor of the great Cosimo as ruler of Florence. . . .

After I had come to Italy with the distinguished
Eberhardus Probus, in our time the first Duke of Würt-
temberg, I entered Florence with him in April 1482.
Whenever I would praise to the duke the remarkable
nobility of the Medici family, as to tell the truth I certainly should have done, he would wish to converse
with Lorenzo himself. When Lorenzo discovered this—
I do not know who told him—he grasped the hand of
the stranger with great kindness and took us all to his
home, and showed us everything worth seeing: first, the
well-built stables for the horses, then the arsenal furnished with all the equipment of war, and after this
the individual chambers hung with the most precious
tapestries and covered with beautiful carpets, and on
the lofty ceiling a grove planted with trees, the gardens
of Hesperides and the golden apples. And when I

praised his library to the skies, he answered very courteously, as this sweetest of men used to do, that "his greatest treasures were his children rather than his books."

I beg you, most holy Father, to permit me, the lowliest of men, a man of the people, to speak to you somewhat more freely. How powerfully, do you think, was I moved by both admiration and the greatest joy when I heard that you, the noblest son of the best and wisest prince, the divine Lorenzo de' Medici, had ascended amid universal acclaim to the highest dignity of the papal throne, and, like a high priest, I immediately remembered that paternal saying as a true prophecy!

For what blossom of the Laurentian laurel could be more precious than you, not only to the Roman people but to all the world? What greater treasure could be imagined than your ineffable reign, in which all riches flow upon us like the golden sands of Pactolus, in which all the best letters, and everything that is good in human affairs, are honoured? Your father sowed the seeds of all ancient philosophy, which now in you, his son, grow to maturity, so that in your reign we may be allowed to reap their fruit in all the languages, Greek, Latin, Hebrew, Arabic, and Chaldean. For at this time books are dedicated to your Holiness in these languages, and all those things which were most wisely begun by your father are more fruitfully accomplished under your authority.

Considering, therefore, that scholars lacked only the Pythagorean works, which still lay hidden, dispersed here and there in the Laurentian Academy, I believed that you would hardly be displeased if I should make public the doctrines which Pythagoras and the noble Pythagoreans are said to have held, so that these works which up to now have remained unknown to the Latins may be read at your happy command. Marsilio has prepared Plato for Italy, Lefèvre d'Étaples has restored Aristotle for the French, and I, Reuchlin, shall complete the group, and explain to the Germans the Pythagoras who has been reborn through my efforts, in the work which I have dedicated to your name. But this task could not be accomplished without the cabala of the Jews, because the philosophy of Pythagoras had its origins in the precepts of the cabala, and when in the memory of our ancestors it disappeared from Magna Graecia, it lived again in the volumes of the cabalists. Then all these works were almost completely destroyed. I have therefore written *On the Cabalistic Art,* which is symbolical philosophy, so that the doctrines of the Pythagoreans might be made better known to scholars. About these doctrines I affirm nothing, but I simply present a dialogue between Philolaus Junior, a Pythagorean, and Marranus, a Moslem, who came together from their various travels in an inn at Frankfort to listen to Simon the Jew, a man highly trained in the cabala. . . .

In this brief compendium by your humble servant, Reuchlin, you have, most holy Pope Leo, the opinions and doctrines contained in the symbolical philosophy of Pythagoras and the cabala of the wise ancients. Although they are few in number, these doctrines offer to scholars an opportunity to investigate and speculate much more fully. As a man of mediocre talents and little prudence, I should not have dared to judge these, nor have I judged them wisely. But I submit this entire book to your authority, in whose judgment the censure of the whole world is united, so that you may reject what is displeasing, and then I shall rejoice that the rest has pleased you. You will be able to determine that I have undertaken this task for our own sake and for that of the commonwealth, and I trust that it will not seem to you wholly without merit, since my labour may make ideas which were hitherto unknown accessible to our people. Through their reading of these works, I may attempt in half a year to lighten, if I cannot escape it entirely, this five-year-long war, which, as you know, my enemies have waged against me. Then, finally, you will have some work of mine at hand to make you think of me more kindly, when my enemies strive to cut off or to avert your paternal spirit from me.

For they will not cease, I know, to besiege your pious ears with whispers, now through hired agents, and again by means of letters like those which, as I mentioned above, were sent to you in October from Cologne, bearing both a false accusation and a title that lies about the author. It is not the well-beloved city of Cologne or its venerable university that commits this crime, but only a part of it, and indeed its dregs, a remarkable offscouring of hostile spirits, the least part of the city and the more foolish and violent, who assert to your Holiness things that are not true, and who do this against the apostolic prohibitions and against the peace established by the emperor. You can see how audaciously, in these same letters, they presume to dictate laws to you, as if they were Solons, and to instruct you, who are the fount of law, how you must proceed to judge me according to their command and will, in order to beat me down into the dirt—as if my innocence were not held as proved by almost the whole world.

I cannot bring myself to suspect, therefore, that you will put your faith in these men who, in contempt of the apostolic prohibition and your censures, and hardly observing the process of law, have burned my book while the case was pending. But you will believe instead the more important men of Germany, greater in every higher judgment, that I have caused no scandal, that I have prepared no occasion of ruin for any of the German people, who are joined to me in fellowship by a common language. . . . Indeed, you have been made more certain of my innocence, piety, faith, and integrity by the letters, sealed and worthy of trust, which have been written by very many of the most distinguished rulers of the broad territories of our nation, by magistrates, and by the German people, and by the most holy bishops of our dioceses, and by the towns and cities. You have in hand testimonies concerning my innocence, which were sent to you three or four times by the invincible Maximilian, Emperor of the Romans, and from the most reverend Cardinal, my Lord of Gurk. . . .

If you will remember the testimony and the oaths of all those men everywhere whom I have mentioned, and also if you will order the decrees of the judges to be read in your presence, you will surely find me far from guilty of any charge made by my accusers. Almost the whole city of Rome leaps to proclaim my innocence, and all the learned men of all nations, from whom I daily receive letters declaring that I have never been an occasion of scandal to any man in my writings, but rather that in various languages I have striven to establish the Church in the Holy Spirit, which, through the diversity of all languages, has assembled the peoples in the unity of faith. These men observe truly that I, first of all, brought Greek to Germany, and that I, before anyone else in the universal Church, presented and taught the art and studies of the Hebrew language. I trust, therefore, that I shall not hope in vain that my merits will not be displeasing to the future members of the Church, and that you, most blessed Pope Leo, the present judge of deeds rather than words, will justly restore peace and tranquillity of soul to me, because of my many and difficult labours for the orthodox faith. . . . If then you do not wish me to surrender to the constant persecution of the wicked in this life, I shall rejoice most heartily to seem worthy of your confidence, I who have suffered such great wrongs for our Christ.

From *Johann Reuchlins Briefwechsel*, ed. L. Geiger (Tübingen, 1875); trans. M.M.M.

Gargantua's Advice to Pantagruel

FRANÇOIS RABELAIS

1532

PANTAGRUEL studied very hard, you may be sure of that, and profited greatly from it; for he had a two-fold understanding, while his memory was as capacious as a dozen casks and flagons of olive oil. And while he was residing there, he received one day a letter from his father, which read as follows:

My very dear Son:

Among all the gifts, graces, and prerogatives with which that sovereign plastician, Almighty God, has endowed and adorned human nature in its beginnings, it seems to me the peculiarly excellent one is that by means of which, in the mortal state, one may acquire a species of immortality, and in the course of a transitory life be able to perpetuate his name and his seed. This is done through that line that issues from us in legitimate marriage. By this means, there is restored to us in a manner that which was taken away through the sin of our first parents, of whom it was said that, inasmuch as they had not been obedient to the commandment of God the Creator, they should die, and that through their death, the magnificent plastic creation which man had been should be reduced to nothingness. By this means of seminal propagation, there remains for the children that which was lost to the parents, and for the grandchildren that which, otherwise, would have perished with the children; and so, successively, down to the hour of the last judgment, when Jesus Christ shall have rendered to God the Father His specific realm, beyond all danger and contamination of sin; for then shall cease all begettings and corruptions, and the elements shall forgo their incessant transmutations, in view of the fact that the peace that is so desired shall then have been consummated and perfected, and all things shall have been brought to their period and their close.

It is not, therefore, without just and equitable cause that I render thanks to God, my Saviour, for having given me the power to behold my hoary old age flowering again in your youth: for when, by the pleasure of Him who rules and moderates all things, my soul shall leave this human habitation, I shall not feel that I am wholly dying in thus passing from one place to another, so long as, in you and through you, my visible image remains in this world, living, seeing, and moving among men of honour and my own good friends, as I was wont to do. My own conduct has been, thanks to the aid of divine grace—not, I confess, without sin,

for we are all sinners, and must be continually be-
seeching God to efface our sins—but at least without
reproach.

For this reason, since my bodily image remains in
you, if the manners of my soul should not likewise
shine there, then you would not be held to have been
the guardian and the treasury of that immortality
which should adhere to our name; and the pleasure I
should take in beholding you would accordingly be
small, when I perceived that the lesser part of me,
which is the body, remained, while the better part,
which is the soul, through which our name is still
blessed among men, had become degenerate and bastardized. I say this, not out of any doubt of your virtue,
of which you have already given me proof, but to encourage you, rather, to profit still further, and to go
on from good to better. And I am now writing you, not
so much to exhort you to live in this virtuous manner,
as to urge you to rejoice at the fact that you are so
living and have so lived, that you may take fresh courage for the future. In order to perfect and consummate
that future, it would be well for you to recall frequently the fact that I have spared no expense on you,
but have aided you as though I had no other treasure
in this world than the joy, once in my life, of seeing
you absolutely perfect in virtue, decency, and wisdom,
as well as in all generous and worthy accomplishments,
with the assurance of leaving you after my death as a
mirror depicting the person of me, your father—if not
altogether as excellent and as well formed an image as
I might wish you to be, still all that I might wish, certainly, in your desires.

But while my late father of blessed memory, Grand-
gousier, devoted all his attention to seeing that I should
profit from and be perfected in political wisdom, and

while my studious labours were equal to his desires
and perhaps even surpassed them, nevertheless, as you
can readily understand, the times were not so propitious
to letters as they are at present and I never had an
abundance of such tutors as you have. The times then
were dark, reflecting the unfortunate calamities brought
about by the Goths who had destroyed all fine literature; but through divine goodness, in my own lifetime
light and dignity have been restored to the art of letters, and I now see such an improvement that at the
present time I should find great difficulty in being received into the first class of little rowdies—I who, in
the prime of my manhood, and not wrongly so, was
looked upon as the most learned man of the century.
I do not say this in any spirit of vain boasting, even
though I might permissibly do so—you have authority
for it in Marcus Tullius, in his book on *Old Age,* as
well as in that maxim of Plutarch's that is to be found
in his book entitled *How One May Praise One's Self
Without Reproach*—but I make the statement, rather,
to give you the desire of climbing higher still.

Now all the branches of science have been re-estab-
lished and languages have been restored: Greek, without which it is a crime for anyone to call himself a
scholar, Hebrew, Chaldaic, and Latin; while printed
books in current use are very elegant and correct. The
latter were invented during my lifetime, through divine
inspiration, just as, on the other hand, artillery was
invented through the suggestion of the devil. The world
is now full of scholarly men, learned teachers, and most
ample libraries; indeed, I do not think that in the time
of Plato, of Cicero, or of Papinian there ever were so
many advantages for study as one may find today. No
one, longer, has any business going out in public or
being seen in company unless he has been well polished

in the workshop of Minerva. I see brigands, hangmen, freebooters, and grooms nowadays who are more learned than were the doctors and preachers of my time. What's this I'm saying? Why, even the women and the girls have aspired to the credit of sharing this heavenly manna of fine learning. Things have come to such a pass that, old as I am, I have felt it necessary to take up the study of Greek, which I had not contemned, like Cato, but which I never had had the time to learn in my youth. And I take a great deal of pleasure now in reading the *Morals* of Plutarch, the beautiful *Dialogues* of Plato, the *Monuments* of Pausanias, and the *Antiquities* of Athenaeus, as I wait for the hour when it shall please God, my Creator, to send for me and to command me to depart this earth.

For this reason, my son, I would admonish you to employ your youth in getting all the profit you can from your studies and from virtue. You are at Paris and you have your tutor, Epistemon; the latter by word-of-mouth instruction, the former by praiseworthy examples, should be able to provide you with an education.

It is my intention and desire that you should learn all languages perfectly: first, the Greek as Quintilian advises; secondly, the Latin; and finally, the Hebrew, for the sake of the Holy Scriptures, along with the Chaldaic and the Arabic, for the same purpose. And I would have you form your style after the Greek, in imitation of Plato, as well as on the Latin, after Cicero. Let there be no bit of history with which you are not perfectly familiar. In this you will find the various works which have been written on cosmography to be of great help.

As for the liberal arts, geometry, arithmetic, and music, I gave you some taste for these while you were still a little shaver of five or six; keep them up; and as for astronomy, endeavour to master all its laws; do not bother about divinatory astrology and the art of Lully, for they are mere abuses and vanities.

As for civil law, I would have you know by heart the best texts and compare them with philosophy.

As for a knowledge of the facts of nature, I would have you apply yourself to this study with such curiosity that there should be no sea, river, or stream of which you do not know the fish; you should likewise be familiar with all the birds of the air, all the trees, shrubs, and thickets of the forest, all the grasses of the earth, all the metals hidden in the bellies of the abysses, and the precious stones of all the East and South: let nothing be unknown to you.

Then, very carefully, go back to the books of the Greek, Arabic, and Latin physicians, not disdaining the Talmudists and the Cabalists, and by means of frequent dissections, see to it that you acquire a perfect knowledge of that other world which is man. And at certain hours of the day, form the habit of spending some time with the Holy Scriptures. First in Greek, the New Testament and the Epistles of the Apostles; and then, in Hebrew, the Old Testament.

In short, let me see you an abysm of science, for when you shall have become a full-grown man, you will have to forsake your quiet life and leisurely studies, to master the art of knighthood and of arms, in order to be able to defend my household and to succour my friends in all their undertakings against the assaults of evildoers.

In conclusion, I would have you make a test, to see how much profit you have drawn from your studies; and I do not believe you can do this in any better fashion than by sustaining theses in all branches of science, in public and against each and every comer, and by keeping the company of the learned, of whom there are as many at Paris as there are anywhere else.

But since, according to the wise Solomon, wisdom does not enter the malevolent soul, and since science without conscience is but the ruin of the soul, it behooves you to serve, love, and fear God and to let all your thoughts and hopes rest in Him, being joined to Him through a faith formed of charity, in such a manner that you can never be sundered from Him by means of sin. Look upon the scandals of the world with suspicion. Do not set your heart upon vain things, for this life is transient but the word of God endures eternally. Be of service to all your neighbours and love them as yourself. Respect your teachers, shun the company of those whom you would not want to be like, and do not receive in vain the graces which God has bestowed upon you. And when you feel that you have acquired all the knowledge that is to be had where you now are, come back to me, so that I may see you and give you my blessing before I die.

My son, may the peace and grace of Our Lord be with you! Amen.

From Utopia, this seventeenth day of the month of March.

Your Father,
Gargantua.

When he had received and read this letter, Pantagruel took fresh courage, and was inflamed to profit more than ever from his studies; to such a degree that, seeing him so study and profit, you would have said that his mind among his books was like a fire among brushwood, so violent was he and so indefatigable.

From *The Portable Rabelais*, selected, translated, and edited by Samuel Putnam (New York: The Viking Press, 1946).

The Orphic Lyre

In Praise of Poetry

GIOVANNI BOCCACCIO

c. 1363

THIS POETRY, which ignorant triflers cast aside, is a sort of fervid and exquisite invention, with fervid expression, in speech or writing, of that which the mind has invented. It proceeds from the bosom of God, and few, I find, are the souls in whom this gift is born; indeed, so wonderful a gift it is that true poets have always been the rarest of men. This fervour of poesy is sublime in its effects: it impels the soul to a longing for utterance; it brings forth strange and unheard-of creations of the mind; it arranges these meditations in a fixed order, adorns the whole composition with unusual interweaving of words and thoughts; and thus it veils truth in a fair and fitting garment of fiction. Further, if in any case the invention so requires, it can arm kings, marshal them for war, launch whole fleets from their docks, nay, counterfeit sky, land, sea, adorn young maidens with flowery garlands, portray human character in its various phases, awake the idle, stimulate the dull, restrain the rash, subdue the criminal, and distinguish excellent men with their proper meed

421

of praise: these, and many other such, are the effects of poetry. Yet if any man who has received the gifts of poetic fervour shall imperfectly fulfil its function here described, he is not, in my opinion, a laudable poet. For, however deeply the poetic impulse stirs the mind to which it is granted, it very rarely accomplishes anything commendable if the instruments by which its concepts are to be wrought out are wanting—I mean, for example, the precepts of grammar and rhetoric, an abundant knowledge of which is opportune. I grant that many a man already writes his mother tongue admirably, and indeed has performed each of the various duties of poetry as such; yet over and above this, it is necessary to know at least the principles of the other Liberal Arts, both moral and natural, to possess a strong and abundant vocabulary, to behold the monuments and relics of the ancients, to have in one's memory the histories of the nations, and to be familiar with the geography of various lands, of seas, rivers, and mountains.

Furthermore, places of retirement, the lovely handiwork of nature herself, are favourable to poetry, as well as peace of mind and desire for worldly glory; the ardent period of life also has very often been of great advantage. If these conditions fail, the power of creative genius frequently grows dull and sluggish.

Now since nothing proceeds from this poetic fervor, which sharpens and illumines the powers of the mind, except what is wrought out by art, poetry is generally called an art. Indeed the word poetry has not the origin that many carelessly suppose, namely *poio, pois,* which is but Latin *fingo, fingis;* rather it is derived from a very ancient Greek word *poetes,* which means in Latin exquisite discourse (*exquisita locutio*). For the first men who, thus inspired, began to employ an exquisite style

of speech, such, for example, as song in an age hitherto
unpolished, to render this unheard-of discourse sonorous
to their hearers, let it fall in measured periods; and lest
by its brevity it fail to please, or, on the other hand,
become prolix and tedious, they applied to it the standard of fixed rules, and restrained it within a definite
number of feet and syllables. Now the product of this
studied method of speech they no longer called by the
more general term poesy, but poem. Thus, as I said
above, the name of the art, as well as its artificial product, is derived from its effect.

Now though I allege that this science of poetry has
ever streamed forth from the bosom of God upon souls
while even yet in their tenderest years, these enlightened cavillers will perhaps say that they cannot trust
my words. To any fair-minded man the fact is valid
enough from its constant recurrence. But for these dul-
lards I must cite witnesses to it. If, then, they will read
what Cicero, a philosopher rather than a poet, says in
his oration delivered before the Senate in behalf of
Aulus Licinius Archias, perhaps they will come more
easily to believe me. He says: "And yet we have it on
the highest and most learned authority, that while
other arts are matters of science and formula and tech-
nique, poetry depends solely upon an inborn faculty,
is evoked by a purely mental activity, and is infused
with a strange supernal inspiration."

But not to protract this argument, it is now sufficiently clear to reverent men that poetry is a practical
art, springing from God's bosom and deriving its name
from its effect, and that it has to do with many high
and noble matters that constantly occupy even those
who deny its existence. If my opponents ask when and
in what circumstances, the answer is plain: the poets
would declare with their own lips under whose help

and guidance they compose their inventions when, for example, they raise flights of symbolic steps to heaven, or make thick-branching trees spring aloft to the very stars, or go winding about mountains to their summits. Haply, to disparage this art of poetry now unrecognized by them, these men will say that it is rhetoric which the poets employ. Indeed, I will not deny it in part, for rhetoric has also its own inventions. Yet, in truth, among the disguises of fiction rhetoric has no part, for whatever is composed as under a veil, and thus exquisitely wrought, is poetry and poetry alone.

From *Boccaccio on Poetry*, trans. C. G. Osgood (Princeton: Princeton University Press, 1930).

Music and the Courtier

BALDASSARE CASTIGLIONE

1528

AT THIS they all laughed. And the Count, beginning afresh: "My lords," said he, "you must think I am not pleased with the Courtier if he be not also a musician, and besides his understanding and cunning upon the book, have skill in like manner on sundry instruments. For if we weigh it well, there is no ease of the labours and medicines of feeble minds to be found more honest and more praiseworthy in time of leisure than it. And principally in courts, where (beside the refreshing of vexations that music brings unto each man) many things are taken in hand to please women withal, whose tender and soft breasts are soon pierced with melody and filled with sweetness. Therefore no marvel that in old times and nowadays they have always been inclined to musicians, and counted this a most acceptable food of the mind."

Then the Lord Gaspar: "I believe music," said he, "together with many other vanities, is meet for women, and peradventure for some also that have the likeness of men, but not for them that be men indeed; who ought not with such delicacies to womanish their minds and bring themselves in that sort to dread death."

"Speak it not," answered the Count. "For I shall enter into a large sea of the praise of music and call to rehearsal how much it has always been renowned among them of old time and counted a holy matter; and how it has been the opinion of most wise philosophers that the world is made of music, and the heavens in their moving make a melody, and our soul framed after the very same sort, and therefore lifts up itself and (as it were) revives the virtues and force of itself with music. Wherefore it is written that Alexander was sometime so fervently stirred with it that (in a manner) against his will he was forced to arise from banquets and run to weapon, afterwards the musician changing the stroke and his manner of tune, pacified himself again and returned from the weapon to banqueting. And I shall tell you that grave Socrates, when he was well stricken in years, learned to play upon the harp. And I remember I have understood that Plato and Aristotle will have a man that is well brought up to be also a musician; and declare with infinite reasons the force of music to be to very great purpose in us, and for many causes (that should be too long to rehearse) ought necessarily to be learned from a man's childhood, not only for the superficial melody that is heard, but to be sufficient to bring into us a new habit that is good and a custom inclining to virtue, which makes the mind more apt to the conceiving of felicity, even as bodily exercise makes the body more lusty, and not only hurts not civil matters and warlike affairs, but is a great stay to them. Also Lycurgus in his sharp laws allowed music. And it is read that the Lacedae-monians, which were valiant in arms, and the Cretenses used harps and other soft instruments; and many most excellent captains of old time (as Epaminondas) gave themselves to music; and such as had not a sight in it (as Themistocles) were a great deal the less set by. Have you not read that among the first instructions which the good old man Chiron taught Achilles in his tender age, whom he had brought up from his nurse and cradle, music was one? And the wise master would have those hands that should shed so much Trojan blood to be oftentimes occupied in playing upon the harp? What soldier is there (therefore) that will think it a shame to follow Achilles, omitting many other famous captains that I could allege?

"Do you not then deprive our Courtier of music, which does not only make sweet the minds of men, but also many times wild beasts tame; and whoso savours it not, a man may assuredly think him not to be well in his wits. Behold, I pray you, what force it has, that in times past allured a fish to suffer a man to ride upon it through the tempestuous sea. We may see it used in the holy temples to render laud and thanks unto God, and it is a credible matter that it is acceptable unto Him, and that He has given it unto us for a most sweet lightening of our travails and vexations. So that many times the boisterous labourers in the fields in the heat of sun beguile their pain with rude and carterlike sing-ing. With this the unmannerly countrywoman that arises before day out of her sleep to spin and card, defends herself and makes her labour pleasant. This is the most sweet pastime after rain, wind, and tempest unto the miserable mariners. With this do the weary pilgrims comfort themselves in their troublesome and long voyages. And oftentimes prisoners in adversity, in fetters, and in stocks. In like manner for a greater proof that the tunableness of music (though it be but rude) is a very great refreshing of all worldly pains and griefs, a man would judge that nature had taught it unto nurses for a special remedy to the continual wailings of sucking babes, which at the sound of their voices fall into a quiet and sweet sleep, forgetting the tears that are so proper to them, and given us of nature in that age for a guess of the rest of our life to come."

Here, the Count pausing awhile, the Lord Julian said: "I am not of the Lord Gaspar's opinion, but I believe for the reasons you allege and for many others, that music is not only an ornament, but also necessary for a Courtier. But I would have you declare how this and the other qualities which you appoint him are to be practised, and at what time, and in what sort. Because many things that of themselves be worthy praise, oftentimes in practising them out of season seem most foolish. And contrariwise, some things that appear to be of small moment, in the well applying them are greatly esteemed."

Sir Frederick laughed; afterwards he proceeded on: ". . . I would not our Courtier should do as many do, that as soon as they come to any place, and also in the presence of great men with whom they have no acquaintance at all, without much entreating, set out themselves to show as much as they know, yea and many times that they know not, so that a man would ween they came purposely to show themselves for that, and that it is their principal profession.

"Therefore let our Courtier come to show his music

as a thing to pass the time withal, and as he were enforced to do it, and not in the presence of noblemen, nor of any great multitude. And for all he be so skilful and does well understand it, yet will I have him to dissemble the study and pains that a man must needs take in all things that are well done. And let him make semblance that he esteems but little in himself that quality, but in doing it excellently well, make it much esteemed of other men."

Then said the Lord Gaspar Pallavicin: "There are many sorts of music, as well in the breast as upon instruments; therefore would I gladly learn which is the best, and at what time the Courtier ought to practise it."

"Methink," then answered Sir Frederick, "pricksong is a fair music, so it be done upon the book surely and after a good sort. But to sing to the lute is much better, because all the sweetness consists in one alone, and a man is much more heedful and understands better the feat manner and the air or vein of it when the ears are not busied in hearing any more than one voice; and besides, every little error is soon perceived, which happens not in singing with company, for one bears out another. But singing to the lute with the ditty (methink) is more pleasant than the rest, for it adds to the words such a grace and strength that it is a great wonder. Also all instruments with frets are full of harmony, because the tunes of them are very perfect, and with ease a man may do many things upon them that fill the mind with the sweetness of music. And the music with a set of viols does no less delight a man, for it is very sweet and artificial. A man's breast gives a great ornament and grace to all these instruments, in the which I will have it sufficient that our Courtier have an understanding. Yet the more cunning he is upon them, the better it is for him, without meddling much with the instruments that Minerva and Alcibiades refused, because it seems they are noisome.

Now as touching the time and season when these sorts of music are to be practised, I believe at all times when a man is in familiar and loving company, having nothing else ado. But especially they are meet to be practised in the presence of women, because those sights sweeten the minds of the hearers and make them the more apt to be pierced with the pleasantness of music, and also they quicken the spirits of the very doers. I am well pleased (as I have said) they flee the multitude, and especially of the unnoble. But the seasoning of the whole must be discretion, because in effect it were a matter impossible to imagine all cases that fall. And if the Courtier be a righteous judge of himself, he shall apply himself well enough to the time and shall discern when the hearers' minds are disposed to give ear and when they are not."

From *The Courtier*, trans. Sir Thomas Hoby (1561).

A Complaint by Night of the Lover Not Beloved

FRANCESCO PETRARCA

Alas, so all things now do hold their peace!
    Heaven and earth disturbèd in no thing;
The beasts, the air, the birds their song do cease,
    The nightès car the stars about doth bring;
Calm is the sea; the waves work less and less:

So am not I, whom love, alas! doth wring,
Bringing before my face the great increase
　Of my desires, whereat I weep and sing,
In joy and woe, as in a doubtful case.
　For my sweet thoughts sometime do pleasure bring;
But by and by, the cause of my disease
　Gives me a pang that inwardly doth sting,
When that I think what grief it is again
To live and lack the thing should rid my pain.

Trans. Henry Howard, Earl of Surrey.

On the Death of the Lady Laura

FRANCESCO PETRARCA

In thought I raised me to the place where she
　Whom still on earth I seek and find not, shines;
　There mid the souls whom the third sphere confines,
　More fair I found her and less proud to me.
She took my hand and said: Here shalt thou be
　With me ensphered, unless desires mislead;
　Lo! I am she who made thy bosom bleed,
　Whose day ere eve was ended utterly:
My bliss no mortal heart can understand;
　Thee only do I lack, and that which thou
　So loved, now left on earth, my beauteous veil.
Ah! wherefore did she cease and loose my hand?
　For at the sound of that celestial tale
　I all but stayed in paradise till now.

Trans. J. A. Symonds.

A Ballata

ANGELO POLIZIANO

I went a roaming, maidens, one bright day,
In a green garden in mid month of May.

Violets and lilies grew on every side
   Mid the green grass, and young flowers wonderful,
Golden and white and red and azure-eyed;
   Toward which I stretched my hands, eager to pull
   Plenty to make my fair curls beautiful,
To crown my rippling curls with garlands gay.

I went a roaming, maidens, one bright day,
In a green garden in mid month of May.

But when my lap was full of flowers I spied
   Roses at last, roses of every hue;
Therefore I ran to pluck their ruddy pride,
   Because their perfume was so sweet and true
   That all my soul went forth with pleasure new.
With yearning and desire too soft to say.

I went a roaming, maidens, one bright day,
In a green garden in mid month of May.

I gazed and gazed. Hard task it were to tell
   How lovely were the roses in that hour:
One was but peeping from her verdant shell,
   And some were faded, some were scarce in flower:

Then Love said: Go, pluck from the blooming bower
Those that thou seest ripe upon the spray.

I went a roaming, maidens, one bright day,
In a green garden in mid month of May.

For when the full rose quits her tender sheath,
  When she is sweetest and most fair to see,
Then is the time to place her in thy wreath,
  Before her beauty and her freshness flee.
  Gather ye therefore roses with great glee,
Sweet girls, or ere their perfume pass away.

I went a roaming, maidens, one bright day,
In a green garden in mid month of May.

Trans. J. A. Symonds.

A Carnival Song

LORENZO DE' MEDICI

Fair is youth and void of sorrow;
  But it hourly flies away.
  Youths and maids, enjoy today;
Nought ye know about tomorrow.

This is Bacchus and the bright
  Ariadne, lovers true!
They, in flying time's despite,
  Each with each find pleasure new;
These their Nymphs, and all their crew
  Keep perpetual holiday.

Youths and maids, enjoy today;
Nought ye know about tomorrow.

These blithe Satyrs, wanton-eyed,
    Of the Nymphs are paramours:
Through the caves and forests wide
    They have snared them mid the flowers;
Warmed with Bacchus, in his bowers,
    Now they dance and leap alway.
    Youths and maids, enjoy today;
Nought ye know about tomorrow.

These fair Nymphs, they are not loth
    To entice their lovers' wiles.
None but thankless folk and rough
    Can resist when Love beguiles.
Now enlaced, with wreathèd smiles,
    All together dance and play.
    Youths and maids, enjoy today;
Nought ye know about tomorrow.

See this load behind them plodding
    On the ass! Silenus he,
Old and drunken, merry, nodding,
    Full of years and jollity;
Though he goes so swayingly,
    Yet he laughs and quaffs alway.
    Youths and maids, enjoy today;
Nought ye know about tomorrow.

Midas treads a wearier measure:
    All he touches turns to gold:
If there be no taste of pleasure,
    What's the use of wealth untold?
What's the joy his fingers hold,

When he's forced to thirst for aye?
Youths and maids, enjoy today;
Nought ye know about tomorrow.

Listen well to what we're saying;
Of tomorrow have no care!
Young and old together playing,
Boys and girls, be blithe as air!
Every sorry thought forswear!
Keep perpetual holiday.
Youths and maids, enjoy today;
Nought ye know about tomorrow.

Ladies and gay lovers young!
Long live Bacchus, live Desire!
Dance and play; let songs be sung;
Let sweet love your bosoms fire;
In the future come what may!
Youths and maids, enjoy today!
Nought ye know about tomorrow.

Fair is youth and void of sorrow;
But it hourly flies away.

Trans. J. A. Symonds.

Astolpho's Journey to the Moon

LUDOVICO ARIOSTO

Canto xxxiv

ARGUMENT

In the infernal pit Astolpho hears
  Of Lydia's woe, by smoke well nigh opprest.
He mounts anew, and him his courser bears
  To the terrestrial paradise addrest.
By John advised in all, to heaven he steers;
  Of some of his lost sense here repossest.
Orlando's wasted wit as well he takes,
  Sees the Fates spin their threads, and earthward
    makes.

.　　.　　.

The chariot, towering, threads the fiery sphere,
  And rises thence into the lunar reign.
This, in its larger part they find as clear
  As polished steel, when undefiled by stain;
And such it seems, or little less, when near,
  As what the limits of our earth contain:
Such as our earth, the last of globes below,
Including seas, which round about it flow.

Here doubly waxed the paladin's surprise,
  To see that place so large, when viewed at hand;
Resembling but a little hoop in size,
  When from the globe surveyed whereon we stand,

And that he both his eyes behoved to strain,
  If he would view Earth's circling seas and land;
  In that, by reason of the lack of light,
  Their images attained to little height.

Here other river, lake, and rich champaign
  Are seen, than those which are below descried;
  Here other valley, other hill and plain,
  With towns and cities of their own supplied;
  Which mansions of such mighty size contain,
  Such never he before or after spied.
  Here spacious holt and lonely forest lay,
  Where nymphs forever chased the panting prey.

He, that with other scope had thither soared,
  Pauses not all these wonders to peruse:
  But led by the disciple of our Lord,
  His way towards a spacious vale pursues;
  A place wherein is wonderfully stored
  Whatever on our earth below we lose.
  Collected there are all things whatsoe'er,
  Lost through time, chance, on our own folly, here.

Nor here alone of realm and wealthy dower,
  O'er which aye turns the restless wheel, I say:
  I speak of what it is not in the power
  Of Fortune to bestow, or take away.
  Much fame is here, whereon Time and the Hour,
  Like wasting moth, in this our planet prey,
  Here countless vows, here prayers unnumbered lie,
  Made by us sinful men to God on high.

The lover's tears and sighs; what time in pleasure
  And play we here unprofitably spend;

To this; of ignorant men the eternal leisure,
And vain designs, aye frustrate of their end.
Empty desires so far exceed all measure,
They oe'r that valley's better part extend.
There wilt thou find, if thou wilt thither post,
Whatever thou on earth beneath hast lost.

He, passing by those heaps, on either hand,
Of this and now of that the meaning sought;
Formed of swollen bladders here a hill did stand,
Whence he heard cries and tumults, as he thought.
These were old crowns of the Assyrian land
And Lydian—as that paladin was taught—
Grecian and Persian, all of ancient fame;
And now, alas! well-nigh without a name.

Golden and silver hooks to sight succeed,
Heaped in a mass, the gifts which courtiers bear
—Hoping thereby to purchase future meed—
To greedy prince and patron; many a snare,
Concealed in garlands, did the warrior heed,
Who heard, these signs of adulation were;
And in cicalas, which their lungs had burst,
Saw fulsome lays by venal poets versed.

Loves of unhappy end in imagery
Of gold or jewelled bands he saw exprest.
Then eagles' talons, the authority
With which great lords their delegates invest:
Bellows filled every nook, the fume and fee
Wherein the favourites of kings are blest:
Given to those Ganymedes that have their hour,
And reft, when faded is their vernal flower.

O'erturned, here ruined town and castle lies,
  With all their wealth: "The symbols" (said his
      guide)
  "Of treaties and of those conspiracies,
  Which their conductors seemed so ill to hide."
  Serpents with female faces, felonies
  Of coiners and of robbers, he descried;
  Next broken bottles saw of many sorts,
  The types of servitude in sorry courts.

He marks a mighty pool of porridge spilled,
  And asks what in that symbol should be read,
  And hears 'twas charity, by sick men willed
  For distribution, after they were dead.
  He passed a heap of flowers, that erst distilled
  Sweet savours, and now noisome odours shed;
  The gift (if it may lawfully be said)
  Which Constantine to good Sylvester made.

A large provision, next, of twigs and lime
  —Your witcheries, O women!—he explored.
  The things he witnessed, to recount in rhyme
  Too tedious were; were myriads on record,
  To sum the remnant ill should I have time.
  'Tis here that all infirmities are stored,
  Save only Madness, seen not here at all,
  Which dwells below, nor leaves this earthly ball.

He turns him back, upon some days and deeds
  To look again, which he had lost of yore;
  But, save the interpreter the lesson reads,
  Would know them not, such different form they
      wore.
  He next saw that which man so little needs,
  As it appears—none pray to Heaven for more;

I speak of sense; whereof a lofty mount
Alone surpast all else which I recount.

It was as 'twere a liquor soft and thin,
   Which, save well corked, would from the vase have
      drained;
   Laid up, and treasured various flasks within,
   Larger or lesser, to that use ordained.
   That largest was which of the paladin,
   Anglantes' lord, the mighty sense contained;
   And from those others was discerned, since writ
   Upon the vessel was ORLANDO'S WIT.

The names of those whose wits therein were pent
   He thus on all those other flasks espied.
   Much of his own, but with more wonderment,
   The sense of many others he descried,
   Who, he believed, no dram of theirs had spent;
   But here, by tokens clear was satisfied,
   That scantily therewith were they purveyed;
   So large the quantity he here surveyed.

Some waste on love, some seeking honour, lose
   Their wits, some, scouring seas, for merchandise,
   Some, that on wealthy lords their hope repose,
   And some, befooled by silly sorceries;
   These upon pictures, upon jewels those;
   Those on whatever else they highest prize.
   Astrologers' and sophists' wits mid these,
   And many a poet's too, Astolpho sees.

From *Orlando Furioso*, trans. W. S. Rose.

Love's Justification

MICHELANGELO BUONARROTI

Yes! hope may with my strong desire keep pace,
And I be undeluded, unbetrayed;
For if of our affections none find grace
In sight of Heaven, then wherefore hath God made
The world which we inhabit? Better plea
Love cannot have, than that in loving thee
Glory to that eternal peace is paid,
Who such divinity to thee imparts
As hallows and makes pure all gentle hearts.
His hope is treacherous only whose love dies
With beauty, which is varying every hour:
But, in chaste hearts uninfluenced by the power
Of outward change, there blooms a deathless flower,
That breathes on earth the air of paradise.

       Trans. William Wordsworth.

To Vittoria Colonna: The Model and the Statue

MICHELANGELO BUONARROTI

When divine Art conceives a form and face,
 She bids the craftsman for his first essay
 To shape a simple model in mere clay:

This is the earliest birth of Art's embrace.
From the live marble in the second place
  His mallet brings into the light of day
  A thing so beautiful that who can say
  When time shall conquer that immortal grace?
Thus my own model I was born to be—
  The model of that nobler self, whereto
  Schooled by your pity, lady, I shall grow.
Each overplus and each deficiency
  You will make good. What penance then is due
  For my fierce heat, chastened and taught by you?

Trans. J. A. Symonds.

Mass of Love: A Spanish Ballad

ANONYMOUS

Dawn of a bright June morning,
The birthday of Saint John,
When ladies and their lovers
To hear High Mass are gone.

Yonder goes my lady,
Among them all, the best;
In coloured silk mantilla
And many skirts she's dressed.

Embroidered is her bodice
With gems of pearl and gold.
Her lips of beauty rare
Beguiling sweetness hold.

Faint the touch of rouge
On cheeks of fairest white,
Sparkling blue her eyes
With subtle art made bright.

Proudly church she entered
Radiant as sun above,
Ladies died of envy
And courtiers, of love.

A singer in the choir
His place lost in the creed;
The priest who read the lesson
The pages did not heed,

And acolytes beside him
No order could restore;
Instead of Amen, Amen,
They sang Amor, Amor.

Trans. Anna Pursche in *Translations from Hispanic Poets* (Hispanic Society of America).

A Sonnet

LUIS VAZ DE CAMÕES

Time and the mortal will stand never fast;
    Estrangèd fates man's confidence estrange;
Aye with new quality imbued, the vast
    World seems but victual of voracious Change.

New endless growth surrounds on every side,
   Such as we deemed not earth could ever bear;
Only doth sorrow for past woe abide,
   And sorrow for past good, if good it were.

Now Time with green hath made the meadows gay,
   Late carpeted with snow by winter frore,
And to lament hath turned my gentle lay;
Yet of all change this chiefly I deplore,
   The human lot, transformed to ill alway,
Not chequered with rare blessing as of yore.

Trans. Richard Garnett.

Night of Stars

LUIS DE LEÓN

When I behold the sky
With stars innumerable spangled bright
And then the Earth descry
Encompassèd with night,
Buried in sleep, oblivion infinite,

Sorrow and love arise
And with a burning fever fill my breast,
And ever from mine eyes
The tears flow without rest,
Till my tongue speaks at length, by grief oppressed:

O dwelling of great might,
Temple of lovely light incomparable,

My soul that to thy height
At birth aspired, what spell
Doth in this dark, low prison-house compel?

What mortal folly thus
From truth's possession can remove our sense,
So that, oblivious
Of thy blest gifts, it thence
Strays and seeks tinselled joys and vain pretence?

Man lives imprisonèd
In sleep and recks not of his destiny,
While still with silent tread,
At Heaven's swift decree,
Hour after hour his life doth from him flee.

Ah mortal men, awake
And turn your thoughts intent upon your loss!
Shall souls divine forsake
Such blessings for the cross
Of life unreal and dull delusions dross?

O skyward lift your eyes,
Unto this heavenly eternal sphere!
And you will then despise
The vain delights that here
Offers our life, its every hope and fear;

Petty, if we compare
The fleeting span of this low earthly scene
With that great region where
In noblest forms are seen
What is and what shall be and what hath been.

Who sees the eternal fires
With fixèd laws move on their heavenly way,
How each with each conspires:
Uneven their array,
Yet, varying, they one ordered scheme obey;

How in the moon's clear train,
As she her silver sphere doth onward move,
Goes light of wisdom's rain,
And, gleaming there above,
Follows, serenely fair, the star of love;

But blood-red angry Mars
Chooses unto himself another way,
While, girt with thousand stars,
Jupiter, clear alway,
Benignly calms the heavens with his loved ray;

And yonder in the height
Whirls Saturn, father of the Age of Gold,
And after him the bright
Stars in fair choir enrolled
Their light and all their treasure still unfold;

Who may all this descry
And pleasure still in this vile Earth retain,
Who will not groan and sigh
To rive the imprisoning chain
Wherein, exiled from Heaven, his soul hath lain?

Lo, here dwells sweet content,
Peace reigns, and on a rich and lofty throne
Sits holy love, and blent
Together in its zone
Delight and honour are evermore at one.

Here beauty infinite
Unveils itself, and light, quintessence pure,
Transparent gleams: no night
Its radiance may obscure,
Spring's flowered splendour here is ever sure.

O fields of truth most fair!
O meadows verily ever fresh and bright!
Mines full of riches rare!
O fountains of delight!
Deep valleys with a thousand blessings dight!

Trans. Aubrey FitzGerald Bell.

To the Moon

PIERRE DE RONSARD

Hide this one night thy crescent, kindly Moon;
  So shall Endymion faithful prove, and rest
  Loving and unawakened on thy breast;
So shall no foul enchanter importune
Thy quiet course; for now the night is boon,
  And through the friendly night unseen I fare,
  Who dread the face of foemen unaware,
And watch of hostile spies in the bright noon.
  Thou knowest, Moon, the bitter power of Love;
  'Tis told how shepherd Pan found ways to move,
For little price, thy heart; and of your grace,
  Sweet stars, be kind to this not alien fire,
  Because on earth ye did not scorn desire,
Bethink ye, now ye hold your heavenly place.

Trans. A. Lang.

Of His Lady's Old Age

PIERRE DE RONSARD

When you are very old, at evening
   You'll sit and spin beside the fire, and say,
   Humming my songs, "Ah well, ah well-a-day!
When I was young, of me did Ronsard sing."
None of your maidens that doth hear the thing,
   Albeit with her weary task foredone,
   But wakens at my name, and calls you one
Blest, to be held in long remembering.

I shall be low beneath the earth, and laid
On sleep, a phantom in the myrtle shade,
   While you beside the fire, a grandame grey,
My love, your pride, remember and regret;
Ah, love me, love! we may be happy yet,
   And gather roses, while 'tis called today.

Trans. A. Lang.

Happy Who Like Ulysses

JOACHIM DU BELLAY

Happy who like Ulysses, or that lord
   That raped the fleece, returning full and sage,

With usage and the world's wide reason stored,
　　With his own kin can wait the end of age.
When shall I see, when shall I see, God knows!
　　My little village smoke; or pass the door,
The old dear door of that unhappy house,
　　That is to me a kingdom and much more?
Mightier to me the house my fathers made,
　　Than your audacious heads, O Halls of Rome;
More than immortal marbles undecayed,
　　The thin sad slates that cover up my home;
More than your Tiber is my Loire to me,
　　Than Palatine my little Lyré there;
And more than all the winds of all the sea,
　　The quiet kindness of the Angevin air.

Trans. G. K. Chesterton.

A Sonnet to Heavenly Beauty

JOACHIM DU BELLAY

If this our little life is but a day
　　In the Eternal—if the years in vain
　　Toil after hours that never come again—
If everything that hath been must decay,
Why dreamest thou of joys that pass away,
　　My soul, that my sad body doth restrain?
　　Why of the moment's pleasure art thou fain?
Nay, thou hast wings—nay, seek another stay.

There is the joy whereto each soul aspires,
And there the rest that all the world desires,
　　And there is love, and peace, and gracious mirth;

And there in the most highest heavens shalt thou
Behold the Very Beauty, whereof now
   Thou worshippest the shadow upon earth.

Trans. A. Lang.

Poor Loving Soul

LOUISE LABÉ

When to my lone soft bed at eve returning
Sweet desir'd sleep already stealeth o'er me,
My spirit flieth to the fairy-land of her tyrannous love.

Him then I think fondly to kiss, to hold him
Frankly then to my bosom; I that all day
Have looked for him suffering, repining, yea many long
    days.

O bless'd sleep, with flatteries beguile me;
So, if I ne'er may of a surety have him,
Grant to my poor soul amorous the dark gift of this
    illusion.

Trans. Robert Bridges.

My Lute Awake

SIR THOMAS WYATT

My lute awake! perform the last
Labour that thou and I shall waste,
   The end that I have now begun;

For when this song is sung and past,
  My lute be still, for I have done.

As to be heard where ear is none,
As lead to grave in marble stone,
  My song may pierce her heart as soon;
Should we then sigh or sing or moan?
  No, no, my lute, for I have done.

The rocks do not so cruelly
Repulse the waves continually,
  As she my suit and affection,
So that I am past remedy;
  Whereby my lute and I have done.

Proud of the spoil that thou hast got
Of simple hearts thorough love's shot,
  By whom, unkind, thou hast them won,
Think not he hath his bow forgot,
  Although my lute and I have done.

Vengeance shall fall on thy disdain
That makest but game on earnest pain;
  Think not alone under the sun
Unquit to cause thy lovers plain,
  Although my lute and I have done.

Perchance thee lie withered and old
The winter nights that are so cold,
  Plaining in vain unto the moon;
Thy wishes then dare not be told;
  Care then who list, for I have done.

And then may chance thee to repent
The time that thou hast lost and spent

To cause thy lovers sigh and swoon;
Then shalt thou know beauty but lent,
    And wish and want as I have done.

Now cease, my lute: this is the last
Labour that thou and I shall waste,
    And ended is that we begun;
Now is this song both sung and past:
    My lute be still, for I have done.

Thou Blind Man's Mark

SIR PHILIP SIDNEY

Thou blind man's mark, thou fool's self-chosen snare,
Fond fancy's scum, and dregs of scattered thought;
Band of all evils, cradle of causeless care;
Thou web of will, whose end is never wrought;
Desire, desire! I have too dearly bought,
With price of mangled mind, thy worthless ware;
Too long, too long, asleep thou hast me brought,
Who should my mind to higher things prepare.
But yet in vain thou hast my ruin sought;
In vain thou madest me to vain things aspire;
In vain thou kindlest all thy smoky fire;
For virtue hath this better lesson taught—
Within myself to seek my only hire,
Desiring nought but how to kill desire.

Weep You No More, Sad Fountains

ANONYMOUS

Weep you no more, sad fountains;
　　What need you flow so fast?
Look how the snowy mountains
　　Heaven's sun doth gently waste.
　　But my sun's heavenly eyes
　　　　View not your weeping,
　　　　That now lie sleeping
　　Softly, now softly lies
　　　　Sleeping.

Sleep is a reconciling,
　　A rest that peace begets.
Doth not the sun rise smiling
　　When fair at even he sets?
　　Rest you then, rest, sad eyes,
　　　　Melt not in weeping
　　　　While she lies sleeping
　　Softly, now softly lies
　　　　Sleeping.

In John Dowland's *Third and Last Book of Songs or Airs* (1603).

The Theater of Life

Orfeo

ANGELO POLIZIANO

1472

SCENE IV

ORPHEUS, *at the gate of Hell*

Pity, nay pity for a lover's moan!
  Ye Powers of Hell, let pity reign in you!
  To your dark regions led me Love alone:
  Downward upon his wings of light I flew.
  Hush, Cerberus! Howl not by Pluto's throne!
  For when you hear my tale of misery, you,
  Nor you alone, but all who here abide
  In this blind world, will weep by Lethe's tide.
There is no need, ye Furies, thus to rage;
  To dart those snakes that in your tresses twine:
  Knew ye the cause of this my pilgrimage,
  Ye would lie down and join your moans with mine.
  Let this poor wretch but pass, who war doth wage
  With Heaven, the elements, the powers divine!
  I beg for pity or for death. No more!
  But open, ope Hell's adamantine door!
                              Orpheus enters Hell.

453

PLUTO

What man is he who with his golden lyre
  Hath moved the gates that never move,
  While the dead folk repeat his dirge of love?
The rolling stone no more doth tire
  Swart Sisyphus on yonder hill;
  And Tantalus with water slakes his fire:
The groans of mangled Tityos are still;
  Ixion's wheel forgets to fly;
  The Danaïds their urns can fill:
I hear no more the tortured spirits cry;
But all find rest in that sweet harmony.

PROSERPINE

Dear consort, since, compelled by love of thee,
  I left the light of Heaven serene,
  And came to reign in Hell, a sombre queen;
The charm of tenderest sympathy
  Hath never yet had power to turn
  My stubborn heart, or draw forth tears from me.
Now with desire for yon sweet voice I yearn;
  Nor is there aught so dear
  As that delight. Nay, be not stern
To this one prayer! Relax thy brows severe,
And rest awhile with me that song to hear!

Orpheus stands before the throne.

ORPHEUS

Ye rulers of the people lost in gloom,
  Who see no more the jocund light of day!
  Ye who inherit all things that the womb
Of Nature and the elements display!
  Hear ye the grief that draws me to the tomb!
  Love, cruel Love, hath led me on this way:

Not to chain Cerberus I hither come,
But to bring back my mistress to her home.
A serpent hidden among flowers and leaves
  Stole my fair mistress—nay, my heart—from me:
  Wherefore my wounded life forever grieves,
  Nor can I stand against this agony.
  Still, if some fragrance lingers yet and cleaves
  Of your famed love unto your memory,
  If of that ancient rape you think at all,
  Give back Eurydice!—On you I call.
All things ere long unto this bourne descend:
  All mortal lives to you return at last:
  Whate'er the moon hath circled, in the end
  Must fade and perish in your empire vast:
  Some sooner and some later hither wend;
  Yet all upon this pathway shall have passed:
  This of our footsteps is the final goal;
  And then we dwell for aye in your control.
Therefore the nymph I love is left for you
  When Nature leads her deathward in due time:
  But now you've cropped the tendrils as they grew,
  The grapes unripe, while yet the sap did climb:
  Who reaps the young blades wet with April dew,
  Nor waits till summer hath o'erpassed her prime?
  Give back, give back my hope one little day!—
  Not for a gift, but for a loan I pray.
I pray not to you by the waves forlorn
  Of marshy Styx or dismal Acheron,
  By Chaos where the mighty world was born,
  Or by the sounding flames of Phlegethon;
  But by the fruit which charmed thee on that morn
  When thou didst leave our world for this dread
      throne!
  O queen! If thou reject this pleading breath,
  I will no more return, but ask for death!

PROSERPINE

Husband, I never guessed
   That in our realm oppressed
   Pity could find a home to dwell:
   But now I know that mercy teems in Hell.
   I see Death weep; her breast
   Is shaken by those tears that faultless fell.
   Let then thy laws severe for him be swayed
   By love, by song, by the just prayers he prayed!

PLUTO

She's thine, but at this price:
   Bend not on her thine eyes,
   Till mid the souls that live she stay.
   See that thou turn not back upon the way!
   Check all fond thoughts that rise!
   Else will thy love be torn from thee away.
   I am well pleased that song so rare as thine
   The might of my dread sceptre should incline.

SCENE V

EURYDICE

Ah me! Thy love too great
   Hath lost not thee alone!
   I am torn from thee by strong Fate.
   No more I am thine own.
   In vain I stretch these arms. Back, back to Hell
   I'm drawn, I'm drawn. My Orpheus, fare thee well!
                Eurydice disappears.

ORPHEUS

Who hath laid laws on Love?
   Will pity not be given

For one short look so full thereof?
Since I am robbed of heaven,
Since all my joy so great is turned to pain,
I will go back and plead with Death again!

Tisiphone blocks his way.

TISIPHONE

Nay, seek not back to turn!
  Vain is thy weeping, all thy words are vain.
  Eurydice may not complain
  Of aught but thee—albeit her grief is great.
  Vain are thy verses 'gainst the voice of Fate!
  How vain thy song! For Death is stern!
  Try not the backward path: thy feet refrain!
  The laws of the abyss are fixed and firm remain.

SCENE VI

ORPHEUS

What sorrow-laden song shall e'er be found
  To match the burden of my matchless woe?
  How shall I make the fount of tears abound,
  To weep apace with grief's unmeasured flow?
  Salt tears I'll waste upon the barren ground,
  So long as life delays me here below;
  And since my fate hath wrought me wrong so sore,
  I swear I'll never love a woman more!
Henceforth I'll pluck the buds of opening spring,
  The bloom of youth when life is loveliest,
  Ere years have spoiled the beauty which they bring:
  This love, I swear, is sweetest, softest, best!
  Of female charms let no one speak or sing;
  Since she is slain who ruled within my breast.
  He who would seek my converse, let him see

That ne'er he talk of woman's love to me!
How pitiful is he who changes mind
    For woman! for her love laments or grieves!
    Who suffers her in chains his will to bind,
    Or trusts her words lighter than withered leaves,
    Her loving looks more treacherous than the wind!
    A thousand times she veers; to nothing cleaves:
    Follows who flies; from him who follows, flees;
    And comes and goes like waves on stormy seas!
High Jove confirms the truth of what I said,
    Who, caught and bound in love's delightful snare,
    Enjoys in Heaven his own bright Ganymed:
    Phoebus on earth had Hyacinth the fair:
    Hercules, conqueror of the world, was led
    Captive to Hylas by this love so rare.
    Advice for husbands! Seek divorce, and fly
    Far, far away from female company!

Enter a Maenad leading a train of Bacchantes.

A MAENAD

Ho! Sisters! Up! Alive!
    See him who doth our sex deride!
    Hunt him to death, the slave!
Thou snatch the thyrsus! Thou this oak tree rive!
    Cast down this doeskin and that hide!
    We'll wreak our fury on the knave!
Yea, he shall feel our wrath, the knave!
    He shall yield up his hide
    Riven as woodmen fir trees rive!
    No power his life can save;
    Since women he hath dared deride!
    Ho! to him, sisters! Ho! Alive!

       Orpheus is chased off the scene and slain:
         the Maenads then return.

A MAENAD

Ho! Bacchus! Ho! I yield thee thanks for this!
   Through all the woodland we the wretch have borne:
So that each root is slaked with blood of his:
   Yea, limb from limb his body have we torn
Through the wild forest with a fearful bliss:
   His gore hath bathed the earth by ash and thorn!
Go then! thy blame on lawful wedlock fling!
Ho! Bacchus! take the victim that we bring!

CHORUS OF MAENADS

Bacchus! we all must follow thee!
Bacchus! Bacchus! Ohe! Ohe!

With ivy coronals, bunch and berry,
   Crown we our heads to worship thee
Thou hast bidden us to make merry
   Day and night with jollity!
Drink then! Bacchus is here! Drink free,
And hand ye the drinking-cup to me!
   Bacchus! we all must follow thee!
   Bacchus! Bacchus! Ohe! Ohe!

See, I have emptied my horn already:
   Stretch hither your beaker to me, I pray:
Are the hills and the lawns where we roam unsteady?
   Or is it my brain that reels away?
Let every one run to and fro through the hay,
As ye see me run! Ho! after me!
   Bacchus! we all must follow thee!
   Bacchus! Bacchus! Ohe! Ohe!

Methinks I am dropping in swoon or slumber:
   Am I drunken or sober, yes or no?

What are these weights my feet encumber?
   You too are tipsy, well I know!
Let every one do as ye see me do.
Let every one drink and quaff like me!
   Bacchus! we all must follow thee!
   Bacchus! Bacchus! Ohe! Ohe!

Cry Bacchus! Cry Bacchus! Be blithe and merry,
   Tossing wine down your throats away!
Let sleep then come and our gladness bury:
   Drink you, and you, and you, whiie ye may!
Dancing is over for me today,
Let every one cry aloud Evohe!
   Bacchus! we all must follow thee!
   Bacchus! Bacchus! Ohe! Ohe!

Trans. J. A. Symonds.

A Theatrical Performance

BALDASSARE CASTIGLIONE

1513

TO LUDOVICO CANOSSA

It is some time since I received a letter from your
Excellency, to which I did not reply at first, out of
curiosity to see if you would become my debtor for
more than one letter! At length I must confess that
you have won the day, and in reply I will tell you that
I cannot recollect the precise date on which I gave you
those hundred ducats to send to Naples. But I know
this, that it was when our two lady duchesses left
Rome and I stayed behind for ten or twelve days, in-

tending to go to Naples, and then changed my mind and gave you the money, and returned to Urbino with the Cardinal of Pavia. Now you will remember the whole thing!

I send you my Marine Elegy, which please pass on to M. Pietro Bembo. I beg you to read it and give me your opinion on the poem. I know not if it is worth your perusal, but I know well that it cannot possibly equal your expectations or be worthy of your praise. As for my delays, you are aware how many reasons I have to excuse them. Our comedies have gone off well, most of all the *Calandria*, which was represented in a truly magnificent style, which I need not describe, since you will have heard full accounts from many who were present. But I will tell you this much. The scene represented was an outer street of the town, between the city wall and its last houses. The wall with its two towers was represented in the most natural way possible, rising from the floor of the stage to the top of the hall. One tower was occupied by the pipers, the other by the trumpeters, and between the two there was another finely constructed rampart. The hall itself, where the audience sat, occupied the place of the moat, and was crossed as it were by two aqueducts. The back of the wall above the tiers of seats was hung with the tapestries of the Trojan War. Above these was a large cornice in high relief, bearing the following inscription in large white letters on a blue ground, running the whole length of the hall:

Both in wars abroad and in games at home, Caesar displays his strength, for both alike are fit work for great minds.

From the roof of the hall hung great bunches of foliage, almost hiding the ceiling, and from the rosettes of the vault wire threads were suspended, to which two rows of candelabra in the shape of letters were fastened, from one end of the hall to the other. These thirteen rosettes made thirteen letters, spelling the words *Deliciæ Populi*, and these letters were so large that they held seven or ten torches, which lighted the hall brilliantly.

The scene was laid in a very fine city, with streets, palaces, churches, and towers, all in relief, and looking as if they were real, the effect being completed by admirable paintings in scientific perspective. Among other objects there was an octagon temple in low relief, so well finished that, even if all the workmen in the duchy of Urbino had been employed, it seemed hardly possible to think that all this had been done in four months! This temple was completely covered with beautiful stucco reliefs, the windows were made to imitate alabaster, the architraves and cornices were of fine gold and ultramarine blue, with glass jewels here and there, looking exactly like real gems; there were roundels of marble containing figures, carved pillars, and much more that would take me too long to describe. This temple stood in the centre of the stage. At one end there was a triumphal arch about two yards from the wall, marvellously executed. Between the architrave and the vault an admirable representation of the story of the Horatii had been painted to imitate marble. The two niches above the pillars supporting the arch were filled with little Victories bearing trophies in their hands made of stucco. On the top of the arch stood a most beautiful equestrian statue of a figure in armour, striking a vanquished man at his feet with his spear. To right and left of this rider were two little altars with vases of burning flame that lasted to the end of the comedy.

I will not describe everything, as I feel sure you will

have heard a good deal already; nor will I tell how one of the plays was composed by a child and recited by children, who perhaps put their elders to shame. They certainly acted marvellously, and it was a new thing to see little old men, not a foot high, preserving a gravity and severity of manner worthy of Menander. Nor will I attempt to describe the strange music of these comedies, played by minstrels who were all out of sight, and placed in different corners; but I will come at once to our Bernardo's *Calandro*, which gave the greatest pleasure. And since the prologue arrived very late, and the actor who had to recite it could not learn it by heart in time, another which I had written was recited in its place, and met with general approval. Otherwise little was changed, only a few scenes which, perhaps, were not fit for recitation, but little or nothing else, and it was performed exactly as it is written.

These were the *intermezzi*. First a *moresca* by Jason, who appeared on one side of the stage, dancing in antique armour, looking very fine, with a splendid sword and shield. On the other came two bulls, so lifelike that several of the spectators took them for real animals, breathing fire through their nostrils. The good Jason yoked them to the plough and made them draw it, and then sowed dragon's teeth in the furrows. Presently ancient warriors sprang upon the stage in a way that was, I think, excellently managed, and danced a fiery *moresca*, trying to kill Jason all the while. As they were leaving the stage, they fell upon each other and were slain, without being actually seen to die. Then Jason appeared again, dancing exquisitely with the golden fleece on his shoulders; and this was the first interlude, or *moresca*. The second was a very beautiful chariot of Venus, with the goddess seated and holding a lighted taper in her hand. The car was drawn by two doves,

who certainly seemed to be alive, and who were ridden
by two Amorini with lighted tapers in their hands and
bows and quivers on their shoulders. Four Amorini went
before the car, four followed after, all bearing lighted
tapers in the same manner, dancing a *moresca* and
flourishing their burning torches. Having reached the
end of the stage, they set fire to a door, from which
nine gallants issued all ablaze with light, and danced
another most beautiful *moresca*. The third *intermezzo*
was a chariot of Neptune drawn by two sea-horses with
fish scales and fins, wonderfully well imitated. Neptune
himself rode in the car with his trident, attended by
eight monsters, four before and four behind, all as well
done as it is possible to imagine, and dancing a sword
dance with the chariot all aflame. These beasts were
the strangest creatures in the world, but no one who
did not see them can have an idea what they were like.
The fourth was a car of Juno, also ablaze with light.
The goddess, wearing a crown on her brow and a
sceptre in her hand, appeared seated on a cloud which
encircled the chariot, and surrounded by numberless
heads blowing the winds of heaven. This car was drawn
by two peacocks so beautiful and lifelike that I could
not believe my eyes, and yet I had seen them before,
and had myself given directions how they were to be
made. In front were two eagles and ostriches, behind
two sea-birds and two large parrots, with gaily coloured
plumage. All of these were so well done, my dear Mon-
signore, that I am quite sure no imitation ever came
so near to reality, and they all danced a sword dance
with a grace that it is impossible to describe or imagine.

When the comedy was ended, one of the Amorini,
whom we had already seen, appeared suddenly on the
stage, in the same habit, and explained in a few verses

the meaning of these *intermezzi,* which was a separate thing from the comedy itself.

First of all there was the battle between earth-born brothers, when, as we see today, there is war between those nearest of kin, who ought to live at peace, as set forth in the fable of Jason. Then comes Love, who kindles first mankind and earth, then the sea and air, with his sacred flame, and seeks to drive away war and discord and join the whole world in blessed concord. This indeed, you will say, is rather a hope and devout aspiration, but the vision of war, alas! is all too real for our misfortune! I did not mean to show you the verses that Love sang, but yet I send them, and you can do what you like with them. They were written in great haste, by one who was struggling all the while with painters and carpenters, with actors and musicians and dancers. When the verses were ended Love disappeared. The sound of hidden music, proceeding from four viols, was heard, and then four voices singing a verse to the strains of a beautiful melody, as it were an invocation to Love. So the *festa* ended, after giving the greatest satisfaction and pleasure to the spectators. If I had not praised the whole thing so much, I would have told you what share I had in it; but I will not do this, for fear your Excellency should think that I flatter myself!

In J. Cartwright, *Baldassare Castiglione, His Life and Letters* (New York: E. P. Dutton & Co., 1908).

Lazarillo de Tormes

ANONYMOUS

1554

Your Worship shall understand before all things, that my name is Lazaro de Tormes, son of Thome Gonzales and Antona Perez native of Tejares, a village near Salamanca. I was born within the river called Tormes, whereof I took my surname, as hereafter you shall hear; my father, whom God pardon, had the charge of a mill standing upon that river wherein he supplied the room of a miller about fifteen years. It fortuned on a night my mother, being great with child, was there brought to bed, and then was I born; therefore now I may truly report the river itself to be the place of my nativity. And after the time I came to the age of eight years, there was laid to my father's charge that he had shamefully cut the seams of men's sacks that came thither to grind, wherefore he was taken and imprisoned, and being tormented he confessed the whole matter, denying nothing wherefore he was persecuted. I trust in God that he is now in Paradise, seeing that the Gospel doth say that blessed are such as confess their faults.

About the same time an army was made against the Turks, and my father being then banished for the mishap aforesaid, chanced to be one supplying the room of a muleteer under a knight which went thither, in whose service, like a true and a faithful man, he ended his life. My mother being then a comfortless widow, after the loss of her dear husband, determined to inhabit among such as were virtuous and honest, to be of that number, and therefore came immediately to this noble city, where, after that she had hired a little house, she kept an ordinary table for divers students, and washed shirts for a company of horsekeepers, belonging to the Commander of Magdalena, by means whereof she had occasion to make often resort unto the stables. Where in continuance of time, a black Moor, one of master Commander's men, became to be familiarly acquainted with her, so that for his part he would oftentimes arrive at midnight to our house, and return again betimes in the morning, otherwhiles at noontide, demanding at the door whether my mother had eggs to sell, and so come in prettily without suspicion. At the beginning I was right sorry to see him make repair thither, being afraid to behold his black uncomely visage; but after that I once perceived how only by his resort our fare was so well amended, I could by no means find in my heart to hate him, but rather bear him good will, rejoicing to see him; for he always brought us home with him good round cantels of bread and pieces of broken meat, and in the winter time wood to warm us withal.

To be short, by his continual repair thither, matters went so forward that my mother found good time to bring forth a young blackamoor, whom I daily played withal, and sometimes helped to warm. And I remember very well, that on a time as my stepfather played merrily with his young son, the little child perceiving that my mother and I were white, and his father black as jet, he ran away for fear to my mother, and stretching forth his finger, cried, "*Mamma*, the bug!" Whereat my black stepfather would laugh, and say, "Whoreson, art thou afraid of thy father?" Although I was then but young, I right well marked the child's words, and said to myself, there are many such in the world, which do abhor and flee from others because they cannot see what shape they have themselves.

Within a while after, it pleased fortune that the daily conversation of Zaide (for so was my father's name) came to the ears of him that was steward to master Commander, who made such strait inquiry, that he was advertised how the black Moor did use to steal half the provender that was allowed the horses, yea, horse coverings, sheets, and curry combs, otherwhiles wood and bran; which things indeed he always said were lost, and when nothing could be gotten to serve his turn, he would never stick to unshoe the horses, to get some gain, presenting daily all such gifts to my mother, as a help to bring up my little black brother. Let us never therefore marvel more at those which steal from the poor, nor yet at them which convey from the houses they serve, to present therewith whom they love in hope to attain thereby their desired pleasure, seeing that love was able to encourage this poor bondman or slave to do thus much as I have said, or rather more, which by evident trial was afterwards proved true. For I being examined of the deed, after much threatening was constrained as a child, for fear, to discover the whole matter, confessing how I had sold certain horseshoes to a smith at my mother's commandment. Wherefore my miserable stepfather was by judgment of the law, as the order is there, whipped and larded, and to my mother express commandment was given upon the usual pain of a hundred stripes, no more to enter into the house of the abovenamed Commander, nor yet entertain into hers the unfortunate Zaide.

My sorrowful mother, fearing to throw the helve after the hatchet, determined by all means to keep their commandment, wherefore she entered into service with those which at that time dwelt at the ordinary inn called Solona, so to escape danger and to avoid the dangerous reports of evil tongues, where she suffered much sorrow, and there brought up my black brother, until he was able to run abroad, and that I being a good stripling, could go up and down the town to provide the guests with wine, and candles, and other things necessary. In this mean time, there happened a blind man to come thither to lodge, who thinking me to be a fit man to lead him, desired my mother that I might serve him, wherewith she being right well content, most earnestly prayed him to be a good master unto me, because I was an honest man's son, who in maintaining the faith of Jesus Christ against Turks, died in the battle of Gelves, and how that she trusted in almighty God I would prove as honest a man as he; therefore in any wise that he would be careful over me, being a fatherless child.

"Let me alone then," answered he, "I will not use him as a servant, but as a son."

Then in happy time I began to serve my old and new master. And after we had remained certain days at Salamanca, my blind master perceiving his gain there to be but small, determined to depart thence; and a little before our departure, I went to see my mother.

When I came where she was, we shed both most bitter tears, and she gave me her blessing, saying, "Now, my dear son, I shall see thee no more, therefore be a good child. I pray God be thy help, I do thank the Lord I have brought thee up well hitherto, and I have now put thee to a good master; from henceforth provide for thyself, seeing that I have done my part."

I took my leave and returned in haste to my master,

which tarried for me ready to take his voyage. So we departed out of Salamanca, and came on our way as far as the bridge, at the entrance whereof standeth a beast of stone, fashioned much like a bull. As soon as we came near it, the blind man willed me to approach, saying, "Lazaro, put thine ear to this bull, and thou shalt hear a terrible noise within it."

As soon as he had said the word, I was ready like a fool to bow down my head, to do as he had commanded, thinking that his words had been most true; but the traitorous blind man suspecting how near it my head was, thrusteth forth his arm upon a sudden, with such force, that my sore head took such a blow against the devilish bull, that for the space of three days my head felt the pains of his horns.

Wherefore he was right glad, and said, "Consider now what thou art, thou foolish calf; thou must understand that the blind man's boy ought to know one trick more than the devil himself."

It seemed then immediately that I awaked out of simplicity, wherein I had of long time slept (like a child), and I said to myself, "My blind master hath good reason, it is full time for me to open mine eyes, yea, and to provide and seek mine own advantage, considering that I am alone without any help."

We continued on our journey, and within few days I came to good knowledge, so he perceiving what a ready tongue I had, was right glad, and said, "Neither gold nor silver can I give thee, howbeit, I do mean to teach thee the way to live."

And so certainly he did; for next after God he made me a man, and although he was blind, it was he that gave me sight and that taught me how to know the world. I rejoice to declare unto your Worship these childish toys, that you may see how commendable it is

for a man of low estate to be brought to authority and
exalted, and contrariwise what a shame it is for a man
of dignity and estimation to be pulled down to wretched
misery.

But to return to my blind master, and to show his
nature, I assure you that since the beginning of the
world God never made man more deceitful and crafty.
For in his art and trade of living he far passed all other:
he could recite by heart a hundred long prayers and
more, yea, and the life of all the holy saints; at his
devotion time he used such a loud tunable voice, that
it might be heard throughout the church where he
prated, and besides all that, he could counterfeit a good
devout countenance in praying, without any strange
gesture, either with mouth or eye, as other blind men
are accustomed to use. I am not able to recite a thousand other manner of ways which he had to get money:
he would make many believe that he had prayers for
divers good purposes, as for to make women bring
forth children, yea, and to make men to love their
wives, although they had hated them before never so
much. He would prognosticate to women that were
with child, whether they should bring forth a son or
a daughter: in matters of physic, he would affirm that
Galen never knew half so much as he: also for any
grief, the toothache, or any other disease, there was
never one complained, but that immediately he would
say, do this, do that, seethe such a herb, take such a
root. So that by this his continual practice, he had daily
great resort made unto him (especially of women)
which did faithfully believe all that ever he said; by
them he had great gain, for he won more in a month,
than twenty of his occupation did in a whole year.

Yet for all his daily gains, you must understand that
there was never man so wretched a niggard. For he

caused me not only to die for hunger, but also to want whatsoever I needed. And therefore to confess the truth, if I had not found out means to help myself, I had been buried long since. Wherefore oftentimes I would so prevent him of all his craft, that my portion should prove as good as his; and to bring my matter so to pass I used wonderful deceits (whereof I will recite unto you some), although sometimes my practising of them did cost me bitter pains. This blind man carried always his bread and his victual in a little bag of cloth, which was shut at the mouth with an iron buckle, under a miserable lock and key. At the time of putting his meat in, and taking it out, he would keep such strait account, that all the world was not able to deceive him of one crumb, and therefore there was no help but that I must needs be content with that small allowance that he gave me, which always I was sure to dispatch at two morsels; and as soon as ever he had shut his little lock, he would think then that all were sure, imagining that I had other matters in hand. Then would I boldly unrip and sew up again the side of his covetous sack, using daily to lance one of the sides, there to take out not only bread at mine own pleasure, but also slices of flesh, and sweet *carbonados;* so that by such means I found convenient time to ease the raging hunger which he was cause of. . . .

At dinner or supper time he had always before him a little pot full of wine, which oftentimes I would lay hand on, and after two or three kisses send it him secretly home again. But that happy time continued but a while, for I was wont to leave so little behind me, that he might soon espy the fault, as indeed immediately he did mistrust the whole matter, wherefore he began a new order, not to leave his wine any more at random, but to avoid danger, had always his little pot fast by the ear, so to be sure of his drink. Yet not-withstanding for all this, the adamant stone had never such virtue to draw iron to it, as I had to suck up his wine with a long reed which I had prepared for the purpose: for as soon as the end of my reed had been once in, I might well desire him to fill the pot again.

Yet at the last the crafty blind man chanced to feel me, and being angry, determined to take another way, to place his pot between his legs, covering it still with his hand, so to avoid all former dangers. When he had so done, I being accustomed to drink wine, did long to taste of it, and perceiving that my reed could then no more prevail at all, I devised another kind of fetch, how to make a hole in the bottom of his wine pot, and to stop the same with a little soft wax, so that at dinner time making a show as I were ready to die for cold, I would creep between the blind man's legs, to warm myself at his small fire, by the heat whereof, the wax being little in quantity, would so melt away, that the wine would issue down into my mouth freshly and trim, I being sure to gape upward so just, that one drop should never fall beside. So that when my blind master would taste of his wine, he should never find drop to quench his thirst, whereat he would much marvel, curs-ing and swearing all manner of oaths, yea, wishing the pot and all that was within it at the devil, musing still how his wine should be so consumed away. Then straightways to excuse myself, I would say, "I trust you will not mistrust me, gentle uncle, seeing that the pot came never out of your own hands."

Whereupon then to be well informed of the truth, he began to feel and to grope the pot over so often, that at last he found the spring, and at that time dis-sembled quietly the matter, as if he had perceived nothing.

The next day I began again to prepare myself after my accustomed sort to take my pleasure of his wine, being ignorant of the evil that should ensue, thinking that my master would never have mistrusted me about such a matter, wherefore I was merry and careless. But my cruel master, perceiving after what strange sort I received those sweet drops of wine, which came forth as a quick spring at his pot bottom, my face bent towards heaven, my eyes in manner closed, so to receive with more delight and better taste that pleasant liquor which I thought did preserve my life, the malicious blind man having time of revengement at his will, lifted up the sweet and sour pot (as I may say), and with all his force clapped it so rudely upon my face, that I thought verily heaven above, and all therein, had fallen upon me. The cruel blow was such that it took away my senses, it troubled sore my brains, and my face was all cut with pieces of the broken pot, yea, and some of my teeth were then broken, which as yet is seen, wherefore I never loved him after, howbeit he cherished me daily; yet for all the false love and friendship which he showed, I perceived right well how glad he was that he had so punished me. To make me amends, he washed with wine the wounds which the unhappy pot had made, and after much laughing, said, "What sayest thou to this, my boy, the wine that hath done the hurt shall now heal thee again," and such other merry jests, which I utterly misliked.

As soon as I began to recover, and that my face was in manner healed, I considered with myself, how that with few more such blows the blind man might quickly bring me to my grave. And therefore determined to shorten his days if I could, which thing I went not about immediately, but tarried a due time for mine own safety and advantage. And whereas afterwards I

went about to forget mine anger, and to forgive him
the blow, the evil usage and entertainment which he
daily showed me would in no wise consent thereto.
For still he tormented me with sore blows without any
offence or fault at all. And when any man demanded
why he handled me so cruelly, straightways he would
up and declare the discourse of his pot, saying, "Do
you not think that this child is some innocent?" And
always at the end of his tale these would be his words,
"Who unless it were the devil himself could have
found out such rare pranks?"

The people would much marvel at my invention and,
blessing themselves, would say unto my master, "Punish
him, punish him! God will reward you therefor."

Which thing he did continually, and would have
done without their bidding: wherefore I daily led him
through the worst ways I could possibly find, all for
every spite, minding if I could to do him harm. Where
I might espy stones or mire, I would even through the
thickest; and although I could never escape dry foot,
I was glad with losing one of mine own eyes to put out
both his that never had any. At such times of his sorrows, to be revenged, he would take hold with his
nails on the hinder part of my head, where with his
often pulling he had left very few hairs behind. It
would never prevail me then to say that I could find
no better way, nor yet to swear how I did not lead him
that naughty way maliciously, for he was so subtle that
to my words he would give small credit.

Trans. David Rowland (1576).

The Dignity of Man

The Dignity of Man

GIOVANNI PICO DELLA MIRANDOLA

1486

I HAVE READ, reverend Fathers, in the works of the Arabs, that when Abdala the Saracen was asked what he regarded as most to be wondered at on the world's stage, so to speak, he answered that there was nothing to be seen more wonderful than man. To this opinion may be added the saying of Hermes [Trismegistus]: "A great miracle, Asclepius, is man." But when I thought about the reason for these statements, I was not satisfied by the many remarkable qualities which were advanced as arguments by many men—that man is the intermediary between creatures, the intimate of higher beings and the king of lower beings, the interpreter of nature by the sharpness of his senses, by the questing curiosity of his reason, and by the light of his intelligence, the interval between enduring eternity and the flow of time, and, as the Persians say, the nuptial bond of the world, and by David's testimony, a little lower than the angels. Great indeed as these attributes are, they are not the principal ones, those, that is, which may rightfully claim the privilege of the highest ad-

miration. For why should we not admire the angels
themselves and the most blessed choirs of heaven more?
At last I seem to have understood why man is the most
fortunate creature and thus worthy of all admiration,
and what precisely is the place alloted to him in the
universal chain, a place to be envied not only by the
beasts, but also by the stars, and the Intelligences beyond this world. It is an incredible and wonderful thing.
And why not? For this is the very reason why man is
rightly called and considered a great miracle and a
truly marvellous creature. But hear what this place is,
Fathers, and courteously grant me the favour of listening with friendly ears.

Now the Highest Father, God the Architect, according to the laws of His secret wisdom, built this
house of the world, this world which we see, the most
sacred temple of His divinity. He adorned the region
beyond the heavens with Intelligences, He animated the
celestial spheres with eternal souls, and He filled the
excrementary and filthy parts of the lower world with
a multitude of animals of all kinds. But when His work
was finished, the Artisan longed for someone to reflect
on the plan of so great a creation, to love its beauty,
and to admire its magnitude. When, therefore, everything was completed, as Moses and the *Timaeus* testify,
He began at last to consider the creation of man. But
among His archetypes there was none from which He
could form a new offspring, nor in His treasure houses
was there any inheritance which He might bestow upon
His new son, nor in the tribunal seats of the whole
world was there a place where this contemplator of the
universe might sit. All was now filled out; everything
had been apportioned to the highest, the middle, and
the lowest orders. But it was not in keeping with the
paternal power to fail, as though exhausted, in the last

act of creation; it was not in keeping with His wisdom to waver in a matter of necessity through lack of a design; it was not in keeping with His beneficent love that the creature who was to praise the divine liberality with regard to others should be forced to condemn it with respect to himself. Finally the Great Artisan ordained that man, to whom He could give nothing belonging only to himself, should share in common whatever properties had been peculiar to each of the other creatures. He received man, therefore, as a creature of undetermined nature, and placing him in the middle of the universe, said this to him: "Neither an established place, nor a form belonging to you alone, nor any special function have We given to you, O Adam, and for this reason, that you may have and possess, according to your desire and judgment, whatever place, whatever form, and whatever functions you shall desire. The nature of other creatures, which has been determined, is confined within the bounds prescribed by Us. You, who are confined by no limits, shall determine for yourself your own nature, in accordance with your own free will, in whose hand I have placed you. I have set you at the centre of the world, so that from there you may more easily survey whatever is in the world. We have made you neither heavenly nor earthly, neither mortal nor immortal, so that, more freely and more honourably the moulder and maker of yourself, you may fashion yourself in whatever form you shall prefer. You shall be able to descend among the lower forms of being, which are brute beasts; you shall be able to be reborn out of the judgment of your own soul into the higher beings, which are divine."

O sublime generosity of God the Father! O highest and most wonderful felicity of man! To him it was granted to have what he chooses, to be what he wills.

At the moment when they are born, beasts bring with them from their mother's womb, as Lucilius says, whatever they shall possess. From the beginning or soon afterwards, the highest spiritual beings have been what they are to be for all eternity. When man came into life, the Father endowed him with all kinds of seeds and with the germs of every way of life. Whatever seeds each man cultivates will grow and bear fruit in him. If these seeds are vegetative, he will be like a plant; if they are sensitive, he will become like the beasts; if they are rational, he will become like a heavenly creature; if intellectual, he will be an angel and a son of God. And if, content with the lot of no created being, he withdraws into the centre of his own oneness, his spirit, made one with God in the solitary darkness of the Father, which is above all things, will surpass all things.

Who then will not wonder at this chameleon of ours, or who could wonder more greatly at anything else? For it was man who, on the ground of his mutability and of his ability to transform his own nature, was said by Asclepius of Athens to be symbolized by Prometheus in the mysteries.

From *Oratio de dignitate hominis*, in *Latin Writings of the Italian Humanists*, ed. F. A. Gragg (New York: Charles Scribner's Sons, 1927); trans. M.M.M.

Self-Portrait of a Universal Man

LEON BATTISTA ALBERTI

After 1460?

IN EVERYTHING suitable to one born free and educated liberally, he was so trained from boyhood that among the leading young men of his age he was considered by no means the last. For, assiduous in the science and skill of dealing with arms and horses and musical instruments, as well as in the pursuit of letters and the fine arts, he was devoted to the knowledge of the most strange and difficult things. And finally he embraced with zeal and forethought everything which pertained to fame. To omit the rest, he strove so hard to attain a name in modelling and painting that he wished to neglect nothing by which he might gain the approbation of good men. His genius was so versatile that you might almost judge all the fine arts to be his. Neither ease nor sloth held him back, nor was he ever seized by satiety in carrying out what was to be done.

He often said that not even in letters had he noticed what is called the satiety of all things among mortals; for to him letters, in which he delighted so greatly, seemed sometimes like flowering and richly fragrant buds, so that hunger or sleep could scarcely distract him from his books. At other times, however, those very letters swarmed together like scorpions before his eyes, so that he could see nothing at all but books. Therefore, when letters began to be displeasing to him, he turned to music and painting and exercise.

He played ball, hurled the javelin, ran, leaped, wrestled, and above all delighted in the steep ascent of mountains; he applied himself to all these things for the sake of health rather than sport or pleasure. As a youth he excelled in warlike games. With his feet together, he could leap over the shoulders of men standing by; he had almost no equal among those hurling the lance. An arrow shot by his hand from his chest could pierce the strongest iron breastplate. With his left foot lifted from the ground to the wall of a church, he could throw an apple into the air so high that it would go far beyond the top of the highest roofs. He could hurl a small coin into the air with such force that whoever was with him in the church could hear clearly the sound of the coin ringing against the lofty vaulting. On horseback, holding in his hand one end of a long wand, while the other was firmly fixed to his foot, he could ride his horse violently in all directions for hours at a time as he wished, and the wand would remain completely immobile. Strange and marvellous! that the most spirited horses and those most impatient of riders would, when he first mounted them, tremble violently and shudder as if in great fear. He learned music without teachers, and his compositions were approved by learned musicians. He sang throughout his whole life, but in private, or alone, and especially in the country with his brother or relatives. He delighted in the organ and was considered an expert among the leading musicians. Not a few musicians became more learned by virtue of his advice.

When he had begun to mature in years, neglecting everything else, he devoted himself entirely to the study of letters, and spent some years of labour on canon and civil law. Finally after so many nightly vigils and such great constancy, he fell gravely ill from the exer-

tion of his studies. Since his relatives were neither kind
nor humane to him in his illness, by way of consoling
himself between his convalescence and cure he wrote
the play *Philodoxeos*, putting aside his legal studies—
this when he was only twenty years old. And as soon
as his health permitted, he resumed his studies, intending to complete the law, but again he was seized by
a grave illness as he dragged his life along through
severe labour and extreme poverty. Reduced to a state
of weakness and emaciation, his energies consumed and
almost all the vigour of his body gone, his strength
broken and used up, he became so gravely ill that when
he tried to read the power of his vision seemed to fail,
with rising dizziness and griping pains, and far-off
crashings and whistlings dinned his ears. The doctors
declared that these things came about from the ex-
haustion of his physique, and they advised him again
and again not to persevere in his laborious pursuits. He
did not obey, but in his lust for learning consumed
himself by working late at night. Finally, when he
found his stomach was failing him, he fell into an illness worthy to be remembered. For during that time
the names of his most intimate friends would not come
to him although he knew them from long usage; other
things which he had seen, however, he held in mind
tenaciously.

At length, on the orders of his doctors, he desisted
from those studies which were most fatiguing to the
memory, just when they were about to flourish. But
in truth, because he could not live without letters, at
the age of twenty-four he turned to physics and the
mathematical arts. He did not despair of being able
to cultivate them sufficiently, because he perceived that
in them talent rather than memory must be employed.
At this time he wrote for his brother *On the Advan-*

tages and Disadvantages of Letters, in which booklet, taught by experience, he discussed whatever could be thought about letters. And he wrote at this time for the sake of his soul several little works: *Ephebia, On Religion, Deiphira,* and more of this sort in prose; then in verse, *Elegies* and *Eclogues,* and *Discourses,* and works on love of such a kind as to inculcate good habits in those who studied them and to foster the quiet of the soul.

In the year before he was thirty, moreover, he wrote in his native tongue, for the benefit of his relatives, in order to be of use to those who were ignorant of Latin, some books in Tuscan, the first, second, and third of *On the Family,* which he finished in Rome ninety days after he began them, but these books were uncultivated and harsh, not wholly Tuscan. For because of the long exile of the Alberti family he was educated among foreign peoples and did not possess his native tongue, and it was difficult for him to write with elegance and refinement in a language he had not been accustomed to use. But in a short time, thanks to his great zeal and industry, he mastered it, to such an extent that his fellow citizens, eager to be called eloquent in the Council, confessed that for the occasion they took not a few ornaments from his writings to adorn their own orations.

Besides these he also composed before he was thirty many dinner speeches, especially those facetious ones, "The Widow," "The Deceased," and others like them; many of these, however, because they did not seem to him sufficiently mature in form, although they were very entertaining and occasioned much laughter, he consigned to the flames lest he give occasion to his detractors to accuse him severely of levity. To those who disparaged what he had written, whenever they uttered their opinion in his presence, he gave thanks and received it, rejoicing that their admonition would lead to improvement. He felt, however, that it would be easy for anyone to support the opinion that his writing should be highly approved, and even if it pleased less than he wished, he should not be blamed, since he did not judge himself differently from other authors. For to each one, he said, it was forbidden by his own nature to do better than he was able to do; indeed, it should be considered enough if one fulfilled one's duty with all one's strength and ability.

He was always extremely circumspect in his habits lest they should in any way be subject to suspicion or censure, and he asserted that detractors were the worst evil in the life of man. For he had learned that they wound the reputation of good men not less by jesting and out of sheer pleasure than through indignation and wrath; and that such a wound could not be healed by any remedy because of the treacherous character of the ulcer they had caused. He wished by everything in his life, every gesture and every word, both to be and to seem worthy of the good will of good men; and together with other things, on three especially, he said, every art should be lavished. Art should be added to art lest anything seem to be done artfully when one is walking about in the city, riding a horse, or speaking. For in these things one must watch on all sides in order not to displease anyone greatly.

Although he was affable, gentle, and harmful to no one, nevertheless he felt the animosity of many evil men, and hidden enmities, both annoying and very burdensome; in particular the harsh injuries and intolerable insults from his own relatives. He lived among the envious and malevolent with such modesty and equanimity that none of his detractors or rivals, although very hostile towards him, dared to utter a word about him in the presence of good and worthy men unless it was full of praise and admiration. Even by these envious ones he was received with honour face to face. But, in truth, when he was absent, those who had pretended to love him most slandered him with every sort of calumny, wherever the ears of the fickle and their like lay open. For they took it ill to be exceeded in ability and fame by him who, far inferior to them in fortune, had striven with such zeal and industry. There were even some among his kinsmen (not to mention others) who, having experienced his humanity, beneficence, and liberality, conspired against him most ungratefully and cruelly in an evil domestic plot, and those barbarians aroused the boldness of servants to strike him with a knife, blameless as he was.

He bore injuries of this kind from his kinsmen with equanimity, more in silence than by indignantly resorting to vengeance or permitting the shame and ignominy of his relatives to be made public. He granted them more than enough in praise and recognition. He could not be induced by injuries to hate anyone whom he had once loved, but said that evil men could so easily outstrip good men in doing harm. For he thought it should be considered more suitable for the good to endure injuries rather than to inflict them, and therefore it was not an equal struggle between those unwilling to offend and those who were ready to excite trouble. And so he broke the impetus of the shameless by his patience, and so far as he could, saved himself from calamity solely by the cultivation of virtue. He was commended by good and studious men. He was most acceptable to not a few princes. But because he detested all forms of ambition and adulation he was less pleasing to many than he would have been if he had been closer to more of them.

Among the Italian princes and among foreign kings, witnesses and heralds of his virtue were not lacking. He did not make use of their favour for any revenge, however, although he was continually disturbed by new injuries and could easily have avenged himself. When in the course of time, moreover, it came about that his private fortune was of great value to those by whom he had been gravely injured, he preferred to pay them back with kindness, benefits, and all kinds of philanthropy rather than to take revenge, so that the scoundrels regretted they had injured such a man. When he had given his relatives the first, second, and third books of *On the Family* to read, he resented the fact that among all the Albertis, even the most leisurely, scarcely one could be found who deigned to read even the titles of the books, although those very books were sought out by foreigners; and he could not stomach it when he observed some of them openly making fun of the whole work and of the author's intention as completely inept. As a result of that affront he would have thrown into the fire those three books which he had just finished if certain princes had not prevented him. He conquered his indignation with a sense of duty, however, and after three years he offered to the ingrates a fourth book, which he had added to the first. "If you are honourable you will love me henceforth," he said, "but if you are dishonourable, your dishonour will become offensive to you." By these very books, many uneducated and even crude fellow citizens of his became devoted to letters. He counted them as brothers, and all others eager for learning, and whatever he came to know, he voluntarily communicated to them. He turned over those discoveries of his which were worthy and important to any who could use them. When he heard that a learned man of any kind had arrived, he would at once work his way into a position of familiarity with him and thus from any source whatsoever he began to learn what he was ignorant of. From craftsmen, architects, shipbuilders, and even from cobblers he sought information to see if by chance they preserved anything rare or unusual or special in their arts; and he would then communicate such things to those citizens who wished to know them. He pretended to be ignorant in many things so that he might observe the talents and habits and skill of others. And so he was a zealous observer of whatsoever pertained to inborn talent or the arts.

He wholly despised the pursuit of material gain. He gave his money and goods to his friends to take care of and to enjoy. Among those by whom he believed himself loved, he was not only outgoing about his affairs and his habits but even about his secrets. He never betrayed the secrets of another but remained silent forever. He would not produce the letter of a certain traitor by which he could have gravely harmed that vile enemy, but from time to time, when that evil reviler, the author of the letter, did not desist from his biting, he was moved only to say, smiling, "Tell me, my good man, do you remember having written any letters?" And, turning to a most annoying detractor, he would say, "I shall endure the lies that you tell about me. I shall gladly let you show by your lying what each one of us is like, in whatever you wish. By broadcasting in this way you actually succeed better in revealing your own lack of modesty than in vituperating me shamelessly. By laughing at these absurdities of yours, I bring it about that you accomplish nothing except to displease yourself when you depart from me in a state of frustation."

He was by nature prone to wrath and bitter in spirit

but he could repress his rising indignation immediately
by taking thought. Sometimes he deliberately fled from
the verbose and the headstrong because with them he
could not subdue his wrath. At other times he voluntarily submitted to the bold, in order to grow in patience. He would summon his friends to him, and
while he held continual conversations about letters and
learning with them, and while they were writing, he
would dictate little essays and at the same time would
paint their portraits or model in wax. In Venice he
portrayed the countenances of his friends far away in
Florence, whom he had not seen for a year and months
on end. He used to ask young boys whether they
recognized the portrait he was painting, and said that
nothing could be called skilfully painted if it was not
at once recognized by the young. He copied his own
expression and likeness so that from this painted and
modelled semblance he would be more easily known
to strangers approaching him.

He wrote some books entitled *On Painting*, and in
this very art of painting he created works unheard of
and unbelievable to those who saw them, which, enclosed in a small box, he showed through a tiny opening. You could have seen there great mountains, vast
plains, and the immense bay of an encircling sea, and
then regions far remote from view, even so distant that
one's vision failed. He called these things "demonstrations," and they were such that both the experienced
and the inexperienced insisted that the things seen
were not painted but real and natural. There were two
kinds of "demonstrations," one which he called diurnal,
the other nocturnal. In the nocturnal demonstration
you could see Arcturus, the Pleiades, Orion, and sparkling constellations of this kind; and the moon shone,
rising above the lofty peak of rocks and cliffs, and the

nightly stars gleamed. And in the diurnal demonstration there shone here and there, illuminating widely the immense orb of the earth, a star that glitters after the "early born" Aurora, as Homer says. He inspired admiration in certain distinguished Greeks who were experts in matters relating to the sea. For when he showed them this invented mass of the world through the little opening, as I have said, and asked them what they had seen, they replied, "We saw a fleet of ships in the midst of waves. We shall have it with us before noon, unless that thundercloud to the east of the sun and that threatening tempest harm it as it hastens here. For already we observe the sea quaking, and there are signs of danger in that the sun casts too many sharp rays over the sea."

He applied himself more in his work to investigating things of this kind than to making them known, for he always served genius rather than fame. His mind was never free from meditation and deliberation. He rarely stayed at home out of the public eye without deliberating upon something, and also pondered at dinner between courses. Hence he seemed excessively silent and solitary, and sorrowful in countenance, but he was not at all morose in his manners; on the contrary, among his intimates, even when he was discussing serious matters, he always showed himself agreeable and, though maintaining his dignity, even gay.

There were those who collected many sayings of his, both serious and humorous, which he usually brought forth on the spot and quickly, rather than by premeditation. . . .

We have his letters to Paul the Doctor in which he put in writing the coming disasters of the fatherland years in advance; and he foretold the fortunes of the popes which were to come about in the twelve years following. His friends and intimates relate that the political movements in many other cities and the acts of princes were foretold by him. He had within himself a ray by which he could sense the good or evil intentions of men towards himself. Simply by looking at them, he could discover most of the defects of anyone in his presence. He used all kinds of reasoning and great effort, but in vain, to make more gentle towards himself those whom he had learned at one glance would be inimical. He bore their hostilities calmly, however, as if they were a kind of fatal necessity, and in every dispute he intimated that he would strive more moderately than was perhaps his right, except in returning favours of mutual benefit. He could hardly bear to see anyone exceed him in benevolence, excluding ambition, however, which was so alien to him that he even ascribed his own deeds, worthy of memory, to his elders in his book *On the Family*. And he also put in his own works the titles of others, and there exist whole works devoted to the fame of his friends.

He could endure pain and cold and heat. When, not yet fifteen, he received a serious wound in the foot, and the physician, according to his custom and skill, drew together the broken parts of the foot and sewed them through the skin with a needle, he scarcely uttered a sound of pain. With his own hands, though in such great pain, he even aided the ministering doctor and treated his own wound though he was burning with fever. And when on account of a pain in his side he was continually in an icy sweat, he called in musicians, and for about two hours he strove by singing to overcome the force of the malady and the agony of the pain. His head was by nature unable to endure either cold or wind; but by persistence he learned to bear them, gradually getting used to riding bareheaded in summer, then in winter, and even in raging wind. By some defect in his nature he loathed garlic and also honey, and the mere sight of them, if by chance they were offered to him, brought on vomiting. But he conquered himself by force of looking at and handling the disagreeable objects, so that they came to offend him less, thus showing by example that men can do anything with themselves if they will.

When, to refresh his mind, he went out from home into the marketplace and saw all the artisans hard at work in their shops, often on his return he would at once resume his work as if warned by some grave censor, saying, "We too must exert ourselves in the task we have undertaken." In the spring when he saw the fields and the hills in bloom and noticed all the plants and trees bearing the greatest promise of fruit to come, deep sadness overcame him, and he would reproach himself in these words, "Now you too, Battista, must bring forth some fruit from your studies!" And in the autumn when he saw the fields heavy with the harvest and the trees laden with fruit, he was so afflicted with sadness that he was even seen on occasion to weep from sorrow and heard to murmur, "See, Leo, how on all sides witnesses and accusers of our idleness surround us! For what is there anywhere in nature which in the course of a whole year does not produce something of great advantage to men? But you, what do you have that you can bring forth, by virtue of your profession, for the public good?"

He took extraordinary and peculiar pleasure in looking at things in which there was any mark of beauty or adornment. He never ceased to wonder at old men who were endowed with dignity of countenance, and unimpaired and vigorous, and he proclaimed that he honoured them as "delights of nature." He declared that quadrupeds, birds, and other living things of out-standing beauty were worthy of benevolence because by the very distinction of their nature they deserved favour.

When his favourite dog died he wrote a funeral oration for him.

Whatever was done by man with genius and with a certain grace, he held to be almost divine; and he so respected anything achieved that he insisted even poor writers were worthy of praise. The sight of gems, flowers, and especially pleasant places more than once restored him from illness to good health.

From *Opere volgari di Leon Batt. Alberti*, ed A. Bonucci (Florence: 1843); trans. J.B.R.

St. Thomas More

NICHOLAS HARPSFIELD

c. 1555

THIS EXCELLENT and peerless man, whose life we have to indite, besides all other great and beautiful outward and perpetual arguments that God and nature adorned him withall, was beautified (if such things may add any weight to his commendation, as they do in the eyes and consideration of many) as well by the place of his birth, being born at London, the chief and notable principal city of this our noble realm, as by the heritage and worshipful family whereof he sprang. His father, Master John More, was very expert in the laws of this realm, and for his worthiness advanced to be one of the justices of the king's bench, and to the wor-

shipful degree of knighthood. Who, besides his learning, was endued with many notable and virtuous qualities and gifts. . . . But now to return to his son;
neither was he by his parents, nor by his birth and
place, so much adorned and beautified as he did adorn
and beautify them both and the whole realm beside. . . .

It remains now then . . . that we speak somewhat
of his books, whereby he has consecrated his worthy
name to immortality in this transitory world to the
world's end. . . . Whereof some are written in Latin
only, some in English only, some certain in both
tongues. . . . Among his other Latin books are his
epigrams, partly translated out of Greek, partly so
wittily and pleasantly devised and penned of his own,
as they may seem to be nothing inferior or to yield to
any of like kind written in our days, and perchance
worthy to be set and compared with many like writers
of the old bygone days. These epigrams, as they be
learned and pleasant, so are they nothing biting or
contumelious. . . .

He wrote also most elegantly and eloquently the life
of King Richard the Third, not only in English, which
book is abroad in print, but corrupted and vitiated, but
in Latin also, not yet printed. . . .

But the book that bears the prick and prize of all
his other Latin books of witty intention, for profane
matters, is his Utopia. He paints me it forth so lively
and so pleasantly, as it were an exquisite platform,
pattern, and example of a singular good commonwealth,
as to the same neither the Lacedaemonians, nor the
Athenians, nor yet, the best of all others, the Roman
commonwealth is comparable; full prettily and probably devising the said commonwealth to be in one of
the countries of the new-found lands declared unto him

at Antwerp by Hithlodius, a Portuguese, and one of the
sea companions of Americus Vespucius, that first sought
out and found these lands. Such an excellent and absolute state of commonwealth that, saving the people
were unchristened, might seem to pass any state and
commonwealth, I will not say of the old nations by me
rehearsed, but even of any other even in our time.

Many great learned men, as Budé and John Desmarais, seemed to take the same story as a true story.
And Desmarais upon a fervent zeal wished that some
excellent divines might be sent thither to preach
Christ's Gospel. Yea, then there were among us at home
sundry good men and learned divines very desirous to
take that voyage, to bring that people to Christ's faith,
whose manners they did so well like upon. . . .

Now have we besides other excellent and fruitful
books of his which he made, being prisoner in the
Tower, as his three books of comfort against tribulation, a treatise to receive the blessed sacrament sacra-
mentally and virtually both, a treatise upon the passion, with notable introductions to the same. He wrote
also many other godly and devout instructions and
prayers. . . .

And these be in effect the books he made either in
Latin or English. His English books, if they had been
written by him in the Latin tongue also, or might be,
with the like grace that they now have, translated into
the Latin speech, would surely much augment and increase the estimation and admiration that the world
has already in foreign countries of his incomparable
wit and learning. For which he was even while he
lived throughout all Christendom marvellously esteemed
and renowned, as appears by the writings of sundry
learned men, with many of which he was well acquainted also by reason of his embassies into France

and Flanders, especially with Erasmus and Peter Gilles. Which two persons, when that one Quentin [Metsys], a singular good painter, had set forth and painted at a certain table, Sir Thomas More made thereof certain verses, declaring that he was sorry that himself also was not set at the same table, who did so entirely love them both. The said Erasmus of all men in the world most delighted in the company of Sir Thomas More, whose help and friendship he much used when he had any affairs with King Henry the Eight.

The which king, for the exquisite learning that he well knew, not only by his erudite books, but by good experience of him otherwise, he was adorned withall, for many years used upon the holy days, when he had done his devotions, to send for him into his closet, and there to sit and confer with him, not only in matters and affairs of this realm, but also in astronomy, geometry, divinity, and other faculties. And otherwhiles would he in the night have him onto his roof, there to consider with him the diversities, courses, motions, and operations of the stars and planets. With whom he was, as not lightly with any man more, at other times wonderfully familiar, as we have partly touched before, not only for his learning's sake, but because he was of so merry and pleasant disposition. Whom when he perceived so much in his talk to delight that he could not once in a month get leave to go home to his wife and children, whose company he most desired, and to be absent from the court two days together but that he should be thither sent for again, he, much misliking this restraint of his liberty, began thereupon somewhat to dissemble his nature, and so little and little from his accustomed mirth to disuse himself that he was of them from henceforth at such seasons no more so ordinarily sent for as he was wont to be.

Now for his wise, pleasant, witty talk, and for his other qualities, he had beside his learned friends many others in England as otherwhere, but yet none so dear and so entire to him as was the good and gracious right worshipful merchant Master Antonio Bonvisi. To whom he [More], being prisoner in the Tower, a little before he was arraigned and condemned, wrote a Latin letter with a coal. Wherein among other things he confesses himself that he had been almost forty years not a guest but a continual nursling in Bonvisi's house and the singular favour, help, and aid that he had at all times, especially in his adversities, felt at his hands. And that few did so fawn upon their fortunate friends as Bonvisi did favour, love, foster, and honour him being overthrown, cast down, afflicted, and condemned to prison. And Sir Thomas More was wont to call him the apple of his eye. . . .

But because we are in hand with the books and learning of the said Sir Thomas More, I will now tell you this one thing only, that I have heard him [Bonvisi] report that he would at table and otherwhere wonderfully deeply and like a cleric talk with learned men, as well English as of other countries; and that he once knew when a very excellent learned man (as he was considered), a stranger, being in this realm, chanced to be at the table with Sir Thomas More, whom he knew not. At which table there was great reasoning between the said stranger and others of many great points of learning. At length Sir Thomas More set in a foot, and coped with the said stranger, and demeaned himself so cunningly and so learnedly that the said stranger, who was a religious man, was much astonished and abashed to hear such profound reasons at a layman's hand. And thereupon inquired of such as were nearest at hand to him what his name was, which when he once understood, he had no great pleasure afterwards to encounter any more with him.

And his good blessed disposition and wise behaviour in such kind of disputations is worth the noting. For among all his other virtues, he was of such meekness that, if it fortuned him with any learned men resorting to him from Oxford, Cambridge, or elsewhere (as there did divers, some for desire of his acquaintance, some for the famous report of his wisdom and learning, and some for suits of the universities), to have entered into arguments (wherein few were comparable to him) and so far to have discoursed with them therein that he might perceive they could not without some inconvenience hold out much farther disputation against him; then, lest he should discomfort them (as he that sought not his own glory, but rather would seem conquered than discourage students in their studies, even showing himself more desirous to learn than to teach), would he by some witty device courteously break off into some other matter, and give over.

Of whom for his wisdom and learning had the king such an opinion that, at such times as he attended upon his Highness taking his progress either to Oxford or Cambridge, where he was received with very eloquent orations, his Grace would always assign him, as one that was prompt and ready therein, *ex tempore* to make answer thereunto. His manner was, whenever he had occasion, either here or beyond the sea, to be in any university, not only to be present at the readings and disputations there commonly used, but also learnedly to dispute among them himself.

But now it is time to cease from further treating of his learning and books, saving I think good to be by the way marked and noted how he could possibly write so many and excellent works; either being out of prison, though furnished with books, being so continually travailed in the affairs of the king's council and of his great office, but one great help was the excellence of his wit and memory, which were both twain singular, and one other, that he spared and saved much time that men commonly misspend in eating and sleeping; or being in prison, being as he was, so unfurnished of books. . . .

But yet it shall not be perchance amiss, seeing we have set forth to your sight his excellent learning and some singular qualities of his blessed soul and mind, somewhat also here to interlace to the satisfaction of such as be desirous thereof, before we go farther, of his body also, and of other things thereto belonging.

Then, as he was no tall man, so was he no notably low or little man; all the parts of his body were in as good proportion and congruence as a man could wish. His skin was somewhat white, and the colour of his face drew rather to whiteness than to paleness, far from redness, saving that some little thin red sparkles everywhere appeared. His hair was blackish yellow or rather yellow blackish, his beard thin, his eyes grey and speckled, which kind of eyes do commonly betoken and signify a very good and sharp wit. And they say that such eyes are least encumbered with diseases and faults. His countenance was conformable to his nature and disposition, pleasant and amiable, somewhat resembling and tending to the fashion of one that would laugh.

His voice was neither too boisterous and big, neither too small and shrill. He spoke his words very distinctly and deliberately, without any manner of hastiness or stuttering. And albeit he delighted in all kind of melody, yet he seemed not of nature to be apt and meet to sing himself.

He enjoyed the health of his body full well; and though he was not very strong of body, yet was he able to go through with any labour and pain meet and convenient for him to dispatch his business and affairs. He was very little infested and encumbered with sickness, saving a little before he gave over the office of Lord Chancellor and especially afterward, when he was shut up in the Tower.

And now somewhat to speak of his diet. Being a young man, he used and delighted much in drinking of water. He used very small ale, and as for wine, he did not sip of it only for company's sake and pledging of his friends. He more delighted to feed upon beef, salt meats, and coarse bread, and that very well leavened, than upon fine meats and bread. He loved very well milk and fruit and especially eggs.

It was great pleasure for him to see and behold the form and fashion, the manner and disposition, of divers beasts. There was probably not any kind of birds that he kept not in his house, as he also kept the ape, the fox, the weasel, the ferret, and other beasts that were rare and not common. Besides, if there had been anything brought out of a strange country, or worthy to be looked upon, that was he very desirous to buy, and to adorn and furnish his house withall, to the satisfaction and pleasure of such as came to him, who took great pleasure in the beholding of such things, and himself also with them. . . .

Sir Thomas More was condemned in Westminster Hall, where he and his father before him ministered justice most uprightly to all manner of suitors, and where a few years before there was such a praise, even by the king's commandment (as we have showed) given him, as probably has not been given before to any other.

He was executed at the Tower, and his head (for defending the right head of the Church) by the king's commandment (who rending the unity of the Church, and taking away St. Peter's prerogative and of his successors, had, as I may say, cut off St. Peter's head, and put it, an ugly sight to behold, upon his own shoulders) pitifully cut off. And the said head was set upon London Bridge, in the said city, where he was born and brought up, upon a high pole, among the heads of traitors. A rueful and a pitiful spectacle for all good citizens and other good Christians, and much more lamentable to see their Christian English Cicero's head in such sort, than it was to the Romans to see the head of Marcus Tullius Cicero set up in the same city where he had, by his great eloquent orations, preserved many an innocent from imminent danger and peril, and had preserved the whole city, by his great industry, from the mischievous conspiracy of Cataline and his seditious accomplices.

But yet Sir Thomas More's head had not so high a place upon the pole as had his blessed soul among the celestial martyrs in heaven. By whose hearty and devout intercession and his aforesaid co-martyrs, and of our protomartyr St. Alban, and other blessed martyrs and saints of the realm, I doubt not but God of late has the sooner cast his pitiful eye to reduce us again by his blessed minister and queen, Lady Mary, and by the noble, virtuous, excellent prelate, Cardinal Pole, to the unity of the Church that we had before abandoned. In the which God of his great mercy long preserve the realm. Amen.

From *The Life and Death of Sir Thomas More*, ed. E. V. Hitchcock (London: Early English Text Society, 1932).

Michelangelo Buonarroti

ASCANIO CONDIVI

1553

IT SEEMS to me that nature has endowed Michael Angelo so largely with all her riches in these arts of painting and sculpture, that I am not to be reproached for saying that his figures are almost inimitable. Nor does it appear that I have allowed myself to be too much carried away, for until now he alone has worthily taken up both chisel and brush. Of the painting of the ancients there is no memorial, and to whom does he yield in their sculpture (of which, indeed, much remains)? In the judgment of men learned in the art, to no one, unless we stoop to the opinion of the vulgar, who admire the antique for the sole reason that they envy the genius and industry of their own times. All the same, I have not yet heard anyone say the contrary; this man is so far above envy. Raffael da Urbino, although he desired to compete with Michael Angelo, was often constrained to say that he thanked God he was born in his time, as he acquired from him a style very different from that which he learned from his father, who was a painter, and from his master Perugino. But what greater and clearer sign can we ever have of the excellence of this man than the contention of the princes of the world for him? From the four pontiffs, Julius, Leo, Clement, and Paul, to the Grand Turk, father of him who today holds the Empire. As I have said above, the Sultan sent certain monks of

the Order of Saint Francis with letters begging Michael
Angelo to come and stay with him; arranging by letters of credit for the bank of the Gondi, in Florence,
to advance the amount of money necessary for his
journey, and also that from Cossa, near Ragusi, he
should be accompanied to Constantinople most honourably by one of his grandees. Francesco Valesio
[Francis I], King of France, tried every means to get
him, crediting him with three thousand scudi for his
journey wherever he should go. Il Bruciolo was sent
to Rome by the Signoria of Venice to invite him to
come and dwell in that city, and to offer him a provision of six hundred scudi a year, not binding him to
anything, only that he should honour the republic with
his presence; with the condition also that if he did any
work in her service he should be paid for it as if he
received no pension from them at all. These are not
ordinary doings that happen every day, but new and
out of the common use, and would only happen to
singular and most excellent worth, as was that of
Homer, for whom many cities contended, each one
appropriating him as her own.

He is held of no less account, than by those already
named, by the present pontiff, Julius III, a prince of
supreme wisdom and a lover and patron of all the arts;
but particularly inclined to painting, sculpture, and
architecture, as may be clearly known by the works he
has done in the Palazzo and the Belvedere, and now
has ordered for his Villa Giulia (a memorial and
scheme worthy of a noble and generous soul like his).
It is filled with so many statues, ancient and modern,
so great variety of beautiful stones, precious columns,
plaster work, paintings, and every other kind of ornament, of which I will write another time, as a unique
work, not yet in its perfection, requires. He does not

ask Michael Angelo to work for him. Having respect
for his age, he understands well and appreciates his
greatness; but wishes not to burden him with more
than he is willing to do. This regard, in my judgment,
brings Michael Angelo more honour than all his employment under the other popes. It is, however, true
that in the paintings and architecture that his Holiness is continually having done, he almost always seeks
Michael Angelo's advice and judgment, frequently
sending the artists to seek him at his house. It grieves
me, and it grieves also his Holiness, that by reason of a
certain natural timidity, or let us say respect and reverence, which some call pride, Michael Angelo does
not profit by the good will, kindness, and liberality of
so great a pontiff and so much his friend. As I first
heard from the most Reverend Monsignor di Forlì, his
chamberlain, the pope has often said that (if it was
possible) he would willingly take from his own years
and his own blood to add to the life of Michael Angelo,
that the world might not so soon be deprived of such
a man. I also, having access to his Holiness, heard it
from his lips with my own ears, and more also, that
if he survive him, as in the natural course of life is
probable, he will have Michael Angelo's body em-
balmed and keep it near him, so that it should be as
lasting as his works. He said this at the beginning of
his pontificate to Michael Angelo himself in the presence of many. I do not know what could be more
honourable to Michael Angelo than these words, or a
greater proof of the esteem in which the pope holds
him.

Again the pope showed his esteem plainly when
Pope Paul died and he was created pontiff, in a con-
sistory, all the cardinals then in Rome being present.
He defended Michael Angelo and protected him from

the overseers of the fabric of St. Peter's, who, for no fault of his, as they said, but of his servants, wished to deprive him of, or at least to restrain, that authority given him by Pope Paul by a *motu proprio,* of which more will be said below. . . .

At the request of his Holiness, Michael Angelo designed the façade of a palace that the pope had a mind to build in Rome, a thing new and original to those who have seen it—not bound to any laws, ancient or modern, as in many other works of his in Florence and in Rome—proving that architecture has not been so absolutely treated in the past that there is not room for fresh invention no less delightful and beautiful.

Now to return to anatomy. He gave up dissection because it turned his stomach so that he could neither eat nor drink with benefit. It is very true that he did not give up until he was so learned and rich in such knowledge that he often had in mind the wish to write, for the sake of sculptors and painters, a treatise on the movements of the human body, its aspect, and concerning the bones, with an ingenious theory of his own, devised after long practice. He would have done it had he not mistrusted his powers, lest they should not suffice to treat with dignity and grace of such a subject, like one practised in the sciences and in rhetoric. I know well that when he reads Alberto Duro [Albrecht Dürer] he finds him very weak, seeing in his own mind how much more beautiful and useful his own conception would be. To tell the truth, Alberto only treats of the proportions and diversities of the body, for which one cannot make fixed rules, making figures as regular as posts; and what matters more, says nothing of human movements and gestures. And because Michael Angelo has now reached a ripe old age, he thinks of putting his ideas in writing and giving them to the world. With great kindness he has explained everything minutely to me; he also conferred with Messer Realdo Colombo, an anatomist and most excellent surgeon, a great friend of Michael Angelo's and mine. He sent to Michael Angelo for study the body of a Moor, a very fine young man, and very suitable to the purpose; he was sent to Santa Agata, where I then lived and still live, as it is a quiet place. On this corpse Michael Angelo showed me many rare and recondite facts, perhaps never before understood, all of which I noted down, and hope one day, with the help of some learned man, to publish for the advantage and use of painters and sculptors; but enough of this.

He devoted himself to perspective and to architecture, his works show with what profit. Michael Angelo did not content himself with knowing only the main features of architecture, but wished also to know about everything that could be useful in any way in that profession, such as ties, platforms, scaffolding, and such like; he knew as much of these things as those who profess nothing else, which was exemplified in the time of Julius II, in this wise. When Michael Angelo had to paint the ceiling of the Sistine Chapel the pope ordered Bramante to erect the scaffolding. For all the architect he was he did not know how to do it, but pierced the vault in many places, letting down certain ropes through these holes to sling the platform. When Michael Angelo saw it he smiled, and asked Bramante what was to be done when he came to those holes. Bramante had no defence to make, only replied that it could not be done any other way. The matter came before the pope, and Bramante replied again to the same effect. The pope turned to Michael Angelo and said, "As it is not satisfactory, go and do it yourself."

Michael Angelo took down the platform, and took away so much rope from it that, having given it to a poor man that assisted him, it enabled him to dower and marry two daughters. Michael Angelo erected his scaffold without ropes, so well devised and arranged that the more weight it had to bear the firmer it became. This opened Bramante's eyes, and gave him a lesson in the building of a platform, which was very useful to him in the works of St. Peter's. For all that, Michael Angelo, although he had no equal in all these things, would not make a profession of architecture. On the contrary, when at last Antonio de San Gallo, the architect of St. Peter's, died, and Pope Paul wished to put Michael Angelo in his place, he refused the post, saying that architecture was not his art. He refused it so earnestly that the pope had to command him to take it, and issued an ample *motu proprio,* which was afterwards confirmed by Pope Julius III, now, as I have said, by the grace of God, our pontiff. For these, his services, Michael Angelo would take no payment; so he wished it to be stated in the *motu proprio.* One day, when Pope Paul sent him a hundred scudi of gold by Messer Pier Giovanni, then Gentleman of the Wardrobe to his Holiness now Bishop of Forlì, as his month's salary on account of the building, Michael Angelo would not accept it, saying it was not in the agreement they had between them, and he sent them back. The pope was very angry, as I have been told by Messer Alessandro Ruffini, a gentleman of Rome, then Groom to the Chambers and Carver before his Holiness; but this did not move Michael Angelo from his resolution. When he had accepted this charge he made a new model, both because certain parts of the old one did not please him in many respects, and, besides, if it was followed one would sooner expect to see the end of the world than St. Peter's finished. This model, praised and approved by the pope, is now being followed to the great satisfaction of those who have judgment, although there be certain persons who do not approve of it.

Michael Angelo gave himself, then, whilst still young, not only to sculpture and painting, but to all the kindred arts, with such devotion that for a time he almost withdrew from the fellowship of men, only consorting with a few. So that by some he was held to be proud, and by others odd and eccentric, though he had none of these vices; but (like many excellent men) a love of knowledge and continued exercise in the learned arts made him solitary, and he was so satisfied and took such a delight in them that company not only did not please him but even annoyed him, as interrupting his meditations; he was never less solitary than when alone (as the great Scipio used to say of himself).

Nevertheless he willingly kept the friendship of those from whose wise and learned conversation he could gather any fruit and in whom shone some ray of excellence, such as the most reverend and illustrious Monsignor Polo [Pole], for his rare learning and singular goodness; and similarly my most reverend patron the Cardinal Crispo, finding in him besides his many excellent qualities a rare and excellent judgment. . . .

More particularly he loved greatly the Marchesa [Vittoria Colonna] of Pescara, of whose divine spirit he was enamoured, being in return loved tenderly by her. He still possesses many letters of hers, full of an honest and most sweet love, such as issued from her heart. He has written to her also many and many sonnets, full of wit and sweet desire. She often returned to Rome from Viterbo and other places, where she had gone for her pastime and to spend the summer, for no other reason than to see Michael Angelo; and he bore her so much love that I remember to have heard him say [that] nothing grieved him so much as that when he went to see her after she passed away from this life he did not kiss her on the brow or face, as he did kiss her hand. Recalling this, her death, he often remained dazed as one bereft of sense. He made at the wish of his lady a naked Christ, when He was taken down from the Cross, and His dead body would have fallen at the feet of his most holy Mother, if it were not supported by the arms of two little angels; but she, seated under the cross with a tearful and sorrowful face, raises to heaven both hands with her arms outstretched, with this cry, which one reads inscribed on the stem of the Cross: "Little you reck how much His blood hath cost." The Cross is like that which was carried in procession by the Bianchi at the time of the plague of 1348, and afterwards placed in the Church of Santa Croce, at Florence. He also made for love of her a drawing of a Jesu Christ on the Cross, not as if dead, as is the common use, but with a divine gesture. Raising His face to the Father, He seems to say, "Eli, Eli." The body does not hang like a corpse, but as if still living, suffering and contorted by the bitter agony of His death.

And as he greatly delighted in the conversation of the learned, so he took pleasure in the study of the writers of both prose and poetry. He had a special admiration for Dante, delighting in the admirable genius of that man, almost all of whose works he knew by heart; he held Petrarca in no less esteem. He not only delighted in reading, but occasionally in composing too, as may be seen by some sonnets that are to be found of his, and which give a very good idea of his invention and judgment. Concerning some of them, there have been published *Lectures and Criticism by Varchi*. But he wrote these sonnets more for his pleasure than because he made a profession of it, always belittling himself, accusing himself of ignorance in these matters.

Likewise, with deep study and attention, he read the Holy Scriptures, both the Old and the New Testaments, as well as those who have expounded them, such as the writings of Savonarola, for whom he always had a great affection, keeping always in mind the memory of his living voice. He has also loved the beauty of the human body, as one who best understands it; and in such wise that certain carnal-minded men, who are not able to comprehend the love of beauty unless it be lewd and shameful, have taken occasion to think and speak evil of him, as if Alcibiades, a youth of perfect beauty, had not been purely loved by Socrates, from whose side he arose as from the side of his father. I have often heard Michael Angelo reason and discourse of Love, and learned afterwards from those who were present that he did not speak otherwise of Love than is to be found written in the works of Plato. For myself I do not know what Plato says of Love, but I know well that I, who have known Michael Angelo so long and so intimately, have never heard issue from his mouth any but the most honest of words, which had the power to extinguish in youth every ill-regulated and unbridled desire which might arise. By this we may know that no evil thoughts were born in him. He loved not only human beauty, but universally every beautiful thing— a beautiful horse, a beautiful dog, a beautiful country, a beautiful plant, a beautiful mountain, a beautiful forest, and every place and thing beautiful and rare after its kind, admiring them all with a marvellous love; thus choosing the beauty in nature as the bees gather honey from the flowers, using it afterwards in their works, as all those have done who have ever made a noise in painting. That old master who had to paint a Venus was not content to see one virgin only, but studied many, and, taking from each her most beautiful and perfect feature, gave them to his Venus; and, in truth, whoever expects to arrive at any excellence in art without this method of study, by which a true theory of beauty may be acquired, is greatly mistaken.

All through his life Michael Angelo has been very abstemious, taking food more from necessity than from pleasure, especially when at work, at which time, for the most part, he has been content with a piece of bread, which he munched whilst he laboured. But latterly he has lived more regularly, his advanced age requiring it. I have often heard him say, "Ascanio, rich man as I have made myself, I have always lived as a poor one." And as he took little food so he took little sleep, which, as he says, rarely did him any good, for sleeping almost always made his head ache, and too much sleep made his stomach bad. When he was more robust he often slept in his clothes and with his buskins on; these he has always used for fear of the cramp, from which he continually suffered, besides other reasons; and he has sometimes been so long without taking them off that when he did so the skin came off with them like the slough of a snake. He was never miserly with his money, nor did he hoard it, contented with enough to live honestly. So, although works from his hand were sought for more and more by the gentry and rich people with large promises, yet he has rarely satisfied them; and when he has done so, it has been from friendship and good will rather than for hope of reward. . . .

Michael Angelo is of a good complexion; his figure

rather sinuous and bony than fleshy and fat; healthy above all by nature, as well as by the use of exercise and his continence of life and moderation in taking food; nevertheless as a child he was feeble and sickly, and as a man he had two illnesses. He has suffered much for several years in the passing of urine, which trouble would have turned into a stone if he had not been relieved by the care and diligence of the before-mentioned Messer Realdo. Michael Angelo has always had a good colour in his face. His figure thus: he is of middle height, broad, with the rest of the body in proportion, rather slight than otherwise. The shape of his skull in front is round, so that the height above the ear makes more than a half circle, a sixth part, so that the temples project somewhat beyond the ears, and the ears beyond the cheekbones, and the cheekbones beyond the rest of the face; the skull in proportion to the face must be called large. The front view of the forehead is square, the nose a little flattened, not naturally, but because, when he was a boy, one Torrigiano de' Torrigiani, a brutal and proud fellow, with a blow almost broke the cartilage, so that Michael Angelo was carried home as one dead; for this Torrigiano was banished from Florence, and he came to a bad end. Michael Angelo's nose, such as it is, is in proportion to the forehead and the rest of the face. His lips are thin, the lower one somewhat the thicker, so that seen in profile it sticks out a little. The chin goes well with the above-mentioned parts. The forehead in profile is almost in front of the nose, which is little less than broken, except for a small hump in the middle. The eyebrows have few hairs; the eyes are rather small than otherwise, the colour is that of horn, but changing, with sparkles of yellow and blue; the ears in proportion; the hair black, and beard also, but in this his seventy-ninth year plentifully sprinkled with grey; his beard is forked, four or five fingers long and not very thick, as may partially be seen in his portraits. Many other things remain to be said, but I have left them out because of the hurry in which I bring out these writings, hearing that others wish to reap the reward of my labours, which I confided to their hands; so, if it should ever happen that another should undertake this work again, or write this same life, I hereby offer to tell him all I know, or most lovingly to give it to him in writing. I hope before long to bring out some of Michael Angelo's sonnets and madrigals, which I have for a long time collected, both from himself and from others, that the world may know the worth of his imaginations, and how many beautiful conceits were born in his divine spirit. And with this I make an end.

From *The Life of Michael Angelo Buonarroti*, in C. Holroyd, *Michael Angelo Buonarroti* (London: Duckworth & Co., 1911).

On Himself and His Life

GIROLAMO CARDANO

1575

I AM a man of medium height; my feet are short, wide near the toes, and rather too high at the heels, so that I can scarcely find well-fitting shoes; it is usually necessary to have them made to order. My chest is somewhat narrow and my arms slender. The thickly fashioned right hand has dangling fingers, so that chiromantists have declared me a rustic; it embarrasses them to know the truth. The line of life upon my palm is short, while the line called Saturn's is extended and deep. My left hand, on the contrary, is truly beautiful, with long, tapering, well-formed fingers and shining nails.

A neck a little long and inclined to be thin, cleft chin, full pendulous lower lip, and eyes that are very small and apparently half-closed, unless I am gazing at something; . . . such are my features. Over the eyebrow of my left eye is a blotch or wart, like a small lentil, which can scarcely be noticed. The wide forehead is bald at the sides where it joins the temples. My hair and beard were blond; I am wont to go rather closely clipped. The beard, like my chin, is divided, and the part of it beneath my chin always was thick and long, seeming to have a more abundant growth thereunder. Old age has wrought changes in this beard of mine, but not much in my hair.

A rather too shrill voice draws upon me the censure of those who pretend to be my friends, for my tone is harsh and high; yet when I am lecturing it cannot be heard at any distance. I am not inclined to speak in the least suavely, and I speak too often.

I have a fixed gaze as if in meditation. My complexion varies, turning from white to red. An oval face, not too well filled out, the head shaped off narrowly behind and delicately rounded, complete a picture so truly commonplace that several painters who have come from afar to make my portrait have found no feature by which they could so characterize me, that I might be distinguished. Upon the lower part of my throat is a swelling like a hard ball, not at all conspicuous, and coming to me as an inheritance from my mother.

My bodily state was infirm in many respects: by nature; as the result of several cases of disease; and in the symptoms of weakness which displayed themselves.

My head is afflicted with congenital discharges coming at times from the stomach, at times from the chest, to such an extent that even when I consider myself in the best of health, I suffer with a cough and hoarseness. When this discharge is from the stomach, it is apt to bring on a dysentery and a distaste for food. More than once I believed I had had a touch of poison, but I shortly and unexpectedly recovered.

Another trouble was a catarrh or rheum of the teeth, through the effects of which I began to lose my teeth, several at a time, from the year 1563 on. Before that I had lost but one or two. Now I have fourteen good teeth and one which is rather weak; but it will last a long time, I think, for it still does its share.

Indigestion, moreover, and a stomach not any too strong were my lot. From my seventy-second year, whenever I had eaten something more than usual, or had drunk too much, or had eaten between meals, or eaten anything not especially wholesome, I began to feel ill. I have set forth a remedy for the foregoing in the second book of my treatise *On Guarding the Health*.

In my youth I was troubled with congenital palpitation of the heart, of which I was absolutely cured by medical skill. I had hemorrhoids also, and the gout, from which I was so nearly freed that I was more frequently in the habit of trying to call it back when it was not present than of getting rid of it when I had it. . . .

It was my custom—and a habit which amazed many —when I had no other excuse for a malady, to seek one, as I have said, from my gout. And for this reason I frequently put myself in the way of conditions likely to induce a certain distress—excepting only that I shunned insomnia as much as I could—because I considered that pleasure consisted in relief following severe pain. If, therefore, I brought on pain, it could easily be allayed. I have discovered, by experience, that I cannot be long without bodily pain, for if once that circumstance arises, a certain mental anguish overcomes me, so grievous that nothing could be more distressing. Bodily pain, or the cause of bodily distress—in which there is no disgrace—is but a minor evil. Accordingly I have hit upon a plan of biting my lips, of twisting my fingers, of pinching the skin of the tender muscles of my left arm, until the tears come. Under the protection of this self-chastisement I live without disgracing myself.

I am by nature afraid of high places, even though they are extensive; also of places where there is any report of mad dogs having been seen.

At times I have been tormented by a tragic passion so heroic that I planned to commit suicide. I suspect that this has happened to others also, although they do not refer to it in their books. . . .

It is my custom to remain in bed ten hours, and, if I am well and of fair and proper strength, to sleep eight hours; in periods of ill health I can sleep but four or five hours. I arise at the second hour of the day. If insomnia troubles me, I get up, walk around the bed, and count to a thousand many times. I also diet, cutting down on my food by more than half. At such times I make small use of medication beyond a little poplar ointment or bear's grease or oil of water lilies. With this I anoint seventeen places: the thighs, the soles of my feet, the cervix, the elbows, the wrists, the temples, the regions of the jugular, heart, and liver, and last of all my upper lip. I was especially troubled with early morning wakefulness.

Breakfast was always a lighter meal than dinner.

After my fiftieth year I was satisfied in the morning with bread steeped in broth, or even, at first, with bread and water, and with those large Cretan grapes called Zibbibos or red raisins. Later in the day I followed a more varied menu, desiring for the midday meal simply an egg yolk with two ounces of bread or a little more, and a mild draught of sweet wine, or none at all. Or if the day happen to be Friday, or Saturday, I try a small piece of meat with bread and cockle broth or crab soup. I consider nothing better than firm young veal, beaten tender with the back of a butcher knife and pot-roasted without any liquors save its own. In this dish I take great satisfaction; it has a way of drawing its own drippings, than which nothing is better; and thus the meat is far more juicy and much richer than meat roasted on a spit.

For supper I order a dish of beets, a little rice, a salad of endive; but I like even better the wide-leafed spiny sow-thistle, or the root of white endive. I eat more freely of fish than of meat, but only wholesome fresh fish. I love firm meat, the breast of veal or of wild boar roasted, and finely cut with sharp knives. And it seems good to me to eat my meal by the fire. At this repast I delight also in sweet new wine, about six ounces with double, or even more, the amount of water. I find especially good the wings, livers, and giblets of young fowl and pigeons.

I am especially fond of river crabs, because, while my mother carried me, she ate so many of them. Likewise I delight in cockles and oysters. I prefer fish to meat, and eat them with much more benefit than the latter: sole, turbot, flatfish, gudgeon, land turtles, chub, mullet or red mullet, roach, sea bream, the merluce or seacod, the spigola or wolf-fish, tilefish, and grayling. . . .

l take great delight in honey, in cane sugar, dried grapes, ripe grapes, melons—after I learned of their medicinal properties—figs, cherries, peaches, and fruit syrup; nor do these cause me the least distress, even at my present age. Above all, I find olive oil delicious, mixed with salt and ripe olives. Garlic does me good; and bitter rue has always seemed to have special properties, both when I was a boy and since I am grown, of protecting my health, and besides, serving as an antidote against all poisons. By experiment I have found *absinthium Romanum*, or wormwood, beneficial.

I was never immoderately addicted to venery, nor have I been harmed much by excesses in this respect; now, however, it plainly results in abdominal nervousness. . . .

Vowing to perpetuate my name, I made a plan for this purpose as soon as I was able to orient myself. For I understood, without any doubt, that life is twofold: the material existence common to the beasts and the plants, and that existence which is peculiar to a man eager for glory and high endeavour. In the former, I realized that nature had failed me, that my desire had been left ungranted; as for the latter, I knew there would be nothing by reason of which I would dare to hope—neither resources, nor power, nor firm health, nor strength, nor family, nor any special devotion to labour. I did not have a wide knowledge of the Latin tongue, nor friends, nor anything from my parents except an endowment of misery and scorn.

After a few years I was inspired by a dream to a hope of attaining this second way of life—the way of fame. Only I did not clearly see how, except in so far as I was helped, as it were, by a miracle to the understanding of the Latin tongue. But in truth I was recalled by my sane reasoning from any great aspiration towards such fame, perceiving that nothing was emptier than that hope, not to mention my simple resolve.

"How," said I, "will you write what will be read? And what remarkable facts do you know that readers care for? In what style will you write, or with what choice of diction, so that you may hold the attention of those readers? Can it be that any would read? May it not be that the course of ages will see such a constant accumulation of writings that those early books may be scorned, not to say neglected? Will they endure for even a few years? How many—a hundred, a thousand, ten thousand? Show me a case; is there one such book among thousands?

"And since all things will come to naught—even as there was a beginning will there be an end—even though, as the academic philosophers want to believe, the world may again be renewed, does it make any difference whether the end is after ten days, or after ten times countless thousands of years? None either way, and it is all one in eternity!

"Meanwhile, will you torment yourself with hope, will you be tortured with fear, will you be exhausted by strivings? Whatever of sweet life is left, you will lose —oh, excellent idea!" . . .

Yet did not Caesar, Alexander, Hannibal, Scipio, Curtius, and Herostratus prefer this hope of enduring fame before all others, even at the risk of infamy, the price of torture, and the cost of very life itself? . . .

It is scarcely surprising, therefore, that I, urged on by love of fame, seek it; what *is* surprising is that I can still seek it, realizing all these matters which I have just considered. But be that as it may, an unshakable ambition remains. It was, I grant, a fatuous purpose in Caesar and these others; yet my desire is for renown, so many things to the contrary, so many obstacles in my way; and it is a desire not so much foolish as stubbornly fixed.

Yet have I never longed for praise and honours; indeed, quite the contrary, I have spurned them, wishing it to be known only that I had lived, and having no concern that it be known what manner of man I was.

As for my descendants, I know how fraught with uncertainty this hope for fame may be, and I realize how little we may foresee its consequences. Therefore I have lived my life as best I might; and in some hope of the future, I have scorned the present. If I must excuse my present manner of life, let me say that I now continue to exist as well as I can. For this course seems but honourable; and even if any hope I have for fame should fail me, my ambition is worthy of praise, inasmuch as longing for renown is but natural. . . .

From my early youth I persistently held to this purpose—that I should make it my duty to care for human life. The study of medicine seemed to point more clearly to such a career than did the study of law, as being more appropriate to the end I had in view, and as of more common concern to all the world in every age. I deemed medicine a profession of sincerer character than law, and a pursuit relying rather upon reason and nature's everlasting law than upon the opinions of men. . . .

An account of this nature is by its own character a most difficult thing to write, and so much the more for me as I reflect that those who have been wont to read the autobiographical books of writers are not used to seeing such a straightforward narrative set down as I purpose to publish. . . .

I have accustomed my features always to assume an expression quite contrary to my feelings: thus I am able to feign outwardly, yet within know nothing of dissimulation. This habit is easy if compared to the practice of hoping for nothing, which I have bent my efforts towards acquiring for fifteen successive years, and have at last succeeded. And now, trained to pretences of a sort, I sometimes go forth clad in rags, but just as often elegantly dressed; sometimes I am taciturn, and sometimes talkative; sometimes gay, sometimes sad. From these moods all things acquire double aspects. . . .

I am lacking in reverence and have a far from continent tongue; and I have such a quick temper that I am often shamed and embarrassed thereby. Though I may be led to repent, I have nevertheless paid heavy penalties, as I have elsewhere stated, for my sins; even so I atoned for the debaucheries of that Sardanapalian life I led the year I was rector of the University at Padua. Yet wisely and patiently to have carried and corrected one's fault is praise even in disgrace, and virtue even in sin. Necessity may pardon me for speaking thus in my own praise; yet even if I were inclined to pass over in silence the gifts of God towards me, I should be an ingrate indeed to complain of the loss which I suffered without acknowledging the kind of life I was leading at the time. Frankness is, moreover, the simpler course, inasmuch as my personal affairs are not as highly esteemed as men commonly value their own interests—vain, empty affairs like those great clouds seen in the wake of the sunset which are meaningless and soon pass away. If anyone would like to pass unprejudiced judgment on these actions and to reflect how easy it is to yield, he will understand in what spirit of mind, and urged by what necessity, or by what occasion I acted, and with what great grief I was afflicted through those deeds of my youth. . . .

This I recognize as unique and outstanding among my faults—the habit, which I persist in, of preferring to say above all things what I know to be displeasing to the ears of my hearers. I am aware of this, yet I keep it up wilfully, in no way ignorant of how many enemies it makes for me. So strongly are our natures fettered to long-standing habits! Yet I avoid this practice in the presence of my benefactors and of my superiors. It is enough not to fawn upon these, or at least not to flatter them.

I used to be just as immoderate in living when I well knew what course was most expedient to follow, and what I ought to do; scarcely another man could be found so obstinate in a fault of the sort. . . .

Truly the cause of a great part of my misery was the stupidity of my sons, connected as it was with actual shame, the folly of my kinsfolk, and the jealousy existing among them, which was a vice peculiar to our family. Indeed, it is a fault common to many a group!

From my youth I was immoderately given to gambling; and in this way I became known to Francesco Sforza, a prince of Milan, and made many friendships for myself among the nobles. And since for many years —almost forty—I applied myself assiduously to gambling, it is not easy to say how greatly the status of my private affairs suffered, and with nothing to show for it. The dice turned out to be far worse, and once my sons were instructed in the attractions of games of chance, our home too frequently was thrown open to gamblers. For this gaming habit I have naught but a worthless excuse to offer—the poverty of my early life, a certain shrewdness in hazards, and something of skill in play.

This is mortal frailty, then, but some will not admit

it; others are even intolerant of it. Are they better, or wiser?

What if one should address a word to the kings of the earth and say, "Not one of you but eats lice, flies, bugs, worms, fleas—nay, the very filth of your servants"? With what an attitude would they listen to such statements, though they be truths? What is this complacency, then, but an ignoring of conditions, a pretence of not being aware of what we know exists, or a will to set aside a fact by force? And so it is with our sins and everything else foul, vain, confused, and untrue in our lives. On a rotting tree are rotten apples! It is nothing new that I proclaim; I merely lay bare the truth. . . .

I name, among the trials of my life, the indulgence of the flesh, distracting entertainments, disease, impotency, the disparagements of my rivals, issues none too felicitous, law suits, attacks, the threats of the powerful, the suspicion of certain men, the distractions of a family, the failure of many projects; and finally, the contrary advice either of true friends, or of men in the guise of friends, and the hazards which beset me on account of my many unorthodox views. . . .

In misfortune, however, I am by no means steadfast, since certain afflictions which I was forced to meet were more than I could bear. For these exigencies I overcame nature by a scheme of my own. In the moments when my spirit was afflicted with the most insupportable grief, I would strike my thighs with rods, or bite my left arm sharply and quickly. Often I fasted. I was relieved much by weeping, if weep I could, but very often I was unable. . . .

To the duties of life I am exceptionally faithful, and particularly in the writing of my books, to such an extent that even though the most attractive opportunities have been offered, I have not abandoned my undertaking, but continued to adhere to my original purpose. I had observed that my father's habit of relinquishing one aim in life for another had been a mighty obstacle to his success. . . .

Among the things which please me greatly are stilettos, or *stili*, for writing; for them I have spent more than twenty gold crowns, and much money besides for other sorts of pens. I daresay the writing materials which I have got at one time and another could not be bought for two hundred crowns. Besides these, I take great pleasure in gems, in metal bowls, in vessels of copper or silver, in painted glass globes, and in rare books.

I enjoy swimming a little and fishing very much. I was devoted to the art of angling as long as I remained at Pavia, and I am sorry I ever changed.

The reading of history gives me extraordinary satisfaction, as well as readings in philosophy, in Aristotle and Plotinus, and the study of treatises on the revelations of mysteries, and especially treatises on medical questions.

In the Italian poets, Petrarca and Luigi Pulci, I find great delight.

I prefer solitude to companions, since there are so few men who are trustworthy, and almost none truly learned. I do not say this because I demand scholarship in all men—although the sum total of men's learning is small enough; but I question whether we should allow anyone to waste our time. The wasting of time is an abomination. . . .

Though I was born in most troublesome times, and have been subjected to the influence of so many experiences; though in my many journeys I have met men not simply strangers to religion, but indeed the enemies of religion, I have not lost my faith; and this I must attribute more to a miracle than to my own wisdom; more to divine providence than to my own virtue. Steadfastly, in fact from my earliest childhood, I have made this my prayer: "Lord God, in Thine infinite goodness grant me long life, and wisdom, and health of mind and body." Wherefore it is no marvel if I have ever been most devoted to religion and to the worship of God.

Indeed, it seems that I have been the recipient of other gifts as well—such things, however, as are apparently more another's needs than my own. At all times I have enjoyed a certain health, in spite of my complaints. I have become more learned, so to speak, in matters to which I gave little study, and in which I had no schooling, than in subjects for which I had resorted to teachers. Where duty was concerned, I was somewhat more assiduous; I fought against my son's death and that terrible grief; yet he was bound to die, and in that same year the infant he had left came near to dying, so that my son would have had no issue, but my grandson—his child—lived and still lives.

Yet why moan on? Why compare mortal wretchedness and pain to the joys of those who have won immortality? If he had never existed at all! Or if he had not perished at that time, would he have lived forever? What difference, then, to me if I have suffered some loss? Oh, senseless soliloquies of men! Oh, unutterable delirium!

Not only do I keep ever in mind the divine majesty of God, but turn my meditation as well upon the blessed Virgin Mary, and holy Saint Martin; for I had been warned in a dream that under his aegis I should lead a quiet existence and enjoy long life.

From *De Vita Propria Liber*, trans. Jean Stoner (New York: E. P. Dutton & Co., 1930).

IV. THE BOOK
OF NATURE

The Arts and Nature

The Art of Building

LEON BATTISTA ALBERTI

1450

Oᴜʀ ᴀɴᴄᴇsᴛᴏʀs have left us many and various arts tending to the pleasure and conveniency of life, acquired with the greatest industry and diligence: which arts, though they all pretend, with a kind of emulation, to have in view the great end of being serviceable to mankind, yet we know that each of them in particular has something in it that seems to promise a distinct and separate fruit: some arts we follow for necessity, some we approve for their usefulness, and some we esteem because they lead us to the knowledge of things that are delightful. What these arts are, it is not necessary for me to enumerate; for they are obvious. But if you take a view of the whole circle of arts, you shall hardly find one but what, despising all others, regards and seeks only its own particular ends: or if you do meet with any of such a nature that you can in no wise do without it, and which yet brings along with it profit at the same time, conjoined with pleasure and honour, you will, I believe, be convinced that architecture is not to be excluded from that number. For it is certain, if you examine the matter carefully, it is inexpressibly delightful, and of the greatest convenience to mankind in all respects, both public and private; and in dignity not inferior to the most excellent. But before I proceed further, it will not be improper to explain what he is that I allow to be an architect: for it is not a carpenter or a joiner that I thus rank with the greatest masters in other sciences; the manual operator being no more than an instrument to the architect. Him I call an architect who, by a sure and wonderful art and method, is able, both with thought and invention, to devise and, with execution, to complete all those works which, by means of the movement of great weights and the conjunction and amassment of bodies, can, with the greatest beauty, be adapted to the uses of mankind: and to be able to do this, he must have a thorough insight into the noblest and most curious sciences. . . .

It is my opinion that beauty, majesty, gracefulness, and the like charms consist in those particulars which, if you alter or take away, the whole would be made homely and disagreeable. If we are convinced of this, it can be no very tedious inquiry to consider those things which may be taken away, increased, or altered, especially in figures and forms; for every body consists of certain peculiar parts, of which if you take away any one, or lessen, or enlarge it, or remove it to an improper place, that which before gave the beauty and grace to this body, will at once be lamed and spoiled. From hence we may conclude, to avoid prolixity in this research, that there are three things principally in which the whole of what we are looking into consists; the number, and that which I have called the finishing, and the collocation. But there is still something else besides, which arises from the conjunction and connection of these other parts, and gives the beauty and grace to the whole: which we will call congruity, which we may consider as the original of all that is graceful and handsome. The business and office of congruity is to put together members differing from each other in their natures in such a manner that they may conspire to form a beautiful whole: so that wherever such a composition offers itself to the mind, either by the conveyance of the sight, hearing, or any of the other senses, we immediately perceive this congruity; for by nature we desire things perfect, and adhere to them with pleasure when they are offered to us. Nor does this congruity arise so much from the body in which it is found, or any of its members, as from itself, and from nature, so that its true seat is in the mind and in reason: and accordingly it has a very large field to exercise itself and flourish in, and runs through every part and action of man's life, and every production of nature herself, which are all directed by the law of congruity; nor does nature study anything more than to make all her works absolute and perfect, which they could never be without this congruity, since they would want that consent of parts which is so necessary to perfection.

But we need not say more upon this point, and if what we have here laid down appears to be true, we may conclude beauty to be such a consent and agreement of the parts of a whole in which it is found, as to number, finishing, and collocation as congruity—that is to say, the principal law of nature—requires. This is what architecture chiefly aims at, and by this she obtains her beauty, dignity, and value. The ancients, knowing from the nature of things that the matter was in fact as I have stated it and being convinced that if they neglected this main point they should never produce anything great or commendable, did in their works propose to themselves chiefly the imitation of nature, as the greatest artist at all manner of compositions; and for this purpose they laboured, as far as the industry of man could reach, to discover the laws upon which she herself acted in the production of her works, in order to transfer them to the business of architecture. Reflecting therefore upon the practice of nature as well with relation to an entire body, as to its several parts, they found from the very first principles of things that bodies were not always composed of equal parts or members; whence it happens that, of the bodies produced by nature, some are smaller, some larger, and some middling: and considering that one building differed from another, upon account of the end for which it was raised, and the purpose which it was to serve, as we have shown in the foregoing books, they found it necessary to make them of various kinds. Thus from an imitation of nature they invented three manners of adorning a building and gave them names drawn from their first inventors. One was better contrived for strength and duration: this they called Doric; another was more tapered and beautiful: this they named Corinthian; another was a kind of medium composed from the other two, and this they called Ionic. Thus much related to the whole body in general. Then, observing that those three things which we have already mentioned—namely, the number, finishing, and collocation —were what chiefly conduced to make the whole beautiful, they found how they were to make use of this from a thorough examination of the works of nature, and, as I imagine, upon the following principles. The first thing they observed, as to number, was that it was of two sorts, even and uneven, and they made use of both, but in different occasions: for, from the imitation of nature, they never made the ribs of their structure,

that is to say, the columns, angles, and the like, in uneven numbers; as you shall not find any animal that
stands or moves upon an odd number of feet. On the
contrary, they made their apertures always in uneven
numbers, as nature herself has done in some instances,
for though in animals she has placed an ear, an eye,
and a nostril on each side, yet the great aperture, the
mouth, she has set singly in the middle. But among
these numbers, whether even or uneven, there are some
which seem to be greater favourites with nature than
others, and more celebrated among learned men: which
architects have borrowed for the composition of the
members of their edifices, upon account of their being
endued with some qualities which make them more
valuable than any others.

From *The Architecture of Leon Batista Alberti,* tr. James Leoni
(London, 1755).

Nature, Art, and Science

LEONARDO DA VINCI

ON PAINTING

I AM FULLY conscious that, not being a literary man,
certain presumptuous persons will think that they
may reasonably blame me, alleging that I am not a
man of letters. Foolish folks! Do they not know that
I might retort, as Marius did to the Roman patricians,
by saying that they who deck themselves out in the
labours of others will not allow me my own. They will
say that I, having no literary skill, cannot properly express that which I desire to treat of; but they do not

know that my subjects are to be dealt with by experience rather than by words; and [experience] has been the mistress of those who wrote well. And so, as mistress, I will cite her in all cases.

The mind of the painter must resemble a mirror, which always takes the colour of the object it reflects and is completely occupied by the images of as many objects as are in front of it. Therefore you must know, O painter! that you cannot be a good one if you are not the universal master of representing by your art every kind of form produced by nature. And this you will not know how to do if you do not see them, and retain them in your mind. Hence as you go through the fields, turn your attention to various objects, and in turn look now at this thing and now at that, collecting a store of divers facts selected and chosen from those of less value. . . .

If you contemn painting, which is the only imitator of all visible works of nature, you will certainly despise a subtle invention which brings philosophy and subtle speculation to the consideration of the nature of all forms—seas and plains, trees, animals, plants, and flowers—which are surrounded by shade and light. And this is true knowledge and the legitimate issue of nature; for painting is born of nature—or, to speak more correctly, we will say it is the grandchild of nature; for all visible things are produced by nature, and these her children have given birth to painting. Hence we may justly call it the grandchild of nature and related to God.

The eye, which is called the window of the soul, is the principal means by which the central sense can most completely and abundantly appreciate the infinite works of nature; and the ear is the second, which acquires dignity by hearing of the things the eye has seen.

If you, historians or poets or mathematicians, had not seen things with your eyes you could not report of them in writing. And if you, O poet, tell a story with your pen, the painter with his brush can tell it more easily, with simpler completeness and less tedious to be understood. And if you call painting dumb poetry, the painter may call poetry blind painting. Now which is the worse defect? to be blind or dumb? Though the poet is as free as the painter in the invention of his fictions, they are not so satisfactory to men as paintings; for, though poetry is able to describe forms, actions, and places in words, the painter deals with the actual similitude of the forms, in order to represent them. Now tell me which is the nearer to the actual man: the name of man or the image of man? The name of man differs in different countries, but his form is never changed but by death.

And if the poet gratifies the sense by means of the ear, the painter does so by the eye—the worthier sense; but I will say no more of this but that, if a good painter represents the fury of a battle, and if a poet describes one, and they are both together put before the public, you will see where most of the spectators will stop, to which they will pay most attention, on which they will bestow most praise, and which will satisfy them best. Undoubtedly painting, being by a long way the more intelligible and beautiful, will please most. Write up the name of God [Christ] in some spot and set up His image opposite and you will see which will be most reverenced. Painting comprehends in itself all the forms of nature, while you have nothing but words, which are not universal, as form is, and if you have the effects of the representation, we have the representation of the effects. Take a poet who describes the beauty of a lady to her lover and a painter who represents her and you will see to which nature guides the enamoured critic. Certainly the proof should be allowed to rest on the verdict of experience. You have ranked painting among the mechanical arts, but, in truth, if painters were as apt at praising their own works in writing as you are, it would not lie under the stigma of so base a name. If you call it mechanical because it is, in the first place, manual, and that it is the hand which produces what is to be found in the imagination, you too, writers, who set down manually with the pen what is devised in your mind. And if you say it is mechanical because it is done for money, who falls into this error—if error it can be called—more than you? If you lecture in the schools, do you not go to whoever pays you most? Do you do any work without pay? Still, I do not say this as blaming such views, for every form of labour looks for its reward. And if a poet should say, "I will invent a fiction with a great purpose," the painter can do the same, as Apelles painted Calumny. If you were to say that poetry is more eternal, I say the works of a copper-smith are more eternal still, for time preserves them longer than your works or ours; nevertheless they have not much imagination. And a picture, if painted on cop-per with enamel colours, may be yet more permanent. We, by our arts, may be called the grandsons of God. If poetry deals with moral philosophy, painting deals with natural philosophy. Poetry describes the action of the mind, painting considers what the mind may effect by the motions [of the body]. If poetry can terrify people by hideous fictions, painting can do as much by depict-ing the same things in action. Suppose that a poet ap-plies himself to represent beauty, ferocity, or a base, a foul, or a monstrous thing, as against a painter, he may in his ways bring forth a variety of forms; but will the painter not satisfy more? are there not pictures to be seen, so like the actual things, that they deceive men and animals? . . .

The painter strives and competes with nature. . . .

ON ANATOMY

I wish to work miracles. It may be that I shall possess less than other men of more peaceful lives, or than those who want to grow rich in a day. I may live for a long time in great poverty, as always happens, and to all eternity will happen, to alchemists, the would-be creators of gold and silver, and to engineers who would have dead water stir itself into life and perpetual motion, and to those supreme fools, the necromancer and the enchanter.

And you, who say that it would be better to watch an anatomist at work than to see these drawings, you would be right, if it were possible to observe all the things which are demonstrated in such drawings in a single figure, in which you, with all your cleverness, will not see or obtain knowledge of more than some few veins, to obtain a true and perfect knowledge of which I have dissected more than ten human bodies, destroying all the other members, and removing the very minutest particles of the flesh by which these veins are surrounded, without causing them to bleed, excepting the insensible bleeding of the capillary veins; and as one single body would not last so long, since it was necessary to proceed with several bodies by degrees, until I came to an end and had a complete knowledge: this I repeated twice, to learn the differences.

And if you should have a love for such things you might be prevented by loathing, and if that did not prevent you, you might be deterred by the fear of living in the night hours in the company of those corpses, quartered and flayed and horrible to see. And if this did not prevent you, perhaps you might not be able to draw so well as is necessary for such a demonstration; or, if you had the skill in drawing, it might not be combined with knowledge of perspective; and if it were so, you might not understand the methods of geometrical demonstration and the method of the calculation of forces and of the strength of the muscles; patience also may be wanting, so that you lack perseverance. As to whether all these things were found in me or not, the hundred and twenty books composed by me will give verdict Yes or No. In these I have been hindered neither by avarice nor negligence, but simply by want of time.

OF THE ORDER OF THE BOOK

This work must begin with the conception of man, and describe the nature of the womb and how the foetus lives in it, up to what stage it resides there, and in what way it quickens into life and feeds. Also its growth and what interval there is between one stage of growth and another. What it is that forces it out from the body of the mother, and for what reasons it sometimes comes out of the mother's womb before the due time.

Then I will describe which are the members, which, after the boy is born, grow more than the others, and determine the proportions of a boy of one year.

Then describe the fully grown man and woman, with their proportions, and the nature of their complexions, colour, and physiognomy.

Then how they are composed of veins, tendons, muscles, and bones. This I shall do at the end of the book. Then, in four drawings, represent four universal conditions of men. That is, Mirth, with various acts of laughter, and describe the cause of laughter. Weeping in various aspects with its causes. Contention, with various acts of killing; flight, fear, ferocity, boldness, murder, and everything pertaining to such cases. Then represent Labour, with pulling, thrusting, carrying, stopping, supporting, and such like things.

Further I would describe attitudes and movements. Then perspective, concerning the functions and effects of the eye; and of hearing—here I will speak of music—and treat of the other senses.

And then describe the nature of the senses.

This mechanism of man we will demonstrate in . . . figures; of which the three first will show the ramification of the bones: that is, the first one to show their height and position and shape; the second will be seen in profile and will show the depth of the whole and of the parts and their position; the third figure will be a demonstration of the bones of the backparts. Then I will make three other figures from the same point of view, with the bones sawn across, in which will be shown their thickness and hollowness. Three other figures of the bones complete, and of the nerves which rise from the nape of the neck, and in what limbs they ramify. And three others of the bones and veins, and where they ramify. Then three figures with the muscles and three with the skin, and their proper proportions; and three of woman, to illustrate the womb and the menstrual veins which go to the breasts. . . . .

ON NATURE AND EXPERIENCE

And you, O Man, who will discern in this work of mine the wonderful works of nature, if you think it would be a criminal thing to destroy it, reflect how much more criminal it is to take the life of a man; and if this, his external form, appears to thee marvellously constructed, remember that it is nothing as compared with the soul that dwells in that structure; for that indeed, be it what it may, is a thing divine. Leave it then to dwell in His work at His good will and pleasure, and let not your rage or malice destroy a life—for indeed, he who does not value it, does not himself deserve it.

The soul can never be corrupted with the corruption of the body, but is in the body as it were the air which causes the sound of the organ, where when a pipe bursts, the wind would cease to have any good effect.

Experience, the interpreter between formative nature and the human race, teaches how that nature acts among mortals; and being constrained by necessity cannot act otherwise than as reason, which is its helm, requires her to act.

Experience does not err; only your judgments err by expecting from her what is not in her power. Men wrongly complain of Experience; with great abuse they accuse her of leading them astray, but they set Experience aside, turning from it with complaints as to our ignorance, causing us to be carried away by vain and foolish desires to promise ourselves, in her name, things that are not in her power; saying that she is fallacious. Men are unjust in complaining of innocent Experience, constantly accusing her of error and of false evidence.

Why did nature not ordain that one animal should not live by the death of another? Nature, being inconstant and taking pleasure in creating and making constantly new lives and forms, because she knows that her terrestrial materials become thereby augmented, is more ready and more swift in her creating than time in his destruction; and so she has ordained that many animals shall be food for others. Nay, this not satisfying her desire, to the same end she frequently sends forth

certain poisonous and pestilential vapours upon the vast
increase and congregation of animals; and most of all
upon men, who increase vastly because other animals
do not feed upon them; and, the causes being removed,
the effects would not follow. This earth therefore seeks
to lose its life, desiring only continual reproduction; and
as, by the argument you bring forward and demonstrate,
like effects always follow like causes, animals are the
image of the world.

From *The Literary Remains of Leonardo da Vinci,* ed. J. P.
Richter (London: Sampson Low, etc., 1883).

[*The following letter, described as "a copy of a letter
sent by the infidel called Leonardo from Genoa," probably dictated by Leonardo and sent to the Sultan
Bajazid II in 1502 or 1503, was recently discovered in
the Turkish archives in Ankara.*]

I, your servant, as I have pondered on the problem
of the mill, have found, with the Lord's help, that by a
device of art, one could construct a mill which works
without water and by the wind alone; this could be
constructed with less difficulty than a mill in the sea.
This mill is not only easier for the crew to handle, but
it will also work wherever it stands.

Besides this, the Lord—may He be praised!—has
inspired me with a device for drawing water up out of
a ship without a rope or string, by means of a machine
which spins by itself.

I, your slave, have been informed that you intended
to construct a bridge from Galata to Stamboul [i.e.,
over the Golden Horn], but that you could not do it
because no expert could be found. I, your slave, know
how to do it. I shall build it as high as an arch, so
that no one will be prepared to walk over it because it

will be so high. I thought, however, of building a wooden structure, and then pumping out the water, and putting the bridge on piles. Thus I shall make it possible for a sailing ship to pass underneath it. And I shall construct a drawbridge of a kind which can, if one so desires, reach the coast of Anatolia. But since the water is in constant motion, the edges will be worn away. Therefore I shall use a trick, so that the water will pass underneath without damaging the edge. And the sultans who succeed you will be able to restore it at small expense.

God willing, you will believe these words and send instructions, being sure of the everlasting services of this your servant.

This letter was written on the third of July. That was four months ago.

In Nachrichten der Akademie der Wissenschaften in Göttingen; Phil.-hist. Klasse, 1952, No. 1.

The Casting of the "Perseus"

BENVENUTO CELLINI

c. 1560

ABANDONED thus to my own resources, I took new courage, and banished the sad thoughts which kept recurring to my mind, making me often weep bitter tears of repentance for having left France; for though I did so only to revisit Florence, my sweet birthplace, in order that I might charitably succour my six nieces, this good action, as I well perceived, had been the beginning of my great misfortune. Nevertheless, I felt convinced that when my Perseus was accomplished, all these trials would be turned to high felicity and glorious well-being.

Accordingly I strengthened my heart, and with all the forces of my body and my purse, employing what little money still remained to me, I set to work. First I provided myself with several loads of pinewood from the forests of Serristori, in the neighbourhood of Montelupo. While these were on their way, I clothed my Perseus with the clay which I had prepared many months beforehand, in order that it might be duly seasoned. After making its clay tunic (for that is the term used in this art) and properly arming it and fencing it with iron girders, I began to draw the wax out by means of a slow fire. This melted and issued through numerous air vents I had made; for the more there are of these, the better will the mould fill. When I had finished drawing off the wax, I constructed a funnel-shaped furnace all round the model of my Perseus. It was built of bricks, so interlaced, the one above the other, that numerous apertures were left for the fire to exhale at. Then I began to lay on wood by degrees, and kept it burning two whole days and nights. At length, when all the wax was gone, and the mould was well baked, I set to work at digging the pit in which to sink it. This I performed with scrupulous regard to all the rules of art. When I had finished that part of my work, I raised the mould by windlasses and stout ropes to a perpendicular position, and, suspending it with the greatest care one cubit above the level of the furnace, so that it hung exactly above the middle of the pit, I next lowered it gently down into the very bottom of the furnace, and had it firmly placed with every possible precaution for its safety. When this delicate operation was accomplished, I began to bank

it up with the earth I had excavated; and, ever as the
earth grew higher, I introduced its proper air vents,
which were little tubes of earthenware, such as folk
use for drains and such-like purposes. At length I felt
sure that it was admirably fixed, and that the filling-in
of the pit and the placing of the air vents had been
properly performed. I also could see that my work
people understood my method, which differed very
considerably from that of all the other masters in the
trade. Feeling confident, then, that I could rely upon
them, I next turned to my furnace, which I had filled
with numerous pigs of copper and other bronze stuff.
The pieces were piled according to the laws of art, that
is to say, so resting one upon the other that the flames
could play freely through them, in order that the metal
might heat and liquefy the sooner. At last I called out
heartily to set the furnace going. The logs of pine were
heaped in, and, what with the unctuous resin of the
wood and the good draught I had given, my furnace
worked so well that I was obliged to rush from side
to side to keep it going. The labour was more than I
could stand; yet I forced myself to strain every nerve
and muscle. To increase my anxieties, the workshop
took fire, and we were afraid lest the roof should fall
upon our heads; while, from the garden, such a storm
of wind and rain kept blowing in, that it perceptibly
cooled the furnace.

Battling thus with all these untoward circumstances
for several hours, and exerting myself beyond even the
measure of my powerful constitution, I could at last
bear up no longer, and a sudden fever, of the utmost
possible intensity, attacked me. I felt absolutely obliged
to go and fling myself upon my bed. Sorely against my
will having to drag myself away from the spot, I turned
to my assistants, about ten or more in all, what with

master-founders, hand-workers, country fellows, and my own special journeymen, among whom was Bernardino Mannellini of Mugello, my apprentice through several years. To him in particular I spoke: "Look, my dear Bernardino, that you observe the rules which I have taught you; do your best with all dispatch, for the metal will soon be fused. You cannot go wrong; these honest men will get the channels ready; you will easily be able to drive back the two plugs with this pair of iron crooks; and I am sure that my mould will fill miraculously. I feel more ill than I ever did in all my life, and verily believe that it will kill me before a few hours are over." Thus, with despair at heart, I left them and betook myself to bed.

No sooner had I got to bed than I ordered my serving maids to carry food and wine for all the men into the workshop; at the same time I cried, "I shall not be alive tomorrow." They tried to encourage me, arguing that my illness would pass over, since it came from excessive fatigue. In this way I spent two hours battling with the fever, which steadily increased, and calling out continually, "I feel that I am dying." My housekeeper, who was named Mona Fiore da Castel del Rio, a very notable manager and no less warmhearted, kept chiding me for my discouragement; but, on the other hand, she paid me every kind attention which was possible. However, the sight of my physical pain and moral defection so affected her that, in spite of that brave heart of hers, she could not refrain from shedding tears; and yet, so far as she was able, she took good care I should not see them. While I was thus terribly afflicted, I beheld the figure of a man enter my chamber, twisted in his body into the form of a capital S. He raised a lamentable, doleful voice, like one who announces their last hour to men condemned to die upon the scaffold, and spoke these words: "O Benvenuto! your statue is spoiled, and there is no hope whatever of saving it." No sooner had I heard the shriek of that wretch than I gave a howl which might have been heard from the sphere of flame. Jumping from my bed, I seized my clothes and began to dress. The maids, and my lad, and everyone who came around to help me, got kicks or blows of the fist, while I kept crying out in lamentation, "Ah! traitors! enviers! This is an act of treason, done by malice prepense! But I swear by God that I will sift it to the bottom, and before I die will leave such witness to the world of what I can do as shall make a score of mortals marvel."

When I had got my clothes on, I strode with soul bent on mischief towards the workshop; there I beheld the men whom I had left erewhile in such high spirits, standing stupefied and downcast. I began at once and spoke: "Up with you! Attend to me! Since you have not been able or willing to obey the directions I gave you, obey me now that I am with you to conduct my work in person. Let no one contradict me, for in cases like this we need the aid of hand and hearing, not of advice." When I had uttered these words, a certain Maestro Alessandro Lastricati broke silence and said, "Look you, Benvenuto, you are going to attempt an enterprise which the laws of art do not sanction, and which cannot succeed." I turned upon him with such fury, and so full of mischief, that he and all the rest of them exclaimed with one voice, "On then! Give orders! We will obey your least commands, so long as life is left in us." I believe they spoke thus feelingly because they thought I must fall shortly dead upon the ground. I went immediately to inspect the furnace, and found that the metal was all curdled; an accident which we express by "being caked." I told two of the hands to cross the road and fetch from the house of the butcher Capretta a load of young oak wood, which had lain dry for above a year; this wood had been previously offered me by Madame Ginevra, wife of the said Capretta. So soon as the first armfuls arrived, I began to fill the grate beneath the furnace. Now oak wood of that kind heats more powerfully than any other sort of tree; and for this reason, where a slow fire is wanted, as in the case of gun foundry, alder or pine is preferred. Accordingly, when the logs took fire, oh! how the cake began to stir beneath that awful heat, to glow and sparkle in a blaze! At the same time I kept stirring up the channels, and sent men upon the roof to stop the conflagration, which had gathered force from the increased combustion in the furnace; also I caused boards, carpets, and other hangings to be set up against the garden, in order to protect us from the violence of the rain.

When I had thus provided against these several disasters, I roared out first to one man and then to another, "Bring this thing here! Take that thing there!" At this crisis, when the whole gang saw the cake was on the point of melting, they did my bidding, each fellow working with the strength of three. I then ordered half a pig of pewter to be brought, which weighed about sixty pounds, and flung it into the middle of the cake inside the furnace. By this means, and by piling on wood and stirring now with pokers and now with iron rods, the curdled mass rapidly began to liquefy. Then, knowing I had brought the dead to life again, against the firm opinion of those ignoramuses, I felt such vigour fill my veins that all those pains of fever, all those fears of death, were quite forgotten.

All of a sudden an explosion took place, attended by a tremendous flash of flame, as though a thunderbolt

had formed and been discharged amongst us. Unwonted
and appalling terror astonished everyone, and me more
even than the rest. When the din was over and the
dazzling light extinguished, we began to look each other
in the face. Then I discovered that the cap of the
furnace had blown up, and the bronze was bubbling
over from its source beneath. So I had the mouths of
my mould immediately opened, and at the same time
drove in the two plugs which kept back the molten
metal. But I noticed that it did not flow as rapidly as
usual, the reason being probably that the fierce heat
of the fire we kindled had consumed its base alloy.
Accordingly I sent for all my pewter platters, porringers,
and dishes, to the number of some two hundred pieces,
and had a portion of them cast, one by one, into the
channels, the rest into the furnace. This expedient succeeded, and everyone could now perceive that my
bronze was in most perfect liquefaction, and my mould
was filling; whereupon they all with heartiness and
happy cheer assisted and obeyed my bidding, while I,
now here, now there, gave orders, helped with my own
hands, and cried aloud, "O God! Thou that by Thy
immeasurable power didst rise from the dead, and in
Thy glory didst ascend to heaven!" Even thus in a
moment my mould was filled; and, seeing my work
finished, I fell upon my knees, and with all my heart
gave thanks to God.

After all was over, I turned to a plate of salad on a
bench there, and ate with hearty appetite, and drank
together with the whole crew. Afterwards I retired to
bed, healthy and happy for it was now two hours
before morning, and slept as sweetly as though I had
never felt a touch of illness. My good housekeeper, without my giving any orders, had prepared a fat capon for

my repast. So that, when I rose, about the hour for breaking fast, she presented herself with a smiling countenance and said, "Oh, is that the man who felt that he was dying? Upon my word, I think the blows and kicks you dealt us last night, when you were so enraged, and had that demon in your body as it seemed, must have frightened away your mortal fever! The fever feared that it might catch it too, as we did!" All my poor household, relieved in like measure from anxiety and overwhelming labour, went at once to buy earthen vessels in order to replace the pewter I had cast away. Then we dined together joyfully; nay, I cannot remember a day in my whole life when I dined with greater gladness or a better appetite.

After our meal I received visits from the several men who had assisted me. They exchanged congratulations, and thanked God for our success, saying they had learned and seen things done which other masters judged impossible. I too grew somewhat glorious, and, deeming I had shown myself a man of talent, indulged a boastful humour. So I thrust my hand into my purse and paid them all to their full satisfaction.

That evil fellow, my mortal foe, Messer Pier Francesco Ricci, majordomo of the duke, took great pains to find out how the affair had gone. In answer to his questions, the two men whom I suspected of having caked my metal for me, said I was no man, but of a certainty some powerful devil, since I had accomplished what no craft of the art could do; indeed they did not believe a mere ordinary fiend could work such miracles as I in other ways had shown. They exaggerated the whole affair so much, possibly in order to excuse their own part in it, that the majordomo wrote an account to the duke, who was then in Pisa, far more marvellous and full of thrilling incidents than what they had narrated.

From *The Life of Benvenuto Cellini*, trans. J. A. Symonds (London: G. Newnes, Ltd., 1888).

On Landscape Painting

KAREL VAN MANDER

1603-1604

YOU YOUNG PAINTERS, who have sat for a long time bent double, so wrapped up in your incessant work in art that you have become almost half blind, and have almost deadened and closed your senses because, in your eagerness to learn, you always want to know more: Stop! You have pulled the plough long enough. Free yourself today from the yoke of work, for the strongest man needs rest and the bow cannot always be stretched taut.

Look yonder, how swiftly the golden ball of the sun rises! It is already aflame as we stand looking elsewhere. See, before us the hunters with their hounds run through the green, bedewed fields, and see how the falling dew reveals in deeper green the marks of their footsteps and the direction in which they are going.

Look there, the distant image of the landscape has the appearance of air, and almost dissolves in air, and the lofty mountains look like moving clouds. From both sides we see the ditches and furrows of the fields run, as in a river bed, towards the background from the point of vision, and fade away. Do not let it trouble you to observe this, for it lets your background recede in strong perspective.

I recommend that you pay attention to foreshortening and diminution, as one sees it in life. Although there is no construction which requires strict rules, yet you must still know how to guide your eyes accurately by the horizon or point of vision—that is, by the highest waterlines; everything that is below them one sees from above, and the rest one sees as distorted, from below.

You should not put in the background too faintly, or be as delicate with the shadows as with the lights. You must think about the masses of blue air, which lie between them and paralyse the eye, and bring to nothing the effort for clear comprehension. You should make it seem as though the sun shone through the clouds only thinly here and there and diffused its light over the cities and mountains.

You should, moreover, render darkness, and let the cities be shadowed by clouds, sometimes completely, sometimes only half; you should take care that the mirrorlike surface of the water is not deprived of the colours of the heavens; besides, it is pretty to let the dispersing clouds above dissolve after the old fashion, and sometimes to show the sunshine.

You must also seek to portray with colours snow, hail, rainfall, frost, rime, steaming, and dreary fogs, all the things that are necessary to depict melancholy winter days, in such a way that the eye will not often be drawn further than one can throw a stone, to see gateways, houses, towns, and villages.

It is proper that our foreground should be strong, in order to let the other grounds recede, and that we take care to bring something large towards the front, as did Brueghel and other painters of great fame, to whom one may award the palm in what concerns landscape. For in the work of these men who are worthy of honour, there are often powerful tree trunks in the foreground. Let us follow them enthusiastically in this. . . .

There are few Italians who paint landscapes; these, however, are of consummate artistic skill and have almost no peers. They often let us see a vista of perspective effect and grounds firmly fitted into one another, and cities, as in what we see . . . in the especially great Titian, whose work in wood-engraving serves to instruct us here, also in what we see of the painter of Brescia [Geronimo Muzziano, 1528-92].

Besides these, I might name as a competitor with respect to beautiful colours and the artistic content of painting and engraving, the gifted Brueghel; in these pictures he shows us, when he was in the cragged Alps, how, without much trouble, to portray the view downward into valleys which make one dizzy, the sheer cliffs, the cloud-kissing pines, the far and distant prospects and rushing streams.

But in the happy time of spring one has to give attention to decorating in colours like the noble jewels, and to painting the earth carefully in emerald or sapphire green with their nuances, straight across the meandering curves of the crystal-clear, murmuring brooks, which flow between green and grassy banks.

On the one side sits Ceres with yellow ears of grain, on the other side the field of unripe oats in which Eurus moves in play, as he makes the field a sea of green billows and softly rustling movement. Here grows vetch, there buckwheat, yonder clover, red and blue flowers, wheat, and the wholesome flax with the colour of heaven.

Also ploughed fields with long furrows drawn across them or sometimes fields with harvested grain. Today the meadows and fields have canals, hedgerows, and curving paths, and then I do not know what kind of curious shepherds' huts and peasant villages we should build, with walls and roofs in hollow cliffs, and trees and tree trunks.

Do not make these huts of handsome red bricks, but rather out of pieces of earth, rushes, straw, rags, and stonework, plastered and moss-grown in a special way, and towards the rear paint our blue shrubs which should seem to grow whiter on the blue ground, so that they stand out against the dry blue, as well as correctly drawn, light tree trunks turning inward, and one close behind the other.

One should only stipple the smallest tree trunks. Yet before we hasten on to our trees in the foreground, let us climb a way up the steep cliffs, the cliffs moistened with wet lips by the drifting clouds which wash their highest summits. In general, their colour is light grey, and often they raise their bare peaks out of the midst of a dense forest of fir trees.

See how the stones hang like icicles on the rocks, irregular and green with moss, in this waterfall, and how the water rushes drunkenly through the twisting paths helter-skelter until it falls below; now you wise serpents of art, see how these mastic trees grow here and how strangely they lie! Who could dream of such a thing!

To paint the lovely structure of trees requires effort, whether it be a small shrub or a towering tree. Often they may be yellow, but sometimes green; also one should show the foliage turning upward from below. But to avoid dullness, you should not make the foliage too small, and when you paint your foliage, let it be so constructed as to be run through with little slender branches, some of which should be curved lightly upward and some downward.

It would be good if you would learn your story from books or poems beforehand—in whatever way pleases you—so as to arrange your landscape in accordance with it. Yet above all do not forget to place small figures next to the great trees, and to set your little world in motion, here to ploughing, there to mowing, there to loading a wagon, here and there to fishing, walking, running, and hunting.

From *Das Lehrgedicht*, ed. and trans. into German by R. Hoecker (Haag: M. Nijhoff, 1916); trans. M.M.M.

The Art of Paracelsus

PARACELSUS

c. 1520

SINCE YOU, O Sophist, everywhere abuse me with such fatuous and mendacious words, on the ground that being sprung from rude Helvetia I can understand and know nothing: and also because being a duly qualified physician I still wander from one district to another; therefore I have proposed by means of this treatise to disclose to the ignorant and inexperienced: what good arts existed in the first age; what my art avails against you and yours against me; what should be thought of each; and how my posterity in this age of grace will imitate me. Look at Hermes, Archelaus, and others in the first age: see what Spagyrists [alchemists] and what Philosophers then existed. By this they testify that their enemies, who are your patrons, O Sophist, at the present time are but mere empty forms and idols. Although this would not be attested by those who are falsely con-

sidered your authentic fathers and saints, yet the ancient
Emerald Table shows more art and experience in Philosophy, Alchemy, Magic, and the like than could ever
be taught by you and your crowd of followers. If you
do not yet understand, from the aforesaid facts, what
and how great treasures these are, tell me why no prince
or king was ever able to subdue the Egyptians. Then
tell me why the Emperor Diocletian ordered all the
Spagyric books to be burned (so far as he could lay
his hands upon them). Unless the contents of those
books had been known, they would have been obliged
to bear still his intolerable yoke—a yoke, O Sophist,
which shall one day be put upon the neck of yourself
and your colleagues.

From the middle of this age the Monarchy of all the
Arts has been at length derived and conferred on me,
Theophrastus Paracelsus, Prince of Philosophy and of
Medicine. For this purpose I have been chosen by God
to extinguish and blot out all the phantasies of elaborate and false works, of delusive and presumptuous
words, be they the words of Aristotle, Galen, Avicenna,
Mesva, or the dogmas of any among their followers.
My theory, proceeding as it does from the light of
nature, can never, through its consistency, pass away
or be changed: but in the fifty-eighth year after its
millennium and a half, it will then begin to flourish.
The practice at the same time following upon the theory
will be proved by wonderful and incredible signs, so
as to be open to mechanics and common people, and
they will thoroughly understand how firm and immovable is that Paracelsic Art against the triflings of the
Sophists: though meanwhile that sophistical science
has to have its ineptitude propped up and fortified by
papal and imperial privileges. In that I am esteemed
by you a mendicant and vagabond sophist, the Danube

and the Rhine will answer that accusation, though I
hold my tongue. Those calumnies of yours falsely devised against me have often displeased many courts
and princes, many imperial cities, the knightly order,
and the nobility. I have a treasure hidden in a certain
city called Weinden, belonging to Forum Julii, at an
inn—a treasure which neither you, Leo of Rome, nor
you, Charles the German, could purchase with all your
substance. Although the signed star has been applied to
the arcanum of your names, it is known to none but
the sons of the divine Spagyric Art. So then, you wormy
and lousy Sophist, since you deem the monarch of
arcana a mere ignorant, fatuous, and prodigal quack,
now, in this mid age, I determine in my present treatise
to disclose the honourable course of procedure in these
matters, the virtues and preparation of the celebrated
Tincture of the Philosophers for the use and honour of
all who love the truth, and in order that all who despise
the true arts may be reduced to poverty. By this arcanum [incorporeal, immortal substance; also tincture]
the last age shall be illuminated clearly and compensated for all its losses by the gift of grace and the
reward of the spirit of truth, so that since the beginning
of the world no similar germination of the intelligence
and of wisdom shall ever have been heard of. In the
meantime, vice will not be able to suppress the good,
nor will the resources of those vicious persons, many
though they be, cause any loss to the upright. . . .

CONCERNING THE TRANSMUTATION OF METALS
BY THE PERFECTION OF MEDICINE

If the Tincture of the Philosophers is to be used for
transmutation, a pound of it must be projected on a
thousand pounds of melted Sol [gold]. Then, at length,
will a medicine have been prepared for transmuting

the leprous moisture of the metals. This work is a wonderful one in the light of nature, namely, that by the Magistery, or the operation of the Spagyrist, a metal, which formerly existed, should perish, and another be produced. This fact has rendered that same Aristotle, with his ill-founded philosophy, fatuous. For truly, when the rustics in Hungary cast iron at the proper season into a certain fountain, commonly called Zifferbrunnen, it is consumed into rust, and when this is liquefied with a blast fire, it soon exists as pure Venus [the first metal, formed of parts of sulphur, mercury, salt], and never more returns to iron. Similarly, in the mountain commonly called Kuttenberg, they obtain a lixivium [lye] out of marcasites, in which iron is forthwith turned into Venus of a high grade, and more malleable than the other produced by nature. These things, and more like them, are known to simple men rather than to Sophists, namely, those which turn one appearance of a metal into another. And these things, moreover, through the remarkable contempt of the ignorant, and partly, too, on account of the just envy of the artificers, remain almost hidden. But I myself, in Istria, have often brought Venus to more than twenty-four (al. 38) degrees, so that the colour of Sol could not mount higher, consisting of Antimony or of Quartal, which Venus I used in all respects as other kinds.

But though the old artists were very desirous of this arcanum, and sought it with the greatest diligence, nevertheless very few could bring it by means of a perfect preparation to its end. For the transmutation of an inferior metal into a superior one brings with it many difficulties and obstacles, as the change of Jove [tin] into Luna [silver] or Venus into Sol. Perhaps on account of their sins God willed that the Magnalia [great and divine works] of nature should be hidden from men. For sometimes, when this Tincture has been prepared by artists, and they were not able to reduce their projection to work its effects, it happened that, by their carelessness and bad guardianship, this was eaten up by fowls, whose feathers thereupon fell off, and, as I myself have seen, grew again. In this way transmutation, through its abuse from the carelessness of the artists, came into Medicine and Alchemy. For when they were unable to use the Tincture according to their desire, they converted the same to the renovation of men, as shall be heard more at large in the following chapter.

CONCERNING THE RENOVATION OF MEN

Some of the first and primitive philosophers of Egypt have lived by means of this Tincture for a hundred and fifty years. The life of many, too, has been extended and prolonged to several centuries, as is most clearly shown in different histories, though it seems scarcely credible to anyone. For its power is so remarkable that it extends the life of the body beyond what is possible to its congenital nature, and keeps it so firmly in that condition that it lives on in safety from all infirmities. And although, indeed, the body at length comes to old age, nevertheless it still appears as though it were established in its primal youth.

So, then, the Tincture of the Philosophers is a universal medicine, and consumes all diseases, by whatsoever name they are called, just like an invisible fire. The dose is very small, but its effect is most powerful. By means thereof I have cured the leprosy, venereal disease, dropsy, the falling sickness, colic, scab, and similar afflictions; also lupus, cancer, noli-metangere, fistulas, and the whole race of internal diseases, more surely than one could believe. Of this fact Germany,

France, Italy, Poland, Bohemia, etc., will afford the most ample evidence.

Now, Sophist, look at Theophrastus Paracelsus. How can your Apollo, Machaon, and Hippocrates stand against me? This is the Catholicum of the Philosophers, by which all these philosophers have attained long life for resisting diseases, and they have attained this end entirely and most effectually, and so, according to their judgment, they named it the Tincture of the Philosophers. For what can there be in the whole range of Medicine greater than such purgation of the body, by means whereof all superfluity is radically removed from it and transmuted? For when the seed is once made sound all else is perfected. What avails the ill-founded purgation of the Sophists since it removes nothing as it ought? This, therefore, is the most excellent foundation of a true physician, the regeneration of the nature, and the restoration of youth. After this, the new essence itself drives out all that is opposed to it. To effect this regeneration, the powers and virtues of the Tincture of the Philosophers were miraculously discovered, and up to this time have been used in secret and kept concealed by true Spagyrists.

From Theophrastus Bombast of Hohenheim, *The Book Concerning the Philosophers*, in *The Hermetic and Alchemical Writings of . . . Paracelsus the Great*, ed. and trans. A. E. Waite (London: James Elliott & Co., 1894)

𝕾𝕾

A Surgeon in the Field

AMBROISE PARÉ

1537

I WILL here show the readers the places where I have had means to learn the art of surgery, for the better instructing of the young surgeon. And first in the year 1536 the great King Francis sent a great army to Turin to recover the cities and castles which the Marquis of Guast, lieutenant general of the emperor, had taken, where the High Constable of France, the great master, was lieutenant general of the army and Monsieur de Montejan colonel general of the foot, of which I was then surgeon. A great part of the army arrived in the country of Suze; we found the enemy that stopped the passage, and had made certain forts and trenches, insomuch that to hunt them out and make them leave the place we were forced to fight, where there were divers hurt and slain, as well of the one side as of the other. But the enemies were constrained to retire and get into the castle, which was caused partly by one Captain Ratt, who climbed with divers of the soldiers of his company upon a little mountain. There where he shot directly upon the enemies he received a shot upon the ankle of his right foot, wherewith he fell to the ground, and said then, "Now is the Rat taken." I dressed him, and God healed him.

We entered the throng in the city and passed over the dead bodies, and some which were not yet dead we heard cry under our horses' feet, which made my heart relent to hear them. And truly I repented to have forsaken Paris to see so pitiful a spectacle. Being in the city, I entered into a stable, thinking to lodge my own and my man's horse, where I found four dead soldiers, and three which were leaning against the wall, their faces wholly disfigured and neither saw, nor heard, nor spoke; and their clothes did yet flame with the gunpowder which had burned them. Beholding them with pity, there happened to come an old soldier who asked me if there were any possible means to cure them; I told him no. He presently approached them and gently cut their throats without choler. Seeing this great cruelty, I told him he was a wicked man; he answered me that he prayed to God that whensoever he should be in such a case, that he might find someone that would do as much to him, to the end that he might not miserably languish.

And to return to our former discourse, the enemy was summoned to surrender, which they did and went out, their lives only saved, with a white staff in their hands. The greatest part whereof went and got to the Castle of Villane, where there was about two hundred Spaniards. Monsieur the Constable would not leave them behind, to the end that the way might be made free. This castle is seated upon a little mountain which gave great assurance to them within, that one could not plant the ordnance to beat upon it, and were summoned to surrender or that they should be cut in pieces; which they flatly refused, making answer that they were as good and faithful servants to the emperor as Monsieur the Constable could be to the king his master. Their answer heard, we made by force of arm two great cannons to be mounted in the night with cords and ropes by the Swiss and Lansquenets [German Landsknechts], when as the ill luck would have it, the two cannons being seated, a gunner by great negligence set on fire a great bag of gunpowder, wherewith he was burned together with ten or twelve soldiers. And, moreover, the flame of the powder was a cause of discovering the artillery, which made them so that all night they of the castle did nothing but shoot at that place where they discovered the two pieces of ordnance, wherewith they killed and hurt a great number of our people.

The next day early in the morning a battery was made which in a few hours made a breach, which being made they demanded to parley with us but 'twas too late for them. For in the meantime our French foot, seeing them amazed, mounted to the breach and cut them all in pieces, except a fair young lusty maid of Piedmont which a great lord would have kept and preserved for him to keep him company in the night for fear of the greedy wolf. The captain and ensign were taken alive but soon after were hanged upon the gate of the city, to the end they might give example and fear to the Imperial soldiers not to be so rash and foolish as to be willing to hold such places against so great an army. Now all the said soldiers of the castle, seeing our people coming with a most violent fury, did all endeavour to defend themselves; they killed and hurt a great company of our soldiers with pikes, muskets, and stones, where the surgeons had good store of work cut out.

Now at that time I was a freshwater soldier; I had not yet seen wounds made by gunshot at the first dressing. It is true I had read in John de Vigo, in the first book of wounds in general, the eighth chapter, that wounds made by fire did participate of venomosity, by reason of the powder, and for their cure commands to cauterize them with oil of elders scalding hot, in which should be mingled a little treacle. And not to fail, before I would apply of the said oil, knowing that such a thing might bring to the patient great pain, I was willing to know first, before I applied it, how the other surgeons did for the first dressing, which was to apply the said oil the hottest that was possible into the wounds, with tents and setons; insomuch that I took courage to do as they did. At last I wanted oil and was constrained instead thereof to apply a digestive of yolks of eggs, oil of roses, and turpentine. In the night I could not sleep in quiet, fearing some default in not cauterizing, that I should find those to whom I had not used the burning oil dead poisoned; which made me rise very early to visit them, where beyond my expectation I found those to whom I had applied my digestive medicine, to feel little pain, and their wounds without inflammation or tumor, having rested reasonably well in the night. The others, to whom was used the said burning oil, I found feverish, with great pain and tumor about the edges of their wounds. And then I resolved with myself never so cruelly to burn poor men wounded with gunshot.

Being at Turin, I found a surgeon who had fame above all others for the curing of wounds of gunshot, into whose favour I found means to insinuate myself, to have receipt of his balm, as he called it, wherewith he dressed wounds of that kind; and he held me off the space of two years before I could possibly draw the receipt from him. In the end by gifts and presents he gave it me, which was this, to boil young whelps, new pupped, in oil of lilies, with earthworms prepared with turpentine of Venice. Then was I joyful and my heart made glad, that I had understood his remedy, which was like to that which I had obtained by great chance. See then how I have learned to dress wounds made with gunshot, not by books.

My Lord Marshal of Montejan remained lieutenant general for the king in Piedmont, having ten or twelve thousand men in garrison through the cities and castles, who often combatted with swords and other weapons, as also with muskets; and if there were four hurt, I had always three of them, and if there was a question of cutting off an arm or leg, or to trepan, or to reduce a fracture or dislocation, I brought it well to pass. The said Lord Marshal sent me one while this way, another while that way, to dress the appointed soldiers which were beaten as well in other cities as that of Turin, insomuch that I was always in the country one way or other. Monsieur the Marshal sent for a physician to Milan, who had no less reputation in the medicinal art (than the deceased Monsieur le Grand), to take him in hand for an hepatical flux whereof at last he died. This physician was a certain while at Turin to deal with him, and was often called to visit the hurt people, where he always found me, and I consulted with him and some other surgeons. And when we had resolved to do any serious work of surgery, 'twas Ambroise Paré that put his hand thereto, where I did it promptly and with dexterity, and with a great assurance, insomuch that the said physician admired me, to see me so ready in the operation of surgery, seeing the small age which I had. One day discoursing with the said Lord Marshal, he said to him, "Thou hast a young surgeon of age, but he is old in knowledge and experience; preserve him well, for he will do thee service and honour." But the old man knew not that I had dwelt three years in the Hospital of Paris, there to dress the diseased. In the end Monsieur Marshal died with his hepatical flux. Being dead, the king sent Monsieur the Marshal of Annehaut to be in his place, who did me this honour to pray me to dwell with him, and that he would use me as well or better than Monsieur the Marshal Montejan; which I would not do for the grief I had for the loss of my master who loved me intimately, and I him in the like manner. And so I came back to Paris.

From *The Apologie and Treatise*, translated out of Latin and compared with the French by Thomas Johnson (1634).

Anatomy and the Art of Medicine

ANDREAS VESALIUS

1543

THOSE engaged in the arts and sciences, most gracious Emperor Charles, find many serious obstacles to the exact study and successful application of them. In the first place, no slight inconvenience results from too great separation between branches of study which serve for the perfection of one art. But much worse is the mischievous distribution among different practitioners of the practical applications of the art. This has been carried so far that those who have set before themselves the attainment of an art embrace one part of it to the neglect of the rest, although they are intimately bound up with it and can by no means be separated from it. Such never achieve any notable result; they never attain their goal, or succeed in basing their art upon a proper foundation.

I shall pass over all the other arts in silence and confine myself to a few remarks on that which presides over the health of mankind. This, of all the arts which the mind of man has discovered, is by far the most beneficial, necessary, abstruse, and laborious. But in

bygone times, that is to say, [in the West] after the
Gothic deluge and [in the East] after the reign of
Mansor at Bochara in Persia, under whom, as we know,
the Arabs still lived as was right on terms of familiarity
with the Greeks, medicine began to be sore distem-
pered. Its primary instrument, the employment of the
hand in healing, was so neglected that it was relegated
to vulgar fellows with no instruction whatsoever in the
branches of knowledge that subserve the art of medicine. . . .

The triple art of healing, as it is called, cannot at all
be disunited and wrenched asunder, but belongs in its
entirety to the same practitioner; and for the due attainment of this triple art, all the parts of medicine have
been established and prepared on an equal footing, so
that the individual parts are brought into use with a
success proportioned to the degree in which one com-
bines the cumulative force of all. How rarely indeed a
disease occurs which does not at once require the triple
manner of treatment: that is to say, a proper diet must
be prescribed, some service must be rendered by
medicine, and some by the hand. Therefore the tyros
in this art must by every means be exhorted to follow
the Greeks in despising the whisperings of those physicians (save the mark!), and, as the fundamental nature
and rational basis of the art prescribes, to apply their
hands also to the treatment, lest they should rend the
body of medicine and make of it a force destructive of
the common life of man.

And they must be urged to this with all the greater
earnestness because men today who have had an irre-
proachable training in the art are seen to abstain from
the use of the hand as from the plague, and for this
very reason, lest they should be slandered by the masters of the profession as barbers before the ignorant

mob, and should henceforth lack equal gain and honour with those less than half-doctors, losing their standing both with the uneducated commonalty and with princes. For it is indeed above all other things the wide prevalence of this hateful error that prevents us even in our age from taking up the healing art as a whole, makes us confine ourselves merely to the treatment of internal complaints, and, if I may utter the blunt truth once for all, causes us, to the great detriment of mankind, to study to be healers only in a very limited degree. . . .

But when medicine in the great blessedness of this age, which the gods will to entrust to the wise guidance of your divine power, had, together with all studies, begun to live again and to lift its head up from its utter darkness (so much so, indeed, that it might without fear of contradiction be regarded in some academies as having well nigh recovered its ancient brilliance); and when there was nothing of which the need was now so urgently felt as the resurrection of the science of anatomy, then I, challenged by the example of so many eminent men, insofar as I could and with what means I could command, thought I should lend my aid. And lest, when all others for the sake of our common studies were engaged in some attempt and with such great success, I alone should be idle, or lest I should fall below the level of my forebears, doctors to be sure not unknown to fame, I thought that this branch of natural philosophy should be recalled from the dead, so that if it did not achieve with us a greater perfection than at any other place or time among the old teachers of anatomy, it might at least reach such a point that one could with confidence assert that our modern science of anatomy was equal to that of old, and that in this age anatomy was unique both in the level to which it had sunk and in the completeness of its subsequent restoration.

But this effort could by no manner of means have succeeded, if, when I was studying medicine at Paris, I had not myself applied my hand to this business, but had acquiesced in the casual and superficial display to me and my fellow students by certain barbers of a few organs at one or two public dissections. For in such a perfunctory manner was anatomy then treated in the place where we have lived to see medicine happily reborn, that I myself, having trained myself without guidance in the dissection of brute creatures, at the third dissection at which it was my fortune ever to be present (this, as was the custom there, was concerned exclusively or principally with the viscera), led on by the encouragement of my fellow students and teachers, performed in public a more thorough dissection than was wont to be done. Later I attempted a second dissection, my purpose being to exhibit the muscles of the hand together with a more accurate dissection of the viscera. For except for eight muscles of the abdomen, disgracefully mangled and in the wrong order, no one (I speak the simple truth) ever demonstrated to me any single muscles, or any single bone, much less the network of nerves, veins, and arteries.

Subsequently at Louvain, where I had to return on account of the disturbance of war, because during eighteen years the doctors there had not even dreamed of anatomy, and in order that I might help the students of that academy, and that I myself might acquire greater skill in a matter both obscure and in my judgment of prime importance for the whole of medicine, I did somewhat more accurately than at Paris expound the whole structure of the human body in the course

of dissecting, with the result that the younger teachers
of that academy now appear to spend great and very
serious study in acquiring a knowledge of the parts of
man, clearly understanding what invaluable material for
philosophizing is presented to them from this knowledge. Furthermore at Padua, in the most famous gymnasium of the whole world, I had been charged with
the teaching of surgical medicine five years by the
illustrious Senate of Venice, which is far the most
liberal in the endowment of the higher branches of
learning. And since the carrying out of anatomical inquiry is of importance for surgical medicine, I devoted
much effort to the investigation of the structure of man,
and so directed my inquiries, and, exploding the ridiculous fashion of the schools, so taught the subject that
we could not find in my procedure anything that fell
short of the tradition of the ancients. . . .

And that the Muses might the more smile upon this
hope, I have, so far as in me lay, and in addition to
my other publications on this subject—which certain
plagiarists, thinking me far away from Germany, have
put out there as their own—made a completely fresh
arrangement in seven books of my information about
the parts of the human body in the order in which I
am wont to lay the same before that learned assembly
in this city, as well as at Bologna, and at Pisa. Thus
those present at the dissections will have a record of
what was there demonstrated, and will be able to expound anatomy to others with less trouble. And also the
books will be by no means useless to those who have no
opportunity for personal examination, for they relate
with sufficient fullness the number, position, shape, substance, connection with other parts, use, and function
of each part of the human body, together with many

similar facts which we are wont to unravel during dissection concerning the nature of the parts, and also the method of dissection applicable to dead and living animals. Moreover, the books contain representations of all the parts inserted in the text of the discourse, in such a way that they place before the eyes of the student of nature's works, as it were, a dissected corpse.

Thus in the first book I have described the nature of all bones and cartilages, which, since the other parts are supported by them, and must be described in accordance with them, are the first to be known by students of anatomy. The second book treats of the ligaments by which the bones and cartilages are linked one with another, and then the muscles that affect the movements that depend upon our will. The third comprises the close network of veins which carry to the muscles and bones and the other parts the ordinary blood by which they are nourished, and of arteries which control the mixture of Innate Heat and Vital Spirit. The fourth treats of the branches not only of the nerves which convey the Animal Spirit to the muscles, but of all the other nerves as well. The fifth explains the structure of the organs that subserve nutrition effected through food and drink; and furthermore, on account of the proximity of their position, it contains also the instruments designed by the Most High Creator for the propagation of the species. The sixth is devoted to the heart, the *fomes* of the vital faculty, and the parts that subserve it. The seventh describes the harmony between the structure of the brain and the organs of sense, without, however, repeating from the fourth book the description of the network of nerves arising from the brain.

Now in arranging the order of these books I have

followed the opinion of Galen, who, after the account of the muscles, considered that the anatomy of the veins, arteries, nerves, and then of the viscera should be handled. But with very great reason it will be urged, and especially in the case of a beginner in this science, that the study of the viscera ought to be combined with that of the distribution of the vessels, a course I have followed in the *Epitome*. This latter I have made to be as it were a footpath beside the highway of the larger book, and an index of what is set forth in it; and it is honoured with the splendid patronage of his serene Highness Philip, your Majesty's son, and a living embodiment of his father's virtues.

But here there comes into my mind the judgment of certain men who vehemently condemn the practice of setting before the eyes of students, as we do with the parts of plants, delineations, be they never so accurate, of the parts of the human body. These, they say, ought to be learned, not by pictures, but by careful dissection and examination of the things themselves. As if, forsooth, my object in adding to the text of my discourse images of the parts, which are most faithful, and which I wish could be free from the risk of being spoiled by the printers, was that students should rely upon them and refrain from dissecting bodies; whereas my practice has rather been to encourage students of medicine, in every way I could, to perform dissections with their own hands. . . .

Dissection of dead bodies gives accurate instruction in the number, position, and shape of each part, and its particular substance and composition; vivisection sometimes plainly shows the function itself, and sometimes supplies helpful arguments leading to its discovery. Wherefore it is proper that students should first come for training on dead animals, in order that when they afterwards proceed to investigate the action and use of the parts, they may be prompt in their approach to the living animal. And as there are many parts of the body assigned to different actions and uses, nobody ought to be in doubt of the fact that there are manifold ways of dissecting the living animal. . . .

To proceed: the vivisection I promised a little while ago to describe, you should perform on a pregnant sow or bitch. It is better to choose a sow on account of the voice. For a dog, after being bound for some time, no matter what you may do to it, finally neither barks nor howls, and so you are sometimes unable to observe the loss or weakening of the voice. First, then, you must fasten the animal to the operating table as firmly as your patience and your resources allow, in such a way that it lies upon its back and presents unimpeded the front of its neck and the trunk of its body. It is not a difficult matter to get a plank with holes in it suited for fastening the legs; or if there are no holes in it, it is easy to put two sticks beneath the plank and bind the legs to them. Among other details, special attention must be given to the upper jaw, so that it may be firmly fastened to the plank. Do this with a chain or a strong cord fixed in front of the canine teeth, and then tied to a ring in the plank, or a hole, or any other way you find convenient, but so that the neck may be extended and the head motionless, and the animal at the same time free to breathe and cry.

Before the animal is bound in this way my custom is to pass in review for the audience, already well skilled in the dissection of dead bodies, the precise points that are to be observed in the present dissection, lest a wordy account in the middle of the operation should hinder the progress of the work, or the work even be broken off by the necessity for speech.

Then I make a long incision in the throat with a sharp razor, cutting through the skin and the muscles under it right down to the trachea, taking care lest the incision should be deflected and injure some important vein. Then I grasp the trachea in my hand, and, freeing it merely with the aid of my fingers from the muscles that lie upon it, I search out the soporal [i.e., carotid] arteries at its sides and the sixth pair [i.e., the vagus and spinal accessory nerves] of cerebral nerves stretched along it. Then I also examine the recurrent nerves attached to the sides of the trachea, and sometimes I ligature them, sometimes sever them. And this I do first on one side, in order that when the nerve is here tied or cut it may be clearly seen how the middle voice perishes, and how it altogether disappears when both nerves are affected, and how, if I slacken the knot, it again returns. You can quickly examine without much loss of blood, and very nicely hear, what a powerful outward blast the animal produces without voice when the recurrent nerves have been cut with a knife.

Then I pass to the abdomen, and with a sharp strong knife, below the cartilages of the spurious ribs and at the pointed site [i.e., xiphisternum] of the breastbone, I make a single semicircular cut right down to the cavity of the peritoneum; and from the middle of this incision right to the pubis I attempt another, which comes off readily if I insert the knife or razor into the cavity of the peritoneum. In this way, by these two incisions, we shall expose the intestines and the uterus distended with the fetuses. But we must take particular care that one of the audience put his thumb on the vessels which descend below the breastbone and make

for the abdomen. For these are the only vessels up to
now from which much blood flows.

From *De fabrica corporis humani*: Preface, *Transactions of the
Royal Society of Medicine*, June 1932; and Book VII, 19, *Trans-
actions of the Royal Society of South Africa*, June 1932; trans.
B. Farrington.

The Health of the Mind

GIROLAMO FRACASTORO

1544

TO CARLO GUALTARUZZI

Concerning the state of the most illustrious Marchesa
di Pescara [Vittoria Colonna] . . . this, as you know,
is my opinion, that as the body when it tyrannizes over
the mind ruins and destroys all its soundness, so in the
same way when the mind becomes the tyrant, and not
merely the true lord, it wastes and destroys the soundness of the body first, and then their common bond of
union . . . and sins against prudence and charity. For
God wills that, while we are on this pilgrimage and
wayfarers, this companion and minister should be necessary to us. So we ought to take care of it and behave
to it like a true master, who does not deprive his
servant of that which is due to him. God alone knows
the end of things, and when and how it will be good
for us to be delivered from this. It does not belong to
us to bring it about, or to be the cause of it by our
want of care, contrary to the example that God, our
true Lord and Master, showed us in Himself. I have
put forward this little discourse, my lord, because I

fancy that all the Marchesa's sufferings had their origin in this. Not that I do not think that so much intellect will not know and recognize this better than I do, but that the error does not arise in general things, which can be clearly seen and known, but in particular things, and there lies all the difficulty: not in things in which one sees a great departure from the right, but in those where the departure is small and insensible, and, because one does not see it, one does not heed it. Which little, repeated over and over again, becomes great and perceptible, yet, as we do not perceive it ourselves, we go on little by little to our hurt, so difficult is it to find that just mean and balance which is fitting between the master and the servant. On which account, Signor Messer Carlo, I should wish for a physician of the mind to be found, who should minutely calculate and justly balance all the Marchesa's actions, giving to the master what is his and to the servant what belongs to him. And this physician must be wise, and of so much authority that her ladyship would believe and obey him, like the most illustrious and most reverend Cardinal of England [Reginald Pole]. And this beginning once put right, I do not doubt that all the rest will follow. Otherwise, I see that the most beautiful light of this world in some strange way will be extinguished and removed from our eyes, which God avert of His goodness.

In M. F. Jerrold, *Vittoria Colonna with Some Account of Her Friends and Her Times* (London: J. M. Dent & Sons, 1906).

On Nature and Experience

BERNARD PALISSY

DIALOGUE ON AGRICULTURE AND PHILOSOPHY

1563

Reply: I know that every customary folly is taken as a law and virtue but I pay no attention to this, and I do not wish to imitate my predecessors in any way except in what they have done well according to the law of God. I see such great abuses and ignorance in all the arts that it seems as if every order were in great part perverted, and that everyone works the soil without any philosophy and all jog along at the accustomed pace, following the footsteps of their ancestors without considering the nature or the principal causes of agriculture.

Question: You make me more astonished by what you say than I ever was before. To hear you talk it seems that some philosophy is needed by labourers, which I find very strange.

Reply: I tell you that there is no art in the world which requires more philosophy than agriculture, and I say that if agriculture is carried on without philosophy it amounts to a daily violation of the earth and the things it produces; and I marvel that the earth and its products do not cry for vengeance on certain murderers, ignorant and ungrateful, who every day do nothing but waste and ruin the trees and plants, without any consideration. I dare also to tell you that if the earth were cultivated as it should be, one day's work would yield more fruit than two yield as it is now cultivated daily. . . .

Question: I beg you, point out some fault committed in agriculture in order to make me believe what you say.

Reply: When you go through the villages, notice the dunghills of the labourers and you will see that they put them outside their stables, sometimes in a high place, sometimes in a low place, without any care; it is enough for them if the dung is piled up. And then look carefully in the rainy season and you will see that the water which falls on the heaps carries off a black colouring in passing through the dung; and, running into the hollow or down the slope or incline of the place where the heaps are placed, the water which passes through the said heaps carries off the said colouring, which is the chief and indeed the total substance of the dung. Therefore the dung, washed in this way, serves no purpose except for show, and on being carried to the fields it does no good. Is that not a clear case of ignorance, greatly to be regretted?

Question: I won't believe that at all unless you give me another reason.

Reply: You must first understand the reason why one carries dung to the fields and then, having understood the reason, you will easily believe what I have told you. You must admit that when you carry dung to the fields it is in order to restore to them part of what has been removed. For in sowing wheat you hope that one grain will yield many, but that cannot happen without taking some substance from the soil, and if the field has been sown for several years its substance has been carried off with the stalks and kernels. Therefore it is necessary to carry the dunghills, muddy and filthy, and even the excrement and ordure of men as well as of beasts, if it were possible, in order to put back in place the very substance which has been removed. And that is why I say that the dunghills must not be left at the mercy of the rains, because the rains, in passing through the dunghills, carry off the salt, which is the principal substance and virtue of the dung.

Question: You have now told me something that astonishes me more than anything else, and I know that many people make fun of you because you say there is salt in the dunghills. I beg you, give me some good reason for believing this.

Answer: Before, you thought it strange that I told you some philosophy was needed by labourers, and now you ask me for a reason which is related to my first proposition. I shall tell you the reason, but I beg you to respect it as it deserves; on hearing it you will learn a number of things you did not know before. Note, then, that nothing is sown, either good or bad, which does not carry in itself some kind of salt, and when the stalks, hay, and other grasses have rotted, the water passing through them carries off the salt that was in the said stalks, other grasses, or hay. And just as you see that a salted cod or other fish which has soaked for a long time will finally lose all its salty substance, and will at last have no taste at all, similarly you must believe that dunghills lose their salt when they are washed by the rains. And as to what you affirm in saying that dung remains dung, and that on being spread on the soil it will still do much good, I shall give you an example to the contrary. Don't you know that those who extract the essence of herbs and spices draw the substance from the canal, without destroying its form in any way? You will find, however, that in the liquor which they have extracted from the canal they have drawn off its entire savour and odour and its virtue; nevertheless the canal remains in its shape, and has the appearance of a canal as before. But if you eat it you will find in it no odour or savour or virtue. There is an example which ought to make you believe what I have said.

DEDICATION OF THE *Admirable Discourse*
TO ANTOINE DE PONS

1580

The number of my years gives me the boldness to tell you that recently I was observing the colour of my beard which made me think about the short time that remains to me, to finish my course; and that led me to admire the lilies and the wheat of the fields and many kinds of plants which change their green colours into white when they are ready to yield their fruit. And as many trees hasten to flower when they feel their natural and vegetative virtues failing, a like consideration has reminded me that it is written one should take care not to abuse the gifts of God and hide one's talent in the earth; and also that the fool who hides his folly is worth more than the wise man who conceals his wisdom. It is, therefore, just and reasonable that each one should seek to multiply the talents he has received from God, following His commandment. For this reason I have striven to bring to light the things it has pleased God to make me understand, according to the measure with which it has pleased him to endow me, in order to benefit posterity. And it seems that many in fine Latin or some other well-polished language have left many pernicious talents to harm the young and waste their time, and such were a Geber, a *Roman de la Rose*, and a Raymond Lull; and some disciples of Paracelsus and many other alchemists have left books in the study of which many people have lost both their time and their goods. Such harmful books have induced me to scrape the earth for forty years and to dig into its entrails in order to know the things it produces within itself, and in this way I have found grace before God, who has enabled me to know secrets heretofore unknown to men, even to the most learned, as one can know from my writings contained in this book.

I know well that some will make fun of me, saying it is impossible that a man deprived of the Latin language could attain an understanding of natural things; and they will say that I have great temerity in writing against the opinion of so many famous and ancient philosophers, who have written about natural effects and filled all this earth with wisdom. I know also that some will judge by appearances, saying that I am only a poor artisan, and by such talk will try to discredit my writings. In truth there are things in my book which it will be difficult for the ignorant to believe. Despite all these considerations, I have persisted in my enterprise, and in order to cut short all kinds of calumnies and attacks, I have made up a collection in which I have put many admirable and wonderful things that I have drawn from the matrix of the earth, which serve as certain proof of what I say. And there is no man to be found who will not be forced to admit the truth of what I say after he has seen the things I have prepared in my collection, in order to convince those who would not otherwise be willing to have faith in my writings. If by chance there comes some numskull who wishes to ignore the proofs put in my collection, I ask for no judgment except yours, which is sufficient to convince and to overturn all the opinions of those who wish to contradict it. I say this in truth and without any flattery, for just as I had good evidence of the excellence of your mind from the time when you returned from

Ferrara, in your château at Pons, so it has been in these recent days when it has pleased you to talk to me of various sciences, namely philosophy, astrology, and other arts derived from mathematics. This, I say, has led me to value doubly the boldness and capacity of your marvellous intellect; and although the age of many persons diminishes their memory, I find yours increased rather than diminished. I have learned this in the discourse it has pleased you to hold with me. For these reasons I believe there is no lord in this world to whom my work could be better dedicated than to you, knowing well that whereas it would be considered by some as a fable full of lies, by you it will be prized and considered a rare thing. And if there is anything poorly presented or arranged in it, you will know very well how to draw the substance from the matter and to excuse the undue rudeness of the author's language; and in this hope, I beg you most humbly to do me the honour of receiving it as from the hand of one of your most humble servants.

From *Les oeuvres de Bernard Palissy*, ed. Anatole France (Paris, 1880); trans. J.B.R.

Revolutions of the Spheres

The Diurnal Rotation of the Earth

NICOLE ORESME

1377

IT SEEMS to me that, subject to all correction, the said opinion could well be upheld and affirmed, namely, that the earth is moved by a daily movement and that the heavens are not. And I wish first to declare that the contrary cannot be demonstrated by any experience; second, that it cannot be demonstrated by reasons; and third, I wish to present reasons for this movement. . . .

As to the third point, I want to offer persuasions or arguments by which it would seem that the earth is moved as has been said. First, everything that is served by something else should be disposed to receive the good which it obtains from the other by the movement of that which receives; thus we see that each element is moved to its natural place, or is conserved and goes to its place, but its place does not come to it. And then the earth, and the elements of the inferior regions which are served by the heat and the influence of the heavens all around them, ought to be disposed by their movement to receive this benefit duly; just as, to speak familiarly, the object which is roasted at the fire receives the heat of the fire around it because it is turned, and not because the fire is turned around it.

Also in a case where neither experience nor reason demonstrates to the contrary, as has been said, it is more reasonable that all the principal movements of the simple bodies of the universe should be and turn or proceed in one way or in one manner. It could not be, according to the philosophers and astronomers, that all would move from east to west; but if the earth is moved as has been said, all would proceed in one way from west to east; that is to say, the earth making its circuit in a natural day beneath the poles of this movement, and the bodies of the heavens beneath the poles of the zodiac; the moon in a month, the sun in a year, Mars in two years or thereabouts, and the others in like manner. . . .

Further, all the philosophers say that nothing is accomplished by numerous or by large operations which can be done by fewer and smaller operations. Aristotle says (*De caelo*, I, 8) that God and nature never do anything in vain. But if the heavens are moved by a daily movement, it is necessary to assume in the principal bodies of the universe and in the heavens two ways of movement which are contrary to each other: one from east to west and the other from west to east, as has often been said. And with this, it is proper to assume an excessively great speed, for anyone who reckons and considers well the height of distance of the heavens and the magnitude of these and of their circuit, if such a circuit were made in a day, could not imagine or conceive how marvellously and excessively swift would be the movement of the heavens, and how unbelievable and unthinkable.

Thus all the effects that we observe can be caused, and all the appearances saved, by assuming in place of this one little operation, that is to say, the daily movement of the earth, which is very small with respect to the heavens, without multiplying so many operations, which are so diverse and so outrageously large that it would follow that God and nature would have caused and ordained them to no purpose. And this is inconvenient, as has been said. Also, suppose that the entire heavens would be moved by a daily movement and that, with this, the eighth sphere would be moved by another movement, as the astronomers state, it would be proper, according to them, to assume a ninth sphere that is moved only by a daily movement. But supposing that the earth is moved as has been said, the eighth sphere is moved by a single slow movement, and thus in this way it is not necessary to dream or conjecture about a ninth natural sphere, invisible and without stars. For God and nature would have made such a sphere in vain, when in another way all things could be just as they are.

Further, when God performs any miracle, we ought to suppose and hold that He performs it without changing the common course of nature, except in the least possible way. And thus if it could be explained how God lengthened the day or the time of Joshua by arresting the movement of the earth or of the inferior region only, which is so very small and like a point with reference to the heaven, without assuming that the whole universe except this little point has been moved out of its common course and order, and likewise such bodies as the bodies of heaven are, it would be much more reasonable. And this could be explained thus, as appears from the response to the seventh argument which was made against this opinion. And it could be argued in like manner concerning the return of the sun in the time of Ezechias.

It appears thus that it cannot be shown by any experience that the heavens are moved by a daily movement, for it is true that, supposing that the heavens are moved thus and that the earth is not, or that the earth is moved, and the heavens are not, if a bird were in the heavens, and he saw the earth clearly, it would seem to be moved, and if the bird were on earth, the heavens would seem to be moved. And the vision is not deceived in this, for it does not feel or see anything except that movement exists. But the judgment whether the movement is of this body or of that is made by the interior senses, as is said in the *Perspective* [of Witelo], and these senses are often deceived in such cases, as was said above concerning the man who is in a moving ship.

Then it has been shown how it cannot be concluded by reasons that the heavens may be moved. And third, reasons have been offered to the contrary, that it is not so moved. Nevertheless all hold and I believe that it is so moved and that the earth is not: "God has established the sphere of the earth, which shall not be moved"—the arguments to the contrary notwithstanding, for these are persuasions which do not lead to evident conclusions.

But considering all that has been said, it is possible to believe that the earth is so moved and that the heavens are not, and it is not evident to the contrary. And, in any case, it seems on the face of it, as much or more against natural reason, as are either all or some of the articles of our faith. And thus what I have said for fun in this manner could be of value in confuting or reproving those who would attack our faith by rational arguments.

From *Le Livre du ciel et du monde*, ed. A. D. Menut and A. J. Denomy, *Medieval Studies*, 1942; trans. M.M.M.

The Nature of the Universe

NICHOLAS OF CUSA

1440

THE UNIVERSE, then, has no circumference, for, if it had a centre and a circumference, it would thus have in itself its beginning and its end, and the universe itself would be terminated by relation to something else; there would be outside the universe another thing and a place—but all this contains no truth. Thus, since it is not possible that the universe is enclosed between a material centre and a circumference, the world is unintelligible; the universe whose centre and circumference are God. And although our universe is not infinite, nevertheless one cannot conceive of it as finite, since there are no boundaries between which it is enclosed. Thus the earth, which cannot be the centre, cannot be absolutely lacking in movement; for the earth must necessarily have such a movement, that it could still have a movement infinitely less strong. Just as the earth is not the centre of the universe, neither is the circumference of the universe the sphere of the fixed stars, although if one compares the earth to the heavens, the earth seems nearer the centre and the heavens nearer the circumference. Thus the earth is at the centre neither of the eighth nor of any other sphere, and the appearance of the six stars above the horizon does not prove that the earth is at the centre of the eighth sphere. In fact, if it was even at a certain distance from the centre and in the vicinity of the axis passing through the poles, so that in one part it was raised towards one pole and in the other lowered towards the other pole, then, to men situated at a distance from the poles as great as the extent of the horizon, only a half of the sphere would appear, as is clear. Now the centre of the universe is not in the interior of the earth any more than in its exterior; and the earth does not have a centre any more than any of the spheres. In fact, a centre is a point equidistant from a circumference, and it is not possible that there should exist a sphere or a circle so true that one could not find truer ones; thus it is clear also that neither could one find a centre such that one could not find one more true and more precise. Except for God, one would not know how to find precise equidistance to diverse points, because He alone is infinite equality. Thus He who is the centre of the universe, namely God whose name is blessed, He is the centre of the earth and of all the spheres, and of everything in the universe, He who is at the same time the infinite circumference of all things.

Moreover, there are not in the heavens fixed and immobile poles, although the heaven of the fixed stars seems to describe by its movement circles of progressive magnitude, circles smaller than the colures or than the equinoctial and so on for the intermediaries; but, necessarily, every part of the heavens is in movement, although unequally, in comparison with the circles described by the movement of the stars. That is why, as certain stars seem to describe a maximum circle, others seem to describe a minimum; but one does not find a star which does not describe some circle. Therefore, because there is no fixed pole on the sphere, it is evident that one cannot find a mean equidistant from the poles. Therefore there is not, on the eighth sphere, any star which describes by its revolution a maximum circle, for, necessarily, it would be at an equal distance from the poles, and these do not exist; consequently there is none that describes the minimum circle. Therefore the poles of the spheres coincide with the centre, in order that the centre may be nothing else than the pole, that is, the God whom we bless. And because we cannot grasp movement except in relation to something fixed, poles or centres, and because we presuppose those in the measures of movements, it follows that, wandering as we do in conjectures, we find that we err in everything, and we are astonished when, following the rules of the ancients, we do not find the stars in their places. That is because we have considered correct their conceptions of centres, poles, and measures. From these it is manifest that the earth is in movement. And, because we have learned from the movement of the comet, of air, and of fire that the elements move, and that the moon moves less from east to west than Mercury, Venus, or the sun, and so on, it follows that the earth moves still less than all the planets; and yet it is not like a star describing a minimum circle around a centre or a pole, and the eighth sphere, or any other, does not describe a maximum circle, as we have just proved. . . .

What we have said above the ancients did not consider because they were lacking in learned ignorance. It is already clear to us that this earth actually moves although it does not seem to, for we only apprehend movement by means of comparison with a fixed point. For if someone did not know that water runs, and if, finding himself on a ship in the middle of the seas, he did not see the shores, how could he understand that the ship was in motion? And for this reason if someone finds himself on earth, in the sun, or another star, it will always seem to him that he is at the immobile centre and that all the other things are in motion; he will always, without doubt, constitute different poles for himself, some if he is in the sun, others if he is on earth, still others in the moon, and so on. Hence the machine of the universe has, so to speak, its centre everywhere—its circumference nowhere, because God is circumference and centre, He who is everywhere and nowhere.

Also the earth is not spherical, as some have said, although it tends toward sphericity, for the shape of the universe is limited in its parts as well as its movement. When, however, an infinite line is considered to be limited in such a way that there could be no limited form more perfect or one which embraces more properties, then it is circular, since in such a form the beginning coincides with the end. The movement which is more perfect than others is, therefore, circular, and the corporeal form which is the most perfect is the sphere. Therefore every movement of the part is for the perfection of the whole, so that heavy things go towards the earth, and light things upwards, and earth towards earth, water towards water, air towards air, fire towards fire. That is why the movement of everything seeks as much as possible to be circular, and every form to be spherical; we have experience of this in the members of animals, in trees, in the heavens. Hence it comes about that one movement is more circular and more perfect than another, and likewise that forms have differences. . . .

The earth, then, is a noble star, which has a light, a heat, and an influence different from those of all other stars. Just as each differs from every other by its light, its nature, and its influence, so each one communicates to another light and influence, not intentionally, since all the stars move and shine only in order to be in a better way; and then consequently participation occurs. Light shines by virtue of its own nature and not in order that I should see; but consequently participation comes about when I use the light in order to see. Now it is thus that God, whose name is blessed, has created everything; while each object tries to preserve its being, as a gift of God, it does that in communion with other objects. The foot, for example, is not useful only to itself because it serves only in walking, but to the eye, the hands, the body, to the whole of man. And so it is with the eye, the other members, and parts of the world. Plato, in fact, said that the world is an animal; if one conceives God as its soul—without any immersion—much of what we have said will be clear.

And we must not say, because the earth is smaller than the sun and is under its influence, that it is for that reason more vile. In fact the total region of the earth, which extends as far as the circumference of fire, is great. And, although the earth is smaller than the sun, as we know from the shadow and the eclipses, nevertheless we do not know by how much the region of the sun is greater or smaller than the region of the earth; but it cannot be exactly the same, for no star can be equal to another. And the earth is not the smallest star, for she is greater than the moon, as the experience of the eclipses has taught us, and greater even than Mercury, as some say, and perhaps than other stars. Thus from a consideration of size, one cannot conclude that the earth is vile. . . .

Nor from the point of view of place is it true that the earth is vile. Without doubt our place in the world is the habitation of men, of animals and vegetation, and they are in degree less noble than the inhabitants of the solar region and of the other stars. But, although God is the centre and the circumference of all the regions of stars, and from Him proceed the various kinds of nobility which inhabit each region, in order that so many celestial and stellar places should not be empty, and not only the earth, which is perhaps inhabited by lesser beings, nevertheless it does not seem that one could find a nature more noble and more perfect according to this nature than the intellectual nature which inhabits the earth as its own region, even if there are in other stars inhabitants of another kind. For man does not seek another nature, but he seeks to be perfect in his own.

From *De docta ignorantia*, ed. P. Rotta (Bari: Laterza e figli, 1913); trans. J.B.R.

The Revolutions of the Celestial Spheres

NICHOLAS COPERNICUS

1543

FROM THESE and similar reasons it is claimed that the earth is at rest in the centre of the universe and that this is undoubtedly true. But one who believes that the earth rotates will also certainly be of the opinion that this motion is natural and not violent. Whatever is in accordance with nature produces effects which are the opposite of what happens through violence. Things upon which violence or an external force is exerted must become annihilated and cannot long exist. But whatever happens in the course of nature remains in good condition and in its best arrangement. Without cause, therefore, Ptolemy feared that the earth and all earthly things, if set in rotation, would be dissolved by the action of nature, for the functioning of nature is something entirely different from artifice, or from that which could be contrived by the human mind. But why did he not fear the same, and indeed in much higher degree, for the universe, whose motion would have to be as much more rapid as the heavens are larger than the earth? Or have the heavens become infinite just because they have been removed from the centre by the inexpressible force of the motion; while otherwise, if they were at rest, they would collapse? Certainly if this argument were true the extent of the heavens would become infinite. For the more they were driven aloft by the outward impulse of the motion, the more rapid would the motion become because of the ever-increasing circle which it would have to describe in the space of twenty-four hours; and, conversely, if the motion increased, the immensity of the heavens would also increase. Thus velocity would augment size into infinity, and size, velocity. But according to the physical law that the infinite can neither be traversed, nor can it for any reason have motion, the heavens would, however, of necessity be at rest.

But it is said that outside of the heavens there is no body, nor place, nor empty space, in fact, that nothing at all exists, and that, therefore, there is no space in which the heavens could expand; then it is really strange that something could be enclosed by nothing. If, however, the heavens were infinite and were bounded only by their inner concavity, then we have perhaps even better confirmation that there is nothing outside of the heavens, because everything, whatever its size, is within them; but then the heavens would remain motionless. The most important argument, on which depends the proof of the finiteness of the universe, is motion. Now, whether the world is finite or infinite we will leave to the quarrels of the natural philosophers; for us remains the certainty that the earth, contained between poles, is bounded by a spherical surface. Why should we hesitate to grant it a motion, natural and corresponding to its form, rather than assume that the whole world, whose boundary is not known and cannot be known, moves? And why are we not willing to acknowledge that the *appearance* of a daily revolution belongs to the heavens, its *actuality* to the earth? The relation is similar to that of which Vergil's Aeneas says: "We sail out of the harbour, and the countries and cities recede." For when a ship is sailing along quietly, everything which is outside of it will appear to those on board to have a motion corresponding to the movement of the ship, and the voyagers are of the erroneous opinion that they with all that they have with them are at rest. This can without doubt also apply to the motion of the earth, and it may appear as if the whole universe were revolving. . . .

Since nothing stands in the way of the movability of the earth, I believe we must now investigate whether it also has several motions, so that it can be considered one of the planets. That it is not the centre of all the revolutions is proved by the irregular motions of the planets, and their varying distances from the earth, which cannot be explained as concentric circles with the earth at the centre. Therefore, since there are several central points, no one will without cause be uncertain whether the centre of the universe is the centre of gravity of the earth or some other central point. I, at least, am of the opinion that gravity is nothing else than a natural force planted by the divine providence of the Master of the World into its parts, by means of which they, assuming a spherical shape, form a unity and a whole. And it is to be assumed that the impulse is also inherent in the sun and the moon and the other planets, and that by the operation of this force they remain in the spherical shape in which they appear; while they, nevertheless, complete their revolutions in diverse ways. If, then, the earth too possesses other motions besides that around its centre, then they must be of such a character as to become apparent in many ways and in appropriate manners; and among such possible effects we recognize the yearly revolution. If one admits the motionlessness of the sun, and transfers the annual revolution from the sun to the earth, there would result, in the same manner as actually observed, the rising and setting of the constellations and the fixed stars, by means of which they become morning and evening stars; and it will thus become apparent that also the haltings and the backward and forward motion of the planets are not motions of these but of the earth, which lends them the appearance of being actual planetary motions. Finally, one will be convinced that the sun itself occupies the centre of the universe. And all this is taught us by the law of sequence in which things follow one upon another and the harmony of the universe; that is, if we only (so to speak) look at the matter with both eyes.

First and above all lies the sphere of the fixed stars, containing itself and all things, for that very reason immovable; in truth, the frame of the universe, to which the motion and position of all other stars are referred. Though some men think it to move in some way, we assign another reason why it appears to do so in our theory of the movement of the earth. Of the moving bodies first comes Saturn, who completes his circuit in thirty years. After him, Jupiter, moving in a twelve-year revolution. Then Mars, who revolves biennially. Fourth in order an annual cycle takes place, in which we have said is contained the earth, with the lunar orbit as an epicycle. In the fifth place Venus is carried round in nine months. Then Mercury holds the sixth place, circulating in the space of eighty days. In the middle of all dwells the Sun. Who indeed in this most beautiful temple would place the torch in any other or better place than one whence it can illuminate the whole at the same time? Not ineptly, some call it the lamp of the universe, others its mind, others again its ruler—Trismegistus, the visible God, Sophocles' Electra the contemplation of all things. And thus rightly inasmuch as the Sun, sitting on a royal throne, governs the circumambient family of stars. . . . We find, therefore, under this orderly arrangement, a wonderful symmetry in the universe, and a definite relation of harmony in the motion and magnitude of the orbs, of a kind it is not possible to obtain in any other way.

From *De revolutionibus orbium celestium*: I, 8-9, in H. Shapley and H. Howarth, *A Source Book in Astronomy* (New York: McGraw-Hill Book Co., 1929); I, 10, in W. C. Dampier-Whetham, *Cambridge Readings in the Literature of Science* (Cambridge: University Press, 1928).

The New Star

TYCHO BRAHE

1573

LAST YEAR (1572), in the month of November, on the eleventh day of the month, in the evening, after sunset, when, according to my habit, I was contemplating the stars in a clear sky, I noticed that a new and unusual star, surpassing the other stars in brilliancy, was shining almost directly above my head; and since I had, almost from boyhood, known all the stars of the heavens perfectly (there is no great difficulty in attaining that knowledge), it was quite evident to me that there had never before been any star in that place in the sky, even the smallest, to say nothing of a star so conspicuously bright as this. I was so astonished at this sight that I was not ashamed to doubt the trustworthiness of my own eyes. But when I observed that others, too, on having the place pointed out to them, could see that there was really a star there, I had no further doubts. A miracle indeed, either the greatest of all that have occurred in the whole range of nature since the beginning of the world, or one certainly that is to be classed with those attested by the Holy Oracles, the staying of the Sun in its course in answer to the prayers of Joshua, and the darkening of the Sun's face at the time of the Crucifixion. For all philosophers agree, and facts clearly prove it to be the case, that in the ethereal region of the celestial world no change, in the way either of generation or corruption, takes place; but that the heavens and the celestial bodies in the heavens are without increase or diminution, and that they undergo no alteration, either in number or in size or in light or in any other respect; that they always remain the same, like unto themselves in all respects, no years wearing them away. Furthermore, the observations of all the founders of the science, made some thousands of years ago, testify that all the stars have always retained the same number, position, order, motion, and size as they are found, by careful observation on the part of those who take delight in heavenly phenomena, to preserve even in our own day. Nor do we read that it was ever before noted by any one of the founders that a new star had appeared in the celestial world,

except only by Hipparchus, if we are to believe Pliny.
For Hipparchus, according to Pliny (Book II of his
Natural History), noticed a star different from all
others previously seen, one born in his own age. . . .

In order, therefore, that I might find out . . .
whether this star was in the region of the Element or
among the celestial orbits, and what its distance was
from the Earth itself, I tried to determine whether it
had a parallax, and, if so, how great a one; and this
I did in the following way: I observed the distance
between this star and Schedir of Cassiopeia (for the
latter and the new star were both nearly on the meridian), when the star was at its nearest point to the
vertex, being only 6 degrees removed from the zenith
itself (and for that reason, though it were near the
Earth, would produce no parallax in that place, the
visual position of the star and the real position then
uniting in one point, since the line from the centre of
the Earth and that from the surface nearly coincide). I
made the same observation when the star was farthest
from the zenith and at its nearest point to the horizon,
and in each case I found that the distance from the
above-mentioned fixed star was exactly the same,
without the variation of a minute: namely 7 degrees
and 55 minutes. Then I went through the same process,
making numerous observations with other stars. Whence
I conclude that this new star has no diversity of aspect,
even when it is near the horizon. For otherwise in its
least altitude it would have been farther away from the
above-mentioned star in the breast of Cassiopeia than
when in its greatest altitude. Therefore we shall find
it necessary to place this star, not in the region of the
Element, below the Moon, but far above, in an orbit
with respect to which the Earth has no sensible size.
For if it were in the highest region of the air, below

the hollow region of the lunar sphere, it would, when nearest the horizon, have produced on the circle a sensible variation of altitude from that which held when near the vertex. . . .

Therefore, this new star is neither in the region of the Element, below the Moon, nor among the orbits of the seven wandering stars, but it is in the eighth sphere, among the other fixed stars, which was what we had to prove. Hence it follows that it is not some peculiar kind of comet or some other kind of fiery meteor become visible. For none of these are generated in the heavens themselves, but they are below the Moon, in the upper region of the air, as all philosophers testify; unless one would believe with Albategnius that comets are produced, not in the air, but in the heavens. For he believes that he has observed a comet above the Moon, in the sphere of Venus. That this can be the case is not yet clear to me. But, please God, sometime, if a comet shows itself in our age, I will investigate the truth of the matter. Even should we assume that it can happen (which I, in company with other philosophers, can hardly admit), still it does not follow that this star is a kind of comet; first by reason of its very form, which is the same as the form of the real stars and different from the form of all the comets hitherto seen, and then because, in such a length of time, it advances neither latitudinally nor longitudinally by any motion of its own, as comets have been observed to do. For, although these sometimes seem to remain in one place several days, still, when the observation is made carefully by exact instruments, they are seen not to keep the same position for so very long or so very exactly. I conclude, therefore, that this star is not some kind of comet or a fiery meteor, whether these be generated beneath the Moon or above the Moon, but that it is a star shining in the firmament itself—one that has never previously been seen before our time, in any age since the beginning of the world.

From *De nova stella*, trans. J. H. Walden, in Shapley and Howarth, *A Source Book in Astronomy*.

Comrades in the Pursuit of Truth

Padua, August 4, 1597

GALILEO TO KEPLER

I received your book, most learned sir, which you sent me by Paulus Amberger, not some days since, but only a few hours ago. And as this Paulus has notified me of his return to Germany, I would consider myself ungrateful if I did not now send you my thanks in the present letter. I thank you, therefore, and most especially because you have judged me worthy of such a token of your friendship. So far I have read only the introduction of your work, but I have to some extent gathered your plan from it, and I congratulate myself on the exceptional good fortune of having such a man as a comrade in the pursuit of truth. For it is too bad that there are so few who seek the truth and so few who do not follow a mistaken method in philosophy. This is not, however, the place to lament the misery of our century, but to rejoice with you over such beautiful ideas for proving the truth. So I add only, and I promise, that I shall read your book at leisure; for I am certain that I shall find the noblest things in it. And this I shall do the more gladly, because I accepted the view of Copernicus many years ago, and from this standpoint I have discovered from their origins many natural phenomena, which doubtless cannot be explained on the basis of the more commonly accepted hypothesis. I have written many direct and indirect arguments for the Copernican view, but until now I have not dared to publish them, alarmed by the fate of Copernicus himself, our master. He has won for himself undying fame in the eyes of a few, but he has been mocked and hooted at by an infinite multitude (for so large is the number of fools). I would dare to come forward publicly with my ideas if there were more people of your way of thinking. As this is not the case, I shall refrain. The shortness of time and my eager desire to read your book compel me to close, but I assure you of my sympathy, and I shall always gladly be at your service. Farewell and do not neglect to send me further good news of yourself.

Graz, October 13, 1597

KEPLER TO GALILEO

I received your letter of August 4 on September 1. It gave me a twofold pleasure, first, because it sealed my friendship with you, the Italian, and second, because of the agreement in our opinions concerning Copernican cosmography. Since at the end of your letter you invite me in friendly fashion to carry on a correspondence with you, and I myself am impelled to do so, I will not overlook the opportunity of sending you a letter by the present young nobleman. Meanwhile, if your time has permitted, I hope that you have come to study my little book more thoroughly. So a great desire has seized me to hear your judgment of it. For it is my way to urge all those to whom I write to give me their true opinion; believe me, I much prefer the sharpest criticism of a single intelligent man to the thoughtless approval of the great masses.

I could only have wished that you, who have so profound an insight, would choose another way. You advise us, by your personal example, and in discreetly veiled fashion, to retreat before the general ignorance and not to expose ourselves or heedlessly to oppose the violent attacks of the mob of scholars (and in this you follow Plato and Pythagoras, our true preceptors). But after a tremendous task has been begun in our time, first by Copernicus and then by many very learned mathematicians, and when the assertion that the earth moves can no longer be considered something new, would it not be much better to pull the wagon to its goal by our joint efforts, now that we have got it under way, and gradually, with powerful voices, to shout down the common herd, which really does not weigh the arguments very carefully? Thus perhaps by cleverness we may bring it to a knowledge of the truth. With your arguments you would at the same time help your comrades who endure so many unjust judgments, for they would obtain either comfort from your agreement or protection from your influential position. It is not only your Italians who cannot believe that they move if they do not feel it, but we in Germany also do not by any means endear ourselves with this idea. Yet there are ways by which we protect ourselves against these difficulties. . . .

Be of good cheer, Galileo, and come out publicly. If I judge correctly, there are only a few of the distinguished mathematicians of Europe who would part company with us, so great is the power of truth. If Italy seems less a favourable place for your publication, and if you look for difficulties there, perhaps Germany will allow us this freedom. But enough of this. Let me know privately at least, if you do not want to do so publicly, what you have discovered in support of Copernicus.

Now I should like to ask you for an observation; since I possess no instruments, I must appeal to others. Do you own a quadrant on which minutes and quarter-minutes can be read? If so, please observe, around the time of December 19, the greatest and smallest altitude, in the same night, of the middle star of the handle of the Great Dipper. Also, observe about December 26 both altitudes of the polar star. Also, watch the first star around March 19, 1598, in its height at midnight, the second about September 28, also around midnight. If, as I wish, there could be shown a difference between the two observations, of one or another minute, or even of 10 to 15 minutes, this would be proof of something of great importance for all of astronomy. If no difference is shown, however, we shall still earn together the fame of exploring a very significant problem not hitherto examined by anyone [the fixed-star parallax]. This is enough for those who are enlightened! . . . Farewell, and answer me with a very long letter.

Graz, March 16, 1598

KEPLER TO JOHANN HERWART

As to what you wrote about my *Prodromus,* I can certainly believe that the judgment of that mathematician, whoever he may be, is very much like mine. For I have found more than once that if I encounter people who have a good understanding of these matters, but who cannot accept the movement of the earth, I hear that my idea would be excellent, if only the one hypothesis of the earth's movement were true, for then it would come about that all the other theories would work out very well. I myself have given a prominent place in the title of my book to the subject which you consider worthy of a careful treatment. My little book shall indeed be a "herald" of future astronomical treatises.

My plan is this: in the new cosmography the physical arguments for the movement of the earth should be brought together, which if presented separately here and there would find little acceptance. Now in order that my discovery with respect to the five bodies ("Platonic bodies," or five regular solids) may not be hidden under chaff, and my thesis should not be rejected with others as uncertain, I want to publish that discovery separately and see whether it can gain acceptance. For it is this that must bear the weight of successive proofs of possibility from physics, etc.

I plan four cosmological books: 1) concerning the universe, especially the parts of the world which are at rest, and concerning the location and repose of the sun, the order of the fixed stars and their repose, and the unity, etc., of the universe; 2) concerning the planets, a repetition of the conception of the five "Platonic bodies," and an inquiry concerning the movement of the earth, the relationship of movements according to Pythagoras, music, etc.; 3) concerning the heavenly bodies individually, especially the terrestrial globe, and concerning the origins of mountains, rivers, etc.; 4) concerning the relation between the heavens and earth, insofar as these influence each other, and concerning light, the aspects and the physical principles of meteorology and astrology. These works will thus correspond with the first three books of Aristotle's *De caelo,* and the fourth book of his *De generatione.* I have not yet fixed a time for their publication. I see that for this purpose I must zealously study Aristotle, Plato, etc., and, especially for the third book, the cosmographers and the historians of our age. And yet one thing in particular prevents me from setting my hand to this work. It is this: in the old hypothesis we were put in a position, by the doctrine of the eclipses, to measure the spheres of the sun and moon, as to their bodies; with respect to the other heavenly bodies nothing can be determined geometrically. In the new hypothesis of Copernicus we have learned to measure all the planets and all the planetary spheres. But from this we cannot measure the sphere of fixed stars. Copernicus teaches, with the ancient Aristarchus, that the orbit or sphere of the earth is considered*in position as a point in relation to the distance of the fixed stars, as I have shown in my book.

Now I consider it very important, for a treatment of cosmography, to know whether it is so held. As I find nothing in Copernicus except the assertion itself . . . I have sought a method by which either the assertion can be proved or the distance of the earth from the centre of the sun can be determined and ascertained, so that in this way we would be enabled to measure also the most distant heavens. . . .

When this phenomenon is more certainly known (and I could wish that other astronomers would be aware of it), then in the first place the whole of astronomy and geography will have to be presented anew and will have to exhibit the changes which occur in the natural phenomena in consequence of the perceptibility of the distance of the earth from the centre of the universe. Then I shall concentrate on the ideas of physics concerning the origins of that relationship; for one must first determine the "what" from which the "why" is derived. Finally I shall proceed to the elaboration of the subject which I have tackled.

If you think that one could deduce arguments for the movement of the earth from the winds and the movements of the seas, I too have some ideas on these matters. When Galileo, a mathematician of Padua, assured me, without indeed discussing details, that he could, with complete accuracy, derive from the hypothesis of Copernicus the origins of very many natural phenomena, I also thought of the tides. If I think correctly about these phenomena, however, it seems to me that we must not exclude the moon, so far as we can deduce from it the calculation of the tides, and I believe that we can do that. He who ascribes the movement of the seas to the movement of the earth assumes a purely forced movement; but he who lets the seas follow the moon makes this movement in a certain way a natural one.

Raimar Ursus has already done what you write about Phil. Lansberg: he lets the fixed stars and the earth's centre rest, and has the surfaces of the earth circle around their centre, and the sun (the centre of all five planetary orbits) circle around the earth. Magini in Italy has done almost the same, except that he transfers the movement of the surfaces of the terrestrial sphere to the fixed stars. Others do likewise, but in a philosophical rather than an astronomical fashion—Röslin in Alsace and Tycho Brahe in Denmark, who seems to be the first of all. In short, the hypotheses are not new; they are a combination of the old hypotheses and the new ones of Copernicus. But I think in this way: since we astronomers are priests of the most high God with respect to the book of nature, it behooves us not to think of the praise of our abilities, but above all of the glory of God. He who is convinced of this does not publish frivolously anything other than what he himself believes, and he does not boldly change something in the hypothesis, except in order thereby to explain the phenomena more accurately. Also he does not try to outdo the great men, Ptolemy, Copernicus, etc. in the glory of newer discoveries. So, although I am utterly convinced of the truth of the Copernican theory, a wholesome awe prevents me from advancing something different, even though it would win praise for my genius or the favour of men who are in large degree disturbed by the heterogeneity of this theory. Enough for me is the honour of guarding, with my discovery, the door of God's temple, in which Copernicus serves before the high altar.

December 16, 1598

KEPLER TO HERWART

It is no small comfort when I reflect that we should not so much marvel at the vast and almost infinite breadth of the most distant heavens but much more at the smallness of us manikins and the smallness of this our tiny ball of earth and also of all the planets. To God the world is not immeasurable, but we are exceedingly small, compared with this world. . . . But we must not reason from size to special significance. For God, who dwells on high, still looks down upon the humble. And if the planets were the most unimportant part of the world, since the whole planetary system almost vanishes in comparison with the system of fixed stars, so according to the same argument man would belong among the most trifling things in the world, because he can in no way be compared with the earth, as the earth cannot be compared with the sphere of Saturn. Indeed if size were any criterion, the crocodile or the elephant must be dearer to God's heart than man, since these animals surpass men in size. With these and like sugar-coatings this huge morsel of a pill could perhaps be digested.

I can certainly wish for new, large, and properly constructed instruments, and enough of them, but to state where and by what means they are to be procured, this I cannot do. Tycho Brahe has given Mästlin an instrument of metal as a present, which would be very useful if Mästlin could afford the cost of transporting it from the Baltic, and if he could hope that it would travel such a long way undamaged. I believe that with the help of a Maecenas and a Praxiteles, a Kepler (or in his place many another) could also build very delicate and useful instruments. If I were to wish for a master workman, I would not choose a cabinet-maker but a mason and an architect. For with a tower and an observation place round about—that is, with a perpendicular and a hydrostatic level—some sound work could begin. One can really ask for nothing better for the observation of the sun than an opening in a tower and a protected place underneath. For if the rays of the sun enter through an opening and fall obliquely on a plane, they outline, according to optical laws, an ellipse; I would accordingly, if the ellipse were large enough, sketch it out from a high place, in order to learn more from its long and short diameter than I would with all the quadrants, astrolabes, armillaries, rods, and similar instruments. . . .

April 1599

KEPLER TO HERWART

Here is another question: how does the conformation of the heavens influence the character of a man at the moment of his birth? It influences a human being as long as he lives in no other way than that in which the peasant haphazardly ties slings around pumpkins; these do not make the pumpkin grow, but they determine its shape. So do the heavens; they do not give a man morals, experiences, happiness, children, wealth, a wife, but they shape everything with which a man has to do. And yet from the constellation of the birth of a man, the heavens take an infinite number of forms during the course of his life. They never remain the same; so the constellation at birth is a passing one. Now how can something be active which doesn't exist? It is active in so far as it had that position once, a position in which it does not remain. Would there perhaps be some mark of this position on human bodies, or is it related to the light and in this way impressed on the proper soul? And how would it imprint on the soul its destiny which is a nothing? All this would be confirmed by experience, and indeed by the experience of those who are by no means stupid.

Look at the man at whose birth the constellation of the good planets Jupiter and Venus was not favourable. You will see that such a person can be just and wise, but his fate will be less serene and rather sad. I know such a woman [Kepler is thinking of his own wife]. She is praised throughout the whole city for her virtue, chastity, and modesty. She is, however, simpleminded and has a stout body. From earliest youth she was treated harshly by her parents. When she was scarcely grown she was married against her will to a man in his forties. As soon as he died she married another of like age, but of a gayer disposition, yet he was no kind of a husband and spent the four years during which he was married to her being ill. She, who had formerly been rich, married for the third time, a poor and undistinguished man [Kepler]. Her dowry was unjustly held back. . . . In all that she does she is confused and perplexed. She bears children with difficulty, and everything else is the same way. You can thus recognize the same character in the soul, the body, and the fate, and this is in fact analogous to the constellations in such a way that it is impossible for the soul to be the moulder of its whole destiny, since fate is something foreign, which comes from the outside.

In my case, Saturn and the sun work together in the sextile aspect (I prefer to speak of what I know best). Therefore my body is dry and knotty, and not tall. My soul is faint-hearted and hides itself in literary corners; it is distrustful and fearful; it seeks its way through harsh brambles and becomes entangled in them. Its habits are similar. To gnaw bones, to eat dry bread, to taste spiced and bitter things is a joy to me. To walk over rugged paths, uphill and through thickets, is a holiday treat for me. I know no other way of seasoning my life than science; I do not desire any other spice and I reject it if it is offered to me. My fate is precisely similar to this attitude. Where others despair, there opens before me a path to fame and fortune, although not a very great one. For however high I climb, I am always pushed back. While circumstances change, the pattern of my life remains the same. However far I have advanced, I have been vigorously opposed everywhere. Perhaps my mind will meet the same fate, because, challenging the human race, I uphold the movement of the earth, because I "push swiftly and with straining neck the heavy weight of the earth through the universe of stars, while the chorus of the earth's inhabitants protests against it." Yet this can be considered the common fate of all distinguished men. Here

the sayings are appropriate that the beautiful is hard
to conquer, and, in Cicero's well-known words, that
"the gods have placed sweat before virtue."

From *Johann Kepler in seinen Briefen*, ed. M. Caspar and
W. von Dyck (Munich, 1930); trans. M.M.M.

The Starry Herald

GALILEO GALILEI

1610

IN THE present small treatise I set forth some matters
of great interest for all observers of natural phenomena to look at and consider. They are of great interest, I think, first, from their intrinsic excellence;
secondly, from their absolute novelty; and lastly, also
on account of the instrument by the aid of which they
have been presented to my apprehension.

The number of the fixed stars which observers have
been able to see without artificial powers of sight up
to this day can be counted. It is therefore decidedly a
great feat to add to their number, and to set distinctly
before the eyes other stars in myriads, which have
never been seen before, and which surpass the old previously known stars in number more than ten times.

Again, it is a most beautiful and delightful sight to
behold the body of the moon, which is distant from us
nearly sixty semidiameters of the earth, as near as if it
was at a distance of only two of the same measures;
so that the diameter of this same moon appears about
thirty times larger, its surface about nine hundred times,
and its solid mass nearly twenty-seven thousand times

larger than when it is viewed only with the naked eye: and consequently anyone may know, with the certainty that is due to the use of our senses, that the moon certainly does not possess a smooth and polished surface, but one rough and uneven, and, just like the face of the earth itself, is everywhere full of vast protuberances, deep chasms, and sinuosities.

Then to have got rid of disputes about the Galaxy, or Milky Way, and to have made its nature clear to the very senses, not to say to the understanding, seems by no means a matter which ought to be considered of slight importance. In addition to this, to point out, as with one's finger, the nature of those stars which every one of the astronomers up to this time has called *nebulous,* and to demonstrate that it is very different from what has hitherto been believed, will be pleasant, and very fine. But that which will excite the greatest astonishment by far, and which indeed especially moved me to call the attention of all astronomers and philosophers, is this: namely, that I have discovered four planets, neither known nor observed by any one of the astronomers before my time, which have their orbits round a certain bright star, one of those previously known, like Venus and Mercury round the sun, and are sometimes in front of it, sometimes behind it, though they never depart from it beyond certain limits. All which facts were discovered and observed a few days ago by the help of a telescope devised by me, through God's grace first enlightening my mind.

Perchance, other discoveries still more excellent will be made from time to time by me or by other observers, with the assistance of a similar instrument, so I will first briefly record its shape and preparation, as well as the occasion of its being devised, and then I will give an account of the observations made by me.

The Telescope. About ten months ago a report reached my ears that a Dutchman [Jan Lippershey?] had constructed a telescope, by the aid of which visible objects, although at a great distance from the eye of the observer, were seen distinctly as if near; and some proofs of its most wonderful performances were reported, which some gave credence to, but others contradicted. A few days later, I received confirmation of the report in a letter written from Paris by a noble Frenchman, Jacques Badovere, which finally determined me to give myself up first to inquire into the principle of the telescope, and then to consider the means by which I might compass the invention of a similiar instrument, which after a little while I succeeded in doing, through deep study of the theory of refraction; and I prepared a tube, at first of lead, in the ends of which I fitted two glass lenses, both plane on one side, but on the other side one spherically convex and the other concave. Then, bringing my eye to the concave lens, I saw objects satisfactorily large and near, for they appeared one-third of the distance off and nine times larger than when they are seen with the natural eye alone. I shortly afterwards constructed another telescope with more nicety, which magnified objects more than sixty times. At length, by sparing neither labour nor expense, I succeeded in constructing for myself an instrument so superior that objects seen through it appear magnified nearly a thousand times, and more than thirty times nearer than if viewed by the natural powers of sight alone.

First Telescopic Observations. It would be altogether a waste of time to enumerate the number and importance of the benefits which this instrument may be expected to confer, when used by land or sea. But without paying attention to its use for terrestrial objects, I betook myself to observations of the heavenly bodies; and first of all I viewed the moon as near as if it was scarcely two semidiameters of the earth distant. After the moon, I frequently observed other heavenly bodies, both fixed stars and planets, with incredible delight; and, when I saw their very great number, I began to consider about a method by which I might be able to measure their distances apart, and at length I found one. And here it is fitting that all who intend to turn their attention to observations of this kind should receive certain cautions. For, in the first place, it is absolutely necessary for them to prepare a most perfect telescope, one which will show very bright objects distinct and free from any mistiness, and will magnify them at least four hundred times, for then it will show them as if only one-twentieth of their distance off. For, unless the instrument be of such power, it will be in vain to attempt to view all the things which have been seen by me in the heavens, or which will be enumerated hereafter.

From *The Sidereal Messenger*, trans. E. S. Carlos (London, 1880).

V. THE KINGDOM
OF GOD

The Congregation of the
Faithful

The Trial of Jerome of Prague

POGGIO BRACCIOLINI

1416

TO LEONARDO ARETINO

Soon after my return from Baden to Constance, the
cause of Jerome of Prague, who was accused of heresy,
came to public hearing [Council of Constance]. The
purport of my present letter is to give you an account
of this trial, which must of necessity be a matter of
considerable interest, both on account of the importance
of the subject and the eloquence and learning of the
defendant. I must confess that I never saw anyone who
in pleading a cause, especially a cause on the issue of
which his own life depended, approached nearer to that
standard of ancient eloquence which we so much
admire. It was astonishing to witness with what choice
of words, with what closeness of argument, with what
confidence of countenance he replied to his adversaries.
So impressive was his peroration that it is a subject of
great concern that a man of so noble and excellent a

genius should have deviated into heresy. On this latter
point, however, I cannot help entertaining some doubts.
But far be it from me to take upon myself to decide in
so important a matter. I shall acquiesce in the opinion
of those who are wiser than myself.

Do not, however, imagine that I intend to enter into
the particulars of this cause. I shall only touch upon
the more remarkable and interesting circumstances,
which will be sufficient to give you an idea of the learning of the man.

Many things having been alleged against the prisoner
as proofs of his entertaining heretical notions, and the
council being of opinion that the proof was sufficiently
strong to warrant further investigation, it was ordered
that he should publicly answer to every particular of the
charge. He was accordingly brought before the council.
But when he was called upon to give in his answers, he
for a long time refused so to do; alleging, that he ought
to be permitted to speak generally in his defence, before he replied to the false imputations of his adversaries. This indulgence was, however, denied him. Upon
which, standing up in the midst of the assembly—"What
gross injustice is this!" exclaimed he, "that though for
the space of three hundred and forty days, which I
have spent in filth and fetters, deprived of every comfort, in prisons situated at the most remote distances
from each other, you have been continually listening to
my adversaries and slanderers, you will not hear me for
a single hour! The consequence of this is, that while on
the one hand everyone's ears are open to them, and
they have for so long a time been attempting to persuade you that I am a heretic, an enemy of the true
faith, a persecutor of the clergy; on the other hand, I
am deprived of every opportunity of defending myself;
you have prejudged my cause, and have in your own

minds condemned me, before you could possibly become acquainted with my principles. But," says he, "you are not gods but men, not immortals but mortals, liable to error, and subject to imperfection. We are taught to believe that this assembly contains the light of the world, the prudent men of the earth. You ought therefore to be unremittingly careful not to do anything rashly, foolishly, or unjustly. I indeed, who am pleading for my life, am a man of little consequence; nor do I say what I do say through anxiety for myself (for I am prepared to submit to the common lot of mortality) —but I am prompted by an earnest desire that the collective wisdom of so many eminent men may not, in my person, violate the laws of justice. As to the injury done to myself, it is comparatively of trifling consequence; but the precedent will be pregnant with future mischief."

These and many other observations he made with great eloquence; but he was interrupted by the murmurs and clamours of several of his auditors. It was decreed that he should first answer to the charges exhibited against him, and afterwards have free liberty of speech. The heads of the accusation were accordingly read from the desk. When, after they had been proved by testimony, he was asked whether he had any remarks to make in his defence, it is incredible with what skill and judgment he put in his answers. He advanced nothing unbecoming a good man; and if his real sentiments agreed with his professions, he was so far from deserving to die that his principles did not even give just ground for the slightest offence. He denied the whole impeachment, as a fiction invented by the malice of his enemies. Amongst others, an article was read which accused him of being a detractor of the Apostolic See, an oppugner of the Roman pontiff, an enemy of the cardinals, a persecutor of prelates, and an adversary of the Christian clergy. When this charge was read he arose, and, stretching out his hands, he said in a pathetic tone of voice, "Fathers! to whom shall I have recourse for succour? Whose assistance shall I implore? Unto whom shall I appeal, in protestation of my innocence? Unto you? But these my persecutors have prejudiced your minds against me, by declaring that I entertain hostility against all my judges. Thus have they artfully endeavoured, if they cannot reach me by their imputations of error, so to excite your fears that you may be induced to seize any plausible pretext to destroy your common enemy, such as they most falsely represent me to be. Thus, if you give credit to their assertion, all my hopes of safety are lost."

He caused many to smart by the keenness of his wit and the bitterness of his reproaches. Melancholy as the occasion was, he frequently excited laughter, by turning to ridicule the imputations of his adversaries. When he was asked what were his sentiments concerning the sacrament, he replied that it was by nature bread; but that at the time of consecration, and afterwards, it was the true body of Christ, etc., according to the strictest orthodoxy. Then someone said, "But it is reported that you have maintained that there remains bread after consecration." "True," said Jerome, "there remains bread at the baker's." When one of the order of preaching friars was railing against him with uncommon asperity, he said to him, "Hold thy peace, hypocrite!" When another swore by his conscience—"This," said he, "is a very safe mode of deceiving." One man, who was particularly inveterate against him, he never addressed but by the title of ass or dog.

As, on account of the number and importance of the articles exhibited against him, the cause could not be

determined at that sitting, the court was adjourned to
another day, on which the proofs of each article of
impeachment were read over and confirmed by more
witnesses. Then he arose and said, "Since you have attended so diligently to my adversaries, I have a right
to demand that you should also hear me with patience."
Though many violently objected to this demand, it
was at length conceded to him that he should be heard
in his defence. He then began by solemnly praying to
God so to influence his mind, and so to inspire his
speech, that he might be enabled to plead to the advantage and salvation of his soul. He then proceeded
thus. "I know, most learned judges, that many excellent
men have been most unworthily dealt with, overborne
by false witnesses, and condemned by the most unjust
judgments." Illustrating this position by particular instances, he began with Socrates, who was unjustly condemned by his countrymen, and who could not be
persuaded by the dread of the most formidable evils,
imprisonment or death, to avail himself of an opportunity which was presented to him of escaping out of
custody. He then proceeded to mention the captivity
of Plato, the torments endured by Anaxagoras and
Zeno, and the unjust condemnations of many other
Gentiles—the banishment of Rutilius, the unmerited
death of Boethius, and of others mentioned in the writings of that author. He then passed on to the instances
which are recorded in the Jewish history—and in the
first place, he observed that Moses, the deliverer and
legislator of the Jews, was frequently calumniated by
his own countrymen, as a seducer and contemner of
the people. He also instanced Joseph, who was sold
to slavery, in consequence of the envy of his brethren,
and afterwards imprisoned under a groundless suspicion of incontinence. Besides these, he enumerated

Isaiah, Daniel, and almost all the prophets, who were calumniated and persecuted, as despisers of God and sowers of sedition. He also alluded to the trial of Susannah, and of many others, who, notwithstanding the integrity of their lives, perished by unjust sentences. Coming down to the time of John the Baptist and our Saviour, he observed that all are agreed that they were unjustly condemned, upon false charges, supported by false witnesses. He next quoted the case of Stephen, who was put to death by the priests; and reminded the assembly that all the Apostles were condemned to die, as seditious movers of the people, contemners of the gods, and workers of iniquity. He maintained that it was a scandalous thing that one priest should be unjustly condemned by another; that it was still more scandalous that a college of priests should be guilty of this crime; and that it was most scandalous of all that it should be perpetrated by a general council. Nevertheless he proved from history that these circumstances had actually occurred.

Upon these topics he enlarged in so impressive a manner that everybody listened to him with fixed attention. But as the weight of every cause rests upon the evidence by which it is supported, he proved, by various arguments, that no credit was due to the witnesses who deposed against him, more especially as they were instigated to give evidence against him by hatred, malevolence, and envy. He then so satisfactorily detailed the causes of the hatred which he imputed to his prosecutors, that he almost convinced his judges of the reasonableness of his objections against their testimony. His observations were so weighty that little credit would have been given to the depositions of the witnesses for the prosecution in any other cause except in a trial for heresy. He moreover added that he had

voluntarily come to the council, in order to defend his
injured character; and gave an account of his life and
studies, which had been regulated by the laws of duty
and of virtue. He remarked that holy men of old were
accustomed to discuss their differences of opinion in
matters of belief, not with a view of impugning the
faith, but of investigating the truth—that St. Augustine
and St. Jerome had thus differed in opinion, and had
upon some points even held contrary sentiments, without any suspicion of heresy. All the audience entertained
hopes that he would either clear himself by retracting
the heresies which were objected to him, or supplicate
pardon for his errors. But he maintained that he had
not erred, and that therefore he had nothing to retract.

He next began to praise John Huss, who had been
condemned to the flames, calling him a good, just, and
holy man, a man who had suffered death in a righteous
cause. He professed that he himself also was prepared
to undergo the severest punishment with an undaunted
and constant mind, declaring that he submitted to his
enemies, and to witnesses who had testified such shameful falsehoods; who would, however, on some future
day, give an account of what they had said, to a God
who could not be deceived. When Jerome made these
declarations the assembly was affected with the greatest
sorrow; for everybody wished that a man of such extraordinary talents should repent of his errors and be
saved. But he persisted in his sentiments and seemed
to court destruction. Dwelling on the praises of John
Huss, he said that he entertained no principles hostile
to the constitution of the Holy Church, and that he only
bore testimony against the abuses of the clergy, and
the pride and pomp of prelates: for that since the
patrimony of the Church was appropriated first to the
poor, then to strangers, and lastly to the erection of

churches, good men thought it highly improper that it should be lavished on harlots, entertainments, dogs, splendid garments, and other things unbecoming the religion of Christ.

It may be mentioned as the greatest proof of Jerome's abilities that though he was frequently interrupted by various noises, and was teased by some people who cavilled at his expressions, he replied to them all, and compelled them either to blush or to be silent. When the clamour incommoded him he ceased speaking, and sometimes reproved those who disturbed him. He then continued his speech, begging and entreating them to suffer him to speak, since this was the last time they would hear him. He was never terrified by the murmurs of his adversaries, but uniformly maintained the firmness and intrepidity of his mind. It was a wonderful instance of the strength of his memory that though he had been confined three hundred and forty days in a dark dungeon, where it was impossible for him to read, and where he must have daily suffered from the utmost anxiety of mind, yet he quoted so many learned writers in defence of his opinions, and supported his sentiments by the authority of so many doctors of the Church, that anyone would have been led to believe that he had devoted all the time of his imprisonment to the peaceful and undisturbed study of philosophy. His voice was sweet, clear, and sonorous; his action dignified and well adapted either to express indignation or to excite compassion, which, however, he neither asked nor wished for. He stood undaunted and intrepid, not merely contemning, but like another Cato longing for death. He was a man worthy to be held in everlasting remembrance. I do not commend him for entertaining sentiments hostile to the constitution of the Church; but

I admire his learning, his extensive knowledge, the suavity of his eloquence, and his ability in reply. But I am afraid that all these endowments were bestowed on him by nature, in order to effect his destruction.

As he was allowed two days for repentance, several learned men, and amongst the rest the Cardinal of Florence, visited him, with a view of persuading him to change his sentiments and turn from the error of his ways. But as he pertinaciously persisted in his false notions he was condemned as guilty of heresy and consigned to the flames. No stoic ever suffered death with such constancy of mind. When he arrived at the place of execution he stripped himself of his garments and knelt down before the stake, to which he was soon after tied with wet ropes and a chain. Then great pieces of wood, intermixed with straw, were piled as high as his breast. When fire was set to the pile he began to sing a hymn, which was scarcely interrupted by the smoke and flame. I must not omit a striking circumstance, which shows the firmness of his mind. When the executioner was going to apply the fire behind him, in order that he might not see it, he said, "Come this way, and kindle it in my sight, for had I been afraid of it I should never have come to this place." Thus perished a man, in every respect exemplary, except in the erroneousness of his faith. I was a witness of his end and observed every particular of its process. He may have been heretical in his notions, and obstinate in persevering in them, but he certainly died like a philosopher. I have rehearsed a long story, as I wished to employ my leisure in relating a transaction which surpasses the events of ancient history. For neither did Mutius suffer his hand to be burned so patiently as Jerome endured the burning of his whole body; nor did Socrates drink the hemlock as cheerfully as Jerome submitted to the fire.

In Rev. William Shepherd, *The Life of Poggio Bracciolini* (Liverpool: Longman, Rees, etc., 1837).

The Unity of the Church

NICHOLAS OF CUSA

1433

CONCORDANCE is that by reason of which the Catholic Church agrees in one and in many, in one Lord and in the many who are subject to Him. And from one peace-giving Ruler of infinite concordance there flows that sweet concordant spiritual harmony by degrees and progressively into the subordinate and united members, so that there may be one God all in all. For from the beginning we have been predestined to this more than marvellous and harmonious peace in the adoption of the sons of God through Jesus Christ, who descended from heaven in order that He might accomplish all this. This predestination the apostle Paul demonstrates to the Ephesians by that which was proclaimed from the beginning, since a man leaves his father and mother and will adhere to his spouse, and these two shall be one flesh. This sacrament pertains to Christ and the Church.

If then the bond of Adam and Eve is a great sacrament in Christ and in the Church, it is certain that, just as Eve was bone of Adam's bone and flesh of his flesh, so also the Church of the members of Christ is bone of His bone and flesh of His flesh. Therefore Ambrose said in his letter to Irenaeus, in praise of this epistle of Paul: "No epistle of greater blessing than this has been proclaimed to the people of God." And he said that Christ sits at the right hand of the Father, and we shall not all sit there, but we shall sit together in Christ and in His flesh in heaven. In order that we should attain to this most concordant, eternal union through faith, He established a diverse ecclesiastical concordance, ordered by ranks, by giving to it apostles, bishops, and doctors, so that everyone may come to the unity of faith and the source of knowledge. And as the member is not separated from its head which is Christ, who is the head of all, by whom the whole body of the faithful has been joined together, and brought into agreement, and united through the rational harmony of the Word . . . so one temple rises up in the midst of all and there is one abode for all spirits. . . .

Since it is manifest that everything is constituted to be and live through concordance, then in that divine essence where life and being are one in the highest equality, there is the highest and infinite concordance. For where eternal life is, there can be no place for opposition. All concordance, however, is the concordance of differences. . . . Therefore this is the sum of what should be said, that Christ is the Way, the Truth, and the Life, and the Head of all creatures, the Bridegroom and Spouse of the Church, which is founded on Him alone through the concordance of all rational creatures, and is constituted in its own multiplicity according to various ranks and degrees of order. . . .

We should consider that, since the Church is so called from its unity and harmonious congregation, it is composed of a fraternity, to which nothing is essentially so much opposed as division and schism. For although one faith is the bond of its collectivity, yet diversity of opinions without obstinacy may sometimes be compatible with unity. For Cyprian and the whole council of seventy bishops differed in faith from the Catholic Church, but they were not cut off from it, since they did not prefer their own opinion to fraternal unity, because they were without obstinacy, as Augustine agrees in his second book *Against the Donatists*. The judgment of faith is, then, very difficult. Ambrose says in his letter to Constantius: "These are the very sinews and strength of wisdom, not to believe rashly, especially in matters of faith, which has rarely been perfected in man." Therefore this Church militant which is subject to human judgment has within its body many armies which by outward signs do not appear unfaithful, although secretly they are cut off from the agreement of the faith, and they are not expelled or condemned, unless these hidden things have been made known. . . .

The concordance in this body of the Church should, moreover, be investigated in the sign of the Trinity, since there are three great orders in one marvellous relation to one Head, Christ. In the first, the relation of the sacraments may be likened to the divine concordance of Trinity and Unity. In the second, the holy priesthood may be likened to the divine concordance of the angels, who are the ministers of the divine Trinity, since the priests are ministers of the sacraments. In the third, the faithful who are in the pilgrimage of life may be likened to the blessed souls in Paradise. There are the sacraments, which are both illuminating and purifying; there is the pastoral priesthood, which is both purified and purifying; and there is the faithful people, which is purified and does not purify. . . .

In the marvellous hierarchy of the sacraments, Christ, the Head, communicates Himself to all who are sojourning in this life, under a symbol and in an enigma, as is proper to this pilgrimage of life and to our mortality, just as in the Church triumphant He reveals Himself face to face without enigma, since this is appropriate, according to the capacity of each state. And this divine, sacramental communication has a hierarchical order, since there are so many sacraments, as Augustine agrees when he says to Volusian that it is proper to discuss at great length the variety of signs, which, since they pertain to divine things, may be called sacraments. Therefore, among so many and such great sacraments partaking of divinity for our salvation, since they tend finally to the one Christ, the holy order of concordance is manifest constantly in the supreme sacrament of the Eucharist, just as in the Church triumphant all order tends to marvellous concordance in Christ the Head, through whom the whole assembly reposes eternally in God. Thus in this sacrament of that unique Head, Christ, all other sacraments repose as in their end, since it is the sacrament of sacraments. . . .

There follows the order of the priesthood, upon which the mark of the sacraments is imprinted, so that there may be continuity without any division in the centre of the whole Church; and thus the priesthood bears the sign of the sacramental and indelible communion of order and concordance with respect to higher and divine things. And in this priesthood, hierarchy is ordained from the sovereign pontificate even to the laity, according to the description by the great Dionysius of the ecclesiastical hierarchy. And just as man is formed of spirit, soul, and body, so the sacraments of this body of the Church are one spirit, and the priesthood is the soul, and the faithful are the body. As the soul adheres partly to the body and partly to the spirit, and is the means by which the spirit flows into the body, so is the priesthood in relation to the faithful. The whole priesthood is, therefore, as a single soul in one body of the faithful. The priesthood thus becomes the ruling, life-giving, and illuminating force, since these are the light of the world and the salt of the earth. Whence, as Cyprian says in his letter concerning the gambler, the priests are called the salt of the earth, since from all of them the brotherhood may be salted with celestial wisdom.

And there are hierarchical orders in this priesthood in order to animate it. In this governing and presiding office, although all supreme hierarchs who are bishops are equal as to order and episcopal office, there is nonetheless a division by ranks as to governing function. And in this government the hierarchy derives from a certain concordance, which is in one and in many. For there is only one episcopate, in which each bishop holds a share and a differing order with respect to governing function. Undoubtedly all the other Apostles were what Peter was, in a fellowship of equal honour and governing power, but Peter was set above the others, so that there might be unity in concordance, as Cyprian wrote to Novatian. And Jerome said against Jovinian that Peter had been chosen to preside among the Apostles who were equals, so that with an established head the occasion for schism might be removed. Thus just as there is one episcopate, so there is a single office of bishop and one government established hierarchically and by orders. . . .

Since this presiding office was instituted by Christ as Head in order to avoid schism and to preserve the peace and unity of the faithful, so its ranks may be considered figuratively, in the likeness of temporal governments. Thus it is observed, according to Jerome, that, just as an army chooses a captain for itself, and then he, bearing the agreement of all in himself, exists as one governing public person, so a governing bishop is constituted. Therefore, as the commonwealth is the common good of the people, and the common good is the concern of the state, and the state is a multitude of men brought together in any bond of concord, as Augustine writes to Volusian concerning the mutation of divine laws, so one who holds the presiding office in the cure of souls is like one to whom the commonwealth has been committed. Whence all who are subject to his care are considered as united in him who rules them, as if he were one soul and they the body, which the soul has to animate. Thus those who are so united with the pastor constitute the Church, as Cyprian elegantly writes. . . . These, he says, are the Church: the people united to the priest and the flock adhering to their shepherd. Thus you ought to know that the bishop is in the Church and the Church is in the bishop. And if anyone is not united with the bishop, he is not in the Church. . . .

But the episcopacy is arranged in ranks after the fashion described by Pope Leo IX in a letter to two African bishops: "There is one order of bishops, although some take precedence over others either because they hold the cities which are first in rank and considered higher according to the power and laws of the world, or because they possess some privilege of dignity as an honour from the Holy Fathers. For just as all worldly power is divided into these orders of dignities, that is, as the Augustus or emperor is first, then the Caesars, then the kings, dukes, counts, and tribunes, so it is with the ecclesiastical power ordained by the Holy Fathers, according to the blessed Clement, who says: 'In those cities in which formerly among the pagans there were their chief priests and chief doctors of the law, there have been established the primates or patri-

archs, who rightly determine the judgments of the
others, and the larger affairs, and who also rule not
simply one province, but many. Then where there were
the high priests of the pagans, the Christian archbishops
have been established, who rule individual provinces.
. . . But where lesser cities had only priests or counts,
bishops were established. Finally where there were
tribunes of the people, there are priests and the rest of
the lower order of the clergy. Above all these by divine
and human law is set the Roman pontiff.' "

From *De concordantia catholica*, in *Nicolai de Cusa opera omnia*,
Vol. XIV, ed. G. Kallen (Heidelberg, 1939); trans. M.M.M.

The Election of a Pope

POPE PIUS II

1458

TEN DAYS after Calixtus's death the other eighteen
cardinals entered the conclave, while the whole
city waited in suspense for the outcome; though indeed
it was common talk that Aeneas, Cardinal of Siena,
would be pope, since no one was held in higher esteem.

The conclave was held in the apostolic palace at
St. Peter's, where two halls and two chapels were set
apart for it. In the larger chapel were constructed cells
in which the cardinals might eat and sleep; the smaller,
called the chapel of San Niccolò, was reserved for discussion and the election of the pope. The halls were
places where all might walk about freely.

On the day of their entrance nothing was done about
the election. On the next day certain capitulations were

announced, which they agreed should be observed by
the new pope, and each swore that he would abide by
them, should the lot fall on him. On the third day,
after Mass, when they came to the scrutiny, it was
found that Filippo, Cardinal of Bologna, and Aeneas,
Cardinal of Siena, had an equal number of votes, five
apiece. No one else had more than three. On that ballot,
whether from strategy or dislike, no one voted for Guillaume, Cardinal of Rouen.

The cardinals were accustomed, after the result of
the scrutiny was announced, to sit and talk together in
case any wished to change his mind and transfer the
vote he had given one to another (a method called
"by accession"), for in this way they more easily reach
an agreement. This procedure was omitted after the
first scrutiny, owing to the opposition of those who had
received no votes and therefore could not now be
candidates for accession. They adjourned for luncheon,
and then there were many private conferences. The
richer and more influential members of the college summoned the rest and sought to gain the papacy for themselves or their friends. They begged, promised, threatened, and some, shamelessly casting aside all decency,
pleaded their own causes and claimed the papacy as
their right. Among these were Guillaume, Cardinal oi
Rouen, Pietro, Cardinal of San Marco, and Giovanni,
Cardinal of Pavia; nor did the Cardinal of Lerida
neglect his own interests. Each had a great deal to say
for himself. Their rivalry was extraordinary, their energy
unbounded. They took no rest by day or sleep by night.
Rouen, however, did not fear these men so much as
he did Aeneas and the Cardinal of Bologna, towards
whom he saw the majority of the votes inclining. But
he was especially afraid of Aeneas, whose silence he
had no doubt would prove far more effective than the

barkings of the rest. Therefore he would summon now some, now others, and upbraid them as follows: "What is Aeneas to you? Why do you think him worthy of the papacy? Will you give us a lame, poverty-stricken pope? How shall a destitute pope restore a destitute Church, or an ailing pope an ailing Church? He has but recently come from Germany. We do not know him. Perhaps he will even transfer the Curia thither. And look at his writings! Shall we set a poet in Peter's place? Shall we govern the Church by the laws of the heathen? Or do you think Filippo of Bologna is to be preferred?—a stiff-necked fellow, who has not the wit to rule himself, and will not listen to those who show him the right course. I am the senior cardinal. You know I am not without wisdom. I am learned in pontifical law and can boast of royal blood. I am rich in friends and resources with which I can succour the impoverished Church. I hold also not a few ecclesiastical benefices, which I shall distribute among you and the others, when I resign them." He would then add many entreaties, and if they had no effect he would resort to threats. If anyone brought up his past simony as an indication that in his hands the papacy would be for sale, he did not deny that his past life had been tainted with that stain but swore that in the future his hands should be clean. He was supported by Alain, Cardinal of Avignon, who lent him every assistance in his power, not so much because he was a Frenchman siding with a Frenchman as because, at the elevation of Guillaume, he expected to obtain his house in Rome, the church of Rouen, and the vice-chancellorship.

Not a few were won over by Rouen's splendid promises and were caught like flies by their gluttony. And the tunic of Christ without Christ was being sold.

Many cardinals met in the privies as being a secluded

and retired place. Here they agreed as to how they might elect Guillaume pope, and they bound themselves by written pledges and by oath. Guillaume trusted them and was presently promising benefices and preferment and dividing provinces among them. A fit place for such a pope to be elected! For where could one more appropriately enter into a foul covenant than in privies? Guillaume could certainly count on the two Greeks, the Cardinals of Genoa, San Sisto, Avignon, Colonna, and Pavia. The vice-chancellor and the Cardinals of Bologna, Orsini, and Sant' Anastasia were doubtful and seemed likely to accede to him if pushed a little. Indeed they had almost given him definite grounds for hope. Since it now appeared that eleven were agreed, they did not doubt that they would at once get the twelfth. For when it has come to this point, someone is always at hand to say, "I too make you pope," to win the favour that utterance always brings. They thought therefore that the thing was as good as done and were only waiting for daylight to go to the scrutiny.

Some time after midnight the Cardinal of Bologna went hurriedly to Aeneas's cell and, waking him, said, "Look here, Aeneas! Don't you know that we already have a pope? Some of the cardinals have met in the privies and decided to elect Guillaume. They are only waiting for daylight. I advise you to get up and go and offer him your vote before he is elected, for fear that if he is elected with you against him, he will make trouble for you. I intend to take care not to fall into the old trap. I know what it means to have the pope your enemy. I have had experience with Calixtus, who never gave me a friendly look because I had not voted for him. It seems to me expedient to curry favour beforehand with the man who is going to be pope. I offer you the advice I am taking myself."

Aeneas answered, "Filippo, away with you and your advice! No one shall persuade me to vote for a man I think utterly unworthy to be the successor of St. Peter. Far from me be such a sin! I will be clean of that crime and my conscience shall not prick me. You say it is hard not to have the pope well disposed to you. I have no fears on that score. I know he will not murder me because I have not voted for him. 'But,' you say, 'he will not love you, will not make you presents, will not help you. You will feel the pinch of poverty.' Poverty is not hard for one accustomed to it. I have led a life of indigence heretofore; what matter if I die indigent? He will not take from me the Muses, who are all the sweeter in humble fortunes. But I am not the man to believe that God will allow the Church, His Bride, to perish in the hands of the Cardinal of Rouen. For what is more alien to the profession of Christ than that His Vicar should be a slave to simony and lewdness? The divine mercy will not endure that this palace, which has been the dwelling of so many Holy Fathers, shall become a den of thieves or a brothel of whores. The apostleship is bestowed by God, not by men. Those who have conspired to commit the papacy to Rouen are men; and men's schemes are vain—who does not know it? Well has their conspiracy been made in the privies! Their plots too will have to retire, and, like the Arian heresy, their most foul contrivings will end in a most foul place. Tomorrow will show that the Bishop of Rome is chosen by God not by men. As for you, if you are a Christian, you will not choose as Christ's Vicar him whom you know to be a limb of the devil." With these words he frightened Filippo from going over to Rouen.

Next Aeneas went at daybreak to Rodrigo, the vice-chancellor, and asked whether he had sold himself to

Rouen. "What would you have me do?" he answered. "The thing is settled. Many of the cardinals have met in the privies and decided to elect him. It is not for my advantage to remain with a small minority out of favour with a new pope. I am joining the majority, and I have looked out for my own interests. I shall not lose the chancellorship; I have a note from Rouen assuring me of that. If I do not vote for him, the others will elect him anyway, and I shall be stripped of my office." Aeneas said to him, "You young fool! Will you then put an enemy of your nation in the Apostle's chair? and will you put faith in the note of a man who is faithless? You will have the note; Avignon will have the chancellorship. For what has been promised you has been promised him also and solemnly affirmed. Will faith be kept with him or with you? Will a Frenchman be more friendly to a Frenchman or to a Catalan? Will he be more concerned for a foreigner or for his own countryman? Take care, you inexperienced boy! Take care, you fool! And if you have no thought for the Church of Rome, if you have no regard for the Christian religion and despise God, for whom you are preparing such a vicar, at least take thought for yourself, for you will find yourself among the hindmost, if a Frenchman is pope."

The vice-chancellor listened patiently to these words of his friend and completely abandoned his purpose.

After this Aeneas, meeting the Cardinal of Pavia, said to him, "I hear that you too are with those who have decided to elect Rouen. Is this true?" He replied, "You have heard correctly. I have agreed to give him my vote so that I may not be left alone. For his victory is already certain; so many have declared for him." Aeneas said, "I thought you a different man from what I find you. Only see how much you have degenerated from your ancestors! Your father's brother (or was he your mother's?), Branda, Cardinal of Piacenza, when the papacy was beyond the mountains in Germany (for John XXIII, when he appointed the Council of Constance, had carried the Roman Curia across the Alps), never rested till he brought the Holy See back to Italy. It was owing to his diplomacy, devotion, and genius that on the withdrawal of the contestants for the papacy, Martin V, a Roman of the house of Colonna, was elected pope. Branda brought the Apostolic Curia back from Germany to Italy; you, his nephew, are going to transfer it from Italy to France. But Rouen will prefer his own nation to Italy, and a Frenchman will be off to France with the supreme office. You say, 'He is under oath. He will not go outside this province without the decree of the senate, and if he wishes to go we will not consent.' What cardinal will dare oppose him when he is once seated on the apostolic throne? You will be the first, when you have secured some rich benefice, to say, 'Go where you will, Holy Father.' And what is our Italy without the Bishop of Rome? We still have the Apostleship though we have lost the Imperium, and in this one light we see light. Shall we be deprived of this with your sympathy, persuasion, help? A French pope will either go to France—and then our dear country is bereft of its splendour; or he will stay among us—and Italy, the queen of nations, will serve a foreign master, while we shall be the slaves of the French. The kingdom of Sicily will come into the hands of the French. The French will possess all the cities and strongholds of the Church. You might have taken warning from Calixtus, during whose papacy there was nothing the Catalans did not get. After trying the Catalans, are you so eager to try the French? You will soon be sorry if you do! You will see the college filled with Frenchmen and the papacy will never again be wrested from them. Are you so dull that you do not realize that this will lay a yoke upon your nation forever? And what shall I say of this man's life? Are you not ashamed to entrust Christ's office to a slippery fellow who would sell his own soul? A fine bridegroom you are planning for the bride of Christ! You are trusting a lamb to a wolf. Where is your conscience? your zeal for justice? your common sense? Have you so far fallen below your true self? I suppose we have not often heard you say that it would be the Church's ruin if it fell into Rouen's hands? and that you would rather die than vote for this very man? What is the reason for this change? Has he suddenly been transformed from a demon to an angel of light? Or have you been changed from an angel of light to the devil, that you love his lust and filth and greed? What has become of your love for your country and your continual protestations that you preferred Italy above all other nations? I used to think that if everyone else fell away from devotion to her, you never would. You have failed me; nay, more, you have failed yourself and Italy, your country, unless you come to your senses."

The cardinal of Pavia was stunned by these words and, overcome alike with grief and shame, he burst into tears. Then, stifling his sobs, he said, "I am ashamed, Aeneas. But what am I to do? I have given my promise. If I do not vote for Rouen I shall be charged with treachery." Aeneas answered, "So far as I can see, it has come to the point where you will be guilty of treachery whichever way you turn. You now have to choose whether you prefer to betray Italy, your country, and the Church, or the Bishop of Rouen." Convinced by these arguments, Pavia decided it was less shameful to fail Rouen.

When Pietro, Cardinal of San Marco, learned of the conspiracy of the French and had lost hope of getting the papacy himself, actuated alike by patriotism and hatred of Rouen, he began to go to the Italian cardinals, urging and warning them not to abandon their country; and he did not rest till he had gathered all the Italians except Colonna in the cell of the Cardinal of Genoa, revealed the conspiracy that had been made in the privies, and showed them that the Church would be ruined and Italy a slave forever if Rouen should obtain the papacy. He implored them individually to show themselves men, to consult for the good of Mother Church and unhappy Italy, to put aside their enmities for one another and choose an Italian rather than a foreigner for pope. If they listened to him, they would prefer Aeneas to all others. There were present seven cardinals: Genoa, Orsini, Bologna, San Marco, Pavia, Siena, and Sant' Anastasia. All approved Pavia's words except Aeneas, who thought himself unworthy of so exalted an office.

The next day they went as usual to Mass, and then began the scrutiny. A golden chalice was placed on the altar, and three cardinals, the Bishop of Ruthen, the Presbyter of Rouen, and the Deacon of Colonna, were set to watch it and see that there should be no cheating. The other cardinals took their seats, and then, rising in order of rank and age, each approached the altar and deposited in the chalice a ballot on which was written the name of his choice for pope. When Aeneas came up to put in his ballot, Rouen, pale and trembling, said, "Look, Aeneas! I commend myself to you"—certainly a rash thing to say when it was not allowable to change what he had written. But ambition overcame prudence. Aeneas said, "Do you commend yourself to a worm like me?" and without another word he dropped his ballot in the cup and went back to his place.

When all had voted, a table was placed in the middle

of the room and the three cardinals mentioned above turned out upon it the cupful of votes. Then they read aloud the ballots one after another and noted down the names written on them. And there was not a single cardinal who did not likewise make notes of those named, that there might be no possibility of trickery. This proved to be to Aeneas's advantage, for when the votes were counted and the teller, Rouen, announced that Aeneas had eight, though the rest said nothing about another man's loss, Aeneas did not allow himself to be defrauded. "Look more carefully at the ballots," he said to the teller, "for I have nine votes." The others agreed with him. Rouen said nothing, as if he had merely made a mistake.

This was the form of the ballot: the voter wrote with his own hand, "I, Peter (or John or whatever his name was), choose for pope Aeneas, Cardinal of Siena, and Jaime, Cardinal of Lisbon"; for it is permitted to vote for one or two or more, on the understanding that the one first named is the one preferred, but if he does not have enough votes to be elected, the next is to be counted in his place, that an agreement may more easily be reached. But a thing advantageous in itself some men pervert to base ends, as Latino Orsini did on that day. He named seven in the hope that those he named might be influenced by that good turn either to accede to him in that scrutiny or to vote for him in another; although he who has the reputation of a cheat does not gain much by tricks.

When the result of the scrutiny was made known, it was found, as we have said before, that nine cardinals (Genoa, Orsini, Lerida, Bologna, San Marco, Santi Quattro Coronati, Zamora, Pavia, and Portugal) had voted for Aeneas; the Cardinal of Rouen had only six votes, and the rest were far behind. Rouen was petrified when he saw himself so far outstripped by Aeneas, and all the rest were amazed, for never within the memory of man had anyone polled as many as nine votes by scrutiny. Since no one had received enough votes for election, they decided to resume their seats and try the method that is called "by accession," to see if perhaps it might be possible to elect a pope that day. And here again Rouen indulged in empty hopes. All sat pale and silent in their places, as if entranced. For some time no one spoke, no one opened his lips, no one moved any part of his body except the eyes, which kept glancing all about. It was a strange silence and a strange sight, men sitting there like their own statues; no sound to be heard, no movement to be seen. They remained thus for some moments, those inferior in rank waiting for their superiors to begin the accession. Then Rodrigo, the vice-chancellor, rose and said, "I accede to the Cardinal of Siena," an utterance which was like a dagger in Rouen's heart, so pale did he turn. A silence followed, and each man, looking at his neighbour, began to indicate his sentiments by gestures. By this time it looked as if Aeneas would be pope, and some, fearing this result, left the conclave, pretending physical needs, but really with the purpose of escaping the fate of that day. Those who thus withdrew were the Cardinals of Ruthen and San Sisto. However, as no one followed them, they soon returned. Then Jacopo, Cardinal of Sant' Anastasia, said, "I accede to the Cardinal of Siena." At this all appeared even more stunned, like people in a house shaken by unprecedented earthquakes, and lost the power of speech. Aeneas now lacked but one vote, for twleve would elect a pope. Realizing this, Cardinal Prospero Colonna thought that he must get for himself the glory of announcing the pope. He rose and was about to pronounce his vote, with the customary dignity, when he was seized by the Cardinals of Nicaea and Rouen and sharply rebuked for wishing to accede to Aeneas. When he persisted in his intention, they tried to get him out of the room by force, resorting even to such means to snatch the papacy from Aeneas. But Prospero, who, though he had voted for the Cardinal of Rouen on his ballot, was nevertheless bound to Aeneas by ties of old friendship, paid no attention to their abuse and empty threats. Turning to the other cardinals, he said, "I too accede to the Cardinal of Siena and I make him pope." When they heard this, the courage of the opposition failed and all their machinations were shattered.

All the cardinals immediately fell at Aeneas's feet and saluted him as pope. Then they resumed their seats and ratified his election without a dissenting vote. At this point Bessarion, Cardinal of Nicaea, speaking for himself and for the others who had voted for the Cardinal of Rouen, said, "Your Holiness, we approve your election, which we do not doubt is of God. We thought before and still think that you are worthy of this office. The reason we did not vote for you was your infirmity. We thought your gout the one thing against you; for the Church needs an active man who has the physical strength to take long journeys and meet the dangers which we fear threaten us from the Turks. You, on the contrary, need rest. It was this consideration that won us to the side of the Cardinal of Rouen. If you were physically strong, there is no one we should have preferred. But, since God is satisfied, we must needs be satisfied too. God Himself, who has chosen you, will make good the defect in your feet and will not punish our ignorance. We revere you as pope, we elect you again, so far as in our power, and we will serve you faithfully."

Aeneas answered, "Your Eminence of Nicaea, your opinion of us, as we understand it, is much higher than our own, when you attribute to us no defect except that in our feet. We are not ignorant that our imperfection is more general, and we realize that our failings, which might justly have caused us to be rejected as pope, are almost innumerable. As to any virtues, which might raise us to this post, we know of none; and we should declare ourselves utterly unworthy and should refuse the honour offered us if we did not fear the judgment of Him who has called us. For what is done by two-thirds of the sacred college, that is surely of the Holy Ghost, which may not be resisted. Therefore we obey the divine summons, and we praise you, your Eminence of Nicaea, and those who voted with you. If, following the dictates of your conscience, you thought we ought not to be elected as being inadequate, you will still be welcomed by us, who attribute our calling not to this man or that but to the whole college and to God Himself, from whom cometh every good and perfect gift."

With these words he took off the garments he was wearing and put on the white tunic of Christ. When asked by what name he wished to be called, he answered, "Pius," and he was at once addressed as Pius II. Then, after swearing to observe the capitulations that had been announced in the college two days before, he took his place by the altar and was again reverenced by the cardinals, who kissed his feet, hands, and cheek. After that the election of a pope was proclaimed to the people from a high window, and it was announced that he who had been Cardinal of Siena was now Pope Pius II.

The attendants of the cardinals in the conclave plundered Aeneas's cell and meanly carried off all the plate (though it was very modest), his clothes, and his books; and the infamous rabble not only pillaged his house in the city but actually demolished it, taking away even the blocks of marble. Other cardinals, too, suffered losses, for while the people were waiting in suspense, various rumours got about, and as now this cardinal, now that, was reported elected, the crowd would rush to their houses and plunder them. The Cardinal of Genoa, whose name was mistaken for Siena, lost part of his possessions. Though many names were mentioned, none was received with enthusiasm except that of the Cardinal of Siena. When the cry arose that Rouen or Genoa or Lerida (for there were reports of them too) had been elected, all cast down their eyes and cursed the college. Only their personal friends were pleased; the rest shared the general sorrow. But when it was certain that Aeneas had been seated on Peter's throne, there was no one who did not rejoice. You might have seen not men only but the very animals and the buildings of the city exulting. Everywhere was heard laughter and expressions of joy and the cries of men shouting, "Siena! Siena! O happy Siena! Viva Siena!" Though the city was under arms and no one seemed to have confidence in anything but the sword, presently, when the people were told that the papacy had fallen to Aeneas, the aspect of the capital was completely changed. What had a little time before been the city of Mars all at once became the city, I will not say of Venus, the mother of that ancient Trojan Aeneas, but of Peace and Quiet, and joy and tranquillity reigned everywhere.

Meantime the new pope, after taking a little refreshment, was escorted to the basilica of St. Peter and conducted to the high altar, under which lie the bodies of the blessed Apostles. Shortly after, he took his seat according to custom on the high throne and in the apostolic chair itself. There the cardinals and bishops and after them many of the people kissed his feet and reverenced him on his throne as Christ's Vicar. Then after a brief interval, when evening was coming on, they escorted him back to the palace. At nightfall fires blazed at every crossroad and on every tower; singing could be heard; neighbours called to neighbours; everywhere horns and trumpets blared, and there was no spot in all the city which did not share in the general rejoicing. The older men said they had never seen such enthusiasm among the Roman populace.

The next night in a procession that reached from Hadrian's mausoleum to the Church of St. Peter the chief citizens of Rome on horseback and carrying lighted tapers went to the palace to greet the pope.

From *The Commentaries of Pius II*, trans. F. A. Gragg, ed. L. C. Gabel, in *Smith College Studies in History*, Vol. XXII (Oct. 1936-Jan. 1937).

❧

A Preacher of Reform

GIROLAMO SAVONAROLA

1493

WHEN the devil sees that a man is weak, he strikes him with a hatchet in order to make him fall into sin; but if he sees that he is strong, he then strikes him with an axe. If a young girl be modest and well brought up, he throws some dissipated youth in her way, and causes her to yield to his flatteries and fall into sin. Thus the devil strikes her with his axe. Here is a citizen of good repute; he enters the courts of the great lords, and there is the axe so well sharpened that no virtue can resist its strokes. But we are now living in still more evil days; the devil has called his followers together, and they have dealt terrible blows on the very gates of the temple. It is by the gates that the house is entered, and it is the prelates who should lead the faithful into the Church of Christ. Therefore the devil hath aimed his heaviest blows at them, and hath broken down these gates. Thus it is that no more good prelates are to be found in the Church. Seest thou not that they do all things amiss? They have no judgment; they cannot distinguish *inter bonum et malum, inter verum et falsum, inter dulce et amarum;* good things they deem evil, true things false, sweet things bitter, and *vice versa. . . .* See how in these days prelates and preachers are chained to the earth by love of earthly things; the cure of souls is no longer their concern; they are content with the receipt of revenue; the preachers preach for the pleasure of princes, to be praised and magnified by them. . . . And they have done even worse than this, inasmuch as they have not only destroyed the Church of God, but built up another after their own fashion. This is the new Church, no longer built of living rock, namely, of Christians steadfast in the living faith and in the mould of charity; but built of sticks, namely, of Christians dry as tinder for the fires of hell. . . . Go thou to Rome and throughout Christendom; in the mansions of the great prelates and great lords there is no concern save for poetry and the oratorical art. Go thither and see, thou shalt find them all with books of the humanities in their hands, and telling one another that they can guide men's souls by means of Vergil, Horace, and Cicero. Wouldst thou see how the Church is ruled by the hands of astrologers? And there is no prelate nor great lord that hath not intimate dealings with some astrologers, who fixeth the hour and the moment in which he is to ride out or undertake some piece of business. For these great lords venture not to stir a step save at their astrologer's bidding. . . .

But in this temple of theirs there is one thing that delighteth us much. This is that all therein is painted and gilded. Thus our Church hath many fine outer ceremonies for the solemnization of ecclesiastical rites, grand vestments and numerous draperies, with gold and silver candlesticks, and so many chalices that it is a majestic sight to behold. There thou seest the great prelates with splendid mitres of gold and precious stones on their heads, and silver crosiers in hand; there they stand at the altar, decked with fine copes and stoles of brocade, chanting those beautiful vespers and masses, very slowly, and with so many grand cere-monies, so many organs and choristers, that thou art struck with amazement; and all these priests seem to thee grave and saintly men, thou canst not believe that they may be in error, but deem that all which they say and do should be obeyed even as the Gospel; and thus is our Church conducted. Men feed upon these vanities and rejoice in these pomps, and say that the Church of Christ was never so flourishing, nor divine worship so well conducted as at present . . . likewise that the first prelates were inferior to these of our own times. . . . The former, it is true, had fewer gold mitres and fewer chalices, for, indeed, what few they possessed were broken up to relieve the needs of the poor; whereas our prelates, for the sake of obtaining chalices, will rob the poor of their sole means of support. But dost thou know what I would tell thee? In the primitive Church the chalices were of wood, the prelates of gold; in these days the Church hath chalices of gold and prelates of wood. These have introduced devilish games among us; they have no belief in God, and jeer at the mysteries of our faith! What doest Thou, O Lord? Why dost Thou slumber? Arise, and come to deliver Thy Church from the hands of the devils, from the hands of tyrants, the hands of iniquitous prelates. Hast Thou forsaken Thy Church? Dost Thou not love her? Is she not dear unto Thee? O Lord, we are become the despised of all nations; the Turks are masters of Constantinople; we have lost Asia, have lost Greece, we already pay tribute to the Infidel. O Lord God, Thou hast dealt with us as a wrathful father, Thou hast cast us out from Thy presence! Hasten then the chastisement and the scourge, that it may be quickly granted us to return to Thee. *Effunde iras tuas in gentes.* Be ye not scandalized, O my brethren, by these words; rather, when ye see that the righteous desire chastisement, know that it is because they seek to banish evil, so that the kingdom of our blessed Lord, Jesus Christ, may flourish in the world. The only hope that now remains to us, is that the sword of God may soon smite the earth.

"Advent Sermon," in P. Villari, *Life and Times of Girolamo Savonarola* (London: T. Fisher Unwin, 1896).

Savonarola, A Portrait

FRANCESCO GUICCIARDINI

1509

AND so there was shamefully put to death [1498] Fra Girolamo Savonarola, of whose character it would not be inappropriate to speak at greater length because neither in our age nor even in that of our fathers and grandfathers was there ever seen a man of religion so well schooled in many virtues or with such great reputation and authority as he. Even his adversaries confess that he was most learned in many disciplines, notably in philosophy, which he mastered so well and so used for every purpose that it seemed as if he himself had created it; but above all in holy scripture in which it is believed there had been none equal to him for some centuries. He had the soundest judgment not only in letters but even in the active affairs of this world, all of which he was much interested in, as his sermons reveal, in my opinion. In the art of preaching he far surpassed others of his age by virtue of these gifts, adding to them an eloquence which was not artificial or forced but natural and easy. By it he gained such a great hearing and reputation that it was marvellous when one considers that he had preached so many years continuously not only during Lent but on many holidays of the year in a city full of the most subtle and even fastidious talents, and where preachers, even if excellent, usually become wearisome after no more than one or two Lents. These virtues were so clear and manifest in him that both his adversaries and his disciples and followers agree on this point.

But the point of controversy and difference of opinion concerns the goodness of his life. Here it should be noted that if there was in him any defect, it was none other than the dissimulation caused by pride and ambition, because whoever observed his life and habits over a long period could not find there even a trace of avarice, or voluptuousness, or any other cupidity or frailty but, on the contrary, evidence of a most pious life, full of charity, full of prayer, full of observation not of the superficialities but of the very marrow of

divine worship. And even in his trial, although his detractors hunted zealously, there was not found the
slightest little defect to be noted in this regard. The
works he performed for the enforcement of good morals
were most holy and marvellous, and in Florence there
was never such goodness and piety as in his time. After
his death she behaved in such a way as to prove that
all that was good had been introduced and supported
by him. For in his time they gambled no more in public
and even in private with fear; there stood locked the
taverns which were wont to be the haunt of all corrupt
and depraved youths; sodomy was extinguished and
humbled; women for the most part put aside disrepu-
table and seductive garments. The children had almost
all recovered from dishonourable habits and been restored to a holy and normal way of life. Being through
his efforts assembled in companies under the direction
of Fra Domenico, they frequented the churches, wore
their hair short, pursued with stones and insults dishonourable men and gamblers and women with too
seductive clothing. They went about during the carnival
gathering up dice, playing cards, cosmetics, indecent
pictures and books, and burned them publicly in the
piazza of the Signoria, having first celebrated on that
day, which was wont to be a day of a thousand iniq-
uities, a procession of great holiness and piety. Old
men all turned to religion, to masses, to vespers, to
sermons, confessed and communicated often; and on
the day of the carnival an enormous number of persons
confessed. There was much giving of alms, many acts
of charity. Every day he encouraged those who, having
put aside pomps and vanities, were restored to the
simplicity of living piously and like Christians. For this
purpose he called for laws concerning the ornaments
and garments of women and children, but these were

so strongly opposed by his adversaries that they were never passed in the council except the ones for children, and even those were not observed.

Through his preaching a very great number became friars in his order, of every age and rank, some noble youths and from the first families of the city, some men of age and reputation: Pandolfo Rucellai who was a member of the Council of Ten and chosen as orator before King Charles VIII; Messer Giorgio Antonio Vespucci and Messer Malatesta, canons of Santa Lipe-rata [Reparata] good men of learning and dignity; Master Pietro Paolo of Urbino, a doctor of repute and good habits; Zanobi Acciaiuoli, most learned in Greek and Latin letters; and many similar ones. Thus there was not a convent like it in Italy; and he directed the young men in their studies, not only Latin but also Greek and Hebrew, in such a way as to create hope that they would become the ornaments of religion. And having done so much for the advantage of spiritual things, he did no less for the good of the city and the public benefit.

When Piero de' Medici had been expelled and a meeting of all the citizens called, the land was shaken to its foundations, and the friends of the old regime were in such great alarm and peril that it seemed im-possible they would not be maltreated, and in great numbers, because Francesco Valori and Piero Capponi were not adequate to defend them; and this would have been a great calamity for the state, since many were good men, wise and rich, and of great families and relationships. After this, disunion sprang up among those who ruled, as was seen in the example of the Twenty, and they split up, in order to be more equal in reputation and to seek the primacy, each for him-self. There followed crises and public meetings, the expulsion of citizens, and more than one change; and perhaps in the end a forcible return of Piero with the final extermination and ruin of the city. He [Savonarola] alone put an end to this violence and agitation, introduced the Great Council, and so put a bridle on all those who wished to make themselves great. He put into effect the appeal to the Signoria which acted like a bit in the preservation of the citizens. He established general peace, which was nothing else than seizing the opportunity to punish those of the Medicean state under pretext of seeking out the old ways.

These things were without doubt the salvation of the city, and as he most truly said, to the advantage both of those who were presently ruling and of those who had ruled in the past. And his deeds were so good in effect and some of his predictions so well borne out that many have for a long time believed that he was in truth sent by God and that he was a prophet, notwithstanding his excommunication, trial, and death. I am in doubt about it, and I have not made up my mind in any respect; and I reserve judgment, if I live that long, until the time when all will be made clear. But I am certain of this, that if he was good, we have seen in our times a great prophet; if he was bad, still a very great man, because, in addition to his learning, if he knew how to act such a great role for so many years, and so publicly, without ever being discovered in a single imposture, one must confess that he possessed a most profound judgment, and talent, and power of invention.

There were put to death with him, as we have said, Fra Domenico and Fra Silvestro. Of these, Fra Domenico was a man of greatest simplicity and goodness of life, and such that, if he erred, it was through simplicity and not malice: Fra Silvestro was considered more astute and more in touch with the citizens, but nevertheless, according to the trial, he was not conscious of any dissimulation. But they were put to death to satisfy the madness of their enemies, who were popularly called in these times "the mad ones."

From *Storie Fiorentine*, ed. R. Palmarocchi (Bari: Laterza e figli, 1931); trans. J.B.R.

The Lutheran Revolt

ALFONSO DE VALDÉS

Brussels, 31st August, 1520

TO PIETRO MARTIRE D'ANGHIERA

That which you would fain learn from me, as to the origin and progress of the Lutheran sect, which has recently sprung up among the Germans, I am now about to write to you, if without elegance, at least with accuracy, relating things conscientiously, as I have heard them from persons worthy of credit.

I think you are already aware that Pope Julius II had begun to erect, in the city of Rome, a temple dedicated to the Prince of the Apostles, at incredible expense, and exceeding in the vastness of its proportions all similar structures, with good reason thinking it indecorous that the Prince of the Apostles should be meanly lodged, particularly since men, from religious motives, repair thither from all parts of the world. And this greatest and most magnanimous of men would have finished the mighty work had he not been taken off by death during the process of its erection.

Leo X succeeded him, who, not having adequate

funds to defray the large outlay, sent throughout Christendom the amplest absolutions, or pardons, commonly called indulgences, for those who should contribute offerings for the erection of the temple; he thought that by such means he should clear an immense sum of money, getting it especially from the Germans, whose veneration for the Church of Rome was singularly loyal. But as there is nothing firm and stable in human affairs—nothing that is not destroyed either by the damage brought by time or by the malice of men—so it is a fact that these indulgences have brought it to pass that Germany, which surpasses in religion every other Christian nation, may now actually see itself left behind by them all.

For as a certain Dominican was preaching in Wittenberg, a city in Saxony, and urging the people to purchase these pontifical indulgences, from which this friar himself netted no mean profits, an Augustinian monk, of the name of Martin Luther, and the author of this tragedy, came forward, possibly moved by envy of the Dominican, and published certain printed propositions, in which he affirmed that the Dominican attributed to his indulgences effects much greater than the Roman pontiff either did or could concede. The Dominican, having read the propositions, was inflamed with wrath against the Augustinian, and the dispute between the monks was exasperated both by injurious expressions and by arguments—the one defending his sermon, and the other defending his propositions; so that the Augustinian, with the characteristic audacity of the wicked, began to disparage the papal indulgences, and to say that they had been devised, not for the welfare of the Christian body, but to satisfy sacerdotal avarice; and from this point the monk proceeded to discuss the powers of the Roman pontiff.

Here you have the first scene of this tragedy, which we owe to monkish animosity. For since the Augustinian envies the Dominican, and the Dominican, in his turn, the Augustinian, and both of them the Franciscan, what else shall we expect but the gravest dissensions? And now let us come to scene the second.

Frederick, the Duke of Saxony, and Albert, the Cardinal Archbishop of Mainz, were, as Electors, colleagues in the election of Roman emperors; the former, who was not on the best of terms with the latter, had heard that Albert made much money by these indulgences, the prelate and the pope having agreed to share the money thus obtained between them. In the meanwhile the duke, who sought an opportunity to deprive the archbishop of these gains, did not let slip that presented by an audacious monk, who, ready for any bad action, had stood forward to declare war against the pontifical indulgences. Accordingly, the duke seized upon all the money in the hands of the so-called commissaries, which had been collected in his duchy, saying that "he intended to appoint a man, one of his subjects, in Rome, to present that money to the fabric of St. Peter, who should, at the same time, see to the proper expenditure of the other sums which had been collected for that purpose in other parts of Germany." But the pontiff, on whom it devolves to guard the liberties of the Church, and not to permit profane princes to intermeddle in things solely within the province of the Roman pontiff, warned the duke once and again, both by letters couched in the most affectionate terms, and by nuncios specially sent to Germany, that he should not act so injuriously to the apostolic seat, but should refund the confiscated moneys, which the duke obstinately refused to do; whereupon the pontiff, going to the other extreme, declared him excommunicated.

Then the Augustinian, having gained the duke's favour, assured him, with great hardihood, that such a sentence was invalid, because iniquitous, for the Roman pontiff could excommunicate no one unjustly; and he began, through printed circulars, which were spread with facility and rapidity throughout all Germany, to publish many and grave things against the Roman pontiff and the Romanists. Luther, moreover, exhorted the Duke of Saxony not to be driven, by dread of the papal anathema, from the determination he had once formed. Furthermore, he declared that the temper of the Germans was getting irritated by long contemplation of the worse than profane habits of the Romanists, and that they had secretly begun to devise how to loosen and shake off the yoke of the Roman pontiff, which was accomplished when Luther's writings were first published, and received with general admiration and applause. Then the Germans, showing their contempt for the Romanists, evinced at the same time their intense desire, and they demanded it too, that there should be convened a general council of all Christians, in which, those things being condemned, against which Luther had written, better order might be established in the Church. Would to God that this had been realized! In the meanwhile the pontiff obstinately guards his rights and fears lest Christians should hold a meeting; for (to speak freely) his particular interests, which might possibly be endangered by a general council, weigh more with him than the welfare of Christendom. He is also anxious to have Luther's writings suppressed without discussion, and has sent a Legate *a latere* to Maximilian, to procure, amongst other things, that silence be imposed on Luther by the emperor's authority and that of the whole Roman empire.

They then convened a general diet, an Imperial

parliament, at Augsburg, a celebrated city of Germany, where Luther appeared, having been summoned by an Imperial decree, and where he defended his writings with great power; whereupon Cajetan had to enter upon the arena. Cajetan—for such was the legate's name—alleged that "a monk ought not to have a hearing, who had written so many blasphemies against the Roman pontiff." And the Estates of the Empire, in their turn, declared "that it was an iniquitous thing to condemn a man unheard, or without having previously convinced him and compelled him to retract those very writings which he declared himself ready to defend. That if this Cajetan (a man, as you know, profoundly versed in polemics) could convince Luther, they were ready (both the emperor and the Estates of the Empire) to pass sentence on him." Thus Cajetan, seeing that he should make no progress unless he combatted Luther face to face, which he had attempted once but came off unsuccessfully, departed, leaving the affair unsettled. Luther was dismissed with greater glory than that with which he had been received—with a victor's joy. Alas! that human relations are so prone to ill: relying upon the Duke of Saxony's protection, he wrote and published, with fresh vigour, new dogmas opposed to the apostolic institutions.

The pope, seeing that he could, neither by caresses nor by warnings, cause the deserved punishment to be imposed upon the blasphemous monk, in order that he might not diffuse the poison which he scattered on every side with impunity, and that all might flee the man declared a heretic and schismatic, launched a most severe bull, as they call it, against Luther and Luther's partisans.

Luther, much more irritated than dismayed by this proceeding (oh, shame!), proclaimed the pontiff himself a heretic and schismatic, and issued a pamphlet, entitled *De captivitate babylonica ecclesiae* (*The Babylonian Captivity of the Church*), in which—Eternal God!—he combats the decrees and statutes of councils and popes, and with what artifices! In it he affirms that John Huss was iniquitously condemned by the Council of Constance, and that he, Luther, would defend as orthodox all those propositions of his which had been condemned. And not content with this, he publicly burned all the books on Roman law that he could find in Wittenberg, saying that "they perverted and contaminated the Christian religion, and that for this reason they ought to be destroyed."

The report of these events, spread throughout all Germany, excites to such an extent the minds of the Germans against the apostolic seat that if the prudence and piety of the pontiff, or the good star of our emperor, in conjunction with a general council, do not come to the relief of these evils, I fear, and I do very much fear, that this evil will spread so widely as to be absolutely incurable. It has appeared to me to be my duty to describe these things, writing them here on the spot, and I hope by so doing to gratify you. Farewell.

Worms, 13th May, 1521

From Brussels I have already written to you as to the origin of the Lutheran party and its progress up to that time. I will describe in this letter the events which have since transpired. The Electors and other Orders of the Roman Empire, having been convened at this city of Worms, the emperor, desirous that this affair of Luther's should be treated before every other, proposed that this man's folly should be repressed by the authority of the whole Roman Empire, that others might

be prevented from becoming his followers. Well, notwithstanding that he obtained this only by persevering
effort, nothing more resulted from it but that Luther
was summoned, under a safe-conduct and the emperor's
pledged faith, that he would hear him prior to any
adverse decision against him. For they said that it was
iniquitous to condemn a man without hearing him, and
that the emperor's dignity and piety were engaged
that, should Luther retract his errors, those other subjects should be recognized, upon which he had written
so learnedly and in such a Christian manner, and that
Germany should, by the authority of the emperor, be
relieved from the burdens and tyrannies of the apostolic
seat.

The emperor, finding his power thus restricted, commanded that Luther should come and appear in person
before him and the other Orders of the Empire. Being
asked there, "If those were his books which were everywhere published under his name, and whether he
would retract what he had written in them, or not?"
he replied that all of them were his books—the titles
of which at his request they read—and that he was
unwilling to deny them, and that he never had denied
them. But that as to the second part of the question
which had been addressed to him, to know whether he
was willing to retract what he had written, he begged
the emperor would grant him time to deliberate; which
was conceded him by the emperor until the following
day.

Upon that very day, the emperor and the Electors
of the Roman Empire and the other Orders being
present, Martin Luther being commanded to appear to
answer to the second part of the question which had
been addressed to him on the previous day, after a
long and diffuse oration in Latin and in German, Luther

said that he could retract nothing contained in his books, unless it were proved by the New Testament, or by the testimony of the Old Testament, that he had erred and written impiously. And when he was again pressed that he should respond without paraphrase with a categoric Yes or No, "whether he would abide by the decrees and constitutions of the councils?" he replied that he would retract nothing, nor could he abide by the decrees of the councils, since those councils occasionally contradicted each other.

Whereupon the emperor commanded him to retire and, having dissolved the assembly for that day, summoned the Prince Electors for the following day, and showed them a rescript, in his own handwriting, in which he declared what seemed to him right to be done in this affair. He asked them if they were all of his opinion, to wit, that the severest edicts should be issued against Luther and the Lutherans, and that the books of that madman should be burned. But the Electors, and other Orders of the Empire, some of whom had imbibed Luther's poison, and others who declared that Luther should by no means be condemned before the Germans were liberated from the burdens and tyrannies of the Romanists, as they called them, begged the emperor, with great importunity, that at the least Luther should be privately admonished that he should retract what he had written against the constitutions of the Church. As the emperor conceded this point to them, they during three days admonished the hardened Luther, but in vain; and, seeing their utter failure, they subscribed the emperor's decree.

This done, the emperor, being unwilling to break his word publicly pledged for his safe-conduct, warned Luther by a published document that he should leave Worms on the day following, and that he should flee,

within twenty days, to some place that might serve
him as a refuge. Luther obeyed. The emperor, then, as
well by his own authority as by that of the Prince
Electors, and of all the Orders of the Roman Empire,
having published an awful edict against Luther and
the Lutherans, and against his writings, commanded
that all the writings of Luther that could be found
should be solemnly burned, and that, following his
example, the same should be done throughout the other
cities of Germany.

Here you have, as some imagine, the end of this
tragedy, but I am persuaded that it is not the end, but
the beginning of it. For I perceive that the minds of the
Germans are greatly exasperated against the Romish
See; and they do not seem to attach great importance
to the emperor's edicts; for since their publication
Luther's books are sold with impunity at every step and
corner of the streets and marketplaces. From this you
may easily conjecture what will happen when the emperor leaves.

This evil might have been cured, with the greatest
advantage to the Christian republic, had not the pontiff
refused a general council, had he preferred the public
weal to his own private interests. But whilst he obstinately stands upon his right, though possibly from
a pious motive, or stopping his ears, he is anxious that
Luther be condemned and burned at the stake, I see
the whole Christian republic hurried to destruction,
unless God Himself succour us. Farewell.

In B. B. Wiffen, *Life and Writings of Juan de Valdés* (London:
B. Quaritch, 1865).

An Anabaptist View of the Church

PETER RIDEMAN

1540

WE CONFESS also that God hath, through Christ, chosen, accepted, and sought a people for Himself, not having spot, blemish, wrinkle, or any such thing, but pure and holy, as He Himself is holy. Therefore is such a people, community, assembly, or Church gathered and led together by the Holy Spirit, which from henceforth ruleth, controlleth, and ordereth everything in her, leading all her members to be of one mind and intention (so that they want only to be like Christ, to partake of His nature, and diligently to do His will), cleaving to Him as a bride and spouse to her bridegroom, yea, as one body with Him, one plant, one tree, bearing and giving one kind of fruit, as Paul saith, "As many as are led by the Spirit of God, they are the children of God," and again, "The same Spirit assureth us that we are children of God."

Since, then, the Church is an assembly of the children of God, as it is written, "Ye are the temple of the living God," as God hath said, "I will dwell in them and walk in them; and I will be their God and they shall be my people," "Wherefore come out from among them, and be ye separate, saith the Lord, and touch no unclean thing; and I will receive you, and will be your father, and ye shall be my sons and daughters." The children of God, however, become His children through the unifying Spirit. Thus it is evident that the

Church is gathered together by the Holy Spirit: also that she hath being and is kept in being by Him, and that there is no other Church apart from that which the Holy Spirit buildeth and gathereth.

Therefore is the assembly of the unjust and sinners, whores, adulterers, brawlers, drunkards, the covetous, selfish, vain, and all those who lie in word and deed, no Church of God, and they belong not to Him; as Paul saith, "If any man have not the Spirit of Christ he is none of his." Thus is not only their assembly not a Church of Christ, but none of them can be or continue therein unless he repent of his sins, as David saith, "The sinner shall not stand in the congregation of the righteous." After him John also saith, "There shall in no wise enter into it anything that defileth, neither that worketh abomination and lies; but they which are written in the living book of the Lamb. But outside are dogs, sorcerers, and whoremongers, idolators, murderers, and whosoever loveth and maketh a lie.". . .

Community, however, is naught else than that those who have fellowship have all things in common together, none having aught for himself, but each having all things with the others, even as the Father hath nothing for Himself, but all that He hath He hath with the Son, and again, the Son hath nothing for Himself, but all that He hath, He hath with the Father and all who have fellowship with Him.

Thus all those who have fellowship with Him likewise have nothing for themselves, but have all things with their Master and with all those who have fellowship with them, that they might be one in the Son as the Son is in the Father.

It is called the community of saints because they have fellowship in holy things, yea, in those things whereby they are sanctified, that is in the Father and the Son, who Himself sanctifieth them with all that He hath given them. Thus everything serveth to the betterment and building up of one's neighbour and to the praise and glory of God the Father. . . .

Now because it is a testament of the recognition, knowledge, and grace of God, baptism is also, according to the words of Peter, the bond of a good conscience with God, that is, of those who have recognized God. The recognition of God, however, cometh, as hath been said, from hearing the word of the Gospel. Therefore we teach that those who have heard the word, believed the same, and have recognized God, should be baptized—and not children. . . .

Since then we must be born of God, and are children of Christ and not of Adam, we must consider carefully how the birth of Christ came to pass, which, as we have said above, took place in faith through the working of the Holy Spirit. Now, whosoever is to be born of his nature and character must also be born of God that he may be His child, together with Christ, as also Peter saith, "Being born again, not of corruptible, but of incorruptible seed, namely of the word of truth."

This birth, however, taketh place in this wise. If the Word is heard and the same believed, then faith is sealed with the power of God, the Holy Spirit, who immediately reneweth the man and maketh him live (after he had been dead in sin) in the righteousness that standeth before God, so that the man is formed a new creature, a new man after God's likeness, or is renewed therein. Thus, whosoever is born in this wise, to him belongeth baptism as a bath of rebirth, signifying that he hath entered into the covenant of the grace and knowledge of God. . . .

Thus we say, and must say and confess, that not we

but all baptizers of children have forsaken the Church and community of Christ and separated themselves and the same. They have fallen away, and are become so corrupt that they neither know nor recognize what the true Church of Christ is and in what way she proveth herself the Church of Christ. To which thing, if one asks them and tell them, they give the answer, "The saints did that, who had the Holy Spirit. But we are not able to do so." They know not that the Church of Christ is a house of the Holy Spirit, and that none is therein unless he hath the same, as also Paul saith, "If any man have not the Spirit of Christ, he is none of His."

Since then God hath chosen this Church for Himself and separated her from all nations that she might serve Him with one mind and heart through the one child-like Spirit, there is, as hath been said, no more a servant therein but only children. Nor have they separated themselves, but God hath separated them from all other peoples, and hath therefore also given them a sign of the covenant, that is baptism, whereby they receive all who surrender themselves to God into the Church. . . .

Thus, we have not turned away from the Church of Christ, but to it; but we have left the soiled and impure assembly, and would wish that all men did so too. Therefore we call to repentance and tell whoever is willing to hear to harden not his heart and so bring the wrath of God upon him. Whosoever will not repent, however, and cleave to the true ordinances of God, but remaineth in his sins, we must let go his way and leave him to God. . . .

Governmental authority hath been ordained by God because of the turning aside of the people, in that they turned away from him and walked according to the flesh. For God saith, "My Spirit shall not always strive with men, for they are flesh." For this reason, after the flood, He ordained governmental authority for them to be a rod of the anger and vengeance of God, to shed the blood of those who have shed blood. . . .

Now because in Christ our King is the full blessing of God—yea, He is himself the blessing—all that was given in wrath must come to an end and cease in Him, and hath no part in Him. But governmental authority was given in wrath, and so it can neither fit itself into nor belong to Christ. Thus no Christian is a ruler and no ruler is a Christian, for the child of blessing cannot be the servant of wrath. Thus, in Christ, not the temporal, but the spiritual sword, doth rule over men, and so ruleth that they deserve not the temporal sword, therefore also have no need of it.

From *Account of Our Religion, Doctrine, and Faith*, trans. K. E. Hasenberg (London: Hodder & Stoughton, 1950).

An Appeal to the Council of Trent

REGINALD POLE

1546

MOST reverend Fathers, As the matters to be dealt with in this sacred congress for God's glory and the Church's good increased, we who bore the office of presidents and legates of the Apostolic See thought it our bounden duty often to use words of exhortation or of warning. Nor must we change our way in this second session, which, we hope, has been given as a happy beginning to the council.

All the more willingly shall we fulfil this duty, be-

cause when we exhort you to do what befits so great a
gathering or, on the contrary, warn you, we are exhorting or warning ourselves, who are in the same bark
with you, and are exposed with you to the same
dangers and the same storms. We bestir ourselves, I
say, to watch, lest on the one hand we run on the
rocks, which certainly are all too many in these matters,
or on the other hand by our sloth we are stormbeaten
and wrecked by the very flood of affairs; but rather
steadied by faith and hope, we may steer our course
where the harbour of safety may most clearly show
itself to the glory of God in Christ Jesus.

Therefore, that we may begin as we should, all be
warned in this beginning: each of us should above all
things keep before his eyes the things that are expected
of this holy council. Each one will easily see therein
what is the duty resting upon him. To put it briefly,
these duties are what are contained in the bull sum-
moning the council, viz., the uprooting of heresies, the
reformation of ecclesiastical discipline and of morals,
and lastly the external peace of the whole Church.
These are the things we must see to, or rather for which
we must untiringly pray in order that by God's mercy
they may be done. This again, at the outset of the
council and before all else, must be made an admonition to each and all of us who have here foregathered
—and especially to us who are presiding in this sacred
office—lest at any time we should think the many ills
now oppressing the flock of Christ could be withstood
either by any one of us who have come here or by the
whole council, even if all the pastors of the whole
earth were met. If, indeed, we think the thing can
be accomplished by us, or by any other than by Christ
Himself, whom God the Father has made the sole
Saviour and Shepherd and to whom He has given all

power, we shall err in the very foundation of all our actions, and we shall provoke still further the divine wrath.

To the former evils which have come upon us because we left the well of living waters, we shall have added the greater sin of wishing to heal these ills by our own power or prudence, so that justly it may be said of us what the prophet in the Name of God spoke in accusation of the chosen people: "This people hath wrought two evils. They have left me, the well of living water, and they have dug to themselves cisterns that cannot hold water" (Jer. 2:13). These cisterns are all the counsels which spring from our prudence without the breathing of the divine Spirit. They cannot hold the people in godliness and obedience as cisterns hold water. But the more we toil to pen the waters by these devices the more rapidly and floodlike shall they flow from us and leave us. This may we learn from our experience in many places and in these latter years. And this may warn us that there is one only way left for curing these ills. First we must acknowledge that all our remedies are useless, and indeed are more powerful to strengthen than to destroy these evils. Secondly, we who have the office of Fathers must act in everything by faith and hope and place our trust in the power of Christ, whom God the Father calls His right hand, and in the Wisdom of Christ, who is the Wisdom of the Father, whose ministers in all things we acknowledge ourselves to be. . . .

Therefore what, in His great love of God the Father and in His mercifulness towards our race, Christ did, justice itself now enacts of us that we should do. Before the tribunal of God's mercy we, the shepherds, should make ourselves responsible for all the evils now burdening the flock of Christ. The sins of all we should take upon ourselves, not in generosity but in justice; because the truth is that of these evils we are in great part the cause, and therefore we should implore the divine mercy through Jesus Christ.

If any should think that in calling ourselves, who are the shepherds, a cause of the evils burdening the Church, we are using undue bitterness and exaggeration of speech, rather than the truth, facts themselves which cannot lie will bear us witness. Let us therefore scan for a moment the evils burdening the Church and, at the same time, our own sins.

Yet who can count these sins? Like the other evils, they outnumber the sands of the seashore and raise their voice to the very heavens. We must therefore narrow this so great a mass of evils within the limits set by this council itself, which is called to cure the greatest of them, viz., the three we have named above: (1) heresy; (2) the decline in ecclesiastical morals; and (3) internal and external war.

Since the Church has been beset for many years by these woes, let us now look and think what is their source—and if we gave them birth or increase. Consider, then, the birth of these heresies which in these days are everywhere rife. We may indeed wish to deny that we have given them birth, because we ourselves have not uttered any heresy. Nevertheless wrong opinions about faith, like brambles and thorns, have sprung up in the God's-garth entrusted to us. Hence, even if, as is their wont, these poisonous weeds have spread of themselves, nevertheless if we have not tilled our field as we ought—if we have not sowed—if we took no pains at once to root up the springing weeds—we are no less to be reckoned their cause than if we ourselves had sowed them; and all the more since all these have their beginning and increase in the tiller's sloth. Here, therefore, the tillers of God's-garth should examine themselves, should question their conscience what pains they have taken in tilling and sowing. Whoever will do this, especially in these days when so few have a care to till God's-garth, will, we think, have no doubt that the guilt of these heresies spreading in the Church is upon him. But we have said enough by way of warning about what comes under the first heading.

Let us come to the second, which embraces the breaking down of right living and what is called "abuses." Herein no good is served by a long inquiry as to who are the causes of these evils, seeing that we cannot even name any other causes but ourselves.

Therefore let us approach the third, which embraces in itself the hindrances to the Church's peace, as wars domestic or external. These, indeed, have already disturbed and still disturb the Church's peace. We will say of them that if these wars are (and God shows by most sure signs that they are) His scourges to chasten us because we cannot deny that we are guilty under the two former heads—even of these wars we cannot deny that we ourselves are the chief cause. We are of opinion that God sends these scourges to punish our sinning and to turn our gaze towards these very sins by which we greatly offend His majesty.

Here, if anyone would estimate in what ways the Church has been troubled by war, let him deliberate within himself what are those things especially in which the Church suffers most because of wars. Nor does it matter whose wars they are—whether the intestine wars of our own princes, or the external wars of the Turks which in past years have wrought such havoc on us, or of those who have given up obedience to their shepherds and indeed have driven them from their sees. In a word, all that is to be said of every kind of war, whether men have taken up arms against us, have driven the shepherds from their churches, have thrown the Orders into confusion, have set laymen in the place of bishops, have robbed Church property, have hindered the preaching of God's Word, we may sum up in this: if they are willing to read the Book of the Abuses of Shepherds, the greater number of those who claim this name will find it stated in the clearest terms that there is none of these things which has not been done by themselves. It will be found that our ambition, our avarice, our cupidity, have wrought all these evils on the people of God; and that, on account of this, shepherds are being driven from their churches, and the churches starved of the Word of God, and the property of the Church, which is the property of the poor, stolen, and the priesthood given to the unworthy and to those who differ from lay folk only in dress (if even in that!). Which of these things can we deny having done during these latter years? If, then, the Turks and the heretics do the same to us, what else are we witnessing than our crimes and at the same time the just judgment of God—a judgment, indeed, full of mercy? If He punished us as we deserved, we should have been long since as Sodom and Gomorrah.

Why do we recall these things? To shame you? Far from it; but rather, my beloved Fathers and brethren, to admonish you—and our own selves first of all—how to avoid these scourges which now rain on us, and even greater evils which await us unless we repent; so that we may escape God's fearful judgment—fearful indeed to those who will not repent and especially to those who hold authority. "For a most severe judgment shall be for them that bear rule" (Wisd. of Sol. 6:5). We see judgment beginning with the house of God. Now that the priests are cast out and trodden underfoot, what does this signify if not the divine judgment on us? This is what Christ foretold in saying that His priests are the salt of the earth, but that if the salt lose its savour it is good for nothing more than to be cast out and to be trodden underfoot (Matt. 5:13). All these things we are now suffering. If like our fathers we were suffering for justice's sake, we should be blessed. But because the salt has lost its savour we are suffering justly yet not for the sake of justice. . . .

Let us therefore come back to those whom we undertook to admonish; and especially those bishops who have come here with mandates from their princes. We therefore admonish them that they serve their princes with all loyalty and zeal, but as becomes bishops. They must serve them as the servants of God and not as servants of men. The Apostle says, "Be not the servants of men" (I Cor. 7:22). Let them first serve the one King Christ to whom God the Father has given all power; and then on His account let them serve all and especially princes: "Honour to whom honour is due, and tribute to whom tribute" (I Cor. 7:33). We exhort them to serve their princes unto honour; as the very words of their commissions declare, in which nothing is set forth that is not unto honour and to the common good. In a word, let them so serve that their first care will be for the honour of God and the profit of this council, which has been summoned for the common good. All those who must give their judgment here before God, His angels, and the whole Church, we exhort that they speak without human respect; but still more that we speak without hatred of anyone, even should he represent one of our opponents or private or public enemies.

Finally, we desire and exhort in the Lord that we keep ourselves from all strife amongst ourselves. It is this which grieves and repels the Holy Spirit, without whom we can do naught to the good of peace or the Church. "For whereas," says the Apostle, "there are among you contentions, are you not men and walk you not as men?" (I Cor. 3:3). Now when he calls them men, he means devoid of the Spirit of God.

In everything pertaining to the reformation of the Church, for which purpose we have forgathered, we should imitate Him who first made it. Of His entrance on the work the prophet says in the person of God, "Behold my Servant, whom I have chosen: my beloved in whom my soul delights. I have given my Spirit unto Him. He will deliver judgment to the Gentiles. He shall not strive nor cry aloud. The bruised reed He shall not break; the smoking flax He shall not quench."

This spirit of peace, of charity, of meekness, we should show towards all and in the sight of all; but especially in this sacred council to which we have come that by the grace of this Spirit an end may be put to the disputes that for so long have rent the Church.

From *Eirenikon*, trans. Vincent McNabb, *Dublin Review*, Vol. 198 (1936).

The True Kirk and Its Signs

JOHN KNOX

1560

As WE BELIEVE in one God, Father, Son, and Holy Ghost, so do we most constantly believe that from the beginning there has been and now is, and to the end of the world shall be, one Kirk, that is to say, one company and multitude of men chosen of God, who rightly worship and embrace Him by true faith in Christ Jesus, who is the only head of the same Kirk, which also is the body and spouse of Christ Jesus; which Kirk is catholic, that is, universal, because it contains the elect of all ages, of all realms, nations, and tongues, be they of the Jews, or be they of the Gentiles, who have communion and society with God the Father, and with His Son Christ Jesus, through the sanctification of His Holy Spirit; and therefore it is called the communion, not of profane persons, but of saints, who, as citizens of the heavenly Jerusalem, have the fruition of the most inestimable benefits, to wit, of one God, one Lord Jesus, one faith, and one baptism, out of the which Kirk there is neither life nor eternal felicity. And therefore we utterly abhor the blasphemy of them that affirm that men which live according to equity and justice shall be saved, what religion that ever they have professed. For as without Christ Jesus there is neither life nor salvation, so shall there none be participant thereof but such as the Father has given unto His Son Christ Jesus, and they that in time come unto Him, avow His doctrine, and believe into Him; we comprehend the children with the faithful parents. This Kirk is invisible, known only to God, who also knows whom He has chosen, and comprehends as well (as is said) the elect that be departed, commonly called the Kirk Triumphant, and they that yet live and fight against sin and Satan, as shall live hereafter.

Because that Satan from the beginning has laboured to deck his pestilent synagogue with the title of the Kirk of God, and has inflamed the hearts of cruel murderers, to persecute, trouble, and molest the true Kirk and members thereof, as Cain did Abel, Ishmael Isaac,

Esau Jacob, and the whole priesthood of the Jews, Christ Jesus himself, and His Apostles after Him; it is a thing most requisite that the true Kirk be discerned from the filthy synagogues, by clear and perfect notes, lest we, being deceived, receive and embrace, to our own condemnation, the one for the other. The notes, signs, and assured tokens whereby the immaculate spouse of Christ Jesus is known from the horrible harlot, the Kirk malignant, we affirm are neither antiquity, title usurped, lineal descent, place appointed, nor multitude of men approving an error; for Cain, in age and title, was preferred to Abel and Seth; Jerusalem had prerogative above all places of the earth, where also were the priests lineally descended from Aaron; and greater number followed the scribes, pharisees, and priests, than unfeignedly believed and approved Christ Jesus and His doctrine; and yet, as we suppose, no man of sound judgment will grant that any of the forenamed were the Kirk of God. The notes therefore of the true Kirk of God we believe, confess, and avow to be, first, the true preaching of the word of God, into the which God has revealed Himself unto us, as the writings of the prophets and Apostles do declare. Secondly, the right administration of the sacraments of Christ Jesus, which must be annexed unto the word and promise of God, to seal and confirm the same in our hearts. Last, ecclesiastical discipline uprightly ministered, as God's word prescribes, whereby vice is repressed and virtue nourished. Wheresoever then these former notes are seen, and of any time continue (be the number never so few above two or three), there, without all doubt, is the true Kirk of Christ, who, according unto His promise, is in the midst of them. Not that universal, of which we have before spoken, but particular, such

as was in Corinth, Galatia, Ephesus, and other places,
in which the ministry was planted by Paul, and were of
himself named the kirks of God; and such kirks, we
the inhabitants of the realm of Scotland, professors of
Christ Jesus, profess ourselves to have in our cities,
towns, and places reformed, for the doctrine taught in
our kirks is contained in the written word of God, to
wit in the books of the Old and New Testaments. In
those books we mean, which of the ancient have been
reputed canonical, in the which we affirm that all
things necessary to be believed for the salvation of
mankind, is sufficiently expressed. The interpretation
whereof, we confess, neither appertains to private nor
public person, neither yet to any kirk, for any pre-
eminence or prerogative, personal or local, which one
has above another, but appertains to the Spirit of God,
by the which also the Scripture was written. When
controversy then happens, for the right understanding
of any place or sentence of Scripture, or for the reformation of any abuse within the Kirk of God, we
ought not so much to look what men before us have
said or done, as unto that which the Holy Ghost uniformly speaks within the body of the Scripture, and
unto that which Christ Jesus Himself did, and commanded to be done. For this is a thing universally
granted, that the Spirit of God, which is the spirit of
unity, is in nothing contrarious unto Himself. If, then,
the interpretation, determination, or sentence of any
doctor, kirk, or council repugn to the plain word of
God, written in any other place of the Scripture, it is a
thing most certain, that theirs is not the true understanding and meaning of the Holy Ghost, although that
councils, realms, and nations have approved and received the same. For we dare not receive or admit any

interpretation which repugns to any principal point of our faith, or to any other plain text of Scripture, or yet unto the rule of charity.

From "The Confession of Faith," in *The Works of John Knox*, ed. David Laing (Edinburgh, 1846-1864).

Freedom of the Will

On Free Will

ERASMUS OF ROTTERDAM

1524

A MONG the difficulties which not infrequently arise in the Holy Scriptures, there is perhaps no more inescapable labyrinth than the question of free will. For this problem has marvellously exercised the wits of theologians, both ancient and modern, as it once did those of the philosophers, but, it seems to me, with greater effort than results. In our day the controversy has been renewed by Carlstadt and by Eck, but in a moderate way; this question was soon agitated more violently by Martin Luther, one of whose theses concerns free will. Although his assertion has not been unanswered, I am intervening in my turn, at the urging of my friends, in the hope that my little work may contribute to the progress of truth.

Now I know that certain people will shut their ears and protest: "The world is turned upside down! Erasmus dares to oppose Luther! This is the mouse going into battle against the elephant!" To pacify them, if I may be allowed a moment's silence, I shall simply repeat by way of preface one single well-established

677

fact: I have never accepted the doctrines of Luther. No one should then be shocked to see me affirm publicly a difference of opinion such as this which can divide one man and another; still less am I prevented from contesting one of his opinions and especially from engaging in a temperate discussion with him, inspired only by a desire to seek out the truth. Certainly I do not think that Luther can be scandalized if someone disagrees with him, since he himself has not hesitated to attack not only the opinions of all the doctors of the Church, but the doctrines taught by all the schools, all the councils, and all the popes; what he does openly and without disguise should not be imputed to me as a crime by his friends, if I disagree with him in my turn.

On the other hand, to avoid anyone's interpreting this controversy as a gladiatorial combat, I shall take issue with but a single thesis of his, with no other aim than to make the truth more clearly manifest, if it is possible, by comparing the Scriptural texts and the arguments; such an inquiry has always been considered especially honourable for learned men. The affair will be conducted without abuse, both because this is more fitting for Christians, and because in this way the truth may be attained more surely, as it is often lost in the violence of argument. . . .

Let us then suppose that it is true in a certain sense, as Wyclif has taught and as Luther has asserted, that whatever is done by us is done not by free will but by pure necessity; what is more inexpedient than to publish this paradox to the world? Again, let us suppose that in a certain sense it is true, as Augustine says somewhere, that God works both good and evil in us, and rewards His own works in us and punishes His own evil works. What a door to impiety this pronouncement would open to countless mortals, if it were spread abroad in the world, especially in view of the great sloth, indifference, and wickedness of men, and their ineradicable proclivity to all kinds of impiety! What weak man would keep up the perpetual and weary struggle against the flesh? What evil man would strive to amend his life? Who could persuade his soul to love with all his heart a God who prepared a hell flaming with eternal tortures where He may avenge on wretched men His own misdeeds, as if He delighted in human tortures? . . .

Now since Luther no longer accepts the authority of any doctor, however highly approved, but declares that he holds to the canonical writings, I accept with joy this lightening of my labour. For the authors are innumerable, both among the Greeks and among the Latins, who have treated of free will either deliberately or casually. It would not be a small matter to collect all that each of these has said for or against free will; to explain the meaning of each passage, to develop and demonstrate their arguments, would be a long and painstaking task—and also useless as far as Luther and his friends are concerned, for not only do they differ among themselves, but sometimes they are unfaithful to their own doctrine. But although we may allow as much importance as Luther does to the testimonies and solid arguments drawn from the Holy Scripture, yet I would like to invite the reader to pass in review the numerous procession of the most eminent doctors, who have received until our days the agreement of so many centuries, and the greater number of whom can invoke, in addition to their admirable knowledge of sacred literature, the piety of their lives. Some of them rendered to the doctrine of Christ, which they defended in their works, the testimony of their blood. This is the case, among the Greeks, with Origen, Basil, Chrysostom, Cyril, John of Damascus, and Theophylactus; among the Latins, with Tertullian, Cyprian, Arnobius, Hilary, Ambrose, Jerome, and Augustine, not to mention after them, Thomas, Duns Scotus, Durand, Capreolus, Gabriel, Aegidius, Gregory, and Alexander, whose power and dialectical ability no one, in my opinion, should reject; and I shall not forget, moreover, the authority of so many theological faculties, councils, and sovereign pontiffs. From apostolic times to this day no one has ever claimed the right to deny all efficacy to the free will, with the sole exceptions of Manichaeus and John Wyclif, for Lorenzo Valla, who seems to share a little in their opinion, does not have great authority among the theologians. Although the Manichaean doctrine has been the object of reprobation and of universal ridicule, yet I scarcely think that it is less profitable to piety than that of Wyclif. For the Manichaean doctrine refers all good or bad works to two natures working in man, but we are responsible for our good works to the Author of Creation, and there remains to us also the resource of imploring against the powers of darkness the help of the Creator, to the end that with His aid we may sin more lightly and do good more easily. But with Wyclif who refers everything to necessity alone, what remains for our prayers and our efforts?

Then, to return to what I said above, if in the course of this discussion my arguments seem to balance those on the opposite side, the reader may consider and judge for himself if there is reason to give the advantage to the doctrine established by so many learned men, orthodox Christians, so many saints, martyrs, and theologians, both ancient and modern, or to the private judgment of one individual or another. This is not to say that I give more weight, as in human assemblies, to the opinions of the greater number or to the authority of those who are speaking. I know that it often happens that the majority vanquishes the better part. I know that it is not always the best causes which attract the greatest numbers. I know that in the search for truth one can always find something to add to the efforts of the ancients. I believe that it is equally true that the authority of the Scriptures alone surpasses the united opinions of all men. But the controversy here does not concern the value of the Scriptures; both parties accept and venerate the same books. The conflict concerns the meaning of the Scriptures. And if its interpretation owes something to intellect and learning, whose intellect is more acute and more penetrating than that of the Greeks? Or where are there found men more familiar with sacred letters? . . . And if in this debate one regards sanctity of life more than erudition, see what champions can be lined up on the side of free will! But let us abandon this comparison, which the jurisconsults consider odious. For I do not wish to compare certain of these heralds of the new Gospel to the ancient doctors.

Now I hear the objection: "What need is there for interpretation when the Scripture is entirely clear?" But if it is so clear, why have such eminent men groped so blindly and for so many centuries in such an important matter, as our adversaries claim? If there is no obscurity in the Scriptures, what need was there for prophecies in apostolic times? This, you may say, was a gift of the Holy Spirit. But I hardly know whether, like the gift of healing and the gift of tongues, this gift of prophecy has not also ceased. If it has not ceased, it should be asked to whom it has passed. If to everyone, then all interpretation is uncertain. If it passed to no one, then today, when so many obscurities baffle learned men, no interpretation will be certain. If I claim that it passed to those who succeeded the Apostles, then some will protest that for many centuries the successors of the Apostles did not possess the apostolic spirit. Yet of these men we may very probably assume, other things being equal, that God infused His spirit into those to whom He entrusted His mission, just as we may believe it more probable that grace was given to the baptized, rather than to the unbaptized. . . .

My book is already half finished, if I have convinced my reader of the point which I have advanced: namely, that it would be better not to discuss these matters too scrupulously, especially in front of the crowd. If this is so, the demonstration to which I am going to apply myself becomes superfluous. Yet I hope that the truth will triumph everywhere, and that it will spring forth from the collation of Scriptures like fire from the rubbing of flints. In the first place, it cannot be denied that there are in the sacred Scriptures many texts which seem to establish clearly the doctrine of free will, and some others which seem to destroy it utterly. But it is evident that the Scripture cannot contradict itself, since it has issued wholly from the same spirit. We shall begin, therefore, by presenting the texts which confirm our opinion, then we shall try to explain those which seem to us to oppose it. Here we define free will as a power of the human will, by virtue of which man can apply himself to all that concerns eternal salvation or can turn away from it. . . .

So far we have confined ourselves to comparing the passages of the Scripture which support free will and those which, on the contrary, seem to suppress it entirely. But since the Holy Spirit, who is the author of the whole of Scripture, cannot contradict Himself, we are then constrained, whether we will or not, to seek some moderate conclusion. Since each of the two opposed opinions is based on the same Scripture, it is clear that the defenders of each have examined the Scripture from their own particular points of view, and have read it in the light of the end that they pursue. Some have considered how slothfully men strive for piety and then what a great evil is despair, and while they tried to find a remedy for these evils, they fell imprudently into another error, by granting too much to human free will. But other authors, considering how great an enemy of true piety is the confidence of man in his own powers and merits, and how intolerable is the pride of those who praise themselves for their good works, and who go so far as to sell them to others, according to measure, as one sells oil and soap, in their anxiety to avoid this evil, the opponents of this pride have cut free will in half, saying that a good work cannot be done, or they have killed it entirely by invoking the absolute necessity of all things.

Doubtless to Luther and his followers it seems absolutely necessary, for the simple obedience of the Christian soul, that man should depend wholly on the will of God, that he should place all his hopes and his confidence in His promises, and recognizing his own wretchedness, should admire and adore the boundless mercy of Him who freely grants us so many blessings, that he should submit wholly to the will of God, whether He wishes to save him or damn him; that man should take no credit for his own good works but render all glory to the divine grace, remembering that man is only the living organ of the Holy Spirit, purified and consecrated by His free goodness, guided and ruled by His inscrutable wisdom. There is nothing here that anyone can attribute to his own powers, and yet one may expect with confident faith the reward of eternal life, not because his good works have merited it, but because it has seemed good to the divine charity to promise it to His faithful. The role of man is to pray to God assiduously that He will grant and increase in us His spirit, to render thanks to Him if any good work is done in us, to adore His power in all things, to marvel at His wisdom, and to love His goodness everywhere.

To me also this position appears eminently praiseworthy, for it agrees with the Holy Scriptures, and with the testimony of those who by baptism have truly died to the world and been buried with Christ, so that by mortifying the flesh they may afterwards live and act in the spirit of Jesus, in whose body they are planted by faith. . . . I applaud all this gladly, until it becomes extravagant.

For when I hear it said that human merit is so null that all works of men, however pious, are sinful; that our will has no more power than the clay in the hand of the potter; that everything we do or will derives from an absolute necessity, my spirit is assailed by many scruples. First, how shall we understand all the texts in which we read that the saints, who were full of good works, observed justice, that they walked justly before God, that they turned neither to the right nor to the left, if all the actions of even the most pious men are sinful, and so sinful that without the divine mercy he for whom Christ died would be plunged into hell? Why do we hear so often of reward, if there is no merit? On what grounds would one dare to praise the obedience of those who submit to divine commands, and condemn the disobedience of those who do not submit? Why does the Scripture so often mention judgment, if no account is taken of our merits? Or why are we obliged to present ourselves before the sovereign Judge if everything is done in us by pure necessity and nothing according to our free will?

And I repeat again this other thought: What is the purpose then of all these warnings, precepts, threats, exhortations, and innumerable demands, if we do nothing, but if God, according to His immutable will, works everything in us, wills it, and accomplishes it. God commands us to pray without ceasing, to watch, to struggle, and to contend for the reward of eternal life. Why does He wish to be prayed to endlessly for that which He has already decreed to grant or not to grant, since being immutable He cannot change His decrees? Why does He command us to seek by so many labours that which He has already decided to grant us freely? We are afflicted, we are despised, we are mocked, we are put to death; it is thus that the grace of God contends in us, it is thus that it vanquishes, that it triumphs. The martyr suffers atrocious things, and yet no merit is imputed to him; still more, it is claimed that he sins if he exposes his body to punishment in the hope of heavenly life. But why would God, who is all merciful, wish to deal thus with the martyrs? Would we not consider a man cruel who, having decided to give largess freely to a friend, would give it only after seeing him tortured to the point of despair?

But when one comes before the mystery of the divine counsels, one is obliged to adore that which one has not the right to scrutinize. The human mind says: "This is the Lord; He can do all that He wills, and since by nature He is infinitely good, what He wills can only be excellent." One says also in a manner praiseworthy enough that God crowns His gifts in us, and that His benefits will be our reward; that in His free goodness He deigns to impute to us that which He has worked in us in such a way that thus we could be said to pay the price of immortality. But I ask myself how those men can be in agreement with themselves who so exaggerate the mercy of God toward the good that they make Him almost cruel with regard to others. It is not difficult for pious ears to admit the goodness of Him who imputes to us His own good; on the other hand, it is difficult to explain how it is just (I do not say merciful) to condemn to eternal punishments those in whom He has not deigned to work good. For it would have been impossible for them to do anything good by themselves since either they had no free will, or if they had, it was one which could only serve the ends of sin. . . .

In my opinion, one could so define free will as to avoid that abusive confidence in our merits, and the other difficulties which Luther avoids, and also those which I have noted above, and all without losing those advantages which Luther praises. This solution seems to me to be manifest in the doctrine which attributes entirely to grace the first impulsion which stimulates the soul, but which leaves to the human will, when it does not lack divine grace, a certain place in the unfolding of the act. Since all things have three parts, a beginning, a development, and a completion, those who hold this doctrine ascribe the two extremes to grace, and admit that free will does something only in the development. But even this it does in such a way that two causes work together in the same individual act: namely, the grace of God and the will of man. Grace is the principal cause, and the will is the secondary cause, which can do nothing without the principal cause, while this cause suffices in itself alone. Thus fire burns by its natural virtue, although the principal cause of the burning of the fire is God, who acts through the

fire and who would be sufficient alone, whereas the
fire could do nothing without this cause, if it were
withdrawn. By reason of this working together, man
owes all his salvation to the reception of divine grace,
since the share which pertains directly to the free will
is so small, and it even derives finally from the grace
of God, who in the beginning created the free will, and
then delivered it, and restored it to health. Thus those
men would be reassured—if they can be reassured—
for whom man can have no good which he does not
owe to God. . . .

On the other hand, those who deny absolutely the
existence of free will, and claim that everything is done
by pure necessity, assert that God produces in all men
not only good works but also bad. It follows, then, that
if man has no claim to be considered the author of his
good works, he also cannot be regarded as the author
of his bad works. This conclusion, which seems manifestly to attribute injustice and cruelty to God, which
is most abhorrent to pious ears (for God would not
exist if He had in Him anything vicious or imperfect),
finds defenders nonetheless, who uphold this cause
which is so little defensible. They say: "Since God is,
what He does can only be the best and most beautiful.
If you contemplate the order of the universe, even those
things which are bad in themselves are good there, and
show forth the glory of God. Nor does it pertain to any
creature to judge the designs of the Creator, but he
should on the contrary submit himself entirely to God;
if he sees then that God condemns this one and that
one, he should not murmur, but embrace that which is
pleasing to God, and at the same time persuade himself
that what He does is for the best and could only be
for the best." On the other hand, who would support
the man who says to God: "Why have you not made

me an angel?" Would not God justly answer him: "Shameless one, if I had made you a frog, what would you have to complain about?" Similarly if a frog demanded of God: "Why am I not a peacock with many-coloured plumage?"—would He not justly reply to him: "Ingrate, I could have made you a mushroom or an onion, while as it is, you jump, you drink, and you sing." Finally, if a basilisk or a viper would say: "Why have you made me an animal which no one can see and which is poisonous to everyone, instead of a sheep?"—what should God reply? Perhaps simply: "Because I have found it good and in accord with the beauty and harmony of the universe. There is no more injustice in your case than for the flies, mosquitoes, and other insects whose organization seems a great marvel to those who examine it.". . .

But let us stop reasoning with these people who are deprived of reason, and take up our discussion of man, whom God has created in His image and likeness, whose goodness is the source of all creation. Yet we see that certain men are born with well-made bodies, with excellent minds, as if they were predestined to virtue, while others possess monstrous bodies, or suffer from terrible maladies, and still others have minds so stupid that they are indistinguishable from animals, and that certain men surpass even the beasts in beastliness, and that some have souls so naturally inclined to evil that they seemed to be seized by a fatal power, and that others are completely mad and demoniac. How shall we in these circumstances explain the divine justice and mercy? Shall we repeat with Paul: "O the depths, etc."? This would be better, in my opinion, than to judge in bold and wicked fashion those counsels of God which are inscrutable to men. Nevertheless it would still be very difficult to explain why God crowns with immortal glory the good that He has done in some men, and why He punishes with eternal penalties the evil that He has done in others. To defend this paradox it is necessary to appeal to many other paradoxes, and to draw up the whole line of battle against the opposite side.

They most excessively exaggerate original sin, in which they claim that the most splendid powers of human nature have been so corrupted that of themselves they can do nothing but remain ignorant of God and hate Him, and that no one, even if he is justified by faith, can do anything that is not a sin. They claim that this very inclination to sin left in us by the sin of our first parents is already a sin, and that it is so invincible that not even the man justified by faith can fulfil any divine commandments, but that so many precepts of God have no other purpose than to magnify the divine grace which bestows salvation on man without regard to merits. . . . If God has burdened man with so many commandments which have no other purpose than to make him hate God the more and condemn Him more severely, do they not make God more unmerciful than Dionysius, the tyrant of Sicily, who purposely made many laws which he expected most persons would not observe, if no one compelled them, and for a while overlooked offences until he saw that almost everyone had violated his laws, and then he began to punish the offenders? Thus he made everyone hate him. . . .

Luther seems to delight in this kind of extravagance so that he might, as the saying goes, split the evil knot of others' excesses with an evil wedge. The temerity of those who sell not only their merits but also those of all the saints is excessive. And for what kind of works? Incantations, the recitation of psalms, abstinences, fastings, vestments, and titles? But Luther only drove out this nail with another by asserting that there are no merits of the saints at all, and that all the works of pious men are sins leading to eternal damnation, unless faith and God's mercy come to their aid. Again one side makes a profit out of the confessions and reparations by which they have wonderfully ensnared the consciences of men, and also out of Purgatory, concerning which they hold some paradoxical notions. Their opponents correct this vice by claiming that confession is an invention of Satan (the more moderate deny that it should be enforced), and that no satisfaction for sins is necessary, since Christ has paid the ransom for all our sins, and finally that there is no Purgatory.

Likewise, the one party declares that even the constitutions of any petty prior are binding under pain of damnation, and they do not hesitate to promise eternal life to those who obey them. And the opposing party combats this excess by declaring that all the decrees of the popes, the councils, and the bishops are heretical and anti-Christian. If the one group exalts the power of the Holy See beyond all measure, the other speaks of the sovereign pontiff in terms which I should not dare to repeat. Similarly, those on the one side say that the vows of monks and priests bind a man under pain of Hell forever, while the others say that such vows are impious, that it is not necessary to make them, and that if one has made them it is not necessary to keep them.

It is from the collision of such excesses that the lightnings and thunders arise which today violently shake the world. And if each side continues to defend its exaggerations so bitterly, I foresee such a struggle between them as that between Achilles and Hector, who since they were so equal in savagery could only be separated by death. There is a popular saying that in order to straighten a curved stick it is necessary to bend it to the other side; this is perhaps applicable in the reformation of morals, but I am not sure that it should be applied in the case of doctrine. In exhorting or dissuading men, I can see that there is sometimes a place for exaggeration, as to give confidence to the timid, you might aptly say: "Never fear, God speaks and does all things in you." And on the other hand, to humble the wicked insolence of man, you might usefully say that man is nothing but sin; and against those who claim to make their teaching equal to the canonical Scriptures, you would doubtless profitably say that man is nothing but a lie.

But when axioms are proposed in the search for truth, I do not think that such paradoxes, which are not far from enigmas, should be used. For my part I prefer moderation. Pelagius seemed to attribute too much to free will, and Scotus still more, but Luther first mutilated it by cutting off its right arm, then not content with this he throttled free will and destroyed it altogether. For myself, I prefer the doctrine of those who allow something to free will, and at the same time acknowledge the greater share of grace. For it does no good to avoid the Scylla of pride in order to fall into the Charybdis of despair or indifference; or to set a dislocated limb in such a way that you dislocate it on the other side, instead of putting it back in its proper place. And it is no use to attack the enemy in front of you at the risk of receiving a surprise attack from behind.

One should then accept this moderate solution: that there may be some good works, although imperfect, but for them man cannot arrogate anything to himself; there will be some merit, but its achievement is owing to God. The life of man is so full of weakness, vice, and sin that if anyone contemplates it he will easily lose his conceit, even if we do not assert that man, however justified, can only be sinful, especially since Christ speaks of a rebirth, and Paul, of the "new man." But why, you say, should anything be allowed to free will? In order to charge with something by way of deserts the wicked who willingly reject the grace of God, in order to spare God the reproaches of cruelty and injustice, to deliver ourselves from despair, so that we may be incited to effort. Such are the reasons which have led almost all men to admit free will, but as inefficacious without the perpetual grace of God, so that we may not arrogate anything to ourselves. But someone may say: "Of what value is free will, if it is not efficacious?" And I answer: "Of what value is man as a whole, if God works in him as does the potter in clay, or as He would in a stone?"

Now if this matter has now been sufficiently demonstrated to be such that it is not expedient, so far as piety is concerned, to investigate it more deeply than is necessary, especially among the unlearned; if I have shown that this opinion is based on more numerous and more evident texts of the Holy Scripture than the other; if it is plain that the Holy Scripture is obscure and figurative in many passages, or even at first glance seems to be in conflict with itself, and that, for this reason, whether we wish to or not, we must depart from it somewhat verbally and literally, and we must modify the sense by interpretation; and if, finally, there are set forth the many inconveniences, I will not say absurdities, which would follow if free will were once entirely taken away; and if it were openly brought about, by the acceptance of this doctrine of which I have spoken, that none of those things would be lost which Luther has discussed piously and in a Christian manner—supreme love of God, the abolition of confi-

dence in our merits, works, and efforts, and the trans-
ference of these to God and His promises—I would
now ask the reader to weigh this and say whether he
would think it just to condemn this judgment of so
many doctors of the Church, approved by the consent
of so many ages and peoples, and to take in its place
certain erroneous opinions which now convulse the
Christian world? If these latter opinions are true, I
candidly confess the slowness of my wits in not being
able to understand them. Certainly I do not knowingly
resist the truth, and from my heart I favour the true
freedom of the Gospel, and I detest whatever is opposed
to the Gospel. I do not here assume the role of a judge,
as I have said, but that of one who discusses a question
thoroughly, and yet I can truly affirm that in discussing
this matter I have maintained the religious point of
view, which was formerly required of judges appointed
to consider these capital cases. Although I am an old
man, it will not shame or anger me to learn from a
young man, if he teaches me more evident doctrines
with evangelical gentleness. Here I know that I shall
hear: "Let Erasmus learn to know Christ and be strong;
let him give up his human wisdom, for no one who
does not have the Spirit of God understands these
things." If I do not yet understand what Christ is, I
have certainly wandered far afield up to now. Yet I
should certainly like to learn what spirit has guided so
many doctors and Christian people. For it is probable
that the people understand what the bishops, who do
not understand this new doctrine, have been teaching
them for now almost thirteen centuries. I have finished;
let others judge.

From *De libero arbitrio diatribe sive collatio*, ed. L. von Walter
(Leipzig, 1910); trans. M.M.M.

The Bondage of the Will

MARTIN LUTHER

1525

THAT I have been so long answering your *Diatribe on Free Will*, venerable Erasmus, has happened contrary to the expectation of all, and contrary to my own custom also. For hitherto I have not only appeared to embrace willingly opportunities of this kind for writing, but even to seek them of my own accord. Someone may, perhaps, wonder at this new and unusual thing, this forbearance or fear, in Luther, who could not be roused up by so many boasting taunts, and letters of adversaries, congratulating Erasmus on his victory, and singing to him the song of triumph— What that Maccabee, that obstinate assertor, then, has at last found an antagonist a match for him, against whom he dares not open his mouth!

But so far from accusing them, I myself openly concede that to you, which I never did to anyone before: that you not only by far surpass me in the powers of eloquence, and in genius (which we all concede to you as your desert, and the more so as I am but a barbarian and do all things barbarously), but that you have damped my spirit and impetus, and rendered me languid before the battle; and that by two means. First, by art: because, that is, you conduct this discussion with a most specious and uniform modesty, by which you have met and prevented me from being incensed against you. And next, because, on so great a subject, you say nothing but what has been said before: therefore you say less about, and attribute more unto, free will than the Sophists have hitherto said and attributed (of which I shall speak more fully hereafter). So that it seems even superfluous to reply to these your arguments, which have been indeed often refuted by me, but trodden down, and trampled under foot, by the incontrovertible book of Philip Melanchthon, *Concerning Theological Questions*—a book, in my judgment, worthy not only of being immortalized, but of being included in the ecclesiastical canon; in comparison of which, your book is, in my estimation, so mean and vile that I greatly feel for you for having defiled your most beautiful and ingenious language with such vile trash; and I feel an indignation against the matter also, that such unworthy stuff should be borne about in ornaments of eloquence so rare; which is as if rubbish, or dung, should be carried in vessels of gold and silver. And this you yourself seem to have felt, who were so unwilling to undertake this work of writing; because your conscience told you that you would of necessity have to try the point with all the powers of eloquence; and that, after all, you would not be able so to blind me by your colouring, but that I should, having torn off the deceptions of language, discover the real dregs beneath. For, although I am rude in speech, yet, by the grace of God, I am not rude in understanding. And, with Paul, I dare arrogate to myself understanding, and with confidence derogate it from you; although I willingly, and deservedly, arrogate eloquence and genius to you, and derogate it from myself. . . .

The "form" of Christianity set forth by you, among other things, has this: "that we should strive with all our powers, have recourse to the remedy of repentance, and in all ways try to gain the mercy of God; without

which, neither human will nor endeavour is effectual";
also, "that no one should despair of pardon from a God
by nature most merciful."

These statements of yours are without Christ, without
the Spirit, and more cold than ice, so that the beauty
of your eloquence is really deformed by them. Perhaps
a fear of the popes and those tyrants extorted them
from you, their miserable vassal, lest you should appear
to them a perfect atheist. But what they assert is this:
that there is ability in us; that there is a striving with
all our powers; that there is mercy in God; that there
are ways of gaining that mercy; that there is a God,
by nature just, and most merciful, etc. But if a man
does not know what these powers are, what they can
do or in what they are to be passive, what their efficacy
or what their inefficacy is, what can such an one do?
What will you set him about doing?

"It is irreligious, curious, and superfluous," you say,
"to wish to know whether our own will does anything
in those things which pertain unto eternal salvation,
or whether it is wholly passive under the work of grace."
But here you say the contrary: that it is Christian piety
to "strive with all the powers"; and that "without the
mercy of God the will is ineffective."

Here you plainly assert that the will does something
in those things which pertain unto eternal salvation,
when you speak of it as striving; and again you assert
that it is passive when you say that without the mercy
of God it is ineffective. Though, at the same time, you
do not define how far that doing, and being passive, is
to be understood—thus designedly keeping us in ignorance how far the mercy of God extends, and how
far our own will extends; what our own will is to do,
in that which you enjoin, and what the mercy of God
is to do. Thus that prudence of yours carries you along;

by which you are resolved to hold with neither side and to escape safely through Scylla and Charybdis, in order that, when you come into the open sea and find yourself overwhelmed and confounded by the waves, you may have it in your power to assert all that you now deny, and deny all that you now assert. . . .

In this book, therefore, I will push you, and the Sophists together, until you shall define to me the power of free will and what it can do; and I hope I shall so push you (Christ willing) as to make you heartily repent that you ever published your *Diatribe*.

This, therefore, is also essentially necessary and wholesome for Christians to know: that God foreknows nothing by contingency, but that He foresees, purposes, and does all things according to His immutable, eternal, and infallible will. By this thunderbolt free will is thrown prostrate and utterly dashed to pieces. Those, therefore, who would assert free will must either deny this thunderbolt, or pretend not to see it, or push it from them. But, before I establish this point by any arguments of my own, and by the authority of Scripture, I will first set it forth in your words.

Are you not then the person, friend Erasmus, who just now asserted that God is by nature just and by nature most merciful? If this be true, does it not follow that He is *immutably* just and merciful? That as His nature is not changed to all eternity, so neither His justice nor His mercy? And what is said concerning His justice and His mercy must be said also concerning His knowledge, His wisdom, His goodness, His will, and His other attributes. If therefore these things are asserted religiously, piously, and wholesomely concerning God, as you say yourself, what has come to you that, contrary to your own self, you now assert that it is irreligious, curious, and vain to say that God foreknows of necessity? You openly declare that the immutable *will* of God is to be known, but you forbid the knowledge of His immutable *prescience*. Do you believe that He foreknows against His will or that He wills in ignorance? If, then, He foreknows, willing, His will is eternal and immovable, because His nature is so; and, if He wills, foreknowing, His knowledge is eternal and immovable, because His nature is so. . . .

How copious an orator! And yet you understand nothing of what you are saying. In a word, you treat this discussion as though it were some matter, between you and me only, about the recovering of some money that was at stake, or some other trivial thing, the loss of which, as being of much less consideration than the general peace of the community, ought not so to concern anyone, but that he may yield, act, and suffer upon the occasion in any way that may prevent the necessity of the whole world being thrown into a tumult. Wherein, you plainly evince that this peace and tranquility of the flesh are, with you, a matter of far greater consideration than faith, than conscience, than salvation, than the Word of God, than the glory of Christ, than God Himself! Wherefore let me tell you this, and I entreat you to let it sink deep into your mind: I am, in this discussion, seeking an object solemn and essential; nay, such, and so great, that it ought to be maintained and defended through death itself; and that, although the whole world should not only be thrown into tumult and set in arms thereby, but even if it should be hurled into chaos and reduced to nothing. If you cannot receive this, or if you are not affected by it, do you mind your own business, and allow us to receive it and to be affected by it, to whom it is given of God.

For, by the grace of God, I am not so great a fool or madman as to have desired to sustain and defend this cause so long, with so much fortitude and so much firmness (which you call obstinacy), in the face of so many dangers of my life, so much hatred, so many traps laid for me; in a word, in the face of the fury of men and devils—I have not done this for money, for that I neither have nor desire; nor for vainglory, for that, if I wished, I could not obtain in a world so enraged against me; nor for the life for my body, for that cannot be made sure of for an hour. Do you think, then, that you only have a heart that is moved by these tumults? Yet I am not made of stone, nor was I born from the Marpesian rocks. But since it cannot be otherwise, I choose rather to be battered in temporal tumult, happy in the grace of God, for God's Word's sake, which is to be maintained with a mind incorrupt and invincible, than to be ground to powder in eternal tumult, under the wrath of God and torments intolerable! May Christ grant, what I desire and hope, that your heart may not be such—but certainly your words imply, that, with Epicurus, you consider the Word of God and a future life to be mere fables. For, in your instructions, you would have us, for the sake of the popes, the heads, and the peace of the community, to put off, upon an occasion, and depart from the all-certain word of God: whereas, if we put off that, we put off God, faith, salvation, and all Christianity together. How far different from this is the instruction of Christ—that we should rather despise the whole world! . . .

"Who," you say, "will endeavour to amend his life?" I answer, "No man! No man can!" For your self-amenders without the Spirit, God regardeth not, for they are hypocrites. But the Elect, and those that fear God, will be amended by the Holy Spirit; the rest will perish unamended. Nor does Augustine say that the works of *none*, nor that the works of *all* are crowned, but the works of *some*. Therefore there will be *some* who shall amend their lives.

"Who will believe," you say, "that he is loved of God?" I answer, "No man will believe it! No man can!" But the Elect shall believe it; the rest shall perish without believing it, filled with indignation and blaspheming, as you here describe them. Therefore there will be *some* who shall believe it.

And as to your saying that "by these doctrines the floodgate of iniquity is thrown open unto men"—be it so. They pertain to that leprosy of evil to be borne, spoken of before. Nevertheless, by the same doctrines, there is thrown open to the Elect, and to them that fear God, a gate unto righteousness—an entrance into heaven, a way unto God! But if, according to your advice, we should refrain from these doctrines, and should hide from men this Word of God, so that each, deluded by a false persuasion of salvation, should never learn to fear God, and should never be humbled, in order that through this fear he might come to grace and love; then, indeed, we should shut up your floodgate to purpose! For in the room of it, we should throw open to ourselves and to all, wide gates, nay, yawning chasms and sweeping tides, not only unto iniquity, but unto the depths of hell! Thus we should not enter into heaven ourselves, and them that were entering in we should hinder. . . .

God has promised certainly His grace to the humbled: that is, to the self-deploring and despairing. But a man cannot be thoroughly humbled until he comes to know that his salvation is utterly beyond his own powers, counsel, endeavours, will, and works, and absolutely depending on the will, counsel, pleasure, and work of another, that is, of God only. For if, as long as he has any persuasion that he can do even the least thing himself towards his own salvation, he retain a confidence in himself and do not utterly despair in himself, so long he is not humbled before God; but he proposes to himself some place, some time, or some work, whereby he may at length attain unto salvation. But he who hesitates not to depend wholly upon the good will of God, he totally despairs in himself, chooses nothing for himself, but waits for God to work in him; and such a one is the nearest unto grace. . . .

These things, therefore, are openly proclaimed for the sake of the Elect; that, being by these means humbled and brought down to nothing, they might be saved. The rest resist this humiliation; nay, they condemn the teaching of self-desperation; they wish to have left a little something that they may do themselves. These secretly remain proud, and adversaries to the grace of God. This, I say, is one reason: that those who fear God, being humbled, might know, call upon, and receive the grace of God. . . .

This is the highest degree of faith—to believe that He is merciful, who saves so few and damns so many; to believe Him just, who according to His own will makes us necessarily damnable, that He may seem, as Erasmus says, "to delight in the torments of the miserable, and to be an object of hatred rather than of love." If, therefore, I could by any means comprehend how that same God can be merciful and just who carries the appearance of so much wrath and iniquity, there would be no need of faith. But now, since that cannot be comprehended, there is room for exercising faith, while such things are preached and openly proclaimed: in the same manner as, while God kills, the faith of life is exercised in death. . . .

As to the other paradox you mention, that "whatever is done by us is not done by free will but from mere necessity." Let us briefly consider this, lest we should suffer anything most perniciously spoken to pass by unnoticed. Here then, I observe, that if it be proved that our salvation is apart from our own strength and counsel, and depends on the working of God alone (which I hope I shall clearly prove hereafter, in the course of this discussion), does it not evidently follow that when God is not present with us to work in us, everything that we do is evil, and that we of necessity do those things which are of no avail unto salvation? For if it is not we ourselves, but God only, that works salvation in us, it must follow . . . that we do nothing unto salvation *before* the working of God in us. . . .

But again, on the other hand, when God works in us, the *will*, being changed and sweetly breathed on by the Spirit of God, desires and acts, not from *compulsion*, but *responsively*, from pure willingness, inclination, and accord; so that it cannot be turned another way by anything contrary, nor be compelled or overcome even by the gates of hell; but it still goes on to desire, crave after, and love that which is good; even as before it desired, craved after, and loved that which was evil. This, again, experience proves. How invincible and unshaken are holy men, when, by violence and other oppressions, they are only compelled and irritated the more to crave after good! Even as fire is rather fanned into flames than extinguished by the wind. So that neither is there here any willingness, or free will, to turn itself into another direction, or to desire anything else, while the influence of the Spirit and grace of God remain in the man.

In a word, if we be under the god of this world, without the operation and Spirit of God, we are led captives by him at his will, as Paul saith. So that we cannot will anything but that which he wills. For he is that "strong man armed," who so keepeth his palace that those whom he holds captive are kept in peace, that they might not cause any motion or feeling against him; otherwise the kingdom of Satan, being divided against itself, could not stand; whereas Christ affirms it does stand. And all this we do willingly and desiringly, according to the nature of *will*: for if it were forced, it would be no longer *will*. For compulsion is (so to speak) *unwillingness*. But if the "stronger than he" come and overcome him, and take us as His spoils, then, through the Spirit, we are His servants and captives (which is the royal liberty), that we may desire and do, willingly, what He wills.

Thus the human will is, as it were, a beast between the two. If God sit thereon, it wills and goes where God will: as the Psalm saith, "I am become as it were a beast before thee, and I am continually with thee." If Satan sit thereon, it wills and goes as Satan will. Nor is it in the power of its own will to choose, to which rider it will run, nor which it will seek; but the riders themselves contend, which shall have and hold it. . . .

I shall here draw this book to a conclusion, prepared if it were necessary to pursue this discussion still further. Though I consider that I have now abundantly satisfied the godly man, who wishes to believe the truth without making resistance. For if we believe it to be true that God foreknows and foreordains all things; that He can be neither deceived nor hindered in His Prescience and Predestination; and that nothing can take place but according to His will (which reason herself is compelled to confess), then, even according to the testimony of reason herself, there can be no free will in man, in angel, or in any creature!

From *The Bondage of the Will*, trans. Henry Cole, corrected by H. Atherton (Grand Rapids, Mich.: Wm. B. Eerdmans, 1931).

Free Will and Predestination

JOHN CALVIN

1537

SINCE we have seen that the domination of sin, from the time of its subjugation of the first man, not only extends over the whole race, but also exclusively possesses every soul; it now remains to be more closely investigated, whether we are despoiled of all freedom, and, if any particle of it yet remain, how far its power extends. But that we may the more easily discover the truth of this question, I will first set up by the way a mark, by which our whole course must be regulated. The best method of guarding against error is to consider the dangers which threaten us on every side. For when man is declared to be destitute of all rectitude, he immediately makes it an occasion of slothfulness; and because he is said to have no power of himself for the pursuit of righteousness, he totally neglects it, as though it did not at all concern him. On the other hand, he cannot arrogate anything to himself, be it ever so little, without God being robbed of His honour, and himself being endangered by presumptuous temerity. Therefore to avoid striking on either of these rocks, this will be the course to be pursued: that man, being taught that he has nothing good left in his possession, and being surrounded on every side with the most miserable necessity, should nevertheless be instructed to aspire to the good of which he is destitute, and to the liberty of which he is deprived; and should be roused from indolence with more earnestness than if he were supposed to be possessed of the greatest strength. The necessity of the latter is obvious to everyone. The former, I perceive, is doubted by more than it ought to be. For this being placed beyond all controversy, that man must not be deprived of anything that properly belongs to him, it ought also to be manifest how important it is that he should be prevented from false boasting. For if he was not even then permitted to glory in himself, when by the divine beneficence he was decorated with the noblest ornaments, how much ought he now to be humbled, when on account of his ingratitude he has been hurled from the summit of glory to the abyss of ignominy? At that time, I say, when he was exalted to the most honourable eminence, the Scripture attributes nothing to him, but that he was created after the image of God; which certainly implies that his happiness consisted not in any goodness of his own, but in a participation of God. What then remains for him now, deprived of all glory, but that he acknowledge God, to whose beneficence he could not be thankful when he abounded in the riches of His favour? and that he now at least by a confession of his poverty glorify Him, whom he glorified not by an acknowledgment of His blessings? It is also no less conducive to our interest than to the divine glory that all the praise of wisdom and strength be taken away from us; so that they join sacrilege to our fall, who ascribe to us anything more than truly belongs to us. For what else is the consequence, when we are taught to contend in our own strength, but that we are lifted into the air on a reed, which being soon broken, we fall to the ground. Though our strength is placed in too favourable a point of view, when it is compared to a reed. For it is nothing but smoke, whatever vain men have imagined and pretend concerning it. Wherefore it is not without reason that that remarkable sentence is so frequently repeated by Augustine, that free will is rather overthrown than established even by its own advocates. It was necessary to premise these things for the sake of some who, when they hear that human power is completely subverted in order that the power of God may be established in man, inveterately hate this whole argument, as dangerous and unprofitable: which yet appears to be highly useful to us, and essential to true religion. . . .

Now when I assert that the will, being deprived of its liberty, is necessarily drawn or led into evil, I should wonder if anyone considered it as a harsh expression, since it has nothing in it absurd, nor is it unsanctioned by the custom of good men. It offends those who know not how to distinguish between necessity and compulsion. But if anyone should ask them whether God is not necessarily good, and whether the devil is not necessarily evil, what answer will they make? For there is such a close connection between the goodness of God and His divinity that His deity is not more necessary than His goodness. But the devil is by his fall so alienated from communion with all that is good that he can do nothing but what is evil. But if anyone should sacrilegiously object that little praise is due to God for His goodness, which He is constrained to preserve, shall we not readily reply that His inability to do evil arises from His infinite goodness and not from the impulse of violence? Therefore if a necessity of doing well impairs not the liberty of the divine will in doing well; if the devil, who cannot but do evil, nevertheless sins voluntarily; who then will assert that man sins less voluntarily, because he is under a necessity of sinning? This necessity Augustine everywhere maintains, and even when he was pressed with the cavils of Celestius, who tried to throw an odium on this doctrine, he confidently expressed himself in these terms: "By means of liberty it came to pass that man fell into sin; but now the penal depravity consequent on it, instead of liberty, has introduced necessity." And whenever the mention of this subject occurs, he hesitates not to speak in this manner of the necessary servitude of sin. We must therefore observe this grand point of distinction, that man, having been corrupted by his fall, sins voluntarily, not with reluctance or constraint; with the strongest propensity of disposition, not with violent coercion; with the bias of his own passions, and not with external compulsion: yet such is the pravity of his nature that he cannot be excited and biased to anything but what is evil. . . . From these passages the reader clearly perceives that I am teaching no novel doctrine, but what was long ago advanced by Augustine with the universal consent of pious men, and which for nearly a thousand years after was confined to the cloisters of monks. But [Peter] Lombard, for want of knowing how to distinguish necessity from coaction, gave rise to a pernicious error. . . .

It has now, I apprehend, been sufficiently proved that man is so enslaved by sin as to be of his own nature incapable of an effort or even an aspiration towards that which is good. We have also laid down a distinction between coaction and necessity, from which it appears that while he sins necessarily, he nevertheless sins voluntarily. But since, while he is devoted to the servitude of the devil, he seems to be actuated by his will rather than by his own, it remains for us to explain the nature of both kinds of influence. There is also this question to be resolved, whether anything is to be attributed to God in evil actions, in which the Scripture intimates that some influence of His is concerned. Augustine somewhere compares the human will to a horse, obedient to the direction of his rider: and God and the devil he compares to riders. "If God rides it, He, like a sober and skilful rider, manages it in a graceful manner: stimulates its tardiness, restrains its immoderate celerity, represses its wantonness and wildness, tames its perverseness, and conducts it into the right way. But if the devil has taken possession of it, he, like a foolish and wanton rider, forces it through pathless places, hurries it into ditches, drives it down over precipices, and excites it to obstinacy and ferocity." With this similitude, as no better occurs, we will at present be content. When the will of a natural man is said to be subject to the power of the devil, so as to be directed by it, the meaning is, not that it resists and is compelled to a reluctant submission, as masters compel slaves to an unwilling performance of their commands; but that, being fascinated by the fallacies of Satan, it necessarily submits itself to all his directions. For those whom the Lord does not favour with the government of His Spirit, He abandons in righteous judgment to the influence of Satan. . . .

The covenant of life not being equally preached to all, and among those to whom it is preached not always finding the same reception, this diversity discovers the wonderful depth of the divine judgment. Nor is it to be doubted that this variety also follows, subject to the decision of God's eternal election. If it be evidently the result of the divine will that salvation is freely offered to some and others are prevented from attaining it, this immediately gives rise to important and difficult questions, which are incapable of any other explication than by the establishment of pious minds in what ought to be received concerning election and predestination: a question, in the opinion of many, full of perplexity; for they consider nothing more unreasonable than that of the common mass of mankind some should be predestinated to salvation and others to destruction. But how unreasonably they perplex themselves will afterwards appear from the sequel of our discourse. Besides, the very obscurity which excites such dread not only displays the utility of this doctrine, but shows it to be productive of the most delightful benefit. We shall never be clearly convinced as we ought to be, that our salvation flows from the fountain of God's free mercy, till we are acquainted with his eternal election, which illustrates the grace of God by this comparison, that He adopts not all promiscuously to the hope of salvation, but gives to some what He refuses to others. Ignorance of this principle evidently detracts from the divine glory and diminishes real humility. But, according to Paul, what is so necessary to be known never can be known, unless God, without any regard to works, chooses those whom He has decreed. "At this present time also, there is a remnant according to the election of grace. And if by grace, then it is no more of works: otherwise, grace is no more grace. But if it be of works, then it is no more grace: otherwise, work is no more work." If we need to be recalled to the origin of election to prove that we obtain salvation from no other source than the mere goodness of God, they who desire to extinguish this principle do all they can to obscure what ought to be magnificently and loudly celebrated, and to pluck up humility by the roots. In ascribing the salvation of the remnant of the people to the election of grace, Paul clearly testifies that it is then only known that God saves whom He will of His mere good pleasure, and does not dispense a reward to which there can be no claim. They who shut the gates to prevent anyone from presuming to approach and taste this doctrine do no less injury to man than to God; for nothing else will be sufficient to produce in us suitable humility, or to impress us with a due sense of our great obligations to God. Nor is there any other basis for solid confidence, even according to the authority of Christ, who, to deliver us from all fear, and render us invincible amidst so many dangers, snares, and deadly conflicts, promises to preserve in safety all whom the Father hath committed to His care. Whence we infer that they who know not themselves to be God's peculiar people will be tortured with continual anxiety; and therefore that the interest of all the faithful, as well as their own, is very badly consulted by those who, blind to the three advantages we have remarked, would wholly remove the foundation of our salvation. And hence the Church rises to our view; which otherwise, as Bernard justly observes, could neither be discovered nor recognized among creatures, being in two respects wonderfully concealed in the bosom of a blessed predestination, and in the mass of a miserable damnation. But before I enter on the subject itself, I must address some preliminary observations to two sorts of persons. The discussion of predestination, a subject of itself rather intricate, is made very perplexed, and therefore dangerous, by human curiosity, which no barriers can restrain from wandering into forbidden labyrinths and soaring beyond its sphere, as if determined to leave none of the divine secrets unscrutinized or unexplored. As we see multitudes everywhere guilty of this arrogance and presumption, and among them some who are not censurable in other respects, it is proper to admonish them of the bounds of their duty on this subject. First, then: let them remember that when they inquire into predestination they penetrate the inmost recesses of divine wisdom, where the careless and confident intruder will obtain no satisfaction to his curiosity, but will enter a labyrinth from which he will find no way to depart.

For it is unreasonable that man should scrutinize with impunity those things which the Lord hath determined to be hidden in Himself; and investigate, even from eternity, that sublimity of wisdom which God would have us to adore and not comprehend, to promote our admiration of His glory. The secrets of His will which He determined to reveal to us He discovers in His Word; and these are all that He foresaw would concern us, or conduce to our advantage. . . .

Predestination, by which God adopts some to the hope of life and adjudges others to eternal death, no one, desirous of the credit of piety, dares absolutely to deny. But it is involved in many cavils, especially by those who make foreknowledge the cause of it. We maintain that both belong to God; but it is preposterous to represent one as dependent on the other. When we attribute foreknowledge to God, we mean that all things have ever been, and perpetually remain, before His eyes, so that to His knowledge nothing is future or past, but all things are present: and present in such a manner that He does not merely conceive of them from ideas formed in His mind, as things remembered by us appear present to our minds, but really beholds and sees them as if actually placed before Him. And this foreknowledge extends to the whole world and to all the creatures. Predestination we call the eternal decree of God, by which He hath determined in Himself what He would have to become of every individual of mankind. For they are not all created with a similar destiny; but eternal life is foreordained for some, and eternal damnation for others. Every man, therefore, being created for one or the other of these ends, we say, he is predestinated either to life or to death.

From *Institutes of the Christian Religion*, trans. John Allen (New Haven, 1816).

True Christian Piety

The Brethren of the Common Life

THOMAS A KEMPIS

Early fifteenth century

SUCH WAS the inclination amongst the people to hear the Word of God that the Church could scarcely contain the crowd that came together. Many left their food, and, being drawn by a hunger after righteousness, postponed their urgent business and ran together to hear his discourses: he often delivered two sermons in one day, and sometimes continued preaching for three hours or more when fervency of spirit took hold upon him. He preached in the chief cities of the diocese of Utrecht, Deventer, and Zwolle; in Kempen often, and in Utrecht itself before the assembled clergy; in the country of Holland at Leyden, Delft, and Ghent; in Amsterdam (where he delivered his first sermon in the vulgar tongue) and in various other towns and well-known villages where he hoped to gather fruit and to bring forth new children for God. Blessed be God, who sending His Holy Spirit from Above kindled the hearts of His faithful people, and mightily increased them, so that from the seed of a few converts there grew many companies of devout brethren and sisters who served

712

God in chastity; and to them several monasteries of monks and holy nuns owed the origin of their godly life.

It is the great glory of Master Gerard [Groote] that by his preaching so great a tree was planted and watered, a tree which after his death, though but newly set in the ground, ceased not to flourish in the field of the Lord. Although this religious order and these communities of devout persons were first planted in the nearer parts of Holland, Gelders and Brabant, they afterwards spread rapidly to the more remote regions of Flanders, Frisia, Westphalia, and Saxony, for God prospered them, and the sweet savour of their good reputation reached even to the Apostolic See.

Now the venerable Master Gerard, being filled with the Holy Ghost, and perceiving that by little and little the number of his disciples was increasing and that they were burning with zeal for heavenly warfare, took due care and forethought that the devout might come together from time to time into one house for mutual exhortation, and that they might deal faithfully with one another of the things pertaining to God and to the keeping of the law of Charity: and he ordained that if any should wish to abide continually together, they should earn their own living by the labour of their hands, and, as far as might be, live in common under the discipline of the Church. He allowed none to beg in the public ways unless compelled by evident necessity, nor toilsomely to go round from house to house to obtain alms, but rather he ordered them to remain at home, and, as St. Paul taught, to be diligent in the labour of their hands, but not to engage in any business which might hinder their devotion in the hope of greater gain, lest at the instigation of the devil there might be given to the weak some occasion of falling back into their former naughty ways.

He had it in mind to build a monastery for clerks of the Order of Regular Canons, for he wished to move some of those clerks who followed him and were fitted for such a life to take the religious habit in order that they might serve as an example to other devout persons, and show the way of holiness to any clerks or lay folk that came from elsewhere.

He was moved to institute this religious order chiefly by the especial love and reverence he had for that venerable John Ruysbroek, the first prior of Grünthal, and for the other brethren in the same place, who lived the religious life and were without reproach. These were they whom he had visited in person in Brabant; in them he observed, and from them derived, a mode of life greatly tending to edification by reason of their deep humility and the wearing of a simple garb.

But although he busied himself with all diligence to find a place and a monastery fitted for the religious life, he could not accomplish the end which he desired, for death was beforehand with him; yet in the sight of God the King immortal, invisible, the Founder of all things, the intention was counted as if it were the fulfilment of his design, and he bequeathed his desire to build a religious house to those most beloved disciples whom he had converted, exhorting them not to let so great a purpose fall into forgetfulness when he was dead, but to unite in lending their aid and counsel in carrying it out so as to further the glory of God. Some of these disciples were they who dwelt in the monastery of Windesheim, and also they who with the help of God first founded the house of Agnietenburg near Zwolle. . . .

When I had come to study in Deventer, in the days of my youth, I sought the way to the Regulars at Windesheim, and having found there the Canons Regu-

lar, amongst whom was my brother, I was led by his
advice to approach that most reverend man Master
Florentius [Radewyns], who was vicar of the Church
of Deventer, a devout priest, whose most excellent fame
had already reached the Upper Provinces, and had
drawn my mind to love him: for a great multitude of
scholars used to praise him for his conduct of holy
things. Both his appearance and his words confirmed
his righteous reputation, and he was in favour in the
sight of all men, for indeed he was a true worshipper
of God and most devoted in his reverence for our Holy
Mother the Church.

When I came into the presence of the reverend
Father he kept me for a while with him in his house,
being moved thereto by fatherly affection; and he
placed me in the school, and besides this gave me the
books which he thought I needed. Afterwards he obtained for me a lodging, at no cost to myself, with a
certain honourable and devout matron, who often
showed kindness to me and many other clerks. So being
associated with this man who was so holy, and with the
Brothers of his Order, I had their devout lives daily in
my mind and before my eyes, and I took pleasure and
delight in the contemplation of their godly conduct,
and in the gracious words which proceeded from the
mouths of these humble men. Never before could I
recollect to have seen such men, so devout and fervent
were they in the love of God and of their neighbour.
Living in the world, they had no part in the life thereof,
and seemed to take no heed to worldly business. Remaining at home, they laboured carefully in copying
books, being instant continually in sacred study and
devout meditation. In the hours of labour they had
recourse to ejaculatory prayer for their consolation; in
the morning, having said Matins, they went to the

church, and during the celebration of Mass they poured forth as an offering to God the first fruits of their mouth and the aspirations of their heart, and, prostrating the body, lifted up their pure hands and the eyes of their soul to Heaven, seeking by prayer and lamentation to reconcile God to them through the Saving Host.

The first founder and the spiritual ruler of this notable community was Master Florentius, who was adorned with virtue and filled with divine wisdom and understanding in his knowledge of Christ, because he, with his priests and clerks, humbly imitated the manner of the apostolic life. These men, therefore, having one heart and mind in God, brought every man what was his own into the common stock, and, receiving simple food and clothing, avoided taking thought for the morrow. Of their own will they devoted themselves to God, and all busied themselves in obeying their rector or his vicar, and, holding holy obedience as the highest rule, strove with all their strength to conquer self, to resist the passions, and to break down their own will, and besides this they sought earnestly to be gravely admonished for any acts of omission and neglect. For this reason there was in them much grace and true devotion: and they edified many by their words and example; likewise, by patiently abiding the mockery of the world, they led many to despise the same, and those who had formerly contemned them and considered their life—which was without honour—as a folly, afterwards being converted to God, and, having experienced the grace of devotion, were compelled by their consciences to confess openly that these men were truly servants and friends of God.

From *The Founders of the New Devotion*, trans. J. P. Arthur (London: Kegan Paul, Trench, Trübner & Co., 1905).

Members of One Body
ERASMUS OF ROTTERDAM

1501

LET THIS excellent learning and paradoxes of the true Christian faith be sure and steadfast with thee, that no Christian man may think that he is born for himself: neither ought to have the mind to live to himself: but whatsoever he hath, whatsoever he is, that altogether let him ascribe not to himself, but unto God the author thereof, and of whom it came, all his goods let him think to be common to all men. The charity of a Christian man knoweth no property: let him love good men in Christ, evil men for Christ's sake, which so loved us first when we were yet His enemies, that He bestowed Himself on us altogether for our redemption: let him embrace the one because they be good: the other nevertheless to make them good: he shall hate no man at all, no more verily than a faithful physician hateth a sick man. Let him be an enemy only unto vices: the greater the disease is, the greater cure will pure charity put thereto: he is an adulterer, he hath committed sacrilege, he is a Turk: let a Christian man defy the adulterer, not the man: let him despise the committer of sacrilege, not the man: let him kill the Turk, not the man: let him find the means that the evil man perish such as he hath made himself to be, but let the man be saved whom God made: let him will well, wish well, and do well, to all men unfeignedly: neither hurt them which have deserved it, but do good to them which have not deserved it; let him be glad of all men's commodities as well as of his own, and also be sorry for all men's harms none otherwise than for his own. For verily this is that which the Apostle commandeth: to weep with them that weep, to joy with them that joy, yea let him rather take another man's harm grievouser than his own: and of his brother's wealth be gladder than of his own.

It is not a Christian man's part to think on this wise: what have I to do with this fellow, I know not whether he be black or white, he is unknown to me, he is a stranger to me, he never did aught for me, he hath hurt me sometime, but did me never good. Think none of these things: remember only for what deserving can those things which Christ hath done for thee, which would His kindness done to thee, should be recompensed, not in Himself, but in thy neighbour. Only see of what things he hath need, and what thou art able to do for him. Think this thing only, he is my brother in our Lord, co-heir in Christ, a member of the same body, redeemed with one blood, a fellow in the common faith, called unto the very same grace and felicity of the life to come, even as the Apostle said, one body and one spirit as ye be called in one hope of your calling, one lord and one faith, one baptism, one God, and Father of all which is above all and everywhere, and in all us. How can he be a stranger to whom thou art coupled with so manifold bonds of unity? Among the Gentiles let those circumstances of rhetoricians be of no little value and weight, either unto benevolence or unto malevolence, he is a citizen of the same city, he is of alliance, he is my cousin, he is my familiar friend, he is my father's friend, he hath well deserved, he is kind, born of an honest stock, rich or otherwise. In Christ all these things either be nothing, or after the mind of Paul be all one, and the very self-same thing: let this be ever present before thine eyes and let this suffice thee, he is my flesh, he is my brother in Christ. Whatsoever is bestowed upon any member, reboundeth if not to all the body, and from thence into the head?

We all be members each one of another, members cleaving together make a body. The head of the body is Jesu Christ, the head of Christ is God. It is done to thee it is done to everyone, it is done to Christ it is done to God: whatsoever is done to any one member whichsoever it be, whether it be well done or evil: all these things are one, God, Christ, the body, and the members. That saying hath no place conveniently among Christian men, like with like. And the other saying, diversity is mother of hate: for unto what purpose pertain words of dissension where so great unity is, it savoureth not of Christian faith that commonly a courtier to a town dweller: one of the country to an inhabiter of the city: a man of high degree, to another of low degree: an officer, to him that is officeless: the rich to the poor: a man of honour, to a vile person: the mighty to the weak: the Italian to the German: the Frenchman to the Englishman: the English to the Scot: the grammarian to the divine: the logician to the grammarian: the physician to the man of law: the learned to the unlearned: the eloquent to him that is not facund and lacketh utterance: the single to the married: the young to the old; the clerk to the layman: the priest to the monk: the Carmelites to the Jacobites: and that (lest I rehearse all diversities) in a very trifle unlike to unlike, is somewhat partial and unkind: where is charity which loveth even his enemy: when the surname changed, when the colour of the vesture a little altered, when the girdle or the shoe and like fantasies of men make me hated unto thee? Why rather leave we not these childish trifles, and accustom to have before our eyes that which pertaineth to the very thing: whereof Paul warneth us in many places, that all we in Christ our head be members of one body, endued with life by one spirit (if so be we live in him) so that we should neither envy the happier members, and should gladly succour and aid the weak members: that we might perceive that we ourselves have received a good turn, when we have done any benefit to our neighbour: and that we ourselves be hurt, when hurt is done to our brother: and that we might understand how no man ought to study privately for himself, but every man for his own part should bestow in common that thing which he hath received of God, that all things might redound and rebound thither again, from whence they sprung, that is to wit, from the head.

This verily is the thing which Paul writeth to the Corinthians, saying, As the body is one and hath many members, and all the members of the body though they be many, yet be they but one body: even so likewise is Christ, for in one spirit we be all baptized to make one body, whether we be Jews or Gentiles, whether we be bond or free, and all we have drunk of one spirit, for the body (saith Paul) is not one member but many: if the foot shall say, I am not the hand, I am not of the body: is he therefore not of the body? If the ear shall say, I am not the eye, I am not of the body: is he therefore not of the body? If all the body should be the eye, where is then the hearing: if all the body were the hearing, where then should be the smelling? But now God hath put the members every one of them in the body, as it pleased him: for if all were but one member, where were the body? but now verily be there many members, yet but one body. The eye cannot say to the hand I have no need of thy help, or again the head to the feet, ye be not to me necessary: but those members of the body which seem to be the weaker are much more necessary: and to those which we think to be the viler members of the body we give more abundant honour: and those which be our unhonest members have more abundant honesty, for our honest members have need of nothing. But God hath tempered and ordered the body, giving plenteous honour to that part which lacked, because there should be no division, debate, or strife in the body, but that the members should care one for another indifferently. But it is ye which are the body of Christ and members one depending of another.

From *Enchiridion militis christiani*, trans. William Tyndale? (London: Wynkyn de Worde, 1533).

The Faith of a Christian

MARTIN LUTHER

1520

CHRISTIAN FAITH has appeared to many an easy thing; nay, not a few even reckon it among the social virtues, as it were; and this they do because they have not made proof of it experimentally, and have never tasted of what efficacy it is. For it is not possible for any man to write well about it, or to understand well what is rightly written, who has not at some time tasted of its spirit, under the pressure of tribulation; while he who has tasted of it, even to a very small extent, can never write, speak, think, or hear about it sufficiently. For it is a living fountain, springing up unto eternal life, as Christ calls it in John 4.

Now, though I cannot boast of my abundance, and though I know how poorly I am furnished, yet I hope that, after having been vexed by various temptations, I have attained some little drop of faith, and that I can speak of this matter, if not with more elegance, certainly with more solidity, than those literal and too subtle disputants who have hitherto discoursed upon it without understanding their own words. That I may open then an easier way for the ignorant—for these alone I am trying to serve—I first lay down two propositions, concerning spiritual liberty and servitude:

A Christian man is the most free lord of all, and subject to none; a Christian man is the most dutiful servant of all, and subject to everyone.

Although these statements appear contradictory, yet, when they are found to agree together, they will do excellently for my purpose. They are both the statements of Paul himself, who says, "Though I be free from all men, yet have I made myself a servant unto all" (I Cor. 9:19), and "Owe no man anything but to love one another" (Rom. 13:8). Now love is by its own nature dutiful and obedient to the beloved object. Thus even Christ, though Lord of all things, was yet made of a woman; made under the law; at once free and a servant; at once in the form of God and in the form of a servant.

Let us examine the subject on a deeper and less simple principle. Man is composed of a twofold nature, a spiritual and a bodily. As regards the spiritual nature, which they name the soul, he is called the spiritual, inward, new man; as regards the bodily nature, which they name the flesh, he is called the fleshly, outward, old man. The Apostle speaks of this: "Though our outward man perish, yet the inward man is renewed day by day" (II Cor. 4:16). The result of this diversity is that in the Scriptures opposing statements are made concerning the same man, the fact being that in the same man these two men are opposed to one another; the flesh lusting against the spirit, and the spirit against the flesh (Gal. 5:17).

We first approach the subject of the inward man, that we may see by what means a man becomes justified, free, and a true Christian; that is, a spiritual, new, and inward man. It is certain that absolutely none among outward things, under whatever name they may be reckoned, has any influence in producing Christian righteousness or liberty, nor, on the other hand, unrighteousness or slavery. This can be shown by an easy argument.

What can it profit to the soul that the body should be in good condition, free, and full of life, that it should eat, drink, and act according to its pleasure, when even the most impious slaves of every kind of vice are prosperous in these matters? Again, what harm can ill health, bondage, hunger, thirst, or any other outward evil, do to the soul, when even the most pious of men, and the freest in the purity of their conscience, are harassed by these things? Neither of these states of things has to do with the liberty or the slavery of the soul.

And so it will profit nothing that the body should be adorned with sacred vestments, or dwell in holy places, or be occupied in sacred offices, or pray, fast, and abstain from certain meats, or do whatever works can be done through the body and in the body. Something widely different will be necessary for the justification and liberty of the soul, since the things I have spoken of can be done by an impious person, and only hypocrites are produced by devotion to these things. On the other hand, it will not at all injure the soul that the body should be clothed in profane raiment, should dwell in profane places, should eat and drink in the ordinary fashion, should not pray aloud, and should leave undone all the things above mentioned, which may be done by hypocrites.

And—to cast everything aside—even speculations, meditations, and whatever things can be performed by the exertions of the soul itself are of no profit. One thing, and one alone, is necessary for life, justification, and Christian liberty; and that is the most Holy Word of God, the Gospel of Christ, as He says, "I am the resurrection and the life; he that believeth in me shall not die eternally" (John 9:25), and also, "If the Son shall make you free, ye shall be free indeed" (John 8:36), and, "Man shall not live by bread alone, but by every word that proceedeth out of the mouth of God" (Matt. 4:4).

Let us therefore hold it for certain and firmly established that the soul can do without everything except the Word of God, without which none at all of its wants is provided for. But, having the Word, it is rich and wants for nothing, since that is the Word of life, of truth, of light, of peace, of justification, of salvation, of joy, of liberty, of wisdom, of virtue, of grace, of glory, and of every good thing. It is on this account that the prophet in a whole Psalm (Psalm 119), and in many other places, signs for and calls upon the Word of God with so many groanings and words. . . .

But you will ask, "What is this Word, and by what means is it to be used, since there are so many words of God?" I answer, "The Apostle Paul (Rom. 1) explains what it is, namely the Gospel of God, concerning His Son, incarnate, suffering, risen, and glorified through the Spirit, the Sanctifier." To preach Christ is to feed the soul, to justify it, to set it free, and to save it, if it

believes the preaching. For faith alone, and the efficacious use of the Word of God, bring salvation. "If thou
shalt confess with thy mouth the Lord Jesus, and shalt
believe in thine heart that God hath raised Him from
the dead, thou shalt be saved" (Rom. 9:9); and again,
"Christ is the end of the law for righteousness to everyone that believeth" (Rom. 9:4), and "The just shall
live by faith" (Rom. 1:17). For the Word of God cannot be received and honoured by any works but by
faith alone. Hence it is clear that as the soul needs the
Word alone for life and justification, so it is justified by
faith alone, and not by any works. For if it could be
justified by any other means, it would have no need
of the word, nor consequently of faith.

But this faith cannot consist at all with works; that
is, if you imagine that you can be justified by those
works, whatever they are, along with it. For this would
be to halt between two opinions, to worship Baal, and
to kiss the hand to him, which is a very great iniquity,
as Job says. Therefore, when you begin to believe, you
learn at the same time that all that is in you is utterly
guilty, sinful, and damnable, according to that saying,
"All have sinned, and come short of the glory of God"
(Rom. 3:23), and also, "There is none righteous, no,
not one; they are all gone out of the way; they are
together become unprofitable: there is none that doeth
good, no, not one" (Rom. 3:10-12). When you have
learned this, you will know that Christ is necessary
for you, since He has suffered and risen again for you,
that, believing on Him, you might by this faith become
another man, all your sins being remitted, and you
being justified by the merits of another, namely Christ
alone.

Since then this faith can reign only in the inward
man, as it is said, "With the heart man believeth unto

righteousness" (Rom. 9:10); and since it alone justifies, it is evident that by no outward work or labour can the inward man be at all justified, made free, and saved; and that no works whatever have any relation to him. And so, on the other hand, it is solely by impiety and incredulity of heart that he becomes guilty and a slave of sin, deserving condemnation, not by any outward sin or work. Therefore the first care of every Christian ought to be to lay aside all reliance on works, and strengthen his faith alone more and more, and by it grow in the knowledge, not of works, but of Christ Jesus, who has suffered and risen again for him, as Peter teaches (I Peter 5) when he makes no other work to be a Christian one. Thus Christ, when the Jews asked Him what they should do that they might work the works of God, rejected the multitude of works, with which He saw that they were puffed up, and commanded them one thing only, saying, "This is the work of God: that ye believe on Him whom He hath sent, for Him hath God the Father sealed" (John 6:27, 29). . . .

Hence all we who believe on Christ are kings and priests in Christ, as it is said, "Ye are a chosen generation, a royal priesthood, a holy nation, a peculiar people, that ye should show forth the praises of Him who hath called you out of darkness into His marvellous light" (I Peter 2:9).

From *Luther's Primary Works*, ed. H. Wace and C. A. Buchheim (London: Hodder and Stoughton, 1896).

The Self-Knowledge of a Christian
JUAN DE VALDÉS

c. 1535

WHILST a man studies merely in the books of other men, he becomes acquainted with the minds of their authors, but not with his own. Now, as it belongs to a Christian's duty to know himself, to know the state of being that he possesses as a child of God through Christian regeneration, I am accustomed to say that a Christian's proper study should be in *his own book*. This rightly understood, know, then, that I am accustomed to call my *mind my book;* because in this are contained my opinions, both false and true. In this I discover my confidence and my diffidence, my faith and my unbelief, my hope and my negligence, my charity and my enmity. In this also I find my humility and my presumption, my meekness and my impatience, my modesty and my arrogance, my simple-mindedness and my curiosity, my resolution against the world and my deference to it, my firmness against myself and my own self-love. In this is found whatever I possess of good by the favour of God and of Christ, and whatever evil I have acquired by my natural depravity. This is *my book*.

In this I read at all hours and at all seasons, and there is no occupation whatever that interrupts this reading. Sometimes I occupy myself in examining the opinions I entertain upon Christian subjects—on what I base them, how I understand them, and how I feel them. At other times, I set myself to examine what degree of confidence I have in the promises of God: how far I depend upon Him in all circumstances, and with what alacrity I put in practice what I know to be His will. I consider whether the Christian's faith has its efficacy within me, causing me to change my natural disposition; and whether the Christian life has made me change my former state and manners; because such alteration is Christian renovation and regeneration. I enter at other times into a very strict account with myself, examining how far I love God and Christ; whether I love Him more than myself; and how far I love my neighbours, and whether I love them as well as I love myself. If, then, I perceive that I am going forward, purely directed to the glory of God and of Christ, and to the spiritual and eternal good of my neighbours, I know that I go forward in love. This is the way I study in my *own book*.

The fruit I gain from such perusal is, that I arrive at a much better knowledge of what I am, and of what I am worth in myself, and what through God and through Christ; and so I arrive at a more intimate knowledge of the benefit to be received from Christ. And this is the consequence, that the more constantly I read in this my book, so much the more the life I have by the grace of God and of Christ grows within me, and that which I have as a son of Adam becomes less. When I wish to examine whether my opinions in the Christian faith are false or true, I go forward, comparing them with those which I read those holy men held who wrote the sacred Scriptures. Reading the holy faith of those Christians of the primitive Church, who were acknowledged to be justified and sanctified in Christ and by Christ, I know my own faith and my unbelief, and ask of God that He will increase my faith. Considering, also, the modest and simple manner in which Christian people lived at the first publication of the Gospel, having all things in common, and having no other thought than to know Christ crucified, I know my own modesty and simplicity, my arrogance and vain curiosity, and come to abhor all vanity, embracing simplicity of life.

Finally, comparing my affections and appetites with those I read of in the Holy Scriptures, I know well how lively or how dead they are; and I desire to give them not a single day to live. In this manner Holy Scripture serves me the better to study *my own book,* and the better to understand it. In this manner I comprehend whether my Christian life and my Christian self-denial correspond well or ill, little or much, with my Christian faith and profession. Thus I become a gainer of two things: one is that I do not estimate myself by the opinion men have of me, whether good or ill, but by that which I entertain myself, always referring myself to the opinion which God has of me; the other is that I go on forming my mind, reducing it by the imitation of Christ and His saints to what I know to have been in Him and in them. I have said that *my book is my mind,* and in the study of it, when I examine what I have in it, the benefit I draw from it is to know myself, and to know God and Christ. The same belongs to this study which belongs to all others you can pursue; what at the first was dry and forbidding, when advanced to the middle becomes easy, and has some pleasantness in it, and in the end is most sweet and delicious. Besides, so much greater will be the enjoyment in this than in any other study, as the benefit resulting from it is greater, which you will find if you will make the trial.

In B. B. Wiffen, *The Life and Writings of Juan de Valdés* (London: B. Quaritch, 1865).

The Fervent Spirits

PIETRO PAOLO VERGERIO

1540

TO VITTORIA COLONNA, MARCHESA OF PESCARA

Most Excellent Lady, May the grace, mercy, and peace of God the Father and Jesus Christ, Son of the Father, in truth and love be with you.

Your Excellency knows this was the way St. John saluted that lady whom he called elect. Not without mystery, with great fervour did she come to the knowledge of the Gospel. In this same way do I salute you, who are one of those bright elect lights who set forth these same truths, which are almost hidden in the darkness of this our age. As my chief object in conferring with you by letter is to be stimulated in the service of our Lord God, I see no reason to avoid beginning with so long a salutation. I have taken it from a source where nothing is to be found which is not good, and suitable for every place and season. God does not observe whether we attend to worldly customs or to the rules and ornaments of earthly knowledge, but whether we nourish ourselves with His Word, and say and do all to the glory of His Divine Majesty.

I am now to give you an account of the great joy and consolation I have received these few days past from the most serene Queen of Navarre [Marguerite]. I have passed four long hours at two different times conversing with her about the present state of the Church of God, about the study of divine things, and

on some of the most delightful points of spiritual doctrine, the same subjects which your Excellency desires
we should be always thinking of and conversing about.
These conversations are like rich treasures, worthy of
being preserved and communicated. They are also of
such a nature that imparting them to others enhances
their value. As soon as I had left her Majesty I made
notes of our subjects of conversation, and if I have time
today to revise and transcribe them I will send them
with this dispatch, to show your Excellency how high
the intellect of this queen soars, and how rightly she
speaks and feels of the grace of God and of the power
of His word. Having noted the sum and substance of
her opinions, I ought also to describe the fervour,
eloquence, and marvellous grace with which her Majesty expressed herself. I do not think it would have
been possible to speak better. Here you will say, how
could you understand her, as she generally speaks
French, which I know you do not comprehend? Her
Majesty spoke in French: I do not understand others
who speak in that language, nevertheless I think I
understood her, and lost very few words. I will tell
you why; she knows our Italian tongue though she
does not speak it; she also knows Latin very tolerably,
and pronounces it extremely well. Her Majesty, com-
passionating my slight knowledge of the language, and
wishing to be understood, when she made use of a
French word which she thought I should find difficult,
immediately explained it by an Italian or Latin word.
She pronounces also so distinctly and clearly that she
soon made me comprehend the sense of her words; and
besides this she was speaking on subjects which I have
frequently heard discussed. I think I comprehended
and have rightly noted these conversations, and your
Excellency will see and read them with astonishment,

pleasure, and edification. Blessed be our Lord Jesus Christ, who in these our turbulent times has raised up in various cities and provinces spirits of this kind. I daily meditate on this with wonder and consolation. In this kingdom there is the most serene queen of whom I am speaking; in Ferrara the Lady Renée of France; in Urbino the Lady Leonora Gonzaga; and many others who are filled with the love of Christ. In Rome there is the Lady Vittoria Colonna. This is speaking of your sex only. For my own part I feel convinced that this is the manner in which the holy vineyard, the Church of the Lord, in which there are so many thorns and obscurities, will be purified and enlightened. If God in His goodness goes on raising up such fervent spirits in both sexes, in various cities and provinces, we may awake from the long sleep which has closed our eyes and weighed down our faculties, and be enlightened with a true knowledge of the way to serve God much more than by all the ink in the world (even though we wrote new reformations every day), more than by all the diets which ever assembled. *Emittet verbum suum,* He will send forth his word, to speak of God, and to soften that which was hardened, namely our hearts and minds, which were shut up in the solid ice of error and worldly thoughts. When the Spirit of God breathes on us the ice will thaw, and, carried by the vessels of His grace, we shall pass over the waves of error to eternal truth! Who can restrain or retard our course, and the impetus of the Spirit of God? I commend myself to your Excellency.

In M. Young, *The Life and Times of Aonio Paleario* (London: Bell and Daldy, 1860).

The Livery of Christ

HUGH LATIMER

1552

SEEING the time is so far spent, we will take no
more in hand at this time but this one sentence:
Haec mando vobis ut diligatis vos invicem: for it shall
be enough for us to consider this well, and to bear it
away with us. "This I command unto you, that ye love
one another." Our Saviour himself spake these words
at His last supper, before he was taken. It was His last
sermon that He made unto His disciples, before His departure: it is a very long sermon. For our Saviour doth
like as one that knoweth he shall die shortly; therefore
is desirous to spend that little time that he hath with
his friends in exhorting and instructing them how they
shall lead their lives. Now among other things that He
commanded us this was one: *Haec mando vobis ut
diligatis vos invicem:* "This I command unto you, that
ye love one another." My translation hath, *Haec mando
vobis,* the plural number; the English goeth as though
it singularly were but one: "This is my commandment."
I examined the Greek, where it is in the plural number,
and very well: for there be many things that pertain to
a Christian man, and yet all those things are contained
in this one thing, that is, love; He lappeth up all things
in love. Our whole duty is contained in these words,
"Love together." Therefore St. Paul saith, "He that
loveth another fulfilleth the law": so it appeareth that
all things are contained in this word "love." This love

is a precious thing: our Saviour saith, *In hoc cognoscent omnes quia discipuli mei estis, si dilectionem habueritis ad invicem:* "By this shall all men know that ye are my disciples, if ye shall have love one to another." So that He maketh love His cognizance, His badge, His livery. Like as every lord, most commonly, giveth a certain livery to his servants, whereby they may be known that they pertain unto him; and so we say, "Yonder is this lord's servant," because he weareth his livery: so our Saviour, which is the Lord above all lords, would His servants to be known by their liveries and badge, which badge is love. Whosoever now is endued with love and charity is His servant: him we may call Christ's servant, for love is the token whereby you shall know such a servant that pertaineth to Christ; so that charity may be called the very livery of Christ: he that hath charity is Christ's servant; he that hath not charity is the servant of the devil. For like as Christ's livery is love and charity, so the devil's livery is hatred, malice, and discord. But I think the devil hath a great many more servants than Christ hath; for there be a great many more in his livery than in Christ's livery: there be but very few which be endued with Christ's livery, with love and charity, gentleness and meekness of spirit; but there be a great number of those that bear hatred and malice in their hearts, that be proud, stout, and lofty; therefore the number of the devil's servants are greater than the number of Christ's servants. Now St. Paul showeth how needful a thing this love is: I speak not of carnal love, which is a very beastly love, wherewith the whoremonger loveth his whore; but this charitable love is so necessary, that when a man hath her, without all other things it will suffice him. Again, if a man have all other things and lacketh that love, it will not help him, it is all in vain and lost. St. Paul used it so: "Though I spake with tongues of men and angels, and yet had no love, I were even as sounding brass or as a tinkling cymbal: and though I could prophesy, and understand all secrets and all knowledge; yea, if I had all faith so that I could move mountains out of their places, and yet had no love, I were nothing: and though I bestowed all my goods to feed the poor, and though I gave my body even that I burned, and yet had no love, it profiteth me nothing." These are godly gifts; yet St. Paul calleth them nothing, when a man hath them without charity: which is a great commendation and a great necessity of love, inasmuch that all other virtues be in vain when this love is absent. And there have been some which thought that St. Paul spake against the dignity of faith: but you must understand that St. Paul speaketh here not of the justifying faith, wherewith we receive everlasting life; but he understandeth by this word "faith" the gift to do miracles, to remove hills: of such a faith he speaketh. This I say to the confirmation of this proposition, "Faith only justifieth": this proposition is most true and certain. And St. Paul speaketh not here of this lively justifying faith: for this right faith is not without love: for love cometh and floweth out of faith. Love is a child of faith; for no man can love except he believe: so that they have two several offices, they themselves being inseparable.

St. Paul hath a saying in the thirteenth chapter of the first to the Corinthians, which after the outward letter seemed much to the dispraise of this faith, and to the praise of love: these be his words: *Nunc autem manent fides, spes, caritas, tria haec: major autem horum est caritas:* "Now abideth faith, hope, and love, even these three; but the chief of these is love." There be some learned men which expound this majority, of

which St. Paul speaketh here, for diuturnity. For when
we come to God, then we believe no more, but rather
see with our eyes face to face how He is; yet for all
that love remaineth still, so that love may be called
the chiefest, because she endureth forever. And though
she be the chiefest, yet we must not attribute unto her
the office which pertaineth unto faith only. Like as I
cannot say, the Mayor of Stamford must make me a
pair of shoes, because he is a greater man than the
shoemaker is; for the mayor, though he be the greater
man, yet it is not his office to make shoes: so, though
love be greater, yet it is not her office to save. Thus
much I thought good to say against those which fight
against the truth.

Now, when we will know which be in this livery or
not, we must learn it of St. Paul, which most evidently
describeth charity, which is the very livery, saying:
Caritas patiens est: "Love is patient, she suffereth long."
Now whosoever fumeth and is angry, he is out of this
livery: therefore let us remember that we do not cast
away the livery of Christ our master. When we be in
sickness or any manner of adversities, our duty is to be
patient and suffer it willingly, and to call upon Him
for aid, help, and comfort; for without Him we are
not able to abide any tribulation. Therefore we must
call upon God; He hath promised to help: therefore let
me not think Him to be false or untrue in His promises,
for we cannot dishonour God more than in not believing
or trusting in Him. Therefore let us beware above all
things of this dishonouring God: and so we must be
patient, trusting and most certainly believing, that He
will deliver us when it seemeth Him good, which
knoweth the time better than we ourselves. . . .

You shall not be offended because the Scripture commendeth love so highly; for he that commendeth the

daughter, commendeth the mother; for love is the daughter, and faith is the mother. Love floweth out of faith; where faith is, there is love; but yet we must consider their offices: faith is the hand wherewith we take everlasting life.

Now let us go all into ourselves, and examine our own hearts, whether we be in the livery of God, or no: and when we find ourselves to be out of this livery, let us repent and amend our lives; so that we may come again to the favour of God, and spend our time in this world to His honour and glory, forgiving our neighbours all such things as they have done against us.

And now to make an end. Mark here, who gave this precept of love: Christ our Saviour Himself; when and at what time: at His departing, when He should suffer death. Therefore these words ought the more to be esteemed and regarded, seeing He himself spake them at His last departing from us. God the Almighty give us grace so to walk here in this world charitably and friendly one with another, that we may attain the felicity which God hath prepared for all those that love him! Amen.

From *Sermons*, ed. Rev. G. E. Corrie (Cambridge: Parker Society, 1844).

Good Christian Discipline

JOHN CALVIN

1564

TO THE DUCHESS OF FERRARA

Madame, I believe you have received my last letters, to which I expect an answer in order to acquit myself of my duty respecting the subject on which you had been pleased to write to me. In the meantime I was unwilling to neglect the opportunity of recommending the present bearer to you, that you might learn from him the state of things here, for it is better to assign to him the task of informing you orally than charge the paper with such details, seeing that he is one of the most intimate friends I have, and a man in whom one may repose the most absolute trust. He is a son of the late M. Budé, the king's master of the rolls, who was much renowned for his erudition. For the rest, Madame, you have shown by your decision that a residence at Paris was very little to your taste. It is true that it would have been desirable that you had remained constantly at court for the relief of the poor churches, but I am not surprised that you seek for a quieter manner of life.

Now, since God has brought you back to your own town, it behooves you to redouble your care for administering rightly both your subjects and your household. I know, Madame, how obstinate the people are, and how you have laboured heretofore without much profit, to bring them into subjection. Be that as it will,

I pray you to follow out completely the doctrine of St.
Paul on this head, never to be weary of well doing,
whatever malice you may encounter to damp your
ardour. Above all, let your household be a mirror to
set the example to those who show themselves rather
indocile, and to confound those who are incorrigible
and entirely hardened. To accomplish this, I beg you
to keep a firm hand, to the utmost of your power, to
establish a good discipline for repressing vices and
occasions of scandal.

I do not mean a police with regard to political matters, but also in respect of the Consistory of the church,
and let those who are established to have an eye over
the conduct of others be men fearing God, of holy life,
and such sincerity and straightforwardness that nothing
shall prevent them from doing their duty, having such
a zeal as becomes them in maintaining the honour of
God in its integrity. Now let no one, whatever be his
rank or condition, or in whatever esteem you may hold
him, be ashamed to submit to the order which the Son
of God Himself has established, and bend his neck to
receive the yoke. For I assure you, Madame, that without this remedy there will be an unbridled licentiousness which will engender only confusion. Those who
make some profession of Christianity will be for the
most part dissolute. In one word, there will be a pliant,
and, as it were, many-coloured Gospel, for we see how
everyone flatters himself and is disposed to follow his
own appetites. It is wonderful to see how those that
have voluntarily subjected themselves to the tyranny of
the pope cannot endure that Jesus Christ should bear
gentle rule over them for their own salvation. But it is
true that the devil makes use of this device to bring
the truth of God into opprobrium, to cause pure religion to be contemned, and the sacred name of our

Redeemer blasphemed. Thus, Madame, to have a church duly Reformed, it is more than ever requisite to have people charged with a superintendence to watch over the morals of each; and that no one may feel himself aggrieved in giving an account of his life to the elders, let the elders themselves be selected by the church, as nothing can be more reasonable than to preserve to it this liberty, and this privilege will tend also to produce greater discretion in the choice of fitting men, and approved of as such by the Consistory.

I am persuaded, Madame, that you have aided our brother de Colonges with your authority in establishing some such order. But knowing to how much corruption the courts of princes are subject, I have thought that it would not be superfluous to exhort you to maintain it. Nay, it is right that you should be reminded of one thing: namely, that at all times the devil has striven by sinister reports and defamation to render the ministers of the gospel contemptible, in order that they may become the object either of aversion or of disgust. For that reason all the faithful should be carefully on their guard against such wiles. For, in fact, to quarrel with their spiritual pasture is something worse than finding fault with their bodily food, since the matter at stake here is the life of their souls. Be that as it will, if there are any who aim, were it but indirectly, to discourage you from pursuing what you have so well begun, you ought to shun them as deadly plagues. And in sooth the devil stirs them up to alienate people by indirect means from God, whose will it is that He should be recognized in the person of His servants.

Above all, Madame, never allow yourself to be persuaded to change anything in the state of the Church, such as God has consecrated it by his blood. For it is He before whom every knee should bend. If to wheedle you they allege that your house ought to be privileged, reflect that they cannot do you more dishonour than in cutting it off from the body of the Church; as on the contrary you cannot be more highly honoured than in having your house purged of all pollutions. Where, I ask you, Madame, ought we to apply the remedies sooner than in the cases where the diseases have most chance to spread? Now only judge if courts are not more apt to break out into all kinds of licentiousness than private families, unless precautions be taken against the evil. I do not say, if there is any subject of scandal among the members of your household, that you, who are the principal member of the church, should be the first to be reminded of it, in order to deliberate in perfect concord how it may be corrected; but what I recommend is that your authority should not interfere to interrupt the course of discipline, since if your domestics were spared, all respect for the Consistory would disappear like water from a leaky vessel

Madame, I pass to another subject. I have long had a great wish to make you a present of a gold piece. Think how bold I am; but because I supposed you had a similar one, I have not ventured hitherto, for it is only its rarity that can give it any value in your esteem. Finally I have delivered it to the bearer to show it to you, and if it is a novelty to you, will you be pleased to keep it? It is the finest present that I have it in my power to make you.

Madame, having very humbly commended myself to your indulgent favour, I will supplicate our heavenly Father to have you in His holy keeping, and increase you in all good and prosperity.

From *Letters of John Calvin*, ed. J. Bonnet, trans. M. R. Gilchrist (Philadelphia: Presbyterian Board of Publication, 1858).

※

The Lord's Labour

ST. TERESA OF AVILA

HER SECOND FOUNDATION

1567

OCCUPIED as I was with all these anxieties, I determined to seek the help of the Fathers of the Company [the Jesuits], who were thought a great deal of in that place—that is, in Medina. As I said in writing of my first foundation, I had for many years been in touch with them on spiritual matters, and they had done me so much good that I am always particularly devoted to them. I wrote to the Rector there, and told him what our Father General had commanded me: he happened for a great many years to have been my confessor, as I have said, though I did not then give his name, which was Baltasar Alvarez; he is now Provincial. He and the others said they would do what they could in the matter, and they did a great deal to obtain the consent of the town, and of the prelate, which is always difficult when a monastery is to be founded in poverty. So the negotiations took some days.

In order to further them, a cleric went there, who was a great servant of God, greatly detached from all worldly things and much given to prayer. He was chaplain in the convent where I was living, and the Lord had given him the same desires as He had given me, and so he has helped me greatly, as will be seen later: his name was Julián de Avila. I now had the licence, but I had neither a house nor so much as a farthing for buying one. And as for credit to go upon, how could a gadabout like myself have any unless the Lord gave it? However, the Lord provided, for a girl of excellent character, for whom there had been no room at St. Joseph's, knowing that another house was being founded, came to ask to be received into it. She had a little money—very little, not enough for buying a house, but only for renting one and for helping us to make the journey to Medina; so we found a house and rented it. Without any other support than this, we left Avila—two nuns from St. Joseph's and myself, and four from the Incarnation (the convent of the Mitigated Rule, where I had lived before St. Joseph's was founded), with our Father Chaplain Julián de Avila.

When this became known in the city there was a great deal of uncharitable talk. Some said I was mad; others, that this folly would soon come to an end. The Bishop, as he has since told me, thought it the height of folly, although at the time he did not tell me this, or do anything else to upset me, for he was very fond of me and would not cause me distress. My friends had told me so repeatedly, but I took little notice of them, for what they were dubious about seemed to me so easy that I could not persuade myself it could fail to turn out well. Before ever we left Avila, I had written to a Father of our Order, called Fray Antonio de Heredia, asking him to buy me a house. He was at that time Prior of a monastery of our Order there, called St. Anne's. He took up the matter with a lady who was very much devoted to him and who had a house in an excellent situation, though the whole of it, except for one room, was in a very dilapidated state. She was good enough to promise to sell it to him, and they arranged

it without her asking him for a deposit or any other
security than his word: had she done otherwise we
should have been helpless, but the Lord was preparing
the way for us. The house was almost falling down:
so much was there to be done to it that while it was
being repaired we had to hire another. . . .

We arrived at Medina del Campo at midnight on the
eve of the festival of Our Lady in August. In order not
to disturb anyone, we alighted at the monastery of St.
Anne and went to the house on foot. It was a great
mercy on the part of the Lord that we met no one, for
it was just at that time that they were shutting in
the bulls which were to take part in the next day's
bullfight. We were so much absorbed in our task that
we thought of nothing else; but the Lord, who always
remembers those desirous of serving Him—and we certainly had no other aim than that—delivered us from
all danger.

Having reached the house, we entered the courtyard.
The walls seemed to me in a very tumbledown condition and by day they appeared worse still. The Lord
must have been pleased that the blessed Father should
have become blind or he would have seen that it was
not fitting to put the Most Holy Sacrament in such a
place. When I looked at the porch I saw that we should
have to remove some of the earth from it; there were
holes in the roof; and the walls were not plastered.
The night was nearly over and we had only a few
hangings—I believe altogether there were three. These,
in view of the length of the porch, were of no use at
all. I did not know what to do, for I saw that it would
not be seemly to put an altar there. But it was the
Lord's will that it should be done at once, for by His
providence the lady's steward had a great deal of

tapestry belonging to her and also a blue damask bed-spread, and she had said that we were to be given whatever we wanted, for she was very good to us.

When I saw how well we were provided for, I praised the Lord, and the others all did the same. We did not know what to do for nails, and it was not a time at which we could buy any. So we started to look round the walls; and at last, after some trouble, we collected a sufficient number. Then the hanging was begun, while we nuns set to work to clean the floor; and we all worked so quickly that, by daybreak, the altar was set up and the bell hung in a gallery, so that Mass was said immediately. There was no need for us to do more before taking possession. But we did not stop there; we had the Most Holy Sacrament reserved, and through the chinks of the door, which was opposite the altar, we were able to see the Mass—it was the only way we could do so.

So far I was very pleased, for it gives me the greatest joy when I see one more church in which there is reservation of the Most Holy Sacrament. But my joy was of short duration. For, when Mass had been offered, I went to look at the courtyard through a window and saw that its walls had partly fallen down, so that many days would be necessary before they could be repaired. Oh, God help me! What anguish filled my heart when I saw His Majesty turned out into the street, and in times so full of peril as these, on account of those Lutherans!

Together with these thoughts came others, concerning all the difficulties which might be put in our way by those who had spoken ill of us, for I clearly realized that they had done so with good reason. It seemed to me impossible for us to go any farther with the work we had begun; for, just as previously everything had seemed easy to me, when I had reflected that it was being done for God's sake, so now temptation began to intensify its hold upon me as if I had never received any favours from Him at all. All I could think of was my own weakness and lack of power. What good result could I hope for when I was relying on anything so miserable as myself? If I had been alone, I believe I could have endured it better; but to think that my companions would have to return to their houses, after all the opposition they had encountered before leaving, was a terrible trial to me. I thought that, as the beginning of our enterprise had gone wrong, I must have been mistaken in supposing that the Lord would help us. To all this was added the fear that what I had learned in prayer might have been an illusion; and this was not the least of my distresses, but the greatest, for it caused me the most terrible fear that the devil might have been deceiving me. Oh, my God! What it is to see a soul whom Thou art pleased to allow to suffer! When I recall this affliction and other trials that I have endured while making these foundations, I really do not think that any of my physical trials, numerous though they have been, are worthy of the least remembrance by comparison with this.

Greatly as all these troubles oppressed me, I said nothing about them to my companions, for I had no wish that they should be more distressed than they were already. So I bore this trial alone until the evening, when the Rector of the Company sent one of the Fathers to see me, and he gave me great encouragement and comfort. I did not tell him all my troubles but only the grief I felt at our finding ourselves in the street. I began to discuss with him the question of searching for a house which we could lease, at whatever cost, so that we could move there while our repairs were being done here; and when I saw how many people were coming to visit us, and that none of them had observed our folly, I began to feel comforted. This was by the mercy of God; had they done so, the Most Holy Sacrament would certainly have been taken from us. I realize now how foolish I was and how careless they were not to consume the Host; but I thought that, if this were done, it would be all up with us.

But, try as we would, we could find no house to let anywhere, and this caused me extreme distress both by night and by day. For, although I always left men to keep guard over the Most Holy Sacrament, I was afraid they might go to sleep; and so I used to get up in the night, and look at it through the window, for, when the moon was very bright, I could see it easily. During all these days many people were visiting us, and not only did they not think our foundation at all a bad one but it gave them great devotion to see Our Lord once more in the porch; and His Majesty, never weary of humbling Himself for our sakes, did not seem to want to leave it.

At the end of a week, a merchant, who was living in a very good house, saw what we needed and told us we could have the upper part of his house and live there as if it were our own. It had a very large gilded hall, which he gave us for a church, and a lady, called Doña Elena de Quiroga, a great servant of God, who was living near the house we had bought, said that she would help me so that I could at once begin to build a chapel in which the Most Holy Sacrament might be placed and also try to find us accommodation so that we could be enclosed. Other people gave us abundant alms, so that we had more than enough to eat, but it was this lady who helped me most.

With all this happening, I began to be easier in my mind; for we were completely enclosed where we were, and we began to say the Hours, while the good Prior took up the matter of the house with all speed, and went to great trouble about it. He said that, in spite of everything, it would not be finished for two months; but it was so well done that we were able to stay there with reasonable comfort for several years. Since then our Lord has gone on improving things for us.

While I was there, I was continually preoccupied about monasteries for friars; and, having no friars, as I have said, I did not know what to do. So I resolved to discuss the matter in the strictest confidence with the Prior there, and see what advice he would give me. I did this: he was very glad when he heard of it and promised me that he would be the first to join us. I took that for a joke and told him so; for although, besides being a learned man, he was a good friar, given to recollection, very studious, and fond of his cell, he did not seem to me to be at all the man for the beginning of an enterprise of this kind; he had not sufficient spirituality, nor could he have endured the necessary privations, being delicate in health and not accustomed to them. But he reassured me most earnestly and told me that for a long time the Lord had been calling him to a stricter life, that he had already resolved to go to the Carthusians, and that they had assured him that they would receive him. Nonetheless, though very glad to hear this of him, I was not quite satisfied: I asked him, therefore, to let us wait a while so that he might practise the things which he would have to promise to do. He did so; a year passed, during which time he experienced so many trials and persecutions from false witnesses that it seemed as if it was the Lord's intention to prove him. He himself bore it all so well, and made such steady progress, that I praised our Lord, for it seemed to me that His Majesty was preparing him for this new life.

Shortly afterwards there happened to arrive a young Father who was studying in Salamanca. With him was a companion, who told me great things about the life which that Father was leading. His name is Fray Juan de la Cruz. I praised our Lord; and, when I spoke to the friar, I liked him very much; he told me that he too was preparing to go to the Carthusians. I described to him what I had in view and begged him earnestly to wait until the Lord gave us a monastery, pointing out what a great blessing it would be, if he were destined for a higher life, that he should lead it within his own Order, and how much better service he would thus render to the Lord. He gave me his word to do this provided there were no long delay. When I saw that I had two friars to make a beginning with, the thing seemed to me settled, although I was still not quite satisfied with the Prior. So for this reason, and also because I had as yet no place to begin in, I waited for some little time.

The nuns continued to win good opinions in the town, and aroused much devotion—I believe deservedly, for none of them had any other aim than to see how each could best serve our Lord. In every detail they followed the same procedure as had been adopted at St. Joseph's at Avila, the Rule and Constitutions for all our convents being one and the same. The Lord began to call some to take the habit, and so numerous were the favours which He granted them that I was amazed. May He be blessed forever. Amen. For, in order to love, He seems only to wait to be loved Himself.

THE SIMILITUDE OF THE WATERED GARDEN

The beginner must think of himself as of one setting out to make a garden, in soil most unfruitful and full of weeds, in which the Lord is to take His delight. His Majesty uproots the weeds and will set good plants in their place. Let us suppose that this has already been done—that a soul is determined to practise prayer and has already begun to do so. With God's help, we have now to be good gardeners and make these plants grow, and to water them carefully, so that they may not die, but may produce flowers which shall give out great fragrance and refresh this our Lord, so that He may often come into the garden to take His pleasure and have His delight among these virtues.

Let us now consider the way in which this garden can be watered, so that we may know what we shall have to do, how much labour it will cost us, if the gain will be greater than the labour, and for how long this labour must be borne. It seems to me that the garden can be watered in four ways: by taking the water from a well, which is hard work for us; or by a waterwheel and buckets, when the water is drawn by a windlass (I have sometimes drawn it in this way: it is not such a hard one as the other and gives more water); or by a stream or a brook, which waters the ground much better, for it saturates it more thoroughly and there is less need to water it often, so that the gardener's labour is much less; or by heavy rain, when the Lord waters it and it costs us no work at all, a way incomparably better than any of the others.

And now I come to my point, which is the application of these four methods of watering by which the garden is to be kept fertile and without which it will be ruined. In this way I think I can explain something about the four degrees of prayer to which the Lord, of His goodness, has occasionally brought my soul. May He also, in His goodness, grant me to speak in such a way as to be of some profit to one of those who commanded me to write this book, and whom in four months the Lord has brought to a point far higher than that which I have reached in seventeen years. He prepared himself better than I, and thus his garden, without labour on his part, is watered by all these four means, though he is still receiving the last watering only drop by drop; such progress is his garden making that soon, by the Lord's help, it will be submerged. I shall be glad for him to laugh at my explanation if he thinks it foolish.

Beginners in prayer, we may say, are those who draw the water from the well; this, as I have said, is very hard work, for it will fatigue them to keep their senses recollected, which is extremely difficult because they have been accustomed to a life of distraction. Beginners must accustom themselves to pay no heed to what they see or hear, and they must practise this during hours of prayer; they must go away by themselves and in their solitude think over their past life—we must all do this, in fact, whether we are at the beginning of the road or near its end. There are differences, however, in the extent to which it must be done, as I shall show later. At first it causes distress, for beginners are not always sure that they have repented of their sins (though clearly they have, since they have determined to serve God so faithfully). Then they have to endeavour to meditate upon the life of Christ, which fatigues their minds. Thus far we can make progress by ourselves—with the help of God, of course, for without that, as is well known, we cannot think a single good thought.

That is what is meant by beginning to draw water from the well—and God grant there may be water in it! But that, at least, does not depend on us: our task is to draw it and to do what we can to water the flowers. And God is so good that when, for reasons known to His Majesty, perhaps to our great advantage, He is pleased that the well should be dry, we, like good gardeners, do all that in us lies, and He keeps the flowers alive without water and makes the virtues grow. By water here I mean tears—or at least, if there are no tears, tenderness and an interior feeling of devotion.

What, then, will a person do here who finds that for many days he experiences nothing but aridity, dislike, and distaste, and has so little desire to go and draw water that he would give it up entirely did he not remember that he is pleasing and serving the Lord of the garden; if he were not anxious that all his service should not be lost, to say nothing of the gain which he hopes for from the hard work of continually lowering the bucket into the well and then drawing it up without water? It will often happen that, even for that purpose, he is unable to lift his arms—unable, that is, to think a single good thought, for working with the understanding is of course the same as drawing water from the well.

What, then, as I say, will the gardener do here? He will rejoice and take new heart and consider it the greatest of favours to work in the garden of so great an Emperor; and as he knows that he is pleasing Him by doing so (and his purpose must be to please, not himself, but Him), let him render Him great praise for having placed such confidence in him, because He sees that, without receiving any recompense, he is taking such great care of that which He had entrusted to him; let him help Him to bear the Cross and remember

how He lived with it all His life long; let him not wish
to have his kingdom on earth or ever cease from prayer;
and so let him resolve, even if this aridity should persist his whole life long, not to let Christ fall with His
Cross.

From *The Complete Works of St. Teresa of Jesus*, trans. E. A.
Peers (London and New York: Sheed and Ward, 1946).

The Obscure Night of the Soul

ST. JOHN OF THE CROSS

Upon an obscure night
Fevered with love in love's anxiety
(O hapless-happy plight!),
I went, none seeing me,
Forth from my house where all things quiet be.

By night, secure from sight,
And by the secret stair, disguisedly,
(O hapless-happy plight!)
By night, and privily,
Forth from my house where all things quiet be.

Blest night of wandering,
In secret, where by none might I be spied,
Nor I see anything;
Without a light or guide,
Save that which in my heart burnt in my side.

That light did lead me on,
More surely than the shining of noontide,

Where well I knew that one
Did for my coming bide;
Where He abode, might none but He abide.

O night that didst lead thus,
O night more lovely than the dawn of light,
O night that broughtest us,
Lover to lover's sight,
Lover with loved in marriage of delight!

Upon my flowery breast
Wholly for Him, and save Himself for none,
There did I give sweet rest
To my belovèd one;
The fanning of the cedars breathed thereon.

When the first moving air
Blew from the tower and waved His locks aside,
His hand, with gentle care,
Did wound me in the side,
And in my body all my senses died.

All things I then forgot,
My cheek on Him who for my coming came;
All ceased, and I was not,
Leaving my cares and shame
Among the lilies, and forgetting them.

Trans. Arthur Symons.

ACKNOWLEDGMENTS

The editors wish to thank the following for their kind permission to reprint excerpts from the works listed below:

G. Bell & Sons, Ltd., London, *Lives of the Most Eminent Painters, Sculptors and Architects* by Giorgio Vasari, translated by Mrs. Jonathan Foster.

Ernest Benn, Ltd., London, *Life and Times of Girolamo Savonarola* by P. Villari, translated by Linda Villari.

Josephine L. Burroughs, translation of *Platonic Theology* by Marsilio Ficino, in *The Journal of the History of Ideas.*

Cambridge University Press, New York, *Cambridge Readings in the Literature of Science* by W. C. Dampier-Whetham; and *Literary Remains of Albrecht Dürer*, translated by Sir William Martin Conway.

Carnegie Endowment for International Peace, New York, *The Spanish Origin of International Law* by J. B. Scott.

The Clarendon Press, Oxford, *Luis de León; A Study of the Spanish Renaissance* by Aubrey FitzGerald Bell; and *Poems in Classical Prosody* by Robert Bridges.

Columbia University Press, New York, and J. S. Schapiro, *Social Reform and the Reformation* by J. S. Schapiro.

Crown Publishers, Inc., New York, Samuel Putnam's translations of *The Works of Aretino*, copyright 1926 by Pascal Covici.

Crown Publishers, Inc., and The Viking Press, Inc., New York, *The Portable Rabelais*, selected, translated, and edited by Samuel Putnam, copyright 1946 by Samuel Putnam (adapted from his original translation in *The Complete Works of Rabelais*, copyright 1929 by Covici-Friede, Inc.).

J. M. Dent & Sons, Ltd., London, *Vittoria Colonna* by M. F. Jerrold.

Dodd, Mead & Company, Inc New York, *The Collected Poems of G. K. Chesterton;* and *Poems* by Arthur Symons.

The Dublin Review, London, *Eirenikon* by Reginald Cardinal Pole, translated by Vincent Joseph McNabb.

Gerald Duckworth & Co., Ltd., London, *Michael Angelo Buonarroti* by C. Holroyd.

E. P. Dutton & Co., Inc., New York, *De Vita Propria Liber* by Girolamo Cardano, translated by Jean Stoner, copyright 1929 by E. P. Dutton & Co., Inc.; and *Baldassare Castiglione, His Life and Letters*, translated by Julia Cartwright.

B. Farrington, translations of *De fabrica corporis humani*, by Andreas Vesalius, in *Transactions of the Royal Society of Medicine*, and *Transactions of the Royal Society of South Africa.*

Hakluyt Society, London, *Pilgrimage of Arnold von Harff*, translated by Malcolm Letts.

Harvard University Press, Cambridge, *Early Economic Thought* by Arthur Eli Monroe; and *Florentine Merchants in the Age of the Medici* by Gertrude R. B. Richards.

William Heinemann, Ltd., London, *Poems by Arthur Symons.*

The Hispanic Society of America, New York, *Translations from Hispanic Poets.*

Hodder & Stoughton, Ltd., *Luther's Primary Works,* translated by H. Wace and C. A. Buchheim.

John Lane, The Bodley Head, Ltd., London, *Dante, Petrarch, Camoëns, CXXIV Sonnets,* by Richard Garnett; and *The Fugger News Letters,* edited by Victor von Klarwill.

Longmans, Green & Co., Ltd., London, and the Executors of the late F. M. Nichols, *Epistles of Erasmus* by F. M. Nichols; and Longmans, Green & Co., Ltd., and the Representatives of the late Andrew Lang, *Ballads and Lyrics of Old France* by Andrew Lang.

Sampson Low, Marston & Co., Ltd., London, *The Literary Remains of Leonardo da Vinci* by J. P. Richter.

McGraw-Hill Book Company, Inc., New York, *A Source Book in Astronomy* by H. Shapley and H. Howarth, copyright 1929 by McGraw-Hill Book Company, Inc.

John Murray, Ltd., London, *Baldassare Castiglione, His Life and Letters,* translated by Julia Cartwright.

The New York School of Social Work, formerly The New York School of Philanthropy, *Concerning the Relief of the Poor* by Juan Luis Vives, translated by Margaret M. Sherwood.

Princeton University Press,

Princeton, *Boccaccio on Poetry* by C. G. Osgood.

G. P. Putnam's Sons, New York, *Petrarch, the First Modern Scholar and Man of Letters* by J. H. Robinson and H. W. Rolfe.

Routledge and Kegan Paul, Ltd., London, *The Founders of the New Devotion* by Thomas a Kempis, translated by J. P. Arthur; and *The Life and Letters of Ogier Ghiselin de Busbecq,* translated by Charles Thornton Forster and F. H. B. Daniell.

Sheed & Ward, Inc., New York, and Sheed & Ward, Ltd., London, *The Complete Works of St. Teresa of Jesus,* translated and edited by E. Allison Peers.

Smith College, Northampton, Mass., "The Commentaries of Pius II," translated by Florence A. Gragg, with notes by Leona Gabel, published in *Smith College Studies in History.*

Society of Brothers, Bromdon, Bridgnorth, Shropshire, *Account of Our Religion, Doctrine and Faith* by Peter Rideman, translated by Kathleen Hasenberg.

The University of Chicago Press, Chicago, *The Renaissance Philosophy of Man,* edited by E. Cassirer, *et al.*

The Viking Press, Inc., New York, Samuel Putnam's translation of *The Ingenious Gentleman Don Quixote de la Mancha* by Miguel de Cervantes Saavedra, copyright 1949 by The Viking Press, Inc.

A. P. Watt & Son, London, and Miss Dorothy Edith Collins, *Collected Poems of G. K. Chesterton.*